American Orators
of the
Twentieth Century

American Orators
of the
Twentieth Century

CRITICAL STUDIES AND SOURCES

EDITED BY

Bernard K. Duffy
and Halford R. Ryan

GREENWOOD PRESS

NEW YORK
WESTPORT, CONNECTICUT
LONDON

Library of Congress Cataloging-in-Publication Data

American orators of the twentieth century.

 Bibliography: p.
 Includes index.
 1. Political oratory—United States—History—20th
century. 2. Orators—United States—Biography.
3. Speeches, addresses, etc., American—History and
criticism. I. Duffy, Bernard K. II. Ryan, Halford R.
PN4193.P6A44 1987 808.5'1'0973 86–10003
ISBN 0–313–24843–5 (lib. bdg. : alk. paper)

Library of Congress Catalog Card Number: 86–10003
ISBN: 0–313–24843–5

First published in 1987

Greenwood Press, Inc.
88 Post Road West, Westport, Connecticut 06881

Printed in the United States of America

The paper used in this book complies with the
Permanent Paper Standard issued by the National
Information Standards Organization (Z39.48–1984).

10 9 8 7 6 5 4 3 2 1

CONTENTS ————————————————

PREFACE _____

The focus of this book is on American political oratory of the twentieth century. Its companion volume, *American Orators before 1900: Critical Studies and Sources*, focuses on pre–twentieth century speakers. In both works, we define political oratory as discourse that treats the constitutional, social, theological, moral and partisan political concerns of the American people in a free and open society. This book assembles fifty-eight essays on the oratorical careers of influential men and women and points to the materials students and scholars of public address require for their research.

Political discourse concerns scholars of politics and government, rhetoric and public address, U.S. history, journalism, the electronic media, and other related subjects. The roots of this multidisciplinary interest reach back to Aristotle, who observed that rhetoric exists at the nexus between politics and ethics. One reason why political discourse continues to interest a diverse group of scholars is that it exemplifies the rhetorician's craft. Political oratory reflects the remarkably subtle and complex rhetorical choices speakers make. The principal allure of political oratory as a study is its continued significance in modern life. One has only to read a sampling of the essays in this book to appreciate how oratory has continued to be a potent means of persuasion.

We use the term *orators* in the title of the book because the careers and reputations of the individuals considered have been established and influenced by their oratory. The term fits some of the figures represented in this book better than others. A number of speakers examined in this book have spoken for ignoble causes or have given unsound advice to their listeners. Orators of this century—of every other century—have appealed to the best and worst inclinations of their audiences. To put the matter in terms Richard Weaver used in his interpretation of Plato's *Phaedrus*, some orators have moved their audiences toward the good, some have moved them toward the bad, and some have failed to move them at all. We have included speakers from all three categories because they have contributed to the history of American public address. It would be intellectually dishonest and academically unwise to exclude any type from critical review.

This book, through the careful work of its contributors, provides knowledgeable and frank appraisals of the methods and effects of oratory. We believe that criticism of great orators as well as of those who abused the public trust or were unsuccessful in their attempts at persuasion is vitally important to the proper understanding of the role oratory plays in a democratic society.

Readers will also see many opportunities for additional research, for the speaking careers of several figures represented in the book are ongoing, and others, even some famous speakers, have not received much previous scholarly attention. Nor has the last word been written about any speech just because it has already been examined.

We hope that this book will prove useful to all who consult it and that it will stimulate and guide future research on the important and fascinating topic of American political oratory in the twentieth century.

We wish to thank those individuals who helped us formulate our plans for this book and carry them through to completion. Marilyn Brownstein, acquisitions editor at Greenwood Press, recognized the need for a reference work on American rhetoric and deftly guided us in the beginning stages of our work. Cynthia Harris, history editor, assisted us as we prepared the volume for submission, and Mildred Vasan, politics and law editor, Lisa Reichbach, production editor, and Beverly Miller, copy editor, helped bring the work to a successful conclusion. The book reflects their professional editorial experience.

A good deal of the planning for the book was done during the summer of 1984 when Bernard Duffy attended a National Endowment for the Humanities Summer Seminar, "Ciceronian Rhetoric and Its Influence on Modern Writing," directed by James J. Murphy at the University of California-Davis. He thanks the endowment and Professor Murphy for their support of this undertaking.

G. William Koon, head of the Department of English at Clemson University, is owed a debt of gratitude for allocating departmental resources to support this project and for providing a graduate assistant, John Turlington, who carefully proofread the thirty or so manuscripts we received in the summer of 1985 and who helped compile a list of rhetorical terms for the glossary. We are grateful for the secretarial assistance of Pearl Parker, Julie Harmon, and Kim Hunter and for the suggestions of Mark Winchell, Edward Willey, and Richard Leeman, who read the introduction.

Without the scholars who wrote the fifty-eight entries, this book would not exist. Although they represent varied disciplines—speech, history, political science, and government—and are accustomed to the subtle stylistic differences that characterize discourse in their specialties, they tailored their writing to the style and format we believe befits the encyclopedic nature of the entries in this book. We trust that those who use this book will appreciate and applaud their efforts, as we do.

We thank the Speech Communication Association and the American Political

Science Association for carrying a call for contributors in their respective publications.

For whatever sins of omission or commission are detected herein, we nominate contritely the traditional nostra culpa. And finally, we dedicate this book to our wives and children.

AN INTRODUCTION TO AMERICAN POLITICAL ORATORY IN THE TWENTIETH CENTURY _____

Rhetoric, particularly political rhetoric, has long been a target of derision for journalists, academics, and politicians themselves. At a time when popular wisdom suggests that voters no longer vote on issues but rather on image and that the business of government is conducted in smoke-filled rooms rather than in public forums, it is perfectly consistent to add that oratory, an anachronistic political art in which politicians sometimes address issues, has seen its day. Oratory survives, some critics say, because there are still occasions that demand it, but it is not an art that is uniquely adapted to the medium of television and has therefore waned in importance as a political instrument. If William Jennings Bryan were to deliver his "Cross of Gold" speech today, television would probably air only a few minutes of it. Although Soviet television dared to broadcast live Gorbachev's entire five and a half hour address to the Twenty-seventh Soviet Congress, one wonders who among the Russian public watched.

Where, one might ask, are the Lyceum and Chautauqua circuits of today, which in the previous century provided great edification and pleasure to audiences who listened by the hour to the leading lights of their times? Where are the great congressional orators, such as Calhoun, Webster, and Hayne, in a day when congressmen have been known to address the television camera in the House of Representatives even when no other legislator is present in the chamber to hear them? Where are the great stump speakers such as the "little giant," Stephen Douglas, in an era when it is easier to get a rural audience to attend a farm foreclosure auction than a political speech?

There is no question that oratory is very different today than it was in the nineteenth century and that oratory has changed, in part to suit radio, film, and television, but it would be a great mistake to assume that oratory is any less important today than it was a century ago. In fact, in terms of the size of its audiences and the magnitude of its effects, it is more significant. Any medium that reproduces spoken discourse affects it. If it were not for the print medium, oratory of the last century would undoubtedly have been different. Some speeches, especially ceremonial ones, were meant to be read, as well as heard, which is one reason why oratory attained a literary status it does not enjoy today. Edward Everett's address at the Gettysburg ceremony was printed and distributed beforehand as a work of literary accomplishment. Lincoln's Gettysburg Address, initially viewed as lackluster, acquired its fame only after being reported by the press, reprinted in textbooks, and recited by schoolchildren. Nor does there seem any doubt that Clarence Darrow intended his courtroom oratory in the Scopes trial to affect the national public through the work of journalists such as Baltimore's H. L. Mencken, who covered the celebrated trial.

Like the print media, the electronic media have also altered the nature and effectiveness of oratory, though they have not diminished its importance, except as literature. The advent of radio in the early 1920s quickly changed the face of political oratory. Franklin D. Roosevelt first used the new medium as governor of New York to blunt the effect of the upstate Republican-controlled newspapers and used it with even greater effectiveness as president in his famous fireside chats. Roosevelt inadvertently cleared the way for demagogues such as Huey Long, who presented his Share the Wealth program over the air, and Father Coughlin, who used the airwaves to broadcast his antisemitism. Had it not been for radio, it is difficult to imagine how Roosevelt could have quelled so quickly the banking crisis that confronted him during the first days of his presidency. The print medium could not have projected Roosevelt's quiet and soothing reassurances, which successfully persuaded the public to stop their run on the banks.

Television has, if anything, increased the influence of oratory on the public. The poison of Joseph McCarthy's speeches in Congress spread so rapidly in part because the public found the witch hunt absorbing television drama. Richard Nixon's nationally televised "My Side of the Story," the so-called Checkers speech, worked to restore public confidence in the embattled vice-presidential candidate. The Kennedy-Nixon debates brought issues and images of the candidates to the public and, arguably, tipped the balance of the campaign. By covering the March on Washington and Martin Luther King's historic "I Have a Dream" speech, television helped to mobilize the support of the nation and to influence Congress to pass the Civil Rights Act of 1964.

Television has not always worked to the benefit of orators. The presidential news conferences, which were fascinating when John F. Kennedy bantered with the press, were painful during Carter's struggle with the politically disastrous Iranian hostage situation. As other examples of speeches that did not help their authors, one remembers Lyndon Johnson's speech declaring he would not run for a second term as president, Nixon's dissembling press conferences on Watergate, and Jimmy Carter's ill-conceived fireside chat and speech on the energy situation. By increasing the size of their immediate audiences, the electronic media have increased the potential risks and rewards of political oratory.

Throughout the twentieth century, both before and after the advent of the electronic media, oratory has continued to be an effective instrument of political persuasion. In the early years of the century, a generation witnessed far-reaching reform movements, started and sustained by the speeches of preachers, populists, socialists, and suffragists. Theodore Roosevelt's speech, "The Man with the Muckrake," has been said to characterize the Progressive *zeitgeist* of late nineteenth- and early twentieth-century America. Encouraging reformism while warning against sensationalism, it was a speech that, like many others in the nineteenth century, preached a standard for public thought and conduct. Woodrow Wilson's speeches, especially those that pleaded for U.S. neutrality in World War I and, after the war, asked for support of the League of Nations, also took the high road of morality. Less well remembered but also significant was the senator from Idaho, William Borah's, emotionally charged speech against the League of Nations, which successfully sealed its fate in the Senate.

Eugene Debs helped create the Red Scare by preaching socialism during the 1910s, and Hoover deftly sold his ideal of American individualism in his speeches during the 1920s. The Great Depression brought an extraordinary need for leadership and rhetoric that in some senses surpassed that of the previous three decades of the century. Within the depression decade were many remarkable examples of political oratory. Roosevelt's First Inaugural Address, with such resounding phrases as "the only thing we have to fear is fear itself" and "the money-changers have fled from their high seats in the temples of our civilization," was the opening gambit of a New Deal rhetoric that was as bold as the program it promoted. The depression created a situation in which political opportunists could promote their schemes for social salvation and at the same time catapult themselves into positions of national prominence. As Father Coughlin and Huey Long took their appeals to the nation through the instrument of radio, another demagogue, Eugene Talmadge, used his oratorical prowess to control the politics of a state.

World War II presented new rhetorical challenges. From Roosevelt's war address, which declared December 7, 1941, "a date which will live in infamy," to Douglas MacArthur's speech on the U.S.S. *Missouri* accepting the Japanese surrender, the nation's leaders realized that it took more than armaments and industrial strength to win a war or keep the peace; it took a national resolve sustained by rhetoric.

Even before the war had ended, the seeds of a new war had been sown, a war in which words and an arms race largely took the place of conventional hostilities. No generation is more aware of the efficacy of political rhetoric than the one that saw the superpowers plunge headlong into the cold war. Only shortly after the terms of the Yalta Agreement had been sold to the Congress and public, some Republicans alleged that Roosevelt had forged private agreements with Stalin that were not in the interests of the nation. The cold war profoundly affected domestic politics. The right wing of the Republican party tendentiously divided the world into two camps: true patriots and those who were soft on communism.

Not only to Republican hardliners but to a great many other Americans, Truman's dismissal of MacArthur during the Korean war provided dramatic evidence of the Democratic administration's failure to deal resourcefully and decisively with the red menace. Truman in his "Far Eastern Policy" speech failed to provide a convincing argument for MacArthur's dismissal, while MacArthur in his winning address before a joint session of Congress effectively made the case against the administration's policy of a politically limited war and bid the nation farewell with the evocative line, "Old soldiers never die, they just fade away." Joseph McCarthy's witch hunt merely coalesced and focused long-standing right-wing Republican fears and hostilities toward communists and their alleged fellow travelers in the Democratic party.

The cold war fervor helped sweep Eisenhower into office, and though Eisenhower's career as a speaker was undistinguished, his farewell address, in which he warned against the "military-industrial complex," left a significant impact on the political dialectics of the times. In John F. Kennedy the nation found a politician who was an unusually accomplished orator. Kennedy's presidential campaign rested more upon the strength of his oratory than any of his predecessors since Franklin Roosevelt. One remembers his speech to the Houston Ministerial Association, in which he deftly responded to the question of how his religious convictions would affect his presidency. Most critics agree that Kennedy's Inaugural Address ranks among the best of all other presidential inaugurals, and few who heard it have forgotten the high-minded appeals he couched in such antitheses as, "Ask not what your country can do for you, ask what you can do for your country." The brinksmanship diplomacy practiced during the Kennedy administration produced a corresponding rhetoric. Kennedy's speech during the Berlin crisis, in which he solemnly identified with the citizens of Berlin by declaring "Ich bin ein Berliner," and his arms quarantine of Cuba speech during the Cuban missile crisis are two examples in this genre.

The civil rights movement of the 1950s and 1960s brought before the public concerns that had been expressed earlier in the century by such articulate spokespersons for the cause of black Americans as W. E. B. Du Bois and Anna Howard Shaw. The rhetoric of nonviolence coupled with a symbolically persuasive civil disobedience accelerated the civil rights movement and resulted in a new level of equality for more than a fifth of the American population and a more just society for all Americans.

The escalation of the war in Vietnam resulted in a generation of protest rhetoric from outside and within the political establishment. It brought the political career of even so consummate a politician as Lyndon Johnson to an end. The antiestablishment sentiment that arose in response to the Vietnam War was given added dimension by blacks, Hispanics, and women who spoke out for greater social equality. Chicano leaders such as Cesar Chavez and women's rights advocates Ti-Grace Atkinson, Betty Friedan, Shirley Chisholm, and Barbara Jordan made their voices heard in a socially turbulent decade.

Richard Nixon divided the nation further by blaming antiwar protestors for the administration's failure to negotiate an end to the war. His speeches on the

Vietnam War were classic examples of the divisive scapegoating that was the hallmark of his political rhetoric. Waging his second campaign on the theme of law and order, Nixon inadvertently established the basis for the ironic assessment of his own moral conduct as the Watergate hearings headed by Sam Ervin unfolded evidence that the Watergate Hotel break-in was sanctioned at the "highest level."

Jimmy Carter reclaimed the presidency for the Democratic party by running against the Washington establishment and promising to bring morality back to government. But Carter did not realize that the promise of morality was a necessary, but not a sufficient, condition for leadership. Once in office, he failed to adapt his rhetoric and create an inspiring vision for the future of the nation. Portentously he confessed in his Inaugural Address that he had no new dream to present, and his presidential rhetoric dwelled pessimistically on the nation's mounting economic and foreign policy problems, punctuated by the Iranian hostage situation.

Most recently a rhetoric based on more conservative and traditional American values has appealed to the public by challenging some of the tenets of the New Deal and the Great Society. Ronald Reagan, dubbed the "great communicator," has articulated his conservative ideology with remarkable success. Reagan has benefited greatly from the support of a group of preachers and politicians who together form the leadership of the new religious Right. Anticommunist evangelists of the 1950s such as Billy Hargis set the stage for the intermingling of religion and politics in the political sermons of Jerry Falwell and Jesse Helms.

Although the Democratic party seems as emasculated in the 1980s as the Republican party did in the wake of Watergate a decade ago, Mario Cuomo's performance as keynote speaker at the 1984 Democratic National Convention suggests that a compelling speech can still be made in the interests of liberalism. And Jesse Jackson's presidential campaign revealed that the highly charged rhetoric of a minority leader can once again attract a national constituency.

Who in surveying the course of American politics and civic life during this century cannot be struck by the importance of oratory? Although the media have affected the nature of oratory, it seems plain that the most important political symbols are still contained in speeches. That oratory has changed as society has changed simply provides evidence of its durability. Although there are other means to effect political change besides oratory, a skillful orator and sometimes a single speech can alter the course of historical events or the personal destiny of the speaker.

By examining the most significant speeches of recent history, one learns a great deal about the spirit of the times, the speakers, and their audiences. The analysis and criticism of oratory reveals both the timely and the universal appeals that move people. Rhetorical theorist Chaim Perelman observed that to understand an audience, one must know how to persuade them. In studying public address, one comes to understand the nature of historical audiences, and, to the extent that all audiences are moved by similar passions, logical sensibilities, and ideas, one learns a great deal about human nature—a key purpose of any humanistic study.

The second major concern of this introductory essay is to explain our design for the book and to discuss the basic rhetorical concepts that inform most of the essays. This book is about twentieth-century American orators and their orations. It places before the researcher a rich repository of rhetorical essays. Each essay, written as an encyclopedia article, reveals the essentials about the speaker's oratorical career and provides the information necessary for further scholarship. In analyzing their subjects, the contributors offer rhetorical explanations that use both history and the theory of persuasion to lay the groundwork for understanding the orators and their persuasive discourse.

To assemble a book with entries that fit our design, we asked the contributors to write case studies. In the main, we believe the case study is the best means of revealing the rhetorical relationship of the speaker, the speech, and the audience. In this book, the case study approach is actually applied at two levels. At the broader level, the essayists have produced fifty-eight case studies on prominent American orators. Within each of these studies, one will discover many abbreviated case studies of the orators' most important addresses. The speaker entries conform to a consistent format and analysis. They open with brief introductions, which place the orators in historical perspective by emphasizing their oratorical training, the causes they espoused, the general effects of their rhetoric, and whether they contributed to the theory and practice of rhetoric. The core of each essay is a critical examination of each individual's speaking. This criticism is based primarily on a close reading of the most important speech texts and is often supported by illustrative quotations from the speeches themselves, which convey a sense of the orator's own language. As appropriate, each essayist considers rhetorical topics such as the orator's persuasive techniques, style, and delivery, as well as how the speeches were prepared and whether the orator utilized speech writers. Whenever possible, the critics assess the speaker's impact on the American social, legal, and political scene and discuss causes and movements that figured prominently in the speaker's oratory. Each essay closes with a summary evaluation of the orator's negative or salutary influence on American values and democracy.

The essayists employ a variety of rhetorical explanations in these case studies. Especially for the readers who are not specialists in rhetoric, it is useful to summarize this theory since it has provided the basic questions that virtually all of the entries address. Many of the entries reflect a neo-Aristotelian approach to rhetorical criticism based on Aristotle's *Rhetoric*, written around 325 B.C. The perspective of critics who use Aristotle's theories is distilled in his famous declaration: ''Rhetoric may be defined as the faculty of observing in any given case the available means of persuasion'' (1355b26). Accordingly, a neo-Aristotelian critic is concerned about the nature of the speaker's arguments, the *logos* or logical appeals, the *pathos* or the attempts to stir the audience's emotions, and finally the means the speaker employed to enhance the audience's perception of his goodwill, good sense, and good moral character—for these comprise Aristotle's conception of *ethos*, or the proof of the speaker's character. Also traceable to Aristotle is the critic's attempt to assess the relative success or failure of the speaker's persuasive efforts: did the speaker employ the appropriate means of persuasion? If the modern reader does not put too fine a point upon it, Aristotle's division of oratory into three branches is useful in delineating the kinds of orations twentieth-century orators delivered.

Deliberative oratory denotes legislative or political speaking in a sense widely cast. Many of the orators examined in this book figured prominently in political oratory at the state and national levels, from governorships to Congress to the White House. Other orators never sought elective office, but the activists and demagogues, as well as the advocates for civil rights and for racism, were orators in the best or worst traditions of deliberative speaking, which "urges us either to do or not to do something" (1358b9). Forensic speaking, the oratory of the courtroom, is represented by several figures who achieved prominence because of their advocacy or defense of causes or who started their careers as effective advocates at the bar before they advanced to the political arena. Indeed many of these forensic speakers gained valuable speaking and training experiences in collegiate debate.

Aristotle's third division of oratory is *epideictic*, denoting discourse of praise or blame. Such ceremonial discourse often displays the speaker's virtuosity and in many instances celebrates the values that undergird and sustain society. An after-dinner speech, a Fourth of July oration, or a speech honoring those who fell in battle are loose modern equivalents. As useful as Aristotle's categories are in understanding the types and purposes of oratory, they tend to fracture in the face of modern oratorical practice. Aristotle did not account for pulpit persuasions, which are discussed in this book, or such distinctive forms of oratory as the presidential inaugural address, which uses the occasion of ceremonial speaking but seeks the purposes of deliberative oratory. The point is not whether Aristotle's tripartite division of oratory accurately portrays the practice of persuasion in the twentieth century but whether it aids in classifying and clarifying the kinds of oratory treated in this book, and it usually does so acceptably well.

Other essays suggest the influences of Cicero and Quintilian, who are to the Roman tradition in rhetoric what Aristotle is to the Greek tradition. Cicero, followed by Quintilian, spoke of the five classical canons of rhetoric, whose exact origins are obscure. Each canon, or rule, dealt with an important aspect of rhetorical theory and practice. *Inventio*, or invention, described the process by which the speaker brought into being the words and ideas of the speech. *Dispositio*, disposition or arrangement, denoted how the speaker arranged the arguments to achieve the best effect. Cicero recommended an introduction to stimulate the audience's attention and allay their prejudices, a narrative of facts pertinent to the case that could be used to put the audience in a receptive mood, a division to state the speaker's thesis and establish the elements of his argument, a confirmation that supplied the proof, a refutation that anticipated and attacked opposing arguments and a conclusion to arouse the audience to belief or action. For example, Richard Nixon effectively deployed the Ciceronian pattern of *dispositio* in his famous "My Side of the Story" speech in 1952. *Elocutio* was the style of the speech. Franklin D. Roosevelt's war message, Martin Luther King's "I Have a Dream" speech and John F. Kennedy's Inaugural Address exemplify how *elocutio* can be shaped by metaphor, analogy, antithesis, rhetorical rhythm and rhyme, vivid imagery, alliteration, assonance, and anaphora. *Memoria* referred to the orator's ability to remember the oration and the mental process of relying on images to help invigorate ideas and facilitate the flow of words. The use modern speakers make of the teleprompter underscores the importance—without giving the appearance of doing so—of this classical canon. When Ronald Reagan addressed Britain's Parliament, some members were amazed by his lack of reliance on a written speech text until they realized that what they thought to be protective shields were teleprompters. *Actio* reflected the need to attend to the delivery of the speech. It embraced such concerns as gestures, platform appearance and bearing—Cicero cautioned orators not to expectorate in public—voice management, and the importance of eye contact with the audience. The vestiges of Cicero's and Quintilian's rhetorical theories can be discerned in several entries.

The utilization of ghost writers, which concerns some critics of rhetoric more than others, is not a modern phenomenon. During the Golden Age of Athens (the fifth to fourth century B.C.), a group of men functioned as logographers, literally "word writers," or speech writers. Antiphon and Lysias plied this trade with remarkable adaptations to the individual nature of their clients and, although he avoided mentioning it in his rhetorical writings, Isocrates was also an important and effective logographer. To suggest further the public awareness and fascination with the practice, Asphasia, Pericles' mistress, was reputed to have written the funeral oration he delivered. More typically, logographers were hired for a fee to compose speeches for their clients to use in the Athenian courts. Like their modern counterparts, the speech writers were handsomely paid, did not deliver the speeches themselves, and circumspectly eschewed the political limelight. When appropriate, contributors to this book have assayed the extent to which the speakers wrote their own speeches or relied on the help of speech writers.

Modern rhetorical theorists such as Kenneth Burke, Richard Weaver, and Chaim Perelman have added to the richness of rhetorical writings both in reflecting on classical theory and in applying completely new approaches. Modern contributions to rhetorical theory are too numerous and varied to be easily summarized. But the individual essays comprising this book do offer examples of how modern rhetorical theory can help one analyze and interpret contemporary oratory.

Following the critical rhetorical essay is the "Information Sources" section. This section supplies the sources the researchers used in writing their essays and serves as a research aid. In "Research Collections and Collected Speeches," the first subdivision of "Information Sources," each essayist identifies and discusses major speech resources pertaining to the speaker. The books, anthologies, and collected works in which complete and authoritative speech texts may be found are listed; these collections and works are coded with an abbreviation so that the locations of the speech texts can be indicated easily. In "Selected Critical Studies," each researcher lists critical essays, case studies, and theses and dissertations that shed significant light on the related speech activities of the orators. Frequently one or more of these important studies is written by the author of the entry. In "Selected Biographies," each researcher delineates the works illuminating the speaker's persuasive practices. The entry closes with "Chronology of Major Speeches." These speeches are coded and cross-referenced with the anthologies and other sources of speeches listed in "Research Collections and Collected Speeches." The speeches that comprise the chronology are discussed in the entry and form the core materials for the essay.

A chapter on Basic Research Sources in American Public Address and A Glossary of Rhetorical Terms appear at the end of the book. The glossary defines classical and technical speech terms, as well as modern rhetorical terminology, which may not be encountered in general parlance.

The Contributors List describes the professional association, teaching duties, and relevant publications of the contributors. Since in some cases the contributors indicate in the bibliography that they possess such useful research materials as voice recordings and speech texts that may not be readily obtained, they consented to help those researchers who may wish to contact them for special assistance.

Two main principles guided the selection of speakers included in this book. Within space constraints, we attempted to match a list of speakers we wished to have covered with those scholars who were best equipped and qualified to write the essays. Among the most important considerations that led us to include some lesser-known figures were: the existence of enough speech texts, critical studies, and secondary works, which in turn suggested the degree of previous scholarly interest in an individual orator. Thus four general classes of speakers are included in this book. First, we included Theodore Roosevelt and Woodrow Wilson and then all of the presidents from Herbert Hoover forward. The other presidents were excluded not because they did not merit rhetorical attention but because of one or more of the pragmatic considerations discussed above. Second, we endeavored to include great congressional speakers who eloquently addressed the important issues of their day. Third, we tried to include a variety of individuals from among the ranks of citizens who did not attain high offices but whose voices are well remembered for their impact. In general we tried to include only speakers who attracted national attention. A panoply of people are thus represented: socialists, feminists, advocates for civil rights and black power, for the Right and the Left, populists, activists, demagogues, and segregationalists. Fourth, we included a spectrum of representative religious figures. If, therefore, one does not find within these pages one's favorite orator, we ask consideration of Benjamin Franklin's appeal at the Constitutional Convention of 1787: "On the whole, sir, I can not help expressing a wish that every member of the convention who may still have objection to it, would, with me, on this occasion, doubt a little of his own infallibility, and to make manifest our unanimity, put his name to this instrument."

American Orators
of the
Twentieth Century

SPIRO THEODORE AGNEW
(1918–   ), thirty-ninth vice-president of the United States

BERNARD L. BROCK

Agnew was an outspoken, paradoxical politician who advanced by being in the right place at the right time. In high school, he was shy and did not participate in sports or any other school activities, though he received good grades and was considered intelligent. He showed a flair for rhetoric and wrote speeches for his father, who was active in Baltimore's Greek community. After high school, Agnew studied chemistry at Johns Hopkins University for three years before he dropped out and enrolled in Baltimore Law School. In 1941 he was drafted into the army. His career there was not outstanding except that he began to show signs of leadership by acting decisively under pressure. After the war, he completed law school and held a number of jobs, including private law practice. Agnew, who unlike his father had not been involved in the Greek community, switched from the Democratic to the Republican party and in 1957 was appointed to the zoning board of appeals in Baltimore County.

His performance in this initiated a pattern: he would gain an office and perform well; become controversial and lose support; and finally move to a higher position. This pattern was surprising since he was in a state and county where Democrats outnumbered Republicans three to one, but he always opposed a Democrat after the party had experienced a divisive primary campaign. In this manner Agnew moved from county zoning board to county executive, to governor, and finally to vice-president. On October 10, 1973, however, this pattern was broken; Agnew resigned as vice-president and pleaded *nolo contendere* to accepting cash payments for construction contracts while in office both in Maryland and Washington. Agnew passed from the public eye, having left behind a stormy political career.

SPIRO AGNEW AS CONTROVERSIAL POLITICAL PERSUADER

Through his electric speaking style and his understanding of the media's role in political communication, Spiro Agnew became a controversial political figure. Early in his career, Agnew discovered that he gained public and media support because he spoke better than his opponents. On one occasion when Agnew and his opponent, a poor speaker, were at the same meeting, Agnew confronted him and forced a brief exchange in front of reporters. This and other experiences demonstrated that Agnew recognized the importance of media coverage. In 1960, after running last in a five-candidate race for judge, he observed that he had ultimately benefited in that he never could have bought $50,000 worth of coverage for the $5,000 his campaign had cost. Further, Governor Agnew lunched regularly with important reporters and tried out new ideas to influence their coverage and to assess their reactions.

Agnew's work on the county zoning board of appeals should have provided an early warning of the course of his political career. He frequently challenged established members, asked embarrassing questions and demanded that past practices be changed. The alienation Agnew created for himself among Democrats, however, was offset by public attention. He continued this pattern in 1960 when he decided to run against three sitting judges at a time when such a maneuver was politically unacceptable. He did this against the advice of his closest friends. Two factors—his uncompromising nature and impatience to get ahead—appeared to lead Agnew into turbulent political controversies.

In his next position, as Baltimore county executive, Agnew's strong desire for personal control brought about further controversy. Civil rights and urban renewal were central issues. In 1963, civil rights demonstrations found their way to Baltimore County to integrate the Gwynn Oak Amusement Park. Agnew's position was that the demonstrators were "morally right" but should wait for legislation to handle the matter. Lippman reports that he said, "I urge mature consideration of the desirability of a peaceful transition period . . . we need a calm dispassionate approach to these changes lest there be setbacks to gains that are imminent." The ultimate resolution was to Agnew's credit. Through personal intervention and negotiation, the park was integrated, demonstrations were held to a minimum, and charges filed against people were dropped.

With the issue of urban renewal, Agnew was less successful. He proposed a bond issue with matching federal funds to renew a rundown section of black housing. He insisted that private enterprise could not undertake such a large rejuvenation project, and he continued to push this project though it went against the feelings of his constituency, who feared it would bring more blacks into the community. Agnew was controversial because he had to implement his plan and could not compromise with his opponents. While county executive, Agnew's stormy leadership continued, and controversy increased. Confrontation was beginning to characterize the leadership he had advanced by his abrupt speaking style and his ability to capture headlines.

In 1967 while governor of Maryland, Agnew's approach to politics became evident as crises intensified. He had been elected governor with the support of liberals and blacks against a racist Democrat, and generally he had a liberal record on fiscal reform, air and water pollution, crime, urban renewal, and support to black schools. But when students from Bowie College, who had come to the capital to discuss the rundown college conditions, refused to leave at the end of the day, Agnew, who had not met with them because they had bypassed the college president, had them arrested for failing to leave a public building at closing time. This reaction to a technical violation of law provided a hint to his response in April 1968 after four days of fires and looting following the Martin Luther King, Jr., assassination.

When Baltimore calmed down, a furious Agnew assembled the city's major black leaders to remind them of their civic responsibilities. Agnew started by saying he did not bring them there for "the assignment of blame and excuses." He then accused them of indirectly supporting "a reckless stranger to this city, carrying the credentials of a well-known civil rights organization [who] characterized the Baltimore police as 'enemies of the black man.' " He argued, "Those fires were kindled at the suggestion of the advocate of violence." Agnew continued his attack: "Tell me one constructive achievement that has flowed from the madness of the two priests of violence, Stokely Carmichael and Rap Brown. They do not build—they demolish." Only half of the black leaders remained to hear Agnew conclude with the challenge, "Let us publicly and promptly renounce any who counsel or condone violence." Agnew, who had attacked the political Right in his campaign for governor, was now attacking those who had elected him. He had gained a reputation for being liberal, but his pers   onal rigidity and his absolute law and order position not only made him appear conservative but also undermined his support with the electorate, making it impossible for him to run successfully for reelection as governor. This was never challenged because before his term ended, Agnew had been elected vice-president to Richard Nixon.

In his new position, Agnew frequently found himself in the center of controversy, diverting attention away from Nixon's problems. Just as in 1960 Nixon had attacked Eisenhower's enemies, in the 1968 presidential campaign Agnew attacked candidates Hubert Humphrey and George Wallace and emphasized the issues of law and order and Vietnam. The first crisis centered around Agnew's reply when reporters asked if he had been assigned to take the hard line. Lippman reports that Agnew responded, "It's all relative, if one is soft on communism and law and order, maybe the other man looks hard line. When I see this peace-at-any-cost line, Mr. Humphrey looks a lot like Neville Chamberlain and that makes Mr. Nixon look like Winston Churchill." Agnew's set speeches were effective, but his off-the-cuff comments, such as "squishy soft on communism," "if you've seen one slum, you've seen them all," and "the fat Jap," attracted controversy to Agnew and potentially undermined his effectiveness. Nixon, however, who had felt Eisenhower had not adequately supported him, frequently told Agnew he was doing a good job. Appropriately, the campaign climaxed with an editorial attack from the *New York Times* and Agnew's response. The *Times* said Agnew was unfit to be vice-president because of "clear and repeated conflicts of interest." Agnew vehemently denied the charge and demanded a retraction. Richard Nixon and Spiro Agnew's dramatically close election quieted the storm for a brief period while he assumed vice-presidential duties.

After the election and inauguration, Agnew maintained a low profile. During this period, he was the administration's spokesman on a variety of issues: problems of the cities, aid to colleges, the space program, the Vietnam War, welfare, and school busing. Little attention was focused on him personally, partially because his rhetoric was less strident but also because this was the test period for the Nixon administration. But Agnew soon would move to the center of the Vietnam controversy as he defended Nixon's policy and diverted attention away from Nixon himself.

In October 1969, the national debate over Vietnam policy intensified, and antiwar critics called a "Moratorium Day," a symbol for increased rejection of Nixon's Vietnam policy. Immediately Agnew led the administration's counter-attack. In "Masochism versus the Facts," Agnew charged that "a spirit of national masochism prevails, encouraged by an effete corps of impudent snobs who characterize themselves as intellectuals." His rhetoric followed the harsh, judgmental style found in his speeches after Martin Luther King's assassination and during the presidential campaign. Agnew received strong criticism from antiwar protestors as well as Democratic and Republican senators, but when he received support from President Nixon, he followed his speech one week later with "Impudence in the Streets." Agnew's rhetoric now escalated in intensity as he condemned "merchants of hate," "parasites of passion," and "ideological eunuchs" and adopted a scapegoat strategy: "We can . . . afford to separate them [antiwar leaders] from our society—with no more regret than we should feel over discarding rotten apples from a barrel." Agnew advanced the administration's Vietnam policy until November 3, 1969, when President Nixon presented on national television his policy of Vietnamizing the war.

Nixon's speech was followed by commentary from network guests whom Agnew thought hostile toward the president and his policy, so Agnew escalated his attack. On November 13, 1969, in his speech "The Responsibility of Television," Agnew blasted the networks: "And in the networks' endless pursuit of controversy, we should ask what is the end value—to enlighten or to profit?" He diverted attention away from the Nixon administration when he said, "Perhaps the place to start looking for a credibility gap is not in the offices of the government in Washington, but in the studios of the networks in New York." Agnew closed, "We would never trust such power over public opinion in the hands of an elected government." Agnew received attacks from all quarters, but at the same time Nixon's popularity increased. So on November 20, 1969, in "The Power of the Press," he extended his criticism to the press: "I am merely raising these questions so that the American people will become aware of . . . growing monopolization of the voices of public opinion on which we all depend—for our knowledge and for the basis of our views." Agnew focused his attack on the *New York Times* and *Washington Post*. He was no longer attacking radical youth but had brought into the controversy a major institution of society, the media, in his effort to divert attention away from Nixon and his Vietnam policy. Nixon was obviously interested in Agnew's campaign because Pat Buchanan, the president's media specialist, worked with Agnew throughout this period. An important sign of Agnew's success was the fact that television commentary following Nixon's speeches was reduced, and newspapers were less critical of his policies.

In 1970 as the midterm election approached, Agnew assumed the role of attacking Nixon's critics and defending his policies. When Senators Mark Hatfield and George McGovern introduced an amendment to end the Vietnam war, Agnew labeled it a "blueprint for the first defeat in history of the United States and for chaos and communism for the future of South Vietnam." Agnew continued to operate in the center of Nixon's administration and became a major element in maintaining congressional support after the election. He did this by labeling administration critics "rad-libs." Agnew also argued that partisan and divisive campaigns are fundamental to the political process. After the 1970 campaign, Agnew again slipped into the background.

Agnew once more became the center of controversy and briefly diverted attention away from the president's problems. As the Watergate scandal began to envelop Richard Nixon's presidency, rumors circulated that Agnew was under criminal investigation. Agnew strongly denied the allegations until on October 18, 1973, he pleaded *nolo contendere* to accepting cash payments for construction contracts. Agnew, who had left behind a series of political controversies, could no longer shield President Nixon and his policies, and he moved into private life.

INFORMATION SOURCES

Research Collections and Collected Speeches

No library contains all of Agnew's papers and speeches. The National Archives has his vice-presidential papers, and the *Congressional Record* includes his official statements while vice-president. The *Baltimore Sun* and the *New York Times* provided fairly complete coverage of his political career in Baltimore and as vice-president.

Agnew: The Coming of a Household Word. Edited by Robert W. Peterson.   A
    New York: Facts on File, 1972.
Coyne, John R. *The Impudent Snobs: Agnew vs. the Intellectual Establish-*   IS
    ment. New Rochelle, N.Y.: Arlington House, 1972.
Frankly Speaking. Ed. Spiro T. Agnew. Washington D.C.: Public Affairs   FS
    Press, 1972.
Lucas, Jim G. *Agnew: Profile in Conflict.* New York: Charles Scribner's   APC
    Sons, 1970.

Selected Critical Studies

Brock, Bernard L. "Spiro Agnew's Diversionary Rhetoric." *Speaker and Gavel* 7 (1970):
    85–86.
King, Andrew A., and Anderson, Floyd Douglas. "Nixon, Agnew, and the 'Silent
    Majority': A Case Study in the Rhetoric of Polarization." *Western Speech* 35
    (1971): 243–55.

Lowry, Dennis T. "Agnew and the Network TV News: Before/After Content Analysis." *Journalism Quarterly* 48 (1971): 205–10.

Meyer, Timothy F., and Cronen, Vernon E. "Agnew Meets the Student Dissenters: An Experimental Study of Ego-Involvement and Argumentation." *Journal of Communication* 22 (1972): 263–76.

Mowe, Rebecca. "Student Dissidents: Strategic Role in Nixon's Consensus Style." *Speaker and Gavel* 8 (1970): 8–12.

Selected Biographies

Agnew, Spiro T. *Go Quietly . . . or Else*. New York: William Morrow, 1980.

Albright, Joseph. *What Makes Spiro Run*. New York: Dodd, Mead, 1972.

Cohen, Richard M., and Witcover, Jules. *A Heartbeat Away*. New York: Viking Press, 1974.

Lippman, Theo, Jr. *Spiro Agnew's America*. New York: W. W. Norton, 1972.

Marsh, Robert. *Agnew the Unexamined Man: A Political Profile*. New York: Random House, 1972.

Witcover, Jules. *White Knight: The Rise of Spiro Agnew*. New York: Random House, 1972.

CHRONOLOGY OF MAJOR SPEECHES

See "Research Collections and Collected Speeches" for source codes.

"Black Leaders of Baltimore," Baltimore, April 11, 1968; *APC*, pp. 54–60.

"Masochism versus the Facts," New Orleans, Louisiana, October 19, 1969; *A*, pp. 40–47; *IS*, pp. 248–53; *FS*, pp. 25–36; *APC*, pp. 109–11.

"Impudence in the Streets," Harrisburg, Pennsylvania, October 30, 1969; *A*, pp. 49–53; *IS*, pp. 257–61; *FS*, pp. 44–51.

"The Responsibility of Television," Des Moines, Iowa, November 13, 1969; *A*, pp. 55–61; *IS*, pp. 265–70; *FS*, pp. 63–72.

"The Power of the Press," Montgomery, Alabama, November 20, 1969; *A* pp. 65–70; *IS*, pp. 270–74; *FS*, pp.78–88.

"Blueprint for Defeat," Miami Beach, Florida, August 17, 1970; *A*, pp. 113–16; *IS*, pp. 252–55.

"Definition of 'Radical-Liberal,' " Albuquerque, New Mexico, September 15,1970; *A*, pp. 125–29; *IS*, pp. 374–78.

TI-GRACE ATKINSON
(1939–   ), radical feminist

_____ BEATRICE K. REYNOLDS

Ti-Grace Atkinson is a political theorist and orator of the women's movement. She identified issues for the movement such as abortion, sex, and lesbianism, and she related these to the theory of women's oppression she espoused in her speeches. As an active participant in the National Organization for Women (NOW) since 1967 and the Feminists, a radical organization she helped found in 1968, she soon became disillusioned with the movement and was one of its most avid critics. Prompted by what she considered ideological conflicts and value differences, she resigned in October 1968 as president of the New York chapter of NOW and subsequently from all her other elected offices in NOW. Her disillusionment with the leaders and the leadership of the Feminists caused her to resign from that organization in 1970, and in 1971 she quit the Daughters of Bilitis when her friend Ruth Simpson was forced from the presidency.

As a critic of the movement, she attacked the goals of NOW as well as some of the feminists whom she called "phonies." She saw the movement in 1968 as "low-class intellectually" because it was more concerned with opportunism than equal employment rights for women. Four years later, she said that the movement was nonexistent since it had accomplished nothing. On January 4, 1971, she told the Daughters of Bilitis in New York City at the dedication of the first Lesbian Center in America in her speech "Strategy and Tactics: A Presentation of Political Lesbianism" that "the movement itself, so far, has neither demonstrated itself as political nor organized itself to effect major change."

ATKINSON AS PERSUADER

As a speaker, Atkinson exerted influence on the feminist movement rather than on the public. A prescient feminist, she made abortion a key issue. She politicized sex and invented the concepts of radical feminism and political lesbianism, which helped her develop a theory of the oppression of women and a political position. As a radical feminist, she viewed women as a political class oppressed by men, the enemy, and argued that women's oppression is biologically and psychologically based. Political lesbianism is a concept that postulates the significance of lesbianism to feminism because any woman who chooses to affiliate with other women in an effort to achieve common goals is technically a lesbian. Lesbianism as a sexual choice was another issue in the movement, and Atkinson did not propose that.

Atkinson considered herself a representative of the movement as she thought it ought to be. Her differences with the liberal NOW group, founded in 1966, became more pronounced as the movement advanced into its second stage, which Rosenwasser had labeled action and reaction. NOW was egalitarian in its goals, and women who believed that economic independence would permit them full identity and freedom were drawn into the group. Atkinson defined the goals as political ones. She wanted to effect major change in American society, not just the acquisition of power positions for women or jobs that were held predominantly by men. Thus she clashed with Betty Friedan and other liberal feminists who accused the radical feminists of attempting to take over the movement and of using a man-hating rhetoric and sex-class warfare that prevented women who merely wanted equality from joining NOW. Atkinson was conscious that her goals for the movement differed from those advocated by NOW, so while a member, she qualified her spoken remarks by first stating the general position of the movement and then her own, thus distinguishing the two.

Although she spoke to college students and was a keynote speaker at national conferences, women's groups constituted her chief audiences. Among her most significant speeches were "Abortion: Paper Number II" and "Vaginal Orgasm as a Mass Hysterical Survival Response." She also gave important addresses at Notre Dame University and Catholic University, in which she created such key issues for the movement as abortion and prostitution and in which she politicized sex, feminism, and lesbianism. Her oratorical goal was to persuade women to commit themselves to effect changes in society. She did this through her deliberate selection of subject matter, language, tone, reasoning, proofs, and structure of ideas and arguments. Both her inventive process and organization reflected her academic background and professional training in the fine arts and philosophy. For example, she often made the analogy of the artist to his or her art in order to explicate concepts otherwise difficult for the audience to comprehend. In "Abortion: Paper Number II," she defined the reproduction function of a woman as the "only innate function which distinguishes women from men." She discussed that function as "property" and explained it by using the example of the sculptor and "his capacity to sculpture": "The sculptor controls the function [sculpturing]: he can choose not to exercise it at all; he can experiment with it . . . ; he can destroy a work in process of the operation of his capacity upon it; he can complete a work." Her skills in philosophical reasoning are easily recognized in the tightly structured arguments she used in her speeches, especially when she developed her conceptual analysis of the sex role theory of women's oppression. Once the audience had become more enlightened on feminist issues, her tasks as a speaker changed, for then she was able to develop other aspects of the movement, and, in doing so, her speeches became less philosophical argumentatively and freer stylistically.

The political analysis of the oppression of women was her major subject. She developed different aspects of her theory in each of the speeches she delivered since she began speaking in 1967, including those previously mentioned and others such as those given at Juniata College and the University of Rhode Island. Her themes were patriarchy or the male domination of women and political institutions that reinforced the female role: motherhood, sexual intercourse, family, marriage, love, and religion. These institutions, she argued, should be destroyed because they perpetuate the oppression of women. Her strategy was to make men and male behavior the enemy. She also attacked what people accepted as American cultural values, and she violated the belief and value systems of her audiences. As a speaker, Atkinson created dissonance in the minds of the auditors by creating moral conflicts for them. She asked the women not simply to set aside the values they placed on sexual relations, family, marriage, childbearing, and religion but to destroy those institutions. Essentially she asked them to restructure their value hierarchies, an extremely difficult task for many women to accomplish since so many were traditionalists bound to the value system they had been conditioned to accept. Because of her radical position as a political activist in the movement, Atkinson was considered a militant feminist.

Atkinson made abortion a key issue in the movement. When she spoke in 1967 to the National NOW Conference in Washington, D.C., on abortion, she argued that the reproductive function and the fetus were the property of the woman. Liberty and freedom of choice for a woman to determine her life were the major issues; thus any interference with that property was unconstitutional. As president of the New York chapter of NOW, she seized the opportunity to popularize the abortion issue when she spoke at the Governor's Commission for the Study of Abortion on February 29, 1968. Reproduction as an issue was crucial to the development of the sex role theory of the oppression of women, for it was the woman's capacity to bear children that defined her role as a person.

Two months later, she addressed her first public audience, which included males and females, at the National Committee on Human Rights, in Philadelphia on April 5, 1968. The committee had asked her to speak on sex. In "Vaginal Orgasm as a Mass Hysterical Survival Response," she shocked her audience because she not only spoke publicly on the taboo subject of sexual intercourse but also argued that sexual relations were yet another way for men to oppress and exploit women. The language she used was atypical of her other speeches and was considered unfeminine by some, but she believed it appropriately described the situation.

Her college speeches illustrate her audience analysis techniques because she found it more difficult to speak to youthful groups who could not easily identify with oppression and who did not understand feminist issues. She solved the rhetorical problem of making feminism relevant to college women by personalizing much of the information in tone, choice of language, ideas, topics, and examples. She explicated feminism in relation to her theory of oppression by using current examples, drawn from her own experiences and from those of college women, and by providing the necessary background information on the movement, which served as a context in which she could develop her themes.

Her speech at the University of Rhode Island, "Movement Politics and Other Sleights of Hand," on March 4, 1970, is an excellent example of her audience adaptation technique. She first traced the movement from its inception in 1966 to the present by highlighting the issues and citing the women's organizations that had formed to pursue goals left unfulfilled by NOW; she then presented her theory of women's oppression, which she developed more fully in this address. In her closing remarks, she told the students, "You can't survive within marriage, and you can barely subsist outside of it. In fact, you have no choice at all, a fact which more and more women daily are acting upon. You can only organize. . . . I also want to mention some of the instances of extensions of women's oppression in your own situation." She then discussed the situation by posing rhetorical questions about the university's segregation policies that discriminated against women. She concluded her speech with an account of an Amazon legend, from which she drew morals.

Atkinson spoke at other colleges, including Juniata College, where she first discussed political lesbianism in "The Sacrificial Lambs." A year later, she returned as a guest of the philosophy department. Her Juniata II series of speeches in early 1970 are important because they exemplify not only her ability to adapt to youthful audiences but also her strategies and techniques as a feminist orator who could persuade by being informative. Atkinson gained the most notoriety by delivering speeches at Notre Dame University on October 15, 1970, and at Catholic University on March 10, 1971. At Notre Dame, her attack on the Catholic church, which was interpreted as questioning the virginity of the Virgin Mary, created such a furor that Catholic University president Clarence C. Walton banned her from speaking on the college grounds in Washington, D.C. In a court contest over free speech versus the church's right to determine its speakers, a battle the student government won, Atkinson thus was permitted to speak by court order. Addressing an audience of about 800, she discussed her controversial speech and then attacked the church for collaborating with fascism. She concluded the speech with five indictments against the church—murder, conspiracy, enslavement, prostitution, and rape—and to each she repeatedly responded "Guilty!" In the midst of the address when she made remarks about the speech she gave at Notre Dame University, a member of the audience walked up the aisle and unsuccessfully attempted to slap her. Atkinson used this incident to plead with her audience for sympathy.

Atkinson projected prostitution into the movement when she spoke to some 200 women in New York City for the National Conference on Christians and Jews on May 28, 1970. She was applauded when she told the audience that they should "support the prostitutes as a model of the new independent woman" and that "the prostitutes were the most honest women left in America" because they "charge for services rather than submitting to marriage contracts which force them to work for life without pay." Prostitution, she argued, was a political institution because "it is a false alternative posed by men for women to the female role." It served as a "political symbol" to the traditional role of female, which historically was the only profession available to unattached women, and furthermore, it was vital to any economic and political analysis of the "structure of the male-female relationship." Critics questioned whether her statements about prostitutes alienated women or built the movement.

More that 500 women came out to "Speak for Change," sponsored by the Older Women's Liberation (OWL) at Marymount Manhattan College, New York City, on June 2, 1972. In an ad-lib version of her written text, "The Older Woman a Stockpile of Losses," Atkinson called older women the "garbage of society" and asked why the movement had not wanted to deal with them; rather, she argued that older women were essential to the women's movement for their leadership and for their ability to help effect change in society.

Atkinson's rhetoric was specifically feminist, which is unlike other genres of public discourse. It was rhetoric designed to shock the audience in terms of subject matter, ideas, issues, and language and to create moral conflict. Unlike other feminist orators, she did not dwell on the history of the first feminist wave, and she dismissed the suffragists for failing to deal with political institutions such as marriage, sex, motherhood, and their relationship to equality. Essentially equality cannot exist until those institutions are abolished. In her speech "The Equality Issue," she told the Juniata College audience that the suffragist movement was "racist" and "class structured." Unlike other feminists, she did not use the analogy of blacks to women in order to argue that women were slaves. However, like many other feminist speakers and writers, she spoke from personal experiences, such as her arrest in 1972, and about contemporary events involving college students. In "Violence in the Women's Movement," August 4, 1971, she mentioned the assassination of gangster Joseph Columbo in part of her speech by referring to him as a "sister."

Atkinson was not a trained orator, but she learned the art through experience. She also learned the importance of audience analysis and adaptation and what goals she could accomplish in a restricted period of time. Utilizing her knowledge and training as a writer and artist, she always thought about the rhetorical choices she made in developing her speeches, which she prepared by writing with a critical eye toward the ideas and arguments, structure, language, and tone. Although she wrote her speeches, she usually set aside her texts and extemporized. Her soft, well-modulated, clear, calm voice, and genteel manner of speech were antithetical to her radical subject matter and her treatment of it.

Atkinson found herself in a paradoxical situation: she was a feminist orator in a movement she thought was nonexistent, nonpolitical, and not dedicated to effecting major change. Nonetheless, she successfully created critical issues for the movement and thus effected change in it. Whereas she was successful as a political persuader, she was a failure because she was unable to convince her audience to change their deeply rooted beliefs and value systems in order to take the action she advocated. She criticized members of the movement for being "low-class intellectually," yet she addressed them as though they valued logical reasoning. Hers was a lone voice in the movement, but it was a resounding one.

INFORMATION SOURCES

Research Collections and Collected Speeches

The *New York Times* and the *Washington Post* provide background information regarding the rhetorical situation for some of Atkinson's famous speeches.

Atkinson, Ti-Grace. *Amazon Odyssey*. New York: Links Publishers, 1974.   *AO*

Selected Critical Studies

Campbell, Karlyn Kohrs. "The Rhetoric of Women's Liberation: An Oxymoron." *Quarterly Journal of Speech* 59 (1973): 74–86.
———. "Femininity and Feminism: To Be or Not to Be a Woman." *Communication Quarterly* 31 (1983): 101–07.
Hope, Diane Schaich. "Redefinition of Self: A Comparison of the Rhetoric of the Women's Liberation Movement and Black Liberation Movements." *Today's Speech* 23 (1975): 17–25.
Reynolds, Beatrice K. "An Interview with Ti-Grace Atkinson: Her Speeches and Speechmaking." *Today's Speech* 21 (1973): 3–10.
Rosenwasser, Marie J. "Rhetoric and the Progress of the Women's Liberation Movement." *Today's Speech* 20 (1972): 45–56.

CHRONOLOGY OF MAJOR SPEECHES

See "Research Collections and Collected Speeches" for source codes.

"Abortion: Paper Number II," Washington, D.C., November 18, 1967; *AO*, pp. 1–3.

"Vaginal Orgasm as a Mass Hysterical Survival Response," Philadelphia, April 5, 1968; *AO*, pp. 5–7.

"Juniata I: The Sacrificial Lambs," Huntingdon, Pennsylvania, February 20, 1969; *AO*, pp. 25–37.

"Juniata II: The Equality Issue," Huntingdon, Pennsylvania, February 19, 1970; "Metaphysical Cannibalism or Self-Creativity," February 20, 1970; "Lesbianism and Feminism," February 21, 1970; "The Political Woman," February 21, 1970; *AO*, pp. 65–93.

"Movement Politics and Other Sleights of Hand," Kingston, Rhode Island, March 4, 1970; *AO*, pp. 95–108.

"Individual Responsibility and Human Oppression including Some Notes on Prostitution and Pornography," New York City, May 28, 1970; *AO*, pp. 117–30.

"Strategy and Tactics: A Presentation of Political Lesbianism," New York City, January 4, 1971; *AO*, pp. 135–89.

Speech at Catholic University, Washington, D.C., March 10, 1971; *AO*, pp. 191–97.

"On Violence in the Women's Movement," New York City, August 4, 1971; *AO*, pp. 199–211.

"The Older Woman a Stockpile of Losses," New York City, June 2, 1972; *AO*, pp. 223–26.

ALBERT JEREMIAH BEVERIDGE
(1862–1927), U.S. senator, biographer, Pulitzer Prize winner
MICHAEL DENNIS McGUIRE

Albert J. Beveridge was famous as an orator while yet too young to begin his political career. In school he practiced oratory declaiming from McGuffey's *Readers*, and he polished his delivery perched on tree stumps amid the fields of his family's Illinois farm. To develop his oratorical prowess further, he chose to attend DePauw University (then called Indiana Asbury University), known for the preeminence of its debating and literary societies. Beveridge was so successful in oratorical contests at school that he was invited to make campaign speeches for Indiana Republicans in 1884, a year before he finished college.

In the fall of 1886, he, moved to Indianapolis and joined the law firm of McDonald, Butler, and Mason. While working as a clerk, first for no pay at all, Beveridge taught himself with sufficient speed and ease to be admitted to the bar in 1887. He distinguished himself as a trial lawyer and won national acclaim for his handling of some cases. His success at the bar was attributed not only to his effective, if highly emotional, pleading but to thorough preparation, mastery of legal issues, awesome grasp of details, and capacious memory. He became a famous, energetic, sought-after campaign speaker for Indiana Republicans. Fortuitous circumstances and the calling in of past campaign favors allowed Beveridge to win the Republican nomination for the U.S. Senate in 1899, and the Indiana legislature elected him to that post on January 17 of that year, whence he began the first of his two terms of service.

Although Beveridge was a highly admired and busy ceremonial orator throughout his adult life, his most famous and important speeches are two political orations that presaged his senatorial rhetoric and his political career. In 1898, Beveridge launched the Republican campaigns in Indiana with "The March of the Flag," which brought him considerable favorable national attention. He argued its themes in the causes of Republican candidates in every district of Indiana that fall, and it therefore contributed directly to his election to the Senate the next year. During 1899 Beveridge traveled to the Philippines, and on January 9, 1900, he argued to the Senate in support of his resolution to declare that the Philippines were the property of the United States. These two speeches typify Beveridge's rhetoric. He was the most extreme advocate of U.S. imperialism, and for that he is best remembered.

Beveridge never realized his ambition to be president of the United States and lost his bids to be reelected to the Senate after 1911. He never ceased campaigning for his beliefs, however, and even followed them away from the Republican party to campaign for Theodore Roosevelt's Progressive party. After his role in government was basically over (a fact he never faced), Beveridge turned his talents and energies to scholarly writing, producing the four-volume *Life of John Marshall*, which remains the definitive work on America's first chief justice.

A. J. BEVERIDGE: RHETORICAL STAR OF EMPIRE

A. J. Beveridge was the sole architect of his imperialistic rhetoric. His habit was to work hard on speech texts, revising and polishing them until he was satisfied. He shared his drafts with a group of friends who may have influenced him slightly, but most of his inner circle disclaimed any significant influence. Four people in particular were close to Beveridge and counted as friends and advisers. Novelist David Graham Phillips, who modeled his political novels after Beveridge's life was his confidant and adviser until his untimely death in 1911. Newspaper magnate John C. Shaffer helped Beveridge with strategy even before the 1898 campaign and longed to see Beveridge in the White House. George Perkins, financier and partner of J. P. Morgan, was Beveridge's friend and backer throughout his career. Editor and author Albert Shaw, whose ambitions for U.S. expansion paralleled Beveridge's, was his correspondent, contact person, and a frequent audience and critic for Beveridge's writing. As early as his DePauw years, however, Beveridge developed the habits of rewriting and polishing orations, sometimes for several years, and there is no doubt that his speeches and writing were his own compositions.

Beveridge's stamp is best remembered and most strikingly impressed upon his foreign policy addresses, particularly "The March of the Flag." This speech revealed his flamboyancy: his theatrical, intense delivery and his often outrageous style, which were the quintessence of his rhetorical legacy as most critics have reconstructed it. The speech demonstrated the campaigner, the public persuader, and it contained the theme that shaped all of Beveridge's rhetoric, even his more measured, evidenced arguments in the Senate: the characterization of Americans as God's chosen people on this continent and on other continents by their hegemony. Beveridge believed that Americans were "a people imperial by virtue of their power, by right of their institutions, by authority of their Heaven-directed purposes—the propagandists and not the misers of liberty." He believed in the divinely ordained mission of spreading the American way (as he understood it) across the world. In recommending this mission to Americans, Beveridge relied heavily on two techniques that paved the path for the flag's march.

First, he faced the problem of any other rhetorician attributing God's blessing to the advocacy of his cause. Like other debaters who occasionally lacked proof, he resorted to the rhetorical question as an argumentative technique:

Have we no mission to perform, no duty to discharge to our fellow man? Has God endowed us with gifts beyond our deserts and marked us as the people of His peculiar favor, merely to rot in our selfishness, as men and nations must, who take cowardice for their companion and self for their deity—as China has, as India has, as Egypt has? Shall we be as the man who had one talent and hid it, or as he who had ten talents and used them until they grew to riches? And shall we reap the reward that waits on our discharge of our high duty; shall we occupy new markets for what our farmers raise, our factories make, our merchants sell—aye, and, please God, new markets for what our ships shall carry?

The blend in those questions of the divine with the practical, of high mission with gross national product, exemplifies Beveridge's ability to place a panoply of justifications in rhetorical questions.

Second, Beveridge was not at all abashed by arguing his beliefs with assertions. He enjoyed both rhetorical question and assertion of rectitude to answer practical or principled objections from opponents:

The Opposition tells us that we ought not to govern a people without their consent. I answer, the rule of liberty that all just government derives its authority from the consent of the governed, applies only to those who are capable to self-government. We govern the Indians without their consent, we govern our territories without their consent, we govern our children without their consent. How do they know that our government would be without their consent? Would not the people of the Philippines prefer the just, humane, civilizing government of this Republic to the savage, bloody rule of pillage and extortion from which we have rescued them?

Slightly later he asserted:

They ask us how we shall govern these new possessions. I answer: Out of local conditions and the necessities of each case methods of government will grow. If England can govern foreign lands, so can America. If Germany can govern foreign lands, so can America. If they can supervise protectorates, so can America. Why is it more difficult to administer Hawaii than New Mexico or California? Both had a savage and an alien population; both were more remote from the seat of government when they came under our dominion than the Philippines are today.

In such a fashion, Beveridge dispensed with objections based on practicality and different arguments based on principle. It was a duty to spread liberty by ruling over others, and certainly the United States was needed by those incapable of governing themselves.

Beveridge's purpose was to advocate the further march of the flag and to show its feasibility and its divine approval. He was not blind to other, earthly sanctions, however. For him, the further acquisition of territory was the continuation of U.S. history:

The march of the Flag! In 1789 the flag of the Republic waved over 4,000,000 souls in thirteen states, and their savage territory. . . . The timid minds of that day said that no new territory was needed, and, for the hour, they were right. But Jefferson, through whose intellect the centuries marched; Jefferson, who dreamed of Cuba as an American state; Jefferson, the first Imperialist of the Republic—Jefferson acquired that imperial territory which swept from the Mississippi to the mountains, from Texas to the British possessions, and the march of the flag began! The infidels to the gospel of liberty raved, but the flag swept on!

Beveridge traced the historical acquisitions of territory by the United States, which he viewed as natural, and he noted that there have always been opponents, "but the people's judgment approved the command of their blood, and the march of the flag went on!" He anchored his extremist claims in the mainstream of American thought and policy by connecting his rhetoric to historical precedents and to Thomas Jefferson's ideas. Even in these human, historical connections, Beveridge could not resist using religious allusion and sanction by describing the "infidels to the gospel of liberty" or describing the population as "4,000,000 souls."

At this point, we may observe two characteristic assumptions of Beveridge that have not been highlighted but that occur in "The March of the Flag" and dominate the speeches that remain to be examined. First, Beveridge was a racist who thought of an "Anglo-Saxon impulse" that characterized not only Jefferson but what he referred to as the rest of the American race. Second, he saw correctly that the flag was marching westward, inexorably tramping the path toward Southeast Asia. To the former issue he brought a nineteenth-century understanding; to the latter, a twentieth-century will. His speech in the Senate on Philippine policy in January 1900 perfectly illustrates his rhetoric of foreign policy.

Four months before the Senate convened in January 1900, Beveridge returned from a trip to the Philippines, after which he made no public statements. It was so out of character for him that Beveridge wrote to Perkins and complained that the press had taken to calling him "the Sphinx." But he was remaining true to his character, his cause, and his ambition. He was waiting to shape America's destiny with policy proposed to the Senate and to advance his own political star with rhetoric on the floor. So planned was his performance that he introduced his resolution that the Philippines be declared a territory of the United States on January 4 and stipulated that the motion be tabled until January 9, when he would speak in its behalf. Such behavior seems to justify the charges of some critics that Beveridge's rhetoric was theatrical and contrived. The speech was a highly emotional continuation of themes raised in "The March of the Flag."

Beveridge's romantic racism is clear from the introduction to the conclusion of his speech on the Philippines: "We will not abandon our opportunity in the Orient. We will not renounce our part in the mission of our race. And we will move forward to our work [advancing the march of the flag] . . . with gratitude for a task worthy of our strength, and thanksgiving to Almighty God that He has deemed us worthy of his work." Both historical precedent and fortunate circumstance turn the attention of the United States to the Philippines to see a "*providential* conjunction of all the elements of trade, of duty, and of power." Moreover, Beveridge observed, the past successes of the English in the Pacific show that "our constructing race" is well suited to dominate the region. Further, it is the duty of this superior race to manage the affairs of the Philippines, though some Americans do not grasp this. Hinting at the wisdom he had acquired from personal experience, Beveridge explained: "It will be hard for Americans who have not studied them to understand the people. They are a barbarous race, modified by three centuries of contact with a decadent race. The Filipino is the South Sea Malay, put through a process of three hundred years of dishonesty in dealing, disorder in habits of industry and cruelty, caprice, and corruption in government. It is barely possible that 1,000 men in the archipelago are now capable of self-government in the Anglo-Saxon sense." Beveridge followed that anti-Spanish condescension with an argument for gradualism in introducing democracy to the Philippines, an argument he supported with the opinions of American businessmen living in the Philippines, urging " 'the necessity of conferring your benefits on these people quite gradually.' " The loss of American lives in fighting in the Philippines for their beliefs makes the group sacred, but the beliefs in self-government are not literally but spiritually mandated by the Declaration of Independence and U.S. history. The higher duty is direction: *"But, Senators, it would be better to abandon the Philippines, and count our blood and treasure already spent a profitable loss, than to apply any academic arrangement of self-government to these children.* They are not yet capable of self-government. How could they be? They are not a self-governing race; they are Orientals, Malays, instructed by Spaniards in the latter's worst estate." Beveridge, then, saw Anglo-Saxons as a God-empowered race whose duty included the gradual bestowing of democracy upon lesser races.

With nothing but Europe to the East (forgetting Cuba), Beveridge saw the flag's further march necessarily turned to the Pacific. He also grounded this vision in the argument that because Europeans were getting everything they needed from their colonies, "Our increasing trade must be with Asia." The Philippines were crucially important because they "give us a base at the door to all the East." With the burden to the Filipinos temporarily put aside, Beveridge advanced the argument dearest to his heart: "These islands are a self-supporting, dividend-paying fleet, permanently anchored at a spot selected by the strategy of Providence, commanding the Pacific. And the Pacific is the ocean of the commerce of the future. Most future wars will be conflicts for commerce. The power that rules the Pacific, therefore, is the power that rules the world. And with the Philippines, that power will be the American Republic."

To dominate was always both divinely dictated and historically justified for Beveridge. He neatly expressed these themes with his characteristic devices of rhetorical question and parallelism or repetition of introductory clauses in his challenge to the Senate:

What will history say of us? Shall it say that we renounced our holy trust, left the savage to his base condition, the wilderness to the reign of waste, deserted duty, abandoned glory, forgot our sordid profit even, because we feared our strength and read the charter of our powers with the doubter's eye and the quibbler's mind? Shall it say that, called by events to captain and command the ablest, noblest race of history in one of history's largest works, we declined that great commission? Our fathers would not have had it so. No! They founded no paralytic government, incapable of the simplest acts of administration. They planted no sluggard people, passive while the world's work calls. They established no reactionary Nation. They unfurled no retreating flag. The flag has never paused in its onward march.

Echoing himself, Beveridge continued his appeal to the Senate to expand U.S. rule in the rest of the world by grasping the ocean of the future, the Pacific, and its key territories. It was a claim he advanced repeatedly, in the speeches already considered and in other addresses, such as "The Command of the Pacific" (1902) and his famous "The Star of Empire."

In September 1900, the Republican campaign for the western vote was beginning, and Beveridge launched the effort with his "The Star of Empire" speech in Chicago. " 'Westward the Star of Empire takes its Way,' " he opened. Explaining that the Empire is what Washington, Jefferson, and Justice Marshall had meant, Beveridge asserted the need for the United States to bring Cuba under "the star of the empire of liberty and law, of commerce and communication, of social order and the Gospel of our Lord." He argued that the United States must and would "civilize the world." The months intervening between his speech to the Senate on the Philippines and this effort had seen the emergence of many counterarguments, and Beveridge attempted to deal with them by a point-by-point attack. He concluded, however, as usual, that "the institutions of every nation follow its flag." The task before the United States was to achieve hegemony in the Pacific. Beveridge's foreign policy speeches, then, advocated U.S. expansion into the Pacific and justified, in fact sanctified, that expansion by connecting it with God's chosen race and its duty and the historic visions of Jefferson, Washington, Hamilton, and Marshall, among others. These speeches show the intense involvement of Beveridge with imperialism as a political movement. He was neither cause nor effect of that movement but perhaps its sharpest, most eloquent voice. At the dawn of the twentieth century, when people still believed in the nineteenth century, Beveridge stood to speak the mind of the indomitable Americans who, having tamed a continent, were prepared to take a world. Lest we accept that one-sided view of him, however, we should consider at least one case of his advocacy regarding domestic affairs. Beveridge was not a blind or even nearsighted man, and he found time and concern to argue about what still needed to be tamed at home.

For most of three days in January 1907, Beveridge spoke in the Senate supporting a bill to regulate child labor. Never was he more specific, better prepared, or more emotionally stirring than in those debates. He demanded humane legislation in an area the national government was afraid to touch for years after his service. Critics who have claimed that Beveridge dealt only in generality and superficiality have overlooked his extensive efforts in behalf of decent legislation to regulate big business at home. Sadly, this may prove only that he was a worse racist than already suggested because his arguments often rested on the premise that white Americans must protect our race by protecting Anglo-Saxon youth.

In January 1907, Beveridge began his lengthy addresses to the Senate on child labor, "one of the gravest conditions confronting this Republic." As one might predict, he did not speak against children working. He pointed out, in fact, that agricultural labor would not be affected by the pending legislation and that he believed work (especially farm work) is good for children because it helps them to mature. But he provided a list of testimonials against the twelve to fourteen hour workdays children spent in coal mines and textile mills, which might have made Karl Marx blush with envy and pride. This series of speeches was detailed and well evidenced. Beveridge established that the cases of abuse and negligence he reviewed were not isolated, unrepresentative examples but a general rule. He related the arguments of his opposition on key issues by proving that children were compelled to work long hours at low wages generally and that this was a national issue. Yet in this socially progressive message, Beveridge used his standard ground of argument: "Mr. President, we might waive consideration of the ruin of the children themselves (millionaire manufacturers must get still more blood-made millions); but we are confronted with a far graver consequence—the deterioration of the race, the production of a degenerate class in this Republic." Citing by parallel England's problems with child labor, which were followed by losses at war and the inability to recruit healthy, serviceable, young men, Beveridge argued that abusive child labor would lead to an impotent American race. The seat of the damage, he argued, was his blessed Anglo-Saxon race:

The children of the white working-people of the South are going to the mill and to decay, the negro children are going to school and are in the way of improvement. It is not in the power of any man to keep "superior" by asserting superiority. I am glad to see the negro children going to school, but it is enough to wring the heart to think that day by day you are permitting a system to go on which is steadily weakening the white race for the future and steadily strengthening the black race for the future.

For three days Beveridge pressed the issue of child labor, presenting evidence and cogent argumentation. Without apologizing for his racism, it must be said that Beveridge had a social conscience that was years ahead of his own time.

Beveridge might well have become president of the United States but did not. His advocacy of an aggressive foreign policy was in reality no more radical than Theodore Roosevelt's. His dream of empire was possible, if not sensible, at the time he had it. His very early (1904) warning about the "gray-clad, militant figure standing on the frozen shores of the [Pacific] Ocean" may have been grounded in a prescient geopolitical understanding of world affairs. He was unsuccessful against the isolationist mind; two world wars later, anyone who has studied history or politics must wonder if that was a loss, a tragedy.

INFORMATION SOURCES

Research Collections and Collected Speeches

Students of Beveridge's career can consult the Albert J. Beveridge Papers, Library of Congress, which contains over 300 boxes of correspondence, newspaper clippings, speech drafts, and more. Many of Beveridge's speeches have been published, and his magazine articles and books are readily available.

American Forum: Speeches on Historic Issues: 1788–1900. Edited by Ernest   AF
  Wrage and Barnett Baskerville. New York: Harper and Brothers,
  1960.
American Public Addresses, 1740–1952. Edited by A. Craig Baird. New   APA
  York: McGraw-Hill, 1956.
Beveridge, Albert J. *The Meaning of the Times and Other Speeches*. Edited   MT
  by Albert Shaw. 1908; rpt. Freeport, New York: Books for Libraries
  Press, 1968.
Modern Eloquence. Vol. 1. Edited by Thomas B. Reed. Philadelphia: John   ME
  D. Morris and Co., 1900.

Selected Critical Studies

Bowers, Claude G. *Beveridge and the Progressive Era*. Cambridge: The Riverside Press,
  1932.
Ross, Herold Truslow. "Albert J. Beveridge." In *A History and Criticism of American
  Public Address*, vol. 2. Edited by William Norwood Brigance. New York:
  McGraw-Hill, 1943.
———. "Albert J. Beveridge at DePauw." Unpublished manuscript, 1935, DePauw
  University Archives.
———. "The Education of an Orator." *Quarterly Journal of Speech* 18 (1932): 70–
  82.
———. "The Oratorical Career of Albert Jeremiah Beveridge." Ph.D. dissertation,
  University of Iowa, 1932.

Selected Biographies

Braeman, John. *Albert J. Beveridge: American Nationalist*. Chicago: University of Chicago Press, 1971.

CHRONOLOGY OF MAJOR SPEECHES

See "Research Collections and Collected Speeches" for source codes.

Speech to the Middlesex Club of Massachusetts, Boston, April 27, 1898; *MT*, pp. 37–46.

"The March of the Flag," Indianapolis, Indiana, September 16, 1898; *AF*, pp. 352–57; *MT*, pp. 47–57.

"The Republic That Never Retreats," Union League Club, Philadelphia, Pennsylvania, February 13, 1899; *ME*, pp. 70–72.

Speech on Philippine policy, Washington, D.C., January 9, 1900; *APA*, pp. 202–10; *MT*, pp. 58–88.

"The Star of the Empire," Chicago, September 25, 1900; *MT*, pp. 118–43.

Speech opening the Republican campaign for the Pacific slope, San Francisco, September 15, 1902; *MT*, pp. 188–99.

Speeches to the U.S. Senate supporting child labor laws, January 23, 28, 29, 1907; *MT*, pp. 308–67.

"The Meaning of the Times," Yale University, New Haven, Connecticut, January 17, 1908; *MT*, pp. 420–31.

WILLIAM EDGAR BORAH
(1865–1940), U.S. senator

_____ CARL R. BURGCHARDT

William E. Borah was one of the last public speakers in the United States to be compared favorably to the giants of the nineteenth century such as Daniel Webster, Henry Clay, and John Calhoun. Perhaps more than most of his contemporaries, Borah deserved the title "orator." Although his formal education was interrupted and relatively undistinguished, he began the study and practice of oratory at an early age. Borah participated in rhetorical activities at schools and social organizations in Illinois and Kansas, and he gave his first political speech in Illinois at a James Blaine rally in 1884. After practicing law briefly in Kansas, Borah moved to Boise, Idaho, in 1890, where he established his legal office and became active in state politics. His political career in Idaho was founded on his oratorical abilities. After several unsuccessful attempts, he was elected to the U.S. Senate in 1907. Although he was an active and well-known political speaker in Idaho, it was his courtroom oratory that first won him national attention. Borah's 1907 summation in the murder trial of William D. Haywood caused a sensation, particularly his emotional peroration: "I saw murder—no, not murder, a thousand times worse than murder; I saw anarchy wave its first bloody triumph in Idaho."

Borah served in the Senate continuously for thirty-three years. As chairman of the Senate Committee on Foreign Affairs from 1924 to 1933, he used the office as a platform for promulgating his isolationist ideology. Although his positions were almost always controversial, colleagues, journalists, and the public admired his rhetorical prowess.

Because of his reputation, Borah received hundreds of invitations to speak each year. He went on national speaking tours to influence public opinion and exert political pressure on other legislators. He maintained contact with his constituents through extensive public appearances each summer. Borah had the ability to explain clearly the issues of the day, and Idaho voters appreciated him for his educational and entertainment value, as well as the national publicity he brought to their state. His relative independence from the state and national Republican parties allowed Borah to win reelection five times in the politically unpredictable Idaho of his day. Despite his prominence and electoral successes, Borah did not seek the presidency until 1936, but his rhetorical appeals were not well calculated to win his party's nomination.

SENATOR BORAH: THE GREAT OPPOSER

Borah's practice of continually opposing legislative initiatives earned him the label Great Opposer, a role he relished. His most famous opposition occurred during the 1918–1920 debate over the League of Nations, in which he delivered twenty-five speeches against the Treaty of Versailles in the Senate. His November 19, 1919, oration contained a summary of his case against the league and was hailed as a masterpiece. The celebrated "Little Americans" section of the speech reveals the depth of emotion and personal commitment Borah felt in objecting to the league: "Call us little Americans if you will, but leave us the consolation and the pride which the term American, however modified, still imparts." In a related area, Borah gave major speeches in 1925 and 1926 against U.S. partic- ipation in the World Court, which he argued was intertwined with the league. One of his most controversial stands was his opposition to the soldiers' bonus bill. He maintained that the measure was extravagant and that it insulted the veterans to put their service on the "sordid level of money." Many thought his Senate speeches against the Soldier's Bonus bill when it was introduced in 1921 and 1922 were critical in building public support for defeating it. After the onset of the Great Depression, Borah was a major antagonist to Franklin D. Roosevelt's National Recovery Administration (NRA). He criticized the NRA in the Senate in 1933, 1934, and 1935. In his 1933 debate with Senator Robert Wagner, Borah called the proposed NRA "a very advanced step toward the ultra concentration of wealth in the country" because it suspended antitrust laws. Another of Borah's Senate causes was his opposition to several proposed antilynching measures. He objected to the Wagner-Van Nuys bill in 1938 on moral and constitutional grounds. This influential speech electrified the Senate and was counted by many as one of the finest of his career. Borah's last, great, Senate oration was delivered on October 2, 1939. He opposed any effort to repeal the Neutrality Act embargo on the shipment of arms to belligerent nations because it would bring the United States into the war, which Borah viewed as "nothing more than another chapter in the bloody volume of European power politics."

Despite Borah's reputation as a negative voice of protest, he participated in a number of constructive efforts, including support of the federal income tax, the campaign for the outlawry of war, and leadership in bringing about the Washington Disarmament Conference. His most eloquent constructive orations, however, were on other topics. Borah's 1911 speech in support of the direct election of senators, for instance, was called one of the greatest Senate speeches of the decade by the *New York Times*. Borah was praised for his frank discussion of black disfranchisement and for his analysis of the Constitution. Another positive effort was his campaign for the United States to recognize the Soviet government. His Senate speeches of 1922, 1923, and 1931 were recognized as significant in changing public attitudes. The 1922 speech on the Soviet Union captured the spirit of his case: "I care nothing for theories or doctrines over there; I see only 170,000,000 Russian people . . . struggling in almost blinded madness to be free of the inhumanities and the cruelties of the past.''

In response to the depression, Borah was a strong advocate of national programs for relief. A reporter for the *Baltimore Sun* recorded this description of Borah's emotional debate with Senator Simeon Fess over the La Follette-Costigan bill: "Borah, his shaggy hair falling over his face, his unbuttoned coat flapping as he moved excitedly before his desk, his resonant voice ranging from a low whisper to a shout, made an impassioned plea for direct Federal aid to save millions from hunger. It was masterful oratory.''

Although Borah did not record many of his thoughts about rhetorical theory, philosophy, or technique, his discourse displayed several strong characteristics. The first was his practice of careful preparation. In a 1911 speech entitled "Lincoln the Orator," Borah said, "The first qualification of an orator is that he be master of his subject. The second that his subject be master of him.'' Borah followed this advice by spending months preparing for important addresses. Although his staff assisted him with research, he did his own speech writing. Before giving a Senate speech, he often tested his ideas by addressing outside audiences or writing articles for the popular press. Another characteristic of Borah's rhetoric was his superb sense of timing. He saved his speeches for the moment when his message would have the greatest impact. Moreover, Borah believed the effectiveness of his rhetoric came from sensitivity to his audience. As he commented in 1937, "No man was ever persuasive in his study room. If he is effective, it is because his audience helps him.'' With the exception of radio addresses, Borah never used a manuscript during the height of his career, believing them to be too restrictive: "If you don't get any new thought while on your feet, you'd better sit down.'' Borah's speeches were usually concise. He once joked that "a man can tell all he knows in forty minutes.''

Despite the fact that Borah usually advocated controversial, minority positions, he was not disliked by his colleagues. Quite the contrary, he was respected for his sincerity, intellectual integrity, and moral courage. His rhetorical practices went a long way toward creating this goodwill. Borah attacked principles, institutions, and political abstractions in his speeches but rarely individuals. He was courteous and tactful in debate, generally allowing for questions and comments during the course of a Senate speech. Borah did not use sarcasm often, a device he thought was used to bolster untenable positions. He believed that the speaker should strive for clarity and integrity of thought and avoid appeals to prejudice or distorting statements.

Borah's rhetoric was based on a limited number of well-defined tenets. On the domestic front, Borah opposed monopoly, private privilege, concentration of political and economic power, bureaucracy, and government extravagance. He favored agriculture and rural life, particularly that of the West, the Constitution, especially the First Amendment, states' rights, and patriotic pride. Concerning foreign policy, Borah opposed all international, political commitments, such as the League of Nations and the World Court, because he believed they would violate the freedom and values of the United States and would lead to war. In addition, he was against secret diplomacy of any kind. On the other hand, Borah favored international economic cooperation and the national aspirations of struggling nations. He also advocated a vigorous role for the Senate in controlling foreign policy, provided that decisions were made in the open, with public participation and opinion as a guide.

Borah's speeches were usually organized well, with a logical structure and strong transitions. His legal training manifested itself in his skill at marshaling evidence. His speeches advanced a small number of main points, each supported with extensive evidence. He tended to use authority, such as the Constitution and the works of the founding fathers, more than other types of support. Borah used inductive logic almost exclusively, with historical analogy being one of his usual tools. In refutation, he often relied on counterexamples to undermine an opponent's generalization. Borah also used emotional appeals in his rhetoric, which were based on the positive values of patriotism, law and order, peace, Christianity, home ownership, freedom, justice, honor, duty, tradition, and reverence for great leaders of the past, especially Washington. Negative values included fear of war, secrecy, waste, loss of control, barbarism, oppression, and imperialism.

Typically Borah's style was lucid, simple, and direct. Since he tended to pyramid evidence to prove a point, much of his discourse was workmanlike but not sublime. However, Borah was capable of using metaphors, imagery, and vehement expression to underscore a point or convey his moral indignation, and many passages were memorable. Other stylistic devices characteristic of Borah were varied sentence length and form, parallel structure, anaphora, and rhetorical questions.

Borah's physical appearance was imposing. He had a large head and a strong chin, divided by a pronounced cleft. His thick, brown hair was worn long in the Western style. His features were described as rugged, massive, or rough-hewn. His leonine appearance was at least partly responsible for the complimentary nickname of Lion of Idaho. He looked like a senator and orator, which doubtless contributed to the impact of his messages.

Oratory was the life's blood of Borah's career. His law practice in Idaho prospered because of his ability to deliver dramatic, impassioned jury speeches. His position in Idaho politics was based on his abilities as a campaign orator. His fame in the Senate rested on brilliant deliberative speaking. He maintained public attention through national speaking tours. The most persistent and damaging criticism of Borah was that his career was nothing but oratory, that he never followed through on his rhetorical pleas, a charge that prompted Hiram Johnson to dub Borah "our spearless leader." But Borah thought being an orator was enough in itself. He believed that public awareness, engendered through discourse, was the best means for solving or preventing social problems. Thus, society needed senators like Borah to educate the public and to be vigilant against encroachment by monopoly, government centralization, or foreign entanglements. In his November 9, 1911, eulogy to Abraham Lincoln, Borah said that orators were no less than "tribunes of the people. Without them the public conscience would become sluggish and the wisest measures sometimes fail. They arouse public interest. They organize public thought. They call forth and direct the invincible moral force of an entire nation." Borah maintained that a tribune had the moral obligation to speak the truth, even on controversial or unpopular issues. Thus, in his own career, he claimed to eschew personal political advantage in favor of voting for what he believed was in the best interest of the people. Although he felt honor bound to carry out specific campaign pledges, he voted according to his own conviction on unspecified issues. In Borah's words, "I hold with Burke that I owe my constituents my time and energy, but that I owe my judgment only to myself. My constituents elect me to exercise my own best judgment." The interesting paradox to this position was that Borah's controversial, outspoken, independent image was exactly what his constituents prized most in Idaho. Given such a situation, Borah's precise positions were less important than the proper kind of moral posture.

It is difficult to determine with precision the impact of Borah's rhetoric on legislation and social movements. Certainly his discourse played an important role in bringing about the defeat of the League of Nations and impeding participation in a World Court. He was the point man for destroying the bonus bill, blocking antilynching legislation, and obtaining official recognition of the Soviet Union. He was a leader in the fight for the Seventeenth Amendment, and he made several notable expositions on constitutional law. Whatever one thinks of Borah's political causes, Edward Angly's assessment is undeniable: "It is through oratory that Senator Borah has earned an enduring fame in the story of his country."

INFORMATION SOURCES

Research Collections and Collected Speeches

Many of Borah's published speeches have been highly edited or polished. For original materials, researchers must turn to manuscript collections. The William E. Borah Papers (1890–1907) are located in the Idaho State Historical Society, Boise. The Library of Congress houses his Senate papers. Also of interest are the William E. Borah Scrapbooks, held by the University of Idaho in Moscow. Microfilm copies of the scrapbooks are at the Library of Congress.

Borah, William E. *American Problems: A Selection of Speeches and Proph-*   AP
    ecies by William E. Borah. Edited by Horace Green. New York:
    Duffield and Co., 1924.
———. *Bedrock: Views on Basic National Problems.* Edited by Sherman   B
    F. Mittell. Washington, D.C.: National Home Library Foundation,
    1936.

————. *Haywood Trial: Closing Argument of W. E. Borah*. Boise, Idaho: *H*
Statesman Shop, [1907].

Congressional Record.   *CR*

Selected American Speeches on Basic Issues (1850–1950). Edited by Carl *SAS*
G. Brandt and Edward M. Shafter, Jr. Boston: Houghton Mifflin,
1960.

Selected Critical Studies

Braden, Waldo W. "The Bases of William E. Borah's Speech Preparation." *Quarterly Journal of Speech* 33 (1947): 28–30.

————. "How Borah Handled Senatorial Heckling." *Southern Speech Journal* 12 (1947): 58–61.

————. "The Political Speaking of William E. Borah." In *American Public Address: Studies in Honor of Albert Craig Baird*. Edited by Loren Reid. Columbia: University of Missouri Press, 1961.

————. "A Rhetorical Criticism of Invention of William E. Borah's Senate Speeches on the League of Nations, 1918–1920." Ph.D. dissertation, University of Iowa, 1942.

————. "William E. Borah's Senate Speeches on the League of Nations, 1918–1920." *Speech Monographs* 10 (1943): 56–67.

Cooper, John Milton, Jr. "William E. Borah, Political Thespian." *Pacific Northwest Quarterly* 56 (1965): 145–53.

Grover, David H. *Debaters and Dynamiters: The Story of the Haywood Trial*. Corvallis: Oregon State University Press, 1964.

Nielsen, Stephen F. "Constitutional Government as Viewed by William E. Borah: A Study of Speeches on Selected Issues." Ph.D. dissertation, Southern Illinois University, 1968.

Whitehead, Albert Edward. "The Oratorical Career of William Edgar Borah." Ph.D. dissertation, University of Wisconsin, 1944.

————. "The Oratory of William Edgar Borah." *Quarterly Journal of Speech*: 32 (1946): 292–97.

————. "William E. Borah." In *A History and Criticism of American Public Address*. Edited by Marie Kathryn Hochmuth. New York: Longmans, Green, 1955.

Selected Biographies

Johnson, Claudius O. *Borah of Idaho*. Seattle: University of Washington Press, 1967.

McKenna, Marian C. *Borah*. Ann Arbor: University of Michigan Press, 1961.

CHRONOLOGY OF MAJOR SPEECHES

See "Research Collections and Collected Speeches" for source codes.

Haywood trial summation, Boise, Idaho, July 26, 1907; *H*.

Seventeenth Amendment speech, Washington, D.C., February 16, 1911; *CR*, February 16, 1911, pp. 2645–57.

Lincoln address, Larue County, Kentucky, November 9, 1911; *AP*, pp. 31–42.

Speech against the League of Nations, Washington, D.C., November 19, 1919; *AP*, pp. 105–30; *B*, pp. 46–50; *CR*, November 19, 1919, pp. 8781–84; *SAS*, pp. 391–404.

Bonus bill speech, Washington, D.C., July 14, 1921; *AP*, pp. 8–15; *CR*, July 14, 1921, pp. 3764–66.

Speech for recognition of the Soviet Union, Washington, D.C., May 31, 1922; *AP*, pp. 241–76; *CR*, May 31, 1922, pp. 7904–09.

Speech against the World Court, Washington, D.C., December 18, 1925; *CR*, December 18, 1925, pp. 1071–77.

Speech for federal relief, Washington, D.C., February 10, 1932; *CR*, February 10, 1932, pp. 3668–73.

Speech against the National Recovery Administration, Washington, D.C., June 7, 1933; *CR*, June 7, 1933, pp. 5162–67.

Speech against the antilynching bill, Washington, D.C., January 7, 1938; *CR*, January 7, 1938, pp. 138–43.

Speech against repeal of the arms embargo, Washington, D.C., October 2, 1939; *CR*, October 2, 1939, pp. 66–75.

WILLIAM JENNINGS BRYAN
(1860–1925), orator and statesman

DONALD K. SPRINGEN

William Jennings Bryan dominated every national convention of the Democratic party from 1896 to 1924. Few would quarrel that the explanation for this power came principally from his superb oratory. His strength as a speaker came primarily from his ability to simplify an issue, project great sincerity of motives, and, above all, deliver his words with quality of tone and power of projection. He could reach 30,000 people in the open air without a mechanical device and still maintain conversational effectiveness.

Bryan, called The Great Commoner, was actually born to a well-to-do, politically prominent family on March 19, 1860, in Salem, Illinois. He received his early education from his mother, who taught him the rudiments of speech making. His father, a circuit judge, excelled at speech making and was in demand as an orator in the surrounding area. Both parents believed that oratory was necessary to achieve recognition in their Illinois community.

Bryan's early training from his mother in public speaking was continued when he entered Salem High School and, later, Whipple Academy. He joined the literary and debating society, Sigma Pi, at Illinois College and graduated as valedictorian and class orator in 1881. In twelve debate contests in which he debated for Sigma Pi, he won six and lost six, and, for all his prowess as a speaker throughout his high school and college career, he usually finished second. After graduation, he enrolled at Union College of Law in Chicago and completed his work in 1883.

From 1883 to 1887, Bryan practiced law in Jacksonville, Illinois, home of Illinois College. He left Jacksonville and moved his family to Lincoln, Nebraska, in June 1888. The Democrats welcomed him, but the problem was that there were so few of them because Nebraska was solidly Republican. Bryan nevertheless immediately began to campaign for Nebraska's Democratic candidates in 1888 and was instrumental in their victories. By 1891 he was elected to represent the First Congressional District of Nebraska.

Bryan soon discovered that the Nebraska farmer of the 1890s had the same problems that had plagued the Illinois farmer of the 1870s and 1880s (and remain problems in the 1980s): large mortgages because of expanded acreage, high interest and freight rates, declining prices, rising costs, and—worst of all—below-normal rainfall. Neither Republican nor Democrat spoke for the farmer in the late 1800s. Bryan found an audience thirsty for a spokesman to get its message to Washington. In his first address in Lincoln, he compared the tariff to a cow fed by farmers and milked by eastern industrialists who returned nothing to the farmer but higher interest rates. The Nebraska farmers howled with agreement. They had found their spokesman.

BRYAN AS THE GREAT COMMONER

As a congressman on March 16, 1892, Bryan delivered what is considered his first great speech against the theory of protection: "The man who justifies protection as a principle must prove three things: He must prove that the principle is right, that the policy is wise, and that the tax is necessary." This speech propelled Bryan into the national limelight, demonstrating his ability to argue effectively. Newspapers heaped praise upon his speaking, and 100,000 copies of the speech were distributed. Many wondered when this congressman would run for president. He had advanced every important argument against the protection theory in this speech.

The tariff address was scheduled to last for one hour but stretched to three. Bryan asserted that tariff reform was the immediate task of the Fifty-second Congress. He adopted the posture of defender of the average American who, he asserted, ultimately provides the country with its wealth, its defense, and its future. Bryan interspersed emotional appeals with appeals to logic. As he spoke, his rich baritone voice rang through the galleries. Jeffersonian principles were a prominent theme as he urged Congress to enact laws from which "all the people" could benefit. Bryan delineated tariff reform not from the viewpoint of manufacturing lobbyists but from the viewpoint of the consumer. Said Bryan, "The Democratic Party says, 'Hands off, and let home industry live.' "

By 1893 Bryan was considered a national leader of the silver movement, promoting free and unlimited coinage at a sixteen-to-one ratio. The significant August 16, 1893, speech opposing the repeal of the silver issue clause of the Sherman Act before a special session of Congress firmly ensconced him in this role. Sounding like "the great commoner," he referred to the "great mass of our people": "The President has been deceived. He can no more judge the wishes of the great mass of our people by the expressions of these men than he can measure the ocean's silent depths by the foam upon its waves."

Bryan's congressional career officially ended on March 4, 1895. Before its close, however, on September 1, 1894, he joined the race for U.S. senator from Nebraska's First District. Between September 28 and November 6, 1894, Bryan delivered more than eighty speeches. He debated twice in his campaign (on October 16 and 17), and these debates augmented his growing reputation as a speaker. The first debate, on the money issue, attracted an audience of 5,000. The second, on the tariff, drew 15,000. Bryan always spoke in the voice of the plain people and against big business, but superb oratory does not guarantee election, especially for a Democrat in an overwhelmingly Republican state. His subsequent defeat crystallized his conviction that U.S. senators should be elected by popular vote and not by the state legislatures. Bryan had received 75 percent of the popular vote to John M. Thurston's 2 percent. In spite of this defeat,

Bryan assumed leadership of the Nebraska Democratic party, mainly because of his oratory.

With the conclusion of his congressional career on March 4, 1895, Bryan was out of a job. At this time, he decided to enroll in several lecture bureaus. His first fees were $50 a lecture, but they quickly rose to $100 and beyond. He was soon speaking four or five times a week at $200 per appearance all over the United States. Bryan never used speech writers. As a young man, he memorized his speeches; later he outlined them and spoke extemporaneously. His wife stated that if the subject were familiar to him, he spoke entirely without notes. He kept his gestures simple and natural. If a copy of a lecture were required for publication, he actually dictated the speech to a secretary without using notes. Bryan may not have used a speech writer, but Mary, his wife, who loved politics, did much of the research for his quotations and historical references. They read the same books and talked politics.

As the National Democratic Convention approached in 1896, Bryan wondered how he could become one of the Nebraska delegates. For a few days, he was just an outsider, and then the gold delegation from Nebraska was rejected, and Bryan got his seat. In the preceding sixteen months, Bryan had spoken again and again on the issue of the hour—silver. He knew his chances for the nomination were not unreasonable. A clear choice was not apparent. Bryan, in fact, carefully courted the Democratic presidential nomination every way he could for the sixteen months before the convention. He sent Governor John Altgeld of Illinois several of his speeches, but Altgeld considered Bryan a superficial thinker who failed to understand the implications of the money issue. Bryan, at thirty-six years of age, was ultimately to win the nomination by smooth political maneuvering, oratorical superiority, and luck. After all, he was almost not even seated as a delegate. Another bit of luck was the convention hall. Although containing a floor area of five and a half acres and seating 20,000 persons, it was well suited to the carrying power of Bryan's voice. Bryan, who could reach 30,000 people in the open air without a microphone, was to find Chicago's Exhibition Hall to his liking.

It was almost midnight by the time Bryan gave the most important speech of his life on July 9, 1896. Six feet tall, slim, handsome, magnetic, and believing every word he said, Bryan thrilled his audience. He meant to get the nomination for president. The late hour and the audience demanded something other than arguments. Bryan's prose was moving, inspiring, and reminiscent of Patrick Henry when he told the delegates that the people of the West had been ignored long enough: "We have petitioned, and our petitions have been scorned; we have entreated, and our entreaties have been disregarded; we have begged, and they have mocked when our calamity came. We beg no longer; we petition no more. We defy them." It was a beautifully adapted speech. It was short, rich in rhythm, full of frontier images of school houses and country churches, and filled with just enough content about silver and gold to impress a tired audience that the speaker knew his subject. What probably lasted in the minds of his largely Christian audience was not just his final words but those words coupled with his gestures. On paper that famous line reads: "You shall not press down upon the brow of labor this crown of thorns; you shall not crucify mankind upon a cross of gold." But Bryan's gestures gave it an emotional impact. They beheld Christ himself as Bryan raised his hands to the sides of his head and, with fingers spread inward, moved them slowly down to his temples as he uttered, "crown of thorns." When he reached "cross of gold," his arms formed the cross, and the symbol of his body, combined with the words of this young man, transfixed 20,000 people. Twenty-five minutes of cheering, stomping, and pounding followed. It had been a long day. It was now past midnight, and people went wild. The convention adjourned. Bryan was not nominated until late the next day, and it took five ballots before he overcame his opponents. The free silver resolutions were adopted 628 to 301. Subsequently the populists and the National Silver party endorsed his nomination.

The myths surrounding Bryan's great speech are almost as numerous as those describing Lincoln's address at Gettysburg. Bryan was as familiar with most of the phrases he used on July 9, 1896, as he was with the Bible. He had spoken them over and over for the past sixteen months. It is not true that a great occasion filled with high emotion produced a great spontaneous extemporaneous oration that became a historical legend. The nomination did not follow the speech but came late the next day. The speech, nevertheless, was a work of art and served its purpose well. In adaptation to a difficult occasion and audience situation and in power of delivery, it has probably never been equaled, certainly in American political life.

In his 1896 campaign for the presidency, Bryan traveled 18,000 miles; he delivered 600 speeches to nearly 5 million people in 27 states. His only weapon was his eloquence. Eastern Democrats, industrialists, bankers, and the press shunned him. Instead he appealed to the people. He led his audiences to make judgments about his opponents. He then invited them to shout out their opinions by asking questions that prompted partisan answers. He elevated his discussions to the moral plane of right or wrong. The atmosphere would crackle with revivalist fervor. He appealed directly to the heart of his supporters with "crossroads" speaking. He cried out that the hour was timely and that the personal courage of the people was required to thwart the adversary. These dramatic tactics characterized Bryan's speeches throughout his life. On November 3, 1896, however, such techniques did not stop William McKinley's victory with 271 electoral votes to William Jennings Bryan's 176. With only 50,000 more votes, properly distributed, Bryan could have won the presidency.

In 1900, the Democratic party again nominated Bryan as a candidate for president of the United States. On August 8, 1900, in Military Park, Indianapolis, before a crowd of 50,000 people, Bryan delivered an extraordinary acceptance speech. He used 10,000 words to oppose the rise of imperialism. Again he phrased the question as a moral dilemma. He declared that the divine commission to go into the world to preach the gospel was not a sanction to conquer foreign lands. Again he used figurative language: "Imperialism finds no warrant in the Bible. The command, 'Go ye into all the world and preach the gospel to every creature,' has no Gatling gun attachment. When Jesus visited a village of Samaria and the people refused to receive him. . . . Suppose he had said: 'We will thrash them until they understand who we are.' How different would have been the history of Christianity!'' On this occasion Bryan spoke as a reasoning statesman rather than a fiery orator. He was unsuccessful for the second time in his bid for the presidency, but the nation is indebted to him because he defined imperialism in such a manner that it was discredited as an ideal U.S. foreign policy.

Over a lifetime, Bryan bent his skill to agitate successfully and steadfastly for the popular election of senators, the income tax, the requirements of publication of ownership and circulation of newspapers, the creation of the Department of Labor, national prohibition, and woman suffrage. None of these progressive reforms could have been accomplished without his popular appeal. When he was nominated in 1908 for the third time as the Democratic party's candidate for president, his rallying cry still was, "Let the people rule." On August 12, 1908, in his acceptance speech entitled, "Shall the People Rule?" Bryan pledged to make the will of the American people his guide if he were elected president.

After his defeat on November 3, 1908, many thought Bryan was politically dead, but he wielded considerable power in the 1912 election when he fought to secure the presidential nomination for Woodrow Wilson. Bryan served almost two years as secretary of state under Wilson and in this position helped Wilson promote his New Freedom legislation. The personal persuasion he had mastered after years of campaigning should be considered as important as well as his great skill in public speaking. Bryan, however, buttonholed only the progressives and reformers in Congress. Oscar W. Underwood of Alabama, a rival whom Bryan hated and had labeled a conservative Democrat years before, was now majority leader of the House. Although Bryan helped somewhat, it was Underwood, the conservative, who saw to it that the constructive acts of Woodrow Wilson raced through Congress in record time. Bryan, not always the "Prince of Peace," went to Alabama and campaigned for Underwood's opponent. Underwood, finally victorious, drew great applause from his Alabama audiences by stating that Bryan, then serving as secretary of state, had no business leaving Washington and conducting a strenuous five-month campaign in Alabama against a fellow Democrat.

In spite of his political forays out of Washington, Bryan was a good secretary of state and worked hard for international peace. Typical of his speeches as secretary of state was the important address on the hundredth anniversary of the Treaty of Ghent, which he delivered May 10, 1913, at the Astor Hotel in New York City. With eloquent optimism, Bryan stated that no other nation would outstrip the United States in its work for peace because it had the mingled blood of all nations in its veins: "This nation is linked by ties of blood to the other nations of the earth and, therefore, we have at its maximum the restraining influence of blood and kinship that keeps us from engaging in war with any other country in the world.'' Woodrow Wilson genuinely liked Bryan, and when war came and pacifist Bryan resigned, Wilson was truly sorry.

In 1916, Bryan went into semiretirement. When the Democrats met in 1916 to nominate Wilson for a second term, Bryan attended as a journalist but was neither a delegate nor an alternate. He increasingly turned his attention to the issues of prohibition and woman suffrage. He made no speeches in the 1920 campaign for James Cox and Franklin Roosevelt.

Bryan viewed a party in complete chaos in 1923–1924. Wilson was near death, and aspiring candidates were everywhere. Bryan made no major speeches during this political period, but he appeared at the convention promoting progressive, dry candidates. Bryan feared Oscar Underwood, a wet, because he might carry the South, ally himself with Al Smith, and carry the East. By labeling Underwood a wet, a reactionary, and, later, a tool of Wall Street and by ignoring Underwood's courageous stand against the Ku Klux Klan, Bryan damaged the presidential hopes of a fellow Democrat who had been Woodrow Wilson's chief ally in progressive domestic legislation. The charm had gone out of Bryan's tongue. He was old, tired, surly, petulant, and unreasoning. As the convention came to a close after John Davis had been nominated on the 103d ballot, Bryan could be blamed for at least part of the confusion and discouragement among Democrats.

By 1925, diabetes was slowly taking Bryan's energy. The last debate of his life was not political but over religious fundamentalism—a debate fought in the Scopes trial with Clarence Darrow, now sixty-eight and almost as well known as Bryan. The clash was tremendous. Darrow sought truth through the scientific method and reason, and Bryan believed in biblical orthodoxy. When Bryan took the stand as an expert on the Bible, it was probably the gravest miscalculation of his long career. When Jonah and the whale were discussed, Darrow began to bore in: ''But you believe He made them—that He made such a fish and that it was big enough to swallow Jonah?'' ''Yes, sir,'' said Bryan, '' . . . one miracle is just as easy to believe as another.'' The trial ended July 23, 1925. Three days later and before he could deliver his final speech, Bryan died in his sleep.

William Jennings Bryan is frequently adored or scorned. Surely he was without a rival from 1895 to 1900 in the field of political oratory. From 1900 until his death in 1925, he remained one of the most prominent and powerful political and platform speakers in the United States. He was the most dominating personality both backstage and on stage in the Democratic party between Grover Cleveland and Woodrow Wilson. Bryan did not originate the ideas of populism, but he promoted them and thus has been called the founder of the modern Democratic party.

INFORMATION SOURCES

Research Collections and Collected Speeches

The most extensive collection of primary material on Bryan is his personal papers in the Division of Manuscripts, Library of Congress, Washington, D.C. Other useful primary material on Bryan can be found at the same source in the papers of Grover Cleveland, Josephus Daniels, and Woodrow Wilson.

Two helpful collections of primary material outside the Library of Congress are the John Peter Altgeld Papers, Illinois Historical Society, Springfield, helpful for Bryan's early political career, and the Oscar Wilder Underwood Papers at the Alabama Department of Archives and History, Montgomery, helpful for Bryan's later career.

Bryan, William Jennings. *Speeches of William Jennings Bryan.* 2 vols. New   *SWJB*
    York: Funk & Wagnalls Co., 1909.

New York Times.   *NYT*

Selected Critical Studies

Bennett, W. Lance, and Haltom, William. "Issues, Voter Choices, and Critical Elections." *Social Science History* 4 (1980): 379–418.
Grant, Philip A., Jr. "William Jennings Bryan and the Presidential Election of 1916." *Nebraska History* 16 (1982): 531–42.
Phillips, Myron G. "William Jennings Bryan." In *A History of American Public Address*, vol. 2. Edited by William Norwood Brigance. New York: McGraw-Hill, 1943.
Schlup, Leonard. "Bryan's Partner: Arthur Sewall and the Campaign of 1896." *Maine Historical Society Quarterly* 16 (1977): 189–211.
———. "Charles A. Towne and the Vice Presidential Question of 1900." *North Dakota History* 44 (1977): 14–20.
Springen, Donald K. "Labor's Political Allies." In *The Rhetoric of Protest and Reform: 1878–1898.* Edited by Paul Boase. Athens: Ohio University Press, 1980.
———. "The Democrats: Techniques in Destruction, Bryan vs. Underwood." *Southern Speech Communication Journal* 36 (1970): 152–63.
Wood, Margaret. "William Jennings Bryan." In *American Public Address: Studies in Honor of Albert Craig Baird.* Edited by Loren Reid. Columbia: University of Missouri Press, 1961.

Selected Biographies

Bryan, William Jennings, and Bryan, Mary Baird. *The Memoirs of William Jennings Bryan.* Philadelphia: John C. Winston Co., 1925.
Clements, Kendrick A. *William Jennings Bryan: Missionary Isolationist.* Knoxville: University of Tennessee Press, 1982.
Coletta, Paolo E. *William Jennings Bryan*, Vol. 1: *Political Evangelist, 1860–1908*; Vol. 2: *Progressive Politician and Moral Statesman, 1905–1915*; Vol. 3: *Political Puritan, 1915–1925.* Lincoln: University of Nebraska Press, 1964–1970.
Koenig, Louis W. *Bryan.* New York: G. P. Putnam's Sons, 1971.

CHRONOLOGY OF MAJOR SPEECHES

See "Research Collections and Collected Speeches" for source codes.

Speech on the tariff, Washington, D.C., March 16, 1892; *SWJB*, 1: 3–77.

Speech on bimetallism, Washington, D.C., August 16, 1893; *SWJB*, 1: 78–145.

Speech on an income tax, Washington, D.C., January 30, 1894; *SWJB*, 1: 159–79.

"Cross of Gold," Chicago, July 9, 1896; *SWJB*, 1: 238–49.

Speech on imperialism, Indianapolis, Indiana, August 8, 1900; *SWJB*, vol. 2: 17–49.

"The Value of an Ideal," Lecture delivered at numerous Chautauquas and college gatherings beginning in 1901; *SWJB*, 2: 235–60.

"The Prince of Peace," Lecture delivered at many Chautauquas and religious gatherings in America, beginning in 1904; also in Canada, Mexico, Tokyo, Manila, Bombay, Cairo, and Jerusalem; *SWJB*, 2: 261–90.

"Shall the People Rule?" Denver, Colorado, August 12, 1908; *SWJB*, 2: 100–19.

"Lincoln as an Orator," Springfield, Illinois, February 12, 1909, hundredth anniversary of Lincoln's birth; *SWJB*, 2: 419–25.

Treaty of Ghent anniversary speech, New York City, May 10, 1913; *NYT*, May 10, 1913, p. 2.

JAMES EARL CARTER
(1924–   ), thirty-ninth president of the United States

_____ RICHARD W. LEEMAN and MARTIN W. SLANN

The question most asked about Jimmy Carter as an orator has been how someone who came out of nowhere in 1976 to win the presidency could lose it so miserably in 1980. How could he become such a failure as a communicator when only four years earlier he had been considered an oratorical wizard? The answer is that Carter did not change his rhetoric stylistically or substantively in those four years but that the oratory that served him so well as a first-term campaigner was inappropriate for him as president. In *The Symbolic Uses of Politics* Murray Edelman has argued persuasively that Americans want their political leaders to create an image of leadership—regardless of the reality. The case of President Jimmy Carter supports Edelman's theory.

Carter came to the presidency with a background quite different from other modern presidents and presidential aspirants. The product of a small town in the Deep South, he was a one-term former governor of Georgia. He attended the Naval Academy and served with the U.S. Navy seven years. He was assigned to the Polaris program until his father's death, when he resigned his command to take over the Carter family peanut warehouse. In his presidential campaign he billed himself as a farmer, businessman, nuclear engineer, and former governor. He had neither Washington political experience nor a legal background.

JIMMY CARTER AS CAMPAIGNER AND PRESIDENTIAL PERSUADER

Carter's oratorical roots lay in his background as an engineer, his extensive campaigning for governor and then president, and his religious faith. In *A Government as Good as Its People*, Carter estimated that he gave some 3,300 speeches as governor and presidential aspirant. Missing from that total are the numerous speeches he gave as two-time campaigner for governor. Carter campaigned for governor just as he later did for president: by extensive and exhaustive traveling, speaking primarily to small and medium-sized audiences. With this background, even as president, Carter felt more comfortable addressing small audiences; he particularly enjoyed question and answer periods. He did best when discussing specific policies; with more formal, stylized speeches given to larger audiences or in front of a television camera, he was ill at ease. He also had difficulty articulating broad, cohesive political philosophy.

The plain style of Carter's rhetoric suggested a man of sincerity, honesty, and quiet competence. His soft-spoken style complemented his direct promises and statements, such as "I will never lie to you," or "Why not the best?" Carter demonstrated his sincerity by incorporating references to his religious faith in his political rhetoric, startling many of his campaign audiences with his straight-forward pronouncements that "I'm a devout Christian," or "The most important thing in my life is Jesus Christ." He confirmed his sincerity with unanticipated and often out-of-place smiles, as well as by a grammar marred by extended complex sentences, sentence fragments, and fractured syntax.

Carter's plain style was appropriate to the substance of his message. His speeches developed two recurring themes: pragmatic realism and the idea that the people are a national source of strength. In the first, he frequently pointed out that choices are difficult, the world complex, and success often limited. This theme often led to unusual oratorical claims. For example, his 1976 acceptance speech, delivered July 15 in New York City, included the statement, "Our party's not been perfect," hardly typical of convention rhetoric. Clearly Carter borrowed some of this rhetoric of limits from Jerry Brown's "small is beautiful/ less is more" campaign, but the general themes of limitation and pragmatic realism are also in his gubernatorial oratory.

The second theme in Carter's campaign was an almost mystical evocation of the *volk*, or the people, in which Carter portrayed Americans as the wellspring of goodness and morality. If only the Central Intelligence Agency had reflected the American people, he argued in his acceptance speech, it would not have marched down its foolish and immoral path. He had found his two years of campaigning a "humbling experience" as he had come to realize that power rests with the people, not the "power brokers." This concept of the people culminated in his claims that "it's time for the people to run the government and not the other way around" and that as president, he would try to form "a government as good as its people." Carter's rhetoric treated these dual themes of the world's complexity and the people's basic goodness and strength as complementary. As a presidential candidate, he claimed, "I recognize the dif-ficulty," but "with your help" the difficulties could be met. When he said that "as president I want you to help me," he was not simply using a rhetorical trope. He was in fact calling on the people to be the solution.

In 1976 this rhetoric worked well. After an era in which a pay any price approach had led to Vietnam and an imperial presidency had culminated in Watergate, Americans were willing to listen to an orator who talked of limits, honesty, basic morality, and quiet strength. Carter also enjoyed the advantage of running against a similarly plain-styled speaker.

To be sure, Carter's rhetoric did not meet with universal acclaim. He won in 1976 by a very close margin, and even during the campaign certain questions about him had already been raised by the press and the public. Some people voiced concern about his religion and how it might affect his work as president. Some critics thought him overly moral and preachy, and others wondered what Carter really believed. The claim that he was trying to be all things to all people received extended play in the media. Still others complained that he made exaggerated claims. The media particularly criticized Carter's assertion that he would never lie and his biographical claim that he had been a nuclear physicist. In spite of these reservations, the public accepted Carter as a sincere, honest, compassionate person who would guide the ship of state with a steady hand.

Carter's Inaugural Address, given in Washington, D.C., on January 20, 1977, and written almost entirely by himself, pursued the theme of realism. He argued that "even our great nation has its recognized limits and that we can neither answer all questions nor solve all problems." Instead, "we must simply do our best." Dramatically, and unexpectedly, Carter also proclaimed his limits as president. "I have no new dream" he said, "but rather urge a fresh faith in the old dream." These presidential limits held a critical place in Carter's rhetoric because they underscored the importance of the people. "A President may sense and proclaim that new spirit, but only a people can provide it," Carter stated. Furthermore, he suggested that "your strength can compensate for my weakness, and your wisdom can help to minimize my mistakes." Critics noted not only the pronounced theme of limitations in that phrase but also the awkwardness of its formulation. Strict parallel structure would change "help to minimize my mistakes" to "compensate for my stupidity."

Both the domestic and foreign press noted the Inaugural for its brevity and its spiritual tone. The speech was "notably lacking in the kind of idealistic fervor and self-certainty one associates with the 1960's and early 1970's," wrote the *Washington Post*. Contrasting Carter and Kennedy's Inaugurals, the *Times* of London judged that although Carter's speech lacked "idealistic fervor," it was widely perceived to be a "moralistic speech," "spiritual in tone," one granting almost "mystical properties" to the "American people." In general, the U.S. and European press reacted in much the same fashion as the *New York Times*, which noted that there was "nothing memorable" in the speech, but "we liked the melody," and Americans would have to wait and see how his presidency performed. Interestingly, these commentaries echoed those of the Georgian press from his gubernatorial inaugural six years earlier. After that Inaugural, a leading columnist for the *Atlanta Constitution* wrote, "Frankly, the state will not know for several months which is the real Carter. There are clues leading in all directions."

Throughout his four years as president, Carter pursued his major theme of pragmatic realism, which emphasized the complexity of the world and the resulting limits of what can be accomplished. He cautioned repeatedly that "these measures will not be easy, nor will they be popular," "there are no easy answers," and "to be secure we must face the world as it is." Even the January 23, 1980, Washington announcement of the Carter Doctrine, which emphatically drew the line against further Soviet expansion, included the caveat, "Our material resources, great as they are, are limited. Our problems are too complex for simple slogans or for quick solutions. We cannot solve them without effort and sacrifice." His penchant for realism led him to make unexpected admissions while president just as he had as campaigner. As presidential contender, he revealed that he had lusted in his heart. As president, in his April 18, 1977, speech "The Moral Equivalent of War" televised from Washington, D.C., he offered candidly, "Many of you have suspected that some supplies of oil and gas are being withheld. . . . You may be right, but suspicions about the oil companies cannot change the fact that we are running out of petroleum." For a president to admit that he did not know something as significant as the withholding of oil supplies—in a prepared speech, not an extemporaneous press conference—speaks tellingly of Carter's candor: it was a kind of painful honesty. In his "New Foreign Policy" address, a commencement speech at Notre Dame on May 22, 1977, he reported, "We are trying to get other nations, both free and otherwise, to join us in this effort." A rhetor less concerned with accuracy and more attentive to the image of his leadership would have reworded that sentence, perhaps saying "We [or I] call on all nations to join us in this effort," as had John Kennedy in his Inaugural Address.

Carter's theme of realism reached its apex on August 14 in his 1980 acceptance speech in New York, in which he noted: "I'm wiser tonight than I was four years ago. . . . I think I'll be a better president in the next four years just continuing what we are doing." He left to the electorate the task of deciphering what it was we were "continuing" that would make us better and to wonder whether perhaps there was not a better method for educating a person to be president. Yet Carter's declaration of being wiser echoed closely a similar claim in his 1976 acceptance speech—that he had learned much while campaigning. What sounded impressive coming from a campaigner, however, raised eyebrows when enunciated by a president.

Similarly, Carter continued to place his faith in the *volk*. His energy speeches called for sacrifice and effort on the part of the ordinary person. His foreign policy was one "rooted in our moral values, which never change." The Panama Canal treaties should be passed, he argued from the Oval Office on February 1, 1978, because they are fair and Americans are essentially a great, generous, strong, and fair people. "We have profound moral commitments," he told the Congress, "which are deeply rooted in our values as a people." Although most politicians and all presidents pay lip-service to the myth of the people, Carter seems to have had a deep faith in it. Both the pervasiveness of the myth in his rhetoric and the substantive ways in which he involved the myth in his speeches suggest this conclusion. Additionally, his faith in the people seemed to echo clearly his Christian belief in basic human goodness.

If, however, people are basically good, they also sin. In his "Moral Equivalent of War" speech, Carter argued that Americans must change their energy consumption habits. "We must not be selfish or timid," he argued, implying quite clearly that Americans had been both. Indeed later in the speech he said that to continue present policy would be simply to "drift along." His "Crisis of Confidence" speech exemplified this predicament in which Carter placed himself. When he argued that the solution would be found in the people, he implied logically that the problem could be found there too. When Carter said that his successes would be the people's successes, he invited them to consider his failures as their failures. In the summer of 1979, Carter went to Camp David to revitalize his energy program but ended up contemplating his presidency. Upon his return to Washington, he delivered his July 15 "Crisis of Confidence" speech in which he not only apologized for his own failures but also told the public that as a moral community they had failed too. One of those problems, Carter claimed, was that they were not confident enough. A second problem was that "too many of us now tend to worship self-indulgence and consumption." "Why," he wondered, "have we not been able to get together as a nation to resolve our serious energy problem?" This dualistic view of the people was not new in the Carter presidency. His celebrated "Law Day" speech delivered in Athens, Georgia, to the University of Georgia Law School on May 4, 1974, inveighed against the special interests and warned of the selfishness of the people and contains the seeds of his "Crisis of Confidence" speech. Even his 1976 acceptance speech cautioned that "all of us must be careful not to cheat each other," and he used his Farewell Address to issue once more a warning against such selfishness.

Carter combined the themes of selfishness and limits to suggest a kind of minimalism; for example, "because this is not a mandatory control plan, I cannot stop irresponsible corporations from raising its prices or a selfish group of employees from using its power to demand excessive wages." Addressing U.S. energy policy, Carter insisted that "once again, the selfishness of the few will block action which is badly needed to help our entire nation. . . . unless you speak out." Repeatedly Carter's speeches implied that he was powerless to solve the nation's problems and that many of those problems were fundamentally rooted in the nation's selfishness.

Carter's style sprang from a native dislike, or distrust, of rhetoric. James Fallows, Carter's leading speech writer for the first two years of his administration, claimed that Carter "didn't think it was important to give effective speeches." He apparently thought that sincerity was sufficient, that rhetoric was simply embellishment, which at its worst obscured reality. As a result, he spurned many of the rhetorical practices other presidents had used faithfully. For example, he generally avoided extensive speech rehearsal. He first read the speech into a cassette, played it back, and then read it once more. Reportedly he bristled when his speaking style was criticized. While he practiced rather extensively for his debates with Gerald Ford, he was too busy with presidential duties to do the same for the debate against Ronald Reagan.

James Fallows made famous the claim that "Carter thinks in lists, not arguments." According to Fallows, when Carter edited a speech, he generally cut the explanatory and argumentative material and replaced it with what he considered "meat," which was presented in a list of topics. Carter's speeches were in fact often a compilation of lists. The "Moral Equivalent of War" laid out six guidelines for foreign policy; the speech for the Panama Canal treaties unfolded in a question and answer format. The problem with this style was not simply that Carter had many lists but that his method of arrangement often seemed haphazard. In "New Foreign Policy," he appended three minor goals regarding China, Latin America, and South Africa after he presented his six guidelines—almost as if they were afterthoughts. The Panama Canal speech revealed similar problems. Carter appeared to have given no thought to the order of the question and answers. In his speech following the failed rescue mission of the Iranian hostages, Carter accurately identified the major arguments, criticisms, and questions that would arise and answered them. To hear it, however, was to listen to a series of responses answering a set of implied questions. The speech lacked an overall vision of the United States, the hostages, and Iran. Where other rhetors would have more dramatically focused attention back toward a "criminal Iran," Carter merely said that the United States would "continue to hold . . . Iran responsible." The lack of an overall vision was endemic to Carter's oratory. According to Fallows, for a major address that was to clarify the U.S. foreign policy direction, Carter essentially stapled together two memos: one by foreign policy adviser Zbigniew Brzezinski and one by Secretary of State Cyrus Vance. Given their contrary viewpoints on that subject, the resulting speech quite naturally sounded schizophrenic.

Carter's language reflected his concern with reality and limitations and his lack of concern with rhetoric. His speeches were written in complex sentences, many beginning with conjunctions. By using the passive voice, Carter divorced himself linguistically from events that he thus implied were beyond his control. For example, in his Panama Canal Treaty speech, he equivocated: "What they regard as the last vestige of alleged American colonialism is being removed." Carter also strove for a rhetoric of realism through an informality of expression. He frequently used commonplaces such as "the first thing I would like to do," "I'm glad to announce to you," "you can see this is a vital and continuing process," or "these efforts will cost money, a lot of money." His Inaugural walk down Pennsylvania Avenue, his speeches given in cardigan sweaters, and his softball games manifested his informality. At times his inclination to express ideas colloquially worked effectively in his speeches. In the speech on the Panama Canal treaties, he rejected the "we bought it, it's ours" argument on the ground that the United States had been paying annuities to the Panamanians since the canal's inception. As Carter phrased it, "You do not pay rent on your own land." On other occasions his taste for the informal resulted in problems. Hamilton Jordan notes that before his debate with Reagan, Carter discussed using the "Amy and Nuclear War" conversation in which his twelve-year-old daughter, Amy, had discussed her concerns about nuclear war. Carter felt that the conversation illustrated the poignancy of the issue; his advisers correctly predicted that the public would perceive it as trite.

This is not to say that Carter never used figures of speech or attempted formal diction; however, his syntactical and semantic proclivities frequently made the trope or scheme less than effective. Carter's use of hyperbole was particularly unfortunate. Scarcely two hours after his advisers had discussed with him his tendency to exaggerate, Carter said, "I want to thank Chancellor Schmidt for the superb welcome they've given us. I've never met any other world leader who has been of more assistance." On New Year's Eve in 1978, Carter toasted the shah of Iran saying, "And there is no leader with whom I have a deeper sense of personal gratitude and personal friendship." One year later the shah was gone, and the Iranian populace remembered well the "devil Carter's" friendliness with the shah. Carter also used hyperbole to heighten perception of a problem. The energy crisis was therefore the "greatest challenge our country will face during our lifetime"; the Soviet invasion of Afghanistan was the "most serious threat to peace since the Second World War." His use of exaggeration to draw distinctions between himself and Reagan led to charges of meanness in the 1980 campaign.

Carter's delivery also reinforced his theme of pragmatic realism. Observations in the press almost universally recognized this characteristic. They repeatedly noted that he was somber and soft-spoken, had avoided histrionics with a reflective tone, had been serious and unsmiling, and had spoken in a determined fashion, attempting to convince more by persuasion than exhortation. While generally content with his delivery, however, the press almost invariably asked whether Carter would be able to accomplish what his oratory had set on the table.

Jimmy Carter's rhetoric typically demonstrated the honesty, sincerity, and compassion that led to his election in 1976. By 1980, however, his rhetoric of reality was describing a continuing energy problem, a painful hostage crisis, and a weak economy. Rather than creating an image of leadership, his rhetoric of the people and his message that the people were the solution came to imply that the people were the cause of the nation's problems. Carter's rhetoric of limitations provided little hope for the solution of those problems. His plain style of rhetoric, with its accompanying informality and realism, gave a clearer sense of the present than a vision for the future. As James Fallows noted, Carter's Achilles heel was his "inability to convert himself from a good man to an effective one."

INFORMATION SOURCES

Research Collections and Collected Speeches

The Carter Library is in the process of being established at Emory University, Atlanta. Along with other Carter papers, the archives will include drafts of some of his major addresses.

Atlanta Constitution.	*AC*
Carter, Jimmy. *A Government as Good as Its People*. New York: Simon and Shuster, 1977.	*GGP*

————. *Public Papers of the President, Jimmy Carter*. Washington, D.C.:   PP
    Government Printing Office, 1977–1981.
Windt, Theodore. "Jimmy Carter." In *Presidential Rhetoric (1961–1980)*.   PR
    Dubuque, Iowa: Kendall/Hunt Publishing Co., 1980.

Selected Critical Studies

Bitzer, Lloyd, and Rueter, Theodore. *Carter v. Ford: The Counterfeit Debates of 1976*.
    Madison: University of Wisconsin Press, 1980.
Hahn, Dan F. "Flailing the Profligate: Carter's Energy Sermon of 1979." *Presidential
    Studies Quarterly* 10 (1980): 583–87.
————. "The Rhetoric of Jimmy Carter, 1976–1980." *Presidential Studies Quarterly*
    14 (1984): 265–88.
————, and Gustainis, J. Justin. "Anatomy of an Enigma: Jimmy Carter's State of the
    Union Address." *Communication Quarterly* 33 (1985): 43–49.
Jamieson, Kathleen Hall. *Packaging the Presidency*. New York: Oxford University Press,
    1984.
Patton, John H. "A Government as Good as Its People: Jimmy Carter and the Restoration
    of Transcendence to Politics." *Quarterly Journal of Speech* 63 (1977): 249–257.
Sudol, Ronald A. "The Rhetoric of Strategic Retreat: Carter and the Panama Canal
    Debate." *Quarterly Journal of Speech* 65 (1979): 379–91.

Selected Biographies

Carter, Jimmy. *Keeping the Faith: Memoirs of a President*. New York: Bantam Books,
    1982.
————. *Why Not the Best?* Nashville: Broadman Press, 1975.
Fallows, James. "A Passionless Presidency." *Atlantic Monthly* 243 (May 1979), 33–48,
    and (June 1979), 75–81.
Glad, Betty. *Jimmy Carter: In Search of the Great White House*. New York: W. W.
    Norton, 1980.
Johnson, Haynes Bonner. *In the Absence of Power*. New York: Viking Press, 1980.
Jordan, Hamilton. *Crisis: The Last Year of the Carter Presidency*. New York: G. P.
    Putnam's Sons, 1982.
Powell, Jody. *The Other Side of the Story*. New York: Morrow, 1984.

CHRONOLOGY OF MAJOR SPEECHES

See "Research Collections and Collected Speeches" for source codes.

"Law Day Speech," Athens, Georgia, May 4, 1974; *GGP*, pp. 30–42 (edited).

Announcement Speech, Washington, D.C., Dec. 12, 1974; *AC*, Dec. 13, 1974, p. 18A;
GGP, pp. 43–50 (edited).

1976 Acceptance Speech, New York City, July 15, 1976; *GGP*, pp. 125–34.

Inaugural Address, Washington, D.C., January 20, 1977; *PP*, pp. 1–4.

"Report to the American People (First Fireside Chat)," Washington, D.C., February 2,
1977; *PP*, pp. 69–77.

The Energy Problem ("The Moral Equivalent of War"),Washington, D.C., April 18,
1977; *PP*, pp. 656–62; *PR*, pp. 238–42.

"A New Foreign Policy," South Bend, Indiana, May 22, 1977; *PP*, pp. 954–62; *PR*, pp. 242–47.

"The Panama Canal Treaties," Washington, D.C., February 1, 1978; *PP*, pp. 258–63; *PR*, pp. 248–53.

Address of the Camp David Agreement, Washington, D.C., September 18, 1978; *PP*, pp. 1533–37; *PR*, pp. 254–58.

SALT II, Washington, D.C., June 18, 1979; *PP*, pp. 1087–92; *PR*, pp. 258–63.

Energy and National Goals ("A Crisis of Confidence"), Washington, D.C., July 15, 1979; *PP*, pp. 1235–41; *PR*, pp. 264–70.

State of the Union (Carter Doctrine), Washington, D.C., January 23, 1980; *PP*, pp. 194–200; *PR*, pp. 270–76.

Address on the Iranian rescue attempt, Washington, D.C., April 25, 1980; *PP*, pp. 772–73; *PR*, pp. 276–78.

1980 acceptance speech, New York City, August 14, 1980; *PP*, pp. 1532–40.

Farewell Address, Washington, D.C., January 14, 1981; *PP*, pp. 2889–93.

JOHN JAY CHAPMAN
(1862–1933), Socratic gadfly

DANIEL ROSS CHANDLER

Born on March 2, 1862, in New York City, John Jay Chapman was a descendant from Huguenot, Dutch, and English ancestors. In autumn 1874, the twelve-year-old youth moved to Concord, New Hampshire, and entered St. Paul's School, where the Reverend Dr. Henry Augustus Coit exerted a persistent persuasion that provoked John's breakdown and withdrawal. Chapman matriculated at Harvard College during September 1880. He debated in the Harvard Union and when he graduated in 1884, he participated as the Ivy Orator in the commencement ceremonies. During these eventful years, Chapman's father experienced financial collapse and subsequently died. Ralph Waldo Emerson died when John was a sophomore, and the prominent Concord sage became the young man's enduring inspiration. Steeped in New England puritanism, inspired by abolitionist ancestors, disciplined with excellent American education, and familiar with sophisticated European culture, John evidenced a passionate temperament, brilliant mind, distinctive individuality, and splendid literary sensitivity.

Following graduation, he toured Europe during the summer and entered Harvard Law School in October 1885. Within himself Chapman experienced a fear-filled, tormented existence; dominated by a tyrannical conscience, he aggravated an unexplained guilt that required sacrifice and purgation. Enraged with jealousy, he attacked a competitor in romance; overcome with remorse, John removed his coat and waistcoat, wrapped his suspenders about his wrist, and thrust the offending left hand into a blaze until the limb was consumed. The young woman's uncle separated John from Minna Timmons during a two-year interval, attempting to frustrate and postpone their engagement. After Chapman graduated from Harvard Law School and secured admission to the New York bar, he and Minna became engaged in March 1889 and married in July 1889. On Christmas Eve 1896, Minna bore their third child and then died in January. In April 1898, Chapman married his second wife, Elizabeth Chanler, whose substantial wealth removed further financial problems.

CHAPMAN'S LITERARY-RHETORICAL CAREER

Between his marriage and physical breakdown near the century's end, Chapman participated aggressively in governmental reform and political agitation. Sustaining his personal commitment and fulfilling his social responsibility, he traveled around New York in a cart and harangued street-corner crowds. The

Wall Street lawyer described the colorful 1897 mayoralty campaign in his extraordinary book, *Causes and Consequences*. Then during winter 1901, he suffered from grippe and a severe collapse. Turning his interest from practical
politics toward literary criticism, he published an essay, "The Young Shakespeare: A Study of Romeo," in the November 1896 *Atlantic Monthly*. In 1897
this magazine carried his two-part essay, "Emerson Sixty Years After." A sequel
to *Causes and Consequences*, entitled *Practical Agitation*, appeared during 1900.
Concentrating upon drama, Chapman wrote five plays between 1908 and 1911.
These plays were followed in 1913 by *William Lloyd Garrison*, which presented
Chapman's conviction that within a conspiracy of silence, Garrison enunciated
the single thought that everyone comprehended, although the abolitionist's pronouncement was misunderstood. In 1910 he published his perceptive and provocative criticism of American education, *Learning and Other Essays*. With an
undiminished appreciation for education, literary criticism, religion, and social-
political problems, Chapman championed the classics, emphasized liberal studies, challenged scientism, and renounced ineffective learning. He contended that
when a person becomes estranged from historic humanist traditions, the individual relinquishes the capacity for expressing spiritual realities. In 1915 he
published eighteen essays as *Memories and Milestones*; approximately half these
articles analyzed education, religion, art, and drama, while the remainder were
imaginative portraits describing prominent Americans. That same year, 1915,
Chapman's longest book, *Greek Genius and Other Essays*, presented studies
describing Euripides, Shakespeare, and Balzac.

During the decade he spent recovering from his collapse, a convalescing
Chapman pondered the power that religion provides in human personality, and
he matured from a pathetic self-immolation toward an enlightened self-surrender.
He studied similarities between an experimental scientist examining the unfath-
omed universe, a faithful devotee following the will of God, and a philosopher
contemplating a unity within the world's contradictory appearances. Through
the creative arts, Chapman concluded, an individual experiences the "ideal
world" and perceives "life as a totality." Although the critic concurred with
Emerson that a self-reliant individual is God's active agent in reforming the
world, Chapman concluded that a prerequisite for experiencing spiritual strength
is relaxation and self-surrender. Individuals demonstrate spiritual power through
submission before God, and they discover faith as a coherence between articulate
beings expressing themselves through their conduct and language. From these
philosophical ponderings were produced Chapman's *Notes on Religion* (1915)
and *Letters and Religion* (1924). In *Notes on Religion*, Chapman renounced the
assertion that an authoritarian or institutionalized church can serve as an intermediary between a person and God, and he distinguished between Jesus's teachings and the corrupted teachings presented by the Catholic ecclesiastical
establishment. The critic considered the numerous dogmas, rituals, and theo-
logies as awkward attempts to articulate religious experience. Like Emerson, he
repudiated the church's command for obedience that would dominate an indi-

vidual's mind or conscience. As a reflection of the humanist tradition, *Letters and Religion* presents an individualistic credo that provides meaning and purpose to the creative arts and genuine religion. Chapman concluded that religious faith is the inexpungable residue of otherwise transient mystical experiences. Rejecting scientism, he maintained that no comprehensive knowledge or methodological system yields ultimate truth. Through his religious writings Chapman contended that although dogmatists and doctrinaires reason their way to certainty and attempt an intellectual conformity, a person who remains humble before the universe's mysteries will never force one's religious experiences or convictions on another individual.

Speech making was secondary but complementary throughout his distinguished literary career. Chapman presented "The Unity of Human Nature" before the graduating seniors at Hobart College in 1900, when he received an honorary degree; and he gave "Art and Art Schools" in 1914 at the Yale School of Fine Arts. An address delivered before the New York Society for Ethical Culture was revised and published as "Ethical Culture" in 1914. He delivered "American Universities and the Post-Victorian Age" before the Princeton Chapter of Phi Beta Kappa during 1923. At Columbia University in 1931, he presented two lectures, "Our Universities" and "Trends in Popular Thought," which appeared in 1932 in his *New Horizons in American Life*.

Chapman's Coatesville address remains his most memorable. The speech stemmed from tragic events that moved him profoundly. On August 12, 1911, a black man named Walker killed a security guard, was wounded, and was taken under police guard to the Coatesville, Pennsylvania, Hospital. A crowd stormed the hospital, dragged Walker outside, bound the man to his cot, and placed the terrified victim upon a burning rubbish heap. When the flames burned the binding ropes and Walker attempted escape, the crowd recaptured him and returned him to the blaze. Newspapers wrote that for hours playful children kicked Walker's burned torso. Eventually the remains were placed in a carton and taken to the morgue.

Chapman became incensed when Walker's burning was reported, and when the first anniversary of the dramatic event approached, he decided to visit Coatesville and perform penance. Leaving his Islesboro, Maine, home and pausing momentarily in New York City, he discussed his decision with a friend before venturing forth alone. On August 15, 1912, the *Coatesville Record* published an announcement describing a public prayer meeting memorializing Walker's burning that Chapman intended to conduct the following day. The newspaper reported that the service would contain prayer, readings from the Scriptures, and Chapman's short speech. When the appointed hour arrived, four persons gathered: the speaker, his New York friend, an antislavery black woman visiting Coatesville, and a suspected spy. Biographer Hovey explained that Chapman appeared in Coatesville as neither a reforming agitator nor a belated abolitionist but as "a critical witness to report his experience." Chapman willingly endangered his life, recognizing that his premeditated rhetorical act might transform sincere penance into a turbulent race riot and deprive his statement of inward and symbolic meaning.

Without speaking a single sentence, Chapman expressed the spiritual strength emanating from a committed conscience. His solitary confession and eloquent testimony asserted that the universe is never ultimately indifferent and that a resource within the human conscience requires personal accountability. Attempting to perform penance through his physical presence, the speaker became an incarnate witness whose symbolic testimony provoked a nation's troubled conscience. He confessed guilt and expressed contrition so that a complete community might become redeemed, reconciled, and restored. Within the Emersonian tradition that applauds the unattached, committed intellectual confronting social problems as an independent literary critic, Chapman assuaged a corporate guilt through his vicarious atonement and substitutionary offering. Chapman's physical presence in Coatesville demonstrated his conviction that by responding ethically, a single individual confirms the human superiority that separates people from animals, that a human who has been wounded sometimes sympathizes with a special sensitivity when another person suffers, and that by passing through an invisible flame, the human spirit becomes purified.

Although Chapman contended that humans never comprehend absolute truth or final answers, he recognized that profound reality seldom becomes expressed verbally. He recognized that during certain moments an individual's inner resources become unified; during these special times, consciousness becomes concentrated, and individuals respond completely. These moments demonstrate Chapman's unyielding conviction that creative artists, as complete persons and skilled performers, must respond to human existence with their entire being. His evocative Coatesville speech demonstrated this uncompromised conviction through a rhetorical phenomenon in which the speaker, speech, and situation merged and became coherent.

How persons are remembered sometimes suggests how their lives enrich the human community. In his *Lucian, Plato and Greek Morals* (1931), Chapman argued that Plato's greatness came not from his accomplishments as a philosophical thinker and moral teacher but through his achievements as a poet and literary artist. Following Chapman's death on October 4, 1933, writers analyzed the intellectual stature that characterized this unconventional and unorthodox thinker's mind. Scholars studied the restless critic who perceptively analyzed American culture. Hovey concluded that Chapman's published and unpublished writings establish that the author's intellectual sophistication approximated the education employed by an excellent humanities professor. In the May 22, 1929, *New Republic*, Edmund Wilson described Chapman's intense spirit, exceptional literary gifts, and systematic thought and concluded that Chapman constituted "an American Classic." In England on August 14, 1930, the *Times Literary Supplement* described Chapman as an articulate individual in whom thoughts were action, inevitably brimming with faith in human destiny, and superbly qualified to communicate America's meaning and purpose. Observers generally concluded that Chapman was distinctly different from others, that he challenged individuals to think critically and creatively, and that he transcended convention and custom when he articulated his themes and theses.

Just as Socrates troubled the Athenians by his probing, Chapman strengthened the principle and practice of individual freedom of thought and expression. Following his own perspective in political and literary criticism, he was affiliated with no specific school of thought but became instead the finest writer in the United States on significant literature during his generation. He epitomized and antedated the methods employed by the emerging muckrakers. More than a dissatisfied dissident whose interests turned toward social and literary criticism, Chapman was an exceptionally discerning and fluent man of letters whose extended and diverse experiences equipped him to perform perceptively as a distinguished critic probing the American mind. If he failed to keep pace with his contemporaries, perhaps Chapman, like Henry David Thoreau, simply followed the beat of a different drummer.

INFORMATION SOURCES

Research Collections and Collected Speeches

The essential resource for conducting scholarly studies examining John Jay Chapman remains the Chapman Papers, Houghton Library, Harvard University. This collection contains extensive published and unpublished material, such as letters, journals, manuscripts, commonplace books, offprints, scrapbooks, pamphlets, and clippings. Even before Chapman's death in 1933, most of his book were out of print.

Chapman, John Jay. "American Universities and the Post-Victorian Age." *Princeton Alumni Weekly*, April 18, 1923, pp. 581–83. *PAW*

———. *Learning and Other Essays*. New York: Moffat, Yard, and Company, 1910. *LOE*

———. *Memories and Milestones*. New York: Moffat, Yard, and Company, 1915. *MM*

———. *New Horizons in American Life*. New York: Columbia University Press, 1932. *NHAL*

———. "The Unity of Human Nature." In *Representative Phi Beta Kappa Orations*. Edited by Clark S. Northup. New York: Elisha Parmele Press, 1930. *RPBKO*

———. *The Selected Writings of John Jay Chapman* Edited by Jacques Barzun. New York: Farrar, Straus, and Cudahy, 1957. *SWJJC*

Selected Critical Studies

Barzun, Jacques. "Against the Grain: John Jay Chapman." *Atlantic Monthly* 179 (1947): 120–24.

Brown, Stuart Gerry. "John Jay Chapman and the Emersonian Gospel." *New England Quarterly* 35 (1952): 147–80.

Burdick, Norman R. "The 'Coatesville Address': Crossroads of Rhetoric and Poetry." *Western Journal of Speech Communication* 42 (1978): 73–82.

Hovey, Richard B. "John Jay Chapman: The Early Years." Ph.D. dissertation, Harvard University, 1950.

O'Connor, William Van. "Emerson, Chapman, and Righteous Individualism." *Revue de langues vivantes* 31 (1955): 442–47.

Stocking, David. "The Ideas of John Jay Chapman." Ph.D. dissertation, University of Michigan, 1950.

Wilson, Edmund. "John Jay Chapman." *New Republic* 59 (1929): 28–33.

———. "John Jay Chapman: The Mute and Open Strings." In *The Triple Thinkers*. New York: Oxford University Press, 1948.

Wister, Owen. "John Jay Chapman." *Atlantic Monthly* 153 (1934): 595–99.

Selected Biographies

Bernstein, Melvin Herbert. *John Jay Chapman*. New York: Twayne Publishers, 1964.

Hovey, Richard B. *John Jay Chapman: An American Mind*. New York: Columbia University Press, 1959.

Howe, M. A. DeWolfe. *John Jay Chapman and His Letters*. Boston and New York: Houghton Mifflin Company, 1937.

CHRONOLOGY OF MAJOR SPEECHES

See "Research Collections and Collected Speeches" for source codes.

"The Unity of Human Nature," Hobart College, Geneva, New York, June 20, 1900; *LOE*, pp. 175–90; *RPBKO*, pp. 254–62.

"Coatesville Address," Coatesville, Pennsylvania, August 16, 1912; *MM*, pp. 225–32; *SWJJC*, pp. 255–58.

"Ethical Culture," New York Society for Ethical Culture, New York City, 1914; *MM*, pp. 149–62.

"Art and Art Schools," Yale School of Fine Arts, New Haven, Connecticut, June 8, 1914; *MM*, 3–16.

"American Universities and the Post-Victorian Age," Princeton University, Princeton, New Jersey, April 7, 1923; *PAW*, pp. 581–83.

"Our Universities," Columbia University, New York City, November 1931; *NHAL*, pp. 1–28.

"Trends in Popular Thought," Columbia University, New York City, November 1931; *NHAL*, pp. 31–51.

CESAR ESTRADA CHAVEZ
(1927–   ), labor leader and minority activist
——————————————— JOHN C. HAMMERBACK and RICHARD J. JENSEN

In the early spring of 1962, Cesar Chavez moved from San José to Delano, California, to begin organizing farmworkers into an effective union, a task that most other labor leaders considered impossible. California farmworkers typically had been illiterate, indigent, and migratory, and growers had easily broken all farmworkers' unions since 1903. Further diminishing Chavez's chances of success, he initially lacked coworkers, personal wealth, political power, or formal education past the seventh grade. He appeared to be no match for the wealth and power of California agribusiness, yet through preparation, perseverance, public address, and perhaps prayer, the quiet and unassuming Chavez would succeed where others had failed.

His readings of Saint Thomas Aquinas, Saint Paul, Gandhi, and books on Mexican-American history stimulated his intellectual growth and suggested persuasive strategies. Winthrop Yinger reports in *Cesar Chavez: The Rhetoric of Nonviolence* that from Paul, Chavez learned the importance of face-to-face communication: "St. Paul must have been a terrific organizer, as he would go and talk with the people right in their homes, sit with them and be one of them." At the beginning of his career he felt awkward and nervous when speaking before groups. Soon, however, he began speaking frequently at various homes. In an interview published in the July 1966 issue of *Ramparts* magazine he recalled often lying awake at night after a meeting, "going over the whole thing, playing the tape back, trying to see why people laugh at one point, or why they were for one thing or against another." He saw public address as necessary to organize workers. Jacques Levy in *Cesar Chavez: Autobiography of La Causa* quotes Chavez as saying that "there are some very simple things that have to be done, certain key things that nobody can do without, like talking to people." He concluded that if one persisted in presenting one's message, the audience would respond. As a community service organization speaker, he also learned that clear illustrations and examples were more effective in communicating ideas than was philosophizing. According to biographer Peter Matthiessen, Chavez felt that to reach listeners "You have to draw a simple picture and color it in."

Chavez expanded his commitment to persuasive discourse and achieved striking successes as a Chicano leader and a labor leader. In 1962 the National Farm Workers Association was founded in Fresno, California, with Chavez as president. From its beginning, his labor union, later named the United Farm Workers, was closely identified with the civil rights movement and its techniques of aggressive nonviolence. Consisting mainly of Mexican-Americans, his farm-labor group played a major role in creating the Chicano protest movement. A wide variety of Americans shared the opinion of him expressed in *Look* magazine: "At a time when many American radicals are saying that nonviolence—as an instrument for social change—died with Martin Luther King, it is reassuring to meet a man of faith who preaches and gets results." As Chavez attracted national attention, he gained a reputation as the most persuasive union leader in a generation.

CHAVEZ AS LABOR RHETOR

Chavez's perseverance with public address resulted largely from his millennial interpretation of contemporary history, an interpretation based on his beliefs in God, the injustices suffered by the poor, the need to organize workers, and the power of public address. A devout Roman Catholic, he accepted the orthodox position that the church is a powerful moral and spiritual force in the world and that Christ's model of nonviolence is admirable. As the 1960s ended, he shared his view of contemporary reforms: "People are not going to turn back now. The poor are on the march: black, brown, red, everyone, whites included. We are now in the midst of the biggest revolution this country has ever known." Consisting primarily of disadvantaged members of racial minorities, the UFW was "unlike other unions in that it sought to alter the conditions of human life." In "Letter from Delano" in 1969, Chavez stated his convictions that "our cause is just, that history is a story of social revolution, and that the poor shall inherit the land." In his interview with *Look* of April 1, 1969 he could announce with assurance: "We will win, we *are* winning, because ours is a revolution of mind and heart, not just economics." Just as irreconcilable labor-management disputes can often be settled by an impartial third-party arbiter, he envisioned a human arbiter of his struggle for justice: public opinion. In the *Christian Century*, February 18, 1970 he confidently forecasted: "I contend that not only the American public but people in general throughout the world will respond to a cause that involves injustice."

A brief examination of Chavez's extensive public communication, which eventually included speeches, letters, interviews, fasts, marches, boycotts, proclamations, and religious and ethnic icons, will illustrate his prominent rhetorical characteristics and substantial themes. The key to understanding his rhetorical behavior is found in the relationship between his theory and practice of reform rhetoric.

In March 1966 Chavez issued his *El Plan De Delano* (the plan of Delano), in which he referred to the plan as his blueprint "for the liberation of farm workers of the United States of North America, affiliated with the unique and true union of farm workers . . . seeking social justice in farm labor with those reforms that they believe necessary for their well-being as workers." Because farmworkers must be granted their "basic God-given rights as human beings," Chavez asked for support from all political groups, particularly the Christian church. He announced that all farmworkers "across the country—the Mexicans, Filipinos, Blacks and poor whites; the Puerto Ricans, the Japanese, the Indians, the Portuguese and the Arabs" would unite in a nonviolent movement to improve the lives of farm workers.

On February 14, 1968, in response to potential violence in the fields, Chavez began a twenty-five day fast as an act of penance, recalling farm workers to the nonviolent roots of their movement. During the fast he prepared a document, "The Mexican-American and the Church," which was presented at the Second Annual Mexican-American Conference in Sacramento, California, March 8–10, 1968. Chavez called the church a "moral movement." He noted how Protestant ministers worked in the movement at its beginning, while the Catholic church initially either ignored the workers or worked against them. Chavez pleaded for the Catholic church, a servant to the poor, to use its tremendous power to improve human lives: "We don't ask for more cathedrals. We don't ask for bigger churches or fine gifts. We ask for its presence with us, beside us, as Christ among us. We ask the Church to sacrifice with the people for social change, for justice, and for love of brother. We don't ask for words. We ask for deeds. We don't ask for paternalism. We ask for servanthood."

At the completion of his fast on March 10, 1968, a religious service and fiesta were held. The 8,000 to 10,000 people present heard a speech written by Chavez read in both English and Spanish. Chavez was too weak to read it. Described as "a compilation or model of the strategy and mind of Cesar Chavez," the brief statement began by thanking people for their support during the fast. Chavez proclaimed that people were not gathered that day as much to end a fast as to observe the fact that "we are a family bound together in a common struggle for justice. We are a Union family celebrating our unity and the nonviolent nature of our movement." He explained that he had undertaken the fast "because my heart was filled with grief and pain for the suffering of farm workers. The Fast was first for me and then for all of us in this Union. It was a Fast for nonviolence and a call to sacrifice." He concluded by explaining that farmworkers faced rich and powerful opponents, but they were not invincible: "We have something the rich do not own. We have our own bodies and spirits and the justice of our cause as our weapons." The use of those weapons was vital: "It is how we use our lives that determines what kind of men we are. . . . I am convinced that the truest act of courage, the strongest act of manliness is to sacrifice ourselves for others in a totally non-violent struggle for justice. To be a man is to suffer for others. God help us to be men."

Chavez also employed public letters to reach his opponents as well as his potential supporters. In a widely anthologized letter to E. L. Barr, Jr., the president of the California Grape and Free Fruit League, Chavez quoted from Martin Luther King, Jr.'s, "Letter from Birmingham Jail" to describe why farmworkers were resorting to strikes and boycotts in their battle against the growers: "Injustice must be exposed, with all the tension its exposure creates, to the light of human conscience and the air of national opinion before it can be cured.'' Chavez concluded that farmworkers' suffering locked them ''in a death struggle against man's inhumanity to man in the industry that you represent. And this struggle itself gives meaning to our life and ennobles our dying.''

Chavez's speech at the Montopolis Community Center in Austin, Texas, on February 6, 1971, was representative of many of his other addresses. Five thousand listeners, including supporters of *La Raza* and strikers against the Economy Furniture Company, heard opening words that set his persuasive tone of graciousness: ''Friends, sisters, honored guests, I'm extremely pleased to be here in Austin and in Texas. I've heard so much of the warm Texas hospitality, and let me tell you that I really know what you mean when you say, when you hear in California—about Texas hospitality. . . . I think that everyone that I have come in contact with in this day and a half has been extremely gracious and courteous and friendly.'' Later in the speech he acknowledged generously that ''there's so many good people that must be thanked''—Texas legislators, county commissioners, people who met him at the airport. Former U.S. senator from Texas Ralph Yarborough, listening in the audience, was a long-time friend of the farmworkers and ''a great man.'' Although he predicted a Chicano would someday be elected governor of a southwestern state, he hastened to add benevolently that he intended ''no offense to the present governors of the various southwestern states.''

Chavez began by briefly discussing the Economy strike and then urging a boycott of Montgomery Ward until the store discontinued its line of Economy furniture. These immediate issues ushered in a lengthy explanation of the broader issues of what, how, and why nonviolent tactics succeeded in a right cause. Maintaining that workers possess an ''inherent'' right to join unions in order to reach ''their rightful place in society,'' he argued that the boycott would succeed because it was an ''extension of love from one human being to the other'' and therefore a ''powerful weapon of the poor people and people who struggle for justice.'' This expression of love ''creates a chain reaction that has tremendous consequences for good.'' To demonstrate the influence of the boycott, he used detailed anecdotes to show that children recognized his name and had heard of the farmworkers' boycott against grapes and lettuce. Chavez asserted that once Chicanos were treated as ''human beings,'' they would obtain political power as well as union contracts. His concern for justice extended far beyond Chicanos, however, and he called for attention to needy people regardless of race.

Chavez's conclusion in English began with an emphasis on moral questions: ''The thing that all of us want—and here we're concerned for one another—is to build and not destroy. . . . And really be concerned, really for the dignity of men'' in order to ''change things so we can get justice and dignity for our people.'' Nonviolence was essential, he added, to effect these changes. His conclusion in Spanish, eight paragraphs in which he urged Chicanos to help each other and to stress education of the young, contained little except anecdotes and illustrations. After a lengthy Mexican anecdote ended with one cowboy telling another that he would not cut off the head of a bee because a bee is ''very organized; if I harm it, I'll have thousands of its kind on me soon," he made his point: "That is how we ought to think: a wrong against any one of us is a wrong against us all."

Throughout Chavez's rhetorical career his oral delivery—his use of voice and body—reinforced his persona as a gentle advocate who emphasizes content over personality. Levy reported that his speeches were "soft, sweetened by a Spanish accent," and Matthiessen that "what is striking in his gentle voice is his lack of mannerisms." The September 2, 1973 *London Times* noted that he "overwhelmed the listener with his gentleness." Yinger, who heard Chavez speak three or four dozen times between 1965 and 1976, described his "conversational tone of delivery. He does not punctuate his ideas with shouts, indeed, he seldom raises his voice at all." Speaking slowly, deliberately, calmly, and gently, Chavez appeared to trust the persuasive power of his arguments and explanations.

Chavez relied on lucid explanations and arguments, illustrated with plentiful facts, simple anecdotes, and concrete examples. He added clarity to his case through abundant transitions and a simple style. Elevating his message and himself above purely practical, pragmatic, or selfish interests, he stressed moral issues and treated opponents generously. His case for supporting his union fit into his broader argument that racial minorities, in particular Mexican-Americans, were being swept toward the economic, social, and political justice they deserved. His calm delivery further focused attention on his message rather than on himself. Not neglecting rhetorical concerns, he adapted his topics to his audiences and pressing issues.

Chavez's discourse persuaded Anglos as well as Mexican-Americans. For Chicanos, he employed conventionally powerful patterns, forms, and appeals: folk sayings and *dichos* or maxims; anecdotes and stories or *cuentos*; Spanish formality, graciousness, and respect, as illustrated by his warm and respectful acknowledgments in introductions, and familial and religious themes and images, which surfaced in his references to God and his examples of and quotes about Mexican, Mexican-American, and southwestern families. To Anglo idealists in the idealistic 1960s, moreover, he was also an ideal spokesman—one with a case built on abundant facts and high moral principles. That case, because it was presented so calmly and clearly, appeared to trust the good judgment of all listeners.

INFORMATION SOURCES

Research Collections and Collected Speeches

Although there is no centralized collection of Chavez's speeches and writings, there are collections at the San Joaquin Farm Workers Collection, Special Collections Department, Fresno State University; the Labor History Archives, Wayne State University, Detroit, Michigan; the Chicano Studies Library, Arizona State University; Tempe, Arizona; and at other colleges and libraries. Speeches and interviews also appear in the

Catholic Worker, *El Grito*, *El Malcriado*, the *Fresno Bee*, the *Los Angeles Free Press*, *Movement*, *National Catholic Reporter*, *Playboy*, *Ramparts*, and the *Christian Century* and *Look*. Examples of his discourse appear in virtually every collection of Chicano literature.

Aztlan: An Anthology of Mexican American Literature. Edited by Luis Val-   CEP
    dez and Stan Steiner. New York: Vintage Books, 1972.

Cortes, Carlos E.; Ginsburg, Arlin I.; Green, Allan W. F.; and Joseph,   TPEA
    James A. *Three Perspectives on Ethnicity in America*. New York:
    G. P. Putnam's Sons, 1976.

La Causa Politica: A Chicano Politics Reader. Edited by F. Chris Garcia.   LCP
    Notre Dame: University of Notre Dame Press, 1974.

Pain and Promise: The Chicano Today. Edited by Edward Simmen. New   PPCT
    York: Mentor Books, 1972.

Tice, Robert. "The Rhetoric of La Raza." Unpublished manuscript, Chicano   RLA
    Studies Collection, Hayden Library, Arizona State University,
    Tempe, Arizona.

Yinger, Winthrop. *Cesar Chavez: The Rhetoric of Nonviolence*. New York: CCRN
    Exposition Press, 1975.

Selected Critical Studies

Hammerback, John C., and Jensen, Richard J. "The Rhetorical Worlds of Cesar Chavez and Reies Tijerina." In *Hispanic Voices*. Edited by Robert W. Mullen. Lexington, Mass.: Ginn Custom Publishing, 1984.

Hammerback, J. C., and Jensen, Richard J. "The Rhetorical Worlds of Cesar Chavez and Reies Tijerina." *Western Journal of Speech Communication* 44 (1980): 166–76.

Hammerback, John C.; Jensen, Richard J.; and Gutierrez, Jose Angel. "Teaching the 'Truth': The Righteous Rhetoric of Cesar Chavez." In *A War of Words: Chicano Revolt in the 1960s and 1970s*. Westport, Conn.: Greenwood Press, 1985.

Selected Biographies

Day, Mark. *Forty Acres: Cesar Chavez and the Farm Workers*. New York: Praeger Publishers, 1973.

Dunne, John Gregory. *Delano*. New York: Farrar, Straus, and Giroux, 1971.

Levy, Jacques E. *Cesar Chavez: Autobiography of La Causa*. New York: Norton, 1975.

Matthiessen, Peter. *Sal Si Puedes: Cesar Chavez and the New American Revolution*. New York: Random House, 1969.

Taylor, Ronald B. *Chavez and the Farm Workers*. Boston: Beacon Press, 1975.

CHRONOLOGY OF MAJOR SPEECHES

See "Research Collections and Collected Speeches" for source codes.

"The Organizer's Tale," Delano, California, July 1966; *CEP*, pp. 297–302.

"The Plan of Delano," Delano, California, March 1966; *TPEA*, pp. 379–82.

"The Mexican-American and the Church," Sacramento, California, March 9–10, 1968; *LCP*, pp. 143–46.

Statement by Cesar Chavez on the conclusion of a fast for nonviolence, Delano, California, March 10, 1968; *CCRN*, pp. 46–47.

Letter from Delano, 1969; *PPCT*, pp. 29–32.

"Chavez in Austin, Texas," Austin, Texas, February 6, 1971; *RLA*, pp. 1–18.

SHIRLEY CHISHOLM
(1924–   ), U.S. congresswoman, 1972 presidential candidate, educator

_____ SUSAN DUFFY

In her first address before the U.S. House of Representatives on March 26, 1969, Shirley Chisholm stated unequivocably: "Our children, our jobless men, our deprived, rejected and starving fellow citizens must come first. For this reason, I intend to vote No on every money bill that comes to the floor of this House that provides any funds for the Department of Defense." Such unaffected candor, directness, and humanitarianism characterized Chisholm's political oratory of the 1960s and 1970s and sustains her career in the professoriate in the 1980s. Her debate experience while a student at Brooklyn College markedly influenced her style of speaking, which is aggressive, quick, and incisive; each speech easily fit the mold of a debate case. The former nursery school teacher, who pushed for reform in education, emerged as the candidate for the New York State Assembly in 1963. She was a diminutive, black woman, fluent in Spanish, which gave her tremendous credibility with the large Hispanic constituency in her Twelfth District, who refused to be controlled by the black, male-dominated power brokers of the Black Caucus and the Democratic political machine. She was and has remained "unbought and unbossed," a slogan from her congressional campaign, which she also chose as the title of her 1970 autobiography. Her experience as a speech writer for other New York assemblymen accorded her a political savvy that allowed her to introduce two revolutionary bills in the New York State Assembly: one that established SEEK, a program designed to identify disadvantaged youths while they were still in high school and offer them an opportunity to go to college, and a second that changed the discriminatory practice of revoking tenure for female teachers whose careers were interrupted by pregnancy. Chisholm's frankness and her ability to champion successfully the cause of out-groups made her a candidate for the Twelfth New York Congressional District in 1967 by unanimous endorsement of a citizens' screening committee and gave testament to her comment: "I have a way of talking that does something to people." During her four years as a representative in the New York Assembly and her terms of office in the Ninety-first to Ninety-seventh Congresses, Chisholm became one of the foremost female orators in the United States. She earned this reputation not because she was black or a woman during the turbulent period of civil rights advocacy when tokenism to both groups was perceived as a means of appeasement but because she was strong, understood her audience and their needs, and was politically and morally persuasive.

CHISHOLM AS CONSUMMATE DEBATER

In her speeches, Chisholm argued convincingly to change the status quo and presented virtually impenetrable prima facie cases. She defined the problem, provided the rationale for change, and usually offered a solid plan with clear advantages. She relied heavily on governmental statistics as points of refutation against the government and was particularly caustic in her statements criticizing the Nixon administration. She continually challenged the president to live up to the promises he made in his State of the Union Address, press conferences, and other public addresses. In "It Is Time to Reassess Our National Priorities," her first speech as a freshman congresswoman, she quoted Nixon's promise to make cities livable and indicted him for cutting the Head Start program so the Defense Department would have funding for missile development. The administration claimed two more years of intervention in Vietnam would require a high level of defense spending. Chisholm sardonically turned it into a litany of emotional appeals:

Two more years, two more years of hunger for Americans, of death for our best young men, of children suffering the lifelong handicap of not having a good education when they are young . . . Two more years of high taxes . . . Two more years of too little being done to fight our greatest enemies—poverty, prejudice and neglect—here in this country. Two more years of fantastic waste in the Defense Department, of penny pinching on social programs. Our country cannot survive two more years, or four, or these kinds of policies. It must stop—this year—now.

Each point built to a crescendo and riveted the attention of the audience. In her autobiography Chisholm provides a revealing description of her rhetorical style: "When I get on a platform, I am transformed; I have even been called Messianic." Yet she did not want for humor, acerbic though it was. She began the "National Priorities" speech with a comment clearly intended to display her irritation at being denied committee assignments for which she felt particularly well suited and did so masterfully with the humor and style that characterized her oratory: "Apparently all they know here in Washington about Brooklyn is that a tree grows there. I can think of no other reason for assigning me to the House Agriculture Committee."

Chisholm never abandoned her role of educator when she entered politics. Her speeches repeatedly emphasized children, education, and governmental neglect of minorities and coalesced in the charge that the "government has lost touch with the people." As a black woman politician in the 1960s and 1970s, one might expect Chisholm to make black civil rights a dominant, if not exclusive, theme. She did not. She used examples of American Indians, Chicanos, and Spanish-speaking migrants before using examples of blacks in order to deflect charges that she was a representative voice of the black community only. She saw herself clearly as representing all of the diverse constituencies in the Twelfth

District, which could have served as a microcosm for minority groups in the United States. She stated strongly her genuine concern for all minorities, as well as for whites, in "Economic Injustice in America Today," one of the speeches she delivered with various modifications during her presidential campaign. Her characteristic three-pronged attack, which used statistics, pathos appeal, and repetition, is evident:

Ask the Chicanos in East Los Angeles in which 35% of the housing is substandard whether President Nixon's announcement of . . . 2 million housing starts in 1971 had anything to do with improvement of housing in East Los Angeles. Or talk to the Spanish-speaking migrant worker . . . about the abundance of good health and medical care which this Administration proclaims: That . . . worker knows that infant and maternal mortality among his or her people is 125% higher than the national rate: that influenza and pneumonia death rates are 200% higher . . . that death from tuberculosis and infectious disease is 260% higher; and life expectancy itself for migrant workers is 49 years—compared with the 67.5 years for the members of the silent majority.

She went on to use the same statistical attack on the administration's gross neglect of black ghettos and finally shifted her emphasis to unemployment of all groups in Seattle. Chisholm used epithets as "devil terms." For example, she called the sales tax "the enemy of the poor person." She identified villians, such as the "honor roll of wealthy Americans," who avoid paying income tax, and Nixon, who travels to Peking when "he doesn't have time to walk ten blocks from the White House . . . and look at the lives people are living under Phase II [of his economic program]."

When she announced her candidacy for the presidency on January 25, 1972, Chisholm said emphatically that she was not the candidate of black America, the women's movement, political bosses, or special interests: "I am the candidate of the people." Yet it was precisely black groups and feminist groups, vying to use her as a champion of their causes, and black politicians, who by failing to give her a firm endorsement undermined her campaign. From the outset Chisholm carried the burden of refutation, repeatedly answering the question: "Are you a serious candidate?" The press implied that she was not—that she was running merely as a symbol of blacks and feminists. In "Women in Politics," an important speech given after the campaign, she expressed her belief that though she was not a token candidate for either group, her candidacy "forced the other candidates to deal with issues relating to women."

In *The Good Fight*, an account of her presidential campaign, Chisholm noted that the majority of her campaign speeches were ad-libbed, which suggests her virtuosity as an extemporaneous and impromptu speaker. "If any of them survive," she cautioned, "it must be in the form of films or tape." *The Good Fight* contains the text of two prepared speeches: "Economic Justice for Women," which outlined discrimination against women in the workplace and was adapted throughout the campaign to meet audience demands of the myriad groups she addressed, and "The Cost of Care," which addressed the need for adequate health care for all people, an issue overshadowed, through no fault of Chisholm, by feminist and black concerns during the campaign. Afterward she lamented the fact that feminist groups wanted her to address only feminist issues such as abortion and equal rights and that both black and feminist groups suffered from a tunnel-vision approach to her campaign.

Chisholm's relationship with the press corps was generally amicable. Her sincerity, pointed humor, and command of the issues she addressed in both English and Spanish made for effective coverage in the print media—when she was covered, for she had to file suit against the Federal Communications Commission for equal time on the major television networks. Despite her good relations with them, she voiced strong objections to the press and feminists who chose not to take her candidacy seriously but saw it as a futile exercise. She took both groups to task in "Women in Politics" and charged that in her campaign the press looked for fanatical feminists screaming obscenities at rallies but ignored conservative-looking women with liberal views who were willing to testify before hearings on equal employment. She chided feminists for disparaging traditional roles of women and promoting a feminist paranoia: "Not all sexual advances are sexual. Children are more than a pile of dirty diapers, and families, while they have often restricted women, have also provided warmth, security and love."

Chisholm was keenly aware of the sociological and psychological situation in which blacks, other minorities, and women found themselves. She recognized and understood the lower-class wariness of embracing the black or feminist movement wholeheartedly. She acknowledged that most social movements are led by the "better educated and better-off." The feminist movement found most of its leaders in the educated, white middle class, but she cautioned them to recognize the diversity of the women on the fringe who also had feminist ideals. In "Economic Justice for Women," she made an analogy between women and blacks and pointed to the bias and oppression to which whites subjected both groups. Although she criticized many hard-line feminist positions, she still became an unofficial spokeswoman for feminist groups.

Where did this leave her with the black community? Her association with the largely male Black Caucus was tempestuous. Chisholm was not a candidate to be manipulated on any issue, particularly a racial one. Her candidacy was viewed by many black leaders as self-serving and detrimental to their efforts in promoting black male politicians. She accused prominent black figures of male chauvinism and petty jealousy but recognized the dilemma her candidacy caused in the black community and outlined it sensitively in "Women in Politics":

To black and Chicano women picketing a restricted club or insisting on the title Ms. are not burning issues. . . . Women of color . . . are subject to additional and sometimes different pressures . . . the black experience in America has not been an unbridled success for black men. . . . There have been times when discrimination and the economic situation were such that it was easier for a black woman to get a job than her husband. Because of this, anything that might be construed as anti-male will be viewed skeptically by a black woman.

Shirley Chisholm was, and continues to be, influential in the United States as a political figure, feminist, and educator. She is an excellent impromptu speaker whose competence, integrity, sense of purpose, and sincerity are readily conveyed in her speaking, which is crisp and aggressive but not abrasive. Always a woman of her convictions, even when they went against party or special interests, she used appeals to ambition, optimism, individual dignity, helpfulness, and democracy to sustain her cries for change. Many see Chisholm as a borderline radical feminist or black leader, but her oratory clearly revealed her moderation, even conformity, and above all her call to educate the American people.

There is no indication that Chisholm relied heavily on speech writers. She took pride in her ability to move an audience with rational argumentation and strong evidence and lived by her assertion, "I always mean what I say." There is a bluntness that characterizes Chisholm's speech, but it does not carry a concomitant coldness. Her oratory manifests deep concern for her constituents and for all other Americans. She has lent credibility and dignity to the black and feminist movements in the United States and remains an accomplished orator with an important mission.

INFORMATION SOURCES

Research Collections and Collected Speeches

The voluminous material written about Shirley Chisholm is widely scattered and virtually inaccessible except through congressional indexes, computer data bases, and the reference sources on American women and Afro-American history. The Schomburg Center for Research in Black Culture, New York Public Library, has a large clippings file on Chisholm, as well as films and tapes in the audiovisual department. A bibliography of works by and about Chisholm is being prepared for the American Library Association and should be available by 1987. Few works address her oratory specifically. There is one unpublished dissertation and one master's thesis on this subject. Chisholm's written account of her presidential campaign provides excerpts of speeches and two full texts of speeches. She also includes several texts of position papers, written and circulated during her campaign, but does not indicate if they were delivered.

American Rhetoric from Roosevelt to Reagan: A Collection of Speeches and   ARRR
       Critical Essays. Edited by Halford Ross Ryan. Prospect Heights,
       Ill.: Waveland Press, 1983.
Chisholm, Shirley. *The Good Fight.* New York: Harper & Row, 1973.   TGF
Representative American Speeches, 1968–1969. Edited by Lester Thonssen.   RAS
       New York: H. W. Wilson Company, 1969.   1968–69

Representative American Speeches, 1971–72. Edited by Waldo W. Braden.   *RAS*
    New York: H. W. Wilson Company, 1972.   *1971–72*
Representative American Speeches, 1972–73. Edited by Waldo W. Braden.   *RAS*
    New York: H. W. Wilson Company, 1973.   *1972–73*

Selected Critical Studies

Handle, Margaret Jean. "A Critical Analysis of Selected Speeches on Women's Rights
    by Representative Shirley Chisholm." Master's thesis, California State University
    at Long Beach, 1976.
Williamson, Dorothy Kay. "Rhetorical Analysis of Selected Modern Black Spokespersons
    on the Women's Liberation Movement." Ph.D. dissertation, Ohio State Univer-
    sity, 1980.

Selected Biographies

Chisholm, Shirley. *Unbought and Unbossed*. Boston: Houghton Mifflin, 1970.
———. *The Good Fight*. New York: Harper & Row, 1973.
Brownmiller, Susan. *Shirley Chisholm: A Biography*. Garden City, N.Y.: Doubleday,
    1971.
Haskins, James. *Fighting Shirley Chisholm*. New York: Dial Press, 1975.
Hicks, Nancy. *The Honorable Shirley Chisholm, Congresswoman From Brooklyn*. New
    York: Lion Books, 1971.

CHRONOLOGY OF MAJOR SPEECHES

See "Research Collections and Collected Speeches" for source codes.

"It Is Time to Reassess Our National Priorities," Washington, D.C., March 26, 1969;
RAS 1968–69, pp. 68–72.

"For the Equal Rights Amendment," U.S. House of Representatives, Washington, D.C.,
August 10, 1970; *ARRR*, pp. 222–26.

"Economic Justice for Women," a campaign speech modified and delivered to several
audiences during late 1971 and early 1972; *TGF*, pp. 188–92.

"The Cost of Care," campaign speech delivered originally in Philadelphia and then to
several other audiences during late 1971 and early 1972; *TGF*, pp. 193–99.

"Economic Injustice in America Today," Newark College of Engineering, Newark, New
Jersey, April 15, 1972; *RAS 1972–73*, pp. 27–36.

"Women in Politics," Houston, Texas, February 9, 1973; *RAS 1972–73*, pp. 79–85.

"Vote for the Individual, Not the Political Party," New York City, June 24, 1978; *Vital
Speeches*, August 15, 1978, pp. 670–71.

FRANK CHURCH
(1924–1984), U.S. senator, Idaho

LOCH K. JOHNSON

Frank Church of Boise, Idaho, exhibited uncommon interest and prowess in oratory even as a boy. His poor health was a strong contributor to this direction. Chronic bronchitis often forced him to bed, where he spent his hours immersed in U.S. history books and political biographies and often listened to Idaho Senator William Borah on the radio, speaking in deep, rich tones and with an old-fashioned, ornate style. Impressed by Borah, a popular Republican and chairman of the prestigious Senate Foreign Relations Committee, the young Church studied the senator's written speeches.

As Church matured, his voice grew strong and sure, his diction became more sophisticated, and his knowledge of public affairs increased. His reputation as a public speaker spread throughout Idaho during his high school days: he was a champion debater in his senior year, won first place in an American Legion national contest, and was referred to in the newspapers as the "Boy Orator of the Snake River." During World War II, his commanding officer, a brigadier general, was so struck by his voice that he had Lieutenant Church read aloud in the evenings to other officers. Following the war, Church attended Stanford University, where he won the esteemed debating prize, the Medaille Joffre.

Church completed his law degree at Stanford and returned to Boise to practice law and teach speech at the local college. In 1956, he ran as a Democrat for a U.S. Senate seat—brazenly at age thirty-two—against the entrenched Republican incumbent, Herman Welker. Church won the election by 40,000 votes though Eisenhower carried Idaho by 60,000. Fate had helped him, for Welker fell ill during the campaign. Nevertheless, his handsome appearance, his great energy that carried him into every corner of the state, and his oratory won him many votes.

In national politics, his speaking skills attracted wider attention. Still in his thirties, Church was chosen by Democratic leaders in 1960 to be the keynote speaker at the party's national convention in Los Angeles. He became widely regarded as among the top three or four speakers in the Senate; his speeches on the floor sometimes recaptured the great oratory of a century before.

CHURCH AS POLITICAL PHILOSOPHER

Church was a loner in the U.S. Senate. The clubby, joke-telling, backslapping, logrolling, good-old-boy style that characterizes much of how this institution works was for the most part unappealing to the Phi Beta Kappa intellectual from

Stanford. He was earnest, courtly, independent, and at times distant. His strategy was not to twist arms but to apply logic, analysis, and rhetorical skills to win the day. His colleague and, for a brief time, mentor in the Senate in the early days, Lyndon B. Johnson, was the archetypical cajoler and nose counter; for Church, though, the more natural approach was to speak his piece. Its sheer persuasiveness would be sufficient. Besides, he sometimes said privately, perhaps with undue innocence, all senators are sovereign and would decide their votes based on the merits of the case. "This is a Senate; a Senate of equals; of men of individual honor and personal character, and of absolute independence," said another senator famous as an orator, Daniel Webster. "We know no masters; we acknowledge no dictators." The words might well have been Church's, for this he believed and practiced. He would study an issue closely and state his views in a carefully prepared and well-rehearsed speech. His fellow sovereigns could then accept or reject his philosophy on its merits.

Church's philosophizing often focused on the subject closest to his heart, U.S. foreign policy. Although his theme was almost always one of nonintervention, he was far from a strict isolationist in the tradition of so many other western senators. He supported the United Nations, the North Atlantic Treaty Organization, and other collective-security arrangements. He was, though, deeply wary about U.S. involvement in the ferment and revolution of developing nations. He frequently urged that the foreign adventure be made subordinate to the resolution of domestic problems. Above all, he reminded audiences again and again that the United States did not possess the wealth and the power to mold the world to its own liking. "The sooner we learn to impose some reasonable restraint on our own tendency to intervene too much in other people's affairs," he said to an audience in 1972, "the happier land we will have and the less burden we will place upon our own people to undertake sacrifices that are not really related to their own good or the good of their country."

Although nonintervention was the dominant theme in his career, this view was not initially part of his rhetoric. It evolved as the world began to change dramatically in the early 1960s. When first elected, he was, like many other successful politicians and Americans at that time, a cold warrior. His campaign speeches of 1956 spoke repeatedly of the necessity to halt the spread of communism. In a 1970 interview, he spoke about these early statements: "I was convinced, as nearly everybody was convinced, that the Cold War policies of the United States were absolutely sound. Our duty, as we conceived it then, was to quarantine Communism and to protect the world from the further extension of the Communist system." His most important early speech, the 1960 keynote address at the Democratic National Convention, was suffused with this worldview.

Three events moved him away from this interventionist policy designed to quarantine, or contain, the Soviet Union. First, the Sino-Soviet split of 1962 and other indications of fragmentation in the Soviet bloc led Church to the conclusion that nationalism, not communism, was the dominant political force in the world. Second, he became a member of the Foreign Relations Committee, led by senior senators, most notably chairman J. William Fulbright (Democrat-Arkansas), who had come to this view even earlier and who had a profound influence on the young senator. Last, and most significant, the war in Vietnam came to embody in his mind the disastrous consequences of the cold war mentality—the great loss of American blood and treasure in what was essentially for Church a civil war best left for the Vietnamese to resolve.

Around 1964, Church began to argue strongly and regularly against U.S. interference in a world of revolutionary turmoil. He began to compare the office of the presidency to a Roman Caesardom, demanding a restoration of the congressional role in foreign affairs in order to prevent further excesses from the executive branch such as the concealed escalation in Vietnam. "The Roman Caesars did not spring full blown from the brow of Zeus," he warned his colleagues in the stately (critics would say stilted) prose that was his cachet, "they stole their powers away from an unsuspecting Senate." He began to see U.S. foreign policy in Asia as no less aggressive than the policies of U.S. opponents. The Vietnam War elevated him, along with Fulbright, George McGovern (Democrat, South Dakota), and a few other senators to the status of a well-known national figure, a leader of the rising dissent against the controversial war. Henceforth, Church devoted more and more attention to a criticism of U.S. involvement abroad.

This criticism reached a crescendo when Church was appointed chair of the Senate Select Committee on Intelligence Activities, established in 1975 to investigate the Central Intelligence Agency (CIA). The findings of his committee seemed to confirm his worst suspicions about U.S. interventionism abroad—from assassination plots against foreign leaders to a staggering array of covert operations designed to influence affairs in other lands. As he traveled in the primary states in search of his party's presidential nomination in 1976, his voice often trembled at high levels of emotion as he spoke of the committee's revelations. Standing before the congregation of the Reverend Jesse Jackson in Chicago, he left the set speech in his briefcase and, fueled by shouts of "yes!" and "amen!" his voice rose in a fiery appeal for black support. He had found a CIA, he said, that "had forgotten we are a Christian nation and that was conspiring to murder foreign officials in little countries . . . that couldn't possibly threaten the safety or security of this great nation." He spoke of the civil war in Angola: "If anything should be clear from the recent history of Africa, from the long, long struggle of black Africa to be free, that lesson is that no independent African state—and particularly one that has suffered under the dictatorial control of the Portuguese for centuries—is going to long remain dominated by any foreign power, the Russians or anybody else. . . . Let the Angolans decide their own destiny! They have a right to self-determination, and this country does not have to meddle in their affairs."

A few weeks later, Church presented a similar theme in what he considered his most important speech: the official announcement in Idaho of his presidential candidacy. Normally Church outlined in conversation with his staff speech writer the essence of what he wished to say in an address; the writer would prepare a draft, and the two would work through it, virtually word by word, with Church usually making many changes, perhaps adding a favorite quotation and, his greatest writing talent, making the prose more vivid. In contrast, the announcement speech was one of the few Church drafted himself, with only minor changes in the final version coming from his advisers. He labored over it for days and, as always for his major addresses, virtually memorized it, having spoken the words aloud over and over again to himself and to close aides.

The night before the announcement, he had a trial run before Idaho supporters crowded into a small meeting hall in downtown Boise. His left foot forward, his right hand in the pocket of his suit jacket, his left hand raised in gestures as he spoke, Church came close to mesmerizing a once-boisterous crowd. The effect of his rich voice and a rising pitch of emotion in his delivery, coupled with a compelling sense of outrage over CIA excesses, cast a spell over the room. All were caught up in his appeal for a return to traditional U.S. values. He assailed a "leadership of weakness and fear" that allowed "the most powerful agencies of our government—the CIA, the FBI, and the IRS—to systematically ignore the very laws intended to protect the liberties of the people." His voice at full volume, his body trembling in apparent anger, Church declared, "Runaway bureaucracy must be harnessed once more to the reins of the law. For let it be remembered that in America the people are sovereign, and the government is their servant still!"

The next day in Idaho City, the actual announcement speech was less magical; the close confines of the small hall the night before had amplified the force of his ringing declarations. The outdoor version nevertheless brought the crowd of 2,500 spectators to their feet on several occasions. It was quintessential Church: he rarely looked at his text; his voice rose with emotion, his gestures emphatic; his theme, one of distrust for a government grown arrogant at home and intrusive abroad; his remedy, a reduction in presidential power, an increase in legislative power—in a word, a restoration of the checks against abuse that were so dear to the founders.

"The greatest insight of our Founding Fathers was their recognition of the dangers of unlimited power exercised by a single man or institution," Church often reminded audiences, "their greatest achievement was the safeguards against absolute powers which they wrote into our Constitution." In his career, Church spoke as a populist, a voice of dissent, and a constitutional philosopher. He was a key leader in the institutional revolution on Capitol Hill to bring Congress back into the making of U.S. foreign policy. His eloquent criticism of the war in Indochina, his uncovering of abuses by the intelligence agencies, and his warnings about the "apostles of interventionism" made Americans more sensitive to the fragility of their own democracy and helped stir a vital national debate, one that continues still, about the purposes and limits of U.S. involvement abroad. There lies the legacy of this man who could illuminate with his mind and inspire with his tongue.

INFORMATION SOURCES

Research Collections and Collected Speeches

The papers of Frank Church have been gathered and are being organized at Boise State University, Boise, Idaho. The best sources for his Idaho campaign speeches are the *Boise Idaho Statesman* and the *Lewiston Morning Tribune*.

American Rhetoric from Roosevelt to Reagan: A Collection of Speeches and   ARRR
    Critical Essays. Edited by Halford Ross Ryan. Prospect Heights:
    Waveland Press, 1983.
Boise Idaho Statesman.   IS
Church, Frank. "Of Presidents and Caesars: The Decline of Constitutional   ILR
    Government in the Conduct of American Foreign Policy," *Idaho
    Law Review* 6 (Fall 1969): 1–15.
———. "Covert Action: Swampland of American Foreign Policy," *Bulletin*   BAS
    of the Atomic Scientists 32 (February 1976): 6–9.
———. The Public Papers and Addresses of Frank Church.Boise State   PPA
    University, Boise, Idaho.
Congressional Record.   CR
Lewiston Morning Tribune.   MT
Proceedings of the Democratic National Convention. Washington, D.C.:   PDNC
    Democratic National Committee, 1961, 1977.
The Senate's War Powers. Edited by Eugene P. Dvorin. Chicago: Markham   SWP
    Publishing, 1971.

Selected Critical Studies

Johnson, Loch K. "Operational Codes and the Prediction of Leadership Behavior: Senator
    Frank Church at Midcareer." In *A Psychological Examination of Political Leaders*.
    Edited by Margaret G. Hermann. New York: Free Press, 1977.
———. *The Making of International Agreements: Congress Confronts the Executive*.
    New York: New York University Press, 1984.
———. *A Season of Inquiry: The Senate Intelligence Investigation*. Lexington: University
    Press of Kentucky, 1985.

CHRONOLOGY OF MAJOR SPEECHES

See "Research Collections and Collected Speeches" for source codes.

American Legion National High School oratorical contest, Charleston, South Carolina, 1941; *PPA*.

Keynote address to the Democratic National Convention, Los Angeles, July 11, 1960; *PDNC*, pp. 21–30.

"Vietnam," Washington, D.C., October 8, 1969; *ARRR*, pp. 193–205; *CR*, October 28, 1969, pp. 31955–58.

"Policy for Latin America," Washington, D.C., April 10, 1970; *CR*, April 10, 1970, pp. 11211–17.

"Of Presidents and Caesars," Stanford University, Palo Alto, California, April 20, 1970; *CR*, April 30, 1970, pp. 13563–66; for an earlier draft, see *ILR*, pp. 1–15.

"Cooper-Church Amendment," Washington, D.C., May 13, 1970; *CR*, May 13, 1970, p. 15400; *SWP*, pp. 12–14.

"Farewell to Foreign Aid," Washington, D.C., October 29, 1971; *CR*, November 22, 1971, pp. 42724–26.

"Illusions about Peace," Washington, D.C., January 24, 1973; *CR*, February 15, 1973, pp. 4281–82.

"Foreign Aid Illusion," Washington, D.C., October 2, 1973; *CR*, October 2, 1973, pp. 32595–98.

"CIA," Washington, D.C., November 11, 1975; *CR*, November 11, 1975, pp. 35786–88.

"Covert Action," Washington, D.C., December 16, 1975; *BAS*, pp. 6–9.

Presidential campaign speech, Reverend Jesse Jackson's Congregation, Chicago, February 15, 1976; *PPA*.

Announcement of presidential candidacy, Idaho City, Idaho, March 18, 1976; *CR*, March 22, 1976, pp. 7322–23; *IS* 19 March 1976, p. 1; *MT* 19 March 1976, p. 1.

Campaign address on national television, Washington, D.C., April 19, 1976; *PPA*.

Foreign policy keynote address, Democratic National Convention, New York City, July 13, 1976; *PDNC*, pp. 278–80.

"Nuclear Weapons," American University, Washington, D.C., September 7, 1976; *CR*, September 29, 1970, pp. 33414–16.

"War or Peace," Boise State University, Boise, Idaho, January 28, 1982; *PPA*.

THE REVEREND CHARLES E. COUGHLIN
(1891–1979), the voice of Royal Oak

CHARLES HENRY WHITTIER

At the height of his popularity in the early 1930s, Charles E. Coughlin commanded an estimated radio audience of some 30 million. By the end of the decade, his influence had declined precipitously. In 1942 he was silenced by his ecclesiastical superiors. His death in 1979 was barely reported, but his impact on a critical period of U.S. history exercises a continuing fascination. He was the first to discover the possibility of radio as a source of political power and revenue, and he foreshadowed the present era of television evangelists.

Born in 1891, the year of Pope Leo XIII's social justice encyclical *Rerum Novarum*, Coughlin was ordained a Roman Catholic priest in the Basilian Order at Toronto in 1916. In college and parish work alike, he revealed his natural flair for drama, developing oratorical skills and expressive gestures in his delivery. In 1918 he became a secular priest. Called to Detroit in 1923, he formed a lifelong friendship with Bishop Gallagher, later his loyal patron. The canonization of Saint Therese of Lisieux in 1925 brought both men closer, and Coughlin was named to the newly founded Shrine of the Little Flower at Royal Oak, twelve miles north of Detroit. His eloquence helped build up the shrine's outreach, particularly after his first radio broadcast in 1926. Despite the onset of the Great Depression, money poured in from great numbers of people for his new church.

COUGHLIN AS THE RADIO PRIEST

Coughlin was already the center of political controversy by the late 1920s as a result of his attacks on bolshevism, socialism, and corporate greed. By 1930 he had become a national figure as a result of overwhelming public response to his call for social and economic justice. His messages were broadcast by CBS to sixteen stations in twenty-three states. In 1931 he broke with CBS and proceeded to establish an independent chain of stations, eventually extending from California to Maine and costing some $14,000 a week, all paid by voluntary contributions.

His assault on big business, Wall Street bankers, and federal passivity in the face of growing distress won him wide support from lower and lower-middle-class citizens, rural and urban. His charismatic tone, conveyed with vibrant and decisive authority, heightened his appeal. "If the promoter and financier and industrialist believed in the doctrines of Jesus Christ," he charged, "he would no more exploit his fellow man than he would sell the Master for thirty pieces

of silver." He condemned prohibition, birth control, pacifism, and internationalism, while championing the unemployed and assailing President Herbert Hoover for inactivity. In 1932, in testimony before the U.S. House Ways and Means
Committee in support of a bonus for World War I veterans, he was bitterly
critical of Hoover. His controversial stance was magnified when he vigorously
defended Mayor Jimmy Walker of New York against charges of corruption, was
sharply criticized by Cardinal O'Connell of Boston (to whom he responded with
equal sharpness in 1934), and found himself invited to the Democratic convention
by the governor of New York, Franklin D. Roosevelt.

Coughlin quickly became a confidant and supporter of Roosevelt and embraced
the cry "Roosevelt or Ruin!" (later, "Roosevelt and Recovery"). His influence
on Roosevelt's program has been variously evaluated. He appears to have played
a major role in drafting the First Inaugural, despite the denials of some. Roosevelt's famous reference to the moneychangers having fled the temple seems
to echo Coughlin's "the unscrupulous moneychangers stand indicted." Increasingly Coughlin sought national influence in the face of growing disenchantment
on the part of the president and his advisers. Coughlin's praise of Roosevelt as
one who sought "to make the Christian experiment" (in the New Deal) did not
mollify the president's irritation, especially after the revelation that Coughlin
had been involved in silver speculation while urging a silver standard.

Coughlin turned to direct political action in 1934, founding the National Union
for Social Justice on the broad principles of the "social encyclicals" of Leo XIII
and Pius XI. He saw the organization as a third force between communism and
unbridled capitalism, appealing (he declared) to "every lover of liberty who
desires to eradicate the cancerous growths of decadent capitalism and avoid the
treacherous pitfalls of red communism." The eventual break with Roosevelt was
foreshadowed by disagreements over the World Court, Mexico, the Wagner Act,
and policies directed to the depression. In 1935 General Hugh Johnson attacked
Coughlin's right as a priest to participate in politics, even likening him to Hitler.
Coughlin responded by asserting his right as a citizen to speak out on public
issues.

During a national tour in 1935, Coughlin met with Roosevelt at Hyde Park,
but relations were strained. Their final meeting was in 1936 preceding Coughlin's
denunciation of the president as a "liar" (for which he later, pressured by his
ecclesiastical superiors, made a public apology). In that year Coughlin threw
his support to the Union party of Congressman William Lemke, in alliance with
Francis Townsend (of the Townsend Plan) and the Reverend Gerald L. K. Smith,
a disciple of Huey Long. In a major speech in June over CBS radio, he proclaimed
"both old parties" to be "the banker's party," denounced "the dole standard
of Roosevelt, the gold standard of Landon," and was "constrained to admit that
'Roosevelt *and* ruin' is the order of the day because the money changers have
not been driven from the temple." During a campaign marked by much bitterness,
Coughlin announced that he would quit broadcasting if the Union party failed
to win 9 million votes. His speeches were increasingly marked by vaguely anti-

Semitic innuendo, associating the Rothschilds' "god of gold" with "the theory of the European Jew," denouncing "the Bernard *Manasses* [*sic*] Baruchs of Wall Street."

The result of the election gave Lemke 882,479 votes (out of over 45 million cast) and not a single congressional seat. The failure of the movement has been attributed to many factors, including Coughlin's egocentric leadership and excessive personal influence. Coughlin himself appears to have soured on the spoken word after 1936, turning more and more to his publication, *Social Justice*. Despite renewed pressure from the Holy See, Coughlin resumed his broadcasts in 1938, forming the Christian Front, openly anti-Semitic in its writings and policy. In 1940 he repudiated the Front but upheld its social ideals. By that time radio stations across the land were dropping his program. In 1942 *Social Justice* ceased to publish, and Archbishop Mooney of Detroit ordered Coughlin to stop his political writing and all other nonreligious activities. Obedient as always to church authority, he faded imperceptibly from the national scene during the decades left to him.

The distinctive appeal of Father Coughlin's oratory lay in his ability to blend the twin rhetorics of Americanism and popular Christianity. Proclaiming an essential harmony between the American's creed and the Apostles Creed, a conviction rooted in American civic piety, accepted by Protestant and Catholic alike from the earliest days of the Republic, Coughlin went on to incorporate many themes peculiar to the American past: conspiratorial (his fear of the money power, international bankers of wealth and power, echoing the tone of anti-Masonic and anti-Catholic populism in the last century) and moralistic (invoking traditional values and the utopian promise of their fulfillment). In these respects, he stands in the mainstream of American revivalism, including its emphasis on activism and reformism. His evident appeal to Protestants and others, despite his unlikely identity as a Roman Catholic priest, derived in large measure from these factors. As modern as today's mass media and as American as the mingling of religion and politics, he became an outstanding political manipulator of his time in the New World, rivaling Roosevelt in his ability to communicate with an unseen audience. "Radio broadcasting," he once said, "must not be high hat. It must be human, intensely human. It must be simple."

In Coughlin's case, the medium, if not identical with the message, was crucial in its shaping. His technique, as many have noted, was essentially aural, not visual, combining, in Raymond Swing's famous phrase, the "minimum explicitness" with "the maximum of feeling." The combination of aggrieved resentment and religious zeal proved irresistible to millions. Intoxicating to hear, he elicited wild enthusiasm in response. His speeches, most of which read poorly today, require the sound of his voice, a voice filled with passionate intensity, for their effect to live again. Might they have carried the same excitement if his audience could have seen him, or would his appeal have been weakened?

He shared with Roosevelt a warmly charismatic personality and the use of homely metaphor drawn from everyday life, but seldom could he replicate the intimate tone of the fireside chat. Rather the public oratory of Hitler comes to mind as a striking parallel. Coughlin's speeches, like Hitler's, tended to be rambling, even disorganized, more tirade than discourse. Also like Hitler's, his speeches were strongly emotional, vivid, repetitious, and evocative, seeking dramatically to arrest the attention of his hearers. "Moscow is here!" he cried (speaking of the Calles regime in Mexico). "The league of the godless is encroaching while we sit idly by." Often sentimental, even blatantly so, his heavily anecdotal style embellished a human interest appeal directed chiefly to the heart. In "the mystery of love," he could rhapsodize over children: "O little curly-headed boy, rest sweetly on the throne of your mother's breast . . . the angels which hover about your throne tonight will sing perchance in holy glee; will weep perchance in sorrow." In this way his social and economic views were persuasively argued alongside and even within his religious and doctrinal message. Thus, he could link Purgatory and the oil situation, the Way of the Cross and prohibition, Americanism and Christianity, citing Scripture to his purposes, sacred and secular.

The phenomenon Coughlin represented deserves thoughtful consideration by those who track the course of religion and politics in the United States. Among the first public figures to make effective use of the mass media, he was for a time the most popular voice on radio, articulating the anxieties and the hopes of millions in a period of widespread economic distress. For those who heard him gladly, his message was inspirational rather than propagandist. The "Sixteen Points" of Coughlin's Union of Social Justice were reasonably coherent. Yet he showed an ability to manipulate through hate and fear. As time passed, his speeches reflected a thinly veiled appeal to bigotry in the guise of piety. Lacking any real power base, he was able by oratory alone to create the illusion of mass power through the media, an illusion that, given other circumstances, might have taken a more ominous turn.

Although he vigorously denied all sympathy with fascism or with religious prejudice, his nationalism seemed increasingly to echo certain themes of National Socialism, particularly his ever more strident references to the "Jewish race" and to "communistic Jews." A constantly moving target in his public stance, he was inclined to be reassuring to Jewish representatives in private and then appeal to anti-Jewish feeling in his public speeches—asserting, for example, in the fall of 1938 that "so-called anti-Semitism" was caused by the supposed silence of American Jews in the face of communism. The policy of *Social Justice* in publishing *The Protocols of the Elders of Zion* and in plagiarizing from a speech by Dr. Goebbels belied his reassurances. His references to Jews have a chilling effect when read today in the light of the Holocaust.

As Priest of the Radio, he gained the love and trust of millions of Americans, chiefly through the charisma of his personality manifest in the power of the spoken word. His tragedy lay in the erosion of that influence by ambition, opportunism, and demagoguery. He is both example and warning of the ambiguities inherent in the merging of patriotism with religion, often a source of national strength and civic virtue but a source in perennial danger of distortion and abuse.

INFORMATION SOURCES

Research Collections and Collected Speeches

The Library of Congress, Washington, D.C., has an extensive collection of Father Coughlin's discourses—sermons, lectures, and other addresses—published as delivered, from 1931 on, many by the Radio League of the Little Flower and bearing Bishop Gallagher's imprimatur.

American Rhetoric from Roosevelt to Reagan: A Collection of Speeches and   ARRR
  Critical Essays. Edited by Halford Ross Ryan. Prospect Heights,
  Ill.: Waveland Press, 1983.
A Series of Lectures on Social Justice. Royal Oak, Mich.: Radio League of   ASL
  the Little Flower, 1936.
"Am I an Anti-Semite?" Nine Addresses on Various Isms. Detroit: Condon   NAVI
  Printing Co., 1939.

Selected Biographies

Bennett, David Harry. *Demagogues in the Depression: American Radicals and the Union Party, 1932–1936.* New Brunswick: Rutgers University Press, 1969.
Brinkley, Alan. *Voices of Protest: Huey Long, Father Coughlin, and the Great Depression.* New York: Knopf, 1982.
The Fine Art of Propaganda. Edited by Alfred McClung Lee and Elizabeth B. Lee. New York: Harcourt and Brace, 1939.
Marcus, Sheldon. *Father Coughlin: The Tumultuous Life of the Priest of the Little Flower.* Boston: Little, Brown, 1973.
Spivak, John L. *Shrine of the Silver Dollar.* New York: Modern Age, 1940.
Tull, Charles L. *Father Coughlin and the New Deal.* Syracuse: Syracuse University Press, 1973.

CHRONOLOGY OF MAJOR SPEECHES

See "Research Collections and Collected Speeches" for source codes.

"What Prevents a Just and Living Wage?" Royal Oak, Michigan, November 25, 1934; *ASL*, pp. 34–35.

"Merchandisers of Murder," Royal Oak, Michigan, December 16, 1934; *ASL*, pp. 72–83.

"A Reply to Hugh Johnson," Royal Oak, Michigan, March 11, 1935; *ASL*, pp. 219–31.

"A Third Party," Royal Oak, Michigan, June 19, 1936; *ARRR*, pp. 68–75.

"Persecution—Jewish and Christian," Royal Oak, Michigan, November 20, 1938; *NAVI*, pp. 34–46.

"A Chapter on Intolerance," Royal Oak, Michigan, December 11, 1938; *NAVI*, pp. 89–107.

"Is Christ the Messiah?" Royal Oak, Michigan, December 18, 1938; *NAVI*, pp. 108–21.

MARIO CUOMO
(1932–   ), governor of New York

DAVID HENRY

When Mario Cuomo moved to the podium to deliver the keynote address at the 1984 Democratic National Convention, it is unlikely that many outside the Northeast knew what to expect of the New York governor's performance. By the time he finished speaking, however, few who followed U.S. politics would not know of Cuomo and associate his name with any list of the party's prospective presidential nominees for 1988. Such has been the relationship between Cuomo's oratorical skill and political success throughout his civic life.

Cuomo entered public service in 1972 when New York City Mayor John Lindsay appointed him to resolve a lengthy conflict over proposed low-income housing in the city's Forest Hills section. To mediate the concerns of both the project's proponents and the Forest Hills residents, Cuomo spent months in public and private deliberations acting variously as advocate, auditor, and conciliator. His deftness as conciliator helped achieve a compromise solution and led to his entry into elective politics in 1974 when he sought the Democratic nomination for state lieutenant governor. Although Cuomo was unsuccessful in that campaign, newly elected Governor Hugh Carey appointed him New York secretary of state, a position that increased his prominence and resulted in frequent invitations to address audiences throughout the state. In his speaking engagements, he introduced, tested, and refined the themes and tactics that would form the center of later campaigns. The process took time, however, and was marked by rhetorical and political failures, the most notable being an ill-fated race for mayor of New York City against Ed Koch in 1977.

Cuomo vowed not to repeat the mistakes of that campaign, which he later described as amateurish. After serving as Carey's lieutenant governor, in the 1982 contest for the Democratic gubernatorial nomination Cuomo campaigned aggressively, performed brilliantly in a series of debates with Koch, and convinced the electorate to adopt the "family of New York" theme that had been central to his strategy. In the subsequent general election campaign, the most expensive in state history, he defeated Republican Lewis Lehrman and pledged to remain in Albany for his full four-year term. Consequently when Walter Mondale approached him two years later to propose that he become Mondale's vice-presidential running mate, Cuomo declined. He was receptive, though, to the invitation to deliver the party's keynote address, for he recognized that the convention afforded the best opportunity yet to express the political philosophy that had evolved from his experiences and that undergirded his public discourse.

CUOMO AND THE RHETORIC OF PROGRESSIVE PRAGMATISM

Cuomo's experience with the Forest Hills controversy reaffirmed his conviction that in human affairs, the "truth is often found at neither Scylla nor Charybdis, but somewhere near the middle of the straits." Two elements of his observation are instructive: Cuomo's recognition of the need to seek a middle ground in disputes involving legitimate claims by two sides and his insistence that the ultimate decision be guided by a mutually acceptable truth. Cuomo has identified the resulting political philosophy alternatively as progressive pragmatism, a family kind of politics, or an adherence to traditional Democratic principles. Regardless of the label, four themes drawn from the perspective recur in Cuomo's oratory: work, family, faith, and order. The philosophy, emanating equally from the traditions of American liberalism and the exigencies of political reality, is unified by what Cuomo calls in his *Diaries* "reasonableness. Not an addiction to ideology or pat phrases or canned solutions, but an intelligent application of general principles to specific situations." Programs "and policies change," he asserted in his 1985 Chubb Fellowship lecture at Yale, "our principles don't." The concept of reasonableness and the balancing of principle with practicality permeate Cuomo's speeches. By examining the oratorical techniques used in an array of selected speeches, one discovers a rhetorical method as unique as Cuomo's philosophy. Particularly important are Cuomo's role in the communication process, his approach to the audience, and his blending of style and argument.

Cuomo believes public speakers should write their own speeches. Rather than editing manuscripts submitted by a staff of speech writers, Cuomo drafts his texts, discusses them with his advisers, and edits to final copy. The process is an extension of his academic background and his ongoing reading and writing habits. A graduate of St. John's preparatory school, college, and law school, where he later taught, his speeches reflect the careful reasoning and judicious use of precedent or example expected of lawyers. Simultaneously Cuomo's affinity for the literary raises his texts to a level well above that of a logical but dry legal brief. At least since his involvement in the Forest Hills controversy and continuing through his 1982 campaign for governor, Cuomo has kept a diary in which he records regularly his thoughts on matters both public and personal. Those thoughts are often prompted by his reading, for despite the constraints of his schedule, he makes time to read often. His reading influences his oratory insofar as he believes that wide reading is essential to writing and speaking well.

Recognizing his commitment to progressive pragmatism or a family kind of politics helps illuminate Cuomo's approach to the audience. At one level, he demonstrates consistently his talent for promoting speaker-audience identification. The common bond of family frequently forms the center of such appeals. If "my election proves anything," he contended in his gubernatorial inaugural address, January 1, 1983, "it proves how very much the system was able to do" for the people. He offered the story of his family. His immigrant parents had arrived at Ellis Island penniless, but through hard work and faith they had built a family, lived in dignity, and seen "one of their children go from behind their little grocery store . . . to occupy the highest seat in the greatest state of the greatest nation in the only world we know." But, he assured, "this is not a personal story. This is the story of us all." For those who made New York history "taught us above all things the idea of family. Mutuality. The sharing of benefits and burdens—fairly—for the good of all. It is an idea essential to our success." The ideal is balanced, however, by recognition of the need for order and acceptance of the rule of law. To the Police Conference of the State of New York, on March 24, 1982, he bemoaned "a society that's gone lawless," a phenomenon observable "everywhere. In every part of our society there's a loss of discipline, a lack of respect for authority, for the rule, for the necessity to defer to the rule." Given the state's protection of the lieutenant governor, he continued, "I and my family should be safe in New York City. Yet my daughter got attacked twice by the same guy down the block from our house at four-thirty in the afternoon in broad daylight." The experience and his recognition of it as a microcosm of a critical problem for police and public alike led to his pledge that "when I become governor, the first priority for me will be to do everything we possibly can to bring down the crime rate."

When circumstances require it, however, identification is replaced by a second trait of his relationship to his audiences: he challenges their fundamental assumptions and beliefs. The single remedy to the rising crime rate he rejected in his Police Conference address was the death penalty: "I don't believe it works." Although the majority of the audience disagreed with him, he spelled out his opposition to the death penalty as rooted in the conviction that it merely provided proponents with an easy answer to a complex problem. He urged as an alternative the hiring of more law enforcement personnel, the construction of more prisons, and better management of the correctional system. Cuomo asked his listeners to consider the options because, in spite of their shared concerns, on the death penalty "I think . . . you're wrong, and I feel that deeply." In what conservative critic John Tagg nominated as the one election year speech with potential earth shaker status, Cuomo faced a similar rhetorical problem when he spoke on "Religious Belief and Public Morality" at the University of Notre Dame on September 13, 1984. He began by stressing his family's allegiance to the church's teachings. "But," Cuomo continued referring to his wife, "not everyone in our society agrees with me and Matilda." As he had to the police officers on the death penalty, he offered to an audience overwhelmingly opposed to his view an alternative, middle ground on abortion. In so doing, he returned to his speaker-audience identification strategy by justifying such a course as "in the American-Catholic tradition of political realism."

Cuomo packaged the Notre Dame argument in a series of analogies designed to make his theme more palatable to a potentially hostile audience, thus exhibiting a third characteristic of his speech making: the use of analogy, metaphor, and related figurative techniques to construct his arguments and embellish his prose.

He portrayed the middle-ground alternative on abortion, for example, as analogous to the church's decision in the mid-nineteenth century not to campaign for the abolition of slavery. In neither instance can the church's moral commitment be questioned, Cuomo maintained, but in both it is essential to recognize that "there was and is not one, clear, absolute route that the church says, as a matter of doctrine, we must follow."

Audience attention rather than immediate adherence had also been an aim of Cuomo's keynote speech. Adaptation of a favorite Reagan metaphor served his purpose. Recognizing the potential for alienating a general public enamored of its president by attacking directly the incumbent, he invited both the immediate and television audiences to view the nation not as President Reagan's "shining city on a hill," but as "a tale of two cities." While all may be well in the city the president sees "from the portico of the White House and the veranda of his ranch," Cuomo maintained, in another "part of the city there are more poor than ever, more families in trouble, more people who need help but can't find it." Metaphor explained as well as identified the problem as Cuomo turned to a frontier theme to differentiate between Democratic and Republican attitudes. Because they accept the Darwinian notion of survival of the fittest, "Republicans believe the wagon train will not make it to the frontier unless some of our old, some of our young, and some of our weak are left behind by the side of the trail. . . . We Democrats believe that we can make it all the way with the whole family intact."

Although the Republican view found overwhelming favor with the 1984 electorate, Cuomo shunned suggestions that he and other Democrats adjust their assumptions. He recalled in his Yale address Galileo's forced retraction of his theory that, contrary to conventional wisdom, the earth moved around the sun. As instructed, Galileo knelt before his inquisitors and denied publicly his theory, but as he rose he said quietly, *E pur si muove* ("But it still moves"). Despite the Reagan landslide, Cuomo determined to remain an advocate of a family kind of politics. In promoting his philosophy of progressive pragmatism, he would undoubtedly engage and challenge his audiences with appropriately stylized arguments penned by his own hand.

INFORMATION SOURCES

Research Collections and Collected Speeches

Cuomo, Mario. *Diaries of Mario M. Cuomo: The Campaign for Governor.*   DMMC
    New York: Random House. 1984.
———. "A Tale of Two Cities." *Vital Speeches of the Day*, August 15,   VS
    1984, pp. 646–49.

Selected Critical Studies

Abraham, M. Katie. "A Rhetorical Analysis of Governor Cuomo's Keynote Address to
    the 1984 Democratic National Convention." Paper presented at the annual meeting
    of the Speech Communication Association, Denver, Colorado, November 9, 1985.

Barnes, Fred. "Meet Mario the Moderate." *New Republic*. April 8, 1985, pp. 17–20.

Broder, David. "Meet Mario Machiavelli." *Washington Post National Weekly Edition*, August 16, 1984, p. 4.

Brownstein, Ronald. "The Democrats: The Lessons of 1984." *National Journal*, July 20, 1985, pp. 1666–70.

Canavan, Francis. "The Cuomo Thesis." *Human Life Review* (Winter–Spring 1985): 84–91.

Dionne, E. J. "Cuomo: The Old Liberalism." *New York Times Magazine*, October 31, 1982, pp. 22, 24, 66–69, 84–85, 92.

Henry, David. "Toward 'A Family Kind of Politics': Rhetorical Interaction in Mario Cuomo's Keynote Address." Paper presented at the annual meeting of the Speech Communication Association, Denver, Colorado, November 8, 1985.

Oreskes, Michael. "Rising Voice in Democratic Ranks." *New York Times*, July 17, 1984, p. A17.

Tagg, John. "Understanding Mario Cuomo." *National Review*, February 8, 1985, pp. 25–32.

Selected Biographies

Cuomo, Mario. *Forest Hills Diary*. New York: Random House. 1974.

CHRONOLOGY OF MAJOR SPEECHES

See "Research Collections and Collected Speeches" for source codes.

"On Family," address to the Romulus Club, Buffalo, New York, 1975; *DMMC*, pp. 7–10.

Speech to Police Conference of the State of New York, Albany, New York, March 24, 1982; *DMMC*, pp. 413–19.

Inaugural address, Albany, New York, January 1, 1983; *DMMC*, pp. 455–61.

"A Tale of Two Cities," Democratic Convention Keynote Address, San Francisco, July 16, 1984; *New York Times*, July 17, 1984, p. A16; *VS*.

"Religious Belief and Public Morality," Notre Dame, Indiana, September 13, 1984; *New York Times*, September 14, 1984, A21; *Human Life Review* (Winter–Spring 1985): 26–40.

"On Politics and Principles," Yale University, New Haven, Connecticut, February 15, 1985; *New York Times*, February 16, 1985, p. 26.

CLARENCE SEWARD DARROW
(1857–1938), lawyer, political activist, author

_____ WILLIAM LASSER

Clarence Seward Darrow was one of the most gifted trial lawyers in U.S. history, and of his many assets his gift for oratory was perhaps the greatest. Born in 1857 in Kinsman, Ohio, Darrow decided after an uneventful scholastic career to enter the bar. Both his decision to become an attorney and his subsequent involvement in politics were based in part on his love of speech making and of hearing the approving cheers of a large crowd. "Young men are ambitious to get into the law game," he wrote later, "largely because it is a showy profession, and is one that lets a man enjoy the limelight." In a career that spanned over fifty years, Darrow accepted an endless series of unpopular cases and causes. He is best known for his defense of evolution in the famous Scopes (Monkey Trial) case of 1925 and for his eloquent defense of the child killers Leopold and Loeb in 1924. Darrow spent the last decade of his life writing and lecturing to huge crowds on such themes as "Why I Am an Agnostic," "The Myth of the Soul," "The Futility of the Death Penalty," "Prohibition," and "Is Man Fundamentally Dishonest?" Darrow's reputation for oratory was so great that upon his own death, his eulogist decided merely to read the eulogy that Darrow had composed upon the death of former Illinois governor John Peter Altgeld forty years before.

THE LAWYER AS ORATOR

In his long and distinguished career, Darrow gave hundreds of speeches. He was at his best in court, facing a judge or jury, pleading for a cause he believed right or for a client who (like all others) deserved justice. His orations drew huge crowds. When he delivered his final argument in the Leopold and Loeb case, one newspaper reported that the audience fought to hear him speak. Like all other great orators, Darrow combined appeals to logic with appeals to emotion and relied heavily on establishing a personal identification between himself and his audience. He was also capable of fine tuning his oratorical style to suit any occasion, in court or out.

Darrow was not above using every trick in the lawyer's repertoire to rhetorical advantage, but his effectiveness came more from his passionate belief in the arguments he made and in the issues he stood for. His devotion to the criminal law stemmed from what crime and criminals could teach about human nature. "Strange as it may seem," he wrote of his attraction to criminal law, "I grew to like to defend men and women charged with crime. It soon came to be something more than winning or losing a case. I sought to learn why one man goes one way and another takes an entirely different road. . . . I was dealing with life, with its hopes and fears, its aspirations and despairs.'' All of Darrow's famous cases involved issues of great importance to Darrow; he took the Leopold and Loeb case, for example, because it provided an opportunity for him to argue against capital punishment, and he offered his services in defense of Scopes because he could fight fundamentalism. Other important cases involved freedom of speech and the rights of workers. When Darrow spoke, therefore, he could speak from the heart; his passion was authentic and convincing.

Darrow's technique in preparing for a major speech was to immerse himself in books, becoming familiar not only with the issues of the cases but with a wide range of knowledge that might be relevant to the case at hand. Then he would sketch a handful of notes on a yellow pad and proceed to speak virtually extemporaneously for hours on end. Just as some lawyers dictate their speeches to stenographers without making written notes first, concluded a colleague, Darrow dictated his speeches directly to the judge or jury: ''He knew all the facts of the case thoroughly when he started to sum up, and with his knowledge of those facts he drew upon his tremendous store of knowledge and gave his address just as the atmosphere of the courtroom demanded.''

In many ways, Darrow's greatest speech was his summation in the famous murder trial of Richard Loeb and Nathan Leopold in 1924. The two boys, aged seventeen and eighteen, respectively, had attempted to commit ''the perfect crime'': kidnapping, murder, and ransom. The case attracted national attention because the two boys were wealthy, brilliant, and successful, with every door open to them; because the crime was committed without apparent malice or motive, simply for the sake of a thrill; and because the crime was bizarre. Fourteen-year-old Bobby Franks, chosen at random, was enticed into a rented car in broad daylight, killed with a chisel, driven around Chicago for some twenty miles, stripped, and left in a culvert. Afterward, Loeb told newspaper reporters that, as a reader of mystery novels, he had figured out the crime and led them around to gather evidence.

Darrow, at age sixty-seven, agreed to take the case because it provided an opportunity to argue against the death penalty and because the boys faced what he called hatred and malice masquerading as justice. In addition, he was convinced that if the defendants had not been connected with wealthy (and Jewish) families, any state's attorney would have agreed to a plea of guilty and punishment of life in prison. Accordingly Darrow waived a jury trial (being afraid of exposing his clients to the fury of the public), pleaded the boys guilty, and stood before a lone judge asking for a sentence of life in prison. ''We are asking the court to save their lives,'' Darrow said, ''which is the least and the most that a judge can do.''

As an example of forensic rhetoric, the speech is a masterpiece. Darrow addressed himself directly to the judge, who would later pass sentence. He appealed to precedent, to reason, and above all to emotion. ''Your Honor, if these boys hang, you must do it.'' Darrow immediately introduced the major theme of his speech: Leopold and Loeb were not only children but diseased children; they were not responsible for their actions and should be treated with compassion. He deliberately referred to them as children, or boys, and called them "Dickie" and "Babe," despite the prosecutor's preference for "Richard" and "Nathan." In the deepest sense, they were not in control of their actions: "somewhere in the infinite processes that go to the making up of the boy or man something slipped," Darrow told the judge. The crime was "one of those things that happened, and it calls not for hate but for kindness, for charity, for consideration." But what did the state propose? That they be "led out . . . across the bridge waiting to be hanged. Not a chance to get away. Handcuffed . . . Penned in like rats in a trap." Unlike the murder of Bobby Franks, which was "the senseless act of immature and diseased children," the execution of Leopold and Loeb would be cruel, premeditated murder: "You may stand them up on the trap door of the scaffold, and choke them to death, but that act will be infinitely more cold-blooded, whether justified or not, than any act that these boys have committed or can commit."

Darrow described the murder of Bobby Franks in great detail, to show above all that it could be the act of only sick, irresponsible minds. But it was the future act of the state, not Leopold and Loeb's act, on which he focused the judge's attention. Appealing to the sympathies of the judge, Darrow succeeded in personalizing the act of execution, making it not the unemotional dispatching of a pair of murderers but the specific act of killing two children, causing even more pain to them and their families. Turning the normal conventions of a criminal trial upside down, Darrow focused not on the past but on the future and cast the state in the role of criminal and the boys as victims. The prosecution-as-cold-blooded-murderers motif was sharpened by Darrow's focus on Joseph P. Savage, assistant state's attorney, whose declamations on behalf of the death sentence were particularly emphatic. Darrow ridiculed Savage ("Did you pick him for his name or his ability or his learning?"); patronized him ("Why, when my friend Savage is my age," he tells the judge, "or even yours; he will read his address to this court with horror"); mocked him ("Mr. Savage, with the immaturity of youth and inexperience, says that if we hang them there will be no more killing"). Savage, like the defendants, was young, but his action could not be explained away by disease.

Darrow's plea was a sustained cry for compassion, for justice, not just for Leopold and Loeb but for their families, for Darrow himself ("If the state in which I live is not kinder, more humane, more considerate, more intelligent than the mad act of these two boys, I am sorry that I have lived so long"). Even more, his plea was for the court to recognize that Leopold and Loeb's act was but one part of a larger tragedy that envelops humanity itself. "Where is the man who has not been guilty of deliquencies in youth?" he asks. "How many men are there today . . . even state's attorneys—who have not been guilty of some mad act in youth? And if they did not get caught, or if the consequences were trivial, it was their good fortune." "For God's sake, are we crazy?" Darrow asked. "In the

face of history, of every line of philosophy, against the teaching of every religion-
ist and seer and prophet the world has ever given us, we are still doing what our
barbaric ancestors did when they came out of the caves and the woods.''

In the end, said Darrow, ''I am pleading for the future. I am pleading for a
time when hatred and cruelty will not control the hearts of men, when we can
learn . . . that all life is worth saving, and that mercy is the highest attitude of
man.'' ''If I can succeed,'' he concluded, ''my greatest reward will be that I
have done something for the tens of thousands of other boys . . . who must tread
the same road in blind childhood . . . ; that I have done something to help human
understanding, to temper justice with mercy, to overcome hate with love.'' At
the end, wrote one reporter, ''tears were streaming down the judge's face.''
Leopold and Loeb were sentenced to life in prison.

Another courtroom performance of great oratorical interest was Darrow's
confrontation with William Jennings Bryan at the Scopes Monkey Trial in Dayton, Tennessee, in July 1925. Darrow's client was Thomas Scopes, a school
teacher charged with the criminal act of teaching in the public schools a ''theory
that denies the story of the divine creation of man as taught in the Bible.'' The
trial showcased the clash between Darrow—the believer in reason, progress, and
liberalism—and Bryan—the leader of the Christian fundamentalist movement
and the prime sponsor of antievolution laws such as the one at issue in the Scopes
case. The two men had clashed before in the newspapers, but now they met face
to face. For Darrow, the fight was between education and ''religious fanaticism.''
The case was one of the first to be broadcast to the nation by radio. The trial
itself was strange. Darrow's only sustained speech was his opening argument,
delivered while the jury was absent; his scientific witnesses were forbidden to
testify, so he called instead Bryan himself as an ''expert'' on the Bible; and in
the end, he asked the jury for a guilty verdict so as to permit a speedy appeal
to the higher courts. Scopes was convicted and fined $100; eventually the con-
viction was reversed on a technicality.

Darrow's performance at Dayton was a perfect example of his talent for striking
precisely the right tone and adopting the right strategy to achieve his objectives.
Throughout the trial, Darrow's approach was to convey an attitude of scorn and
contempt for fundamentalism in general and for Bryan in particular. He spoke
with continual but low-key sarcasm that kept Bryan—and the judge—constantly
off balance. At the beginning, he announced, ''This case we have to argue is a
case at law, and hard as it is for me to bring my mind to conceive it, almost
impossible as it is to put my mind back in the nineteenth century, I am going
to argue this case as if it were serious, and as if it were a death struggle between
two civilizations.'' Midway through the trial, Darrow demanded that a sign
proclaiming ''Read Your Bible'' be taken down. ''We might agree to get up a
sign of equal size on the other side and in the same position reading 'Hunter's
Biology,' or 'Read your evolution,' '' Darrow suggested. When one of Scopes's
fourteen-year-old students reported that his teacher distinguished animals from
people by saying that ''man had reasoning power, that these animals did not,''

Darrow commented, "There is some doubt about that." Yet beneath this affected tone of contemptuous indifference, Darrow seethed. He objected when the judge opened court with a prayer; he nearly brought a contempt citation down on himself when the court refused to allow his expert witnesses to testify.

Darrow's strategy revealed itself in full only on his cross-examination of Bryan, in which the agnostic progressive led the old fundamentalist through a series of questions designed ostensibly to show that the Bible admitted of different interpretations on many issues and could not be read literally. Darrow's questioning was relentless; he had combed the Bible for every possible contradiction, omission, and redundancy. Darrow pressed Bryan on whether he believed that Jonah was swallowed by a whale. It was a big fish, said Bryan. "But in the New Testament it says whale, doesn't it?" countered Darrow. And in a later exchange: "But do you believe He made them—that He made such a fish and that it was big enough to swallow Jonah?" Bryan: "Yes, Sir. Let me add: one miracle is just as easy to believe as another." Darrow: "It is for you." Bryan: "It is for me." Darrow: "Just as hard?" Bryan: "It is hard to believe for you, but easy for me." "The only thing is," Bryan concluded, "you have a definition of fact that includes imagination." "And you have a definition that excludes everything but imagination," replied Darrow. The questioning went on until Darrow asked whether the serpent was made to crawl upon his belly because he had tempted Eve. "I believe that," said Bryan. "Have you any idea how the snake went before that time," asked Darrow. "Do you know whether he walked on his tail or not?" At last Bryan could take no more. "The only purpose Mr. Darrow has is to slur at the Bible," he told the judge. "I want the world to know that this man, who does not believe in a God, is trying to use a court in Tennessee . . . to slur at it, and while it will require time, I will take it." "I object to your statement," said Darrow. "I am examining you on your fool ideas that no intelligent Christian on earth believes." The judge adjourned the court and permitted no further questioning, and the trial ended. Bryan left the stand humiliated; a few days later, he suffered a fatal heart attack.

One other courtroom speech should be noted. In 1912, after defending in an extraordinarily bitter California labor case involving arson and murder, Darrow found himself accused of jury tampering. The charge was entirely unfounded; the prosecution's case rested on the testimony of Bert Franklin, who had committed the attempted bribery and who implicated Darrow in order to save himself from a prison term. Apparently the prosecution sought to compel Darrow to reveal incriminating evidence about several important labor leaders with whom he had worked in several cases. After a long, tiring trial, Darrow addressed the jury in his own defense.

The speech is a marvelous example of the appeal to the ethos of the speaker. Darrow began by telling the jury, "I am a stranger in a strange land. . . . I think I can say that no one in my native town would have made to any jury any such statement as was made of me by the district attorney in opening this case." Then he set out the heart of his defense: "I am on trial because I have been a lover of the poor, a friend of the oppressed, because I have stood by labor for all these years, and have brought down upon my head the wrath of the criminal interests in this country. . . . These men are interested in getting me.'' After a long, detailed review of the evidence in the case, Darrow concluded with a similar appeal: ''I have tried to be the friend of every man who lived. I have tried to help in the world. I have had love for my fellow-men. I have done the best I could.'' The bribery charge was particularly upsetting to Darrow because he had indeed built for himself a reputation as an honest man. Often, as here, he relied on that reputation in his arguments in court. The appeal worked. Given the state's weak case and Darrow's masterful presentation, the jury was out only thirty-four minutes before returning a verdict of not guilty.

One final speech should be noted because it is probably the finest of the many speeches he delivered out of court: Darrow's funeral oration in memory of John Peter Altgeld. Altgeld was the governor of Illinois in the 1890s and is best remembered for his pardon of several anarchists convicted of murder after a bomb went off at a meeting in Haymarket Square, Chicago, in 1886. Altgeld was Darrow's friend, mentor, and ideological soul-mate from their meeting in 1888 until Altgeld's death in 1902.

In delivering the funeral oration, Darrow struck a very different tone than is evident in his combative courtroom orations. Still, like many of Darrow's other speeches, it demonstrated Darrow's knack for adopting the right tone for the occasion. Darrow spoke in reverential tones; the effect is stately, even Lincoln-esque. Throughout his tone was controlled, his sentences short, his cadence balanced. He used parallel structure, repitition, and an even, rhythmic structure to preserve the quality of awe and devotion that filled the speech. ''My dear, dead friend,'' Darrow concluded, ''long and well have we known you, devotedly have we followed you, implicitly have we trusted you, fondly have we loved you. . . . But, though we lay you in the grave and hide you from the sight of man, your brave words will speak for the poor, for the oppressed, the captive and the weak; and your devoted life inspire countless souls to do and dare in the holy cause for which you lived and died.'' The speech was a simple, elegant statement of love for the man and at the same time an expression of sympathy for what the man had stood for. This juxtaposition of personal tribute to Altgeld and a more general statement of Altgeld's (and Darrow's) political and personal philosophy gave the speech its special flavor. Altgeld, Darrow said simply, ''was one of the rarest souls who ever lived and died. His was a humble birth, a fearless life and a dramatic, fitting death. We who knew him, we who loved him, we who rallied to his many hopeless causes, we who dared to praise him while his heart still beat, cannot yet feel that we should never hear his voice again.'' Altgeld was ''a soldier in the everlasting struggle of the human race for liberty and justice on earth.'' He was ''a lover of his fellow man''; a man ''of kindness, of charity, of infinite pity to the outcast and weak''; a ''wise and learned lawyer.'' ''He so loved justice and truth and liberty and righteousness that all the terror that the earth could hold was less than the condemnation of his own conscience for an act that was cowardly or mean.'' In the end, concluded Darrow, switching suddenly to the second person, ''your brave words will speak for the poor, the oppressed, the captive and the weak; and your devoted life inspire countless souls to do and dare in the holy cause for which you lived and died.'' This was surely as much Darrow's own creed as it was Altgeld's, and like all his other rhetoric, Darrow's farewell to his friend gets its strength above all from the inner truths Darrow drew out of his own convictions.

INFORMATION SOURCES

Research Collections and Collected Speeches

The Clarence Darrow Papers are located in the Library of Congress, Washington, D.C.

Attorney for the Damned. Edited by Arthur Weinberg. New York: Simon   AD
    and Schuster, 1957.

Selected Critical Studies

Jackson, James H. ''Clarence Darrow's 'Plea in Defense of Himself.' '' *Western Journal of Speech Communication* 20 (1956): 185–95.
Maloney, Martin. ''The Forensic Speaking of Clarence Darrow.'' *Speech Monographs* 14 (1947): 111–16.
———. ''Clarence Darrow.'' In *A History and Criticism of American Public Address*. Edited by Marie Kathryn Hochmuth. New York: Longmans, Green, 1955.
Ravitz, Abe C. *Clarence Darrow and the American Literary Tradition*. Cleveland: Western Reserve, 1962.
Sanbonmatsu, Akira. ''Darrow and Rorke's Use of Burkeian Identification Strategies in *New York vs. Gitlow* (1920).'' *Communications Monographs* 38 (1971): 36–48.

Selected Biographies

Allen, Leslie H. *Bryan and Darrow at Dayton*. New York: Russell and Russell, 1967.
Darrow, Clarence. *The Story of My Life*. New York: Charles Scribner's Sons, 1932.
Stone, Irving. *Clarence Darrow for the Defense*. Garden City, N.Y.: Doubleday, 1941.
Tierney, Kevin. *Darrow: A Biography*. New York: Thomas Y. Crowell, 1979.
Weinberg, Arthur, and Weinberg, Lila. *Verdicts Out of Court*. Chicago: Quadrangle Books, 1963.

CHRONOLOGY OF MAJOR SPEECHES

See ''Research Collections and Collected Speeches'' for source codes.

Oration at the funeral of John Peter Altgeld, Chicago, March 14, 1902; *AD*, pp. 542–46.

Darrow in his own defense, Los Angeles, August 15, 1912; *AD*, pp. 491–531.

Defense of Leopold and Loeb, Chicago, July 31, 1924; *AD*, pp. 16–88.

Scopes evolution case, Dayton, Tennessee, July 20, 1925; *AD*, pp. 174–228.

EUGENE V. DEBS
(1855–1926), labor spokesman and socialist presidential candidate
_____ CRAIG ALLEN SMITH

At fifteen, Eugene V. Debs left school in Terre Haute to work on the railroad. He became secretary of the local Brotherhood of Locomotive Firemen and rose rapidly in the union, serving as associate editor (1878) and editor in chief (1880) of the *Firemen's Magazine* and as grand secretary and treasurer of the Brotherhood of Locomotive Firemen. Frustrated by the union's lack of progress, he served a term in the Indiana legislature beginning in 1885, to which he did not seek reelection. In 1893, disillusioned with both legislative deliberations and trade unions, Debs founded the American Railway Union (ARU), an industrial union of all railroad workers.

In its first year, the ARU won a major victory over the Great Northern Railroad, and membership boomed. But when this influx undermined the discipline and organization of the ARU, the union engaged in a disastrous 1894 strike against the Pullman Car Company. On the grounds that the strike impeded transportation of the mail, federal injunctions against assisting the strike were issued, and President Grover Cleveland sent troops (against the wishes of Illinois governor John Altgeld). With the strike broken, Debs was sentenced to six months in prison for violating the injunction. Frustrated with legislative debate, trade unions, and an industrial union and confined to the solitude of his cell, Debs read about socialism. He emerged from Woodstock jail a believer in the class struggle.

Still hopeful of economic reform through democracy, Debs organized the Social Democratic party of the United States in 1897 and was its 1900 presidential nominee. In 1901 the various socialist factions formed the Socialist party, as whose 1904 presidential candidate Debs polled some 400,000 votes. In 1905 Debs joined with rival socialist Daniel DeLeon and mineworkers' leader "Big Bill" Haywood to found the Industrial Workers of the World (IWW). The IWW sought to organize all workers, regardless of trade or industry, into one big union. Initially enthusiastic, Debs resigned from the IWW in 1908 because of his distaste for its violent tactics. Debs was the Socialist party candidate for president again in 1908 (receiving about 420,000 votes). The 1912 presidential race boasted a strong field: incumbent President Taft, Theodore Roosevelt, Woodrow Wilson, and Debs. In this august company, Debs polled about 6 percent of the vote (about 900,000 votes).

In 1917 the Socialist party denounced the war and U.S. involvement in it as capitalist exploitation. The federal government, already concerned about socialists, monitored Debs's activities carefully. When Debs criticized support for the war effort in a 1918 Canton, Ohio, speech, he was convicted of violating the Espionage Act and sentenced to ten years in prison. While a prisoner, Debs again ran for president in 1920 and again polled about 900,000 votes. He was pardoned by Republican President Warren G. Harding in 1921. After his release from prison, Debs worked toward the rejuvenation of American socialism, but its association with foreign influence, revolutionary bolshevism, and un-Americanism rendered those efforts largely unproductive. After a prolonged illness, Eugene V. Debs died on October 20, 1926.

DEBS AS A SOCIALIST ORATOR

Debs's rhetorical impact was not confined to his oratory. Few of his presocialist speeches remain. Moreover, his writings for *Appeal to Reason* and the *International Socialist Review* reached considerably wider audiences than did his thousands of speeches. For this reason, students of Debs's rhetorical career should pay close attention to both his writings and his speeches.

The major speeches date from his 1895 release from Woodstock jail to the 1920s. A first group consists of "Liberty" and "The Role of the Courts," which he delivered upon his release from jail. These two speeches mark the first public appearances by Debs the socialist and discuss the notions of liberty, freedom, and arbitrary power in a democratic society.

A second group of speeches, all in 1905, concern the IWW. These include his address at the founding of the IWW, and his discussions "Trade Unionism," "Industrial Unionism," "Class Unionism," and "Revolutionary Unionism." All are largely variations on the theme that the unionization of skilled workers by their individual trades divides workers against one another and therefore exacerbates labor's difficulties.

Debs's speeches accepting Socialist party presidential nominations constitute a third group. It seems clear that Debs harbored no great hope for winning the presidency. Instead he used the electoral arena to demonstrate his confidence in government by the people and to attack what he saw as the control of democratic government in the United States by the capitalist "Republican-Democratic party." These speeches offer little explanation of Debs's utopia beyond worker control of the economy and government.

Finally, the Canton speech was devoted to pacifism. World War I, to Debs, was part of a historical pattern:

The feudal barons of the Middle Ages, the economic predecessors of the capitalists of our day, declared all wars. And their miserable serfs fought all the battles. The poor, ignorant serfs had been taught to revere their masters; to believe that when their masters declared war upon one another, it was their patriotic duty to fall upon one another and to cut one another's throats for the profit and glory of the lords and barons who held them in contempt. And that is war in a nutshell.

He expressed his opposition to the kaiser in a way that transformed the conflict into a class struggle:

Now, after being the guest of Emperor Wilhelm, the Beast of Berlin, he [Theodore Roosevelt] comes back to this country, and wants you to send ten million men over there to kill the Kaiser; to murder his former friend and pal. Rather queer isn't it? And yet, he is the patriot and we are the traitors. . . . I hate, I loathe, I despise junkers and junkerdom. I have no earthly use for the junkers of Germany, and not one particle more use for the junkers in the United States.

Debs went beyond discussing war in class terms to critique a double-standard patriotism:

They [capitalists] are continually talking about your patriotic duty. It is not *their* but *your* patriotic duty that they are concerned about. There is a decided difference. Their patriotic duty never takes them to the firing line or chucks them into trenches.

Debs knew his arrest was imminent. Indeed had he not been arrested for the speech, his argument would have lost considerable force.

Debs's rhetoric is characterized by, first, the polarization of society into capitalists and workers. This allowed him to transcend the self-conceptions of skilled and unskilled workers, whites and blacks, women and men, laborers and farmers. His transcendent and polarizing rhetoric was based on neither individuals nor groups but situations. He frequently spoke of labor leaders who had risen from the rank and file only to be corrupted by the temptations of power, wealth, and prestige. Despite the vehemence of his attacks upon prominent capitalists, he always attributed blame for their behavior to the system in which they lived rather than to individual personal failures.

A second rhetorical feature was Debs's articulation of a radical economic philosophy through the use of traditional American values, symbols, and political processes. No doubt recognizing his listeners' attachment to the dream of private ownership, he stressed the enduring American cultural values of morality, hard work, optimism, progress, inevitable change, freedom, liberty, equality of opportunity, and ethical equality. His pattern was to argue that socialism, more than capitalism, embodied the spirit and ideals of America and Christianity.

Finally, Debs's style was marked by sophisticated vocabulary, eloquent but unstaged diction, and frequent allusions to literature. He combined the worldliness of presidential candidates with the bluntness of fifteen-year-old railroad workers. His direct, logical assaults on capitalists focused his listeners' discontent, rendering them less hostile to their employers as persons, or the nobility and assurance of his disposition created a persona to which the workers could aspire.

Debs was the best-known champion of socialism in the United States. His activities rendered socialism a legitimate subject for democratic debate rather than an anarchic threat. At a time when anarchists like Mikhail Bakunin and John Most threatened the destruction of private property and those who held it, Debs addressed the issue of the public good through traditional democratic methods.

But if Debs were a philosophical thorn in the sides of revolutionary socialists and anarchists, he was a helpful adversary of Samuel Gompers and the American Federation of Labor (AFL). While Gompers sought "trade unionism pure and simple" to win larger pieces of the capitalist pie, Debs advocated industrial unionism and class politics for the overthrow of capitalism. Debs's charge that the AFL sold out workers and perpetuated corporate power posed a major threat to the AFL. But just as the revolutionists rendered Debs's polite socialism more palatable, his threat to private corporations rendered the AFL's capitalist demands more attractive. In this sense, Debs's socialist arguments lubricated negotiations between corporations and the AFL.

The oratory of Eugene V. Debs contributed significantly to the emergence of contemporary America. Respected even by his adversaries, Debs articulated socialist views that resonated with traditional American values of effort, fairness, and morality. If judged purely by his direct effects, Debs was a poor rhetor. He was ineffective in the Indiana legislature, he was unable to avert the Pullman strike, he lost control over the direction of the IWW, he was unable to establish a viable Socialist Labor party, and he was unable either to win the presidency or to be co-opted by a major party. But such a judgment would be too harsh. Debs's pamphlets, articles, and speeches enriched American public dialogue by rendering the attractions of socialism and the vulnerabilities of capitalism discussable issues. During the Great Depression, the public's ability to consider a wide range of alternatives, from Herbert Hoover's laissez-faire policies through Franklin Roosevelt's New Deal to Huey Long's Share Our Wealth plan, contributed to the nation's survival.

INFORMATION SOURCES

Research Collections and Collected Speeches

Researchers interested in Debs's rhetoric can draw upon the resources of both the Debs Foundation and Cunningham Library of Indiana State University, Terre Haute, Indiana. Debs's writings and speeches are available on some one hundred reels of microfilm at the Wisconsin State Historical Collection, Madison, and at the Tamiment Institute, Bobst Library, New York University, New York City.

Debs: His Life, Writings and Speeches. Chicago: Charles H. Kerr, 1908.   *DHLWS*

Eugene V. Debs Speaks. Edited by Jean Y. Tussey. New York: Pathfinder   *EVDS*
    Books, 1970.

Writings and Speeches of Eugene V. Debs. Edited by Joseph M. Bernstein.   *WSEVD*
    New York: Hermitage Press, 1948.

Selected Critical Studies

Brommel, Bernard J. "Eugene V. Debs: The Agitator as Speaker." *Central States Speech Journal* 20 (1969): 202–14.

————. "The Pacifist Speechmaking of Eugene V. Debs." *Quarterly Journal of Speech* 52 (1966): 146–54.

Selected Biographies

Ginger, Ray. *The Bending Cross: A Biography of Eugene Victor Debs*. New Brunswick, N.J.: Rutgers University Press, 1949.

Salvatore, Nick. *Eugene V. Debs: Citizen and Socialist*. Urbana: University of Illinois Press, 1982.

CHRONOLOGY OF MAJOR SPEECHES

See "Research Collections and Collected Speeches" for source codes.

"Liberty," Woodstock, Illinois, November 22, 1895; *WSEVD*, pp. 6–20; *DHLWS*, pp. 327–44.

"The Role of the Courts," Terre Haute, Indiana, November 23, 1895; *EVDS*, pp. 50–52.

"Prison Labor," New York City, March 21, 1899; *WSEVD*, pp. 24–33; *DHLWS*, pp. 345–56.

Acceptance speech, Chicago, Illinois, May 1, 1904; *WSEVD*, pp. 73–76.

"The Socialist Party and the Working Class," Indianapolis, Indiana, September 1, 1904; *WSEVD*, pp. 125–39; *DHWLS*, pp. 357–73.

Founding of the Industrial Workers of the World, Chicago, June 29, 1905; *EVDS*, pp. 111–19.

"Craft Unionism," Chicago, September 23, 1905; *WSEVD*, pp. 171–88; *DHLWS*, pp. 375–99.

"Class Unionism," Chicago, November 24, 1905; *WSEVD*, pp. 189–209; *DHLWS*, pp. 391–425.

"Revolutionary Unionism," Chicago, November 25, 1905; *WSEVD*, pp. 209–23; *DHLWS*, pp. 427–43.

"Industrial Unionism," New York City, December 10, 1905; *EVDS*, pp. 121–44; *DHLWS*, pp. 445–71.

"The Issue," Girard, Kansas, May 23, 1908; *WSEVD*, pp. 293–310; *DHLWS*, pp. 473–91.

Canton speech, Canton, Ohio, June 16, 1918; *EVDS*, pp. 243–79.

Address to the jury, Cleveland, Ohio, September 12, 1918; *EVDS*, pp. 281–88.

Statement to the court, Cleveland, Ohio, September 14, 1918; *WSEVD*, pp. 437–39.

EVERETT McKINLEY DIRKSEN
(1896–1969), Republican U.S. Senate minority leader, 1959–1969

_____ EDWARD L. SCHAPSMEIER

Everett McKinley Dirksen was born in the small town of Pekin, Illinois, in 1896. By the time of his death in 1969, he had become one of the most well-known political figures of his time. He represented the state of Illinois in the U.S. Senate from 1951 to 1969. But during the latter ten years, when he served as GOP minority leader, he undoubtedly became the chief spokesperson for the Republican party. His national recognition and power in the Senate were in no small measure due to his oratorical ability and flair for generating media attention.

DIRKSEN AS POLITICAL ORATOR

The thirty-year-old Dirksen entered politics in 1926 by being elected to the Pekin City Council. Because of his prowess as a stump speaker, he quickly became tabbed as the "talkin'est man in Tazewell County." In 1932, despite a Democratic landslide during the lowest ebb of the Great Depression, Dirksen won a seat in the U.S. House of Representatives. In representing the Illinois Sixteenth Congressional District, Dirksen became known for his dynamic personality, hard work, and skill as a floor debater. In 1944, he made a short-lived bid for the Republican presidential nomination. After contracting an eye disease that partially blinded him for a time, he did not seek reelection to the House in 1948.

Following a spontaneous remission of what was diagnosed as eye cancer, Dirksen ran for the U.S. Senate in 1950. He defeated Scott W. Lucas, the Democratic majority leader. In 1952 he gained instant national notoriety when, in a heated debate over the fair play amendment at the Republican National Convention, the fired-up Taftite pointed his finger at Governor Thomas E. Dewey of New York and declared in taunting terms: "You took us down the path of defeat." This particular convention, in which Dwight D. Eisenhower defeated Robert A. Taft for the GOP presidential nomination, was exciting television drama, and Dirksen emerged a nationally known figure despite the fact his candidate lost.

After the death of Senator Taft, with whom Dirksen had been allied politically, the Illinoisan gravitated toward the modern Republicanism and internationalism of President Eisenhower. Senator Dirksen won reelection in 1956 with Ike's endorsement. In 1957, with White House backing, Dirksen was chosen minority whip, and in 1959 he was elected minority leader.

As leader of the Republican members of the Senate, who were perpetually in the minority from 1959 to 1969, he promoted party harmony by utilizing his discourse from the floor, used radio, television, and the print media to influence public opinion, and combined his talent as a pacifier and mediator to effect compromises with regard to significant legislation. His style was that of a persuader, not one of an arm twister. His self-enunciated motto was, "The oil can is mightier than the sword."

Beginning in 1961, when Eisenhower left the White House, Senator Dirksen teamed up with Charles Halleck of Indiana, the House minority leader, to initiate regular television press conferences in which the duo served as spokespersons for the Republican Joint Congressional Leadership Conference. Dubbed the "Ev and Charlie Show" by columnist Tom Wicker of the *New York Times*, Dirksen and Halleck conducted a freewheeling, extemporaneous press conference that was an innovation in U.S. politics. Senator Dirksen immediately emerged as the star performer. He found television a forum much to his liking. His expressive visage, tousled white hair, infectious smile, and professional stage presence made him an appealing virtuoso by virtue of the likeable image he projected on the television screen. Displaying wit, charm, showmanship, and an innate charisma, Dirksen became a true television celebrity. The intimate nature of the electronic medium allowed him to make use of his wizardry as a raconteur and humorist and to coin ingeniously novel metaphors (labeled *Dirksenisms* by the press corps). Commenting on one of President John Kennedy's New Frontier proposals, Dirksen sallied forth with the quip: "That idea has as much effect as a snowflake on the bosom of the Potomac." In a droll vein Dirksen once characterized democratic government as "an old waterlogged scow. It doesn't move very fast, it doesn't move very far at one time, but it never sinks and maybe that is the reason we have free government today."

When Gerald R. Ford of Michigan defeated Charles Halleck for the position of GOP House minority leader in 1965, the "Ev and Charles Show" was renamed by the media the "Ev and Jerry Show." Jerry Ford was much younger and junior in seniority than Dirksen; thus, Dirksen tended to dominate the show. This was particularly true concerning foreign policy. Whenever Ford voiced any criticism of President Johnson's conduct of the Vietnam War, Dirksen criticized his colleague publicly. After Ford castigated LBJ for his "shocking mismanagement" of the Vietnam War, Senator Dirksen lectured his cohort by sternly admonishing him not to demean the chief executive when a war was on. Dirksen succinctly summarized his strong support of the war in Vietnam with the aphoristic utterance, "I have been mistaken for a falcon instead of a hawk, but I have never been mistaken for a dove."

Whether involved in a debate on the floor of the Senate, addressing a huge crowd at a political rally, or holding forth at a press conference, Senator Dirksen enthralled those listening to him. He mixed theatrics with superb timing while mesmerizing listeners with the mellifluous sound of his rich and resonant vocal intonations. He utilized his sonorous baritone voice as if it were a musical instrument to captivate an audience. By adroitly blending serious thoughts and logical reasoning with humor and quotations from literary sources or great figures of a bygone era, Dirksen appealed to both a hearer's intellect and emotions to convert the person to his cause. In a 1962 cover story in *Time* magazine, his unique brand of elocutionary eloquence was described as follows: "He speaks, and the words emerge in a soft, sepulchral baritone. They undulate in measured phrases, expire in breathless wisps. He fills his lungs and blows word-rings like smoke. They chase each other around the room in dreamy images of Steamboat Gothic."

Because of his unusual talent as a speaker, Dirksen had many laudatory appellations bestowed upon him by contemporary admirers. He was acclaimed as the "Demosthenes of the Senate," "the Senate's Golden Voice," the "Silver Throated Senator," and the "Pagliacci of American Politics."

In addition to the distinction accorded him for his political oratory, Dirksen gained fame among the mass public as a recording artist. He recorded four best-seller, long-play albums: "Gallant Men," "Man Is Not Alone," "Christmas Time," and "Everett Dirksen's America" (the last issued posthumously). These popular recordings, which featured his spoken word as a solo part with a background of music, catapulted him into star status as a show business personality. In 1967, Dirksen was awarded a Grammy by the National Academy of Arts and Sciences for "Gallant Men," which as a gold record album sold over 500,000 copies. The silver-haired Dirksen, with his hoary locks, became a national septuagenerian symbol of the nostalgic past with his deep-toned renditions of poetry and patriotic readings.

As GOP Senate minority leader, Dirksen was involved in two losing legislative fights against actions of the U.S. Supreme Court when he sought to overturn by law the high tribunal's decisions relative to banning prayer in the public schools and its reapportionment decision. With regard to his prayer amendment, which failed of approval in the Senate, Dirksen contended, "I say give Caesar what he requires, but give God a little also."

On two important occasions Senator Dirksen marshaled his minority forces with parliamentary skill and oratorical persuasiveness to achieve legislative successes for Democratic presidents. One was to secure Senate ratification of the 1963 Nuclear Test Ban Treaty, which had been submitted to the upper chamber by President Kennedy. In a remarkable speech that won over some needed votes for two-thirds approval of the treaty preventing atmospheric testing of nuclear devices, Dirksen conceded that most of his constituent mail was in opposition to his Senate colleagues: "So today my statement that I shall support the treaty is an exercise of my independent judgment based upon what I think is best for my country.'' In his Senate speech Dirksen quoted Confucius to provide him with a theme: ''The longest journey begins with the first step.'' The crux of his logic was focused on the fact that future adherence to the test ban treaty was verifiable, and thus Soviet actions could be carefully monitored to prevent deliberate deception. Dirksen referred to John Hershey's account of the atomic bomb destruction at Hiroshima. ''The whole bosom of God's earth was ruptured by a man-made contrivance that we call a nuclear weapon,'' asserted Dirksen. He queried, ''Since then, what have we done? What steps have we taken?'' In a telling personal testament, Dirksen acknowledged: ''One of my age thinks about his destiny a little. I should not like to have written on my tombstone, 'He knew what happened at Hiroshima, but did not take a first step.' '' With rhetorical intensity, Senator Dirksen concluded with an impassioned plea: ''This is the first, single step. It is for destiny to write an answer. It is for history to render judgment. But with consummate faith and some determination, this may be the step that can spell a grander destiny for our country and for the world.''

Another major Senate issue in which Dirksen proved effective in providing a margin of voting success by his participation in floor debate related to the need to invoke cloture in the upper chamber in order to be able to enact the Civil Rights Act of 1964. It was essential that Dirksen deliver key votes to obtain the needed two-thirds vote to cut off the seventy-five-day filibuster being conducted by southern Democrats. Dirksen defined the issue of civil rights in moral terms and stressed the fact that the pending legislation, blocked from Senate consideration, was long overdue. Quoting Victor Hugo's diary entry, ''Stronger than all the armies is an idea whose time has come,'' for a theme, Dirksen went on to proclaim: ''The time has come for equality of opportunity in sharing in government, in education, and in employment. It will not be stayed or denied. It is here.'' He affirmed the essential rightness of the civil rights bill by making references to statements uttered by Thomas Jefferson and Abraham Lincoln, both of whom had avowed the fundamental proposition that all men are created equal. Calling on his colleagues to reaffirm ''this article of faith,'' Dirksen concluded his appeal for votes by proclaiming: ''Today let us not be found wanting in whatever it takes by way of moral and spiritual substance to face up to the issue and vote cloture.''

During the presidency of Lyndon Johnson, Senator Dirksen was able to hold most of his party in line in its firm support of the Vietnam war. Dirksen consistently upheld the moral rightness of the principle of self-determination and the correctness of the United States fighting in its behalf.

In a Senate speech, he enjoined, ''The most basic of these deeply held principles is that no nation has the right to change the international map by external violence. On that principle rests the difference between order and anarchy in a dangerous and feverish world. It is for that principle that our men are fighting and dying right now in the jungles of Vietnam.'' Dirksen never waivered from his hawkish position despite the intensity of the antiwar movement within the country. He won reelection to his fourth, and final, term in the U.S. Senate while standing firm on his conviction that the U.S. military crusade in Vietnam was an honorable war for a noble cause.

Everett Dirksen's great contribution to the democratic process in Congress was his deftness in promoting compromise whenever possible to avoid obstructionism. His goal was to lead the Republican minority to seek the overall general welfare of the nation. With his effective oratory, he could ensnarl an adversary in a web of words or weave a golden bridge of rhetoric to permit an opponent to cross over to his side. In his speeches he was not afraid to take stands on controversial issues when convinced they were factually correct and morally sound. His oral arguments in defense of his position, while engaged in verbal combat, were vigorous but not vindictive, courageous but not cantakerous, clever but not cruel. He was a superb politician whose congressional leadership and statesmanlike stature contributed to the strength and vitality of the two-party system. His oratorical wizardry was a tool he used to persuade political friends and foes alike to join him on a particular vote. To do this he used moral suasion, intellectual arguments, cagy cajoling, or sheer appeals to emotion.

Dirksen's speeches, mostly extemporaneous, in the main were verbal weapons forged in the heat of political battle. They were not aimed at posterity. In his role as a parliamentarian and day-to-day tactician on the floor of the Senate, Dirksen made ample use of his oratorical skill to lead his party in partisan debate in order to influence the course of vital legislation. He was a genius in employing the amendatory process and a giant as a legislator leading the loyal opposition. Dirksen was one of the great minority leaders in the Senate and has secured a niche in congressional history as a master practitioner of minority politics. With civility, calm deliberation, and potent speech making, Senator Dirksen carried the banner of conservative Republicanism and activistic intervention against communist imperialism during an era of liberal welfarism and neoisolationism.

INFORMATION SOURCES

Research Collections and Collected Speeches

The Everett McKinley Dirksen Congressional Leadership Research Center, Pekin, Illinois, contains all of Everett M. Dirksen's papers. Archival sources located at the Dirksen Center most useful for the oratorical-political researcher who seeks notes and texts of speeches, as well as public reaction, include the following portions of the collection: Information File, Joint Republican Congressional Leadership File, Legislative File, Memorabilia File, Press Clippings, Remarks and Releases, and the Working Papers. Also available are oral histories, television kinescopes, sound recordings, and motion picture films.

Congressional Record.   CR

Selected Critical Studies

Cronin, Jean Torcom. "Minority Leadership in the United States Senate, The Role and
    Style of Everett Dirksen." Ph.D. dissertation, Johns Hopkins University, 1973.
"Ev and Charlie: GOP End Men." *Newsweek*, April 24, 1961, pp. 34–36.
"The Ev Show." *Time*, April 20, 1962, pp. 29–30.
Fonsino, Frank J. "Everett McKinley Dirksen, The Roots of an American Statesman."
    Journal of the Illinois State Historical Society 76 (1983): 17–34.
Furlong, William B. "The Senate Wizard of Ooze: Dirksen of Illinois." *Harper's Mag-
    azine* 219 (December 1959): 44–49.
Harkness, Jean S."An Analysis of Senator Everett McKinley Dirksen's Nomination of
    Barry Goldwater for President as an Example of Epideictic Speaking." Master's
    thesis, University of Arizona, 1965.
Hope, Emily Bock. "A Study of the Rhetorical Theory and Practice of Everett McKinley
    Dirksen." Ph.D. dissertation, Southern Illinois University, 1969.
"The Leader." *Time*, September 14, 1962, pp. 27–31.
Schapsmeier, Edward L., and Schapsmeier, Frederick H. "Senator Everett M. Dirksen
    and American Foreign Policy." *Old Northwest, A Journal of Regional Life and
    Letters* 7 (1981–1982): 359–372.
———. "Everett M. Dirksen of Pekin, Politician par Excellence." *Journal of the Illinois
    State Historical Society* 86 (1983): 2–16.
"Senator Dirksen: Vandenberg of the 60's? Role in the Test Ban Treaty Debate." *U.S.
    News & World Report*, September 23, 1963, p. 24.

Selected Biographies

Dirksen, Louella, with Browning, Norma Lee. *The Honorable Mr. Marigold, My Life
    with Everett Dirksen*. New York: Harper & Row, 1971.
MacNeil, Neil. *Dirksen: Portrait of a Public Man*. New York: World Publishing Com-
    pany, 1970.
Penny, Annette Culler. *The Golden Voice of the Senate*. Washington, D.C.: Acropolis
    Books, 1968.
Schapsmeier, Edward L., and Schapsmeier, Frederick H. *Dirksen of Illinois: Senatorial
    Statesman*. Urbana and Chicago: University of Illinois Press, 1985.

CHRONOLOGY OF MAJOR SPEECHES

See "Research Collections and Collected Speeches" for source codes.

"Cloture Motion," Washington, D.C., June 10, 1964; *CR*, June 10, 1964, pp. 13319–
20.

"Civil Rights Act," Washington, D.C., June 19, 1964; *CR*, June 19, 1964, pp. 14509–
11.

"Fair Play Amendment," Chicago, July 9, 1952; *Official Proceedings of the 25th Republican National Convention* (Republican National Committee), pp. 91–94.

"Nuclear Test Ban Treaty," Washington, D.C., September 11, 1963; *CR*, September 11, 1963, pp. 16788–91.

"Goldwater Nomination," San Francisco, July 15, 1964; *Official Proceedings of the 28th Republican National Convention* (Republican National Committee), pp. 301–05.

"Prayer Amendment," Washington, D.C., September 19, 1966; *CR*, September 19, 1966, pp. 831–35.

"Vietnam War," Washington, D.C., May 24, 1967; *CR*, May 24, 1967, pp. 1130–34.

"Reapportionment," Washington, D.C., July 16, 1967; *CR*, July 16, 1967, pp. 1245–48.

WILLIAM EDWARD BURGHARDT DU BOIS
(1868–1963), crusader for civil rights

_____ ALLEN H. MERRIAM

W. E. B. Du Bois was one of the most prominent black speakers in the United States in the first half of the twentieth century. A brilliant writer, respected scholar, and the first black to earn a Ph.D. at Harvard, Du Bois helped found the influential National Association for the Advancement of Colored People (NAACP) in 1909. He emerged a leading voice in the civil rights movement, serving as director of publicity and research and editing the NAACP's official publication, the *Crisis*, from 1910 to 1934. A professor of economics and history at Atlanta University between 1897 and 1910 and chairman of the Sociology Department from 1934 to 1944, he advocated a militant strategy of economic, social, and political reform in contrast to the compromising gradualism espoused by Booker T. Washington. During eight decades of speech making, Du Bois traveled widely and lectured extensively on the themes of racial justice, education, socialism, anticolonialism, and peace. He spoke in most U.S. states and numerous other countries, celebrating his ninety-first birthday with a speech broadcast from Peking, China. A frequent participant at international conferences, Du Bois effectively linked the racial struggle in the United States to liberation movements throughout the world. Increasingly impatient with the slowness of reform in the United States, he renounced the capitalist West and emigrated to Ghana in 1961, leaving a legacy of oratory important for its reasoned criticism of racism and oppression but bitter and alienated from the mainstream of American political discourse.

DU BOIS AS POLITICAL ORATOR

From his youth, Du Bois recognized the power of rhetoric. At his Massachusetts high school graduation in 1884, he spoke on Wendell Phillips's contribution to U.S. democracy. Du Bois studied writing and public speaking at Fisk University in Nashville, achieving success as a debater. Moving to Harvard, he won the Boylston Prize in Oratory and in 1890 was chosen one of six commencement speakers, portraying Jefferson Davis as the personification of evils Du Bois associated with white America: oppressive power, aggression and war, greed and self-centeredness. While at Harvard, Du Bois studied English composition and style under Barrett Wendell, using as a text Adam Sherman Hill's *The Principles of Rhetoric*, a standard Victorian work reflecting eighteenth- and nineteenth-century British rhetorical theory. Wrote Du Bois: ''I believe foolishly perhaps but sincerely that I have something to say to the world, and I have taken English 12 in order to say it well.''

That sentiment gives insight into Du Bois's oratorical style. During his several careers—professor at Atlanta University, propagandist for the NAACP, and later world citizen and promoter of socialism and peace—his speech making remained characterized by reasoned analysis, careful and measured phrasing, attention to historical perspective, and a deliberate, unemotional delivery. His attacks on American capitalism as racist and exploitive were strong and, toward the end of his life, increasingly radicalized, but his oratorical style remained scholarly and moderate. He was a thinking man's agitator.

The publication in 1903 of *The Souls of Black Folk*, a classic of Afro-American literature, propelled Du Bois to the forefront of black leadership in the United States. One idea that stirred considerable public debate was the attack on Booker T. Washington's doctrine of accommodation, gradualism, and manual training as the best route for uplifting blacks, a position outlined in Washington's famous 1895 Atlanta Cotton Exposition Address. Du Bois argued that blacks must demand full political and civil rights immediately and should encourage the highest intellectual development of its exceptional people—"the Talented Tenth" he called them. Urging blacks to lift their sights beyond the narrow limits of vocationalism, Du Bois made effective use of antithesis: "I insist that the object of all true education is not to make men carpenters, it is to make carpenters men.'' The ensuing controversy produced numerous opportunities for Du Bois to lecture on his philosophy of education.

Capitalizing on his newly established prominence, Du Bois assumed a leading role in the Niagara movement, a short-lived effort launched in July 1905 to promote economic self-development, education and literacy, freedom of expression, voting rights, access to public accommodations and jobs—in short, to end all social injustice. Touring on behalf of the fledgling movement, Du Bois gave some of his most forceful oratory, including his "We Claim Our Rights" speech of August 16, 1906, at Harpers Ferry, West Virginia. Following a symbolic barefoot pilgrimage to the site of John Brown's martyrdom in 1859, Du Bois declared: "We claim for ourselves every single right that belongs to a freeborn American, political, civil and social; and until we get these rights we will never cease to protest and assail the ears of America.''

The Niagara Movement soon withered due to internal bickering, overly broad objectives, and organizational weakness. But it had laid the foundation for the emergence in 1909 of the NAACP. The editorship of the *Crisis*, which within a decade had a circulation of over 100,000, enhanced Du Bois' reputation as a leading advocate of liberalism and social change. Speaking in New York City on March 5, 1910, Du Bois made one of his most impassioned calls for human rights: "There is in this world no such force as the force of a man determined to rise. The human soul cannot be permanently chained.'' Alert to the persuasive function of symbolic physical action, Du Bois headed the "silent protest parade" on Fifth Avenue in New York on July 28, 1917, which the NAACP used to protest the murder of some forty blacks in an East St. Louis, Illinois, riot occasioned by the employment of blacks in factories with government contracts.

One of Du Bois' major rhetorical accomplishments was his linkage of the civil rights crusade in the United States with the freedom and anticolonialism movements throughout the world. As early as 1900 in his "Address to the Nations of the World" in London Du Bois prophesied: "The problem of the 20th century is the problem of the color line." He thus anticipated by fifty-five years much of the rhetoric of the Afro-Asian Conference at Bandung, Indonesia, where no white delegates were allowed. Du Bois helped organize four international Pan-Africanism Conferences, held in 1919, 1921, 1923, and 1927. Often called the Father of Pan-Africanism, Du Bois stressed that the struggle for racial justice in the United States sprang from the same moral and political impulses as movements for self-determination and national liberation in the colonies of Europe. "We Must Know the Truth," delivered at the 1947 NAACP convention in Washington, D.C., called for support for the United Nations and socialist development as the best hope for combating poverty and colonialism, which Du Bois blamed on deliberate exploitation by capitalist nations. Appropriately, his last public speech, reporting on efforts to produce an *Encyclopedia Africana* at the behest of Kwame Nkrumah, was given in 1962 at the University of Ghana, Accra.

Du Bois' oratory, like his extensive writings, was generally concisely organized, thoughtfully developed, and largely devoid of rhetorical flourishes. As proof, he would often cite historical examples, references to particular places, events, people and dates, and statistical evidence. He frequently utilized enumeration as an organizational pattern, perhaps reflecting his years as a college lecturer. Du Bois liked to conclude a speech with poetry; Langston Hughes, Arna Bontemps, and Paul Laurence Dunbar were among his favorite poets. And although his style was normally serious and analytical, he could dramatically use satire, as in a 1917 speech when, reminiscent of Jonathan Swift's "A Modest Proposal," he suggested a way to end the race problem: "every white family in the United States might choose a person of Negro descent, invite him to their home, entertain him and then through some quick and painless method kill him. In that way, in a single day, we would be rid of twelve million people who are today giving us so much concern." In his choice of language, Du Bois generally used the terms *Negroes, colored people*, and *black folk* interchangeably.

In the final years of his life, Du Bois's oratory showed a speaker increasingly alienated from American public opinion. Long attracted to the Soviet Union's preachings on the welfare of the proletariat (he visited the Soviet Union four times), Du Bois came to view socialism as the key to human salvation. Addressing an audience of 1,000 at the Soviet Peace Conference in Moscow in 1949, he claimed that private corporate wealth in his homeland had "throttled democracy." Nine years later, in his "prisoners of propaganda" speech, he decried the capitalist mindset that he feared had convinced most Americans that "the making of things and their purchase and sale for private profit is the chief end of living.'' Promoting his critique of capitalism during a campaign for the U.S. Senate from New York State in 1950 on the American Labor party ticket, Du Bois received only about 191,000 votes (3.7 percent) of 5.1 million cast in an election won by Democrat Herbert Lehman. The aging black scholar's message had placed him clearly on the left fringe of American politics.

His admiration for Soviet socialism, outspoken denunciations of U.S. military intervention in Korea, and public pronouncements on behalf of the Peace Information Center brought Du Bois into predictable trouble with the government. Indicted as an unregistered foreign agent but acquitted in 1951, he toured the United States addressing tens of thousands on the threat McCarthyism posed to free speech. In ''I Take My Stand,'' a message sent to a communist conference in London in 1951, Du Bois condemned the anticommunist fervor in the United States: ''No! Enough of this hysteria, this crazy foolishness!''

Ultimately Du Bois's rhetoric produced limited direct effect on U.S. politics. He personified the oratory of alienation; his was a voice crying in the wilderness. He was, after all, a black man in a society whose political structures are largely dominated by whites, an intellectual in a land of populist anti-intellectualism, and a proponent of socialism in a nation where capitalism is almost the state religion. Du Bois's decision to join the Communist party in 1961 marked the culmination of his ideological alienation from politics, just as his emigration to Ghana that year signaled a physical isolation from his homeland.

As a mobilizer of public opinion and a shaper of events, Du Bois cannot be considered a success. Although a brilliant thinker, he lacked the oratorical fervor and personal magnetism of black leaders such as Frederick Douglass, Martin Luther King, Jr., and Jesse Jackson. Eschewing demagoguery, Du Bois maintained throughout his life that he was a social scientist, not a politician. His independence of mind and abrasive personality created continual conflict with associates: he broke with Booker T. Washington over strategies for racial improvement, he criticized Marcus Garvey's Back to Africa campaign as wasteful and ill conceived, he viewed NAACP President Walter White as selfish and egotistical, and he disputed with James Weldon Johnson and eventually resigned from the NAACP because they rejected his call for black self-sufficiency through economic segregation. He confessed in a 1938 Atlanta University Convocation address, ''I was no natural leader of men.''

While failing to mobilize followers into a coherent program of political action, Du Bois' uncompromising hostility to injustice, racial discrimination, and imperialism make him an important bridge between Booker T. Washington and Martin Luther King, Jr. Like other socialists such as Eugene Debs and Norman Thomas, Du Bois failed to convince most Americans, white and black, that private enterprise and the pursuit of wealth was evil. Moreover, his romantic fascination with Soviet socialism seemed to blind him to the oppressive restrictions on human rights in many communist countries. But much of Du Bois' rhetoric sounds hauntingly contemporary as poverty, apartheid, and war remain central issues of political discourse. For enhancing America's understanding of its African heritage, relentlessly exposing the nation's shortcomings, and insisting that crusades against racism, colonialism, and militarism require concerted international effort, Du Bois' speeches merit an enduring place in the history of American oratory.

INFORMATION SOURCES

Research Collections and Collected Speeches

The most useful resource for students of Du Bois's oratory is the two-volume anthology edited by Foner. Extensive collections of works by and about Du Bois can be found in the libraries at Atlanta University, where he taught for twenty-three years, Howard University, and the University of Massachusetts at Amherst. Researchers of his rhetoric will find helpful two recordings that contain interviews, oral histories, and excerpts from his speeches: "The First Half of the 20th Century" (Pacifica Tape Library, Program BB 1719.03a) and "W. E. B. Du Bois—A Recorded Autobiography" (Folkways Records, 1961).

Du Bois, W. E. B. *Against Racism: Unpublished Essays, Papers, Addresses, 1887–1961*. Edited by Herbert Aptheker. Amherst: University of Massachusetts Press, 1985.
————. *The Correspondence of W. E. B. Du Bois*. Edited by Herbert Aptheker. Amherst: University of Massachusetts Press, 1973.
————. *The Emerging Thought of W. E. B. Du Bois; Essays and Editorials from The Crisis*. New York: Simon and Schuster, 1972.
————. *The Souls of Black Folk*. Chicago: A. G. McClurg, 1903.
————. *W. E. B. Du Bois Speaks: Speeches and Addresses*. Edited by Philip S. Foner. 2 vols. New York: Pathfinder Press, 1970.   *DS*
————. *The Writings of W. E. B. Du Bois*. Edited by Virginia Hamilton. New York: Crowell, 1975.
Golden, James L., and Rieke, Richard D. *The Rhetoric of Black Americans*.   *RBA*
   Columbus, Ohio: Charles E. Merrill, 1971.
Masterpieces of Negro Eloquence. Edited by Alice Moore Dunbar. New   *MNE*
   York: Bookery, 1914.
Speeches by Black Americans. Ed. Daniel J. O'Neill. Encino, Calif.: Dick-   *SBA*
   enson, 1971.
The Voice of Black America. Edited by Philip S. Foner. Vol. 2. New York: *VBA*
   Capricorn Books, 1975.

Selected Critical Studies

Aptheker, Herbert. "The Washington-Du Bois Conference of 1904." *Science and Society* 13 (Fall 1949): 344–51.
Harding, Vincent. "W. E. B. Du Bois and the Black Messianic Vision."*Freedomways* 9 (Winter 1969): 44–58.
Johnson, Guy B. "Negro Racial Movements and Leadership in the United States." *American Journal of Sociology* 43 (July 1937): 57–71.
Reid, Ira DeA. "Negro Movements and Messiahs, 1900–1949." *Phylon* 10 (1949): 362–69.

Rudwick, Elliott M. "Du Bois vs. Garvey: Race Propagandists at War." *Journal of Negro Education* 28 (Fall 1959): 421–29.

———. "The Niagara Movement." *Journal of Negro History* 43 (July 1957): 177–200.

Walden, Daniel, and Wylie, Kenneth. "W. E. B. Du Bois: Pan-Africanism's Intellectual Father." *Journal of Human Relations* 14 (1966): 28–41.

Selected Biographies

Broderick, Francis L. *W. E. B. Du Bois: Negro Leader in a Time of Crisis.* Stanford: Stanford University Press, 1960.

Hawkins, Hugh, ed. *Booker T. Washington and His Critics.* Boston: Heath, 1962.

Hughes, Langston. *Fight for Freedom: The Story of the NAACP.* New York: Norton, 1962.

Rampersad, Arnold. *The Art and Imagination of W. E. B. Du Bois.* Cambridge: Harvard University Press, 1976.

Rudwick, Elliott M. *W. E. B. Du Bois; A Study in Minority Group Leadership.* Philadelphia: University of Pennsylvania Press, 1960.

Sterling, Dorothy, and Quarles, Benjamin. *Lift Every Voice: The Lives of Booker T. Washington, W. E. B. Du Bois, Mary Church Terrell, and James Weldon Johnson.* New York: Doubleday, 1965.

CHRONOLOGY OF MAJOR SPEECHES

See "Research Collections and Collected Speeches" for source codes.

"Address to the Nations of the World," First Pan African Conference, London, July 25, 1900; *DS*, 1:125–27.

"We Claim Our Rights," Niagara Movement Conference, Harpers Ferry, West Virginia, August 16, 1906; *DS*, 1: 170–73.

"The Value of Agitation," March 1907; *DS*, 1: 174–78; *VBA*, pp. 49–52.

"Race Prejudice," Republican Club, New York City, March 5, 1910; *DS*, 1: 211–217; *RBA*, pp. 235–39.

"The Problem of Problems," Intercollegiate Socialist Society Convention, December 27, 1917; *DS* 1: 258–67.

"We Must Know the Truth," NAACP Convention, Washington, D.C., June 26, 1947; *DS*, 2: 222–27.

"America's Pressing Problems," Soviet Peace Conference, Moscow, August 1949; *DS*, 2: 235–41.

"I Take My Stand," Communist Party of Great Britain Conference, London, April 29, 1951; *DS* 2: 242–49.

"The Negro and Socialism," Socialist Symposium, 1958; *DS* 2: 297–311.

"Hail Humankind!" Peking, China, February 22, 1959; *DS* 2: 316–21.

DWIGHT DAVID EISENHOWER
(1890–1969), General of the U.S. Army and thirty-fourth president of the United States

_____ RICHARD E. CRABLE

Dwight D. Eisenhower ranks among the nation's great political communicators, although his success was not based on traditional ideas of oratorical excellence. Instead, he created a particular ethos for a people sorely in need of a leader perceived to have those characteristics. The magic that was Eisenhower's seems to have arisen from the interaction of perceptions that he was a common man, Supreme Allied Commander of the military, a warrior for peace, and a U.S. president. He can be compared to George Washington. Perhaps more accurately, both were close to being Renaissance men: able to defend the fort, to play the equivalents of golf and poker, and to organize a government. Americans, it is clear, liked Ike. Yet from a rhetorical perspective, Eisenhower's career was not contingent on oratorical success until VE Day in May 1945.

Eisenhower graduated, slightly above average, from the U.S. Military Academy at West Point in 1915. He subsequently held a variety of military postings, including, during the 1930s, special assistant to General Douglas MacArthur, under whom Eisenhower was reputed to have said that he studied theatrics. His rise in the military during World War II was meteoric: he attained four stars in seventeen months. By a special act of Congress, he was promoted to the new five-star rank of general of the army on December 20, 1944. After the war, he served as army chief of staff from 1945 to 1948. He was president of Columbia University from 1948 to 1952, although he took a leave from Columbia to command the fledgling NATO Army in 1951.

Eisenhower's 1945 return to the United States resulted in a hero's welcome, one apparently hindered only by the war-caused shortage of confetti. In 1946, he was voted the second most admired living person—just behind MacArthur but ahead of President Harry Truman. By mid-1948, polls revealed that he had become the preferred presidential candidate by voters of both parties. As events unfolded, Adlai Stevenson was not the last American to recognize his role as sacrificial lamb to a country that wanted—and liked—Ike.

Eisenhower's success is an interesting rhetorical study because his military prowess, not his oratorical ability, captured public attention. Yet once in the public eye, he wisely and persuasively responded to the speaking situations to which he was summoned. The curious yet easy transitions he made from general to educator to president are explainable in part by the success of the rhetorical strategies he marshaled to maintain "Ike" before the public eye. Beginning shortly after VE Day, the general cultivated and sustained his image.

EISENHOWER AS COMMUNICATOR: WHY WE LIKED IKE

Eisenhower was a great U.S. presidential communicator who went through three major periods of his oratorical career: as a military hero, as a presidential aspirant, and as president of the United States. In the first period, he helped generate an ethos that was to serve him well in the two periods to follow. In the second period, he established himself as a formidable political candidate, and in the final period, he was to bring to fruition the reasons why the nation liked him.

In the first major period of his speaking career, as military hero, he epitomized the necessary combination of greatness in leadership and the humility of the common man. In accepting postwar honors in London's Guildhall, for example, Eisenhower was patently modest: "The only attitude in which a commander may with satisfaction receive the tributes of his friends is in humble acknowledgement that, no matter how unworthy he may be, his position is a symbol of great human forces that have labored arduously and successfully for a righteous cause." At Guildhall, he succeeded in the epideictic form as he isolated for his audiences what was truly important: "No petty differences in the world of trade, traditions or national pride should ever blind us to our identities in priceless values." In Paris, he continued to develop the image of the paradoxical common/great man: "The few words which I shall say to you will be simple words. I should like, with your permission, to use the language of the ordinary soldier." In June of the same year, he quipped to a New York audience who had made him an honorary citizen: "New York simply cannot do this to a Kansas farm boy and keep its reputation for sophistication." The war was over, and even great soldiers were coming home to become common men again.

Eisenhower augmented the image of the great yet common man by portraying himself as a nonpolitical politician. Even as events pushed him closer to politics, he scapegoated (other) politicians as "contentious pygmies." Eisenhower's audiences were in no mood for politics as usual, and the nonpolitician was politically astute enough to realize this. Although the nation was interested in his guidance, it was divided in its perception of his politics. In a Gallup poll taken in July 1947, 22 percent thought he was a Republican, 20 percent thought he was a Democrat, and an overwhelming 58 percent could make no judgment about his party affiliation. After his meeting with the already nominated presidential contender Governor Thomas Dewey, Ike maintained that he still would not identify himself with any political party. To a nation not wanting politics as usual, Eisenhower presented himself as an unusual politician.

At the same time that he generated the paradoxical images of great/common man and nonpolitical politician, Ike also succeeded in creating the image of a peaceful warrior—or, more precisely, a warrior for peace. While being honored at the Waldorf-Astoria, for example, he claimed, "There is no greater pacifist than the regular officer." In 1945 also he accepted the Freedom House award saying, "It is with a sense of special distinction that I accept the annual award of 'Freedom House,' particularly as I note in the citation the words, 'soldier for peace.' It is a title I should like always to be worthy to bear." He furthered his right to the title when at West Point graduation ceremonies he called the "true soldier" a "leader for world cooperation." Later, in his final report as chief of staff, Ike called upon not Congress or the military but American citizens for moral, physical, and economic strength. With the help of these citizens, Eisenhower concluded, the United States would be the "world's most potent influence toward increase of freedom and peace among men—the final security goal of mankind." Here was the citizen-soldier who successfully created the ethos of a man identified with both necessary defense and a desired peace.

The Eisenhower magic, then, was not so much mystical as it was rhetorical. Eisenhower became an embodiment of the force of personal persuasion. As astute observers of the period concluded, his messages did not need to stress content and details because Ike was the message. Who he was and what he stood for became the primary ingredients in his eventual effort to win the presidency. His communication as war hero served as a base for what was to come in the second and third major periods of his rhetorical effort.

In the second period of Eisenhower's rhetoric, headlines and not amusement greeted the completely serious assurance from Senator Henry Cabot Lodge that "General Eisenhower has personally assured me that he is a Republican." Just in time for the primary contests, in January 1952, Ike declared himself a Republican.

Some months before the presidential election of 1952, Adlai Stevenson considered a strategy aimed at speaking to the major issue of the campaign; he contemplated making the pledge to go to Korea. In the end, Stevenson decided against such a promise. Months later, on October 24, 1952, Dwight David Eisenhower's campaign reached what many consider to be its peak with the pledge his opponent several months before had declined to make: he would go to Korea.

In 1952, Senator Karl Mundt, co-chairman of the Republican speakers' bureau, epitomized the year's campaign with a snappy, chemical-sounding formula, K_1C_2, meaning that the campaign revolved around Korea, corruption, and communism. In a real sense, ignoring Eisenhower's ethos itself as a factor, the formula served well to summarize the issues of the campaign. Although studies indicate that Americans value integrity, honesty, and a pursuit of regained innocence, they were confronted with Washington. Although they value peace and tranquility, they were confronted with a war in Korea. Although they value freedom and democracy, they found their world being threatened by communist expansion abroad and accusations of communist infiltration at home. In the context of this affront to American values, the Republicans offered a "new broom" and a "clean sweep" for the nation. Who better to wield the broom than Dwight David Eisenhower, a great/common man, a nonpolitical politician, a warrior for peace?

Yet Korea remained the critical issue. As Emmet John Hughes, the eventual formulator of Ike's pledge, hastens to point out, Stevenson had considered making a pledge to visit Korea, but the idea of an Illinois governor inspecting the battlefield seemed low on dramatic impact. From the Republican candidate's perspective, all that had been agreed upon was that at some unspecified date and in front of some unspecified audience, a foreign policy message of unspecified content should deal with Korea—in some unspecified manner. The result of this lack of specificity was a very specific message penned by Hughes: Eisenhower would go to Korea. Made before a Detroit audience, the pledge offered no concrete assurance; it offered no guarantee of success. It promised that Eisenhower would look into the Korean situation. It offered, in a rhetorical tour de force planned only two days before its utterance, the juxtaposition of Ike against the fears of a nation, and that was enough.

Although Hughes had denied that his last-minute Korean pledge really won over the number of votes accorded it by others, there seems little doubt that Americans wished to leave the Korean problem in the hands of the peaceful warrior, a man who could deal with the entire formula: Korea, communism, and corruption at home. The trusted Eisenhower showed himself to be a formidable political candidate who had little difficulty becoming the thirty-fourth president of the United States.

As president, Ike entered the third of his three major oratorical periods. He began his first Inaugural Address with what he considered "a little private prayer of my own," which he shared with millions. In what may have been a synopsis of the cold war mentality, he observed that the "forces of good and evil are amassed and opposed as rarely before in history." The country was warned that "history does not long entrust the care of freedom to the weak or the timid." Indeed Americans had chosen to entrust their nation and its leadership for world peace to the peaceful warrior. The general displayed his understanding of the interrelationship between the national and international spheres: "Whatever America hopes to bring to pass in the world must first come to pass in the heart of America." Ike claimed that world leadership rested on the base of solving domestic problems and maintaining a national faith.

In the ensuing months, Eisenhower displayed a growing awareness of the threat and promise of the nuclear age. In his first presidential appearance before the UN General Assembly, he discussed the decisions to be made by the body but pledged the United States's "determination to help solve the fearful atomic dilemma''; he promised that the United States would ''devote its entire heart and mind to find the way by which the miraculous inventiveness of man shall not be dedicated to his death, but consecrated to his life.'' A year and a half later, in addressing the nation after returning from the Geneva Conference, Ike extolled the nation as having the ''most shining opportunity ever possessed by Americans.'' He saw the conference as important because ''if we are successful in this, then we will make constantly brighter the lamp that will one day guide us to our goal—a just and lasting peace.''

In his final State of the Union message, Eisenhower dealt with many topics: the value of self-examination, which was the goal of the message, the problem of disarmament, the difficulties of new nations, space exploration and its possible uses for defense, basic farm laws that ''were written 27 years ago,'' inflation, and the need for a balanced budget. ''We live,'' he opined, ''in a storm of semantic disorder in which old labels no longer faithfully describe. . . . We must use language to enlighten the mind, not as an instrument of the studied innuendo and distorter of truth. And we must live by what we say.'' In his final appearance as president before the UN General Assembly in late September 1960, Eisenhower continued his communication for peace and tranquility. On this occasion, his first proposition was that ''only through the United Nations Organization can humanity make real and universal progress toward the goal of peace with justice.'' He talked of earth and countries, he spoke of space, he discussed disarmament, but mostly he argued for worldwide cooperation in the development of a world community. ''Opposed to the idea of two hostile, embittered worlds in perpetual conflict,'' he argued, ''we envision a single world community, as yet unrealized but advancing steadily toward fulfillment through our plans, our efforts, and our collective acts.'' Eisenhower's rhetoric projected an ethos identified with unity, cooperation, and peace.

The similarity between Eisenhower and George Washington becomes apparent in a comparison between their Farewell Addresses, though Washington's was never presented orally. In 1796, Washington reminded the nation why it had been a ''true policy to steer clear of permanent alliances with any portion of the foreign world.'' More than 160 years later, with permanent foreign alliances a fact of life, Eisenhower warned of a potentially dangerous ''permanent domestic alliance.'' Historians credit academician turned ghost writer Malcolm Moos with describing the situation for Ike's Farewell Address and coining the term *military-industrial complex*. The term and its image are still very much with us.

Yet to know what Eisenhower said and what images he attempted to create is not to know everything about him as a speaker. It is amusing to note that Ike identified himself with his national audience partly by villifying instruments of communication such as microphones. In a Detroit speech, for example, he said: ''I get tired of my own voice, and so I think they conceal from me at times that I am expected to battle against one of these microphones.'' In less public battles, he fought the fight of the first "televisable" president: knowing that his glasses caused a glare on the television, he attempted to forgo them by using a tele-prompter. On one important occasion, the teleprompter stalled—and so did Ike's message. Thereafter, he returned to the use of eyeglasses.

In preparing his speeches he used the approach of a war-wizened general; he had a staff create drafts of a message and then tailored them to his own pref-erences. Although he used ghosts—Sherman Adams, James Hagerty, Gabriel Hauge, Emmet Hughes, and others—the message was his own. Consistent with his military background, he expected others to contribute to the minutiae, but the goal and method of the message were his own. Eisenhower saw the efforts of his ghosts, even Hughes's surprise pledge to have Ike go to Korea, as the normal and responsible duty of people who worked for him. Such a reliance, of course, caused problems on occasion such as when Eisenhower failed to agree with everything in his 1957 budget.

The rhetorical problems Eisenhower faced in speech preparation were accen-tuated in his public addresses. Ignoring the appeal of the man and his ethos, judgments about his oratorical ability are consistently unfavorable. Carefully prepared manuscripts were delivered without enthusiasm and with a halting, almost fumbling, manner, which soon became expected. Eisenhower did not seem to be at ease or skillful with either the lectern or the new medium of television. In a perverse complement to delivery, his prose (regardless of the care taken in its creation) seemed lacking. Even Eisenhower's old staff member Hughes had to admit that "the reach of the leader was undeniably long, but his grasp did not seem firm; his manner was kind, but uncertain; his words were benign, but unclear." The convolution, even circularity, of Eisenhower's speak-ing became almost universally recognized.

Perhaps for these problems, Eisenhower did not like personal interviews, although he did succumb to the requests of such personages as Henry Luce. Moreover, Ike was an early master of the staged (yet purportedly impromptu) press conference. Specified questioners were equipped with the desired kind of question. At one press conference, for instance, the press laughed when Eisen-hower responded to a supposedly impromptu question: "Mr. Horner [of the Washington Star], I'm glad you asked that question." Eisenhower, always in control of his military forces, attempted to retain control of the press around him.

Still, despite his staging and posturing, Eisenhower seemed to have had some consistent rhetorical premises for his messages. Based on the recollections of Arthur Larson and confirmed by other speech writers, Eisenhower insisted that a message have a point (some reason for its being given), that it be brief (as he insisted on as a military commander), that it be spoken in such a way that the words do not call attention to themselves, and that it be presented with an acceptable level of dignity. The result was the Eisenhower message, which frequently was called dull and uninspired.

Not surprisingly, Eisenhower's speeches do not appear typically in collections of the great speeches of the contemporary world. With rare exceptions, public address scholars leave his messages out of their anthologies. Indeed, Eisenhower as president most often is ignored in collections of great American presidents. But omissions of the man and his speeches may be a mistake. Clearly Eisenhower was not one of the more colorful presidents, nor was he among the most articulate or exciting. He was, however, a man whose accomplishments should not be dismissed lightly. He provided what the United States needed. He had been first in war when the country was at war; he had been first in peace when the country wished to return to peace; and surely he was first in the hearts of his countrymen when they needed a legitimate hero. Americans may have become mesmerized by a John Fitzgerald Kennedy, but they had liked Ike; they may have become enamored with Ronald Reagan's portrayal of the common man, but they liked Ike because he seemed not to be playing a part. He was the common man who became a military hero and an uncommonly loved American president.

INFORMATION SOURCES

Research Collections and Collected Speeches

Two primary sources of research materials for rhetorical scholars are the Eisenhower Library, Abilene, Kansas, and the Eisenhower Project, Johns Hopkins University, Baltimore, Maryland. Researchers also might find valuable information and files at the libraries of both Columbia and Princeton.

American Rhetoric from Roosevelt to Reagan: A Collection of Speeches and Critical Essays. Edited by Halford Ross Ryan. Prospect Heights, Ill.: Waveland Press, 1983.   ARRR

American Speeches on Twentieth Century Issues. Edited by Ernest J. Wrage and Barnet Baskerville. New York: Harper & Brothers, 1962.   ASTCI

Berquist, Goodwin F. *Speeches for Illustration and Example*. Chicago: Scott, Foresman and Company, 1965.   SIE

Eisenhower, Dwight David. *Collected Papers of Dwight David Eisenhower*. Baltimore, Md.: Johns Hopkins Press, 1970.   CP

———. *Peace with Justice: Selected Addresses by Dwight D. Eisenhower*. Foreword by Grayson Kirk. New York: Columbia Press, 1961.   PWJ

———. *Eisenhower Speaks: Dwight D. Eisenhower in His Messages and Speeches*. Edited by Rudolph L. Treuenfels. New York: Farrar, Straus & Company, 1948.   ES

Selected Critical Studies

Clevenger, Jr., Theodore, and Knepprath, Eugene. "A Quantitative Analysis of Logical and Emotional Content in Selected Campaign Addresses of Eisenhower and Stevenson." *Western Speech Journal* 30 (1966): 144–150.

Crable, Richard E. "Ike: Identification, Argument, and Paradoxical Appeal." *Quarterly Journal of Speech* 63 (1977): 188–195.

————. "The Crisis of Limited Conflict: 'I Shall Go to Korea.' " Paper presented at the annual meeting of the Speech Communication Association, Louisville, Kentucky, 1982.

Freeley, Austin J. *"Ethos*, Eisenhower, and the 1956 Campaign." *Central States Speech Journal* 9 (1958): 24–26.

Haberman, Frederick W. "The Election of 1952: A Symposium." *Quarterly Journal of Speech* 38 (1952): 397–414.

Kennedy, Theodore R. "Eisenhower as Extempore Speaker." *Journal of Communication* 28 (1958): 151–55.

Marlin, Charles Lowell. "Eisenhower before the Press." *Communication Quarterly* 9 (1961): 23–25.

Sillars, Malcolm O. "The Presidential Campaign of 1952." *Western Speech Journal* 22 (1958): 94–99.

Selected Biographies

Childs, Marquis. *Eisenhower: The Captive Hero*. New York: Harcourt, Brace, 1958.

Gunther, John. *Eisenhower: The Man and the Symbol*. New York: Harper & Brothers, 1952.

Hughes, Emmet John. *The Ordeal of Power: A Political Memoir of the Eisenhower Years*. New York: Atheneum, 1963.

Lyon, Peter. *Eisenhower: Portrait of the Hero*. Boston: Little, Brown, 1974.

Parmet, Herbert S. *Eisenhower and the American Crusade*. New York: Macmillan, 1972.

CHRONOLOGY OF MAJOR SPEECHES

See "Research Collections and Collected Speeches" for source codes.

Guildhall address, London, June 12, 1945; *ARRR*, pp. 76–79; *ES*, pp. 15–18.

Address at city hall, New York City, June 19, 1945; *ES*, pp. 40–42.

Address at graduation ceremonies, U.S. Military Academy, West Point, New York, June 3, 1947; *ES*, pp. 219–21.

Address at the American Legion Convention, New York City, August 29, 1947; *ES*, pp. 248–55.

Speech to supporters, Detroit, Michigan, October 24, 1952; *SIE*, pp. 193–94.

First Inaugural Address, Washington, D.C., January 20, 1953; *PWJ*, pp. 25–33.

First address before the UN General Assembly, New York City, December 8, 1953; *PWJ*, pp. 54–65.

Address upon returning from the Geneva Conference, July 25, 1955; *PWJ*, pp. 129–35.

Second Inaugural Address, Washington, D.C., January 21, 1957; *ASTCI*, pp. 313–16.

State of the Union Message, Washington, D.C., January 7, 1960; *PWJ*, pp. 207–26.

SAMUEL JAMES ERVIN, JR.
(1896–1985), U.S. senator from North Carolina

_____ HOWARD DORGAN

In May 1956, *New York Times* columnist Russell Baker reported that a "new raconteur" was reigning in the U.S. Senate. "With Alben W. Barkley's death," declared Baker, "the official office of Senate storyteller passes to Samuel J. Ervin, Democrat of North Carolina. Although he has been in the Senate less than two years," Baker continued, "Mr. Ervin has built up such a repertoire of folk humor as to qualify him to continue the Barkley mission of leavening the pompous business of politics."

Samuel James Ervin, Jr., who liked being called Sam, Jr., and who during the Watergate hearings of 1973 was referred to by hundreds of reporters as "Uncle Sam," came to the Senate after a thirty-two-year career as a North Carolina lawyer and jurist. Born in 1896 and deceased April 23, 1985, ten years after stepping down from the Senate, Ervin descended from Scotch-Irish Presbyterians who settled at the close of Reconstruction in the foothills of the Blue Ridge (Morganton, North Carolina). He followed his Calvinistic father not only into law but into a lifetime of adherence to rigid principles and behaviors and in the process became in the U.S. Senate one of the foremost advocates of strict construction constitutionalism, applying this absolutism to legislative issues on both the Left and the Right, but constantly flavoring his advocacy with folk humor that delighted his fellow solons and the nation at large.

After graduating from the University of North Carolina in 1917, Ervin served two years as a World War I infantryman, was wounded twice, and earned the Purple Heart, Silver Star, Distinguished Service Cross, and the French Fourargere. Following the war, he entered Harvard, gained an LL.B. degree, and began judicial and legislative service in his home state. During this time, he spent a year in the U.S. House of Representatives, filling the unexpired term of his brother Joseph, who committed suicide because of health problems.

SAM ERVIN AS A TALE TELLER ADVOCATE OF TRADITIONALISM

Sam Ervin found his way into the U.S. Senate as a result of another unexpired term. A long-time Ervin colleague, Senator Clyde R. Hoey, died in office, and North Carolina governor William B. Umstead appointed Ervin to the vacated post. It was the summer of 1954, and the Tar Heel jurist landed in the Senate just when national legislators were growing tired of the reckless anticommunist demagoguery of the junior senator from Wisconsin, Joseph McCarthy. In part because of Ervin's extensive experience on the bench and in part because few established senators were eager to serve in a politically vulnerable role of passing judgment on the Wisconsin firebrand, this freshman senator from North Carolina found himself on the select committee that recommended McCarthy's censure.

Ervin's vote for censure, his skillful use of humorous anecdotes in ridicule of McCarthy's antics, and his rousing November 15, 1954, Senate address thoroughly castigating the Wisconsin senator initially endeared him to liberals; but that endearment soon waned as the folksy tale teller established one of the most consistent records of opposition to civil rights, denouncing the 1954 *Brown* decision, signing the Southern Manifesto of 1956, engaging in the filibusters of 1957 and 1960, and arguing vehemently against the Civil Rights Act of 1964 and the Voting Rights Act of 1965. He further disappointed liberals by supporting, through his silence and often his votes, the Vietnam War policies of Lyndon Johnson.

It was not until relatively late in Ervin's senatorial career that he began to win back some of his more liberal admirers, first with his leadership against the big brotherism represented by the growing number of government-gathered and -controlled computerized data banks, next by his opposition to the 1970 District of Columbia crime bill (which Ervin said severely violated due process), and finally by his chairmanship of the Watergate committee. Throughout these defenses of liberal causes, however, Ervin employed the same strict constructionist rationales he used to attack civil rights legislation. Thus the press often spoke of him not as one who defended racism but as one who upheld the Constitution and the civil liberties he believed the instrument protected. "We will not fool history as we fool ourselves when we steal freedom from one man to confer it on another," Ervin proclaimed in the 1963 Senate Judiciary Committee's civil rights hearings. "When freedom for one citizen is diminished, it is in the end diminished for all. It is not the 'civil rights' of some but the civil liberty of all on which I take my stand."

Ervin appeared unable to see the reverse of his argument: that the absolute civil liberties of a majority often result in the loss of civil liberties for a minority. Nevertheless, by avoiding racist rationales and by consistently employing cleaner constitutional arguments, Ervin became, according to Paul Clancy, one of his biographers, "the intellectual darling of the segregationists, the legal crutch upon whom those less informed about constitutional principles and more interested in racist politics leaned for support. He gave their cause a veneer of legal class."

Ervin, however, did not see it that way. He believed he was adhering to a bedrock consistency when he invoked the Constitution to denounce with equal fervor such diverse evils as Joe McCarthy's badgering and browbeating of General Ralph Zwicker, judicial decisions mandating forced busing, the absence of rights for American Indians, federally legislated open occupancy laws, Everett Dirksen's 1966 proposed constitutional amendment to allow prayer in public schools, the Supreme Court's *Miranda* ruling, the Nixon administration's behavior in the Pentagon Papers episode, the equal rights amendment, and the burglarizing of the Watergate headquarters of the Democratic National Committee. Paul Clancy saw in all these battles a certain ideological harmony, but Dick Dabney, another Ervin biographer, saw an inability to note distinctions, an insensitivity to social issues, and an inconsistency in application of principles. "I . . . believe," concluded Dabney, "that he was arrogantly uninformed on the abuses suffered by our Negro citizens—however current he may have been on his Constitutional law. I believe, too, that he was irresponsibly passive in letting [Senator John] Stennis and [Senator Richard] Russell do his thinking for him on Armed Services matters, and that as a result his votes on our involvement [in Vietnam] helped to kill a lot of people—Americans and Vietnamese alike."

Although there has been controversy over Ervin's general merit as a legislator, there has been little disagreement concerning his skills as a speaker, and the one characteristic of Ervin's oratory that received by far the most praise from friends, foes, rhetorical critics, reporters, and the world at large was his brilliant use of folk humor. He seldom made a speech in the Senate or before any other audience in which he did not tell at least one tale, and he sometimes told several, "leavening the pompous business of politics."

Ervin employed folktales not just to entertain, although he confessed great enjoyment in motivating laughter. Instead, he made use of humorous narratives to achieve specific rhetorical objectives, believing that an "ounce of revealing humor often has more power to . . . convince . . . than do many tons of erudite argument." On November 15, 1954, when he stood before his fellow senators to deliver his first major address to that body, he wanted his audience to understand that Joe McCarthy was avoiding his responsibility to defend himself by constantly attacking others. Therefore he told his story of a young lawyer who went to an old lawyer "for advice as to how to try a lawsuit. The old lawyer said, 'If the evidence is against you, talk about the law. If the law is against you, talk about the evidence.' The young lawyer said, 'But what do you do when both the evidence and the law are against you?' 'In that event,' said the old lawyer, 'give somebody hell. That will distract the attention of the judge and the jury from the weakness of your case.' '' McCarthy, alleged Ervin, was following that tactic in his response to charges from his fellow senators.

Next, Ervin wanted to ridicule McCarthy's habit of supporting arguments with quotations taken entirely out of context, so he related his story about a North Carolina mountain preacher who did the same thing, only with Bible quotations:

At that time the women had a habit of wearing their hair in topknots. This preacher deplored the habit. As a consequence, he preached a rip-snorting sermon one Sunday on the text Top Not Come Down. At the conclusion of the sermon an irate woman, wearing a very pronounced topknot, told the preacher than no such text could be found in the Bible. The preacher therefore opened the Scriptures to the 17th verse of the 24th chapter of Matthew and pointed to the words: "let him on the housetop not come down to take anything out of his house." Any practitioner of the McCarthy technique of lifting things out of context can readily find the text "top not come down" in this verse.

Finally, in this maiden speech Ervin told what may have been his most popular folktale and in the process introduced the senators to the North Carolina mountain character they seemed to enjoy the most, Uncle Ephriam Swink. The point Ervin wished to make was that the McCarthy episode threatened to destroy the Senate:

Mr. President, many years ago there was a custom in a section of my country, known as the South Mountains, to hold religious meetings at which the eldest members of the congregation were called upon to stand up and publicly testify to their religious experiences. On one occasion they were holding such a meeting in one of the churches, and old Uncle Ephriam Swink, a South Mountaineer whose body was all bent and distorted with arthritis, was present. All of the old members of the congregation except Uncle Ephriam arose and gave testimony to their religious experiences. Uncle Ephriam kept his seat. Thereupon, the moderator said, "Brother Ephriam, suppose you tell us what the Lord has done for you." Uncle Ephriam arose, with his bent and distorted body, and said, "Brother, he has might nigh ruint me." Mr. President, that is about what Senator McCarthy has done to the Senate."

David Zarefsky argues that Ervin "actually was a blend of two *personae*, the legal scholar and the mountain storyteller." Zarefsky also maintains that in his role as legal scholar, Ervin developed essentially a didactic style, that he was constantly lecturing the Senate and the nation on fundamentals of the U.S. Constitution. Whether holding forth against the equal rights amendment, an invasion of privacy procedure, or any move by the Supreme Court by judicial fiat to change the meaning of the Constitution, Ervin seemed always to be playing the role of kindly teacher, attempting to nurture his reluctant students into a proper appreciation of rights they had been guaranteed. Indeed, he was never more fixed in this role than when on September 20, 1966, he stood in the Senate and helped turn the tide on a proposed constitutional amendment that would have permitted prayer in the nation's public schools.

The original Supreme Court decisions that placed public schools off limits to institutionally sanctioned prayers disturbed Ervin when they were handed down, but faced with the question of the Dirksen amendment, which would have formally allowed classroom prayer, he could not reconcile the proposal with the religious clause of the First Amendment: he decided to take a position he knew would anger many of his constituents. It was with unusual caution, therefore, that he developed his arguments, playing that kindly teacher role at its best as he traced the history of the religious clause, depending heavily on the thoughts of James Madison. It was one of the few Senate speeches in which Ervin did not use humor.

But Ervin also carefully sealed the speech with a declaration of his own spiritual position. "I note with awe the order and regularity of the processes of life and nature," he said. "I observe with reverence that, despite the feet of clay on which he makes his earthly rounds, man is endowed with the capacity to obey conscience, exercise reason, study holy writings, and aspire to righteous conduct in obedience to spiritual laws. On the basis of these things, I affirm with complete conviction that the universe and men are not the haphazard products of blind atoms wandering aimlessly about in chaos, but . . . are the creations of God, the maker of the universe and man." In this fashion he said to North Carolina voters, "I can't support this violation of the Constitution, but don't think I'm not religious."

As was the case in his opposition to this prayer amendment, Ervin's rhetoric treating the dangers of government-generated or corporation-compiled employee data banks was loudly applauded by civil libertarians. The best example of the latter rhetoric can be found in an address he delivered at a national meeting of the American Management Association in New York City, March 6, 1967. "The computer," declared Ervin, "is a wondrous invention," with no evils intrinsic to its design or structure. Nevertheless he did see significant problems relative to its use by both big government and big business. "Too often," he argued, " . . . an agency or organization may seize upon a device . . . with the best intentions in the world of achieving some laudable goal. Giving little thought to alternatives which might be less offensive or blatant, they bow in awe to the expertise of the specialist and too often surrender to him their control of policy. In the process, they may deny the dignity of the individual, the sense of fair play, or the right of the citizen in a free society to privacy of his thoughts and activities."

This, Ervin reasoned, was exactly what was happening in business and government through the accumulation in computerized files of private, sensitive, and largely irrelevant employee information. Quoting questionnaires forced upon job applicants, the senator supplied examples of embarrassing revelations individuals would be compelled to make by responding to statements such as the following: "I am very seldom troubled by constipation. My sex life is satisfactory. At times I feel like swearing. I have never been in trouble because of my sex behavior. I do not always tell the truth. I have not lived the right kind of life." Private industries and governments, Ervin observed, "have a duty to assure that personal data collected and filed is relevant, absolutely necessary for management goals, . . . is cleansed of emotion-charged, subjective, arbitrary judgments, and . . . is not the distillation of unconfronted and unevaluated evidence." "That we enjoy the amount of privacy that we do have," he concluded, "is probably due more than anything to the inefficiency of government and private industry in correlating and assembling all the information they already have."

Students of Ervin's oratory will want to examine at least one or two of his other major addresses: his April 28, 1955, remarks to the Harvard Law School Association of New York City, "Alexander Hamilton's Phantom," in which he charged that the Supreme Court had "usurped the power to nullify acts of congress"; his December 6, 1968, address to the Seventy-third Annual Congress of American Industry, "Separation of Powers," in which he detailed some of his thoughts about the legitimate roles of the executive, judicial, and legislative branches of government; and his February 4, 1974, speech to the Twenty-sixth National Conference on Church and State, "Our Basic Liberties," in which he outlined many of his thoughts on intellectual, political, and religious freedoms.

Ervin never directly attacked civil rights as a discrete concept, choosing instead to oppose this genre of legislation with arguments defensive of civil liberties; nevertheless, students can obtain a succinct view of Ervin as an anti–civil rights advocate by examining his confrontations with Robert Kennedy during the July through September 1963 Senate Judiciary Committee's civil rights hearings.

INFORMATION SOURCES

Research Collections and Collected Speeches

The papers of Samuel James Ervin, Jr., are housed in the Southern Historical Collection, University of North Carolina, Chapel Hill. The collection includes large numbers of speeches, recorded interviews, radio broadcasts, films, minutes of meetings, transcripts of testimony, drafts of legislation, legal briefs, letters, and personal files documenting Ervin's years in the U.S. Senate and his years on the bench in North Carolina. The over five hundred feet of shelf space contain voluminous files relating to Ervin's memberships on the Senate Armed Services, Government Operations, and Judiciary committees, in addition to thousands of documents detailing operations of the Select Committee on Presidential Campaign Activities, 1973–1974 (Watergate). Materials also relate to such specific subjects of Ervin's interest as civil rights, civil liberties, the Equal Rights Amendment, separation of powers, the Vietnam War, and Joseph McCarthy.

Congressional Record	CR
Papers of Samuel James Ervin, Jr., Southern Historical Collection, University of North Carolina, Chapel Hill.	PSE
Vital Speeches.	VS

Selected Critical Studies

Dorgan, Howard. "The Mountain Metaphor of Senator Sam." *North Carolina Journal of Speech and Drama* 11 (Spring 1978): 17–28.

Ervin, Sam J., Jr. *Humor of a Country Lawyer*. Chapel Hill: University of North Carolina Press, 1983.

Zarefsky, David. "Fulbright and Ervin: Southern Senators with National Appeal." In *Public Discourse in the Contemporary South: A New Rhetoric of Diversity*, Edited by Calvin M. Logue and Howard Dorgan. Baton Rouge: LSU Press, in press.

Selected Biographies

Clancy, Paul R. *Just a Country Lawyer*. Bloomington: Indiana University Press, 1974.

Dabney, Dick. *A Good Man: The Life of Sam J. Ervin*. Boston: Houghton Mifflin, 1976.

CHRONOLOGY OF MAJOR SPEECHES

See "Research Collections and Collected Speeches for source codes.

For Censure of Joseph McCarthy, Washington, D.C., November 15, 1954: *CR*, November 15, 1954, pp. 16018–22.

"Alexander Hamilton's Phantom: Supreme Court Has Usurped the Power to Nullify Acts of Congress," New York City, April 28, 1955; *VS*, October 15, 1955, pp. 23–26.

"Shall America's Birthright Be Sold for Pottage?" Atlanta, Georgia, December 11, 1959; *CR*, January 7, 1960, pp. 126–29.

"The Computer: Individual Privacy," New York City, March 6, 1967; *VS* May 1, 1967, pp. 421–26; *CR*, March 8, 1967, pp. 5898–901.

"Separation of Powers," New York City, December 6, 1968; *VS*, January 1, 1969, pp. 189–92.

"Confrontation at Watergate," Washington, D.C., October 3, 1973; *CR* October 3, 1973, pp. 32690–93.

"Our Basic Liberties: Freedom of the Individual," Orlando, Florida, February 4, 1974; *VS*, May 15, 1974, pp. 454–56.

"The Necessity for Integrity in Politics," commencement address, University of Cincinnati, Cincinnati, Ohio, June 9, 1974; *PSE*.

THE REVEREND JERRY FALWELL
(1933–   ), pastor, Thomas Road Baptist Church, Lynchburg, Va
————————————————————— CHARLES R. CONRAD and JAMES R. PENCE

Jerry Falwell is a religious leader with enormous political visibility. Pastor of one of the largest Protestant churches in the United States, the 20,000-member Thomas Road Baptist Church, Lynchburg, Virginia, in 1971 he founded Liberty Baptist University, which became the centerpiece of his television ministry on ''The Old Time Gospel Hour.'' In 1979 he formally entered politics as a founding board member of Moral Majority, Inc. Falwell's religious views are fundamentalist, and his political views are strongly conservative.

Falwell's beliefs are congruent with his background in a middle-class family with deeply held religious beliefs. His father was a successful entrepreneur who had established Lynchburg's first successful trucking firm during the 1920s. Falwell credits his mother with preparing him for his religious conversion in 1952, and when his father drifted into depression and alcoholism, it was she who sustained the family. A rambunctious and popular high school student, Falwell entered Lynchburg College and planned to go on to Virginia Tech to study engineering. His conversion changed those plans, and he transferred to Baptist Bible College, Springfield, Missouri, where he became an outstanding student and effective Christian youth worker.

FALWELL AS POLITICAL-RELIGIOUS RHETOR

Falwell developed in the polity and theology of the Baptist church, which offered every able, dedicated preacher—even those who, like him, did not attend a theological seminary—the opportunity for an immediately successful ministry. In June 1956, Falwell formed the Thomas Road Baptist Church, initiated a daily thirty-minute local radio broadcast, and arranged to preach on television every Sunday night. His radio and television ministries made his name familiar and prepared the way for his door-to-door canvassing, direct-mail campaigns, public rallies, and prayer sessions that helped swell the church's membership. In essence, the Thomas Road church offers members an extended family, an institution designed to meet every spiritual, intellectual, and social need.

During the 1960s the fundamentalism of Thomas Road Church contrasted dramatically with the reformist spirit manifested in mainline Christian denominations. For persons seeking secure religious beliefs amid the secular skepticism of the 1960s, Falwell offered the certainty of Bible-based doctrine and a stable local community. Falwell preached in the evangelical political tradition, which contends that personal morality is a prerequisite for successful democratic government and that religious belief is a prerequisite for personal morality. But like other Baptists since Roger Williams, he also believed strongly in the constitutional concept of separation of church and state. Because of that belief, he had not been active in secular politics.

After the 1972 *Roe v. Wade* Supreme Court decision legalizing abortion, however, Falwell reconsidered his decision to avoid politics. While liberal clergymen in mainline churches praised the decision, Falwell denounced it. He reasoned that there was a contradiction between the beliefs of persons who said they were pro-choice in killing fetuses but opposed to choice when it came to a child praying in public school. He contended that it was nonsense to claim that one personally opposed abortion but did not wish to impose views on others: "That is like saying you are against slavery but do not mind if other people keep slaves." Falwell noted tendentiously that many of the same people who supported abortion and opposed school prayer had advocated admission of the People's Republic of China to the United Nations, supported liberation forces in Angola and South Africa, declared that homosexuals were entitled to full church membership, and averred that capitalism conflicted with biblical justice and love. He expressed concern about the moral and social decline of the United States and started to work actively for the preservation of "America and freedom."

Central to Falwell's political views is the taken-for-granted assumption that religious belief and righteous politics are necessary to one another. When a democratic society begins to make decisions based on a moral code that is not grounded in religious belief, Falwell believes, it destroys its own foundations. Conversely, when religious citizens become complacent and allow their society to move away from religious truth as its guiding principle, they inevitably will lose the ability to live truthful lives. Reviving society demands that religious citizens take every legal step available to reintroduce religious values into governmental decision making, which in turn demands a revival of a social and political spirit among believers. Although Falwell's perspective requires believers to be concerned about virtually every element of society and every political action taken at any level of government, it suggests that the crusade to revive the United States should begin with the four tenets included in the national charter of the Moral Majority, Inc.: (1) pro-life, opposition to abortion and euthanasia; (2) pro-family, "one man for one woman for one lifetime"; (3) pro-moral, opposition to pornography and traffic in illegal drugs; and (4) pro-American, support for a strong national defense and the territorial integrity of Israel.

This all-encompassing view of the political responsibilities of religious persons influences Falwell's rhetoric in three important ways. First, it allows him to speak out on virtually every social and political issue, since religious belief provides all the evidence needed to know the right side of any issue. Second, it encourages him to appear in situations as varied as local Baptist churches, television talk shows, and debates at Oxford University and present the same message to all audiences. Finally, it means that his religious rhetoric (sermons) and his political rhetoric (speeches) are essentially alike. Of course, the tone and style of sermons given during Thomas Road's services are influenced by the norms of Baptist worship, but the substance is the same. Falwell's sermons illustrate fundamentalist religious beliefs with references to social and political situations, while his speeches propose solutions to complex social and political situations based on religious truths. Falwell addresses his rhetoric to believers, to persons who share both his religious beliefs and his assumption that political acts must be consistent with religious truths. Thus he risks inflaming nonbelievers while stimulating believers to even greater resolve.

Perhaps the most effective way to explain Falwell's conception of the dual responsibilities of faith and political-social action is to examine a sermon and a speech that illustrate those ideas. Thomas Road Baptist Church's 1985 Missions Sunday coincided with a highly publicized famine in East Africa, which had been particularly severe in Ethiopia and the Sudan. The television broadcast of the service began with a series of pictures of starving Ethiopian children arranged and narrated in a format that duplicated broadcasts being presented nightly on network news. But unlike the evening news, the lead-in to this broadcast promised a "report full of hope," a message in which "Reverend Falwell will tell you how you can help."

In many ways, the service that followed was typical of those in other Baptist churches. Prayer and religious music were used to establish a context for the sermon, which consisted of a four-part exegesis and application of two biblical texts: Matthew 10:42, which promises eternal reward to persons who minister to children, and Mark 9: 38–43, where Christ chastises his apostles for not supporting the ministries of others and promises rewards for everyone who ministers in his name. These texts, Falwell began, call on Christians to adopt four different attitudes. The first is a supportive attitude toward other Christians and their ministries. "The media ministry in America," Falwell claimed, "is more responsible than any other factor for shaking this nation, turning it toward God and waking it toward Spiritual things." Although some doctrinal differences separate these ministries, each deserves the respect and support that Christ demanded of his apostles: "I am an independent, fundamentalist baptist to the right of Attila the Hun on all issues. Everybody knows that. [But] I don't have the right to tell others either you believe this and teach this or close 'er down."

The second and third attitudes required of Christians directly involve mission activities. A missionary attitude includes being willing to accept help, including constructive criticism, from other Christians and a commitment to help others actively, especially those who are helpless. "We are our brothers' keeper," Falwell proclaimed, whether our brother is a "poor little black helpless, starving bundle [Ethiopian child]" or an unborn American child threatened by abortion. There is, he said, "no more helpless person alive than the unborn," and the fact that unborn children are "daily slaughtered by the thousands" is the "national sin of America." The final attitude required of Christian missionaries is a proper attitude toward sin, one that convicts persons of their sinfulness, leads them to confess and repent of their sins, change their habits, and begin to see themselves as witnesses for Christ.

Although this summary of the content of the sermon illustrates Falwell's theological, philosophical, and political beliefs, to understand the effectiveness of his rhetoric, one must examine the symbolic strategies through which he provides proof for his interpretation of reality. Unlike secular rhetoric, which relies heavily on scientific forms of evidence, fundamentalist political-religious rhetoric grounds claims of "truth" in citations from biblical texts assumed to be inerrant, the credibility of the rhetor, the presentation of testimonies by the faithful, and the strategic use of imagery.

Interspersed throughout the Mission Sunday service were references that helped establish the credibility of Falwell and his associates. The only title used during the service to refer to Falwell and his colleagues was "Dr."; Thomas Road was described as "one of the largest and most active churches in America"; and Falwell explicitly mentioned his thirty years of successful ministry. Even his low-key preaching style accents his credibility. Stereotypical views of Baptist ministers present them as aggressive, perhaps even bombastic purveyors of hell-fire and brimstone. Media depictions of Falwell capitalize on this stereotype by associating him with a wide range of aggressive personae, from the virulent sermons of some television evangelists to violent attacks on abortion clinics. But Falwell presents himself as a meek servant of God. When interviewed, he responds to attacks with promises to pray for the attacker; when pushed to comment on his opponents, he typically describes them as honest and committed but misguided. His preaching style relies primarily on humor and warmth, thus extending this contrast.

For his audience, this style serves three purposes. First, it allows him to personify his message of "loving sinners but hating their sin" and establishes him as a Christian who, like Christ, turns the other cheek in response to attackers. Second, it gives them immediate evidence of the irresponsibility and untrustworthiness of the secular media. The mild, almost tame, minister they see on Sundays is depicted by the secular press as an aggressive demagogue. The contrast prepares them to accept Falwell's claims that secular institutions cannot be trusted, even to provide objective news and factual information. Finally, when Falwell does say un-Christian things about persons with beliefs different from his—as he often does when discussing homosexuals and pro-abortion advocates—his followers can interpret his outbursts as natural, human responses to unfair and unrelenting attacks by the liberal media.

Believers' testimonies provided further evidence of the relationships among Christian faith, clear and simple definitions of political, social, and individual problems and commonsense solutions to those problems. A Christian nurse spoke in a clearly British accent: "It is not a complex problem. Give them [Ethiopian children] food and that's it. Solved. We can all [then] go home." Falwell's sermon began with a prayer in which he thanked God for clear instructions on how to live in the world and how to love and serve others, even when they are outside "our own camp; our own nation." The congregation testified about the truths of a simple faith when they sang together the hymn from which Falwell drew the title of his sermon, "A Cup of Cold Water."

These simple and honest testimonies of faith were contrasted with the dishonesty and duplicity of secular leaders and institutions. In his initial appeal for support of Thomas Road's African mission effort, Falwell explained that after many pleas from Christian groups and politicians alike, he decided to send a fact-finding group to the Sudan to "see if the reports you've all seen in the media are accurate." Like the spies sent into the Promised Land, the Thomas Road group returned and reported that the situation was as desperate as they had been told. But unlike the Hebrew people whose lack of faith prevented them from entering the Palestine, Thomas Road's leaders followed God into the wilderness of East Africa. Because the Christian aid groups active in Ethiopia—not secular experts from the United Nations or International Red Cross—predicted that the next major famine would be in the northeastern Sudan, Falwell decided to focus Thomas Road's efforts there. The program would begin with direct aid, distributed by the Thomas Road–Liberty University group itself in order to ensure that the aid would get to the suffering people instead of being misused by "the Marxist government of Ethiopia" or "stored in a warehouse somewhere." In contrast to the secular media, whose reports could not be believed without independent confirmation, the testimony of believers would also be a reliable guide for the mission effort.

At times Falwell's mistrust of secular institutions leads him to engage in unnecessarily risky rhetorical acts. After his 1985 visit to South Africa, Falwell asserted publicly that apartheid was supported by the mass of black Africans and opposed largely by an intellectual elite out of touch with its constituency (such as Bishop Desmond Tutu). For persons who believe the secular media's descriptions of the situation in South Africa and support efforts to force that government to abandon apartheid, Falwell's claims were perceived as at best nonsense. But Falwell's followers, who expect the secular media to be biased against him and his associates and who expect to discover that secular reports about a foreign situation are distorted, are likely to respond very differently to even the most extreme of Falwell's reports.

The final and most important form of evidence used in the mission service was the recurring image of cup and child. Falwell described the act of giving, symbolized by the cup, as a blessing for the giver and receiver alike. But it is a blessing that God can grant only when both parties have sufficient faith to overcome their human resistance. Givers must believe without question that through giving and receiving gifts, God will be glorified and faith will be exercised. In addition, the recipients must not be so weak that they do not accept the gift. In some cases, their weakness may be physical and can be overcome only by an extra measure of faith on the part of the giver. Many of the Ethiopian children, Falwell repeatedly explained, are too weak to "accept Western food and medicine." Some must be force fed through intravenous injections or, in an instance that Falwell described in graphic detail, by breaking out a child's front teeth so that "she could receive nourishing liquids." When the recipient/child is too weak to receive, the continual act of giving in spite of the receiver's apathy or resistance is the greatest test of the giver's faith.

Sometimes spiritual weakness stands between a recipient and the blessings of acceptance. According to Falwell, pride—faith in things human, including faith in oneself—often keeps people from accepting God's aid. Faith, an unqualified, childlike acceptance of divine gifts, is the prerequisite for receiving the cup; receiving the cup is the only evidence of unqualified, childlike faith. The Mission Service explained this dual conception of receiving the cup through a song and a testimony. The song, entitled appropriately "Fill My Cup Lord," immediately preceded the sermon and offered a prayer that God will provide for all of a believer's needs. The testimony was a story about the gift of a poor Missouri widow who had been saving for years to have running water installed in her home. After hearing Falwell's plea during a television broadcast for donations for even less fortunate people, she sent him a crumpled $20 bill. Although his first reaction was to return the money, he said he remembered Christ's promise that those who give will be blessed and decided to keep it. The next day he received a crumpled $100 bill from the same woman (the remainder of her savings) with an apology for having been so selfish. The next Sunday he told his television audience about the gift of this modern "widow's mite" and immediately received offers from plumbing contractors in Kansas City and St. Louis, who soon completed renovation work on the woman's home "far in excess of what she ever could afford." Through faith, believers obtain the capacity to give and therefore to be blessed. Through accepting the gift, recipients strengthen their faith and have their needs met.

It is on the theological position that personal belief and social action are inextricably bound together that Falwell's political philosophy is based. Christ's ascension sermon challenged all believers to act in ways that will Christianize the world. At the simplest level, this Great Commission involves personal evangelism and enactment of a social conscience, for it is through acting on behalf of others that a believer's faith is revealed and strengthened. At a more fundamental level, it calls on believers to create the kind of social and political climate within which faith can arise, be nurtured, and be exercised. The central element of this strengthening society is a strong family unit. Although Falwell has articulated this view in virtually all of his speeches and writings, it is developed at length in "Strengthening Families in the Nation," delivered in Atlanta on March 26, 1982.

The traditional family, which Falwell tersely defines as "one man for one woman for one lifetime," currently is threatened by five aspects of American culture: economic pressures, which force mothers to forsake care of their children to work outside the home; moral permissiveness, based on the belief that ethical principles are humanistic and changing, not divine and constant; television, which supports concepts of situational ethics and robs family members of the opportunity to communicate meaningfully with one another; "plain busyness," which separates children from their parents; and, most important, secular humanism. The family, and therefore the nation and its citizens, can be saved from these threats only through a revived alliance of parents and churches, acting together to recreate a "nation built upon the Judeo-Christian ethic," a society in which parents can "train up a child in the way he [*sic*] should go and when he is old he will not depart from it. Rebuilding families is just coming back to the old biblical principle of getting them into the Word of God and by precept setting the example before them on a daily basis, letting them see Christ in Mom and Dad, and then that local church becomes the confirmation, the reinforcement center."

Parents and church can do their work only within a society grounded in seven key principles: (1) the principle of the traditional family; (2) the dignity of human life, which entails a reversal of the *Roe v. Wade* decision, an action that has "brought the wrath of God upon this nation;" (3) common decency, which requires a ban on pornography; (4) the work ethic, tempered by compassion for "those who cannot help themselves"; (5) the Abrahamic covenant, God's promise to "deal with nations in relation to how those nations deal with Israel"; (6) God-centered education, including voluntary prayer and the teaching of scientific creationism in the public schools and support for private schools; and (7) support of the divinely ordained institutions of the home, state, and church.

For Falwell, the seemingly simple metaphor of the cup and the child contains a complex, almost all-encompassing view of what society should be. The child symbolizes the traditional family, which in turn represents society. Christ's command to care for the children requires believers to take every possible step to create a social, political, and intellectual context in which every vulnerable child can become a moral and productive adult. In the fullest sense of the phrase, to Jerry Falwell the political is personal; the personal is political. It is a worldview that warrants his active involvement in every facet of society and demands that his social and political action leaves no stone unturned.

INFORMATION SOURCES

Research Collections and Collected Speeches

Although Falwell is an active orator, his speeches are sometimes difficult to locate. Copies of speeches, sermons, and related books are available from Dr. Falwell, Thomas Road Baptist Church, Lynchburg, Virginia. He also makes regular contributions to *The Moral Majority Report*, available in most libraries, and grants interviews to a number of newspersons. The most famous of these was published in March 1981 *Penthouse*. Tapes and transcripts of all of his sermons are available at the Liberty University library, Lynchburg, Virginia.

American Rhetoric from Roosevelt to Reagan: A Collection of Speeches and   ARRR
    Critical Essays. Edited by Halford Ross Ryan. Prospect Heights,
    Ill.: Waveland Press, 1983.
Falwell, Jerry. Thomas Road Baptist Church, Lynchburg, Virginia.   TRC

Moral Majority Report.   *MMR*
"Interview with Jerry Falwell" *Penthouse* (March 1981): 60–66.   *PH*
Liberty University Library, Lynchburg, Virginia.   *LBC*

Selected Critical Studies

Brummett, Barry. "The Representative Anecdote as a Burkean Method, Applied to Evangelical Rhetoric." *Southern Speech Communication Journal* 50(1984): 1–23.

Clabaugh, Gary. *Thunder on the Right.* Chicago: Nelson-Hall, 1980.

Conrad, Charles. "The Moral Majority as Romantic Form." *Quarterly Journal of Speech* 69(1983): 159–70.

Daniels, Tom; Jensen, Richard; and Lichtenstein, Allen. "Resolving the Paradox in Politicized Christian Fundamentalism." *Western Journal of Speech Communication* 49(1985): 248–66.

Hart, Roderick. *The Political Pulpit.* West Lafayette, Ind.: Purdue University Press, 1981.

McGee, Michael. "Secular Humanism," *Critical Studies in Mass Communication* 1(1984): 1–33.

Shiels, Richard. "A Response." *Religion and Intellectual Life* 2(1984): 23–27.

Selected Biographies

DeSousa, Dinesh. *Falwell, Before the Millennium.* Chicago: Regnery Gateway, 1984.
Pingery, Patricia. *Jerry Falwell.* Milwaukee: Ideals Publishing Company.

CHRONOLOGY OF MAJOR SPEECHES

See "Research Collections and Collected Speeches" for source codes.

"America Was Built on Seven Great Principles," multiple presentations; *MMR*, May 18, 1981, p. 8.

"Strengthening Families in the Nation," Atlanta, Georgia, March 23, 1982; *ARRR*, pp. 250–64.

Untitled speech to the Republican National Convention Platform Committee, San Francisco, August 13, 1984; *MMR*, September 9, 1984, pp. 3, 8.

"A Cup of Cold Water," Lynchburg, Virginia, May 12, 1985; *TRC*.

GERALD RUDOLPH FORD
(1913–   ), thirty-eighth president of the United States

Gerald Rudolph Ford took the oath of office as president of the United States on August 9, 1974. The swearing in of the sixty-one-year-old former vice-president and former House minority leader took place in the East Room of the White House. Many in the audience were Ford's friends in Congress in which he had served for twenty-five years as the representative from Michigan's conservative Fifth District.

Ford brought to the presidency talents developed in the House of Representatives: networking among colleagues and politicians, bargaining in committee negotiations, and other interpersonal skills. He was regarded as a good mediator and counselor and was perceived as being honest, loyal, straightforward, and friendly—in all a decent man. He was a dependable but not exceptional professional politician who downplayed the development of a unique public persona.

When he was sworn in as vice-president on December 6, 1973, succeeding Spiro Agnew, who was forced to resign the office, Ford insisted that the ceremony take place in the Capitol where he had hoped to become Speaker of the House. In his address to those assembled he said, "I am a Ford, not a Lincoln," referring to the latter's eloquence but ironically implying his own plainness rather than elegance in defining himself with the two products central to the well-being of his home state of Michigan. Early in his political career, Ford reported that he "never thought of myself as a great orator."

FORD'S PROBLEMS AS PRESIDENTIAL PERSUADER

President Ford selected Nelson Rockefeller to be his vice-president, and for the first time in the nation's history neither the president nor the vice-president had been elected to those offices. In the wake of Watergate, Ford often emphasized character and values in his speeches. Immediately after he recited the oath of office on August 9, 1974, he said in his televised statement to the nation that his first duty was "to make an unprecedented compact with my countrymen. Not an inaugural speech, not a fireside chat, not a campaign speech, just a little straight talk among friends." Before a joint session of Congress on August 12, 1974, he returned to the automobile theme: "Only 8 months ago, when I last stood here, I told you I was a Ford, not a Lincoln. Tonight I say I am still a Ford, but I am not a Model T." After the 1976 presidential campaign, a note to President-elect Jimmy Carter began "Dear Jimmy," and was signed by "Jerry Ford," not President Gerald R. Ford. Throughout his short term in office, he

disassociated himself from the imperial presidency of Richard Nixon as he sought
to restore a sense of decency, trust, and stability to government in a time of
doubt. The first sentence of Carter's 1977 Inaugural Address acknowledged that
effort: "For myself and our nation, I want to thank my predecessor for all that
he has done to heal our land."

Ford's contributions to the literature of the presidency are meager. His speeches
were not models of invention and style. His delivery was not compelling. On
balance his platform appearances did not successfully communicate leadership
qualities. Prior to his formal announcement of candidacy in 1976, his staff
prepared for him an assessment of his strengths and weaknesses as the Republican
candidate. The report noted that as a campaigner and a speech maker, he needed
improvement.

If his character was a strength, his platform skills were not. Reporters noted
that he often mispronounced or stumbled over words. In his political autobiography, Ford himself offered an example from a speech in Alton, Illinois, in
October 1976: at the end of it, "I stumbled over the words 'fly swatter . . . Fly
spotter . . . fly spot.' Finally, I got it right." With a text before him, he departed
from it only for cosmetic alterations that often added adjectives, adverbs, and
conjunctions, which weakened the thrust of the prepared, simple, declarative
sentences. Audiences were not easily energized by war and sports metaphors
delivered lethargically. His staff warned him that he needed to discipline himself,
especially on television, because when he got angry, he tended toward overkill.
To counter the wooden qualities in his style, a professional comedy writer was
hired to inject humor appropriate to Ford's manner.

Since Franklin D. Roosevelt, every president has used speech writers to craft
public statements. Ford was no exception, and his team was led by Robert
Hartmann, a long-time employee. Ford clearly thought well of him, but others
who worked with Hartmann believed that some of Ford's difficulties could be
traced to Hartmann, whose personality was difficult and whose ways were fixed.
Another problem was that the team lacked depth of experience and a sense of
commitment. More than the usual backbiting has been described in public accounts. The problems were never surmounted.

Ford participated in the drafting of messages as the issues and his interest
required. For example, a line in his 1976 State of the Union Address, "1975
was not a year for summer soldiers and sunshine patriots," Ford lifted from
Thomas Paine and insisted that it remain despite staff objections.

The preparation of the 1976 State of the Union Address illustrates the administration's sensitivity to evaluations of Ford's rhetorical efforts. His press secretary often reported to the press the hours that Ford himself had spent on it;
the intense promotion of it was unusual. The address itself sounded better at the
moment of utterance than it read in print, a reflection of the media's influence
on invention and style in the process of composition. On balance the speech was
straightforward, optimistic, and energetic. Some evaluators rank it among Ford's
best efforts.

Three examples follow that illustrate additional dimensions of Ford's rhetorical and political efforts: the pardon of Richard M. Nixon, the war on inflation, and the 1976 campaign, divided into the struggle with Ronald Reagan for the Republican party nomination and the election campaign against Democrat Jimmy Carter.

Ford's first political test was how to dispose of the Nixon problem, a no-win issue for him. He chose to grant a "full, free and absolute pardon" to Nixon "to heal the wounds throughout the United States." The decision opened old sores (his press secretary, Jerry terHorst, promptly resigned), and seriously weakened the "our long national nightmare is over" statement in his Inaugural. Ford clearly hoped to close the book on Watergate, but the public and the press were angry and suspicious; his persona was tested. During the 1976 presidential campaign, Jimmy Carter exploited the pardon, constantly referring to the "Nixon-Ford administration."

When he assumed the presidency, Ford faced severe domestic problems: unemployment, energy (an issue that never captured his interest), and inflation, "Public Enemy No. 1," discussed through a war metaphor, that dominated his public speeches until his 1975 State of the Union Address. Citing Pogo in his analysis of the problem, the people became the enemy—"I have met the enemy and he is us"—and they were to enlist in a WIN program ("Whip Inflation Now"), which stressed volunteerism. Sylvia Porter, chairperson of the Citizen's Action Committee to Fight Inflation, was pleased when the metaphor was discarded: "That wasn't our gimmick! You all know what happened—we were left with the job of building the airplane in the sky."

The metaphor neither explained the problem nor mobilized the country. Given Ford's personal temperament and political caution, the metaphor was inappropriate to him, to his audiences, and to the times. The distance between Ford's imagery and his actions in the name of the imagery raised questions about the authenticity of the analyses. The war metaphor demanded vigorous substantive action, which was not forthcoming. Asking the people to "plant WIN [victory] gardens" did not satisfy their need for action and leadership. Asked to accept the blame and the burden, citizens remained suspicious, dubious, and uncertain about the rhetoric.

Ford had to be nominated by the Republicans meeting in convention before he could meet Jimmy Carter. Ronald Reagan challenged him vigorously in state primaries, testing the strength of his political ideology and his power base. The test continued on the convention floor itself until Ford earned the nomination by 57 votes more than the minimum of 1,130. As his running mate, Ford selected Robert Dole, a conservative acceptable to the Reagan camp. He invited Ronald and Nancy Reagan to share the stage with him when he delivered his acceptance speech. He came prepared with a well-polished text that he had practiced, videotaped, and evaluated. It contained no new ideas, but its language was direct, crisp, and energizing. Delivered flawlessly, it reached beyond the assembled Republicans—an extended Grand Rapids, Michigan, constituency. He said he was one of them: "You at home, listening tonight, you are the people who pay the taxes and obey the laws. You are the people who make the system work. You are the people who make America what it is. It is from your ranks that I come, and on your side that I stand." On that upbeat tone, an unelected incumbent prepared for the 1976 presidential campaign.

Because Ford entered the campaign trailing Carter in the polls, he could not stay in the White House and goad Carter into mistakes. He entered the fray and managed to cut the distance between them.

Three debates, modeled on the 1960 debates and sponsored by the League of Voters, were scheduled: the first on September 23 in Philadelphia centered on domestic and economic issues; the second on October 6 in San Francisco on foreign policy and defense; the third on October 22 in Williamsburg, Virginia, featured an open agenda.

To many observers, Ford had a slight edge in the first debate, and Carter was the stronger in the second and third. In the second debate, Ford, in response to a question, asserted that "there is no Soviet domination of Eastern Europe, and there never will be under a Ford administration." The self-inflicted wound was reflected in the polls, and efforts were made to cut the losses. For five days Ford insisted that no clarification was needed. Finally, on October 12, he agreed that he had erred, but the damage had been done. The gaffe raised questions again about his competence and seriously damaged his chances of overcoming Carter on election day.

On November 2, 1976, Carter beat Ford by a margin of only 2 percent: 49.9 percent to 47.9 percent of the votes cast. In the electoral college Carter got 297 votes, Ford 241. The public's perceptions about Ford could not be changed, and Ford's rhetoric certainly contributed to its judgments. The public's criteria for public discourse had not been met.

INFORMATION SOURCES

Research Collections and Collected Speeches

The Gerald R. Ford Library, Ann Arbor, Michigan, contains rhetorical materials about his political career in the House of Representatives and in the White House. The library holds speech drafts, including the final reading copies, and audiovisual recordings of these addresses, and public reaction mail. The Presidential Speeches and Public Statements series is particularly useful to rhetorical researchers. Secondary sources include oral histories, dissertations, and other aids associated with the presidential library system. Ford's speeches were prepared under the aegis of the Office of Editorial Staff, and speech sources are gathered in the Theis-Orben files. The Gerald R. Ford Foundation offers research grants to support scholarly research based in part on the library's holdings.

Carter vs Ford: The Counterfeit Debates of 1976. Edited by Lloyd Bitzer   CF
    and Theodore Reuter. Madison: University of Wisconsin Press, 1980.

The Great Debates. Edited by Sidney Kraus. Bloomington: Indiana Uni-   TGD
    versity Press, 1979.

Presidential Rhetoric, 1961–1980. Edited by Theodore Windt. 2d ed. Du-   *PR*
buque: Kendall/Hunt, 1980.
Public Papers of the Presidents of the United States. Washington, D.C.:   *PPP*
Government Printing Office.

Selected Critical Studies

Evans, Rowland, and Novak, Robert. "Jerry Ford: The Eisenhower of the Seventies."
Atlantic Monthly (August 1974): pp. 25–32.
Hahn, Dan F. "Corrupt Rhetoric: President Ford and the Mayaguez Affair." *Commu-
nication Quarterly* 28 (1980): 38–43.
Hart, Roderick P. *Verbal Style and the Presidency.* Orlando, Fla.: Academic Press, 1984.
Howell, David; Kronman, Margaret-Mary; and Kronman, Robert. *Jerry Ford and the
Campaign of 1976.* Washington, D.C.: HKJV Publications, 1980.
President Ford: The Man and his Record. Washington, D.C.: Congressional Quarterly,
1974.
Stelzner, Hermann G. "Ford's War on Inflation: A Metaphor That Did Not Cross."
Communication Monographs 44 (1977): 284–97.

Selected Biographies

Barber, James David. *The Presidential Character: Predicting Performance in the White
House.* Englewood Cliffs, N.J.: Prentice-Hall, 1977.
Casserly, John J. *The Ford White House: The Diary of a Speech Writer.* Boulder: Colorado
Associated University Press, 1977.
Ford, Gerald R. *A Time to Heal.* New York: Harper & Row, 1979.
Nessen, Ron. *It Sure Looks Different from the Inside.* Chicago: Playboy, 1978.
Osborne, John. *White House Watch: The Ford Years.* Washington, D.C.: New Republic
Books, 1977.
Reeves, Richard. *A Ford, Not a Lincoln.* New York: Harcourt Brace Jovanovich, 1975.
Vestal, Bud. *Jerry Ford, Up Close.* New York: Coward, McCann & Geogheagan, 1974.
Witcover, Jules. *Marathon: The Pursuit of the Presidency, 1972–1976.* New York: Viking
Press, 1977.

CHRONOLOGY OF MAJOR SPEECHES

See "Research Collections and Collected Speeches" for source codes.

Remarks on Taking the Oath of Office, Washington, D.C., August 9, 1974; *PPP, 1974*,
pp. 1–3.

Address to Joint Session of Congress, Washington, D.C., August 12, 1974; *PPP, 1974*,
pp. 6–13.

Remarks on signing a proclamation granting pardon to Richard Nixon, Washington, D.C.,
September 8, 1974; *PPP, 1974*, pp. 101–103.

"The Economy" before a Joint Session of Congress, Washington, D.C., October 8,
1974; *PPP, 1974*, pp. 1239–47.

State of the Union Address, Washington, D.C., January 19, 1976; *PPP, 1976*, pp. 31–42.

Republican Party nomination acceptance address, Kansas City, Missouri, August 19, 1976; *PPP, 1976*, pp. 2157–63.

HARRY EMERSON FOSDICK
(1878–1969), preeminent preacher

———————————————————————— HALFORD R. RYAN

Upon his retirement in 1946, Harry Emerson Fosdick was regarded by the *Christian Century* as one of the greatest preachers in the American pulpit (the other two were Henry Ward Beecher and Phillips Brooks). Beecher had his Plymouth Church in Brooklyn, Brooks his Trinity Church in Boston, and Fosdick his Riverside Church in New York City. John D. Rockefeller, Jr., built the visually stunning neo-Gothic church, with its 400 foot bell tower housing the largest carillon in the world, on Riverside Drive, for Dr. Fosdick. The nave seated 2,400 people, and overflow crowds were routinely reported for years after its opening in 1930. Although Fosdick initiated his National Vespers radio broadcasts in 1927, they came to be associated with him and the Riverside Church. The National Vespers was heard by over 2 million listeners during its peak years.

Fosdick credited the study of oratory as the contributing factor to his prowess in the pulpit: "I regard my college training in oratory as one of the most useful disciplines I ever received. I cannot overestimate the time it has saved me in developing technique as a public speaker." He had debated in high school, but it was at Colgate University where he mastered the principles and practices of rhetoric, debating, and public speaking. Upon graduation from Colgate in 1900, he took a divinity degree from Union Theological Seminary in 1904 and then a pastorate in a Baptist church in Montclair, New Jersey, where he achieved local recognition as an effective preacher. He became an associate minister of the prestigious First Presbyterian Church, New York City, in 1918. And in 1922, Fosdick became a national religious figure because of a sermon he preached; thereafter famous sermons marked his progress to preeminence in the pulpit.

FOSDICK'S SERMONS AS WATERSHEDS

On May 21, 1922, Fosdick preached "Shall the Fundamentalists Win?" to his First Presbyterian Church congregation, which, with its New York sophistication, perceived nothing out of the ordinary in the sermon's sentiments. However, a liberal member of the church, who also headed a large publicity organization, decided that the sermon should reach a national audience. He sectioned the sermon with captions, deleted Fosdick's conciliatory language, and mailed his editorialized version of the sermon to preachers nationwide. The fundamentalist-modernist controversy, which had been simmering, boiled over.

Fosdick's quarrel with fundamentalism is best given in his own words because this sermon is illustrative of his oratorical training, use of rhetorical devices, and the clarity of his thought and expression. He introduced his sermon by juxtaposing the fundamentalists with the modernists or liberals: "The Fundamentalist program is essentially illiberal and intolerant" and they "are out on a campaign to shut against them [the liberals] the doors of the Christian fellowship." He orally signposted his first argument: "We may as well begin with the vexed and mooted question of the virgin birth of our Lord." He used a historical exposition of religious figures to suggest why one could be a Christian yet not believe in unscientific miracles. Further, he asked the congregation a series of compelling rhetorical questions designed to seek assent to his analysis: "Has intolerance any contribution to make to this situation? Will it persuade anybody of anything? Is not the Christian church large enough to hold within her hospitable fellowship people who differ on points like this and agree to differ until further truth be manifested? The Fundamentalists say not." He moved the listener to his second thought with a smooth transition: "Consider another matter on which there is a sincere difference of opinion between evangelical Christians: the inspiration of the Bible." Again he used historical examples to demonstrate that religious books were the products of men at the time they were written, and he summarized his argument with another series of rhetorical questions. In a similar manner, he discussed the Second Coming of Christ. Having delineated the problem, he proposed two solutions. "The first element," he said, "that is necessary is a spirit of tolerance and Christian liberty. When will the world learn that intolerance solves no problems?" The second solution was "a sense of shame that the Christian church should be quarreling over little matters when the world is dying of great needs." He concluded by asking his congregation to continue to be liberal and tolerant in their beliefs and actions.

This speech had several effects that Fosdick probably did not intend or foresee. It thrust him personally to the forefront of the fundamentalist-modernist controversy. The ensuing debate, led by such leading fundamentalists as Clarence Macartney and William Jennings Bryan, who excoriated Fosdick at the General Assembly of the Presbyterian Church in Indianapolis in 1923, divided the church and led inexorably to the denouement of the Scopes trial in 1925 where the fundamentalists claimed a victory, although it was probably pyrrhic. Fosdick, a Baptist, was given an ultimatum to become a Presbyterian minister or to stop preaching from a Presbyterian pulpit, and so he resigned and preached his valedictory sermon in March 1925.

The next significant speech Fosdick delivered was something of a catharsis for him. During World War I, he had wholeheartedly supported the U.S. war effort. But given the grim statistics of the war, that the profiteers did handsomely well, that the propagandists fabricated the Hun atrocity stories, and that the world was not much safer for democracy, he took second thought on his preaching war from the pulpit. So when he spoke to the assembled delegates and dignitaries of the first six member countries of the League of Nations at the Protestant Cathedral of St. Peter, Geneva, Switzerland, on September 13, 1925, the title of his sermon, "A Christian Conscience about War," was a watershed for him.

The structure of this speech was typical of Fosdick's rhetorical presentations. Taking as his text Matthew 26:52, "All they that take the sword shall perish with the sword," he raised the issue of how Christians could reconcile violence and death with Jesus's teachings. Indeed, Fosdick declared: "If mankind does not end war, war will end mankind." He developed his thesis with two headings. First, he demonstrated the futility of war: "In the history of war we have one more example of a mode of social action possibly possessing at the beginning more of good than evil, which has outgrown its good, accentuated its evil, and become at last an intolerable thing." Lest the point be missed, he offered some sobering statistics—10 million dead soldiers, 13 million dead civilians, and 9 million war orphans. Second, he warned that "our religion has been nationalized." Reminiscent of Lincoln's poignant observation in his Second Inaugural Address about God and sectionalism in the Civil War—"'Both read the same Bible and pray to the same God, and each invokes His aid against the other"— Fosdick condemned the church's covenant with religious nationalism: "We helped to identify religion and patriotism. And so far has this identification gone that now, when war breaks, the one God of all humanity, whom Christ came to reveal, is split up into little tribal deities, and before these pagan idols even Christians pray for the blood of their enemies." In one of the most profound thoughts in the speech, Fosdick revealed the crux of the problem, which applied then as well as now:

Mankind's realest conflict of interest is not between this nation and that, but between the forward-looking, progresssive, open-minded people of all nations, who have caught a vision of humanity organized for peace, and the backward-looking, reactionary, militaristic people of the same nations. The deepest line of conflict does not run vertically between the nations; it runs horizontally through all the nations. The salvation of humanity from self-destruction depends on which side of that conflict wins.

Cognizant that "the Church has come down through history too often trying to carry the cross of Jesus in one hand and a dripping sword in the other," he used his conclusion to issue a clarion call for Christians to pray and to work for "a world organized for peace." The speech was well received by pacifists within and without the pulpit, it buttressed the attractiveness of isolationism, it thoroughly linked Fosdick's name with the peace movement of the 1920s and 1930s, and it was another nova in the growing galaxy of his stellar speeches.

At this point, it may be advantageous to ascertain the nature of Fosdick's oratorical attainments. It was said of Henry Ward Beecher that he was a stump speaker who stumbled into the pulpit and that adage is analogous to Fosdick for it explains why he continued to attract overflow congregations for over two decades. It is true that Fosdick gained publicity from delivering significant sermons that crystallized the pressing moral and theological issues of his time and that he was associated in the public's mind with two of the prestigious pulpits in the United States, but those important factors do not fully explain his Sunday-to-Sunday sermonic successes.

Fosdick knew that an orator had to motivate the audience in order to persuade. Consequently he selected sermon topics with which the audience could identify, and he suggested solutions, set in a Christian context, that people could utilize in their everyday lives. He used oral signposting for smooth transitions to aid the audience in following his logical progression of ideas to their ineluctable conclusion. Although he was criticized by conservative churchmen for not using the Bible enough as proof for his points, Fosdick knew that audiences would be persuaded by logical appeals with which they were familiar and in which they found meaning. Hence, one finds in Fosdick's sermons allusions to novelists, poets, historical examples, contemporary events, and commonsense reasoning comprising the persuasive substance of his rhetoric. Yet his sermons were not so secularized as to be devoid of religious feeling and belief, for as adept as Fosdick was in the art of persuasion, his sermons still evinced a preacher calling man to man and, more important, man to God.

Dr. Fosdick wrote his own sermons. On average, he worked for sixteen hours on a typical Sunday's sermon, and important ones took longer. He usually began preparing a sermon on Monday morning by working in his study until around noon every day until the sermon was essentially finished, by Friday noon. He wrote the speech with an eye toward adjusting his purpose to the audience by relying on his rich repository of readings and personal experiences. The sermon was totally reviewed on Saturday, and Fosdick faced his congregation on Sunday with a thoroughly prepared address.

Fosdick also wrote about the attributes of a rhetorical preacher and a persuasive sermon. His observations, culled from his experiences in the pulpit and on the public platform, are germane to the theory and practice of public speaking. Foremost, Fosdick aimed for effect. He wrote in *On Being Fit to Live With:* "A good sermon is direct personal address, individual consultation on a group scale, intended to achieve results. A sermon should creatively get things done, then and there, in the minds and lives of the audience; it should be a convincing appeal to a listening jury for decision." He believed the problem-solution organizational structure was the most efficacious one. In his famous essay, "What Is the Matter with Preaching?" he revealed his rationale for employing that pattern: "Every sermon should have for its main business the solving of some problem—a vital, important problem, puzzling minds, burdening consciences, distracting lives." This audience-centered oratory made him famous and successful because he realized the motivational drives of people: "There is nothing that people are so interested in as themselves, their own problems, and the way to solve them. That fact is basic. No preaching that neglects it can raise a ripple on a congregation. It is the primary starting point of all successful public speaking." He closed his essay by noting that "preaching is wrestling with individuals over questions of life and death, and until that idea of it commands a preacher's mind and method, eloquence will avail him little and theology not at all."

Fosdick considered his audience's needs in organizing his sermons. Given a twenty to thirty-minute speech, he realized that people tire of listening and that their mental alertness wanes as the sermon waxes. When the audience was most alert, Fosdick used unusually long speech introductions to detail the problem. As he moved from main head to main head in the body of the speech, he progressively devoted less time and material to each point. Indeed, ever the orator, Fosdick cautioned readers of his collection of sermons in *On Being Fit to Live With* that "sermons were not meant to be read, as essays are."

The seeds of Fosdick's next famous address were sown in his "Christian Conscience" sermon and they came to famous fruition in "The Unknown Soldier." Fosdick was the featured speaker at a Protestant peace rally held in New York City on May 7, 1934. The tone of the speech, at times discordant, uncompromising, and ultra, was atypical for Fosdick, so he employed the Ciceronian pattern to organize his persuasive arguments. In the introduction, he used sarcasm to heighten the fact that it was "strange" that Christians were beguiled by the national acclaim given to the Unknown Soldier. In the narration, he spoke of himself as an exemplar of Christian pastors who ministered as he had in World War I: "They sent men like me to explain to the army the high meanings of war and, by every argument we could command, to strengthen their morale." He moved to a well-structured argument section. After describing the folly and waste in nations' sending their best men to die, he exclaimed: "I have an account to settle between my soul and the Unknown Soldier."

His second argument was that nations conscripted their soldiers and that Christian ministers obliged: "If I blame anybody about this matter, it is men like myself who ought to have known better. We went out to the army and explained to these valiant men what a resplendent future they were preparing for their children by their heroic sacrifice. O Unknown Soldier, however can I make that right with you?"

Realizing that his audience might have reservations about his harshness on the ministry, he moved to the refutation section to address those concerns. What about the lyric glory of war? His answer was devastating: "Did you look, as I have looked, into the faces of young men who had been over the top, wounded, hospitalized, hardened up—over the top, wounded, hospitalized, hardened up—over the top, wounded, hospitalized, hardened up—four times, five times, six times? Never talk to a man who has seen that about the lyric glory of war." Moreover, he indicted those, including himself, who blew the rhetorical war trumpet: "The glory of war comes from poets, preachers, orators, the writers of martial music, statesmen preparing flowery proclamations for the people, who dress up war for other men to fight. They do not go to the trenches. They do not go over the top again and again and again." What about the idealism of war? He dispatched that notion: "Fifteen years after the Armistice we cannot be sure who won the war, so sunk in the same disaster are victors and vanquished alike." Last, what if the Unknown Soldier were Christian? Fosdick proclaimed: "We can have this monstrous thing [war] or we can have Christ, but we cannot have both."

His conclusion served as a catharsis for him and as an appeal to his audience:

"I renounce war and never again, directly or indirectly, will I sanction or support another! O Unknown Soldier, in penitent reparation I make you that pledge." Fosdick remained true to his pledge by not actively supporting the war effort in World War II.

The fourth major speech Fosdick delivered was an extension of the kind of theology he preached in the "Christian Conscience" and "Unknown Soldier" sermons. In "The Church Must Go beyond Modernism," November 3, 1935, he gave a theological basis for his famous stands in those earlier sermons. Fosdick saw in modernism's (and his) reaction to fundamentalism, in attempting to make religion meaningful to modern man without sacrificing reason, that it had stressed an intellectual approach to religion at the expense of a spiritual approach.

He dramatically began with a poignant example: "Fifty years ago, a boy of seven years of age was crying himself to sleep at night in terror lest, dying, he should go to hell." That boy was Fosdick. Fosdick preached modernism because "we refused to live bifurcated lives, our intellect in the late nineteenth century and our religion in the early sixteenth." However, modernism had become sterile and complacent. His first point was that "modernism has been excessively preoccupied with intellectualism." He urged the practice of a religion of the heart as well as the mind. Second, modernism had become mired in sentimentality, the belief that the world was getting better every day. Indeed he isolated the crux of the problem: "Underline this: *Sin is real*. Personal and social sin is as terribly real as our forefathers said it was, no matter how we change their way of saying so. And it leads men and nations to damnation as they said it did, no matter how we change their way of picturing it." Moreover, modernism had "even watered down and thinned out the central message and distinctive truth of religion, the reality of God"; finally, it has "too commonly lost its ethical standing-ground and its power of moral attack. . . . Harmonizing slips into compromising."

This sermon was perceived by the fundamentalists to be Fosdick's repudiation of modernism. It was not. Rather, he challenged the church to renew the debate on the role of the Christian church in the mid-twentieth century.

Fosdick wanted his audiences to concentrate on his thoughts, so he eschewed dramatic pulpit theatrics. He tended to read from prepared manuscripts, although this did not appreciably hinder his listeners' receptivity to his ideas. He addressed his congregations in a conversational mode by not overly modulating his rather high-pitched tenor speaking voice. He gestured sparingly, and that helped to maintain a dignified pastoral image.

In summation, Harry Emerson Fosdick was an extremely important speaker and preacher during the first half of the twentieth century. His pulpit oratory at Riverside Church followed in the tradition of Henry Ward Beecher in attempting to free Americans' minds from the "excrescences of a harsh theology." Fosdick preached to even greater audiences than Beecher did through the medium of his National Vespers radio program. He spoke about men's and women's relationships to their fellow human beings and to God, and he advocated solutions that were helpful and meaningful to his audiences' everyday lives. His oratorical training enabled him to craft eloquent and persuasive Christian messages on timeless topics. Consequently Fosdick's sermons speak to the issues of the late twentieth century as cogently and convincingly as they did half a century ago.

INFORMATION SOURCES

Research Collections and Collected Speeches

Fosdick gave his papers to Union Theological Seminary, New York City, where they are gathered in the Fosdick Collection. His sermons are collected in numerous books he published over the years.

American Public Address: 1740–1952. Edited by A. Craig Baird. New York: *APA*
    McGraw-Hill, 1956.
Fosdick, Harry Emerson. *The Secret of Victorious Living: Sermons in Chris-*   *SVL*
    tianity Today. New York: Harper, 1934.
Sermons in American History. Edited by DeWitte Holland. Nashville: Abing-   *SAH*
    don Press, 1971.

Selected Critical Studies

Chandler, Daniel Ross. "Harry Emerson Fosdick: Spokesman for the Modernist Move-
    ment." *Religious Communication Today* 5 (1982): 1–4.
Clark, Robert D. "Harry Emerson Fosdick." In *A History and Criticism of American
    Public Address*. Edited by Marie Kathryn Hochmuth. New York: Longmans,
    Green, 1955.
Crocker, Lionel, ed. *Harry Emerson Fosdick's Art of Preaching: An Anthology*. Spring-
    field, Ill.: Charles C. Thomas, 1971.
———. "The Rhetorical Theory of Harry Emerson Fosdick." *Quarterly Journal of
    Speech* 22 (1936): 207–13.
Fosdick, Harry Emerson. "What Is the Matter with Preaching?" *Harpers Magazine* 158
    (July 1928): 133–41.
MacVaugh, Gilbert Stillman. "Structural Analysis of the Sermons of Dr. Harry Emerson
    Fosdick." *Quarterly Journal of Speech* 18 (1932): 531–46.
McCall, Roy C. "Harry Emerson Fosdick: A Study in Sources of Effectiveness." In
    American Public Address: Studies in Honor of A. Craig Baird. Edited by Loren
    Reid. Columbia: University of Missouri Press, 1961.
Moody, Larry A. "A Bibliography of Works by and about Harry Emerson Fosdick."
    American Baptist Quarterly 1 (1982): 81–98; 2 (1983): 65–88.

Selected Biographies

Fosdick, Harry Emerson. *For the Living of These Days*. New York: Harper & Row,
    1956.
Miller, Robert Moats. *Harry Emerson Fosdick*. New York: Oxford University Press,
    1985.

CHRONOLOGY OF MAJOR SPEECHES

See "Research Collections and Collected Speeches" for source codes.

"Shall the Fundamentalists Win?" New York City, New York, May 21, 1922; *SAH*, pp. 338–48.

"A Christian Conscience about War," Geneva, Switzerland, September 13, 1925; *APA*, pp. 274–82.

"My Account with the Unknown Soldier," New York City, New York, May 7, 1934; *SVL*, pp. 343–52.

"The Church Must Go beyond Modernism," New York City, November 3, 1935; *SAH*, pp. 370–77.

BETTY FRIEDAN
(1921–   ), women's movement activist

———————————————————————————————————— KAREN A. FOSS

Betty Friedan once mentioned that men are reluctant to ask her to dance at parties; they think of her as a monument in the women's movement, and as she put it, "Who wants to dance with a monument?" *Monumental* is indeed a good word to use to describe Betty Friedan's contributions to contemporary feminism. Her book, *The Feminine Mystique* (1963), has been called the book that ignited contemporary feminism, and it clearly catapulted Friedan into the forefront of the women's movement.

Friedan founded and served as first president of the National Organization for Women (NOW) in 1966 and proposed and organized the successful Women's Strike for Equality, held on August 26, 1970, to celebrate the fiftieth anniversary of women's suffrage. In addition, she helped plan an intersession course on women at Cornell University, which became the model for women's studies programs across the country; she was a founding member of the National Abortion Rights Action League (NARAL) and the National Women's Political Caucus (NWPC), designed to support the candidacies of women for political office; and she helped found the First Women's Bank and Trust Company.

Friedan continues her commitment to the women's movement through teaching, lecturing, lobbying, and writing. She has served as a visiting professor at several universities, including Temple and Yale, while continuing to lecture on feminism in the United States and abroad. She has published two additional books about the women's movement. *It Changed My Life* (1976) recounts Friedan's personal journey through the women's movement; *The Second Stage* (1981) suggests new directions for the women's movement. She currently is at work on a book about aging, *The Fountain of Age*.

FRIEDAN AS SPOKESPERSON FOR THE WOMEN'S MOVEMENT

Although the contemporary women's movement has sought to avoid hierarchical patterns of leadership, Friedan clearly has played a leadership role. Her involvement can be attributed in part to forces of history but also to her penchant for organizing and to the effectiveness of her discourse. In an article in the *New York Times Magazine* in 1970, she described her role this way: "I wouldn't say that I started the movement; it surely is a product of historical forces, but if Betty Friedan weren't alive, she'd have to be invented to see the movement through."

Friedan's role in the movement began with *The Feminine Mystique*, in which she argued that women have bought into a "feminine mystique" in which "the highest value and the only commitment for women is the fulfillment of their own femininity" in the roles of wife and mother. The popularity of *The Feminine Mystique* was in part a matter of timing: it captured and helped crystallize the discontent that was increasingly apparent among women. Its success brought with it numerous requests for Friedan to speak on women's issues, which in turn put her in touch with large audiences of women and confirmed her claims about the prevalence of the feminine mystique. She discovered, both in the interaction with her speaking audiences and in the thousands of letters she received in response to *The Feminine Mystique*, a sense of expectancy about the future; many women believed she ought to start an organization for women that could begin to remedy women's unequal status in society. NOW, founded in 1966, was the organization for which women had been waiting, and it launched Friedan's role as an organizer in the movement.

Because of Friedan's early and ongoing involvement with the women's movement, her discourse serves as an indicator of some of the major concerns associated with the resurgence of feminism. She dealt with such issues as the equal rights amendment, abortion, divorce, and the nature and goals of the movement itself. Two rhetorical strategies—identification and redefinition—are prominent in Friedan's discourse and suggest her general approach to issues across the movement.

Identification, the process of establishing common ground and a sense of shared identity among members of a group, is crucial to the success of a social movement. Establishing such a collective identity, however, was especially difficult for the women's movement, since women typically had negative self-concepts and often were unable to see themselves as agents of change and also grew up learning to compete rather than to cooperate with one another. Friedan's efforts to create identification among women are especially strong in *The Feminine Mystique*. She devoted a considerable portion of the book to demonstrating, by reference to numerous women with whom she spoke personally, that large numbers of women unknowingly experienced "the problem that has no name." Showing that others shared the frustrations of the housewife role was a first step toward the creation of a group identity.

Friedan, however, did not stop with pointing out that many women experience difficulties with women's roles. She strengthened the sense of identification among her readers by describing the symptoms of the feminine mystique— nervousness, boredom, and being frantically busy around the house—which many readers could recognize and with which they could identify. She also set up scapegoats, including Freudian psychology and advertising, that she saw as largely to blame for the feminine mystique. The naming of an enemy or scapegoat is another way of building group cohesion because it promotes a joining together against that enemy.

Friedan further developed the theme of women's collective identity in her subsequent speeches and writings. In "Crisis in Women's Identity," delivered the year after *The Feminine Mystique* was published, she continued to emphasize women's power, asserting, "We do not know how strong we could be if we affirmed ourselves as women and joined together, instead of each woman feeling freakish and isolated." In "Tokenism," she focused on how women must assume responsibility for self-definition and how the differences between women and men will not be known "until women have begun to spell their own names." In calling for a nationwide strike to celebrate the anniversary of women's suffrage, Friedan took yet another approach to creating women's identity: a reference to the slogan "Sisterhood Is Powerful." Popular from the beginning of the movement, it essentially is an oxymoron because it captures the seemingly contradictory notions of women and group action. By using this phrase, Friedan reminded her audience of the power they have in collective action and of the fact that this phase of the movement now has a shared history of several years. At the conclusion of the strike, too, Friedan's remarks appropriately summarized the evolution of the process of women's emerging identity: "We faced the enemy and the enemy was us, was our own lack of self-confidence."

One finds the biggest shift in Friedan's use of the strategy of identification in *The Second Stage*, in which she moved from a focus on identification among women to a focus on identification between women and two additional groups—men and the family. She argued that identification with these groups is the bridge to a new vision of society in which the family is the new frontier and men are involved in a "quiet movement" that eventually will converge with women's struggle.

Friedan makes extensive use of the strategy of redefinition to complement her focus on identification. While identification fosters a sense of identity and power among women as a group, redefinition functions largely in Friedan's discourse to provide a more positive and credible image for the women's movement in society at large. Friedan frequently takes concepts associated with the movement that have come to have negative connotations and posits more positive and accurate ways of looking at these concepts. The phrase *sexual revolution* is one to which Friedan returns repeatedly throughout her speeches. In "Tokenism," Friedan broadened the definition of sexual revolution; for her, it did not mean "when and with whom we go to bed" but the "actual relationships between the two sexes." When addressing the organizational meeting of the National Abortion Rights Action League, she again redefined the notion of sexual liberation by arguing that "sex will only be liberated . . . when women become active self-determining people."

Another area in which Friedan continually confronts and redefines common misconceptions of the movement is in regard to men. She makes an effort not to exclude men from the movement, preferring to see feminism as a movement for human liberation. In "Crisis in Women's Identity" in 1964, she discussed how men are not as resistant to the movement as many might believe—that some men "do have a full regard for their wives as human beings." Her speech as

NOW president was even more explicit about the need to consider men as "fellow victims" of the "bind of half-equality we are in now." Even at the NOW Marriage and Divorce conference, at which discussions of the inequalities of marriage, divorce, and custody laws provoked considerable hostility toward men, Friedan made a concerted effort to avoid naming men as the enemy, declaring, "It isn't women against men." Her most complete statement of men's role in the movement, however, is found in *The Second Stage*, in which she suggested that men, not women, may be "at the cutting edge of the second stage." For Friedan, then, redefinition served to create an image of the women's movement as a positive, all-encompassing force for social change. She used redefinition to free the movement from the images of sexually liberated, man-hating women and to substitute the image of a serious movement for productive social change.

Friedan's use of the strategies of identification and redefinition is reinforced by certain stylistic strategies. She bolsters identification—for example, by frequent use of the word *we* to convey a personal identification with all women in the movement. She alludes to her own experiences as a housewife and mother and to her own divorce to show that she also was caught up in the "feminine mystique." Such devices not only helped create a sense of community but gave Friedan considerable credibility within the women's movement as well.

A major stylistic device Friedan uses to enhance her redefinitional strategy is antithesis. She frequently places a traditional notion of society side by side with the perspective offered by the women's movement. Some of the issues she more frequently places in such antithetical constructions include power, the role of men in the movement, and misconceptions about the women's movement. "Crisis in Women's Identity" provides a typical example of both her use of the collective *we* and of antithesis: "We must all say yes to ourselves as women, and no to that outworn, obsolete image, the feminine mystique." Friedan's stylistic strategies, then, encourage group identification and invite the audience to share actively in the process of redefining a range of social issues.

Despite the long-ranging impact of Friedan's discourse on the women's movement, her involvement with feminism has not been free from conflict. A major confrontation occurred over the relationship between lesbianism and feminism and was one of the reasons Friedan stepped down as NOW president in 1970. Friedan believed that if the movement made lesbianism a focus, it would alienate women who had begun to identify with feminism but still feared ridicule from association with it. In addition, the publication of *The Second Stage* also brought a wave of criticism because of Friedan's wish to redefine the movement as one in which men and the family—not only women—would play the crucial roles.

Overall, Betty Friedan's discourse continues to have an enormous impact on the women's movement. It has been a unifying force simply by virtue of her continuous involvement with contemporary feminism since its inception. Furthermore, Friedan consistently has articulated a position of moderation, a stance that has provided the movement with a core set of beliefs with wide appeal and considerable credibility. Her discourse, in a sense, weaves a consistent thread through the movement, giving it structure and direction. Friedan, reflecting on her role in the movement in an article in 1970 in the *New York Times Magazine*, offers an apt summary: "If anything were to be said about me when the history of the movement is written, I'd like it to read, " 'She was the one who said women were people, she organized them and taught them to spell their own names.' "

INFORMATION SOURCES

Research Collections and Collected Speeches

The Schlesinger Library, Radcliffe College, Cambridge, Massachusetts, contains Friedan's papers from about 1940 to 1976. The collection, consisting of file boxes and tapes, is uncataloged, with limited access allowed.

Friedan, Betty. *It Changed My Life: Writings on the Women's Movement.*   ICML
    New York: Random House, 1976.
Kennedy, Patricia, and O'Shields, Gloria Hartmann. *We Shall Be Heard:*   WSBH
    Women Speakers in America, 1828-Present. Dubuque: Kendall/Hunt,
    1983.

Selected Critical Studies

Avalos, Elizabeth Riley. "Concepts of *Power* in Betty Friedan's Rhetoric: An Application
    of Burke's Cluster-Agon Method." Ph.D. dissertation, University of Denver,
    1983.
Dijkstra, Sandra. "Simone de Beauvoir and Betty Friedan: The Politics of Omission."
    Feminist Studies 6 (1980): 290–303.
Fargo, Sondra. "The New Feminism: Madame Bovary Goes Professional." *Tri-Quarterly*
    3 (1965): 180–88.
Foss, Karen A. "Identification Strategies in Betty Friedan's Discourse." Paper presented
    at the annual meeting of the Western Speech Communication Association, Al-
    buquerque, New Mexico, 1983.
Foss, Sonja K. "Betty Friedan's Changing Rhetoric: A New Feminist Vision?" Paper
    presented at the annual meeting of the Western Speech Communication Associ-
    ation, Albuquerque, New Mexico, 1983.

Selected Biographies and Works

French, Marilyn. "The Emancipation of Betty Friedan." *Esquire* (December 1983): 510–
    18.
Friedan, Betty. *It Changed My Life.* New York: Random House, 1976.
———. *The Feminine Mystique.* New York: W. W. Norton, 1963.
———. *The Second Stage.* New York: Summit, 1981.
Gilbert, Lynn, and Moore, Gaylen. *Particular Passions: Talks with Women Who Have
    Shaped Our Times.* New York: Clarkson N. Potter, 1981.
Wilkes, Paul. "Mother Superior to Women's Lib." *New York Times Magazine*, November
    29, 1970, p. 27.

CHRONOLOGY OF MAJOR SPEECHES

See "Research Collections and Collected Speeches" for source codes.

"The Crisis in Women's Identity," San Francisco, 1964; *ICML*, pp. 93–105; *WSBH*, pp. 316–25.

"Tokenism and the Pseudo-Radical Cop-Out: Ideological Traps for New Feminists to Avoid," Ithaca, New York, January 1969; *ICML*, pp. 159–65.

"Abortion: A Woman's Civil Right," Chicago, February 14, 1969; *ICML*, pp. 170–76.

"Call to Women's Strike for Equality," Chicago, March 20, 1970; *ICML*, pp. 192–202.

Strike day, New York City, August 26, 1970; *ICML*, pp. 203–06.

"The Next Step," opening remarks to the organizing conference of the National Women's Political Caucus, Washington, D.C., June 10, 1971; *ICML*, pp. 224–29.

"The Crisis of Divorce," NOW Marriage and Divorce Conference, January 1974; *ICML*, pp. 416–22.

JAMES WILLIAM FULBRIGHT
(1905–   ), U.S. senator from Arkansas

——————————————————— RICHARD E. BAILEY

James William Fulbright was one of the twentieth-century's leading orators. He attended the University of Arkansas at Fayetteville and in 1924 graduated with honors from the College of Arts and Sciences. He participated actively in campus life, particularly in the Free Speech Club and the Literary Society.

He received a Rhodes scholarship and left for England in 1925 to attend Pembroke College, Oxford, where he earned the Bachelor of Arts and the Master of Arts degrees. More significant perhaps than his academic career was the year he spent studying German at the University of Vienna, where he became acquainted with M. S. Fodor. Fodor, a newspaper correspondent, made a grand tour with Fulbright. "From then on," E. W. Kenworthy later observed, Fulbright "was never to be rid of the obsession that knowledge is the key to understanding and that understanding is the key to the successful conduct of foreign affairs." Returning to the United States in 1929, Fulbright earned a law degree from George Washington University and in 1936 accepted a position as a part-time lecturer in law at the University of Arkansas. Three years later he became president of the University and served in that position until 1941.

Fulbright entered politics in 1942 when he ran for the seat in the U.S. House of Representatives vacated by Clyde Ellis. For that campaign he formed an organization that arranged engagements for him in every county in his district. His campaign strategy consisted of delivering a brief lecture, followed by a question and answer period. He did not try to entertain his audiences but analyzed them carefully and spoke directly to their needs and interests. He used that format and approach throughout his political career. He won the congressional seat in the election that followed and after a successful bid for a seat in the U.S. Senate was sworn in as junior senator from Arkansas on January 3, 1945.

Fulbright's career in public office extended over a quarter of a century. Those interested in his rhetoric will remember him for three major contributions: his sponsorship of the Fulbright Resolution, which helped generate support for establishing the United Nations at the end of World War II; his creation of the Fulbright Scholarship Program which provided monies for the largest exchange in history of scholars in all fields from the nations of the world; and his leadership as chair of the Senate Foreign Relations Committee. An examination of these contributions led Tristram Coffin to describe him as a "public philospher."

FULBRIGHT AS A PUBLIC PHILOSOPHER

Two orientations molded Fulbright's political oratory. First, he believed that the public welfare is a politician's primary concern. Second, he considered education the primary means a nation has for realizing its values in the lives of its citizens and for securing peace among nations. These ideals guided him as chair of the Senate Foreign Relations Committee.

Fulbright maintained that he and his colleagues in the Senate, as well as those in the executive branch, seldom disagreed on the ends they sought in fulfilling the responsibilities of their respective offices. Disagreements among them usually centered on conflicts about the means for securing the public welfare. Upon such matters equally honorable people might find themselves in disagreement. He was convinced that these kinds of differences should be resolved through a process of education.

Fulbright believed that education as a rational search for knowledge may lead to an understanding of why people disagree. The twin processes of education and understanding equip politicians to make wise choices for the nation. He was convinced that a search for the truth required thoroughly examining the facts of the matter at issue; identifying the objectives sought; establishing criteria that any policy adopted must meet; and applying these criteria to the solutions proposed by the adversaries. Such a free exchange of ideas could generate accurate and full information about the issues that separated discussants, enabling them to make wise decisions. He also recognized that sometimes a search for the truth would fail to achieve consensus among the parties.

Fulbright addressed this problem in his speech "Old Myths and New Realities," delivered in the Senate on March 25, 1964. He acknowledged the divergences between the world as different people perceive it and the world as it is. If perceptions were reasonably close to objective reality, it would be possible for people to act upon problems rationally. "But when perceptions fail to keep pace with events," he observed, "the gap between fact and perception becomes a chasm and actions become irrational."

In Fulbright's view the process of understanding begins when the parties in a dispute reveal the assumptions in which their individual perspectives are rooted. He believed one needs to identify the tacit assumptions that underlie disagreements and influence what each party will accept as valid argumentation. In this way, discussants become aware of their biases. The second step requires disputants to adopt the perspectives of their adversaries. For fullest understanding, discussants must examine each others' assumptions and evaluate the evidence, supporting them to see if the assumptions correspond with objective reality.

As a philosopher, Fulbright revealed the premises of his political perspectives in private conversation, Senate hearings, and public speeches. To understand his rhetoric, one must first recognize the leading ideas in Fulbright's universe of discourse. First, he believed that nations are primarily organizations established by their constituents for the purpose of creating a society in which people can pursue excellence within secure national boundaries. Second, he maintained that as nations become powers, they tend to abandon the tasks of building societies and to take on the tasks of enlarging their territories and enhancing their national glory. Having become powers, they manifest arrogance in their relations with others, overextend themselves in their aggressive conquests or in the well-intentioned commitments of their resources to underdeveloped nations, and engage in wars that become unlimited in their scope and use of force. Third, Fulbright believed that nationalism is the most powerful force that divides nations in the contemporary world. It has armed nations with weapons capable of destroying the world and has become a divisive influence at a time when technology has made the world a single community. Fulbright also believed that Soviet rhetoric and communism are offshoots of nationalism. The United States, he asserted, should respond appropriately whenever the Soviets actually threaten U.S. security but take less seriously ideological statements designed primarily to influence Russians. The most critical of Fulbright's leading ideas was his belief that since all nations that become powers engage in all-out wars, the greatest dangers confronting humans in the twentieth century are threats to their survival. Since the United States cannot alter the nature of nationalism and since it does not have the power to impose its will on all other nations, the best it can do is to practice the politics of survival. For Fulbright, that meant the United States should avoid actions that could escalate from small conflicts to enlarged wars with the danger of a nuclear exchange.

Fulbright suggested in "The Arrogance of Power," on May 5, 1966, "that nations should engage in an intensive study of the causes of war and their elimination. That study should begin with an examination of the attitudes of our ancestors in an effort to identify the influences that have led nations toward the disastrous conflicts that have marred human history and to search for those factors whose cultivation would assist nations to become societies instead of powers." This new knowledge, as Fulbright conceived it, is the preferred means for a democracy to guarantee security. In sum, Fulbright saw education as essentially a philosophical task—the pursuit of truth in the political arena.

Education for political action began for Fulbright with efforts to acquire knowledge, understanding, and personal wisdom through readings and interviews with those who possess expert knowledge. These included his colleagues on the Senate Foreign Relations Committee when an issue fell within that committee's responsibilities. On such occasions, readings and conversations were often supplemented with hearings. These hearings were not partisan reviews of the perspective Fulbright personally favored. Rather, they brought the leading experts on a dispute to that setting for an open discussion with the members of the committee, a discussion Fulbright hoped would be an educational experience for all involved. His hearings on China, for example, created a forum for the exchange of information and perspectives and their examination by foreign affairs specialists, politicans, and scholars that led to a new appreciation for China and its role in the modern world.

Philosophic discourse has its limitations, and Fulbright recognized that issues exist that divide people and that the more clearly the disputants understand the views held by their antagonists, the more certain and open their conflicts become. On such issues Fulbright's efforts ceased to be objective searches for the truth about a matter and became full-fledged attempts at political persuasion. Fulbright's books—*Prospects for the West, Old Myths and New Realities*, and *The Arrogance of Power*—are persuasive discussions of issues.

Fulbright's speaking on the Vietnam War was the most noteworthy example of the campaign nature of his persuasive endeavors. In "The Higher Patriotism," on April 21, 1966, he noted that he had scheduled the Vietnam hearings as an exercise in public education. The televised hearings were a conscious attempt to exert rhetorical influence on the executive. These were followed by "The Arrogance of Power" speeches of April 21, 1966, April 28, 1966, and May 5, 1966, whose immediate audiences were the student body of the Johns Hopkins School of Advanced International Studies. Fulbright wrote magazine articles, made radio and television appearances, and published the speeches in book form. He designed the messages to educate the constituents of his colleagues and the executive and thus influence their decision-making.

The strength of Fulbright's persuasive messages grew from his ability at presenting perspectives and marshaling evidence and arguments to support his contentions. He oriented his speaking around the leading ideas that constituted the subject matter of his philosophic discussions. His question to his staff and speech writers remained always: "Do we know this statement is a fact?" His central concern in his public discourses, as in private discussion, was the truth-fulness of matters involving the public welfare. He demonstrated the most skill in enthymematic reasoning from ethical and logical materials. Recognizing that all politicians espouse the safety of the nation and the happiness of its people as their common end, Fulbright attempted to persuade his audiences by demonstrating his expertise on the subjects he addressed. The erudition Fulbright exhibited in his speaking made his listeners trust him as a person and trust what he said. "The Arrogance of Power," for example, contained twenty-seven footnotes. He frequently wove the sources of his information into the text of the speech. He was also skillful in demonstrating the virtues of wisdom, prudence, magnificence, and magnanimity in his speaking. He most frequently utilized argument from nature, definition, analogy, example, and authority. He used categorical, alternative, and disjunctive modes of reasoning with equal skill. The dominantly intellectual orientation of his speeches gave them an educational quality. He instructed his audiences about issues, introduced them to his way of looking at problems, and gave them evidence and arguments that supported the legitimacy of his perspective. In addition, Fulbright welcomed an intellectual appraisal of his messages and sought to include question and answer periods at the conclusion of his addresses. In sum, he fashioned his oratory to add to his auditors' knowledge and give them an understanding of the matters at issue. He sought to affect their learning and ultimately their behavior through philosophic discourse adapted to a general audience. His objectives and goals remained the same in his public discourse as in his private discussion. He adjusted only the mode of delivery and the means of transmission to meet different situations and audiences.

Although Fulbright's speeches were not predominantly appeals to his auditors' emotions, they were designed to engage his listeners' feelings. Because his speeches dealt with values essential to the nation's security and happiness, they invariably aroused the emotions of their audiences. "The Arrogance of Power" speeches not only presented his "basic views on politics" and his perception of man's "deeply flawed nature," as Eugene Brown suggests, but also illustrated Fulbright's appeals to the pathos of his audiences. Fulbright aroused fear by showing that the "arrogance of power" tends to lead nations to overextend themselves in ways that lead to their eventual downfall; he aroused anger by illustrating that nations that have become powers forsake their natural role of serving the needs of their people and require their citizens to die for such abstractions as "national pride"; and he aroused shame by showing that the United States had exploited weaker nations while rationalizing its thirst for conquest with high ideals. "Not once," Fulbright noted in "The Arrogance of Power," "has the United States regarded itself as intervening in a Latin American country for selfish or unworthy motives—a view not necessarily shared by the beneficiaries." Fulbright tended to avoid highly emotional appeals, and "The Arrogance of Power" speeches illustrated his relative uncertainty in this area. The powerful emotions he excited in those speeches tended to work against his long-range goals. Their pathetic appeals were relatively uncharacteristic of his oratory. It was the rhetorical technique he was least skillful in using.

Nevertheless, the titles of his major addresses—"Prospects of the West," "Old Myths and New Realities," and "The Arrogance of Power"—demonstrate that Fulbright could select speech titles that succeeded in arousing hope, challenge, and fear. They would not have achieved their successes if their themes had not been embedded in the American value system. Fulbright's preference for the problem-solution method of speech organization and a plain style of delivery reflect the objective nature of his approach to communication about political matters. He often read his speeches from prepared manuscripts. He engaged in little physical movement but varied the pitch, rate, and volume of his delivery. Finally, he characteristically underplayed vocally the emotional impact his words conveyed. Following the advice Aristotle gives in the *Rhetoric*, when Fulbright delivered a sentence charged with pathetic potential, he did so with little visible or audible emotion. He was consistently more interested in getting his auditors to think with him than he was in bringing them to emotionally based decisions.

This observation is reinforced by an assessment of his method of speech preparation. Seth Tillman, one of his later speech writers, noted that Fulbright, after accepting a speaking engagement, discussed with him pertinent facts of time, place, occasion, and audience. Later, after a review of possible topics and themes, they agreed on the general nature of the address and some of the specific ideas that would be included. Tillman provided a draft, which Fulbright read, questioned, corrected, and marked for changes. Tillman then wrote a second draft and submitted it to other members of Fulbright's staff for comment. The staff members did not initial their contributions. Tillman prepared a final draft based on the information he received in this process. Fulbright frequently deviated from the exact words in the manuscript in the act of delivery and began his speeches with extempore remarks oriented to the specific interests of the audience.

In conclusion, a rhetorical assessment of Fulbright's speaking shows that he believed that effective communication is a matter of education—that it involves adding to his auditors' knowledge and helping them to understand the issues. His goals, objectives, and methods were always much the same, regardless of the audience or situation. His oratory was grounded in the search for the truth about the topics he discussed. He demonstrated superior rhetorical skills in his use of ethical and logical appeals. He excelled in stylistic areas but was less certain in the use of pathetic appeals and delivery. The dominantly educational nature of his approach to the communication of political problems led him to engage his audiences intellectually rather than emotionally.

INFORMATION SOURCES

Research Collections and Collected Speeches

The best source of materials for Fulbright is in the combined libraries at Fayetteville, Arkansas; Pine Bluff, Arkansas; and Little Rock, Arkansas. The Ozark Regional Library, Fayetteville, has the most comprehensive collection of Fulbright materials at one site.

Congressional Record.   *CR*

Selected Critical Studies

Bailey, Richard E. "A Rhetorical Analysis of James William Fulbright's Speaking on 'The Arrogance of Power,' " Ph.D. dissertation, Ohio State University, 1968.

————. "Fulbright's Universe of Discourse." *Southern Speech Communication Journal* 36 (Fall 1970): 33–42.

Brower, Brock. "The Roots of the Arkansas Questioner." *Life*, May 13, 1966, pp. 92–117.

Downs, Calvin Wharton. "A Thematic Analysis of Speeches on Foreign Policy of Senator J. W. Fulbright." Ph.D. dissertation, Michigan State University, 1963.

Hyman, Sydney. "The Advice and Consent of J. W. Fulbright." *Reporter*, September 17, 1959, pp. 23–25.

Kalb, Marvin. "Doves, Hawks and Flutters on the Foreign Relations Committee." *New York Times Magazine*, March 9, 1967, pp. 56–82.

Kenworthy, E. W. "The Fulbright Idea of Foreign Policy." *New York Times Magazine*, May 19, 1959, pp. 10, 74, 76, 78.

————. "Fulbright Becomes a National Issue." *New York Times Magazine*, October 1, 1961, pp. 21, 89, 92, 96–97.

McCord, Robert. "Bill Fulbright at Home." *Arkansas Democrat Magazine*, October 2, 1955, pp. 1–4.

Oberdorfer, Don. "Common Noun Spelled F-u-l-b-r-i-g-h-t." *New York Times Magazine*, April 4, 1965, pp. 79–80.

Seib, C. B., and Otten, A. I. "Fulbright: Arkansas Paradox." *Harpers Magazine* (June 1956): 60–66.

"Senator Fulbright." *New Yorker*, May 10, 1958, pp. 31–32.

Selected Biographies

Brown, Eugene. *J. William Fulbright: Advice and Dissent*. Iowa City: University of Iowa Press, 1985.

Coffin, Tristram. *Senator Fulbright: Portrait of a Public Philospher*. New York: E. P. Dutton, 1966.

Fulbright, James William. *The Arrogance of Power*. New York: Vintage Books, 1966.

————. *Old Myths and New Realities*. New York: Vintage Books, 1964.

————. *Prospects for the West*. Cambridge: Harvard University Press, 1963.

Meyer, Karl E., ed. *Fulbright of Arkansas: The Public Positions of a Private Thinker*. Washington, D.C.: Robert B. Luce, 1963.

CHRONOLOGY OF MAJOR SPEECHES

See "Research Collections and Collected Speeches" for source codes.

"The American Agenda," Medford, Massachusetts, May 1, 1963; *Vital Speeches of the Day*, June 15, 1963, pp. 520–26.

"The American Character," Washington, D.C., December 5, 1963; *CR*, December 6, 1963, pp. 23726–28.

"Old Myths and New Realities," Washington, D.C., March 25, 1964; *CR*, March 25, 1964, pp. 6227–32.

"The Cold War," Durham, North Carolina, April 5, 1964; *CR*, April 17, 1964, pp. 7093–97.

"Higher Education," Chicago, March 14, 1966; *CR*, March 29, 1966, pp. 6438–40.

"The Higher Patriotism," Washington, D.C., April 21, 1966; *CR*, April 25, 1966, pp. 8869–74.

"Revolution Abroad," Washington, D.C., April 27, 1966; *CR*, April 28, 1966, pp. 9325–30.

"The Arrogance of Power," Washington, D.C., May 5, 1966; *CR*, May 17, 1966, pp. 10805–10.

MARCUS GARVEY
(1887–1940), black nationalist leader

DOROTHY L. PENNINGTON

Marcus Garvey was born in St. Ann's Bay, Jamaica, in the West Indies, in 1887. During his youth, he traveled and served as an apprentice to a master printer where he learned the skills in writing and expression that were to serve him well later. He competed in an elocution contest in 1910, representing the parish of St. Ann.

Jamaica had been a British possession, and its inhabitants had suffered at the hand of colonial domination. Blacks were not given their full rights and found discrimination and oppression common. As Garvey traveled throughout the Caribbean and Latin America, he observed that blacks in those other places suffered a similar plight. He spent time in England observing the conditions of blacks there and further developing his skills as a journalist.

In the meantime, he had heard of the work of the industrial educator, Booker T. Washington, and his self-help philosophy at Tuskegee school in Alabama. Impressed with these ideas, Garvey corresponded with Washington about a future trip to the United States and to Tuskegee. Garvey did not meet Washington, however, for he died in 1915, one year before Garvey arrived in the United States.

Garvey found blacks in the United States frustrated and disappointed, especially after World War I when black veterans discovered that their military service entitled them to no more equality than they had had as civilians before the war. It was a situation upon which Garvey would capitalize.

MARCUS GARVEY AS A BLACK NATIONALIST LEADER

Along with his public speaking, Garvey's influence was spread through his writing as a journalist. He published the *Black Man*, a monthly magazine, and wrote pamphlets and philosophical papers. Garvey appealed to blacks in North America because of his message, his style, and his charisma. Specifically he provided the concept of an alternative to living in the United States. Although the alternative was never realized, the concept provided hope. The concept he provided was Africa and nationhood. "Africa for the Africans, At Home and Abroad," became the theme around which Garvey rallied blacks. Through the Universal Negro Improvement Association, he provided a program that addressed the pressing needs of blacks during the 1920s: for equality, self-esteem, and a sense of hope.

Garvey effectively timed his message and organization. The success of his appeal in the United States was due to several factors. First, the idea of emigration to Africa by blacks was not new. The free black New Englander Paul Cuffe had overseen the emigration of a group of blacks to Sierra Leone in 1812; Edward Blyden, a West Indian who came to the United States, had emigrated to Liberia in 1851; Martin Delany had led an expedition of blacks to the Niger area of West Africa in 1859; and the famous leader and orator Henry McNeal Turner had proffered the idea of "back to Africa" but with less appeal. But Turner and the others were ahead of their time and were unable to stimulate mass enthusiasm with their idea. Garvey had the advantage of speaking at the propitious historical time. Second, Garvey did not develop this idea exclusively for blacks in the United States. His previous travel in the Caribbean, Latin America, and England had shown him that blacks encountered discrimination and maltreatment wherever they lived outside of Africa. In Garvey's view, peoples of the African diaspora were displaced Africans who shared with Africans on the continent a common family stock. This view contributed to his conclusion about what was required for peoples of African descent to obtain true equality.

Garvey's message had two major themes: the need of blacks for a nation of their own (black nationalism) and the need of blacks for self-esteem and recognition. He employed several rhetorical devices in conveying this message: the syllogism, analogy, metaphor, the personal rhetorical question, pathos, argument from circumstance, invoking the name of God, and audience adaptation, referred to in the rhetoric of black Americans as improvisation. These devices were aided by his persona as the black Moses.

In response to his perception of the need for blacks to be rid of their subservient role, which he had observed in various parts of the world, Garvey advocated black nationalism. First, he based his argument on a rather convincing syllogism: (a) that the United States and other industrialized countries are and would continue to operate on the basis of competition wherein the strongest race would survive, (b) that blacks were the weakest race in these countries, and (c) therefore blacks would not survive. Garvey addressed this theme in several speeches, one of which was the Fourth International Convention speech, given in New York City in 1924: "If we do not organize as a people and face the world with a program of African nationalism, our days in civilization are numbered, and it will be only a question of time when the Negro will be completely and complacently dead." In "God and Man," a speech he gave in 1929, Garvey expressed the same sentiment. It provides a clear example of how he used personal emotional appeal and metaphor:

The man with superior intelligence will survive in this world where intelligence will dominate the affairs of men. And we are in the terrible struggle toward the end. We are fighting like animals. We have reduced all other animals, whose strength could not measure up to the superior intelligence of man. So we are engaged in the battle of man, in the battle of nations. . . . Oh! if I could touch the heart of the Negro—of every black man, woman, and child, to realize how much of a responsibility falls upon your shoulders to make the world what it ought to be for yourselves, for your children, posterity, and your race.

In this example, the metaphor of war provided a vivid way for Garvey's audience to view their struggle, and because of the importance of family in the black culture, Garvey skillfully employed pathos to suggest the effects of what one does on one's children and future generations.

Second, Garvey advanced the theme of nationalism by using analogy. Because other races were associated with their native homeland and system of government, Garvey believed that blacks should return to Africa, their ancestral home. In the Fourth International Convention speech he said, "We want a nationality similar to that of the English, the French, the Italian, the German, to that of the White American, to that of the yellow Japanese; we want nationality and government." Garvey reasoned therefore that it would be through nationhood and self-government that blacks would regain their self-identity and sense of belonging. This was, for Garvey, a necessary condition for achieving equality.

What Garvey thought would be necessary for blacks to achieve self-esteem was the second theme. The treatment accorded blacks had led to their sense of despair and diminishment. They were the dispossessed, the disenfranchised, the despised. Garvey believed, however, that the responsibility for changing this condition rested on their shoulders. Blacks, he believed, would be recognized and remembered to the extent that they made contributions analogous to those made by other races—in industry, science, and the professions. Their self-esteem was in their hands. In a speech he gave in Halifax, Canada, "A Straight Talk to the People," Garvey poignantly asked a rhetorical question:

What is the matter with your mind? Are you different from Rockefeller who discovered oil and became the richest man in the world outside of Henry Ford, the poor boy who visualized the use of propelled mechanism and is the richest man in the world today. You are the same soul, then why should God be blamed down here for you when you are no good. . . . How many of you are living up to the dignity of men? . . . Marconi gave us the wireless telegraph. What are you going to give?

By using rhetorical questions, Garvey caused his audience to feel a sense of involvement and responsibility for ameliorating their condition. Although the example of Rockefeller might have been a distant one for his audience, the juxtaposition of the example of Henry Ford facilitated the ability of his audience to identify; most of his hearers could relate to the concept of a poor economic background. Garvey gave a call to action and warned blacks against idleness and self-pity. He presented them with no choice since their survival depended upon their assuming responsibility for their lives. To make this point to his audience on numerous occasions, he used argument from circumstance; that is, he used cause and effect reasoning to try to persuade his audience to accept his course of action on the ground that no alternative was practical or safe. In his

Fourth International Convention speech, Garvey warned, "The Negro is dying out and is going to die faster and more rapidly in the next fifty years than he has in the past. There is only one thing to save the Negro, and that is an immediate realization of his own responsibilities." For Garvey, the only choice for blacks other than that which he prescribed was racial extinction.

In order to reassure his audience that the course of action he prescribed would lead to positive results, Garvey constantly invoked the name of God. In a speech given in Detroit in 1937, he asserted that God would look upon blacks with favor if they were to take charge of changing their conditions and improving their lives. Garvey sanctioned suprarational forces, thus providing spiritual dynamism to the movement. The constant invocation of the name of God appealed to the religious tradition of the black masses and also contributed to Garvey's charisma. Because he possessed charisma, he could employ exhortation, demanding new obligations on the part of his followers. By persuading his followers that he was speaking on the authority revealed to him from God, Garvey assumed the role of an oracle. Psychologically, the recognition Garvey received was enhanced by the personal devotion of his followers as he embodied their hopes and diminished their despair. His charisma as a leader therefore involved an interaction of three components: his ability to articulate clearly the imperative nature of the obligation of blacks, the despair of many blacks who listened to and followed him, and his sanctioning of suprarational forces. The January 15, 1921, issue of the *Cleveland Advocate* attested to Garvey's charismatic qualities. Commenting on a speech he presented in Cleveland, it noted that he had "a wonderful personality and 'bubbles over' with the elements of leadership." The account observed Garvey's "spell-binding oratory" and "evidences of approbation given by the hand-clapping at the meetings." Garvey used a motion metaphor—that of marching—to help portray an image of himself as a leader. He repeated, using parallel structure, the phrase "we shall march out" in the 1922 Principles of the Universal Negro Improvement Association speech.

As an orator, Garvey was skilled at audience adaptation, or improvisation (responding to what is occurring with a given audience at a given time). That he seldom prepared a text in advance attests to his skill in audience adaptation. He often spoke impromptu, gleaning his topic and remarks from something that had occurred during the earlier portion of the program. For example, in speaking before the conference of the Universal Negro Improvement Association in August 1937, Garvey showed how his theme emerged: "I came as usual without a subject, to pick the same from the surroundings, the environment, and I got one from the singing of the hymn 'Faith of our Fathers.' I shall talk to you on that as a theme for my discourse." This type of adaptation allowed Garvey to tap into the main artery of what an audience was thinking and feeling.

Marcus Garvey's use of the rhetorical devices identified here, his charisma, and his audience adaptation skills contributed to his being a great leader and orator during the 1920s and 1930s. His leadership and spell-binding oratory contributed to his persona of black Moses, as one come to lead his people to the promised land.

Because of legal difficulties, Garvey lost some of his hold on leadership in the late 1920s and saw the possibility of a physical return of blacks to Africa become increasingly remote. His oratory reflected a great sense of vision, and through this vision, the hopes of blacks were extended. In a sense, his audience felt an interconnectedness with him rather than the classical separation between speaker and audience.

In one of his last speeches, recorded in written form, he prophetically and strategically involved his audience by using a question as a title: "Can the Negro Find His Place?" By encouraging audience involvement, Garvey followed the tradition of allowing black audiences to participate in the situation with the speaker. Although no audio recordings of Garvey's speeches are available, one can surmise that he and black audiences engaged in "call and response," spontaneous, alternating verbal interaction between the message of the speaker and the ongoing responses of the audience. The speaker interrupts the sequence of the message to allow for feedback from the audience, a device that provides the speaker with an immediate indication of how he or she is faring with the audience.

Although many of his platforms were political, for Garvey, as for many other popular black speakers, his oratory revealed religious, revivalist roots. Often when Garvey spoke to black audiences, the revivalist spirit was underscored by religious singing or some other form of entertainment. An analysis of Garvey as a prototype of black orators illustrates the difficulty of isolating oratory as a separate entity without investigating how it interacts with other parts of the rhetorical situation to produce a total effect. Integral parts of the black rhetorical situation include the message, music or other forms of entertainment, the charisma of the speaker, spontaneous call and response, and the needs of the audience. Garvey understood and managed these components well in making oratory a central part of his appeal as a black nationalist leader.

INFORMATION SOURCES

Research Collections and Collected Speeches

The Arthur L. Schomberg Collection, New York Public Library, New York City, is a good resource for papers, periodicals, and books regarding Marcus Garvey.

Garvey, Marcus. *The Black Man: A Monthly Magazine of Negro Thought*   BM
    and Opinion. Compiled with an introductory essay by Robert A.
    Hill. Millwood, N.Y.: Kraus-Thomson Organization, 1975.
———. *The Marcus Garvey and the Universal Negro Improvement Asso-*   UNIAP
    ciation Papers. Edited by Robert A. Hill. 3 vols. Los Angeles:
    University of California Press, 1975.

————. *Philosophy and Opinions of Marcus Garvey*. Compiled by Amy   *PO*
Jacques Garvey. Totowa, N.J.: Frank Cass and Company, 1967.
————. *Previously Unpublished Material of Marcus Garvey*. Compiled by   *PUM*
G. K. Osei. Philadephia: 3rd Eye Printers, 1983.

Selected Critical Studies

Aron, Burgit. "The Garvey Movement." Master's thesis, Columbia University, 1947.
Marcus Garvey and the Vision of Africa. Edited by John Henrik Clarke, with the assistance
of Amy Jacques Garvey. New York: Vintage, 1974.
Reid, C. H. "Marcus Garvey: A Social Phenomenon." Master's thesis, Northwestern
University, 1928.
Smith, Arthur (Molefi K. Asante). *Rhetoric of Black Revolution*. Boston: Allyn and
Bacon, 1969.

Selected Biographies

Cronon, Edmund D. *Black Moses*. Madison: University of Wisconsin Press, 1955.
Edwards, Adolph. *Marcus Garvey: 1887–1940*. London: New Beacon Publications, 1967.
Fax, Elton. *Garvey: The Story of a Pioneer Black Nationalist*. New York: Dodd, Mead,
1972.
Martin, Tony. *Marcus Garvey, Hero*. Dover, Mass.: Majority Press, 1983.

CHRONOLOGY OF MAJOR SPEECHES

See "Research Collections and Collected Speeches" for Source codes.

"Principles of the Universal Negro Improvement Association." New York City, November 25, 1922; *PO*, pp. 93–100.

At opening of Fourth International Convention of Negro Peoples of the World, New York City, August 1, 1924; *PO*, pp. 101–9.

"God and Man," Edelweiss Park, Jamaica, July 19, 1929; *PUM*, pp. 3–4.

"Faith of Our Fathers," Toronto, Canada, August 29, 1937; *PUM*, pp. 34–39.

Marcus Garvey addressing the people of Detroit, Michigan; *BM*, December 1937, pp. 9–12.

"A Straight Talk to the People," Halifax, Canada; *BM*, March 1938, pp. 8–11.

"Can the Negro Find His Place?" Toronto, Canada, August 14, 1938; *PUM*, pp. 27–34.

BARRY MORRIS GOLDWATER
(1909–   ), U.S. senator from Arizona and presidential candidate
_____ JOHN C. HAMMERBACK and RICHARD J. JENSEN

In 1964 Barry M. Goldwater, senator from Arizona, capitalized on a grass-roots movement to capture the Republican nomination for president of the United States. Unlike most other successful nominees, his climb to popularity and prominence did not result from legislative accomplishment or from the backing of a large political constituency. Denied these traditional paths to power, he relied on rhetorical discourse. His best-selling book, *Conscience of a Conservative* (a compilation of ideas from earlier speeches), a thrice-weekly newspaper column carried by 200 newspapers, and over 200 speeches a year from 1960 to 1964 carried his message to potential followers. Despite his crushing defeat in the presidential election, he retained his popularity in Arizona and has been routinely reelected to the Senate since 1968. He has periodically faded from public view and then regained center stage through newsworthy acts and statements.

During the Watergate crisis, Goldwater criticized the weakened Nixon administration for its lack of decisive action. In an interview in the *Christian Science Monitor* of April 4, 1973, he bluntly proclaimed that the president had to speak out to remove the nation's doubts about Watergate: "There's a smell to it. . . . Let's get rid of the smell." As President Nixon's situation became more precarious, Goldwater was chosen by his Republican colleagues to tell the president that he could expect little or no support from them in any impeachment trial.

In a similar vein, Goldwater vigorously attacked Jerry Falwell and the Moral Majority when Falwell opposed the nomination of Arizonan Sandra Day O'Connor to the Supreme Court. He publicly challenged Falwell's views and read into the *Congressional Record* of September 15, 1981 a speech in which he objected to the New Right's tendency to combine religion and politics. "One of the great strengths of our political system always has been our tendency to keep religious issues in the background. By maintaining the separation of church and state, the United States has avoided the intolerance which has so divided the rest of the world with religious wars." The spokesman for conservatism had become the opponent of elements of the religious New Right.

GOLDWATER AS CONSERVATIVE SPOKESMAN

Throughout his career in local politics in Arizona, as a U.S. senator, and as a presidential candidate, Goldwater's public discourse has been remarkably consistent in tone and content. He has always been candid, even if the result is to bring discomfort to fellow conservatives like Falwell. In his autobiography he assessed this personal trait: "I have achieved [a] certain prominence as a 'shoot-from-the-hip, tell-it-like it is uncompromising public figure.' " But he refused to alter his actions: "I cannot change what I am, nor would I wish to do so. I am quite aware of the risks in speaking frankly and candidly."

The themes of his public discourse have changed little through the years. His most frequent theme, the need to reduce and to localize governmental activities and responsibilities, rests on his belief expressed in *The Conscience of a Conservative* that the Constitution is an "instrument . . . for limiting the functions of government" and that "freedom today—as always—is dependent upon government confinement." In his 1964 acceptance speech he stated: "Those who seek to live your lives for you, to take your liberties in return for relieving you of your responsibilities—those who elevate the state and downgrade the citizen— must see ultimately a world in which earthly power can be substituted for divine will." A second theme, the need to protect private property, sprang from Goldwater's conviction that to attack property rights is to attack freedom. To keep government from hampering business, he advocated abolishing the graduated income tax, liberalizing depreciation allowances, curtailing union power, ending federal wage controls, and selling public works that compete with private ones.

His third major theme is the pressing need to oppose and defeat communism. In his 1964 acceptance speech, he challenged his communist opponents: "The good Lord raised up this mighty republic to be a home for the brave and to flourish as the land of the free—not to stagnate in the swampland of collectivism—not to cringe before the bullying of communism." In order to confront the communists, he advocated a strong military, opposed disarmament, fought diplomatic recognition of and relations with communist countries, and demanded scrutiny of the policies of the United Nations or any other international body he felt undercut a firm anticommunist policy.

Constructing a psychological environment appropriate for accepting his substantive proposals, Goldwater combated contemporary governmental policies, simplified issues and answers, and championed patriotism. To replace the policies he opposed, he provided simple alternatives based on simplified analyses. For example, when analyzing communism, he instructed his audience at Notre Dame University, February 6, 1962 that one must realize that "the Communist respects just one thing, power." To critics who argued that he oversimplified issues, he replied, in a Los Angeles speech on September 16, 1963: "Some people say that I oversimplify complicated issues. They want complexity, I want understanding." Goldwater added a patriotic tone to his message. In a speech in Houston on July 28, 1961 he professed to fear those "influences at work which would like us to believe that patriotism is outdated" and to prefer a "return to those principles of thrift, industry and person-to-person charity which conquered this hostile continent and made America the goal and beacon light for all men.''

These themes and appeals attracted an audience of like-minded individuals who became his followers. In the early 1960s, he gained a large and committed following from young conservatives on college campuses. *Conscience of a Conservative* became a best-seller at college bookstores, and Goldwater was a popular speaker on campuses. His popularity resulted in part from students' dissatisfaction with governmental control over the individual and from their natural inclination to rebel—in this case against the liberalism often espoused by their professors.

Equally dissatisfied were those who demanded simple and immediate answers to the increasingly complex and seemingly unanswerable domestic and international problems of the United States. Political conservatives who generally wanted increased liberty and responsibilities for individuals and consequently less governmental control also found Goldwater's message inspiring.

Goldwater's most dedicated, zealous followers were on the far Right. United in their fear of the expansion of communism after World War II, they attributed many of communism's gains to internal subversion in the United States and strove to restore an earlier America that emphasized religion, patriotism, and other virtues antithetical to communism. Unlike many other politicians, Goldwater refused to condemn the far Right, and they in turn adamantly supported him.

Goldwater's overlapping constituencies formed much of the loose coalition that made him the leader of conservatism in the 1960s. These supporters became the uncommonly hard-working political machine credited for much of his success in winning the crucial California primary against Nelson Rockefeller. Goldwater's advocacy of a point of view representing mainly the right wing of the party, however, made his defeat in 1964 inevitable. His vulnerability stood out indelibly in the most famous lines in his acceptance speech: ''Extremism in defense of liberty is no vice. . . . Moderation in pursuit of justice is no virtue.'' The ensuing avalanche of criticism brought forth far less conciliation and compromise from Goldwater than would be expected of a presidential aspirant. Throughout that campaign, he was depicted as a trigger-happy extremist who might well lead the United States into nuclear war. Even sixteen year later the unrepentant Goldwater told the 1980 Republican Convention: ''So tonight I want to speak about freedom. And let me remind you that extremism in the defense of liberty is no vice.''

Goldwater's substantive themes and psychological appeals emphasized a single pervasive ideal: rugged individualism. With increased liberty and responsibility, individuals, businesses, and communities could solve their own domestic problems. The United States must represent a collective of rugged individuals by deemphasizing international cooperation, discontinuing conciliatory foreign policies, and challenging communism. Further identifying with his ideal, he lauded the wisdom of the pioneer period of the United States and proposed simple programs that seemed more fitting for that time of romanticized self-reliance.

Goldwater personified his message. The descendant of Arizona pioneer merchants who fought Indians and helped civilize the West, he projected the image of a Westerner who was self-sufficient, brave, and persevering. Fitting into the manly mold of his ancestors, he became an explorer, innovative businessman, sports car driver, ham radio operator, jet pilot, and outdoor photographer. Sun, diet, and exercise kept him tanned, trim, and healthy. These characteristics were consciously communicated through his campaign literature, as when he was pictured sitting in the cockpit of a jet aircraft.

Goldwater also made use of his image in his oratory. He sometimes spoke to audiences of his frontier heritage or his adventurous life, as when on May 8, 1961 in Flint, Michigan he described his grandfather's "courage and fortitude" in crossing the Colorado River under attack by Indians or when on another occasion he confided: "As an officer in the Air Force Reserve, I often fly the immense jet bombers of the Strategic Air Command."

He spoke conversationally and gestured sparingly, befitting a natural man. Critics have described him as having an unpolished delivery, but the fact that he has not sought to change his delivery might suggest his belief that it is effective in enhancing his reputation for straightforward honesty. The style of his speeches further communicated his courage and reinforced his public persona. He told Americans "not to cringe before the bully of Communism." He used such colloquial expressions such as "make no bones about it" and "this is hogwash," and completely ad-libbed comments like "poppycock" and "humbug." Such plain speaking supports the image of the rugged individualist, an honest man who says what he believes.

In his autobiography, Goldwater outlined his views on communication: "Purists in the art of communication maintain that the communicator is responsible both for what he says and what his audience believes it heard him say. That requirement places a heavy responsibility on the communicator, suggests the message must be direct, understandable, and unequivocal: no hedging; no qualifications; no use of language susceptible to more than one interpretation." Yet he also revealed that he could be sensitive to occasion and audience: "Most of my speeches are extemporaneous, based on hastily written notes usually confined to the back of dinner menus, envelopes, napkins, and what have you. I try to gauge the interest and temper of my audience and fashion my words accordingly. When I feel a prepared speech is needed, my friend, Tony Smith, who has worked in my office for many, many years as a press representative, helps me to put together the appropriate words."

Barry Goldwater has fashioned a message of rugged individualism through his heritage, life, appearance, and the delivery, style, and content of his public discourse. This potent message identified him with the values, attitudes, beliefs, and desires of four groups of people in the early 1960s and took him to national prominence. Remaining remarkably consistent in rhetorical substance and manner, the senator is ending his long career as a leading conservative. A large part of his rhetorical legacy will be his creation of an audience that has increased in power and size within and beyond the Republican party. By 1980 Goldwater and others on the Right had helped to pave the way for the smashing rhetorical and electoral triumphs of Ronald Reagan, a conservative whose oratory is strikingly similar to that of the overwhelmingly rejected Republican candidate sixteen years earlier.

INFORMATION SOURCES

Research Collections and Collected Speeches

There is no collection of Goldwater's speeches. *Conscience of a Conservative* is a compilation of ideas from his speeches to that time. Excellent sources for his speech texts are *Vital Speeches of the Day* and especially the *Congressional Record*, into which Goldwater inserted many speech texts.

Congressional Record.   CR
Voices of Crisis: Vital Speeches on Contemporary Issues. Edited by Floyd   VOC
      W. Watson. New York: Odyssey Press, 1967.

Selected Critical Studies

Brooks, William D. "A Field Study of the Johnson and Goldwater Campaign Speeches in Pittsburgh." *Southern Speech Communication Journal* 32 (1967): 273–81.
Dell, George W. "Republican Nominee: Barry Goldwater." *Quarterly Journal of Speech* 50 (1964): 339–404.
Hammerback, John C. "Barry Goldwater's Rhetoric of Rugged Individualism." *Quarterly Journal of Speech* 58 (1972): 175–83.
Wrage, Ernest J. "The Little World of Barry Goldwater." *Western Journal of Speech Communication* 27 (1963): 207–15.

Selected Biographies

Bell, Jack. *Mr. Conservative: Barry Goldwater.* Garden City, N.Y.: Doubleday, 1962.
Cook, Fred. *Barry Goldwater: Extremist on the Right.* New York: Grove Press, 1964.
De Toledano, Ralph. *The Winning Side: The Case for Goldwater Republicanism.* New York: McFadden-Bartell, 1964.
Goldwater, Barry, M. *The Conscience of a Conservative.* New York: McFadden, 1960.
———. *Why Not Victory?* New York: McFadden, 1963.
———. *Where I Stand.* New York: McGraw-Hill, 1964.
———. *With No Aplogies.* New York: Morrow, 1979.

Kessell, John Howard. *The Goldwater Coalition: Republican Strategies in 1964*. Indianapolis: Bobbs-Merrill, 1968.

McDowell, Edwin. *Barry Goldwater: Portrait of an Arizonan*. Chicago: H. Regnery, Co., 1964.

Shadegg, Stephen C. *What Happened to Goldwater? The Inside Story of the 1964 Republican Campaign*. New York: Holt, Rinehart, and Winston, 1965.

CHRONOLOGY OF MAJOR SPEECHES

See "Research Collections and Collected Speeches" for source codes.

Speech delivered to Air War College, Maxwell Air Force Base, Montgomery, Alabama, November 14, 1960; *CR*, January 11, 1961, p. 582.

Acceptance speech at the Republican National Convention, San Francisco, 1964; *VOC*, pp. 115–26.

"To Be Conservative," Washington, D.C., September 15, 1981; *CR*, September 15, 1981 pp. 20589–90.

BILLY GRAHAM
(1918–   ), Christian evangelist

HAL W. FULMER

In 1949, William Franklin ("Billy") Graham, Jr., arrived in Los Angeles to preach the Christian message of sin, repentance, and salvation. Since then, Graham has become recognized as one of the world's foremost evangelists, having preached thousands of sermons in the United States and abroad.

Graham attended the fundamentalist Bob Jones College, Tennessee, and the Florida Bible Institute before receiving his bachelor's degree in anthropology from Wheaton College, Illinois. He began preaching while in Florida, often practicing in nearby woods and swamps. He exhibited speech habits that were hardly enviable. His volume and rate were excessive, his pronunciation betrayed his North Carolina background, and his gestures garnered him the title of "the preaching windmill." Graham later recounted: "I had never been trained as a public speaker. I had to learn the best way I knew."

Graham served as an early leader in the Youth for Christ organization in 1947. In late September 1949, he arrived in Los Angeles to lead a three-week crusade. Eight weeks later, still there, Graham was a national celebrity. Thousands attended his nightly sermons with locally and nationally famous converts. Conservative mogul William Randolph Hearst reportedly telegrammed his newspaper editors to "Puff Graham," and Henry Luce, publisher of *Time* and *Life* magazines, provided extensive coverage of the event and the evangelist.

From Los Angeles, Graham took his crusade throughout the United States, went to London in 1954, and eventually brought his warnings of sin to New York City in 1957. In 1950, he began the "Hour of Decision" radio program, broadcasting a weekly sermon into thousands of homes. He was among the first to hold integrated rallies in the Deep South. In 1966, he traveled to Berlin to address the World Congress on Evangelism. In 1969, Graham went to New York City again and received his first extensive television coverage. On July 4, 1970, he was a principal speaker in Washington, D.C., for "Honor America Day." He went to the Soviet Union in 1982, addressing an international clerical group on a solution to the nuclear threat. In 1985, he was again behind the Iron Curtain, traveling in Rumania as the first foreign evangelist to preach there.

GRAHAM AS EVANGELICAL ORATOR

Billy Graham stands as a bridge between the American evangelical tradition of the eighteenth and nineteenth centuries and the electronic church of the late twentieth century. His evangelical heritage includes George Whitefield, Dwight

Moody, Charles Finney, and Billy Sunday. In the age of televised evangelism, Graham is distinctive. He was a successful evangelist prior to the introduction of television; however, his use of the mass media foreshadowed the electronic church popularized by Jerry Falwell, Jimmy Swaggart, and Robert Schuller. A major contribution to evangelism by Graham was his ability to transfer the religious revival setting to the popular media.

Graham adapted his oratory to the political and social context of his era. As he noted in his 1957 opening sermon in New York City, "We look at international relationships tonight and we see a cold war getting hotter; an arms race gathering momentum all over the world. We are living under the shadow of the hydrogen bomb." The central theme of individual repentance as a solution to this chaos never wavers. To the same New York City crowd, he defined his listeners' deficiency: "Sin means that we have come short of the glory of God. . . . And the Bible says the whole world is infected with this disease. . . . We must face it. We've lost God. . . . We've lost our anchorage, we've lost our mooring."

Four distinctive rhetorical elements are evident in virtually all of Graham's sermons. The first is his technique of recasting biblical Scripture into contemporary metaphors. In a 1969 sermon, "The Other Death," Graham preached the importance of Christ's blood sacrifice as the way of redemption: "You know we have blood banks. . . . Well, there's an eternal blood bank, a heavenly blood bank, that we can apply to by faith, and it will take our guilt and sin away." To suggest the fundamentalist belief that Christ's sacrifice is the only entry into heaven, Graham drew upon the forthcoming Apollo 11 moon mission in "Man in Rebellion": "Suppose our men going on Apollo 11 to the moon in July say, 'We're way off course.' And some men down at Mission Control who are broadminded and tolerant say, 'Oh, it's all right. There are many roads that lead to the moon. Just take the one you're on.' " In "The Giants You Face," Graham explained Goliath's challenge to the Israelites to send their champion to face him in terms of a contemporary conflict: "That would be like President Thieu of South Vietnam challenging Ho Chi Minh in North Vietnam to a personal fight. Whoever won the fight would win the war." Such explanations contemporize old, often familiar, stories into current situations and have filled Graham's sermons from the beginning of his evangelical career.

A second aspect of Graham's oratory is the merging of historical biblical texts with contemporary society. For Graham, biblical Scripture, thousands of years old, is relevant to current conditions, problems, and people. In "Come and Know God," Graham explained current crime and violence through its historical precedent: "Where do you think this violence comes from. . . . Let me tell you, there is nothing new about it. Go back to the Garden of Eden. Cain murdered his brother Abel." In "Truth and Freedom," he explained the continuity of the Christian experience, that is, the link between first-century and twentieth-century individuals: "You've got to come to Christ just as people did two thousand years ago if you're going to get to Heaven." In "Two Sets of Eyes," Graham discussed the journeys of Christ, past and present: "You see, Jesus was passing by and right now Jesus is passing by in New York.'' Graham's message is that the problem of sin and the solution of salvation have not changed in two thousand years.

A third constant of Graham's sermons are his sources and supporting materials. The major one is the Protestant Bible, which Graham accepts as divinely inerrant. Again and again, the phrase ''The Bible says'' echoes throughout his oratory. Graham is comfortable with Scripture from both the Old and New Testaments, using verses to point toward a Christian salvation. In a radio sermon entitled, ''Our Bible,'' he concluded, ''The message of Jesus Christ, our Savior, is the story of the Bible—it is the story of salvation; it is the story of the Gospel; it is the story of life, peace, eternity, and heaven.''

Graham also draws on a large number of other sources to increase his own credibility as a speaker and to confirm various scriptural truths. These sources, primarily historical and contemporary figures, suggest a secular justification of Graham's spiritual message. In a 1959 radio sermon, Graham called for a spiritual ''Nonconformity to the World'' and suggested that ''Patrick Henry with his heroic declaration, 'Give me liberty or give me death,' did more for the cause of freedom than a million who were bent on saving their own skins.'' In ''Changing the Tide of History'' in 1966, Graham turned to a popular media figure to accent his point about America's increasing immorality: ''In reviewing the events of the past 20 years, Walter Lippmann, the well-known American columnist, said, 'We have tried so hard, we meant so well, and we have failed so terribly.' ''

In the 1969 New York City crusade, in only ten sermons Graham cited over thirty different secular sources as support for his claims. Among this divergent group were Dwight D. Eisenhower, Martin Luther King, Jr., Arnold Toynbee, Pope Paul, John Kennedy, John Lennon, Leo Tolstoy, the Beatles, Winston Churchill, V. I. Lenin, Earl Warren, and Ian Fleming. This use of secular testimony for Graham's interpretations and applications of Scripture creates an aura of authority for his claims. In an Aristotelian sense, Graham offers the voices of other, well-known individuals to substantiate his arguments.

Graham's sermons are also consistent in theme. The oratory is rooted in humanity's search for relief from its problems, and the evangelist draws his solution from the application of Protestant scripture. He does not shrink from discussing the secular issues of the day but emphasizes that such problems have a common root: the sinfulness of the individual. In a 1967 radio sermon, ''Social Injustice,'' Graham defended his emphasis on spiritual needs rather than social problems: ''I believe in taking a stand on moral, social, and spiritual issues of our day. . . . I have talked on everything from bad housing to highway safety. However, the social issues of our day have not been the main theme of my preaching.'' He discussed the thrust of his sermons in the same broadcast: ''If only we would begin at the root of our problems, which is the disease of human nature that the Bible calls sin!''

According to Graham, even the threat of nuclear holocaust is not merely a political or ideological problem. In a major address in Moscow in 1982, ''The

Christian Faith and Peace in a Nuclear Age,'' Graham suggested, ''The nuclear arms race is primarily a moral and spiritual issue. . . . The possibility of a nuclear war originates in the greed and covetousness of the human heart.''

Graham has faced three significant issues in his evangelical career, and his responses deserve mention. In the midst of the cold war in the 1950s and 1960s, Graham took a strong anticommunist stand. At times, his political red-baiting overshadowed his theological message of sin and redemption. In 1953 to commemorate Labor Day, Graham delivered a radio broadcast, ''Labor, Christ, and the Cross.'' His conclusion was the traditional need of men and women for Christ's sacrifice. Fused into the message was an interesting array of pro-American and anticommunist rhetoric. His strongest line came in favor of the red-hunters in Washington, D.C.: ''I thank God for men who, in the face of public denouncement and ridicule, go loyally on in their work of exposing the pinks and the reds who have sought refuge beneath the wings of the American eagle.'' A 1965 radio sermon, ''The Ultimate Weapon,'' was devoted entirely to a discussion of communism and how to overcome it. He began the address with a bleak picture: ''As we search the map of the world, we cannot find one place where the West is winning.'' For Graham, communism was a tool of Satan, and the only solution was to be found in a Christian America: ''There is only one philosophical system in the world today that has any possibility of combating the Communist conspiracy and that is a virile, dynamic, orthodox Christianity.'' He concluded: ''The greatest and most effective weapon against Communism today is a born-again Christian.''

At the Berlin Congress on World Evangelism in 1966, his position had mellowed somewhat. He spoke of the spiritual, not political, problems faced by individuals worldwide and ended by saying: ''I no longer speak to laboring men as laboring men—to university students as university students—to Africans as Africans—to Americans as Americans. I speak to all as men in need of redemption and salvation.'' By the time of his Moscow address in 1982, the theme of spiritual salvation had completely replaced his anticommunist appeals. He claimed, ''Our purpose is to rise above narrow national interests and give all of humanity a spiritual vision of the way to peace.'' Graham's views on Vietnam parallel this ideological-theological dichotomy. He initially supported the need to defend American freedom and Christian principles abroad. By 1969 in ''The Other Death,'' Graham saw the war in Southeast Asia not as an ideological conflict but as a result of man's poor relationship with God: ''And we cry, 'Peace, peace, peace, peace!' And we've had fifty-one wars since the Second World War. You see, what man really needs is peace with God. Man is at war with God.''

Closely related to the issue of communism is Graham's position on civil religion, or the worship of Americanism. Especially in his early years, Graham portrayed the United States as the primary protector of Christianity. He acknowledged the religious freedoms associated with a democracy and cited the relationships between noted Americans and their belief in Scripture in ''Our

Bible," quoting William McKinley, Benjamin Harrison, and Robert E. Lee. His principal role, however, has been prophetic, not priestly, challenging the spiritual weaknesses of the United States rather than exclusively celebrating its virtues as a nation. In an address to the North Carolina state legislature in 1971, Graham suggested the United States was en route to "total secularism and total materialism [which] will lead to tyranny and suppression and dictatorship, and that's where we're headed right now. Unless we have a revival of the American spirit and a revival of faith in God, that is where we're going to go."

Graham, however, stops short of deifying the American way. He calls on the United States to repent and to adhere to the precepts of Christianity. Graham sees salvation in the Christ figure, not in the United States. In a 1969 sermon, "The Day to Come," he offered his biggest break with civil religion. In his vision of the end times, he said: "The future ruler of the world is not capitalism or Communism. It's Christ. He's the one who's going to rule."

A final concern of this essay is Graham's position toward the civil rights movement of the 1950s and 1960s. Graham integrated his rallies in the South before *Brown v. Board of Education* in 1954, often in the face of local opposition; however, he refused to participate in marches or rallies exclusively for the civil rights movement. He also refused to propagate a social gospel. Despite attacks by such theologians as Reinhold Niebuhr, he stuck to a theme of individual repentance as the essential element for social change. According to Graham, solutions to social ills can result only from changed individuals. At Berlin in 1966, he rejected the notion that efforts of evangelism should focus on society's problems: "We cannot accept this interpretation of evangelism. Evangelism has social implications, but its primary thrust is the winning of men to a personal relationship with Christ." Therefore, the issue of race for Graham had to be solved by changing individuals first. To the North Carolina legislature, he preached: "There is no nation in the world that has the civil rights laws that we have today. But they have not solved the race problem yet . . . because we have to change attitudes. The heart has to be changed."

Graham envisioned the racial problem as one emanating from peoples' sinful natures and as one that existed worldwide. In "Come and Know God," he noted: "The problem is race. It's not an American problem; it's a world problem. . . . Christ can give us the supernatural power to love a person of another race." Graham's solution to racial tensions was his belief that unity existed in a Christian experience. In "The Other Death," he tendered his proposal: "Thirdly, the blood of Christ makes us all equal. One tongue, one language, one race. . . . That's the solution ultimately to the race problem. One in Jesus, cleansed by the blood."

Possibly Graham has delivered more speeches and been heard by more persons than any other preacher of the twentieth century. He has been criticized by liberals for his cold war rhetoric and more recently by the new religious Right for straddling the political fence. But thirty-six years after his first crusade in Los Angeles, thousands still flock to hear Graham, and millions more watch him on television. He continues to preach the lesson of sin and salvation while his ideological pronouncements have given way to more transcendent spiritual statements. His message of hope is tinged with the emotionalism and urgency one expects of evangelists, but it is mild compared with the fire and brimstone preached by many of the primetime clergy. Most of his sermons discuss problems and solutions, define existing political and social chaos as sin, and offer a way of achieving order and balance in a disordered and confusing world. The social ethic he preaches is "Love your neighbor" and "Love your God." As a dominant figure in twentieth-century religion, Graham has adapted his ministry successfully to this era and its media.

INFORMATION SOURCES

Research Collections and Collected Speeches

A major source of information on Graham is the Billy Graham Evangelical Association, Minneapolis, Minnesota. The association and its archives provide a variety of material on the evangelist's life and oratory. Of special interest are tapes and transcripts of Graham's radio sermons from his "Hour of Decision" broadcasts. The association also has a complete run of *Decision* magazine, which publishes many of Graham's sermons. Additional archives, including audiovisual material, are located at the Billy Graham Center, Wheaton College, Illinois.

Graham, Billy. *The Challenge: Sermons from Madison Square Garden.*   TC
    Garden City, N.Y.: Doubleday, 1969.
Christianity Today.   CT
Radio Messages. [240 radio sermons coded by number]. Minneapolis: Billy   RM
    Graham Evangelical Association.

Selected Critical Studies

Arnold, Bob. "Billy Graham: Superstar." In *On Jordan's Stormy Banks: Religion in the South.* Edited by Samuel S. Hill, Jr. Macon, Ga.: Mercer UP, 1983.
McLoughlin, William G., Jr. *Billy Graham: Revivalist in a Secular Age.* New York: Ronald Press, 1960.
Mitchell, Curtis. *God in the Garden: The Story of the Billy Graham Crusade.* Garden City, N.Y.: Doubleday, 1957.
Streiker, Lowell, and Strober, Gerald. *Religion and the New Majority: Billy Graham, Middle America, and the Politics of the 70's.* New York: Associated Press, 1972.

Selected Biographies

High, Stanley. *Billy Graham.* London: Morrison and Gibb, 1957.
Pollock, John. *Billy Graham: The Authorized Biography.* New York: McGraw-Hill, 1966.
————. *Billy Graham: Evangelist to the World.* San Francisco: Harper & Row, 1979.

CHRONOLOGY OF MAJOR SPEECHES

See "Research Collections and Collected Speeches" for source codes.

"Our Bible," radio sermon, [day and month unknown] 1951; *RM* no. 95.

"Labor, Christ, and the Cross," radio sermon, [day and month unknown], 1953; *RM* no. 30.

"The Christian Answer to the World Dilemma," opening address, New York City crusade, May 15, 1957; *New York Times*, May 16, 1957, pp. 22–23.

"The Ultimate Weapon," radio sermon, [day and month unknown] 1965; *RM* no. 141.

"Why the Berlin Congress?" address to the World Congress on Evangelism, Berlin, May 1966; *CT* 10 (1966): 3–7.

"Social Injustice," radio sermon, [day and month unknown] 1967; *RM* no. 166.

"Come and Know God," opening crusade address, New York City, June 13, 1969; *TC*, 1–16.

"The Other Death," crusade address, New York City, June 14, 1969; *TC*, 17–33.

"The Christian Faith and Peace in a Nuclear Age," address to the Religious Workers for Saving the Sacred Gift of Life from Nuclear Catastrophe, Moscow, May 11, 1982; *CT* 26 (1982): 20–23.

BILLY JAMES HARGIS
(1925–   ), founder and director of Christian Crusade

DALE G. LEATHERS

Billy James Hargis, anticommunist evangelist, has gained national fame for himself and his organization, the Christian Crusade, largely as a result of his remarkable oratorical skills. Hargis, who was abandoned by his parents shortly after his birth in 1925, was reared and ultimately adopted by J. E. and Laura Lucille Hargis in Texarkana, Texas. Billy James Hargis and his hard-working but relatively poor parents were like many of their neighbors in at least one respect: their lives were strongly affected by fundamentalist religious values and conservative political values. In his formative years, young Hargis was heavily influenced in his thinking by politically conservative fundamentalist evangelists such as B. B. Crimn and J. T. McKissick, who convinced Hargis that liberalism is evil and that he would be called by God as a watchman to warn the world of a threat greater than liberalism.

After intermittently attending Ozark Bible College, Bentonville, Arkansas, for eighteen months, Hargis became an ordained minister at the age of eighteen on May 30, 1943. He subsequently assumed pastorates of First Christian churches in Oklahoma and Missouri. For some years, the noted evangelist A. B. Mc-Reynolds had been trying to convince Hargis that he was God's chosen representative to lead the fight against the threat of communism in the United States. By 1950 he convinced Hargis. Hargis resigned his pastorate in Sapulpa, Oklahoma, to found the independent and nondenominational organization incorporated as the Christian Echoes National Ministry, popularly known for many years as Christian Crusade. Christian Crusade initially consisted of a small network of radio stations that Hargis used to warn about the communist threat and to elaborate on Christian Crusade's simple theme: "For Christ and against Communism."

BILLY HARGIS AS ANTICOMMUNIST PERSUADER

Although Hargis struggled during the early years simply to keep Christian Crusade on radio, the growth of the organization from 1960 to 1975 was unprecedented for an anticommunist organization of this type. By 1969, the organization had ten separate divisions, which included two magazines (the *Weekly Crusader* and the monthly *Christian Crusade*), television, books, the Summer Youth University at Manitou Spring, Colorado, and the rapidly expanding radio network. In the early 1970s, Hargis opened his own American Christian College. He described it in his autobiography as a "conservative, evangelical, fundamental, anti-Communist, anti-socialist, pro-American college.'' After three and one-half years of operation, the estimated value of the campus was $3.5 million.

Although he has built a diversified anticommunist operation, Hargis recognizes that his ministry is largely a radio ministry. He claimed in his autobiography, *My Great Mistake*, that at one time his Christian Crusade broadcasts were heard on over 600 radio stations daily and weekly. Christian Crusade radio broadcasts on high wattage stations in Mexico were particularly helpful in reaching large numbers of people in many states.

Hargis also relied heavily on anticommunist rallies held throughout the country. His appeals at rallies were readily accepted because most members of a rally audience were true believers. On some occasions, Hargis teamed up at these rallies with noted anticommunists such as General Edwin Walker. The striking success of the rallies over the years was based almost exclusively on Hargis's ability to move audiences deeply with his fear-oriented messages. One Christian Crusade rally with Hargis and Walker in the Shrine Auditorium in Los Angeles drew 7,500 people. In Hargis's opinion, support for Christian Crusade doubled in 1963 solely as a result of rallies held from coast to coast.

Hargis and Christian Crusade experienced great success in the period from 1960 to 1975; since then has been a troubled time for Hargis, most of it traced to an article in *Time* magazine (February 1976), ''The Sins of Billy James Hargis.'' *Time* asserted that ''Hargis stands accused by former colleagues of committing some of the very sins he has railed against.'' Hargis's alleged sins included having sexual relations with five students from American Christian College. Indeed *Time* alleged that one young couple who had been married by Hargis discovered on their honeymoon that both had slept with him.

The charges could have been fatal to Hargis; one would expect his fundamentalist followers to demand that the personal righteousness of their leader be beyond question. Hargis stressed in a telephone conversation with me on April 16, 1985, that the charges in *Time* were ''catastrophic'' and ''beat me completely.'' He has chosen not to deny directly or to refute individually the charges of sexual misconduct made against him. The immediate impact of the charges was negative. Hargis was forced to resign as president of American Christian College and took a leave of absence as head of his other anticommunist operations. He maintained in his autobiography that his enemies, who were trying to destroy him via ''The Great Smear'' in *Time*, ''wanted all my organizations . . . [but] all they ever got was the college, our Tulsa campus radio station, and our summer school in Colorado. And within two years, the doors of the Tulsa college were closed.'' Within another year Hargis returned from his leave of absence to resume control of Christian Crusade and its auxiliary organizations. The fact that he could return at all serves as a testimonial to his persuasive skills. Nonetheless, the damage done to his personal credibility has had the apparent effect of drastically reducing the scope of activities undertaken by Hargis and Christian Crusade.

In *The Great Mistake*, Hargis enunciated the basic message he used to build

Christian Crusade into a multimillion dollar enterprise in the 1960s and early 1970s:

We started Christian Crusade with a Divine Vision to hold back the forces of anti-Christ Communism by exposing the forces of evil and presenting Jesus Christ as the Hope of the World. We knew then and we know now, that Satan is using Communism to bring about his godless one-world government, the anti-Christ regime, and the Battle of Armageddon.

Hargis recognized that one claim was intrinsically more important than any other claim he would make: the influence of the communist conspiracy in the United States has become so widespread that most institutionalized sources of information are untrustworthy and many of the most important institutions are virtually controlled by communists. Much of what Hargis has said since 1950 has been designed to focus the attention of followers and potential converts on this communist conspiracy claim. More specifically, Hargis has steadfastly maintained for over three decades that the conspiratorial activities of the communists and their allies has resulted in a shocking degree of communist control of the clergy, the press, and many other institutions in the United States.

In his noted address, "Christ the Great Destroyer," Hargis warned, "We have barely scratched the surface of the voluminous record of participation in communist front activity by clergymen. No one knows the exact number of clergymen and front affiliations but thousands have participated." Hargis recently sharpened his attack on liberal religious organizations, which he called tools of the communists and the devil. In "Three Things That Could Happen to America," Hargis stressed, "It is a shame when a religious organization is doing the work of the Devil. . . . But that is exactly what the World Council of Churches and the National Council of Churches are doing."

The free press, too, in the persuasion of Billy James Hargis, is a tool used by the communists to deceive Americans. In fact, Hargis maintains that communists have worked to gain control of the free press in the United States since they recognize that the communist conspiracy must practice widespread deception to be successful. In "A Free Press—Leading America Leftward," Hargis charged that "infiltration of the free press in free nations is a necessary tactic of Communism and is being accomplished easily in America, and in other free nations as well." Hargis has made this type of charge against the free press repeatedly. When he comes under personal attack by the press that he claims is communist infiltrated, Hargis frequently dismisses the charge as a "Communist smear."

Communist conspirators have been so successful, according to Hargis, that U.S. court, transportation, money, and law enforcement systems run the risk of paralysis in the foreseeable future. Even international organizations such as the United Nations are under communist control, he believes. In "We Have Been Betrayed," Hargis maintained that U.S. participation in the United Nations is an act of betrayal since the UN is a communist tool that in fact forces the United States to make reckless expenditures on foreign aid.

The net effect of the actions of the communist conspirators, claims Hargis, is that the patriotic anticommunists in the United States have been turned into villains. The inspired prophets are transformed by communist propaganda into money-grubbing alarmists. The anticommunists are forced to bear such derogatory labels as *extremist*, fright peddler, and *reactionary*. Such treatment presumably stimulated Hargis to deliver "Patriotism Once Revered, Now Smeared." The basic question, said Hargis, is why patriotic American citizens and their loyal Christian patriotic leaders must be smeared. They must bear this burden, in Hargis's view, because "millions upon millions of Americans have believed lies and have taken as truth the evil smear attacks and character-assassination superintended by Communists against American patriots."

In short, Billy James Hargis has exhibited considerable skill in developing an enduring persuasive message that shapes the perceptions of his anticommunist followers. The persuasive nuances and subthemes have changed over the years, but Hargis's carefully contrived message has remained basically the same. The reality he describes for his followers means that they must turn to Hargis or a limited number of other anticommunist leaders for enlightenment. Because of the communists' success in the development of the conspiracy, they have the ability to distort, if not control, information that flows from traditional sources in the United States. Hargis asserts that honest communication would subvert the purposes and undermine the actions of communist conspirators. In short, for communists to prosper, they must deceive. Communists and their followers are perpetrating an evil, conspiratorial plan on Americans. Because communists exert so much control over institutionalized communication in the United States, their potential to deceive is almost beyond comprehension.

Many of the major rhetorical techniques Hargis has used have also been used by other anticommunist evangelists. Hargis has simply refined the techniques and used them with uncommon skill. His most frequent techniques are to establish the urgency of the communist threat for the fundamentalist audience; use the allegation of smear to obviate the need to provide empirical support for his own positions on issues; attack targets or scapegoats to highlight conspiratorial activities of the communists; and raise money with a prayer auction.

Hargis has always been particularly ingenious in his ability to sustain the apparent urgency and immediacy of the internal communist threat in the eyes of his followers. He does so by blaming the communist conspiracy for an almost endless variety of contemporary social problems. He charged in the 1960s and 1970s that communist conspirators were actively involved in the civil rights movement, in mental health programs, and even in the development of rock music, which was designed to corrupt the morals of the nation's youth. Hargis has been no less inventive in the 1980s in linking a variety of threats and problems to the communists. In the July 1984 issue of his *Christian Crusade* newspaper, he charged that the Grenada communist Ministry of the Interior prepared a secret plan to subvert the churches and enslave the population of Grenada. In the December 1985 issue, Hargis offered to send the readers for $5 a copy a new twelve-page research report he had authored, "The Russian Weather War Report." In that report Hargis made the startling assertion that Soviets' attempts to manipulate world weather are "prophecy in fulfillment, leading to the second coming of Christ." In the January 1985 issue Hargis went so far as to warn that evangelist Billy Graham has been "duped once again into serving as a propaganda tool for communists."

Hargis has also mastered the technique of deflecting attacks by his detractors by dismissing them as communist smears. When *Time* magazine accused him of having sexual relations with his own students, he chose not to answer the allegations. He simply referred to the charges as the "great smear."

While Hargis has been adept at dismissing criticism aimed at him as Communist smears, he has always specialized in the selection of targets or scapegoats for his own attacks. Not surprisingly, liberals are his favorite targets. Thus, he said in "A Divine Formula for Victory over Communism" that "communism, at least, is open atheism; but liberalism is concealed atheism." Hargis usually depicts his specific targets as witting or unwitting agents of the communist conspiracy who will be punished by an avenging God. On February 25, 1985, on his Christian Crusade radio program, he focused on one of his favorite targets. Referring to the recent visit of Senator Edward Kennedy to the Republic of South Africa, Hargis warned his listeners: "Senator Kennedy has proven himself to be an absolute idiot in terms of the problems that confront Africa today. He has bought and preached the Communist-party line so long that when he came to southern Africa and denounced the Christian and anti-Communist governments . . . he thus set back the relationship between the United States and mineral-rich South Africa by years." Similarly, in the July 1984 issue of *Christian Crusade*, Hargis published his "Hall of Fame" and "Roll of Shame," listing senators who voted for and against the school prayer amendment bill in spring 1984. Senator Daniel Moynihan (Democrat, New York), who voted against the bill, was dismissed as an "Irish clown," and Senators John Chafee (Republican, Rhode Island) and Claiborne Pell (Democrat, Rhode Island), "put their little minds together to vote against school prayer."

Hargis's greatest skill is probably his ability to raise money at anticommunist rallies by relating salvation to the need to fight communism. His speeches at these rallies build to an intense emotional climax. Orban calls the "prayer auction" the final rhetorical act. Hargis typically begins his appeal for money by crying out, "I pray to God for one man to sponsor my radio program for six months. I know that there is such a man in this audience." If no one rises in the audience, Hargis divides the burden. In Indianapolis, for example, he began by asking who would give $40,000. Getting no takers, he asked two persons to contribute $20,000 each. If he still gets no positive response, he asks four persons to contribute $10,000 each.

Hargis's claim to fame as a money raiser is clearly deserved. He in fact has been notably successful over the years not only in raising money from anticommunist audiences but in obtaining large contributions from single individuals. For example, one woman contributed $27,000 to help pay for the original Christian Crusade headquarters in response to an appeal Hargis made on radio.

The motivational appeal that Hargis uses with greatest skill is fear. By mastering the art of mounting graphic fear appeals, Hargis moved to the forefront among anticommunist orators in the 1960s and 1970s. He recognized that fear can be a great motivator for a fundamentalist audience because the God of the fundamentalist is not only fearfully omnipotent but an avenger. Since human beings by their nature are evil and sinful, the probability of punishment by an avenging god is great. Hargis has been the most inventive of all anticommunist persuaders in articulating the types of sins for which he believes unrepentant sinners will be punished by a vengeful God. On his March 25, 1985, Christian Crusade radio broadcast, he warned that "the new wave of sexually transmitted, incurable diseases is God's plague on sinners." The avenging god is wrathful, claims Hargis, because of sexual promiscuity. Hargis described both the alleged transgression against God's law and God's consequent punishment when he warned his radio audience that "the Creator does not take lightly the hatred and rejection of those whom he has created. They incur his wrath and his wrath against the generation of sex sinners consists of the painful and frequently incurable, sexually transmitted diseases now stalking the sinner victims."

Hargis's delivery has become less animated and emotional over the years. On his Christian Crusade radio broadcasts, he currently exhibits a flat, almost monotone voice. In his telephone conversation with me on April 16, 1985, Hargis maintained that his radio listeners no longer respond positively to attempts to "rouse fear in their hearts." He has therefore consciously modified his style on radio from a bombastic to a subdued delivery with an emphasis on entertainment. In his personal appearances, however, he is still at his best when he emulates one of his idols, Billy Sunday, with the grand sweep and intensity of his gestures and when the urgency of his emotional appeals is reflected in the stridency and sheer volume of his powerful voice. Hargis can still move an audience emotionally and recently did so with a sermon delivered in Kismu, Kenya.

To evaluate the speeches and other persuasive efforts of Billy James Hargis by traditional critical standards is probably neither realistic nor fair. In many instances, it is true, as critic Orban contends, that Hargis overgeneralizes, uses faulty cause-and-effect reasoning, substitutes guilt by association and name calling for factual evidence, and relies on his own role as a Christian minister to sustain the ethical efficacy of his personalized judgments and interpretations of the Bible. For the nontraditional audience Hargis has been reaching for over forty years, however, his persuasion has been undeniably effective.

In fact, Hargis has assumed a central role in shaping the persuasion of the anticommunist movement. Whether he and the movement have been staunch defenders of or serious threats to democratic principles depends on one's perspective. It is true, however, that Hargis has convinced his followers that a communist conspiracy has gained virtual control of traditional sources of information in the United States. In cultivating this view of reality, Hargis by definition makes himself an outcast and even an extremist in the eyes of the out-group. From the perspective of his loyal followers, at least, it is safe to say that Billy James Hargis has formulated a message that is more distinctive and resilient than the message of any other anticommunist evangelist.

INFORMATION SOURCES

Research Collections and Collected Speeches

The Christian Crusade, Tulsa, Oklahoma, and conference facilities at the Rose of Sharon Farm, Neosho, Missouri, contain a plethora of information about Hargis and his oratory. Hargis has a commendable record of working cooperatively with researchers. Rally speeches, sermons, and anticommunist seminars are available in printed form and on tape cassette; complete records of the Christian Crusade newspapers and radio broadcasts since their inception; and the vast myriad of books, pamphlets, and records produced by Christian Crusade may be sampled in person. Researchers should note that it may be difficult, if not impossible, to obtain a precise date of delivery for a given speech because the basic theme in certain speeches is often repeated over the years and because taped speeches sold to the public by Christian Crusade bear no delivery date. Researchers should beware of speeches specially recorded in a studio without an audience. They typically lack the emotional intensity of presentation and crowd response that help make Christian Crusade anticommunist rallies so distinctive.

Communist America . . . Must It Be? Berne, Ind.: Economy Printing Concern, 1960   CAMIB

Christian Crusade Pamphlet Publication of Speeches of Billy James Hargis. Tulsa, Okla., 1961.   CCSBJH

Christ and His Gospel as Preached by Billy James Hargis. Tulsa: Christian Crusade Publications, 1969.   CGBJH

Christian Crusade radio broadcasts.   CCRB

Christian Crusade.   CCMN

40th Anniversary Album: Spiritual and Patriotic Teaching Tapes. Tulsa, Okla.: Christian Crusade Tape Ministry, 1985   FAA

Selected Critical Studies

Leathers, Dale G. "Belief-Disbelief Systems: The Communicative Vacuum of the Radical Right." In *Explorations in Rhetorical Criticism.* Edited by Charles J. Stewart, Donovan J. Ochs, and Gerald P. Mohrmann. University Park: Pennsylvania State University Press, 1973.

———. "Fundamentalism of the Radical Right." *Southern Speech Journal* 33 (1968): 243–58.

———. "The Thrust of the Radical Right." In *Preaching in American History.* Edited by DeWitte Holland. Nashville, Tenn.: Abingdon Press, 1969.

———. "The Thrust of the Radical Right." In *Sermons in American History.* Edited by DeWitte Holland. Nashville, Tenn.: Abingdon Press, 1971.

Orban, Donald K. "Billy James Hargis: Auctioneer of Political Evangelism." *Central States Speech Journal* 22 (1969): 83–96.

Smith, Craig A. "The Hofstadter Hypothesis Revisited: The Nature of Evidence in Politically 'Paranoid' Discourse." *Southern Speech Communication Journal* 42 (1977): 274–89.

Selected Biographies

Hargis, Billy James, and Dudley, Cliff. *My Great Mistake*. Green Forest, Ark.: New Leaf Press, 1985.

Penabaz, Fernando, *Crusading Preacher from the West*. Tulsa, Okla.: Christian Crusade, 1965.

CHRONOLOGY OF MAJOR SPEECHES

See "Research Collections and Collected Speeches" for source codes.

"A Free Press—Leading America Leftward," address delivered periodically at anticommunist rallies throughout the United States since 1959; *CAMIB*, pp. 23–30.

"Christ the Great Destroyer," address delivered at anticommunist rallies; *CAMIB*, pp. 165–76.

"Patriotism Once Revered, Now Smeared," address delivered at anticommunist rallies; *CAMIB*, pp. 41–54.

"We Have Been Betrayed," Washington, D.C., April 20, 1961; *CCSBJH*.

"A Divine Formula for Victory over Communism," *Cathedral of Christian Crusade, Tulsa Oklahoma, summer 1968; CGBJH*.

"Three Things That Could Happen to America," conference center, Rose of Sharon Farm, Neosho, Missouri, summer 1984; *FAA*.

Untitled sermon, Christian Crusade Pastor's Seminar, Kismu, Kenya, January 9, 1985; *FAA*.

JESSE ALEXANDER HELMS
(1922–   ), U.S. senator from North Carolina

——————————————————————————— ROBERT V. FRIEDENBERG

The willingness to speak out in support of positions many characterize as extreme, the unwillingness to compromise, and the intensity of his advocacy have combined to make North Carolina's Republican senator, Jesse Helms, the chief spokesman of the militant conservatism that arose in the United States in the early 1970s. Heirs to the Goldwater conservatism of the 1960s, the more militant conservatives of the 1970s are strong supporters of the free enterprise system, strident critics of big government, and strong anticommunists. Unlike the Goldwater conservatives, the New Right of the 1970s and 1980s has added a religious and moralistic fervor to political dialogue by championing such causes as the pro-life movement, the restoration of prayer to the public schools, and opposition to the equal rights amendment. Jesse Helms has exemplified this fervor in such speeches as "Christians in Politics," frequently claiming that it is time for Christians to redefine the terms of public debate and "to reaffirm the spiritual heritage of the country."

From the outset of his career, Helms has used his abundant communication skills on behalf of conservative causes. Raised in tiny Monroe, North Carolina, Helms engaged in his first political activity as a young radio newsman doing publicity for conservative lawyer Willis Smith, who defeated liberal Frank Graham, president of the University of North Carolina, in an acrimonious 1950 Senate campaign. Helms accompanied Smith to Washington as his administrative assistant but soon returned to North Carolina, where he served as executive director of the North Carolina Bankers Association and won two terms on the Raleigh city council. As a city councilman, Helms advocated conservative positions, and as executive director of the association of bankers, he wrote political editorials for the association's publications.

In 1960 Helms bought part interest in a Raleigh-Durham television station and became the station's daily editorialist. His television editorials were also carried by a seventy-station radio network throughout the state and reprinted in over fifty small town newspapers. Helms called his program of editorial commentary "The Voice of Free Enterprise in Raleigh-Durham." He was militantly conservative, speaking against unions, social security, medicare, and similar programs as unwarranted government intervention into areas best left to free enterprise. An equally militant anticommunist, Helms editorialized against the United Nations, against Henry Kissinger's détente policies with Moscow, and against President Richard Nixon's opening of relations with the People's Republic of China. He supported the establishment of private schools while speaking against the civil rights movement. Helms claims that his experience as an editorialist was his best speech training.

HELMS AS SENATORIAL PERSUADER

By 1972, when he chose to run for the U.S. Senate, Helms's twelve years of editorializing, involving almost 2,800 editorials, had made him well known throughout the state. He brought to that campaign more experience as a journalist, speaker, and media personality than virtually any other individual serving in public office at the time. Helms was the first on-camera personality to move directly from reporting and commenting on the news to making the news as a member of the Senate. Winning election with 54 percent of the vote, Helms benefited from the Nixon landslide of 1972, which saw the president carry North Carolina with over 70 percent of the vote.

Since 1972 Helms has contributed heavily to shifting the national agenda to the right by arguing that public policy should be consistently moral. For example, in his 1973 address, ''Survival of Freedom in an Era of Negotiation,'' delivered in London, he argued that rather than negotiate with the immoral Soviet Union solely on arms control, the United States should link arms negotiation to negotiation over the basic freedoms denied Soviet citizens. Rather than negotiate over the price and quantity of grain that it might sell to the Soviet Union, the United States should link its grain concessions to the Soviets with concessions on their part to introduce free enterprise capitalism into the agricultural sector of their economy. To Helms, negotiations over arms control or grain sales do nothing to alter the immoral nature of the Soviet Union. He feels that it makes little sense to lend tacit support to what he believes is a fundamentally evil society by allowing it to negotiate arms and food agreements unless the United States is able to negotiate changes in the society.

To Helms, the conduct of public policy should be based on Judeo-Christian morality. This is strikingly evident when he speaks about the wide range of pro-family issues. Helms began to offer legislative amendments to prohibit abortion, permit prayer in the public schools, or to eliminate forced busing soon after entering the Senate. By introducing amendments that enabled him to address conservative issues, he hoped to place the issue in the public mind, to provide articulate statements of his positions for the public record, and to force his colleagues in the Senate to take clear positions and vote on issues they might otherwise have ignored. Helms seems to have achieved his first two goals in offering amendments and speaking on their behalf.

The third goal—that of forcing his colleagues to cast votes on issues they might otherwise have ignored—is particularly important. The votes Helms has forced on issues such as abortion, busing, school prayer, and a balanced budget have often been major ones in the reelection campaigns of Senate members. Shortly after Helms entered the Senate, the *Raleigh News and Observer* nicknamed him ''Senator No'' because he so often stood alone. Today approximately twenty members of the Senate identify themselves as conservatives, and many liberals are voting less liberally and more conservatively in recent years than they did in the early 1970s. Many of the conservatives who have joined Helms in the Senate were able to do so in part because they ran against incumbents whose liberal positions were made explicit to the electorate by their votes on Helms's amendments. Hence Helms's amendments and the strong speeches he offered in their support have engendered animosity from many of his Senate colleagues, but more important to Helms, they have demanded and forced a response.

On January 22, 1981, Helms offered and spoke in support of his amendment banning legalized abortion, arguing its immorality. "It is no mere coincidence," he claimed, "that abortion first appeared as public policy in Nazi and Communist dictatorships." He claimed that the Supreme Court decision that since 1973 has legalized abortion is no more than "legalized fiction," ignoring moral principles that date to antiquity. Helms offered extensive medical evidence suggesting that life begins at the moment of conception and then claimed that abortion "violates the sanctity of human life." He views this issue as one where there is a morally correct position that brooks no compromise.

Helms's speeches fall into two basic categories. First are speeches given on the Senate floor that are typically well documented, clearly organized, and characterized by concrete imagery and apt word choice. More formal than his non-Senate speeches, Helms's Senate speeches are designed to enunciate and detail his positions. According to his staff, they are prepared and delivered with a conscious awareness that they are speeches of record.

Helms utilizes ghost writers and receives assistance in preparing his speeches from his staff, although he maintains full control over their text. While his staff tend to be subject matter experts, Helms's background as a journalist and media commentator inclines him to make substantial revisions of the language of his speeches, even in which his staff anticipates are final texts. Although he deals with highly charged issues and often utilizes highly emotional language, his delivery is surprisingly understated. An imposing figure, standing over six feet tall, his high forehead and glasses give him an owl-like, bookish appearance, an impression reinforced by his soft-spoken delivery.

The second category of Helms's speeches he delivers as one of the principal spokesmen of the religious Right. These non-Senate speeches are thematically consistent with those delivered in the Senate but differ markedly from his Senate addresses in several respects. They are less formal, are not as well documented, and rely far more heavily on extended examples, striking analogies, and humorous stories. These differences are deliberate adaptations Helms makes when speaking before largely sympathetic audiences of conservative supporters.

Helms' non-Senate speeches are often jeremiads or jeremiad-like. The distinctive features of the jeremiad have been examined by a variety of scholars, most of whom acknowledge that the jeremiad evidences five major characteristics. First, it involves an attempt to make the individual members of the audience aware of themselves as part of a special or chosen people. Second, it stresses the urgent nature of the problem it seeks to remedy. Third, it condemns a social evil. Fourth, it proposes a solution to the social evil or problem. For the Puritan minister, that proposal was normally a return to the path of righteousness. For the secular orator, it involves asking the audience to return to the values and traditions that have made them a select or chosen people. Finally, speakers close their jeremiads by sharing their vision of a bright future with their audiences of the chosen people.

Helms makes use of the jeremiad form in many of his speeches. He attended church twice a week throughout his boyhood, and his strong religious roots may account for his tendency to use the jeremiad form. His staff notes that this tendency is not anything that Helms or they consciously foster, yet it manifests itself in much of his work. Indeed, even his book, *When Free Men Shall Stand*, is essentially an extended jeremiad. In such speeches as his basic campaign speech, delivered throughout North Carolina during his hotly contested 1984 reelection campaign against Governor James Hunt, his addresses to the Conservative Caucus and the Conservative Political Action Committee, delivered in 1984, his commencement address delivered at Grove City College in 1982, and his address to the Republican National Convention in 1980, the first of his addresses to be nationally televised, Helms has repeatedly utilized the jeremiad form.

In each of these speeches, Helms claimed that Americans are a chosen people. As he said campaigning throughout North Carolina in 1984, "No one is more proud than I of the character of our people. . . . The greatness of Americans lies in our worthy ideas and ideals—our commitment as a people to free enterprise and to liberty and to the fundamental Judeo-Christian moral principles which guided the creation of our Republic." But, Helms claimed, "We have lost our sense of perspective over the last 20 years." After establishing this point, Helms detailed a problem or group of problems, adapted to the audience and issues he wished to address, such as the loss of U.S. military supremacy, its economic plight, the legalization of abortion, or court-mandated busing, all of which he argued had reached crisis proportions.

Helms then consistently condemned liberal politicians, the unrestrained court system, and the liberal press specifically, and all Americans in general, because, as he told the graduates in his 1982 commencement address at Grove City College, "I presume to ask you, on this very special day, to consider the proposition that we become part of what we condone." Americans have tolerated and condoned, he continued, "the liberal elites in the judiciary and in the media particularly, who have carried on for the past three decades a ferocious assault on the fundamental institution of the family." Thus, although specific liberal groups can be identified as foes, Helms has condemned virtually all Americans for tolerating such groups.

Next, he presented a proposal or suggestions for resolving the problems he addressed. Invariably, Helms portrayed his solutions as a return to the Judeo-

Christian moral principles on which the United States was founded. He told North Carolina voters in 1984 that to resolve their problems, they "need only to ponder the history of mankind—history as old as the bible, or as contemporary as the counsel of our founding fathers." Whether it is a hard line in dealing with the Soviet Union, a reduction in federal taxation and spending, or the passage of amendments to prevent abortion or allow prayer in the schools, Helms consistently cast his solutions as the result of the logical application of basic American principles to contemporary problems.

Finally, Helms concluded his jeremiads by sharing his vision of a bright future with his audiences. He closed his speech to the 1980 Republican National Convention in typical fashion by asking his audience to "live each day, mindful that the Lord may be giving us just one more chance to save America. With a genuine spiritual rebirth, we can do it. Let's get about it."

No examination of Helms's political oratory would be complete without noting that he has been a pioneer in raising large sums of money for political communication purposes. The union between Helms and direct-mail wizard Richard Vigerie has bankrolled numerous conservative political action committees, most notably Helms's own Congressional Club. In 1984 Helms spent approximately $15.6 million on his own reelection, more than ever before spent in any single nonpresidential race in the country. This exceeded by over $2 million the previous high spent in California by Senator Peter Wilson in his 1982 election campaign.

Much of Helms's political clout comes from the fact that he can mobilize hundreds of thousands of loyal conservatives throughout the country. Through a variety of like-minded political action committees, conservative groups can mount a formidable campaign against liberal foes or issues on relatively short notice. Undeniably, much of the conservative movement's infrastructure in the 1980s grew out of Helms's early efforts.

In sum, Helms presents a consistent conservative ideology in his rhetoric. In the Senate, his speaking is marked by thorough documentation. His inflexibility has helped to shift the nature of public dialogue in the United States to the right. Moreover, his utilization of direct mail to raise substantial amounts of money has pioneered the way for many conservative groups to field and support candidates. Helms's political rhetoric has contributed appreciably to bringing about the current shift to the right in the public agenda and political leadership of the United States.

INFORMATION SOURCES

Research Collections and Collected Speeches

Rhetorical material concerning Helms has not been conveniently gathered. Helms's Senate office keeps speech manuscripts and will provide manuscripts and information. The University of North Carolina has a collection of Helms's editorials delivered between 1960 and 1972. A variety of organizations, most notably the Raleigh-based Congressional

Club, the Republican National Committee, and the Republican Senatorial Campaign Committee, have materials, including some political advertisements, used in Helms's campaigns.

Congressional Record.   *CR*
Grassroots: The Leadership Quarterly of the Conservative Caucus.   *GLQCC*
Turning Point: Christian America at the Crossroads. Edited by Roger El- *TP*
    wood. Cincinnati: Standard Publishing, 1980.
Vital Speeches of the Day.   *VS*

Selected Critical Studies

Bercovitch, Sacvan. *The American Jeremiad.* Madison: University of Wisconsin Press, 1978.

Clark, Thomas D. "An Analysis of Recurrent Features of Contemporary American Radical, Liberal, and Conservative Political Discourse." *Southern Speech Communication Journal* 44 (1979): 399–422.

Conrad, Charles. "The Rhetoric of the Moral Majority: An Analysis of Romantic Form." *Quarterly Journal of Speech* 69 (1983): 159–70.

Friedenberg, Robert V. "The Contemporary American Jeremiad." Paper presented at the annual meeting of the Speech Communication Association, New York City, November 10, 1980.

Medhurst, Martin J. "Resistance, Conservatism, and Theory Building: A Cautionary Note." *Western Journal of Speech Communication* 49 (1985): 103–15.

Selected Biographies

Ajemian, Robert. "Ideologue with Influence." *Time*, May 4, 1984, pp. 20–21.

Drew, Elizabeth. "Jesse Helms." *New Yorker*, July 20, 1981, pp. 78–95.

Hamrick, Sam. Personal interview, July 9, 1985.

Helms, Jesse. Personal interview, July 9, 1985.

———. *"When Free Men Shall Stand."* Grand Rapids, Mich.: Zondervan Publishing House, 1976.

Lucier, James. Personal interview, July 9, 1985.

Range, Peter. "Thunder from the Right." *New York Times Magazine*, February 8, 1981, pp. 22–85.

Snider, William. *Helms and Hunt: The North Carolina Senate Race, 1984.* Chapel Hill: University of North Carolina Press, 1985.

CHRONOLOGY OF MAJOR SPEECHES

See "Research Collections and Collected Speeches" for source codes.

"Survival of Freedom in an Era of Negotiation," London, September 1, 1973; *VS* 39 (1973), pp. 764–67.

Address to the Republican National Convention, Detroit, Michigan, July 17, 1980; made available by Helms's Senate Office.

"Christians in Politics," n.p., n.d.; *TP*, pp. 176–84.

Commencement address, Grove City College, Grove City, Pennsylvania, May 15, 1982; *VS* 48 (1982), pp. 553–54.

Address to the Conservative Political Action Committee, Washington D.C., March 1, 1984; made available by Helms's Senate Office.

Basic campaign speech, 1984 Senate campaign, with slight variations delivered repeatedly throughout North Carolina, April-November 1984; made available by Helms's Senate Office.

Remarks to Tenth Anniversary Dinner, Conservative Caucus, Washington, D.C., November 29, 1984; *GLQCC* 9 (1985).

HERBERT CLARK HOOVER
(1874–1964), thirty-first president of the United States

JAMES S. OLSON

More than fifty years after his departure from the White House, Herbert Hoover remains a controversial enigma, hated by an older generation of Americans for being an insensitive reactionary, praised by a new generation of conservatives for his prescience, or vaguely recalled as a high-collared irrelevancy by many others. Few other U.S. leaders have had such a meteoric career or such a fall from grace. Internationally renowned as a humanitarian during and after World War I and widely respected during the 1920s for his understanding of the modern industrial economy, Herbert Hoover seemed perfectly suited for the White House, where he hoped to preside over the greatest era of prosperity in the history of the world. The Great Depression shattered his dream and transformed him from hero to the most hated figure of his time in the 1930s. Most Americans held him personally responsible for the collapse of the economy and the suffering of millions. But by the 1950s and early 1960s, Hoover's tenacity, political philosophy, and decades on the public lecture circuit had resurrected his reputation. When he died in 1964, most Americans had come to look upon him as an elder statesman whose traditional fears about the size and power of the federal government had been fulfilled.

Hoover secured international recognition during World War I when he personally organized a massive relief effort to provide food and clothing to millions of displaced people. Through the Commission for Relief in Belgium and the American Relief Administration, Hoover raised more than $4 billion and distributed the money in the form of food and clothing to more than 30 million Europeans. His was a personal crusade to mobilize private monies throughout Western Europe and the United States, and Hoover succeeded by cutting through government red tape and, through hundreds of speeches and articles, appealing to the best voluntary instincts of prosperous people. Despite his stiff, formal appearance and personal diffidence, Hoover was known throughout the world by 1920 as the Great Humanitarian, and both the Republican and Democratic parties were interested in nominating him as their presidential candidate.

As a public speaker, Hoover was never able to overcome his discomfort with crowds and unfamiliar people. His oratory was always matter-of-fact, delivered in a consistent monotone and with stiff, poorly timed hand gestures. Later in his life, Hoover recalled, "I have never liked the clamor of crowds. . . . I intensely dislike superficial social contacts. . . . I was terrorized at the opening of every speech." Politics seemed a strange career for such a private person, but the sweep of events between 1914 and 1920 had thrust him into the spotlight.

Consequently Hoover found speechmaking painful. Although he often allowed close associates like Secretary of the Treasury Ogden Mills or presidential secretary Theodore Joslin to examine speech drafts, Hoover did not rely on a speechwriting team and spent inordinately large amounts of time as secretary of commerce (1921–1929) and president (1929–1933) preparing his remarks. What had carried Hoover so far politically was not, however, the quality of his delivery as much as the substance of his ideas. But his political rise in the 1920s, demise in the 1930s, and resurrection in the 1950s all revolved around a subtle connection between his ideas and the way he related to other people.

HOOVER AS PROGRESSIVE SPOKESMAN

In 1921, the new Republican president, Warren Harding, selected Hoover as secretary of commerce, a position of considerable influence during the 1920s. Hoover turned it into the second most powerful office in the federal government. On more than one thousand occasions between 1921 and 1929, at White House and Commerce conferences and conventions of trade associations, labor unions, farm cooperatives, and professional societies, Hoover delivered the same message again and again, creating a political philosophy known as "American individualism" and outlining his vision of the future.

As Hoover searched for some means of guaranteeing economic growth and preserving entrepreneurial individualism while avoiding industrial dictatorship and bureaucratic tyranny, he looked to the network of self-governing trade associations, labor unions, farm cooperatives, and professional societies that had appeared in the early twentieth century. In emphasizing professional standards, ethical codes of conduct, and rational problem solving, these organizations and economic interest groups provided a national perspective to a capitalist society, overcoming the centrifugal forces inherent in entrepreneurial drive. In Hoover's view, the rise of the associational state had eliminated the need for an oppressive regulatory state. The federal government would promote economic prosperity and supervise the exchanges of power between functional interest groups.

Contrary to historical stereotypes, Hoover did not believe in rugged individualism, nor was he a conservative idealogue or a political reactionary. Instead he was a progressive who believed the federal government should not ignore the fluctuations of the business cycle but was responsible for maintaining stable prices and full employment. To overcome narrow competition and provide some national economic planning, Hoover wanted the federal government to continue to encourage the creation of trade associations, farm cooperatives, labor unions, and professional societies. To improve productivity and increase wages, the federal government would provide business with reliable economic statistics, encourage scientific management, and assist in research and development. The federal government was to be the coordinator of the associational state—promoting the interest of each group, negotiating their differences, and occasionally regulating their activities.

In his speech accepting the Republican nomination for president in 1928, Hoover clearly expressed his beliefs in the associational state and the role to be played by unions, cooperatives, professional societies, and trade associations, with the federal government coordinating their relationships and eliminating

those fluctuations from boom to slump which bring on one hand the periods of unemployment and bankruptcy and, on the other, speculation and waste. Both are destructive to progress and fraught with great hardship to every home. By economy in expenditure, wise taxation, and sound fiscal finance it can relieve the burdens upon sound business and promote financial stability. By sound tariff policies it can protect our workmen, our farmers, and our manufacturers from lower standards of living abroad. By scientific research it can promote invention and improvement in methods. By economic research and statistical service it can promote the elimination of waste and contribute to stability in production and distribution. By promotion of foreign trade it can expand the markets for our manufacturers and farmers and thereby contribute greatly to stability and employment.

That perspective, as well as the prosperity of the 1920s, gave Hoover a landslide victory in the election of 1928. But in that acceptance speech were also the seeds of Hoover's political doom. Few other U.S. presidents have ever offered more ironic words:

One of the oldest and perhaps the noblest of human aspirations has been the abolition of poverty. By poverty I mean the grinding by undernourishment, cold, and ignorance, and fear of old age of those who have the will to work. We in America today are nearer to the final triumph over poverty than ever before in the history of any land. We have not yet reached the goal, but . . . we shall soon with the help of God be in sight of the day when poverty will be banished from this nation.

Less than a year after the speech, the country was mired in the worst depression in its history.

The collapse of the economy caught Hoover, and the rest of the country, by surprise. Although Hoover did more than any previous president to ease the pain of an economic disaster, he was uncomfortable in that role and viewed the Reconstruction Finance Corporation, the Emergency Relief and Construction Act, and the Federal Home Loan Bank system as temporary measures to deal with emergency conditions. As soon as the emergency was over, Hoover expected to have the federal government return to its role as coordinator of the economy rather than major participant.

Hoover's public addresses during his presidency had two major themes: that the depression was an extraordinary situation demanding extraordinary policies and that American society was fundamentally sound. To justify administration policies and create a feeling of unity and voluntary cooperation throughout the country, Hoover used the analogue of war theme in most of his speeches. For Hoover the Great Depression and World War I were similar phenomena, draining national resources and demanding unity. During the 1931 congressional debates over the Reconstruction Finance Corporation Act, Hoover said that "combating a depression is, indeed, like a great war, in that it is not a battle on a single front but upon many fronts. These measures all are a necessary addition to the efficient and courageous efforts of our citizens throughout the nation." On February 5, 1932, in an address to a Republican congressional delegation, Hoover said:

We are engaged in a fight upon a hundred fronts just as positive, just as definite and requiring just as greatly the moral courage, the organized action, the unity of strength, and the sense of devotion in every community as in war.

His speeches between 1930 and 1933 were riddled with such military metaphors as "tactics," "enemy," "fronts," "machine," "attack," and "campaign," all in a desperate, and ultimately unsuccessful, attempt to rally the public behind him. These were metaphors Franklin D. Roosevelt would later use to rally popular support.

Hoover spent a great deal of time during his presidency trying to convince people that the United States was fundamentally sound, that unity and confidence would see the country through the crisis, and that citizens should resist temptations to alter public policy dramatically with massive federal intervention into the economy. While people were worrying about losing their jobs or feeding their children, Hoover was spending inordinate amounts of time in radio addresses and public speeches telling them that all was well. Unfortunately, his radio voice was as unreliable as the economy. Because of his personal shyness and discomfort in any but the most controlled private settings, Hoover's radio persona was dull, expressionless, and cold and did little to build confidence in his listeners' perceptions. Indeed, his radio speeches helped reinforce the growing public sentiment that he was an insensitive, uncaring man. Although he was probably correct that American society was fundamentally sound, the economy was fundamentally unsound, and instead of appearing as a man of confidence and optimism, Hoover became an image of insensitivity to most Americans, one that Democrats exploited in the election campaign of 1932. Herbert Hoover, once the Great Humanitarian, had become the most hated figure in the United States. His talk about confidence, optimism, sacrifice, and unity had become a cruel charade, at least in the minds of most Americans. They handed him the greatest electoral defeat in U.S. history in November 1932.

Hoover had appeared cruel to many Americans because of his refusal to expand the power of the federal government aggressively. He had spent too many years in Europe before and after World War I, had seen too much of war and totalitarianism, and he feared for the future of the United States, worried that big government would come to dominate the culture. But the Great Depression had wasted his dream. While he worried about the future substance of American institutions, 70 million people worried about tomorrow night's meal and the next month's rent. The stark immediacy of their needs had rendered Hoover's fears irrelevant to his own generation.

During the 1940s, 1950s, and 1960s, more and more Americans came to appreciate those fears. Between 1935 and 1960, Hoover traveled widely across the country on the lecture tour, and the major theme of his thousands of speeches was the image of the corporate state in which the federal government had forged alliances with the major economic interest groups. In his view, the federal government must never become a competitive participant with the major functional interest groups in the economy because in addition to the characteristic inefficiency of large political bureaucracies, totalitarian political impulses would accompany direct economic intervention. In "True Liberalism," delivered to the Colorado Young Republicans in Colorado Springs on March 7, 1936, Hoover warned:

It is a false liberalism that interprets itself into dictation by government. Every step in that direction crushes the very roots of liberalism. It is the road not to liberty but to less liberty. That spirit of liberalism is to create free men. It is not the regimentation of men. It is not the extension of bureaucracy. You cannot extend the mastery of government over the daily life of a people without somewhere making it a master of people's souls and thoughts.

If the federal government intervened in the economy, it would commit economic blunders and would resent carrying the burden of political responsibility for those mistakes. The persistence of such resentment could lead to tyranny. Economic elites would be anxious to finance the political campaigns of executive incumbents and their bureaucratic allies and dominate the government. Hoover worried about the day when the federal government functioned in every corner of the economy, burdening small businesses with red tape, imposing irrational tax codes that stifled investment, distributing welfare payments and undermining the work ethic, and allowing big corporations and big labor unions to control major economic decisions.

During the Great Depression, the fear of a massive federal government hurtling out of control was inconceivable to most Americans, but after World War II, when fears of communism, socialism, "Big Brother," "1984," and the "Brave New World" magnified, Hoover began to appear more and more reasonable to the American public. By the time of his death in 1964, he had become a widely respected, if not widely loved, elder statesman.

INFORMATION SOURCES

Research Collections and Collected Speeches

The major research collection on the life and presidency of Herbert Hoover is housed in the Herbert Hoover Presidential Library, West Branch, Iowa. Especially useful are

Hoover's daily written and telephone logs, drafts of major speeches, oral history recollections of his major associates, and a wealth of other documentary sources.

Campaign Speeches of American Presidential Candidates, 1928–1972.   CSAPC
   Edited by Aaron Singer. New York: Irwin Ungar, 1976.
Best, Gary Dean. *The Politics of American Individualism.* Westport,   PAI
   Conn.: Greenwood Press, 1975.
Hoover, Herbert. *Addresses upon the American Road, 1933–1938.* New   AUAR, 1938
   York: Scribners, 1938.
————. *Addresses upon the American Road, 1938–1940.* Stanford: Stan-   AUAR, 1940
   ford University Press, 1940.
————. *Addresses upon the American Road, 1948–1950.* Stanford: Stan-   AUAR, 1948
   ford University Press, 1948.
————. *Addresses upon the American Road, 1948–1950.* New York: AUAR, 1950
   D. Van Nostrand, 1951.
————. *Further Addresses upon the American Road,* New York: D.   FAUAR
   Van Nostrand, 1946.
The Hoover Administration: A Documented Narrative. Edited by William   HA
   S. Myers and Walter H. Newton. New York: Scribners, 1936.
The State Papers and Other Public Writings of Herbert Hoover. 2 vols.   SP
   Garden City, N.Y.: Doubleday 1934.

Selected Critical Studies

Jansky, C. M. "The Contribution of Herbert Hoover to Broadcasting." *Journal of Broadcasting* 1 (1957): 241–49.
Runkel, Howard W. "A President Prepares to Speak." *Western Journal of Speech Communication* 15 (1951): 5–9.

Selected Biographies

Burner, David. *Herbert Hoover. A Public Life.* New York: Alfred A. Knopf, 1979.
Olson, James S. *Herbert Hoover and the Reconstruction Finance Corporation, 1931–1933.* Ames: Iowa State University Press, 1977.
Schwarz, Jordan A. *The Interregnum of Despair: Hoover, the Nation, and the Depression.* Urbana: University of Illinois Press, 1970.
Wilson, Joan Hoff. *Herbert Hoover. Forgotten Progressive.* Boston: Little, Brown, 1975.

CHRONOLOGY OF MAJOR SPEECHES

See "Research Collections and Collected Speeches" for source codes.

NBC radio speech, New York City, June 24,1920, *PAI*, pp. 122–123.

Acceptance speech, Stanford, California, August 11, 1928; *CSAPC*, pp. 7–16.

White House Republican congressional delegation speech, Washington, D.C., February 5, 1932; *SP*, II, p. 112.

"True Liberalism," Colorado Young Republican speech, Colorado Springs, Colorado, March 7, 1936; *AUAR, 1938*, pp. 126–141.

HUBERT HORATIO HUMPHREY
(1911–1978), vice-president of the United States

L. PATRICK DEVLIN

In a public career spanning almost four decades, Hubert H. Humphrey delivered thousands of speeches and sponsored hundreds of bills. He was a Phi Beta Kappa scholar; a reform mayor who cleaned out the rackets and passed the first city law forbidding discrimination in employment; a civil rights spokesman at the 1948 Democratic convention; the first Democratic senator from Minnesota; the originator of many legislative proposals, the most significant of which were the Nuclear Test Ban Treaty, the Food for Peace Program, the Peace Corps, and the 1964 Civil Rights Act; a Senate leader and party whip; the vice-president; and a tireless unsuccessful campaigner who in 1960, 1968, and 1972 sought the presidency.

His father, a rural druggist, contributed to the development of his son's oral nature. "They used to say about Dad—"He never sells you a pill without selling you an idea.'" The Great Depression left its imprint on Humphrey. He wrote in 1962 to a student writing a thesis, "I was a very young man during the depression and surely those cruel and critical years left their imprint on me. I suppose this is one of the reasons I have become a liberal in politics." Humphrey was a debater in high school and college. He reflected, "Debate was very interesting to me. It was competitive and I tend to be a competitive person. . . . It taught me how to organize material and how to pound home a point." At the University of Minnesota, Humphrey received instruction in speech making. His professor recalled: "Hubert got an A. His logical outlines were . . . the best in the class. He had had considerable debate experience. . . . He was older than the average student. He talked fluently . . . and was willing to talk on anything at any time." Despite this praise, his voice was described as harsh and nasal.

With a straight A average and membership in Phi Beta Kappa, he graduated magna cum laude in political science in June 1939 from the University of Minnesota. He then went to Louisiana State University where he completed a master's degree with a thesis titled, "The Political Philosophy of the New Deal."

In 1943, Humphrey ran for mayor of Minneapolis and lost, but he won in 1945. In 1948, he went to the Democratic National Convention in Philadelphia where he delivered an impassioned speech in support of a strongly worded liberal plank in the platform supporting civil rights. His speech helped the delegates adopt this plank by a vote of 651 to 582. He campaigned for the Senate in 1948 by making around 700 speeches. He served with distinction in the Senate from 1948 to 1964, when he was chosen by Lyndon Johnson as his vice-presidential running mate. After becoming the Democratic nominee for president in 1968, he lost the election to Richard Nixon. He returned to the Senate in 1971 and served until his death in 1978.

HUMPHREY AS A LEADING DEMOCRATIC ORATOR

Humphrey understood himself as a communicator. "I am, in a sense, a teacher-preacher," he once stated. He believed that the purpose of political speaking should be to educate and to inspire. Regarding his educational approach to speaking, Humphrey asserted during a 1960 campaign speech in Winona, Minnesota, "My hopes, my dreams, my goals are not limited to winning cheers and gathering votes. My quest and my purpose are to help elevate the level of political thinking in America. I was a teacher once, and I have not lost the sense of mission which every teacher must have—to inspire intelligent, rational, independent thought." In an interview with me, Humphrey disclosed, "You have to give to people. I don't just make a speech. I give a speech. I try to give the people a bit of knowledge or perhaps a useful idea." He also emphasized in the interview his inspirational purpose: "When you're speaking to an audience in most situations, in order to hold that audience's attention you not only need substance and thought in your speech but you need to have certain speaking techniques that are effective, and in my instance, I find that some effort to exhilarate, to inspire is very helpful." During the 1964 campaign when he was running for vice-president, he sought to inspire an audience at the University of Washington with an appeal to compassion:

I believe that if it is all right for we the people to be taught individually that compassion and charity is noble and moral and decent. . . . You have been taught that it is good to share, to be compassionate, to be friendly, to be charitable, to be considerate, that is what Sunday school and church and America and schools are all about. Now if it is all right for individuals to be that way, what's wrong with a government that represents those individuals, a government of the people, by the people and for the people to be that way.

There was an element of excitement about a Humphrey speech. One of his aides stated, "He strives for emotional pull. He wants people to get as excited about an issue as he is. He thinks people ought to care and he seeks to tell them why they should care." This tendency can be appreciated in two of his addresses. To an audience of druggists he was trying to involve in politics, he stated in 1947, "Don't be just a sitter. Get in there! Go to work!" And in 1966, he urged college student listeners to support the Peace Corps when he said, "Join up. We need you. Offer your services."

Humphrey was a patriot, and tributes to the nation filled his speeches. He was a liberal who said much of what he said because of personal experience. To an audience in his boyhood home town of Huron, South Dakota, he declared, "I really believe that America is beautiful. I truly believe that this is the home of the brave. I believe that this is the land of the free. And I believe that this America is literally the greatest opportunity that this world has ever known for anyone who wants to enjoy an opportunity and the privilege of an opportunity.''

He had great faith in his natural speaking ability and resented criticism of his speaking. One assistant said he had the ability to ''make a thirty minute or longer extemporaneous speech with no preparation.'' Another maintained that ''written speeches cramp his natural style.'' He preferred extemporaneous speaking because he believed he composed his thoughts better that way and because he believed extemporaneous delivery was more effective. Humphrey commented on his ability to compose a speech extemporaneously: ''Some people compose their thoughts while sitting in front of a typewriter or at a scratch pad. I find my mind is stimulated by the challenge of an audience or a conversation in my company, and I believe that my composition on my feet is better than my composition sitting at a quiet desk.'' He also believed an extemporaneous delivery was more effective: ''Ability to convince is far greater than a speech delivered from manuscript. People are tired of scripted speeches.'' Humphrey often extemporized from prepared texts. As a phrase-maker, he would pick three or four words and put them together to label a concept and capture the imagination of his audience. His staff called them ''Humphreyisms.'' He called the Goldwater proponents a ''fraction of a faction of reaction.'' He referred to Bulganin and Krushchev as the ''Gold Dust Twins of disaster and despair'' and labeled the leaders of the radical Right as ''Knights of Noisy Negativism.'' Such catchy phrases had an immediate appeal for a specific speech or campaign, although they lacked the sustaining power of memorable phrases.

Humphrey was not satisfied with identifying problems; he doggedly sought solutions. One assistant pointed out, ''He has more solutions than there are problems.'' Humphrey respected positively proposed alternatives. ''It doesn't take a great deal of intelligence to know that something is wrong,'' he said, ''but it is more important to find answers and to find a way to get solutions.'' He rarely attacked without substituting something an alternative. He told an audience of elected officials in 1966, ''I wouldn't stay in public life one day if I didn't think that we were going to be able to do something—some good for this generation and for generations yet unborn. And I am not trying to be sentimental; I mean every single word of it.''

Humphrey was an orator with a clear set of speaking principles. He believed conviction was important: ''The most persuasive technique in political speaking is conviction.'' So too was sincerity: ''There is one quality in a speech which really makes it effective and can compensate for many inadequacies—namely sincerity.'' He also said, ''Education is essentially saturation and persuasion is frequently repetitious pronouncement.''

Humphrey's weaknesses as a speaker were his overexuberance and long-windedness. His speeches were often too long. His wife told him he did not have to be eternal to be immortal, but her advice did no good. In his quest for audience identification, he often brought himself down to the level of the audience and spoke under their level of receptivity. He was more concerned with immediate audiences than with larger unseen audiences. Humphrey enjoyed personal contact and immediate audience interaction. He disliked television, though his twenty-five appearances on *Meet the Press* are still a record for one guest.

Humphrey freely admitted limitations. In a speech to the Upholsterers' Union in 1950, he personalized his limitations: "I don't want you to think I haven't made a lot of mistakes. I have. I have made some terrible mistakes and repent them. Everytime I have made one it never hurt anyone half as much as it hurt me."

Humphrey's speeches at Democratic National Conventions gave him historic prominence. In 1948, he thrust the issue of civil rights to the fore when he emphatically told the assembled delegates, "The time has arrived in America for the Democratic Party to get out of the shadow of States' Rights and to walk forthrightly into the bright sunshine of human rights." In one of the shortest speeches (ten minutes) of his political career, he was successful in getting the convention to adopt a strongly worded platform plank supporting civil rights. Humphrey stated in his speech, "There are some matters which I think must be stated clearly and without qualification. There can be no hedging." To those claiming the issue of civil rights was being rushed, Humphrey answered, "We are 172 years late." In his final appeal, he asked the delegates to approve his plank because "for the millions who have sent us, for the whole two billion members of the human family, our land is now more than ever, the last best hope on earth."

In 1964 in his vice-presidential acceptance speech, Humphrey made Barry Goldwater's extremism the issue when he repeated the refrain "but not Senator Goldwater" as he listed the Goldwater votes against the nuclear test ban treaty, against the Civil Rights Act of 1964, against the establishment of the arms control and disarmament agency, and against the National Defense Education Act. Humphrey compared Goldwater with "most Democrats and most Republicans" eight times during the speech. By the end of his litany of differences, he had the delegates shouting in unison, "but not Senator Goldwater."

In 1968, Humphrey was the battered candidate who did not run in primary campaigns but won the nomination at the embattled Chicago convention. Upon accepting the nomination, he said:

This moment is one of personal pride and gratification. Yet one cannot help but reflect the deep sadness that we feel over the troubles and the violence which have erupted. . . . Surely we have learned the lesson that violence breeds counterviolence and it cannot be condoned, whatever the source. . . . Put aside recrimination and dissention. Turn away from violence and hatred. Believe—believe in what America can do and believe in what America can be, and with the help of the vast, unfrightened, dedicated, faithful majority of Americans, I say to this great convention tonight, and to this great nation of ours, I am ready to lead our country.

Humphrey was ready to lead, but the voters gave the opportunity instead to Richard Nixon.

As a political orator, Humphrey knew that "politics is the art of preaching the preferable while practicing the possible." In a 1959 survey of the U.S. Senate, Tompkins and Linkugel found that Humphrey was the most frequently mentioned by his colleagues as the most effective speaker in the Senate.

Humphrey championed many acts. He was particularly proud of four: the Nuclear Test Ban Treaty, the Food for Peace Program, the Peace Corps, and the 1964 Civil Rights Act. He worked for years for the Test Ban Treaty after setting up the Senate Disarmament Subcommittee. In 1960 he appealed in the Food for Peace speech, "Time is against us, my friends. We must make every effort to seize the opportunity now offered to us, before it is too late. . . . Peace is not passive; it is active. It will not come to those who wait for it, who are afraid to reach out for it, who are too timid to risk little to win much." Humphrey was the congressional father of the Food for Peace program. He believed that rather than spending money to store surpluses, it was better to use the surpluses to help feed the hungry of the world. Humphrey stated at a Jefferson-Jackson Day dinner in Salt Lake City in 1959, "For the last four years, I have been devoting much time to studying this concept of using our abundance more wisely as a tool of international policy and international friendship. . . . We need a program to convert the abundance of our farms and the abundance and the productivity of our soil into economic power for our nation and into uses based on neighborly compassion and humanitarianism." The idea of a Peace Corps was not new when Humphrey introduced it in 1960, but he was its first legislative author and remained its principal sponsor. In the speech to Congress that introduced the bill, he proclaimed, "There is a great body of idealistic and talented young men in this country who are longing to have their energies harnessed. The Peace Corps would tap those vital resources. There is nothing which will build greater people-to-people and government-to-government relationships than to have fine young American men helping the people of the emerging countries to help themselves."

Humphrey worked more strenuously for the civil rights cause than for any other in his life. He introduced his first civil rights bill in 1949 and introduced either a new or modified one in every Congress thereafter. On March 30, 1964, he opened the historical debate in Congress on the Civil Rights Act of 1964 by saying:

I cannot overemphasize the historic importance of the debate we are beginning. . . . If freedom becomes a full reality in America, we can dare to believe that it will become a reality everywhere. If freedom fails here—in America, the land of the free—what hope can we have for it surviving elsewhere? That is why we must debate this legislation with courage, determination, frankness, honesty and—above all—with the sense of the obligation and destiny that has come to us at this time and in this place.

As Senate whip he persuaded some senators to vote for provisions they might ordinarily not have accepted. Humphrey reflected when the 1964 act passed: "It was the culmination of my work, and my own vindication."

Humphrey excelled in campaign oratory even if his presidential campaigns did not succeed. After trying for the vice-presidential nomination in 1956, he ran for the presidency in 1960. There were numerous reasons for his defeat in the 1960 primaries. He was underfinanced and understaffed, and parts of his campaign were amateurish. Emblazoned across the front of his campaign was a phrase that ranks as one of the all-time worst political slogans: "Over the Hump with Humph." Humphrey lost because Kennedy was more appealing.

In 1964, he ran for and won the vice-presidency. Lyndon Johnson and Humphrey had known each other for years, were friends, were philosophically compatible, and each respected the talents of the other. As vice-president, Humphrey was more influential than his predecessors because of the nature of the Johnson-Humphrey relationship. Humphrey had an unfailing loyalty to Johnson, and this got him into trouble when the issue of Vietnam arose during the 1968 campaign.

Humphrey received his party's presidential nomination in 1968, which he achieved by not running in primaries. He came within 500,000 votes out of the 73 million cast in 1968, losing to Richard Nixon.

After a short stint at private life and a return to college teaching, he ran for and won back his own Senate seat from Minnesota by the widest margin of his four Senate elections. In 1971 he returned to the Senate, and in 1972 he again ran for president in an ill-fated effort to prevent his long-time friend, George McGovern, from getting the nomination. Humphrey's efforts failed.

In 1976, he toyed with running for president again, but that autumn he learned that he had terminal cancer. In September, he spoke to the Minnesota AFL-CIO from his heart:

I have some loyalties and I have some priorities. . . . One of my loyalties has been to this great movement and I will tell you why. Not because you are perfect, not because there hasn't been a scoundrel now and then, because none of us is perfect. We have all made mistakes—and God only knows some of us have made too many.

But we judge a movement like this by its overall record and we judge the labor movement on what it has done to lift the standard of living for millions and millions and millions of plain American citizens who today can have their own home, who today have decent working conditions, who today can send their children to a good school.

Be proud of it, dear friends, be proud of it! . . . Just remember this [Humphrey paused and wiped tears from his eyes]: Mom said, "They will take your picture if you wipe your eyes with the Kleenex." Well, that's all right. Take it. The fellow that doesn't have any tears, doesn't have any heart.

On October 25, 1977, Hubert Humphrey returned to the Senate for the last time. It was a day of tribute for Humphrey. President Carter had sent Air Force One to Minnesota to pick him up. Tributes from his colleagues, friends, and even foes flooded him on this day.

Humphrey deserves the eulogy the *Washington Post* gave him in its farewell editorial: "For more than 30 years, one full generation, Hubert Humphrey was there. . . . Hubert Humphrey was ambitious to use national office well—and for the sake of other people. . . . It was his obsession. . . . He was a man of joy and bounce and decency and kindness. . . . He was a good man—a good man who did great things."

INFORMATION SOURCES

Research Collections and Collected Speeches

Most Humphrey speeches have not been published. Speech texts can be found at the Hubert H. Humphrey Institute of Public Affairs, University of Minnesota, Minneapolis. That library contains his papers, speeches, and audiovisual materials. Quotations other than those from speeches, which are fully cited in the text, are from unpublished letters or audio tape interviews with Humphrey or his staff assistants. They can be located in the author's dissertation, "Hubert H. Humphrey: His Speaking Principles and Practices," Wayne State University, 1968.

Democracy at Work. The Official Report of the Democratic National Con-   DAW
      vention, 1948. Compiled by C. Edgar Brown. Philadelphia: Dem-
      ocratic National Committee, 1950.
Hubert Humphrey: The Man and His Dream. Compiled by Sheldon E.   HH
      Englemayer and Robert J. Wagman. New York: Methuen, 1978.
Scott, Robert L., and Brockriede, Wayne. *Rhetoric of Black Power.* New   RBP
      York: Harper & Row, 1969.

Selected Critical Studies

Devlin, L. Patrick. "Hubert H. Humphrey: His Speaking Principles and Practices."
      Ph.D. dissertation, Wayne State University, 1968.
———. "Hubert H. Humphrey: The Teacher-Preacher." *Central States Speech Journal*
      21 (Summer 1970): 99–103.
———. "Hubert H. Humphrey's 1948 Civil Rights Speech." *Today's Speech* 16 (Sep-
      tember 1968): 43–47.
Keele, Gary Dallas. "An Examination of a Concept of Image in Presidential Campaigns:
      The Humphrey-Nixon Campaign of 1968." Ph.D. dissertation, University of
      Southern California, 1977.
Mills, Norbert H. "The Speaking of Hubert H. Humphrey in Favor of the 1964 Civil
      Rights Act." Ph.D. dissertation, Bowling Green State University 1974.
Nordvold, Robert. "Rhetoric as Ritual: Hubert H. Humphrey's Acceptance Address at
      the 1968 Democratic National Convention." *Today's Speech* 18 (Winter 1970):
      34–38.
Sauter, Kevin O'Brien. "The Speaking of Hubert H. Humphrey in the 1968 Presidential
      Campaign." Ph.D. dissertation, Pennsylvania State University, 1984.
Scott, Robert L., and Brockriede, Wayne. "Hubert Humphrey Faces the Black Power
      Issue." In *The Rhetoric of Black Power.* New York: Harper & Row, 1969.

Stelzner, Hermann G. "Humphrey and Kennedy Court West Virginia." *Southern Speech Communication Journal* 37 (Fall 1971): 21–33.

Selected Biographies

Cohen, Dan. *Undefeated: The Life of Hubert H. Humphrey*. Minneapolis: Lerner Publications, 1978.

Griffith, Winthrop. *Humphrey, A Candid Biography*. New York: Morrow, 1965.

Humphrey, Hubert H. *The Education of a Public Man*. Edited by Norman Sherman. Garden City, N.Y.: Doubleday, 1976.

Martin, Ralph G. *A Man for All People: Hubert H. Humphrey*. New York: Grosset & Dunlap, 1968.

Ryskin, Allan H. *Hubert: An Unauthorized Biography of the Vice President*. New Rochelle, N.Y.: Arlington House, 1968.

Sherill, Robert. *The Drugstore Liberal*. New York: Grossman, 1968.

Solberg, Carl. *Hubert Humphrey: A Biography*. New York: Norton, 1984.

CHRONOLOGY OF MAJOR SPEECHES

See "Research Collections and Collected Speeches" for source codes.

Civil rights speech at the 1948 Democratic National Convention, Philadelphia, Pennsylvania, July 14, 1948; *DAW*, p. 192.

Jefferson-Jackson Day disarmament speech, Salt Lake City, Utah, April 25, 1959; *HH*, pp. 195–200.

Food for Peace campaign speech, Wausau, Wisconsin, March 26, 1960; *HH*, pp. 225–28.

Peace Corps speech to Senate, Washington, D.C., June 15, 1960; *HH*, pp. 233–37.

Civil rights speech to Senate, Washington, D.C., March 30, 1964; *HH*, pp. 260–68.

Speech at the 1964 Democratic National Convention, Atlantic City, New Jersey, August 27, 1964; *New York Times*, 28 August 1964, p. 12.

Speech to the National Association for the Advancement of Colored People, Los Angeles, July 6, 1966; *RBP*, pp. 65–73.

Speech at the 1968 Democratic National Convention, Chicago, August 29, 1968; *New York Times*, 30 August 1968, p. 17.

JESSE LOUIS JACKSON
(1941–   ), preacher, civil rights leader, and political candidate

———————————————————————————— J. JUSTIN GUSTAINIS

Jesse Jackson is almost certainly the most prominent black leader living in the United States in the mid–1980s. His national reputation and influence are due in no small measure to his skills as a public speaker.

Jackson has successfully employed rhetoric in a variety of contexts. He was a civil rights activist who worked closely with Martin Luther King, Jr., until King's murder in 1968. He founded Project Breadbasket in Chicago, an organization dedicated to combating poverty among blacks in that city. He is founder and major spokesperson for People United to Save Humanity, better known as Operation PUSH, a civil rights organization begun in Chicago, which now has chapters in many other U.S. cities. As an offshoot of operation PUSH, Jackson formed Project Excel in 1975, designed to motivate black youth away from self-destructive life-styles and toward the united struggle for black equality. In 1984 Jackson sought the Democratic presidential nomination but ran third behind Walter Mondale and Gary Hart. Although his presidential bid was not successful, Jackson's rhetoric galvanized audiences across the country.

JACKSON AS RHETORICIAN

To date, Jackson's rhetoric has been studied by few scholars, but one interesting perspective was provided by Swanson, who examined three of Jackson's speeches: "Know Who Your Enemy Is," given at one of the Project Breadbasket meetings in 1969; "A Way Out," Jackson's 1976 presidential message to the Operation PUSH convention; and "It's Up to You," delivered in 1978 to a conference of young people.

Swanson concluded that the goal expressed in Jackson's rhetoric was that of power for black Americans. Jackson linked that power with such concepts as freedom, self-government, and being a registered voter. For Jackson, power could be achieved only by those who were somebody (as in Jackson's oft-used rhetorical refrain,"I am somebody!"), meaning socially responsible, self-disciplined, registered to vote, and willing to work for freedom together with other like-minded people. In opposition to the "somebodies," for Jackson, is the enemy. Unlike Malcolm X and some other black revolutionaries, Jackson does not automatically categorize all whites as enemies of blacks. Rather, he says, the enemies are people who act in certain ways: they are "perverted," racist, divisive, undisciplined, and hedonistic. Actually Jackson portrays two groups of enemies: one consisting of the white power structure, which oppresses blacks, and the other containing many of today's black youth, who for Jackson are more interested in drugs, alcohol, casual sex, and a life of crime than they are in progress for their own people. According to Swanson, Jackson in these speeches depicted himself in the role of savior, comparing himself indirectly to Moses and Jesus, and characterizing himself as a "watchman," "prophet," and "one who knows."

Jackson's rhetorical style has several discernible roots. He is a black American, and that exerts an influence. He has been trained in the ministry and before that attended several different black churches. Furthermore, he was a close associate of Martin Luther King, Jr., generally held to be the greatest black American orator of the modern age. All of these influences show up to some extent in Jackson's rhetoric, although some of his rhetorical characteristics cannot be clearly attributed to any specific factor in his background.

Specifically, six recurring stylistic devices appear in Jackson's rhetoric.

1. *Black English.* The use of this dialect of English, the nonstandard form known as black English, is no longer a characteristic of Jackson's rhetoric, but it was at one time. In Jackson's early Operation Breadbasket speech given in 1969, some usage of Black English occurs, such as occasional use of *ain't*, the use of *be* for *is* (as when Jackson referred to "historians that be taking everything out of context"), and the use of other nonstandard language, such as "he don't have a problem" and "it was growed."

Black English makes no appearance in Jackson's later speeches, perhaps reflecting Jackson's developing belief that he wanted his audiences to identify with him but not as a man who spoke street talk. And it is likely that Jackson came to realize that use of black English would not win him credibility with white audiences. For whatever reason, Jackson's public speaking from at least 1976 has been characterized by the use of standard American English.

2. *Alliteration.* Alliteration is a common device in rhetoric. It is certainly not unique to Jackson, but he does employ it. He points out, for example, that a mature person is one who can "produce, protect, and provide." He says that blacks must rise "from the marshy meadows of mediocrity." He claims that for blacks to achieve educational excellence, they "must contrast the politics of the five B's—blacks, browns, budgets, busing and balance—with the five A's—attention, attendance, atmosphere, attitude and achievement."

3. *Audience participation.* Jackson frequently invites and encourages his audiences to respond in specific ways when he speaks. The response called for may be verbal or nonverbal. The verbal response, which Jackson most often requests, is to have his audience repeat what he has said. One of Jackson's favorite ways to begin mass meetings of Project Breadbasket and Operation PUSH was to have the audience members repeat after him phrases such as, "I am somebody" and "Down with dope, up with hope." He has used this technique as an ending for speeches as well.

Jackson has sometimes called for his audiences to respond nonverbally in specific ways. During his campaign for the Democratic presidential nomination, he frequently ended speeches by asking those in the audience who were over eighteen but not registered to vote to come to the front of the audience and register. He would then invite the rest of the audience to applaud the new voters. This is reminiscent of a religious revival, where those present who wish to accept Jesus as their personal savior are asked to come forward and declare that desire. This similarity is probably not accidental given Jackson's religious background. His experience as a preacher is also rhetorically manifest in the next factor.

4. *Religious references*. Jackson trained to be a preacher when younger, has preached many sermons, and remains religious. As a result, his speeches frequently contain allusions to Christianity. Sometimes these references consist of quotations or paraphrases from the Bible, as when he says, "God rains on the just and the unjust alike," or when he claims to have a mission "to feed the hungry, to clothe the naked," or when he responds to criticism of his trip to Syria to free a captured American pilot by saying, "It reminds me of the time Jesus healed the blind man. Everybody was complaining except the blind man." On other occasions, Jackson's religious references do not refer to Scripture, as when he simply invokes the deity or when he says, "But President Reagan who [*sic*] asks us to pray, and I believe in prayer—I've come this way by the power of prayer. But we must watch false prophecy."

5. *Repetition*. Jackson makes great use of repetition in his rhetoric. Sometimes he merely says the same word, phrase, or sentence two or three times for emphasis. In other cases he repeats slogans—either slogans already identified with him (such as "I am somebody!" or "Excel!" or "Our time has come.") or slogans he wants the audience to identify with him. In the peroration of his speech at the Democratic National Convention, he began a series of sentences with the word *dream* (as in, "Dream of a new value system. . . . Dream of lawyers more concerned with justice than a judgeship. Dream of doctors more concerned with public health than personal wealth"). He told an audience at Howard University, "Fight for equity. Fight for ethics. Fight for excellence."

6. *Antithesis*. This is Jesse Jackson's most commonly employed rhetorical technique. Antithesis may be defined as the use of contrast to make a rhetorical point, usually within parallel grammatical structure. Jackson's speeches are rife with examples. The references to doctors and lawyers are examples of antithesis as well as repetition. In 1976 he noted how whites could go "from the log cabin to the White House—peanut planter to president" (this illustrates alliteration, as well). In the same address he claimed that blacks had turned "a stumbling block into a stepping stone." In 1978 he told an audience of young blacks, "We cannot be what we ought to be if we push dope in our veins, rather than hope in our brains." Later in the speech he adjured, "You are not a man because you can kill somebody. You are a man because you can heal somebody."

Jackson continued to use antithesis in his presidential campaign rhetoric. He stated frequently that blacks were coming "from the outhouse to the White House." His basic campaign speech contained such statements as "We must feed the world, not fight the world," and "We must be the hope of the free world, not the threat to planet earth.'' Jackson's speech to the Democratic National Convention included at least sixteen uses of antithesis, including ''There is a time to compete, and a time to cooperate,'' ''We must turn from finger-pointing to clasped hands,'' and ''Just because you're born in a slum does not mean the slum is born in you.''

Jackson's rhetoric, compassion, energy, and example have inspired many blacks to a greater participation in the political process and a greater sense of their own self-worth. Jackson has made it clear to them that each is, indeed, ''somebody.''

INFORMATION SOURCES

Research Collections and Collected Speeches

Few of Jackson's speeches have been published, and little rhetorical scholarship has appeared in print. To date, there is no Jackson research collection. According to his representatives at Operation PUSH, Jackson's papers and speech texts remain his own property. Three of his speeches have been collected by Swanson in her dissertation.

Swanson, Georgia May. ''Messiah or Manipulator? A Burkean Cluster Anal-   *MOM*
    ysis of the Motivations Revealed in the Selected Speeches of the
    Reverend Jesse Louis Jackson.'' Ph.D. dissertation, Bowling Green
    State University, 1982.

Selected Critical Studies

Coleman, Larry G.; Dates, Jannette; Gandy, Oscar; and Merritt, Bishetta, eds. *The 1984 Jesse Jackson Presidential Campaign: Design, Style, Coverage and Impact*. New York: Ablex Publishing, forthcoming.
Dates, Jannette, and Gandy, Oscar H., Jr. ''Ideological Constraints on the Coverage of Presidential Candidates: The Jesse Jackson Campaign and the American Press.'' Paper presented at the Speech Communication Association Convention, Chicago, November 2, 1984.
Merritt, Bishetta. ''Jesse Jackson and Television: Black Image Presentation and Affect in the 1984 Democratic Campaign Debates.'' Paper presented at the Eastern Communication Association Convention, Providence, Rhode Island, May 4, 1985.
Starosta, William J., and Coleman, Larry. '' 'Binding Up the Wounds': An Interethnic Rhetorical Analysis of Jesse Jackson's 'Hymietown' Apology.'' Paper presented at the Eastern Communication Association Convention, Providence, Rhode Island, May 4, 1985.

Selected Biographies

Reynolds, Barbara A. *Jesse Jackson: The Man, the Movement, the Myth*. Chicago: Nelson-Hall, 1975.

CHRONOLOGY OF MAJOR SPEECHES

See "Research Collections and Collected Speeches" for source codes.

"Know Who Your Enemy Is," Chicago, 1969; recorded on the record album, *The Country Preacher*, Stax Record Company; *MOM*, pp. 123–36.

"A Way Out," president's address, Operation PUSH Convention, Washington, D.C., 1976; *MOM*, pp. 137–61.

"In Pursuit of Equity, Ethics, and Excellence: The Challenge to Close the Gap," Howard University, Washington, D.C., May 1978; *Phi Delta Kappan* 59 (1978): 191–93.

"It's Up to You," Atlanta, Georgia, June 19, 1978; *MOM*, pp. 162–75.

"You Can Make a Difference," *New York Times*, February 27, 1984, p. A17. (Although this does not represent an actual transcript of a particular Jackson speech, it is the text of his typical campaign address given, with modifications, throughout the 1984 presidential campaign.)

"The Rainbow Coalition," Democratic National Convention, San Francisco, July 17, 1984; *Vital Speeches*, November 15, 1984, pp. 77–81.

LYNDON B. JOHNSON
(1908–1973), thirty-sixth president of the United States

_____ DAVID ZAREFSKY

Seldom is Lyndon Johnson listed among America's greatest political orators. The image that survives is almost a caricature of the old-fashioned politician, in all the worst senses of that term. Johnson's rhetorical skill, most observers agree, was displayed in interpersonal encounters, face to face or over the telephone. In public he was wooden, stilted, artificial—so much portraying the model of rectitude that he seemed afraid of his own extemporaneous expression. Johnson disdained oratory, and he was uncomfortable with and distrustful of the electronic media.

Nevertheless, the nature of the times made the president a public figure, and the exigencies of the Johnson presidency often called for public discourse. Moreover, public address had played a central role in Johnson's early life. His father served briefly in the state legislature, and from an early age Johnson became familiar with the give-and-take of political discussion, legislative speaking, and campaign rallies. He was a successful campus politician at Southwest Texas State Teachers' College through a combination of persuasion and political organization. He taught public speaking in a Houston high school, coaching a debate team to the state finals in 1931. As a congressman, he was an outspoken advocate of the New Deal. Because of the way he defined his role as Senate majority leader and vice-president, Johnson had few occasions for oratory. He found himself in late 1963 in the throes of what has been called "the rhetorical presidency." Many of the key events of the 1960s were shaped by or reflected in Johnson's presidential discourse.

PRESIDENT JOHNSON AS PERSUADER

Johnson took office under irregular circumstances. For domestic and international reasons, it was necessary to demonstrate that the political system could endure even the shock of the Kennedy assassination. Replacing chaos with confidence required that people trust the new man at the helm, and Johnson's own situation required him to find the right stance with respect to President Kennedy—revering him but not so completely subordinating himself to the late president that he was seen as having no substance of his own.

These imperatives shaped Johnson's first major public address as president, the speech on November 27, 1963, to a joint session of Congress. The dominant motif of this speech was its stress on continuity. Johnson appealed for the tax cut and the civil rights bill on the grounds that they would be fitting memorials to the slain president. And his phrase, "let us continue," revealed his intentions not only explicitly but in the obvious allusion to Kennedy's inaugural plea, "let us begin." Johnson had many choices about how to define "continuity"; he regarded it as enactment of the Kennedy legislative program. He thereby influenced the agenda of discussion and set the standard by which he later could be judged as having kept the faith. Moreover, by focusing on the sphere of politics in which he was most adept—congressional deliberation—Johnson managed subtly to suggest that he was a leader not utterly subordinate to Kennedy; after all, the thinker depended upon the doer to get the bills through.

The most pressing domestic issue when Johnson took office was civil rights. Inspired by the moral fervor of the protest demonstrations, Kennedy in 1963 submitted a strong civil rights bill, but it was still languishing in committee at the end of the year. Johnson quickly concluded that he must secure the passage of a bill at least as strong as Kennedy's. During the next few months, public address played but a slight role; the president relied instead on the interpersonal persuasion at which he was most gifted. He met with civil rights leaders and advised them which members of Congress to visit. And he concentrated his own attention on the Senate minority leader, Everett Dirksen (Illinois), whose support he needed to break the southern filibuster. The Civil Rights Act passed Congress in June 1964 and was quickly signed into law.

Following passage, Johnson pursued two rhetorical objectives: to reconcile the South to the law and to shape the future direction of the civil rights movement. In speaking to southerners, he employed a combination of rhetorical strategies. In one respect he met the issue head-on, telling his audiences that the law of the land had been passed by both parties and signed by him and that he was determined to enforce it. At the same time, he sought to mute the significance of the issue, suggesting that outsiders were trying to agitate the South over civil rights in order to divide and subjugate the region but that a bright future lay ahead if only the racial controversy could be put to rest. This mix of appeals is evident in Johnson's October 1964 speech in New Orleans, in which he added an extemporaneous discussion of civil rights to his prepared remarks on other subjects.

Even with the Civil Rights Act in place, the moral force of the civil rights movement outpaced the efforts of the federal government. Again responding to events in the South, Johnson spoke to a joint session of Congress in March 1965 in an appeal for voting rights legislation. This speech is sometimes identified as his most moving public address, conveying the natural eloquence that he so often took care to shield. Two points deserve special mention. First, the president linked together the issues of civil rights, education, and poverty, drawing on the memory of his days as a teacher in rural Texas to describe the web of ignorance, poverty, and discrimination in which young children were caught. Second, the speech was notable because a southern president built to a climax and then dramatically uttered the words of the civil rights anthem, "We Shall Overcome."

In the June 1965 commencement address at Howard University, Johnson tried to shape the civil rights movement's direction rather than merely responding to outside pressure. It was not enough, he said, "just to open the gates of opportunity. All our citizens must have the ability to walk through those gates." Accordingly, policies must be developed to recognize the handicapping legacy of discrimination—the beginnings of the idea of affirmative action. Johnson also tried to leapfrog the movement by proposing a third civil rights act, which would, among other features, ban racial discrimination in housing. Originally requested in a presidential message in April 1966, the act finally passed Congress two years later in the aftermath of the assassination of Martin Luther King.

Race riots from 1964 through 1967 posed a dilemma for Johnson's advocacy of civil rights. He recognized that despite the new laws, many of the riots were founded in legitimate grievances, yet he also knew that disregard for law and order cost him support for civil rights by moderate and conservative whites. He could not reward the rioters, but he could not utterly castigate them either. He emphasized the need for order, called for renewed commitment to the goals of civil rights, and announced the appointment of a commission to study the causes and prevention of riots. Each of these approaches, however, was outflanked, either by radicals or by conservatives. Ultimately it was Johnson's fate to seek to define the civil rights agenda at precisely the time when the old civil rights movement was coming apart.

Johnson inherited the civil rights issue, but the Great Society was his own creation. He began with the issue of poverty, declaring "unconditional war" on the enemy during his January 1964 State of the Union Address. The war metaphor, consciously chosen, affected the nature of the program. It called for an omnibus effort, nationwide in scope, with maximum publicity and centralized administrative direction. Johnson formally proposed this program in a March 1964 message to Congress in which he deplored the "paradox of poverty amidst plenty." Despite the absence of strong pressure groups lobbying for the Economic Opportunity Act, it became law within five months.

The president next moved to set his entire domestic program in a broader framework and to find a term to describe it. Harking back to Roosevelt and Truman, he had tried *better deal*, but that phrase had not gone well. The term *great society* surfaced in several Johnson speeches in the spring of 1964, particularly in the University of Michigan commencement address in May. Johnson appealed to new themes and spoke especially about cities, countryside, and classrooms. Besides the War on Poverty, the key components of the Great Society were federal aid to education and medical care for the aged, each proposed to Congress in a special presidential message and each enacted into law during 1965. But the Great Society also could be characterized by overarching themes: a concern for the quality of life as opposed to a purely materialistic sense of well-being, a balance between continuity and change, acknowledgment of the need for special efforts in behalf of those left behind, an active role for the federal government, and a confidence in the country's ability to achieve its goals. This last theme figured prominently in Johnson's 1965 Inaugural Address, in which he expansively boasted, "Is our world gone? We say farewell. Is a new world coming? We welcome it, and will bend it to the hopes of man." To the 1980s reader, this self-confidence appears as arrogance approaching hubris, but it reflected Johnson's genuine belief that the nation could accomplish whatever it set out to do.

In appealing for his domestic programs, Johnson consistently combined the articulation of a utopian vision—the abolition of poverty, conquest of disease, or attainment of "full educational opportunity"—with conservative appeals at the level of means—programs would not cost much, they would "make taxpayers out of taxeaters," save money in the long run, and benefit everybody. Particularly when such important social goals could be achieved without strain or sacrifice, support for the Johnson programs could be portrayed as a moral imperative. The seeming ease of the effort, captured in the president's oratory, may itself have inflated expectations and led to frustration when all did not turn out for the best. Inflation, racial turmoil, and disappointments in Vietnam and in the cities jolted the national confidence in the future and threatened the Great Society. Nevertheless, Johnson got the last word. In his final Economic Message, in January 1969, he returned to the earlier themes of the Great Society, noting his accomplishments, setting forth the unfinished business for the next president, and even adding more items, such as a guaranteed annual income, which he earlier had criticized.

Some of the same desire to control events that characterized domestic policy can be seen in foreign affairs: in Johnson's telephone diplomacy during the 1964 Panama crisis, in urging a new approach toward Eastern Europe in 1966, and in pursuing a nuclear nonproliferation treaty in 1968. Still, for many, Johnson's foreign policy is synonymous with Vietnam. In this regard, it must be remembered that public opinion supported the president's policy on the war almost all the way through his administration. Opposition did not pass the 50 percent mark until March 1968, and of those opposed then, half wanted a more hawkish course of action. One factor in the retention of public support was a series of presidential addresses that now may seem sterile or irrelevant but were powerfully persuasive in their day.

Johnson's primary goal was to stop aggression. But even that was only a prelude to a more positive and ambitious program: the economic development of all of Southeast Asia. He spelled out his objective in a speech at Johns Hopkins University in April 1965, in which he proposed a $1 billion economic development program once peace was restored to Vietnam. With this appeal, Johnson hoped to regain the support of those few liberals who were dubious of his war aims and to induce the North Vietnamese to abandon an irrational war. Neither result came about, and in his disappointment Johnson made few other references to his hopes for the postwar development of Vietnam.

Besides, the war must be ended first. That required "saving" South Vietnam from communism in order to protect the Third World. Yet Johnson constantly portrayed himself as a man of restraint, refusing, for example, to call up the reserves or to seek a declaration of war. His own explanation is that he was fearful of triggering secret treaties by which the Soviet Union and China would intervene, but it is more plausible that he feared that his domestic programs— on which his claim to history would rest—would become casualties of a national mobilization for war. The paradox of unconditional commitment to objectives and self-restraint as to means was reconciled through an unusual definition of victory. Johnson sought to persuade China and the Soviet Union that wars of liberation fail. U.S. perseverance would be taken as a sign that communism could not triumph. Recognizing that sign, the major communist powers would cease and desist, and then, by Johnson's view, the war would be won. It was this stance that served to lock the United States into a basically inflexible position, heavily dependent on the wishes of the South Vietnamese rather than in control of its own actions.

Events enabled Johnson to escalate the war, pursuing his military objective, all the while proclaiming his action to be a limited response to a specific enemy provocation and repeating his desire for restraint. The attack in the Gulf of Tonkin was a fortuitous event, enabling Johnson to justify military action while proclaiming his self-restraint. Even the nature of Johnson's public address on this occasion displayed his ambivalence: he announced the reprisals in a speech delivered twenty-four minutes before midnight, hardly the time likely to attract a large audience. Subsequent escalations followed a similar pattern. The shelling of U.S. barracks at Pleiku in February 1965 provided the occasion for a reprisal recommended earlier. And so began Operation Rolling Thunder, the sustained bombing of the North—without any public address. The commitment of major increments of U.S. troops was explained in July 1965 as a counter to the North Vietnamese infiltration of regular army units. This time, Johnson announced his action during a midday, midweek press conference, sandwiched between other announcements on unrelated subjects. In each of these escalations, the muted rhetorical response effectively portrayed Johnson as restrained even as he was stepping up the military level of the war.

The message of U.S. staying power in Vietnam was undermined by domestic dissent. How could the United States convince others that wars of liberation fail if it was unwilling to persevere? Johnson at first believed that dissenters were simply misinformed and that administration speakers could set them straight; for this reason he welcomed the national teach-ins in the spring of 1965. But when dissent continued, Johnson sought to co-opt the critics (with the Christmas 1965 bombing pause, for instance) and to compete with them for the headlines. When Senator J. William Fulbright (Democrat, Arkansas) held hearings on the war in February 1966, Johnson accepted a long-standing invitation to speak at Freedom House in New York, where he defended U.S. conduct in Vietnam as consistent with the cause of freedom. Still the opposition continued, and the president began to castigate his critics more directly. He thought that they were giving Hanoi the mistaken impression that the country was deeply divided. In September 1967 it appeared as though Johnson might prevail. In a speech in San Antonio, he set forth a framework for peace negotiations that most Americans thought reasonable, and when North Vietnam spurned this offer, public opinion rallied in support of the president. Seventy percent thought bombing of the North should continue. For their part, administration speakers were confident that the long, difficult struggle would soon pay off.

Then came the Tet offensive, a blow far more serious psychologically than militarily. It cast doubt on the predictions of an end to the war and triggered an intense debate within the administration, which culminated in a dispute over what Johnson would say in a major speech on Vietnam scheduled for March 31. The hawks wanted a major increase in troop commitments and a fighting speech; the doves wanted a halt to the bombing and a cap on the U.S. troop presence. Neither faction achieved its goals completely, but Johnson definitely based the speech on the peace draft. The March 31 speech is a text in which one can find what one seeks. It can be read as a continuation of Johnson's policies in that it did announce an increase in troop levels and a bombing halt that was less generous than previous pauses had been. But it also can be taken as signaling a major change by placing a ceiling on troop levels and unilaterally halting even some bombing of the North without a prior commitment to reciprocity. This latter interpretation, of course, was given added credence when North Vietnam, much to Johnson's surprise, agreed to open negotiations.

The most memorable aspect of the March 31 speech was the surprise peroration. Although virtually assured of renomination and having a good chance of reelection, the politician for whom Washington had been home for thirty-six years was heading back to Texas. He left in his presidential public addresses a record of his times. They were times of great and unpredictable change, of striving for mastery and control of events, of confidence in the country's ability to endure even such great problems.

Johnson sought consensus and induced southerners to acquiesce in civil rights, businessmen in the Great Society, and—at least for a time—liberals in the Vietnam war. But Johnson also gained mastery over issues at precisely the wrong time. He dominated civil rights just when blacks and whites alike weakened their commitment to integration. He championed the Great Society programs only to find the beginnings of national sentiment against big government. He followed the standard liberal course in Vietnam just when liberals were reappraising their basic assumptions about America's place in the world. And Johnson, master of flexibility when it came to tactics, proved to be rigid when it came to goals. Seeking to control the change he professed to welcome, his most basic commitments and values left him unable to master the challenge of change during the 1960s.

INFORMATION SOURCES

Research Collections and Collected Speeches

The best resource for research on the presidential rhetoric of Lyndon Johnson is the Lyndon Baines Johnson Library, University of Texas at Austin. The Johnson Library includes the White House Central Files, the president's appointment books and daily diaries, files of numerous aides, and presidential correspondence. It features an extensive collection of books and articles about Lyndon Johnson and an excellent collection of oral histories by many of the principals in the Johnson administration. Finally, the library has a large collection of microfilms of theses and dissertations about President Johnson, and numerous bibliographies and finding aids.

American Rhetoric from Roosevelt to Reagan: A Collection of Speeches and   ARRR
    Critical Essays. Edited by Halford Ross Ryan. Prospect Heights,
    Ill.: Waveland Press, 1983.
Public Papers of the Presidents: Lyndon B. Johnson. 10 vols. Washington,   PP
    D.C.: U.S. Government Printing Office, 1965–1970.
Presidential Rhetoric. Edited by Theodore Otto Windt, Jr. 2d ed. Dubuque: PR
    William C. Brown, 1980.
To Heal and to Build: The Programs of President Lyndon B. Johnson. New   THB
    York: McGraw-Hill, 1968.

Selected Critical Studies

Bass, Jeff D. "The Appeal to Efficiency as Narrative Closure: Lyndon Johnson and the Dominican Crisis, 1965." *Southern Speech Communication Journal* 50 (Winter 1985): 103–20.

Cherwitz, Richard A. "Lyndon Johnson and the 'Crisis' of Tonkin Gulf: A President's Justification for War." *Western Journal of Speech Communication* 41 (Spring 1978): 93–104.

Logue, Cal M., and Patton, John H. "From Ambiguity to Dogma: The Rhetorical Symbols of Lyndon B. Johnson on Vietnam." *Southern Speech Communication Journal* 47 (Spring 1982): 310–29.

Smith, F. Michael. "Rhetorical Implications of the 'Aggression' Thesis in the Johnson Administration's Vietnam Argumentation." *Central States Speech Journal* 23 (Winter 1972): 217–24.

Turner, Kathleen J. *Lyndon Johnson's Dual War: Vietnam and the Press*. Chicago: University of Chicago Press, 1985.

Zarefsky, David. "Civil Rights and Civil Conflict: Presidential Communication in Crisis." *Central States Speech Journal* 34 (Spring 1983): 59–66.

———. "The Great Society as a Rhetorical Proposition." *Quarterly Journal of Speech* 65 (December 1979): 364–78.

———. "Lyndon Johnson Redefines 'Equal Opportunity': The Beginnings of Affirmative Action." *Central States Speech Journal* 31 (Summer 1980): 85–94.

———. *President Johnson's War on Poverty: Rhetoric and History*. University: University of Alabama Press, 1986.

———. "President Johnson's War on Poverty: The Rhetoric of Three 'Establishment' Movements." *Communication Monographs* 44 (November 1977): 352–73.

———. "Subordinating the Civil Rights Issue: Lyndon Johnson in 1964." *Southern Speech Communication Journal* 48 (Winter 1983): 103–18.

Selected Biographies

Bornet, Vaughn Davis. *The Presidency of Lyndon B. Johnson*. Lawrence: University Press of Kansas, 1983.

Caro, Robert A. *The Years of Lyndon Johnson: The Path to Power*. New York: Knopf, 1982.

Divine, Robert A., ed. *Exploring the Johnson Years*. Austin: University of Texas Press, 1981.

Dugger, Ronnie. *The Politician: The Life and Times of Lyndon Johnson—The Drive for Power, From the Frontier to Master of the Senate*. New York: W. W. Norton, 1982.

Evans, Rowland, and Novak, Robert. *Lyndon B. Johnson: The Exercise of Power*. New York: New American Library, 1966.

Goldman, Eric F. *The Tragedy of Lyndon Johnson*. New York: Knopf, 1969.

Johnson, Lyndon Baines. *The Vantage Point: Perspectives of the Presidency, 1963–1969*. New York: Holt, Rinehart, and Winston, 1971.

Kearns, Doris. *Lyndon Johnson and the American Dream*. New York: Harper & Row, 1976.

Steinberg, Alfred. *Sam Johnson's Boy*. New York: Macmillan, 1968.

CHRONOLOGY OF MAJOR SPEECHES

See "Research Collections and Collected Speeches" for source codes.

Address to Joint Session of Congress, Washington, D.C., November 27, 1963; *PP: 1963–1964*, 1: 8–10; *PR*, pp. 53–55.

State of the Union Address, Washington, D.C., January 8, 1964; *PP: 1963–1964*, 1: 112–118; *PR*, pp. 56–61.

Poverty message to Congress, Washington, D.C., March 16, 1964; *PP: 1963–1964*, 1: 375–80.

Great Society speech, University of Michigan, Ann Arbor, Michigan, May 22, 1964; *PP: 1963–1964*, 1: 704–07; *PR*, pp. 61–64.

Tonkin Gulf announcement, Washington, D.C., August 4, 1964; *PP: 1963–1964*, 2: 927–28; *PR*, pp. 65–66.

Political campaign speech, New Orleans, Louisiana, October 9, 1964; *PP: 1963–1964*, 2: 1281–88.

Inaugural Address, Washington, D.C., January 20, 1965; *PP: 1965*, 1: 71–74.

Voting rights address to Joint Session of Congress, Washington, D.C., March 15, 1965; *ARRR*, pp. 173–180; *PP: 1965*, 1: 281–87; *PR*, pp. 66–72.

Johns Hopkins University address, Baltimore, Maryland, April 7, 1965; *PP: 1965*, 1: 394–99.

Howard University commencement address, Washington, D.C., June 4, 1965; *PP: 1965*, 2: 635–40; *THB*, pp. 217–26.

Announcement of troop increase, press conference, Washington, D.C., July 28, 1965; *PP: 1965*, 2: 794–803 (esp. p. 795); *PR*, pp. 80–85.

Freedom House speech, New York City, February 20, 1966; *PP: 1966*, 1: 208–15.

Civil rights message to Congress, Washington, D.C., April 28, 1966, *PP: 1966*, 1: 461–69.

Vietnam policy speech, San Antonio, Texas, September 29, 1967; *PP: 1967*, 2: 876–881; *PR*, pp. 93–98; *THB*, pp. 123–31.

Renunciation speech, Washington, D.C., March 31, 1968; *PP: 1968–1969*, 1: 469–476; *PR*, pp. 98–106; *THB*, pp. 455–64.

Economic message, Washington, D.C., January 16, 1969; *PP: 1968–1969*, 2: 1311–25.

BARBARA JORDAN
(1936–   ), member of Congress from Texas, public advocate

————————————————————————————————— DAVID HENRY

Barbara Jordan's lifelong oratorical education and commitment to civic involvement led to her emergence as a nationally renowned political advocate in the mid–1970s. Her public speaking training began early. She was the daughter of a baptist minister, whose wife was widely known as an orator in her own right; thus church activities were formative in Jordan's life. One task she considered a source of contentment was the memorization and recitation of selected verse, especially James Weldon Johnson's "The Creation." Her superior declamation of the poem brought her recognition and self-satisfaction. It was a talent that would distinguish her from her peers.

In high school Jordan decided she wanted to be named "Girl of the Year" and believed that she could attain the distinction through success in public speaking. When she finished second in an Elks Club contest, she took note of the successful techniques her opposition employed. The winners, she observed, were "very skilled in histrionics and always very dramatic in their presentations." Sensitized to the importance of dramatics, Jordan proceeded to win local, state, and national versions of the National Ushers Convention Oratorical contest. "Girl of the Year" honors followed. Jordan's competitive speaking continued at Texas Southern University when, upon being told that she could not run for student body president as a freshman, she turned for security to "what was familiar: the prestigious three-by-five cards." Her college debate coach expanded her oratorical repertoire. Although Jordan projected herself well, she was less attentive to analysis and substance, so she began her college forensic career as a first affirmative constructive speaker, while the more challenging task of refutation was left to the young men. By her junior year, however, tutored in the importance of content as well as delivery, Jordan was a formidable competitor. When the Supreme Court's decision in *Brown v. the Board of Education* (1954) allowed her to compete against white students, she traveled to Baylor University for her first integrated contest. She won, and her confidence continued to grow.

After graduating with high honors, Jordan attended law school at Boston University, where she added a final skill that would serve her well as a public advocate. Frustrated by her first examination in criminal law, she complained that the questions were phrased ambiguously, thus making several answers equally correct. Upon reflection she realized that "it was not the answer the professor was trying to pull from me, it was the reasoning." In the past, she had always succeeded by "spouting off" and "speechifying," but at Boston she "had to think and read and understand and reason." The discovery was revelatory. "I cannot," she wrote later, "I really cannot describe what that did to my insides and to my head. I thought: I'm being educated finally."

Jordan's emergence as a political figure was similarly evolutionary. Armed with a law degree, she returned to Texas in 1959. She passed the state bar examinations in Massachusetts and Texas and opened a small legal practice in Houston. In 1960, looking for something to do with her free time, she volunteered her services to the Kennedy-Johnson campaign. Her initial political involvement entailed the organization of a block-worker program, but when a colleague was unable to keep a speaking engagement, Jordan substituted. Local party officials quickly decided that she was too valuable to keep at headquarters, so she became a full-time speaker. After the election, she continued to speak publicly, and her press notices grew. An eloquent black woman with a law degree from Boston University was a phenomenon too rare for the press to ignore, and Houston's black newspapers in particular covered her appearances frequently and prominently. The attention led to her first campaign for the state House of Representatives in 1962. Although she lost, she earned recognition and respect for her power to draw prospective voters to rallies where her speeches impressed her fellow candidates and audiences alike. Success as a rally speaker finally converted to electoral victory in 1966 when the Supreme Court's one man, one vote decision mandated reapportionment, placing Jordan in a newly formed state senate district. Six years later, she campaigned successfully for a seat in the U.S. House of Representatives.

When she arrived in Washington, Jordan possessed oratorical habits and political instincts that would define her performance as a national figure. Through years of recitation and public speaking contests, she had polished her impressive delivery; her legal training and practice had taught her the necessity of careful reading, thinking, and preparation; and her successes had produced a sense of self-confidence that pervaded her presence on the platform.

JORDAN AS CITIZEN-ORATOR

The ideal citizen in the Greco-Roman rhetorical tradition, among other traits, possessed broad knowledge, was intent on doing good works for the city-state, and mastered the techniques of eloquence necessary to effect good deeds. When Barbara Jordan emerged as a central player in national politics on the evening of July 25, 1974, it soon became apparent that she was prepared to assume the responsibilities of the citizen-orator. The House Judiciary Committee's hearings on the prospective impeachment of Richard Nixon provided the forum, but the setting was, in fact, every living room in the United States because the committee had agreed to permit the broadcasting of a fifteen-minute statement by each member. The order of presentation was determined by seniority; Jordan appeared late on the second day. Although initially she had opposed the decisions to offer statements and to televise them, her address captured the imagination of the public and launched her into national prominence. Viewers saw a performance that was the product of a lifetime of training. Key rhetorical features of her statement included her detailed research, the speech's compelling structure, and her confident delivery. The speech had an impact on both the audience and Jordan's career.

When the committee recessed for dinner, Jordan had yet to script her remarks. She returned to her office to cull from her study of constitutional history and judicial opinion on impeachment the principles she deemed most applicable to the Nixon case. Determined to avoid a reflexive assumption of Nixon's culpability, she had listened attentively to the testimony presented to the committee. During the recess, she balanced the data issued in committee sessions with her understanding of the Constitution, and when the committee reconvened, she addressed a nation anxious for the resolution of what had become a prolonged crisis. Three issues, Jordan concluded, needed to be addressed in assessing the appropriateness of impeachment. She considered each serially in a fashion strikingly similar to the dictates of the classical stasis system, which established standard lines of legal argumentation. First, the question had been raised by the president's supporters as to the propriety of the Judiciary Committee's jurisdiction; her reading of relevant law convinced her of the appropriateness of the committee's role. The next question was whether the events surrounding Watergate constituted sufficient grounds to warrant an investigation. Clearly, Jordan said, the answer is yes. Finally, and most important, did the Nixon administration's actions meet the constitutional criteria for impeachment? The bulk of Jordan's analysis rested here. The argument's structure forced assent as she moved smoothly through five criteria drawn from the authority of James Madison, Supreme Court Justice Joseph Story, and the South Carolina ratification convention. Following the delineation of each criterion, Jordan assessed its applicability to the call to impeach Richard Nixon. "If the impeachment provision in the Constitution of the United States will not reach the offenses charged here," she declared, "then perhaps that 18th century Constitution should be abandoned to a 20th century paper shredder." Response from press and public stressed the impressiveness of matter and manner alike in Jordan's appeal. Her "booming voice with her elegant articulations" caught the attention of the *New York Times*'s R. W. Apple, who labeled her statement a "lecture in Constitutional law," a view shared by members of the television audience who wrote to thank her for "explaining the Constitution to us."

One product of her performance was an invitation two years later to deliver one of two keynote addresses at the Democratic National Convention. Not sure that the nation was ready for a black woman keynoter as the party's sole representative, Robert Strauss, chair of the Democratic National Committee, asked Jordan to share the podium with Senator John Glenn of Ohio. The setting called for a traditional ceremonial address dominated by praise of the Democrats and blame of the Republicans. Instead Jordan chose to challenge her party to fulfill the promise of its principles and to nudge it gently by outlining its occasional deviations from the proper path.

Glenn appeared first. The milling, talking, and general chaos television coverage defines as typical of a national political convention continued. Then Jordan spoke. Attention turned to her as she began with the observation that after 144 years of quadrennial Democratic conventions, "there is something different about tonight. There is something special about tonight. What is different? What is special? I, Barbara Jordan, am a keynote speaker." Her presence provided "one additional bit of evidence that the American Dream need not forever be deferred." Eschewing the opportunity to slay Republican dragons and to laud her party's white knights, Jordan assessed the prospects for every citizen's achievement of that dream. While prospective Democratic candidates had spent the spring and early summer dividing the party with disputes over ephemeral issues, she said, the need to address fundamental concerns such as how best to "fulfill the promise of America . . . to create and sustain a society in which all of us are equal," went unattended. The Democratic party was founded on the principles needed to create such a society—equality, diversity, active government, innovation, and a positive vision of the future—but in its zeal to please all, it had lost control of the proper relationship between the government and the people. In a particularly prescient passage, given the salience of government's role as a campaign issue in 1980 and 1984, she warned that public servants have to "strike a balance between the idea that government should do everything and the idea, the belief, that government ought to do nothing. Strike a balance." Although the tone of the admonition was admittedly mild, its inclusion is noteworthy for what it reveals of Jordan's political oratory: conventional expectations rarely dictate the formulation of her speech content. When emotion had controlled much of the argument during the Watergate crisis, she made reason and research her guide. In her keynote address, while the audience awaited a recitation of the party's accomplishments, Jordan offered an agenda of what remained to be done. In the latter instance, Jordan gained adherence to her potentially dissonant perspective, at least in part, because of what Wayne Thompson described as her genius for meeting varied sets of listener expectations without alienating either the convention delegates or the television audience.

Contrary to alienating the public, in fact, the keynote spurred countless requests for Jordan's speaking talents. When the invitation arrived to deliver the Harvard commencement address in 1977, Jordan was contemplating a career change. Since her convention speech she had been inundated with speaking invitations, virtually all of which she had to reject. She accepted those concerned with issues of nationwide import and found herself acting increasingly as a representative at large rather than a congressional delegate from Houston. The speech at Harvard exemplified her developing role.

She had been challenged initially by the letter of invitation that alluded to past commencement speakers' use of the Harvard forum. Learning that Secretary of State George Marshall had announced and promoted the Marshall Plan from that platform, Jordan sent to the Library of Congress for a copy of the plan and attendant data. As she sifted through the material, she waited for inspiration for her own topic to strike. Of all phases of the public address process, she wrote in her *Self-Portrait*, she found topic selection the most difficult. Ultimately following the dictum that one speaks best on issues drawn from experience, Jordan's attention turned to her years in public office. One recurring phenomenon she had observed in her three terms in Congress had been the tendency of her colleagues to proclaim the importance of citizen involvement in civic matters, only to create procedures that effectively precluded participation. Jordan advanced her theme in Cambridge by offering a simple but compelling lecture in the history of the nation's political philosophy. The Declaration of Independence, the Constitution, and the arguments on behalf of the Constitution's ratification, she said, made clear the centrality of the people in governance, yet the system that had evolved had come to exclude public participation beyond the exercise of the vote. And when citizens sought to redress their grievances through the judiciary, resultant Supreme Court decisions had only exacerbated the problem. Between legislative decisions and their judicial reinforcement, the people had come to feel like outsiders, but they "want to be insiders on America. We want control of our lives. . . . And when the government erodes that control, we are not comfortable. We're not comfortable at all." The remedy, she concluded, was as clear as the intentions of the founding fathers: "re-inclusion of the people in their government," for the "stakes are too high for government to be a spectator sport." The speech's impact was immediate. So mobbed were she and her friends that one security guard commented that he had not witnessed such a response to a speaker "since the President" had been there. Which president was irrelevant.

The commencement address's long-term effects were even more important, for its development and the reaction to it reconfirmed Jordan's decision to change the course of her life. She realized that she had developed a national constituency and that to reach it, she "would have to leave elected politics and pursue the platform wherever I could find it." She decided "to free my time in such a way that it could be structured by the country's needs as I perceived them." Jordan eventually accepted the Lyndon Baines Johnson Public Service Professorship in the LBJ School of Public Affairs, University of Texas, which afforded her the opportunity to reflect on those needs and to travel as needed to address them. In 1984, for example, she shared the podium with President Reagan at the National Prayer Breakfast. And when the Democratic party sponsored a retreat a year later to ponder the redirection of the party after its unpropitious performance in the 1984 elections, its leaders turned to Jordan for guidance and inspiration. In all such appearances, she summoned up her rhetorical skills. Her habits of careful preparation and critical thinking ensured that the substance of each speech would be an informed and reasoned argument in support of a perspective Jordan determined the audience needed to hear, not necessarily one they wanted to hear. Her control of language and powerful delivery guaranteed an attentive, appreciative audience. She had become a modern citizen-orator.

INFORMATION SOURCES

Research Collections and Collected Speeches

American Rhetoric from Roosevelt to Reagan: A Collection of Speeches and   ARRR
    Critical Essays. Edited by Halford Ross Ryan. Prospect Heights:
    Waveland Press, 1983.
Contemporary American Speeches: A Sourcebook of Speech Forms and   CAS
    Principles. Edited by Wil A. Linkugel, R. R. Allen, and Richard
    L. Johannesen. 5th ed. Dubuque: Kendall/Hunt, 1982.
Jordan, Barbara, and Hearon, Shelby. *Barbara Jordan: A Self-Portrait.*   BJSP
    Garden City, N.Y.: Doubleday, 1979.

Selected Critical Studies

Apple, R. W. "Party Is United." *New York Times*, July 13, 1976, pp. 1, 24.
———. "Voices of New South Emerge at Hearing." *New York Times*, July 26, 1974,
    pp. 1, 15.
Rosenbaum, David E. "Black Woman Keynoter: Barbara Charline Jordan." *New York
    Times*, July 13, 1976, p. 24.
Thompson, Wayne N. "Barbara Jordan's Keynote Address: Fullfilling Dual and Con-
    flicting Purposes." *Central States Speech Journal* 30 (1979): 272–77.
———. "Barbara Jordan's Keynote Address: The Juxtaposition of Contradictory Val-
    ues." *Southern Speech Communication Journal* 44 (1979): 223–32.

Selected Biographies

Jordan, Barbara, and Hearon, Shelby. *Barbara Jordan: A Self-Portrait*. Garden City,
    N.Y.: Doubleday, 1979.

CHRONOLOGY OF MAJOR SPEECHES

See "Research Collections and Collected Speeches" for source codes.

Statement on impeachment, Washington, D.C., July 25, 1974; *House Judiciary Committee Hearings on Impeachment*, 93d Cong. 2d sess., pp. 110–14.

International Women's Year address, Austin, Texas, November 10, 1975; *BJSP*, pp 215–20.

Democratic National Convention keynote address, New York City, July 12, 1976; *ARRR*, pp. 227–31; *CAS*, pp. 333–38.

Commencement address, Harvard University, Cambridge, Massachusetts, June 1977; *BJSP*, pp. 260–66.

EDWARD MOORE KENNEDY
(1932–   ), U.S. senator from Massachusetts
_____ WILLIAM D. PEDERSON

Ted Kennedy has been a U.S. senator for nearly all of his working life. He has shown versatility in that office through the development of a unique speech-making, negotiating, and homework style. Most knowledgeable observers rank him as the best politician of the Kennedy family and one of the best current U.S. senators. As a skilled debater, competent lawyer, and consummate politician, he is the champion of the liberal wing of the Democratic party. For the most part, his twenty-five-year Senate career has reflected an unusual degree of activity and flexibility. In the pursuit of the presidency, his rhetorical skills and enjoyment of politics contain the potential to transform the direction of the Democratic party from New Deal economics to broader concerns.

Oratory played a primary role in Kennedy's formative years as the son of an ambassador and the grandson of a mayor known for Irish oratory. He won his first elective offices in elementary and junior high school. He nervously lost his first school debate when he was eight years old in a mock presidential campaign in 1940. In high school, he was in the drama club and on the debate team that beat Harvard University's freshman debaters. He graduated with honors in high school public speaking, where he is remembered as a poised, prepared debater who was good at refutation. At Harvard he majored in government and studied speech. His debate training culminated at the University of Virginia Law School where he won the coveted moot court competition with John V. Tunney on April 17, 1959. Kennedy's emphasis on debate rather than law suggests his primary interest in politics.

EDWARD M. KENNEDY AS A PRESIDENTIAL SENATOR

In 1960 Kennedy ran for his first public office by seeking his brother John's old Senate seat. His age and lack of experience were the primary issues in the campaign. With an incredible display of energy, he won his party's convention endorsement over Edward McCormack, the well-respected state attorney-general and nephew of the Speaker of the U.S. House of Representatives. The most dramatic and critical event of the campaign occurred during the primary in the first televised debate before a pro-McCormack crowd at South Boston High School, McCormack's alma mater. The site was shrewdly selected by Kennedy advisers to counteract the possible portrayal of Ted as Goliath and McCormack as David.

During the one-hour confrontation, Ted presented himself as a serious, sophisticated, and polite candidate. He wore no makeup. The highlight of the evening occurred during the final two minute closing statement when the heavily made-up McCormack culminated his assault: "If his name were Edward Moore, with . . . [his] qualifications . . . [his] candidacy would be a joke, but nobody's laughing because his name is . . . Edward Moore Kennedy."

Although both candidates and close observers thought the debate had been a disaster for Kennedy, by the next morning it had become clear that he had won a backlash victory over his overly aggressive opponent. Democrats gave him 69 percent of the vote in the primary. Although he campaigned alone, he relied on the advice, money, and techniques that had worked previously for John. The president rehearsed with him for an hour before his national exposure on "Meet the Press." Ted tended to stress data more than argument in his presentations. He bought more television time than his opponents combined in the general election and continued to identify with his presidential brother. On the other hand, he appeared to have a greater affection for personal campaigning than his brothers.

His personality developed while he was in the Senate. His style is reflected in his maiden legislative speech in support of John's civil rights policies. He made the speech on April 9, 1964, fifteen months after he took his seat, whereas John had given his first speech in the Senate after five months and Robert after only one month. The speech revealed his basic position on civil rights: he sought to place the experience of blacks within the context of discrimination against immigrant groups. He argued that "my brother was the first president of the United States to state that segregation was morally wrong." The speech followed a pattern found in his later ones, taking a very liberal position, admitting the difficulty in it, stating that the benefits outweighed the difficulty, and concluding with an appeal to the better side of human nature. Senator Wayne L. Morse (Democrat, Oregon), a former speech professor and law school dean, termed Kennedy's maiden effort a "truly great speech."

After the 1963 assassination of President John Kennedy, two more tragic events in Ted Kennedy's life followed in the late 1960s. The first is reflected in the eulogy he delivered at the funeral for his brother, Senator Robert Kennedy (New York), in 1968. His eloquence and moving delivery reminded some observers of the great Athenian statesman, Pericles, who eulogized the fallen heroes of the Peloponnesian War, and of General Henry Lee's still-quoted eulogy of George Washington. He captured the spirit of idealism and moral courage that his slain brother represented to many Americans. Although he did not write the text, he worked with Alan Walinsky and Milton Gwirtzman on developing it. Kennedy decided to use a series of quotations from Robert's speeches as the basis of the eulogy. He stressed Robert's social conscience and the importance of private citizens to become involved: "It is from numberless diverse acts of courage and belief that human history is shaped. Each time a man stands up for an ideal, or acts to improve the lot of others, or strikes out against injustice, he sends forth a tiny ripple of hope, and crossing each other from a million different centers of energy and daring those ripples build a current that can sweep down the mightiest walls of oppression and resistance." He did not idealize his brother but characterized him "as a good and decent man who saw wrong and tried to right it, saw suffering and tried to heal it, saw war and tried to stop it." The eulogy concluded with two of Robert's favorite lines from George Bernard Shaw: "Some men see things as they are and say why. I dream things that never were and say why not."

Chappaquiddick is the second tragedy of the late 1960s for Kennedy and the most controversial episode of his life. Kennedy was on Chappaquiddick Island for a cookout for staff secretaries. He left the party with Miss Mary Jo Kopechne and accidentally drove off a narrow road into the water. Miss Kopechne drowned and Kennedy managed to swim ashore. He did not immediately report the accident to the authorities. His seventeen-minute television address in 1969 is the most criticized speech he has delivered to date. Ted Sorenson and Milton Gwirtzman wrote most of the speech, which amounted to a confession, an assumption of responsibility, and an appeal to Massachusetts voters to support him. His decision to appear on television seems to have benefited him more than what he said and how he went about it. By 1971 he was rated in a poll as the third most admired man in the United States.

Although he has experienced failures, tragedies, and setbacks, Kennedy has relied on his sense of humor and flexibility to deal with adversity and disarm opponents. His ability to use humor and to mock himself helps him to establish rapport with audiences. He often uses an ad-lib remark to win a crowd over. His enjoyment of politics and instinct to play has developed into an ability to mock the artificiality of politics in the era of mass communications. Often he seems to enjoy toying with audiences and poking fun at the stock political speech and the phoniness in politics.

On the other hand, he has remained a serious critic. His most mature speeches were delivered during the decade after Chappaquiddick. His lecture in 1970 at the College Historical Society Bicentenary, Trinity College, Dublin, Ireland, drafted in collaboration with David Burke, drew on the conservative ideas of the eighteenth-century political thinker Edmund Burke. In the nuclear age with the capacity of governments to suppress political change, Kennedy presented Burke as an example for those who desire to be "moral but realistic, committed to their own nation but responsible for the condition of all men." In his review of political protest in the United States, which hinted indirectly at the situation in Northern Ireland, Kennedy rejected violence by governments, as well as by oppressed groups: "Change within Western nations will not come about through random acts of violence and disruption, for sheer violence cannot compel fundamental change. Rather it helps defeat those who are serious about change— the forces of humane moderation." His identification with Burke's ideals of moderation and skepticism in political life are consistent themes in his own rhetoric, a facet that many of his critics have overlooked.

Two speeches he delivered during his 1980 presidential campaign demonstrated his ability to inspire audiences and the nation, although he undermined his campaign at the start with overconfidence and a lack of preparation. The fall 1979 interview with Roger Mudd and how he later reacted to it illustrates both the early difficulties in his campaign and his capacity to rebound from personal and political setbacks. He gave the initial interview at his Hyannis Port home while he was unexpectedly left alone there without his family and staff. Although the program earned Mudd a Peabody Award for Excellence, Kennedy developed a reputation as a confused and inarticulate candidate as a result of his responses to questions about Chappaquiddick and why he sought the presidency. His performance crushed public belief in the myth of Kennedy oratory. Close observers, however, knew that Kennedy typically does best with a prepared text after he has done his homework. A direct contrast to this episode occurred earlier in the decade when Senator Sam Ervin (Democrat, North Carolina), the former chairman of the Judiciary Committee and a leading constitutional expert in the U.S. Senate, sent Kennedy before a federal court to present the case against the president's use of the pocket veto. Although without a prepared text or even notes, he drew on his formative debate skills to win the case. Kennedy is a better debater than extemporaneous speaker.

After the Mudd interview, he redefined his campaign in what amounted to a reannouncement speech for the presidency delivered at Georgetown University in January 1980. In the tradition of Edmund Burke, Kennedy chose to challenge President Carter's policies after listening to the State of the Union message: "If the Vietnam war taught us anything, it is precisely when we do not debate our foreign policy, we may drift into deeper trouble. If a president's policy is right, debate will strengthen the national consensus. If it is wrong, debate may save the country from catastrophe." By opposing the Carter doctrine in foreign policy and coming out in favor of wage and price controls, as well as gasoline rationing, he switched his style from that of a moderate forerunner to a liberal challenger of President Carter. The speech was drafted by Carey Parker and Robert Shrum. Kennedy memorized and rehearsed it in the hall where it was given.

The high point of Kennedy's campaign occurred at the Democratic National Convention in its most moving speech in which he proclaimed, "We kept the faith . . . the work goes on, the cause endures, the hope still lives, the dream shall never die." The first draft of the speech was written by Robert Shrum and Carey Parker. Kennedy added to it, and Arthur M. Schlesinger and Ted Sorenson collaborated in polishing the final draft. He rehearsed the thirty-two minute speech twice on the teleprompter in his hotel and once at the convention with a teleprompter. The audience interupted the final victory-in-defeat presentation fifty-one times with strong applause and gave him a twenty-three-minute standing ovation.

His most provocative recent speech was delivered at Hofstra University in 1984 during a symposium on John Kennedy's presidency. Although typically portrayed as an advocate of the Great Society, Kennedy stated that the party must break the "mythology that all the Democrats have to offer is more programs at higher cost for lesser returns.'' In another theme from Edmund Burke, he asserted that the nation ''cannot face our actual problems with an ideology that is always pro-government—or always antigovernment.'' He challenged the party to search for ''new approaches'' to the needs of the country and to ''reinvigorate'' themselves by learning to ''do more with less'' and leading ''a country, not a collection of divided and contending groups.''

INFORMATION SOURCES

Research Collections and Collected Speeches

Congressional Quarterly.	*CQ*
Congressional Record.	*CR*
Kennedy, Edward M. *The Eulogy to U.S. Senator Robert F. Kennedy at* *St. Patrick's Cathedral.* New York City. Worcester: A. J. St. Onge, 1968.	*ERFK*
———. *Our Day and Generation: The Words of Edward M. Kennedy.* Edited by Henry Steele Commager. New York: Simon and Schuster, 1979.	
Levin, Murray B. *Kennedy Campaigning.* Boston: Beacon Press, 1966.	*KC*
Levin, Murray B., and Repak, T. A. *Edward Kennedy.* Boston: Houghton Mifflin, 1980.	*EK*
New York Times.	*NYT*

Selected Critical Studies

Barber, James D. *Presidential Character.* 3d ed. Englewood Cliffs, N.J.: Prentice-Hall, 1985.

Butler, Sherry D. ''The Apologia, 1971 Genre.'' *Southern Speech Communication Journal* 37 (1972): 281–89.

Devin, L. Patrick. ''An Analysis of Kennedy's Communication in the 1980 Campaign.'' *Quarterly Journal of Speech* 69 (1982): 397–417.

Green, Thomas M., and Pederson, William D. ''The Behavior of Lawyer-Presidents.'' *Presidential Studies Quarterly* 15 (1985): 343–52.

Kraus, Sidney; Meyer, Timothy, and Shelby, Maurice, Jr. ''16 Months after Chappaquiddick: Effects of the Kennedy Broadcast.'' *Journalism Quarterly* 51 (1974): 431–40.

King, Robert L. ''Transforming Scandal into Tragedy: A Rhetoric of Political Apology.'' *Quarterly Journal of Speech* 71 (1985): 289–301.

Ling, David L. ''A Pentadic Analysis of Senator Edward Kennedy's Address.'' *Central States Speech Journal* 21 (1970): 81–86.

Randolph, Eleanor. ''The Best and the Worst of the U.S. Senate.'' *Washington Monthly* 13 (1982): 30–43.

Robinson, Michael S., and Burgess, Philip M. ''The Edward M. Kennedy Speech: The Impact of a Prime Time Television Appeal.'' *Television Quarterly* 9 (1970): 29–39.

Scheele, Henry Z. "Evaluations by Experts and Laymen of Selected Political Speakers." *Southern Speech Journal* 33 (1968): 270–78.

Wayne, Stephen J.; Beil, Cheryl; and Falk, Joy. "Public Perceptions about Ted Kennedy and the Presidency." *Presidential Studies Quarterly* 12 (1982): 84–90.

Selected Biographies

Burns, James M. *Edward Kennedy and the Camelot Legacy*. New York: Morrow, 1972.

David, Lester. *Ted Kennedy: Triumphs and Tragedies*. New York: Grosset and Dunlap, 1972.

Honan, William H. *Ted Kennedy: Profile of a Survivor*. New York: Quadrangle Books, 1972.

Lerner, Max. *Ted and the Kennedy Legend: A Study in Character and Destiny*. New York: St. Martin's Press, 1980.

McKenzie, Andrew M. "Senator Edward M. Kennedy and the 1970 Massachusetts Senatorial Campaign." Ph.D. dissertation, Ohio University, 1971.

Lippman, Theo, Jr. *Senator Ted Kennedy: The Career Behind the Image*. New York: Norton, 1976.

CHRONOLOGY OF MAJOR SPEECHES

See "Research Collections and Collected Speeches" for source codes.

McCormack-Kennedy debate, Boston, August 27, 1962; *KC*, pp. 192–93; 209–11.

Maiden U.S. Senate speech, Washington, D.C., April 9, 1964; *CR*, April 9, 1964, p. 7573.

Robert F. Kennedy eulogy, New York City; June 8, 1968 *CR*, p. 16826.

Chappaquiddick apologia, Boston, July 25, 1969; *New York Times*, July 26, 1969, p. 10.

Trinity College lecture, Dublin, Ireland, March 3, 1970; *CR*, March 17, 1970, pp. 7775–77.

Roger Mudd CBS interview, November 4, 1979; *EK*, pp. 179–80.

Georgetown University address, Washington, D.C., January 28, 1980; Devlin, p. 413; *CR*, January 29, 1980, p. 1092.

Democratic National Convention speech, New York City, August 12, 1980; *CQ*, August 16, 1980, pp. 2423–25.

Speech at John F. Kennedy Presidency Symposium, Hofstra University, Hempstead, New York, March 29, 1985; *NYT*, March 31, 1985.

JOHN FITZGERALD KENNEDY
(1917–1963), thirty-fifth president of the United States

THEODORE O. WINDT, JR.

John F. Kennedy was the first television president. It was through television that Americans initially realized his effectiveness as a political communicator, and that is the way most people remember him. His masterful performance in the first television debate with opponent Richard Nixon turned the tide of the 1960 election. Through his nationally televised speeches, which he called "reports to the nation," he led the country from crisis to crisis: from foreign crises in Berlin and Cuba through domestic crises of steel price increases and racial integration. In the end, his assassination brought unprecedented television coverage for four days of his funeral and burial, the murder of his assassin, and images of the country's collective grief.

Prior to the 1960 campaign, Kennedy was little known nationally as an effective speaker. Instead, his reputation rested on his war record as hero of PT boat 109, his family's prominence and fortune, his successful campaigns for the House of Representatives (1946, 1948, 1950) and the U.S. Senate (1952, 1958), and his unsuccessful bid for the Democratic vice-presidential nomination (1956). Above all it rested on his literary accomplishments. His senior thesis at Harvard had been published as *Why England Slept* and had become a best-seller. While recovering from critical spinal surgery, he wrote *Profiles in Courage*, which won the Pulitzer Prize in 1956. But during the 1960 campaign and especially after he entered the White House, Kennedy became recognized, first as an effective speaker and then as a president who could rise to eloquence.

KENNEDY AS A PRESIDENTIAL PERSUADER

John F. Kennedy was to live television what Roosevelt had been to live radio. But television offered greater flexibility than radio and new opportunities that the administration seized upon. They developed a variety of formats adapted to television to present the president and his message in the most favorable light. First, the president used conventional set speeches, the staple of presidential rhetoric, to speak directly to the nation without having his message filtered through the press. On nine separate occasions, Kennedy appeared to deliver a formal, prepared address limited to a single topic, usually an immediate issue or event to which he was reacting. This concentrated rhetorical approach was modeled after Harry Truman's "fire brigade" uses of speeches rather than the broad review of policy that Roosevelt had favored. Second, Kennedy revolutionized press conferences by having them televised live and unedited. Of the seventy-two regular and special news conferences he held, no fewer than sixty-three were televised. In addition, his press conference of July 23, 1962, was carried live to Europe via Telestar; thus he became the first president able to reach out to Europeans in this fashion. Third, Kennedy invented conversations with news correspondents, or the so-called rocking chair interviews. On December 17, 1962, Kennedy sat in his rocking chair in the Oval Office, discussed the problems and accomplishments of his first two years in office, and answered questions from three reporters for an hour of prime time on all three national networks. Finally, the administration allowed a wide range of other television events to bring the message and image of the president to the public, including prerecorded interviews, special tours of the White House, and documentaries of the president working in the White House. In using the new dimensions television offered, the president explored and expanded the ways in which presidential rhetoric could be presented to the public. These efforts set precedents for subsequent presidents and pioneered methods in which presidential rhetoric and political television would merge, become inseparable, and eventually arise as a central and formidable force for the exercise of presidential power.

In accepting the Democratic nomination in 1960, John Kennedy promised to usher in the era of the New Frontier, which he said was "not a set of promises" but a "set of challenges." In seeking his claim to the presidency, Kennedy faced two major challenges: his religion and his underdog status.

Since 1928 when Al Smith, a Catholic, was defeated for the presidency, conventional political wisdom had held that a Catholic could not be elected president. In the West Virginia primary in 1960, Kennedy's Catholicism was a major issue with voters, but he effectively dispatched it on his way to victory over Hubert Humphrey. Early in the 1960 general election, however, a group calling themselves the National Conference of Citizens for Religious Freedom challenged Kennedy's fitness for the presidency because he was a Catholic. On September 12, Kennedy forcefully addressed the issue in a major speech before the Greater Houston Ministerial Association. He presented a rigorous defense of religious tolerance in U.S. politics and offered to resign should his religion ever interfere with his duties as president. The speech effectively put the religious issue to rest, and it was so persuasive that Democrats replayed portions of it throughout the campaign.

The rhetorical high point of the campaign was a series of four televised debates between two candidates Richard Nixon and Kennedy, of which the first was the most important. More than 70 million Americans viewed the first debate on television in which Kennedy demonstrated that he had a grasp of the issues equal to that of Vice-President Nixon, thus diminishing Nixon's claim to superior knowledge of government. Equally important was the contrast in appearances between the two candidates. Nixon looked pale and wan in contrast to the suntanned, vigorous Kennedy. The consensus of those who saw the debate was that Kennedy won. Public opinion polls showed a shift in voters, especially those undecided, toward Kennedy. Although the race remained close, the debates were a turning point in Kennedy's shedding his underdog role and gaining momentum. The election of 1960 was the closest in popular vote in the twentieth century. Although Kennedy won 303 electoral college votes, he defeated Nixon by only one-tenth of 1 percent of the popular vote. Thus, he gained the presidency but not a mandate from the people.

On January 20, 1961, John Kennedy delivered one of the few truly memorable Inaugural Addresses in U.S. history. Although a number of people contributed to the final version, Theodore C. Sorensen was the principal draftsman of the address. Sorensen had been with Kennedy during both his Senate years and the presidential campaign. As a speech writer, he held a unique position. Not only was he the primary writer for most of Kennedy's major speeches, he was also a close adviser, confidant, and at times alter ego. Seldom has a speech writer had as much influence in an administration as Sorensen had in Kennedy's.

Kennedy's reputation as a speaker of uncommon ability rests principally on his Inaugural Address. In substance and style, it is the best representative of his rhetoric. The speech is a mixture of idealism and crisis. Being the first president born in the twentieth century, Kennedy proclaimed that the torch of leadership had been passed to a new generation "born in this century, tempered by war, disciplined by a hard and bitter peace, proud of our ancient heritage." In his most memorable and idealistic phrase, he called upon Americans to "ask not what your country can do for you—ask what you can do for your country." The idealism was counterbalanced by a mood of critical urgency. He described the world he faced in somber words: "In the long history of the world, only a few generations have been granted the role of defending freedom in its hour of maximum danger. I do not shrink from the responsibility—I welcome it." Thus do the two major themes of his administration merge in his Inaugural Address. The speech also bears the indelible imprint of Kennedy's style. Successive paragraphs begin with parallelisms: "Let both sides explore," "Let both sides . . . formulate," "Let both sides seek." Rhythmic alliterations abound: "Bear any burden, pay any price." And finally, the most distinctive device marking the Kennedy style is the balanced and antithetical sentences or phrases: "Let us never negotiate out of fear. But let us never fear to negotiate." This grand style in which language elevates substance inspired a generation of Americans and led the poet Carl Sandburg to remark, "Around nearly every sentence of it could be written a thesis, so packed is it with implications."

The rhetorical euphoria of the Inaugural soon paled in the aftermath of the Bay of Pigs disaster. On April 17, 1961, some fourteen hundred anti-Castro Cubans landed at the Bay of Pigs in Cuba intent on overthrowing Fidel Castro or joining other rebels in the interior of Cuba to fight a guerrilla war against Castro. It ended in abject failure, and the United States was soon implicated in the fiasco for its training, transport, and support of the rebels. President Kennedy took complete responsibility. In a major speech before the American Society of Newspaper Editors on April 20, he said there were three lessons to be learned from the venture. First, "the forces of communism are not to be underestimated, in Cuba or anywhere else in the world." Second, the United States "must take an even closer and more realistic look at the menace of external Communist intervention and domination in Cuba." Finally, the United States faced a "relentless struggle in every corner of the globe that goes far beyond the clash of armies or even nuclear armaments."

This hard-line, conservative, anticommunist mentality dominated Kennedy's rhetoric and actions in foreign policy, especially toward the Soviet Union, during the next year and a half of his administration. It led him, a week after his speech to the newspaper editors, to castigate the press for printing stories in advance about the Cuban invasion and to call for the press to exercise voluntary self-censorship in the interests of national security. It also led him to interpret Premier Nikita Khrushchev's demand for negotiations on Berlin and the two Germanys during their meetings in Vienna in June as a direct military challenge to a U.S. presence in West Berlin. His anticommunism and somber interpretation of his meetings with Khrushchev resulted in his apocalyptic address on the Berlin crisis on July 25. He stated that the United States "cannot and will not permit the Communists to drive us out of Berlin, either gradually or by force," and warned the Soviets that Americans "do not want to fight—but that we have fought before." He called for a doubling of the draft, major increases in the armed forces and reserves, and a rapid buildup and augmentation of the civil defense program, including public and private fallout shelters. This speech was so frightening to Americans that the fallout shelter industry boomed, and a nightmarish debate on the morality of defending one's fallout shelter from others poured forth from television and radio, public platforms and church pulpits. In the wake of the speech, the Berlin wall was built, and both the Soviets and the Americans resumed atmospheric testing of nuclear weapons, but eventually both sides relented and allowed the crisis to subside as they began discussions over the future of Germany and Berlin.

The strained relations between the United States and the Soviet Union hit their zenith in October 1962. Earlier that month, the president had learned that the Soviets had begun to deploy offensive missiles in Cuba. Employing foreign crisis rhetoric, the war genre of presidential rhetoric, Kennedy issued an ultimatum demanding that Khrushchev remove the missiles or risk nuclear war. Three lines of argument constitute this rhetorical genre. First, the president pictured the United States as an innocent and virtuous nation desiring only peace and portrayed the enemy as a thoroughly unscrupulous country bent on aggression and world domination. Second, the president contended that the specific action—in this case, the placing of offensive missiles in Cuba—typified the essentially untrustworthy character of the enemy. Finally, the president demanded unified support from the American people for the policy he announced as a test of their character and loyalty as citizens.

The Soviets, given little advance notice of Kennedy's speech, were caught by surprise. The ultimatum worked, and within weeks the crisis began to be resolved when the Soviets agreed to remove the missiles in exchange for a public pledge that the United States would not invade Cuba and for private assurances that obsolete U.S. missiles would be removed from Turkey. At the time and for some time since, Kennedy's speech and his handling of the Cuban missile crisis— though he ventured where no previous president had ever dared to go in risking nuclear war—were viewd by Americans as a triumphant victory for Kennedy and the major achievement of his administration. That opinion is not so widely held today.

During much of the first two years of his administration, Kennedy was politically defensive and rhetorically reactive. Instead of shaping the direction of public opinion, he found himself responding to specific events. The same held true in his celebrated press conferences, which by their nature placed the president in a reactive position of responding to questions from reporters. Kennedy sought to give some focus to these conferences by beginning each with an opening statement. In addition, his aides sometimes planted questions that the president specifically wanted to answer. His most dramatic press conference occurred on April 11, 1962, and concerned the steel crisis. The day before, U.S. Steel and certain other corporations had announced a six dollar a ton increase in the price of steel, which the president believed violated his economic guidelines. In his opening statement at the press conference, Kennedy denounced the steel companies and used domestic crisis rhetoric to plead his case. He defined the issue as a clash between the president, who represents the public interest, and corporations, who represent only private interests. He argued that he was supported by the majority of Americans (thereby drawing on the rhetorical power of the democratic maxim "majority rules") and claimed that the corporations represented only themselves ("a tiny handful of steel executives"). Finally, he argued that the vast majority of Americans were willing to sacrifice to support the public interest, whereas the corporate executives acted only from the base motives of their "pursuit of private power and profit," which led them to "show utter contempt for the interests of 185 million Americans." This slashing attack, as well as additional actions by the administration, caused U.S. Steel and the other companies quickly to rescind the price increases. But as in other cases during the first two years, Kennedy's rhetoric was reactive, and the result was a return to the status quo.

In 1963, after the Cuban missile crisis and Democratic victories in the Senate off-term elections, Kennedy struck out in bold new directions on the two most critical issues facing the country: civil rights and the nuclear arms race. In both cases, the rhetorical change was dramatic.

Civil rights had been the most pressing domestic issue since the Supreme Court decision in *Brown v. Board of Education* (1954). In September 1962 the federal courts had ordered the University of Mississippi to admit James Meredith, a black applicant. Some citizens of Mississippi resisted, and Kennedy federalized the Mississippi National Guard. On September 30, as rioting broke out on the campus, Kennedy reported to the nation on the situation. He described integration in narrow legal terms, implored the citizens of Mississippi to obey the court's decisions, and called for a return to peace and tranquility.

Less than a year later, however, when he was faced with a comparable situation, Kennedy reacted differently. On June 11, 1963, Governor George Wallace fulfilled a campaign pledge by blocking the entrance to the University of Alabama when several black students, again under court order, sought to enroll. In his televised speech that evening, Kennedy defined civil rights not in the narrow legal sense of the year before but in stirring moral terms. In ringing and indignant eloquence, he declared: "We are confronted primarily with a moral issue. It is as old as the scriptures and as clear as the Constitution." To redress this moral grievance, Kennedy introduced his first civil rights legislation, a bill intended to eliminate racial discrimination in public accommodations. A year later under President Lyndon Johnson, the bill became law and marked the first significant civil rights legislation since the Civil War. In addition, President Kennedy endorsed the historic March on Washington on August 28, 1963, and met that day with leaders of the march to address their concerns over passage of the civil rights bill. These acts and this rhetoric caused the civil rights movement to move in a new direction from reliance solely on judicial decisions to legislative action.

President Kennedy exhibited this same boldness in his approach to the nuclear arms race. On June 10, 1963, he addressed graduates at the commencement exercises at American University, Washington, D.C., and gave the best and most eloquent speech of his administration. His topic was world peace, not "a Pax Americana enforced on the world by American weapons of war" or "the peace of the grave or the security of the slave" but rather a "genuine peace" that "makes life on earth worth living." To pursue this vision of peace, Kennedy summoned Americans to reexamine their attitudes toward peace itself, toward the Soviet Union, and toward the cold war. In the most moving section of the speech, Kennedy declared: "And if we cannot end now our differences at least we can help make the world safe for diversity. For, in the final analysis, our most basic common link is that we all inhabit this small planet. We all breathe the same air. We all cherish our children's future. And we are all mortal." This address and subsequent negotiations in Moscow resulted in an end to atmospheric testing by the two nations and the conclusion of the limited nuclear test ban treaty. The address marked a major change in U.S. foreign policy toward the Soviet Union from one of containment to one of détente, a policy on which presidents Nixon, Ford, and Carter were able to forge new initiatives with the Soviets.

John F. Kennedy's administration is difficult to judge because an assassin's bullet ended it all too quickly. Rhetorically Kennedy brought innovations to the White House with his televised press conferences and other uses of that medium, but he rarely exploited the medium to lead the country through formal speeches. His rhetoric was one of idealism and crisis, all too often the latter. Kennedy returned the grand style to presidential speeches, though his style in press conferences was laconic and cool. He used more diverse genres of presidential rhetoric than other recent presidents but usually in reacting to events rather than in leading the nation. John Kennedy's tragically brief administration was one more of promise than performance. He affected the mood of the United States more than its policies. Thus, he is remembered more for his words than his works.

INFORMATION SOURCES

Research Collections and Collected Speeches

The John F. Kennedy Library, Boston, Massachusetts, has more than 32 million pages in its over 150 collections. In addition to the collection of Kennedy's papers, it holds those of Robert F. Kennedy and other members of the family, oral histories, and collections of materials from the Democratic National Committee from 1960 to 1964.

Campaign Speeches of American Presidential Candidates, 1928–1972. Selected and introduced by Aaron Singer. New York: Frederick Ungar Publishing Co., 1976.   CS

Kennedy, John F. *The Burden and the Glory.* Edited by Allan Nevins with foreword by Lyndon B. Johnson. New York: Harper and Row, 1964.   BG

———. *A Compendium of Speeches, Statements and Remarks Delivered during His Service in the Congress of the United States.* Washington, D.C.: Government Printing Office, 1964.   CSS

———. *The Joint Appearances of Senator John F. Kennedy and Vice President Richard M. Nixon. Presidential Campaign of 1960.* Washington, D.C.: Government Printing Office, 1961.   JA

———. *Kennedy and the Press. The News Conferences.* Edited and annotated by Harold W. Chase and Allen H. Lerman with Introduction by Pierre Salinger. New York: Thomas Y. Crowell, 1965.   NC

———. *The Speeches of Senator John F. Kennedy. Presidential Campaign of 1960.* Washington, D.C.: Government Printing Office, 1961.   PC

———. *Public Papers of the Presidents of the United States. John F. Kennedy.* 3 vols. Washington, D.C.: Government Printing Office, 1962–1964.   PP

———. *To Turn the Tide.* Edited by John W. Gardner with foreword by Carl Sandburg. New York: Harper and Brothers, 1962.   TTTT

Presidential Rhetoric: 1961 to the Present. 3d ed. Edited by Theodore Windt. Dubuque: Kendall/Hunt, 1985.   PR

Selected Critical Studies

Corbett, Edward P. J. "Analysis of the Style of John F. Kennedy's Inaugural Address." *Classical Rhetoric for the Modern Student.* 2d ed. New York: Oxford University Press, 1971. pp. 555–65.

Godden, Richard, and Maidment, Richard. "Anger, Language and Politics: John F.

Kennedy and the Steel Crisis." *Presidential Studies Quarterly* 10 (1980): 317–31.

Hahn, Dan F. "Ask Not What a Youngster Can Do for You: Kennedy's Inaugural Address." *Presidential Studies Quarterly* 12 (1982): 610–14.

Spragens, William C. "Kennedy Era Speechwriting, Public Relations and Public Opinion." *Presidential Studies Quarterly* 14 (1984): 78–86.

Windt, Jr., Theodore Otto. "The Presidency and Speeches on International Crises: Repeating the Rhetorical Past." *Speaker and Gavel* 2 (1973): 6–14.

———. "Seeking Détente with Superpowers: John F. Kennedy at American University." In *Essays in Presidential Rhetoric*. Edited by T. Windt, with Beth Ingold. Dubuque: Kendall/Hunt, 1983.

Selected Biographies

Burns, James MacGregor. *John Kennedy. A Political Profile*. New York: Harcourt, Brace, and World, 1961.

Fairlie, Henry. *The Kennedy Promise*. Garden City, N.Y.: Doubleday, 1972.

Paper, Lewis J. *The Promise and the Performance: The Leadership of John F. Kennedy*. New York: Crown, 1975.

Parmet, Herbert S. *Jack: The Struggles of John F. Kennedy*. New York: Dial, 1980.

———. *JFK: The Presidency of John F. Kennedy*. New York: Dial, 1983.

Schlesinger, Jr., Arthur M. *A Thousand Days*. Boston: Houghton Mifflin, 1965.

Sorensen, Theodore C. *Kennedy*. New York: Harper & Row, 1965.

Walton, Richard J. *Cold War and Counter-Revolution: The Foreign Policy of John F. Kennedy*. New York: Viking, 1972.

CHRONOLOGY OF MAJOR SPEECHES

See "Research Collections and Collected Speeches" for source codes.

Acceptance speech, Democratic National Convention, Los Angeles, July 15, 1960; *CS*, pp. 298–303.

Address before the Greater Houston Ministerial Association, Houston, Texas, September 12, 1960; *CS*, pp. 303–07; *PC*, pp. 206–18. (*PC* contains the questioning period that followed the formal speech.)

"The First Television Debate," Chicago, September 26, 1960; *JA*, pp. 78–92.

Inaugural Address, Washington, D.C., January 20, 1961; *PR*, pp. 9–11; *PP*, pp. 1–3; *TTTT*, pp. 6–11.

Address to the American Society of Newspaper Editors on the Bay of Pigs, Washington, D.C., April 20, 1961; *PR*, pp. 11–14; *PP*, pp. 304–06; *TTTT*, pp. 43–48.

"The Berlin Crisis," Washington, D.C., July 25, 1961; *PR*, pp. 24–30; *PP*, pp. 533–40; *TTTT*, pp. 188–98.

Opening statement at press conference on the steel crisis, Washington, D.C., April 11, 1962, *PR*, pp. 31–33; *PP*, pp. 315–17; *BG*, pp. 194–96; *NC*, pp. 223–28.

"The Cuban Missile Crisis," Washington, D.C., October 22, 1962; *PR*, pp. 36–40; *PP*, pp. 806–09; *BG*, pp. 89–96.

Commencement address at American University, Washington, D.C., June 10, 1963; *PR*, pp. 40–46; *PP*, pp. 459–64; *BG*, pp. 53–58.

Radio and television report on civil rights, Washington, D.C., June 11, 1963; *PR*, pp. 46–49; *PP*, pp. 468–71; *BG*, pp. 181–85.

ROBERT F. KENNEDY
(1925–1968), U.S. senator from New York and U.S. attorney general
_____ MICHAEL P. RICCARDS

Few other political leaders have excited more passionate admiration and more passionate animosity in a relatively brief career than Robert F. Kennedy. To his friends and close colleagues, he was a rare and exciting figure whose message of personal commitment to the disinherited of the earth set him apart from conventional politicians, including his brother John. His major biographer, Arthur M. Schlesinger, Jr., has found him to be the most creative man in American public life. Kennedy's detractors, though, are equally outspoken; for them, Kennedy was a ruthless opportunist, cold and vengeful in his displays of hatred. As his critics see it, he moved from McCarthyism to New Left liberalism, from union busting to civil libertarianism, from being a supporter of assassination attempts abroad to grieving brother of a slain president, and from establishing himself as an advocate of protracted guerrilla war to antiwar activist in a short period of time.

Some of these contradictory views come from how Kennedy's differing interpreters view the role of the United States in the turbulent 1960s. Passionate viewpoints are often refracted through politicians like light is distorted through a prism, and in public life, the first step in attacking an opponent's political position is to discredit his character and integrity. Both acclaim and criticism of Kennedy's life and record, then, are partially due to the positions he identified with and the fierce controversies that even more moderate politicians had to confront in the 1960s. In addition, some of the intense evaluations about Kennedy can be ascribed to his style of rhetoric, his choice of themes, and his overall view of himself as a leader.

Unlike his well-known political contemporaries, such as Hubert Humphrey, Eugene McCarthy, Frank Church, and the Reverend Martin Luther King, Jr., Kennedy as an orator lacked polish and a clear, compelling delivery. Yet few other politicians proved to be as effective as he was in moving people emotionally. Kennedy's career is a testimony that leaders can be effective speakers and still violate the traditional prescriptions for rhetoricians that have dominated Western thought since Aristotle and Quintillian.

KENNEDY AS A POLITICAL LEADER

Schlesinger has described one of Kennedy's early speeches, given at Georgetown University in October 1955 after his visit to the Soviet Union. Kennedy's voice was high pitched, trailed off frequently, and was hard to hear. One Kennedy family friend, Lem Billings, concluded, ''Bobby was the worst speaker. . . . It was just horrifying to hear him.'' To others he was, both on and off the platform, contentious, rude, and argumentative. After the death of his brother John, Robert Kennedy adopted a different public posture. Perhaps out of a recognition that some groups were less receptive to his blunt style or as a by-product of the deep melancholy that overcame him after the tragedy at Dallas, Kennedy was much more contained, even timid, in his presentations. Rather than appearing as the ruthless younger brother, Robert Kennedy seemed vulnerable, a bit weary, hunched over, and even somewhat fragile, especially in the heated campaign primaries of 1968.

It was in the late 1960s, then, that the very different characterizations of Kennedy came most to the forefront. To the Democratic party liberals and reform-minded media people, the Kennedy they admired was an advocate of social change, a voice for the dispossessed in the United States and abroad. A sense of sympathy and of genuine alienation became an increasing part of Kennedy's rhetoric. In part, his speeches reflected the concerns of the 1960s, and being an astute political figure, he caught the dominant public mood about poverty and race, and eventually and hesitantly about the war in Vietnam.

The tone and concerns of Kennedy's speeches had changed markedly from his initial public addresses. Early in his career, Kennedy was preoccupied with a fear of corruption, subversion of old ideals, and a general sense of betrayal. The resentments of a younger brother, the maintenance of the nourished hatreds of Boston Irish, and a self-defining contentiousness created a personality that somehow enabled a millionaire scion to feel akin with the underdog in a way more real than contrived. As attorney general, Kennedy was more willing than his brother John to put the full power of the federal government behind efforts to end racial segregation as a state-sanctioned practice. With the assassination of his brother, Robert Kennedy began to place the Kennedy political network in the service of an ideology different from that espoused in the 1960 campaign. The rhetoric became more idealistic in its treatment of human needs, more passionate about immediate remedy, more universal in application. The Kennedy political philosophy changed from a cold war, nationalistic rhetoric full of Churchillian overtones about courage and confrontation to a call for reason, reform, and even charity. The unvarnished ambition of Joseph P. Kennedy's sons and heirs gave way to an elevated stewardship in which idealism and excitement found its expression in the Kennedy political fortune. With Robert Kennedy's assassination, that latter rhetoric became frozen into what one of the family's closest associates, Theodore Sorensen, called ''the Kennedy legacy'' and which Jacqueline Kennedy wistfully labeled ''Camelot.''

When Robert Kennedy entered his first campaign for public office in the 1964 race for a U.S. Senate seat from New York, he drew large crowds. For many listeners, it was an opportunity to see a likely presidential candidate; Kennedy carried with him a sense of the probable future, a touch of tragedy, and an almost mystical link to what was becoming quickly a mythic past. As a speaker, Kennedy was still rather deficient. His voice was often high pitched, if not shrill, and his Boston accent with its long "a" and added "r" to ending vowels sounded alien in other parts of the country. At times Kennedy seemed to sense that his own presence, with its strong suggestions of his late brother's appearance, was the main message he was communicating. In the New York Senate race, for example, Kennedy said with no rhetorical flourishes again and again that he was for Democrat Lyndon Johnson over the conservative Republican nominee Senator Barry Goldwater. A year later, in the fall of 1965, when he was campaigning for the Democratic candidate for mayor, Abraham Beame, Kennedy's stump appearances were so weak that the Beame people complained openly about one especially listless performance. Victor Lasky records that in an Irish-American section of the Bronx, Kennedy said to a youthful crowd, "The Republican party gave you Herbert Hoover, Harding, Coolidge, and Rockefeller. Everyone boo." Then he noted that the independent conservative candidate, William Buckley, was "going to have school on Saturday. . . . He's going to have the nuns hit you with a ruler. A real loud boo for Buckley."

Kennedy's main attraction, then, was himself as a celebrity, not as a public speaker on the stump or as a rhetorician giving his countrymen phrases that would live on after him. Still, Kennedy's political career was not devoid of issues. Indeed, one can best chronicle his complicated public education by reading his speeches over the years, for as his admirers and his detractors alike acknowledge, his opinions and even his basic inclinations seemed to change dramatically.

Early in his public career, Kennedy developed a favorite family theme: the need for toughness. On February 22, 1958, at Notre Dame University, for example, he reiterated the moral of his early book, *The Enemy Within*. He reminded his audience that the great events in U.S. history were "forged by men who put their country above self-interest—their ideals above self-profit." He had argued in his book, "It seems to me imperative that we reinstill in ourselves the toughness and idealism that guided the nation in the past."

In his work as a staff person on the Senate rackets committee, he focused especially on James Hoffa, the head of the Teamsters Union, and Kennedy developed a near obsession to match his personal toughness with that of the labor leader. For him, Hoffa was a prime example of a corrupt leader who had betrayed his trust. By the mid-1960s, Kennedy warned that many of the young activists with whom he saw himself aligned no longer viewed the union movement in general as a positive force for social change. Addressing the Americans for Democratic Action in Philadelphia on February 27, 1967, he observed, "They think of labor as grown sleek and bureaucratic with power, sometimes frankly discriminatory, occasionally even corrupt and exploitive, a force not for change but for the status quo, unwilling or unable to organize new groups of members, indifferent to the men who once worked the coal mines of Appalachia, a latecomer to the struggles of the grape pickers of California or the farm laborers of the Mississippi Delta.''

Kennedy's emphasis on toughness as a political virtue and as a major rhetorical prescription also showed up in his early attitudes toward civil liberties. He was originally associated with Senator Joseph McCarthy during the latter's campaign against alleged communists and left-wing sympathizers. The senator was also the godfather at his first child's baptism, and even after McCarthy's censure in 1954, Kennedy remained on warm terms with the senator, calling him a complicated character who desperately wanted to be liked.

Kennedy's background and experience led to his appointment as chief counsel of the Senate rackets committee, which was focusing on alleged corruption in organized labor. A belligerent interrogator, Kennedy concentrated on the Teamsters and ended up berating those who invoked the Fifth Amendment's protection against self-incrimination. Later as attorney general, his determined attempts to prosecute Hoffa led even some of his close associates to characterize his action as a personal vendetta rather than a professional investigation of malfeasance and corruption.

By the mid–1960s, Kennedy had aligned himself with segments of the counterculture, and at the University of California at Berkeley on October 22, 1966, he made a major speech defending the Constitution and the right of dissent. He observed that criticism was ''the seminal spirit of American democracy'' and that Americans dissent from ''the fact that millions are trapped in poverty while the nation grows rich. We dissent from the conditions and hatreds which deny a full life to our fellow citizens because of the color of their skin. We dissent from the monstrous absurdity of a world where nations stand poised to destroy one another.''

Another major area in which Kennedy showed considerable change was civil rights. As he remarked, ''I won't say I stayed awake nights worrying about civil rights before I became Attorney General.'' Indeed even in that position, he seemed at first more interested in protecting his brother politically from the civil rights controversy than in providing leadership. But Robert Kennedy, sooner than most of his political contemporaries, came to understand the moral depths of the explosive movement and clearly went on to place the Justice Department and the federal government behind what historian Carl Brauer has called the ''Second Reconstruction.'' On May 26, 1964, in Carrollton, Georgia, Robert Kennedy pointed up the contradictions between a society that is segregated and still asks that men of all races serve in its armed forces. The theme was a familiar one, an argument that John F. Kennedy had used effectively in the 1960 election to point up the unfairness of a religious test for a Catholic candidate for the presidency who had emerged from World War II a hero.

Although race was a major issue in the 1960s, the great controversy that swept up many of Kennedy's activist supporters, and eventually even the senator himself, was the war in Vietnam. Severely estranged from President Lyndon Johnson and then elected to the U.S. Senate from New York, Kennedy used his political base to divorce himself slowly but discernibly from the Vietnam policies of the chief executive. Kennedy's critics were quick to point up that he had been one of the strongest supporters of the commitment of U.S. military personnel to South Vietnam made in his brother's administration. At a press conference while he was in Vietnam in 1962, Kennedy insisted, "We will win in Vietnam and we shall remain here until we do." By 1965, he had become indecisive concerning the war and began to call for deescalation. On February 19, 1966, he made a major speech in the Senate in which he supported political dissent against the president's war policies and went on to advocate a negotiated political settlement: "I believe there is a middle way, that an end to the fighting and a peaceful settlement can be achieved." A year later, on March 2, 1967, Kennedy delivered a second Senate speech deploring the breakdown of peace talks and criticizing Johnson's policy of bombing North Vietnam. That speech went on to consider the immorality of the war in terms rarely used by a mainstream U.S. politician. Kennedy charged that Vietnam had become "a land deafened by the unending crescendo of violence, hatred and savage fury . . . where hundreds of thousands fight, but millions more are innocent bewildered victims of brutal passions and beliefs they barely understand. . . . All we say and all we do must be informed by our awareness that this horror is partly our responsibility."

Yet Kennedy refused to challenge directly President Johnson in his bid for the Democratic party's nomination for the presidency. Finally, after Senator Eugene McCarthy ran a strong second to Johnson in the New Hampshire primary, Kennedy announced on March 16 that he too would run for the nomination, leaving himself open once again to charges of gross opportunism. By the summer of 1968, Kennedy entered the Democratic primaries as both the heir apparent and as the candidate of the Left in his own party. Kennedy's rhetoric reflected both legacies. To those who remembered wistfully his elegant and stylized brother, Robert reminded them of the Kennedy past, the unfulfilled dreams, the spirit of adventure that he proclaimed could embrace the land once again. His most articulate speech and eloquent performance, however, had come years before at the 1964 Democratic National Convention when the party leaders designated time for a memorial to their slain standard-bearer, President Kennedy. For twenty-two minutes, the convention cheered to a frenzy scream, while Robert Kennedy holding back tears stood on the podium appearing almost frail and drawn. He went on to extol his brother's memory and concluded his eulogy with Juliet's prayer for Romeo:

When he shall die
Take him and cut him out in little stars
And he will make the face of heaven so fine
That all the world will be in love with night,
And pay no worship to the garish sun.

Robert Kennedy's political world in 1968 was a far cry from that of his brother's in the brokered convention of 1960 or the bittersweet remembrances of 1964. He reached out in his own campaign to the powerful antiwar, reformist, and civil rights elements that embraced the more activist volunteer segments of the Democratic party. While campaigning in Indiana on April 4, Kennedy learned of the assassination of Reverend Martin Luther King, Jr. Before an angry crowd in a black ghetto in Indianapolis, he recalled the circumstances of his own brother's death and his complex feelings at the time and concluded with a plea for racial understanding. Remembering the wisdom of the ancient Greeks, he implored the group, "Let us dedicate ourselves to what the Greeks wrote so many years ago: to tame the savageness of man and to make gentle the life of the world." Two months later, Robert Kennedy was assassinated while celebrating his victory in the California Democratic primary.

INFORMATION SOURCES

Research Collections and Collected Speeches

The major depository of Robert F. Kennedy's speeches and papers is the John F. Kennedy Presidential Library, Boston, Massachusetts. The library contains a section devoted to RFK memorabilia and film clips. The archives include Robert F. Kennedy's notes, letters, speeches and a variety of personal items.

"An Honorable Profession:" A Tribute to Robert F. Kennedy. Edited by   HP
    Pierre Salinger et al. Garden City, N.Y.: Doubleday, 1968.
Robert F. Kennedy: Apostle of Change. Edited by Douglas Rose. New York: AC
    Trident Press, 1968.

Selected Critical Studies

Anatol, Karl W., and Bittner, John R. "Kennedy on King: The Rhetoric of Control."
    Today's Speech 16 (1968): 31–34.
Broadhurst, Allan R. "Audience Adaptation: The Determining Factor." *Today's Speech*
    11 (1963): 11–13.
Greene, Robert J. "The Kennedy-Keating 'Debate.' " *Today's Speech* 13 (1965): 12–
    13.
Hahn, Dan F., and Gonchar, Ruth M. "Political Myth: The Image and the Issue."
    Today's Speech 20 (1972): 57–65.
Hopkins, Thomas A. "Attorney General Robert F. Kennedy's Blueprint for Civil Rights
    Action." *Today's Speech* 10 (1962): 5–7.
Jamieson, Kathleen H., and Campbell, Karlyn. "Rhetorical Hybrids: Fusions of Generic
    Elements." *Quarterly Journal of Speech* 68 (1982): 146–57.
Rosenwasser, Marie J. "Six Senate War Critics and Their Appeals for Gaining Audience
    Response." *Today's Speech* 17 (1969): 43–50.

Selected Biographies

Brauer, Carl. *John F. Kennedy and the Second Reconstruction.* New York: Columbia
    University Press, 1977.

Kennedy, Robert F. *Just Friends and Brave Enemies*. New York: Harper, 1962.
————. *The Enemy Within*. New York: Harper & Row, 1960.
————. *To Seek a Newer World*. Garden City, N.Y.: Doubleday, 1967.
Lasky, Victor. *Robert F. Kennedy: The Myth and the Man*. New York: Trident Press, 1968.
Navasky, Victor. *Kennedy Justice*. Boston: Atheneum, 1971.
Newfield, Jack. *Robert F. Kennedy: A Memoir*. New York: Berkeley, 1969.
Schlesinger, Arthur M., Jr. *Robert F. Kennedy and His Times*. Boston: Houghton Mifflin, 1978.
Sorensen, Theodore. *The Kennedy Legacy*. New York: Macmillan, 1969.

CHRONOLOGY OF MAJOR SPEECHES

See "Research Collections and Collected Speeches" for source codes.

Speech, West Georgia College, Carrollton, Georgia, May 26, 1964; JFK Library, RFK Collection 1.

Speech to the Democratic National Convention, Atlantic City, New Jersey, August 1964; *HP*, pp. 4–6.

Speech, U.S. Senate, Washington, D.C., February 19, 1966; *AC*, pp. 506–10.

Speech, University of California at Berkeley, Berkeley, California, October 22, 1966; *AC*, pp. 220–21.

Address to the Americans for Democratic Action, Philadelphia, Pennsylvania, February 27, 1967; *AC*, pp. 272–73.

Speech, U.S. Senate, Washington, D.C.; March 2, 1967; *AC*, pp. 517–28.

Statement on the death of the Reverend Martin Luther King, Jr., Indianapolis, Indiana, April 4, 1968; *HP*, pp. 7–8.

MARTIN LUTHER KING, JR.
(1929–1968), Baptist minister, civil rights leader

JOHN H. PATTON

In the study of contemporary rhetorical practice Martin Luther King, Jr. is typically cited as one of the outstanding and exceptional communicators of the twentieth century. Indeed it was largely through his rhetoric that King effectively united social, religious, and political consciousness with respect to civil rights. His sensitivity to the rhetorical nuances of language and the power of rhetorical form is evidenced in both his oral and written compositions.

KING AS AN ORATOR FOR CIVIL RIGHTS

King's speaking, writing, and symbolic social action were all pieces of the same cloth and arose in response to clear urgencies and constraints. One such urgency was the lack of clear and unified public concern over widespread instances of racial discrimination; another, and in some ways an even more critical urgency, was the absence of a positive self-image and sense of direction among blacks. In the period immediately prior to King's leadership, the rhetoric of civil rights was confined mainly to legal proceedings, which moved slowly and incrementally. The inadequacy of this process indicated a need for a rhetorical transformation of the terms on which race relations would be defined. Above all, the situation called for an infusion of moral awareness, which the previous approach to segregation and the piecemeal processes of litigation had seemed unable to supply. Hence, the language of civil rights evolved as the vocabulary of moral suasion. No one was better prepared to articulate the new categories of meaning and the moral-ethical dimensions of civil rights than Martin Luther King, Jr.

Rhetorical critics have long been concerned with the inventive processes of rhetors as they develop arguments, engage audiences, and shape meanings. In King's case, the theological foundation of his rhetoric was paramount. King understood himself as a proclaimer in much the same tradition as some of the Old Testament prophets and, even more, the earliest articulators of Christianity in its incipient beginnings as a minority movement. Consistent with those traditions, he proclaimed an inseparable bond between the realm of God and the realm of humanity, the spiritual and the social, eternal or ultimate moral principles, and the daily practice of social, political policy. While King's reliance on the works of Gandhi and Reinhold Niebuhr is well known, he was equally significantly influenced by the writings of the late nineteenth-century theologian, Walter Rauschenbush, whose *Christianity and the Social Crisis* provided the fundamental framework for the application of theology to social problems. Stephen Oates indicated that King "read Rauschenbush in a state of high excitement. Here was the Christian activism he longed for." This early, formative influence became part of King's pattern of proclamation and provided the skeletal structure for many of King's most significant arguments in the rhetoric of civil rights.

There is an abundance of rhetorical discourse, oral and written, associated with the major issues and events in King's life. The principal documents include *Strength to Love*, a collection of sermons originally delivered to his congregations at Dexter Avenue and later at Ebenezer Baptist Church in Atlanta; *Stride toward Freedom*, his narrative account of the Montgomery bus boycott; "Love, Law, and Civil Disobedience," a pivotal address in 1961 that holds special significance for understanding King's rhetoric as a whole; "Letter from Birmingham City Jail" in 1963 and later that year the "I Have a Dream" oration in Washington, D.C.; and King's speech to the Association of the Bar of New York City in April 1965.

King's rhetorical strategy is a combination of what Edwin Black has termed the genres of exhortation and argumentation. King excelled at both the articulation of principle and the positing of concepts and categories to compete with counterclaims in the minds and hearts of listeners. Resting comfortably in both genres, King's rhetoric displays a method of exhortation by synthesis and of argument by transcendence. The most comprehensive example of King's rhetoric was his speech to the Fellowship of the Concerned in 1961. This speech came at the beginning of civil rights as a national movement, a time of flux and conceptual uncertainty about the meaning and direction of civil protest. King had successfully spearheaded the Montgomery bus boycott in 1958 and adopted the tactic of nonviolent resistance. Here was the moment of transition, ripe with rhetorical potential, for establishing larger and ultimately moral connections between the specifics and immediacy of Montgomery and public issues at the center of social and political experience. The transition required a context, a philosophy, and an overall direction for the future.

King began with a direct discussion of the context and philosophy of civil rights. After linking "the new sense of dignity, a new self-respect, and a new determination" of American blacks with the aspirations of "oppressed people all over the world," King identified the context as a continuing struggle. "The question," he said, "is how will the struggle be waged?" In this definitional statement, King had already subsumed a number of opposing positions. Even his choice of the term *struggle* is vital to his strategy. Struggle operates at a much different symbolic level from conflict, for example. Conflict implies factions and hostility, with little prospect for positive and cooperative resolution. Struggle, by contrast, involves relentless determination, the posing and counterposing of positions in an atmosphere of mutual interaction, buttressed by the expectation of eventual prevalence. King moved quickly to define further the terms of this particular struggle.

"There are three ways," King remarked, "that oppressed people have gen-

erally dealt with their aggression." The first first way is "the method of acquiescence, . . . of surrender"; the second way is the method of "corroding hatred
and physical violence." Each represents an extreme, opposite yet functionally
similar approaches in that they both lead to "many more social problems" than
they solve. Arising between these is the third method, nonviolent resistance,
which is chosen as the way of continuing the struggle for civil rights because
of its fundamental moral quality. King's version of nonviolent resistance appro-
priated certain tendencies of both acquiescence and physical violence without
incorporating their destructive dimensions. So construed, nonviolence becomes
the only option that contains both the moral force necessary for pushing on with
the struggle and the pragmatic potential for gaining results.

King invoked the moral quality of nonviolent resistance in several ways,
primarily by identifying *agape*-love as the life force of such resistance. The form
and function of King's argument about the ethic of love is exactly parallel to
his prior depiction of the method of nonviolence. *Agape*-love arises between and
simultaneously surpasses two polar alternatives. It is more than *eros* or *philia*
in the same sense that nonviolence is more than the options of acquiescence or
violent revolt. The language here operates at both a rational and emotional level.
On the one hand, choosing the ethic of love and nonviolence is an act of
deliberation, a comparative choice comprehensible by the ordinary processes of
cognition; on the other hand, the choice involves a personal commitment both
to the nature of the problem being addressed and to the assumptions that accompany it.

Two of the key assumptions central to the movement as a whole also emerged
in this speech: King's belief that "there is within human nature an amazing
potential for goodness . . . something that can respond to goodness" and the
notion of unjust laws. An unjust law, declared King, "does not square with the
moral law of the universe"; more specifically, it is "a code that the majority
inflicts on the minority that is not binding on itself" and "in which that minority
had no part in enacting or creating." These statements clarify and secure the
grounding for the demonstrations and nonviolent resistance that followed. They
provided not only immediate answers to the question of why there should be a
civil rights movement but also linked the fabric of that movement to comprehensive and ongoing questions of value: the moral law of the universe, the
relation of temporal laws to unbound, eternal principles. One of the functions
of such argument is not only to win adherence and approval but to reduce the
viability of competing arguments. Black calls attention to the dissuasive function
of argument in terms of "the conceptual avenues closed by the discourse as well
as the sequence of inferences implied by it" for speakers and audiences alike.
King's discourse dissuades us against moral cynicism (the problem is too large
and human beings are too corrupt) and against the tendency to rely on temporal
conditions as the defining characteristic of moral and social life.

This speech served as a significant model for the structure and impulse of the
civil rights movement as a whole also because of its display of authentic emotion.

In the final section of the speech, King recreated the feeling and climate within which the movement's theme song, "We shall overcome," evolved. He cited the example of Freedom Rides in the South and the typical ritual that accompanied a departure of a group of students taking a bus to Jackson, Mississippi:

And something within me said, now how is it that these students can sing this, they are going down to Mississippi, they are going to face hostile and jeering mobs, and yet they could sing, "We shall overcome." They may even face physical death. Most of them realized they would be thrown into jail, and yet they could sing, "We shall overcome, we are not afraid." Then something caused me to see at that moment the real meaning of the movement. That students had faith in the future. That the movement was based on hope, that this movement had something within it that says somehow even though the arc of the moral universe is long, it bends toward justice.

This passage was followed with two formulaic repetitions characteristic of black preaching in general and King's sermons in particular. The first was a sequence of three conditional warnings, all beginning with the phrase, "Before the victory is won . . . " and ending with the phrase, " . . . but we shall overcome." The second was a final unconditional affirmation framed in a pair of sentences that take up where the previous ones end. Each began with "We shall overcome because . . . " and supplied quotations to emphasize the ultimate prevalence of the moral law of the universe.

In this passage, which constitutes a prototype reappearing consistently in King's subsequent civil rights rhetoric, emotion was used to evoke belief in the legitimacy and moral justification of the movement. King was not addressing the students and volunteers who enacted the protests in the movement. He spoke to an immediate audience of church leaders for whom the questions of the meaning and justification of the movement were at issue and, by extension, to a public audience concerned about those same issues. Rather than provide abstract definitions, King adopted the strategy of recreation by telling the story of the song "We shall overcome." This dimension of King's strategy exhorted an emotional response, which brought about belief in the nature of the situation at hand. Similarly, the "before the victory . . . but we shall . . . " formulas did not arouse fears or hopes in the audience in an after-the-fact manner but instead intensified the awareness of what was at stake in the movement and the fundamental link between the movement and enduring moral themes. "Love, Law, and Civil Disobedience" was a comprehensive rhetorical archetype of the total body of King's civil rights discourse. The form and content displayed in it was extended in several directions in King's subsequent speeches, letters, and public statements.

The famous "Letter from Birmingham City Jail" of April 16, 1963, was an especially revealing example of argumentative discourse showing King at work in a situation of controversy. There are, in fact, two letters, which must be examined as interacting discourses. Here King addressed multiple audiences at once, responding to his immediate audience in the form of eight Alabama clergymen who had written to him and the black community in Birmingham in an appeal to stop the protests, while keeping a sensitive eye on the larger public who would later read and reflect on his words. There is powerful symbolic significance in the fact that the first letter was authored by eight clergymen representing every major strand of the Judeo-Christian tradition. By implication, King's credibility as clergyman and the theological foundation of the movement were potentially undermined. The letter charged King and the movement with "such actions as incite to hatred and violence, however technically peaceful those actions may be" and urged as a remedy to any discrimination that "a cause should be pressed in the courts and in negotiations among local leaders, and not in the streets."

King had to respond to these charges and in a way that sustained the legitimacy and moral intensity of the movement in the mind of the larger public. He did not argue by denial or direct refutation. His pattern was to argue by redefinition, reinforcement, and transcendence, which he accomplished by extending the boundaries of key terms. He started by providing the background and context of the decision to engage in civil protest, rationally describing a four-step process: "(1) collection of the facts to determine whether injustices are alive; (2) negotiation; (3) self-purification; and (4) direct action." He developed each step with great deliberation to show that when negotiations became impossible, it was necessary and reasonable to move to subsequent stages. He countered the charge of incitement with a narration of deliberation, a process that by its nature reflected caution and care.

Even more strikingly, King reintroduced the central concept of an unjust law. He employed virtually the same language observed in the "Love, Law, and Civil Disobedience" speech and concluded a series of examples of unjust laws with the statement, "I submit that an individual who breaks a law that conscience tells him is unjust, and willingly accepts the penalty by staying in jail to arouse the conscience of the community over its injustice, is in reality expressing the very highest respect for law." He did not deny that in protesting he broke the law, but placed the question of law breaking on a higher plane, making it a matter of conscience. He argued that sacrificing one's liberty was the price of dramatizing the priority of morality over laws that perpetuated the injustices of racial discrimination.

King argued in much the same way in an address to the New York City Bar Association on April 21, 1965. Among other reasons, this speech is noteworthy because King's audience was a powerful group whose influence he hoped to mobilize in support of the pending voting rights bill. As before, he distinguished civil disobedience from uncivil disobedience and used the same language found in the "Love, Law, and Civil Disobedience" speech to define the concept of an unjust law. He responded to criticisms of himself and the movement not by rebutting charges but by building a more comprehensive context based on values and emotion. An especially vivid example is his use of the term *maladjusted*.

Without making a direct claim, King implied that the various criticisms of civil disobedience were accusations that it was a maladjusted form of behavior. He replied, "Certainly we all want to live the well adjusted life in order to avoid neurotic and schizophrenic personalities. But I must honestly say to you tonight, my friends, that there are some things in our nation and in our world of which I am proud to be maladjusted. I call upon all men of good will to be maladjusted until the good society is realized."

After the initial pronouncement, King extended the boundaries of this key term by infusing it with value positions on moral issues and intense feeling. He declared, "I never intend to adjust myself to the madness of militarism and the self-defeating effects of physical violence"; "I never intend to become adjusted to religious bigotry." In a moment of serious exaggeration, he even called for the creation of a new organization: "the International Association for the Advancement of Creative Maladjustment." He then cited examples of moral leaders who historically demonstrated the necessity for such maladjusted persons: "They will be as maladjusted as Abraham Lincoln was, . . . as maladjusted as Thomas Jefferson, . . . they will be as maladjusted as Jesus of Nazareth, who could say to the men and women of his day, 'Love your enemies, bless them that curse you, pray for them that despitefully use you.' Through such maladjustments we may be able to emerge from the bleak and desolate midnight of man's inhumanity to man into the bright and glittering daybreak of freedom and justice." In a remarkable fashion, King had taken one term, *maladjusted*, and turned it from a negative accusation to a completely different direction. By the time he finished transforming the term by tying it to moral causes in history and the personae of Lincoln, Jefferson, and Jesus, it had become a symbolic badge of honor. This typifies King's deft use of language to construct new categories of meaning for his audiences. King's strategy revealed an attempt to open up different, more positive possibilities for interpretation by turning accusatory terms from liabilities into assets.

King's most publicly acclaimed speech, the "I Have a Dream" address in Washington, D.C., in 1963, represents an extension and refinement of the rhetorical strategies observed in the other addresses. The speech was addressed to multiple audiences—some 200,000 gathered at the Washington Monument, a national television audience, and the national and international press. Beyond that, the speech aimed at an implied audience not immediately observable yet permanently present: the essential moral capacity of human nature. In a strikingly intense and dramatic fashion, King reinforced the moral quality of civil rights as an issue in terms that left a virtually lasting mark on the landscape of moral consciousness. He accomplished this by the use of metaphoric constructions to summarize and consummate the civil rights movement.

The speech opened with his reference to the Declaration of Independence as a promissory note to all Americans and the consequent claiming of that note by blacks. Negro citizens had come to cash the check of unalienable rights, yet the check had been returned for "insufficient funds." This economic metaphor allowed King to indict the system and stress the urgency of the moment to enact civil rights legislation. This part of the speech was addressed largely to white America and to those in positions of political power. King followed with a direct appeal to blacks and all those actively involved in the civil rights movement. To them he urged restraint against the temptation to let the movement slip into physical violence which would counteract the moral impulse of "creative protest." Significantly, he reflected an awareness of the "new militancy" in the black community and held that "this must not lead us to a distrust of all white people." Indeed, consistent with the pattern of rhetorical transcendence throughout King's rhetoric, he articulated the concept of mutual destiny among blacks and whites as ultimately unifying them.

The concept of destiny led directly to the most familiar section of the speech: King's repetition of the "I have a dream" and "let freedom ring" phrases. The words "I have a dream" constituted a powerful transformative metaphor and operated at several levels. The notion of a dream implied a moral vision that cast the civil rights movement from the realm of the particular and immediate to the realm of the ideal and ultimate. Dreams are basic to human experience, and visionary dreams are a principal means of defining conditions as they ought to be. Hence, by using this term, King tied the cause of civil rights to a recurrent and fundamental human activity. This also accounts in part for why the phrase "I have a dream" is so well remembered. While we may forget the particulars of some specific dreams, the activity of dreaming itself is deeply ingrained. King reinforced the significance of this activity by linking "I have a dream" to a series of ideal depictions of the future when the dream of civil rights had been fully realized. He spoke of a day in Alabama "when little black boys and black girls will be able to join hands with little white boys and white girls as sisters and brothers" and of living in a nation where his own children would be judged "not by the color of their skin but by the content of their character." It is by no means accidental that King chose to cast children as the vehicles and benefactors of the dream. This gave increased moral intensity to the phrase because the welfare of future generations is a typically powerful source for current sacrifice and dedication.

King ended the speech on an emotional crescendo quoting the words of the spiritual "Free at Last." This served to consummate the entire argument by proclaiming that the realization of the moral vision contained in the dream would bring about true freedom. At the end of this noteworthy address, King retained his role as proclaimer and maintained his rhetorical function consistent with his theological and biblical foundations.

This analysis has disclosed several significant features of King's civil rights rhetoric. First, he used emotion distinctively to create heightened awareness of the conditions of discrimination and belief in the means of nonviolent protest. Second, he employed a strategy of argument by redefinition and transcendence that involved dissuasion of competing claims along with reinforcement of the moral foundation of his approach to civil rights. Third, his discourse reflected keen sensitivity to the power of orality and made use of word formulas and word transformations that accentuate the sense of personal contact with audiences typical of oral traditions. By participating in both genres of exhortative and argumentative discourse with equal ability, King was able to address many different audiences with a sense of clarity and moral urgency. The articulation of ultimate principles in this form is King's enduring rhetorical legacy.

INFORMATION SOURCES

Research Collections and Collected Speeches

Contemporary American Speeches. Edited by Wil A. Linkugel, R. R. Allen,   *CAS*
    and Richard Johannesen. 5th ed. Dubuque: Kendall Hunt, 1982.
Record of the Association of the Bar of the City of New York 20, no. 5 (May   *RAB*
    1965).

Selected Critical Studies

Bitzer, Lloyd F. "The Rhetorical Situation." *Philosophy and Rhetoric* (Winter 1968): 1–12.
Black, Edwin. *Rhetorical Criticism: A Study in Method*. Madison: University of Wisconsin Press, 1978.
Bosmajian, Haig A. "The Letter from Birmingham Jail." In *Language, Communication, and Rhetoric in Black America*. Edited by Arthur L. Smith. New York: Harper & Row, 1972.
Bosmajian, Haig A., and Hamida Bosmajian, eds. *The Rhetoric of the Civil-Rights Movement*. New York: Random House, 1969.
Patton, John H. "Causation and Creativity in Rhetorical Situations: Distinctions and Implication." *Quarterly Journal of Speech* 65 (1979): 36–55.

Selected Biographies

King, Martin Luther, Jr. *Strength to Love*. New York: Harper & Row, 1963.
Lewis, David L. *King: A Biography*. 2d ed. Urbana: University of Illinois Press, 1978.
Oates, Stephen B. *Let the Trumpet Sound: The Life of Martin Luther King, Jr*. New York: New American Library, 1982.
Smith, Kelley M. *Social Crisis Preaching*. Macon: Mercer University Press, 1984.

CHRONOLOGY OF MAJOR SPEECHES

See "Research Collections and Collected Speeches" for source codes.

"Love, Law, and Civil Disobedience," November 16, 1961; *CAS*, pp. 75–85.

"I Have a Dream," Washington, D.C., August 28, 1963; *CAS*, pp. 365–70.

"The Civil Rights Struggle in the United States Today," New York City, April 21, 1965; *RAB*, pp. 3–24.

HENRY ALFRED KISSINGER
(1923–   ), fifty-sixth U.S. secretary of state

EUGENE BROWN

It would be hard to identify another modern public figure who has so thoroughly fascinated his contemporaries as Henry A. Kissinger. His meteoric rise from German refugee to Harvard professor, White House adviser, and, finally, the nation's fifty-sixth secretary of state has given him a certain mystique amid the middle-brow blandness of Nixonian Washington. At the apex of his career in the early and mid–1970s, his every public utterance was dissected and given maximum dissemination by a doting media. Scholars, too, devoted enormous energies to Kissinger, poring over his earlier academic writings for premonitions of global policy. Whether critical or admiring, all agreed that Kissinger is different. No other modern statesman has been as prolific as Kissinger in setting forth his most deeply held political beliefs in a detailed, systematic fashion. Henry Kissinger is thus uniquely able to attempt to translate his ideas, developed in the comparative serenity of academe, to the turbulent, dangerous world of foreign policy.

It seems a curious fact, then, that so little attention has been paid to the role of oratory in Kissinger's remarkable career. That he entertained and acted upon a precise, sophisticated conception of rhetoric as a tool of diplomatic purpose can readily be shown. Yet few observers seem to have grasped the point, preferring to dwell upon the idiosyncrasies of his personality, his role in intragovernmental intrigue, and the high drama of foreign policy initiatives associated with him. Scarcely understood is Kissinger's recurring preoccupation with the necessity for a foreign policy leadership capable of transcending both the cramped vision of the masses and the paralyzing inertia of bureaucracy. Kissinger, wrote his friend and biographer Stephen Graubard, proceeded from a "view of history that emphasized the possibility of choice, the need for doctrine, and the centrality of leadership." True statesmanship, he believed, was essential for a nation to navigate safely the treacherous shoals of international politics. It is of the essence of statesmanship to conceptualize and execute a policy attuned to the impersonal logic of existential reality. Yet that policy must also be supported by the nation in whose name it is effected. It follows that effective statesmanship depends critically on the leader's ability to explain, persuade, and rally popular support for the desired external course. Oratory, then, is to Kissinger among the most crucial in the statesman's repertoire of skills.

KISSINGER AS DIPLOMATIC ORATOR

Because his elevation to the role of statesman required him to put his own theory into practice, Kissinger had displayed an oratorical style that seems to break many of the rules of good speech making, yet the results are unusually arresting and effective. Though never a very dramatic performer, he nonetheless manages to convey a certain air of drama. Although his gravely baritone voice seldom deviates from a flat monotone, he is almost never dull. Although ponderously grave and professorial, he has always been among the most sought-after orators. Yet although he is an apparently mediocre speech maker, he nonetheless succeeded to a remarkable degree in fulfilling his own acid test of statesmanship: the ability to win domestic support for the leadership's foreign policy. The answer to his success lies both in the substance of his speeches and in his unique, memorable style of delivery.

Substantively, Kissinger's speeches invariably bear the mark of meticulous craftsmanship. His speeches, like his prose, are uncommonly lucid and intellectually coherent. Impatient with banal platitudes and disdainful of rhetorical cleverness, Kissinger has developed a distinctive style that features a sophisticated analysis of the topic at hand presented in a strikingly clear manner. Students of effective political oratory would do well to read an assortment of Kissinger's speeches; for sheer clarity, depth, and persuasiveness, they stand as models worthy of emulation. He refuses to sacrifice substantive depth to catchy flamboyance, but he also labors to ensure that the analysis he would have others accept be presented in a manner easily grasped by his diverse audiences.

One of Kissinger's most distinctive rhetorical techniques is the frequent use of what might be termed cadenced obverses, a contrivance by which an arresting rhythm is attained through crisp verbal contrasts. For example, his September 23, 1974, address to the United Nations General Assembly contains these contrapuntal lines: ''We have managed but not advanced; we have endured but not prospered''; and ''We have eased tensions; we are far from reconciliation. If we do not continue to advance, we will slip back.'' Similar obverses occur in nearly all of Kissinger's speeches. Combined with his own naturally cadenced delivery, it greatly enhanced his ability to capture and hold his audiences' attention as he led them through his sophisticated analysis and advocacy of foreign policy issues.

Although all of his speeches bear the unmistakable Kissinger stamp, his many duties required him to turn to two trusted aides, Winston Lord and Peter Rodman, for assistance in preparing his addresses. Young, brilliant (Rodman, wrote Kissinger is his memoirs, ''had written one of the most outstanding undergraduate theses of my tenure as professor at Harvard''), and intimately knowledgeable about the nuances of Kissinger's thinking, the two functioned more as extensions of Kissinger's purpose than as independent sources of substantive or stylistic influence upon him.

On October 8, 1973, in his first year as secretary of state, Kissinger delivered a major address, "The Nature of the National Dialogue," to the Pacem in Terris III conference in Washington. He clearly meant the speech to be more than a mere explication of "the nature of the national dialogue." Rather, it was Kissinger's purpose to frame the terms of that dialogue for his elite audience. Speaking in his ponderous teutonic cadences, Kissinger argued, "It is characteristic of periods of upheaval that to those who live through them they appear as a series of haphazard events." Ever the professor, he insisted that global patterns could be discerned through proper analysis: "We need to define the framework of our dialogue more perceptively and understandingly." He then guided his listeners through a masterfully lucid primer on the nature of foreign policy and a *tour de horizon* of his principal policy goals, stressing the centrality of détente with the Soviet Union. Typically, it was the cogency of his analysis rather than the flamboyance of his delivery that accounted for the speech's influence in the nation's ongoing discussion of its proper world role.

In the summer of 1975, with the nation reeling under the combined blows of Watergate and the Vietnam denouement, Kissinger journeyed to Minneapolis on August 5 to deliver a widely noted address that affords one of the best examples of his approach to rhetorical craftsmanship. Entitled "The Moral Foundations of Foreign Policy," the speech explicitly spelled out Kissinger's long-held conviction on the necessity for domestic consensus on foreign policy goals and thus the centrality of effective oratory in the forging of that consensus. "In a democracy, the conduct of foreign policy is possible only with public support," he intoned. "Therefore your government owes you an articulation of the purposes which its policies are designed to serve—to make clear our premises, to contribute to enlightened debate, and to explain how our policies serve the American people's objectives." Few other U.S. political leaders had ever developed so systematic a view of the instrumental character of rhetoric in the pursuit of higher, strategic goals, and few had ever spelled out their premises, to all who would but listen, with such unadorned candor.

Turning to the issue at hand, he noted, "We have found ourselves doubtful of our virtue and uncertain of our direction" in the wake of the Vietnam tragedy. Concerned that a demoralized public would press for a retreat from global involvements, it was Kissinger's purpose to shore up the nation's self-confidence by stressing its broad contributions to world order in the postwar era. He insisted:

The United States can look back on an extraordinary generation of achievement. We have maintained a stable balance of power in the world. We have preserved peace and fostered the growth of the industrial democracies of North America, Western Europe, and Japan. We helped shape the international trade and monetary system which has nourished global prosperity. We promoted decolonization and pioneered in development assistance for the new nations. . . . The global contribution of one nation—the United States—has been without precedent in human history. Only a nation of strong conviction and great idealism could have accomplished these efforts.

Far from mere cheerleading, Kissinger was struggling against the tide of national self-doubt by reminding the nation of its past successes. Short-term tragedy, he was insisting, must not deflect a nation from its long record of constructive and successful global involvements.

A similar thrust shaped an address he delivered in Cincinnati on October 6, 1975. Entitled "Global Peace, the Middle East, and the United States," the speech included Kissinger's familiar use of rhetorical obverses, such as: "We cannot solve every problem, but few solutions are possible without us." At the heart of his address, though, was his recurring preoccupation with shoring up domestic support for continued U.S. activism abroad. Arguing that "in the Middle East there is a yearning for peace surpassing any known for a generation," Kissinger urged his countrymen to "seize this historic opportunity" rather than retreat from the onerous burdens of global leadership. Kissinger was clearly haunted by the specter of a recrudescent isolationism among Americans; equally clear was his belief that effective oratory could help stem the tide of anti-internationalism that Vietnam had begot. "We Americans have spent the better part of a decade apologizing to ourselves and the world for what we thought we had become," he concluded. "We have spent most of the last three years enmeshed in a national tragedy that caused many to lose sight of what our country has meant, and continues to mean, to the billions abroad who look to the United States as a beacon of freedom and hope."

But even Kissinger's remarkable persuasive powers had their limits. By 1976—his final year in office—his personal popularity was slipping as his foreign policy came under mounting domestic attack. In February 1976, he delivered a major speech in San Francisco that sought to rebut his growing chorus of critics and defend his now-controversial policy toward the Soviet Union. As always, the speech bore the Kissinger signature of cerebral analysis. Added to this familiar trait, though, was something quite unusual for Kissinger: an unmistakable undercurrent of passion and anger. Repeatedly he hit back at his right-wing critics, depicting them as dangerously unsophisticated: "We must not equate tough rhetoric with strong action, nor can we wish away tough realities with nostalgic hopes." He denounced his critics' "facile slogans," "naive and dangerous caricatures," and "malicious" attacks on his policy of détente. By temperament and upbringing, he much preferred reasoned argumentation to vituperative polemic, but this episode demonstrates that Kissinger felt strongly enough about the crucial role of oratory in forging domestic support for foreign policy goals that he would not hesitate to adopt a more strident style when he felt it necessary to do so.

Kissinger stands as an interesting phenomenon in the history of American political oratory. By no means a naturally gifted speaker, his scholarship on diplomacy led him to view rhetoric as an indispensable tool in creating the domestic support he defined necessary to successful foreign policy. However one assesses the merits of his policy, there can be no mistaking the significance of Kissinger's public addresses as self-conscious elements in his sophisticated theory of statecraft.

INFORMATION SOURCES

Research Collections and Collected Speeches

Although Kissinger was a prolific speech maker, with one exception no effort has been made to assemble his speeches, nor is there an existing body of critical studies upon which to build.

Department of State Bulletin   *DSB*
Kissinger, Henry. *American Foreign Policy* 3d ed. New York: Norton, 1977.   *AFP*

Selected Biographies

Graubard, Stephen R. *Kissinger: The Portrait of a Mind.* New York: Norton, 1973.
Mazlish, Bruce. *Kissinger: The European Mind in American Policy.* New York: Basic Books, 1976.
Morris, Roger. *Uncertain Greatness.* New York: Harper & Row, 1977.
Stoessinger, John G. *Henry Kissinger: The Anguish of Power.* New York: Norton, 1976.

CHRONOLOGY OF MAJOR SPEECHES

See "Research Collections and Collected Speeches" for source codes.

"The Nature of the National Dialogue," Washington, D.C., October 8, 1973; *AFP*, pp. 115–30.

"From Coexistence to World Community," New York City, September 23, 1974; *AFP*, pp. 177–94.

"Moral Foundations of Foreign Policy," Minneapolis, Minnesota, August 5, 1975; *DSB*, pp. 161–71.

"Global Peace, the Middle East, and the United States," Cincinnati, Ohio, October 6, 1975; *DSB*, pp. 493–506.

"Permanent Challenge of Peace: U.S. Policy toward the Soviet Union," San Francisco, February 23, 1976; *DSB*, pp. 201–15.

ROBERT MARION LA FOLLETTE, SR.
(1855–1925), governor of and U.S. senator from Wisconsin

PETER AUGUSTINE LAWLER

Robert La Follette served in the U.S. Congress from 1855 to 1891, as governor from 1901 to 1905, and in the U.S. Senate from 1906 to 1925. As governor, he pushed through the Wisconsin legislature a series of largely unprecedented progressive measures that became in many respects the model of reform for the other states and the national government. He is almost always counted among the greatest of the senators, although chiefly on the basis of respect for the obstinate integrity of positions he took in unsuccessful opposition.

La Follette ran for the Republican nomination for the presidency in 1912 and was regarded as a serious, progressive alternative to the renomination of President Taft until Theodore Roosevelt entered the race. La Follette refused to withdraw in Roosevelt's favor, even after being soundly defeated in the primaries by him. He viewed Roosevelt's campaign as one of personal ambition and not progressive principle. La Follette sought the presidency again in 1924 as the candidate of the newly formed Progressive party and received almost 17 percent of the popular vote. This showing was extraordinary for a candidate of a third party in U.S. politics, but it was nonetheless disappointing for La Follette and his supporters. It was not good enough to justify the continuance of their party.

LA FOLLETTE AS POLITICAL ORATOR

La Follette made his mark primarily as a political orator. He is remembered for fighting speeches, for his bitter, uncompromising attacks on those whom he believed threatened the independence and honor of the American individual. His speaking tours were legendary. He was often the major attraction at Wisconsin county fairs. He gave well over one thousand Chautauqua and Lyceum addresses, often several hours in length. He was capable of speaking, in effect, for all day, every day for almost two months at a time. As governor and senator, he believed it was part of his public duty to travel throughout the nation to speak to as many as possible concerning the true causes of their discontent. He delivered various versions of his basic speech, "Representative Government," hundreds of times over a twenty-five-year period.

Although La Follette sometimes seemed to speak extemporaneously, his remarks were almost always based on his own meticulous preparation. He always wrote and polished with care his own speeches. He was known to prepare texts approaching one hundred pages in length. Such a text typically included remarkably detailed statistical evidence supporting its argument, compiled and analyzed by La Follette himself. Only in the last few years of his life, apparently due to failing health, did he delegate his statistical research to others. La Follette's characteristic assertion was that he had demonstrated for all who were not blinded by greed or self-interest that the facts were on his side. He used facts to confirm the righteousness of his moral principle.

As a child, La Follette's dream and ambition was to display his excellence on stage, to move audiences with his beautiful speech. He never lost his early love of reading Shakespeare aloud. Throughout his life, he made time to attend good plays. He acted in college and considered acting as a career, an idea he eventually discarded partly because he was too short for leading roles.

La Follette excelled in declamation but not in debate. He preferred grandeur or dramatic effect to unadorned argument. His awe-inspiring moral earnestness smothered the possibility of ambiguity and prevented self-detachment or levity. There was never any real humor in La Follette's speeches. It was always inappropriate in view of the seriousness of the crisis and the immensity of the evil.

La Follette's victory in the Inter-State Oratorical Contest in May 1879 gave him a regional reputation for oratorical excellence. On the basis of this reputation, he campaigned successfully for his first political office, district attorney, against the organization of the local party boss. The force of this speech, "Iago," came from its reduction of *Othello*'s presentation of a complex and ambiguous set of circumstances and psychological phenomena to what Carl Burgchardt has called a "melodramatic scenario," in which good and evil are starkly and simply contrasted. This forceful reductionism is present in and is a large part of the appeal of La Follette's political oratory.

The substance of his political oratory La Follette traced to an excerpt from a speech he heard given by Judge Edward G. Ryan to the graduating class of the Wisconsin Law School in 1873. La Follette called these words "prophetic" in his *Autobiography* and quoted them often in his speeches:

There is looming up a new and dark power. I cannot dwell upon the signs and shocking omens of its advent. The accumulation of individual wealth seems to be greater than it ever has been since the downfall of the Roman Empire. The enterprises of the country are aggregating vast corporate combinations of unexampled capital, boldly marching, not for economic conquests only, but for political power. For the first time really in our politics money is taking the field as organized power. . . . Already here at home, one great corporation has trifled with the sovereign power, and insulted the state. There is grave fear that it, and its great rival, have confederated to make partition of the state and share it as spoils. . . . The question will arise, and arise in your day, though perhaps not fully in mine, "Which shall rule—wealth or man; who shall fill public stations—educated and patriotic free men, or federal serfs of corporate capital?"

The themes of this remarkable excerpt are most of the key themes of the oratory of Governor and Senator La Follette, which remained remarkably constant from the second half of the 1890s through the 1920s. The history of the United States, according to La Follette, is the decline of democracy and individual freedom and the growth of the power of concentrated, corporate wealth and its special form of privilege. The culmination of this history, La Follette said in 1912 in "The Undermining of Democracy," was the "combination of combinations" through the interlocking of directorates. This combination ushered in "the period of complete industrial and commercial servitude in which we now find ourselves." La Follette changed some of the details of this history over time, but its fundamental message never changed.

Perhaps La Follette's most eloquent expression of this message is found in "The Menace of the Political Machine," delivered at the University of Chicago in 1897:

The existence of the corporation as we have it today was not dreamt of by the fathers. It has become all-pervasive; has invaded all departments of business, all activities of life. By their number and power and consolidation oft-times of many into one, corporations have practically acquired dominion over the business world. The effect is revolutionary and cannot be overestimated. The individual as a business factor is disappearing, his place being taken by many under corporate rule. The business man and the artisan of the past gave to his business an individual stamp and reputation, making high mental worth an essential element in business life. Gathered in corporate employ men become mere cogs in the wheel of complicated mechanism. The corporate is a machine for making money, demanding of its employees only obedience and service, reducing men to the status of private in the regular army.

La Follette spoke of "the fathers," a phrase he often used as part of a rhetorical strategy he almost surely learned from Lincoln. He, following Lincoln, invoked the reverence Americans, like all other people, tend to have for those who gave them their way of life. He also made use of Americans' religion; the "fathers" are implicitly compared with the biblical patriarchs.

The way of life given by the fathers was individual independence and freedom. Lincoln appealed to the fathers' tradition of freedom to oppose what he called the revolutionary or radically new doctrines supporting the unlimited expansion of slavery. La Follette also used this tradition, as a good member of the party of Lincoln, to oppose the new, undreamed of threat to freedom in his time. Individuals were being enslaved by the "revolutionary" force of "corporate rule." They were reduced to "mere cogs" in a machine. They lost their "mental worth" or distinctiveness, their particular sources of pride and honor: "The business man and artisan of the past gave his business an individual stamp and reputation."

The "menace" of La Follette's time was the destruction of the distinction between the individual and the interchangeable parts of a machine. Insofar as individuals still take pride in this distinction, in their freedom and honor, La Follette's oratory will cause them to revolt against corporate rule and its revolutionary effects. La Follette hoped and believed his indignation and obstinacy were shared by the great majority of people. He often said he believed that most men are men of honor.

Ultimately La Follette had less in common with the nationalistic, future-oriented visions of progressives such as Theodore Roosevelt or Woodrow Wilson than with the individualistic tradition of Thomas Jefferson and Andrew Jackson. He inherited the Democrats' opposition to government encouragement of industrial development and its promotion of speculation at the expense of manual labor. The decline of the ways of life of the self-reliant, property-owning farmer and the independent, hard-working "business man who gives honest service in return for righteous profits" must be reversed to restore the moral foundation of republican citizenship. Agriculture, La Follette said to a group of farmers in 1904, provides the foundation of America's "most distinctive way of life" and is "the source of our safest, most conservative citizenship and highest level of intelligence." La Follette's partisanship on behalf of and his assertion of the moral superiority of the independence of the farmer and businessman made his message unattractive to propertyless, dependent wage earners and their unions. It could not become the foundation of a farm-labor coalition.

La Follette himself grew up on a frontier farm, and there, he wrote in his *Autobiography*, he "felt the indignation" of the Granger movement around him. His principal source of support, his loyal constituency in Wisconsin, was composed largely of farmers, many of whom were politically mobilized for the first time by the Granger and populist movements. Their indignation was his indignation. For La Follette, their interests were always in accord with the public good. As a congressman in 1886, for example, he gave a remarkably passionate speech in favor of a tax on oleomargarine, one supported for obvious reasons by Wisconsin's dairy farmers. He called oleomargarine a "monstrous product of greed and hypocrisy." The speech was well received in Wisconsin.

La Follette's persistent opposition to U.S. involvement in World War I and the League of Nations was also in accord with his constituents' interests and prejudices. This opposition brought him considerable and sometimes unfair and abusive criticism, especially from other progressives. But it also seems to have increased his already great popularity in Wisconsin and throughout the rest of the Midwest. Many of La Follette's postwar speeches emphasized the injustice of the peace agreements for the German and Irish peoples. Much of the support La Follette received in his 1924 presidential race in the Midwest, the only section of the country in which he ran well, seems to have been from German and Irish-Americans who were pro-German or anti-British and hence antiwar. This support had little to do with progressivism as it is usually understood.

La Follette's opposition to the league, however, was not simply political expedience. His argument was rooted solidly in his understanding of American principle. Its large measure of integrity is the basis of America's guilty conscience as a global power. American principle seems often to give way in the face of the necessities of international conflict.

La Follette's best antileague speech was given in the Senate on November 18, 1919. He said the covenant establishing the league was "an instrument for the preservation of the status quo . . . couched in the language of idealism and peace." Those fighting for "the cause of human freedom" against imperial tyranny, as did Americans, became "international outlaws." Some argue, La Follette went on, "that the 400,000,000 unwilling subjects of the British empire enjoy better government than they would enjoy if left to govern themselves." He showed the racially based inconsistency of this position by quoting extensively from Lincoln's argument against Stephen Douglas. According to Lincoln, said La Follette, "the Declaration of Independence applies not alone to white men, or the descendants of the English settlers in the colonies, but to all men, white and black, yellow and brown."

La Follette did not share the view of Woodrow Wilson and other progressives that political principles themselves evolved or progressed. With Lincoln and Jefferson, he affirmed the permanent truth of the principles of the Declaration of Independence as the necessary precondition of genuine human progress. He spoke of the restoration, not the creation, of principle. His obstinate attachment to the principles of democracy and individualism caused him to oppose class-based government of any sort, whether the "dictatorship of plutocracy or dictatorship of the proletariat."

La Follette's principled individualism led him to distinguish himself among the other political leaders of his time for his forthright attacks on racism (in the speeches opposing U.S. support of imperialism) and his firm support of women's rights (in speeches favoring women's suffrage). He also gave in the Senate a rather extreme defense of individual rights in time of war that serves as a salutary corrective to patriotic extremism and the Wilson administration's sometimes unnecessary censorship and coercion. He particularly urged citizens to be watchful of "those precedents . . . which, excused on the plea of necessity in war time, become the fixed rule when necessity has passed."

La Follette's reputation as a progressive is based on his promotion of institutional reform in the service of individualistic principle. The most important of these reforms was the direct primary, which he is chiefly responsible for introducing into U.S. politics. He publicly announced his crusade on behalf of the primary in 1897 in "The Menace of the Political Machine." His account of the origins of the menace finds its roots in Jefferson. La Follette replaced the decline in civic spirit Jefferson feared after the Revolutionary War with the real decline he claimed occurred after the Civil War. During that war, he asserted, Americans were willing to sacrifice everything "to preserve a government of the people, by the people, and for the people." After the war, however, they became preoccupied with "material affairs" and ignored their responsibilities as citizens. In their "hot pursuit of fortune," they did not want "to let business go for politics." They became complacent, inattentive, and unassertive. They became easy prey for despots.

They became enslaved by the "impersonal, irresponsible, extra-legal" machine. Just like and in the service of corporate power, it reduces human beings to "cogs." The political machine is part of the pervasive phenomenon of the mechanistic destruction of individual independence. It empties democratic citizenship of its substance. It must "create an artificial interest in the general election'' to induce citizens to make what is in truth a meaningless choice between the two machine-generated candidates.

Having activated the conscience of materialists and the indignation of citizens, La Follette announced the way for the majority to free itself from bondage. The direct primary "is the way to be saved." It "is our final safety." It will provide for "the ultimate overthrow of the machine" and the restoration of "the first principles of democracy."

La Follette taught that the primary would strengthen U.S. political parties by radically purifying them, but purification meant the destruction of their organization. Any dependence on such organization undermines the individual's sense of responsibility. For La Follette, representative government meant government responding in a direct or unmediated fashion to the majority will. The primary, contrary to La Follette's explicit intention but in harmony with the consequences of his principles, has been the principal agency in the gradual disappearance of most of the organization of U.S. political parties.

Another long-term impact of the successful institutionalization of the primary has been to increase the power of the rhetoric of indignation and the politics of obstinacy, La Follette's rhetoric and politics, at the expense of the power of organizationally based coalition building or interest adjustment in U.S. politics. As a result of the McGovern-Fraser commission reforms, La Follette's ultimate solution was finally wholly implemented by the national Democratic party in 1972. The party organization could no longer choose any of the delegates to the national convention.

The first beneficiaries of the reforms were George McGovern and George Wallace, who differed markedly on principle but shared the oratorical strategy of making extreme appeals to antiestablishment indignation. In 1976, Jimmy Carter's seemingly nonpartisan anti-Washington and antiorganization rhetoric of personal sincerity and integrity, which manipulated subtly and effectively Watergate-related anger, produced his surprising primary victories and finally a failed presidency.

This stunning success of La Follette's oratorical project has not led to an improvement in the quality of U.S. government. It has not even led to an improvement in the quality of political oratory. Hyprocrisy and image appeals typically have prevailed over La Follette–type proud integrity and painstaking articulation of progressive principle. Nevertheless, it would have been wrong to have wished for the complete failure of La Follette's oratory. It is a fine example of the nobility of the American idea of freedom. It needs to be moderated but not destroyed by the just demands of self-interest and prudence.

INFORMATION SOURCES

Research Collections and Collected Speeches

The La Follette Family Papers have been deposited at the Library of Congress, Washington, D.C. This collection includes holographs and typed drafts of many of La Follette's speeches, editorials, and articles and bound copies of the addresses he delivered as governor to the Wisconsin legislature and on the floor of the House and the Senate. The only published collection of La Follette's speeches is *The Political Philosophy of Robert La Follette*, a large and varied selection of excerpts from his speeches and writings arranged according to topic; unfortunately, it contains no complete speeches. Another useful and readily available primary source is *La Follette's Autobiography: A Personal Narrative of Political Experiences*, originally published in 1913 and reprinted by the University of Wisconsin Press in 1961.

American Public Addresses 1740–1952. Edited by A. Craig Baird. New   APA
     York: McGraw-Hill, 1956.
La Follette, Robert. *La Follette's Autobiography*. Madison: University of   LA
     Wisconsin, 1913.
———. *The Political Philosophy of Robert La Follette*. Madison: Robert   PPRL
     La Follette Co., 1920.
La Follette Family Papers, Library of Congress.   LFP

Selected Critical Studies

Burgchardt, Carl Robert. "The Will, the People, and the Law: A Rhetorical Biography of Robert M. La Follette, Sr." Ph.D. dissertation, University of Wisconsin, 1982.
Hofstadter, Richard. *The Age of Reform*. New York: Vintage Books, 1955.
Lahman, Carroll P. "Robert La Follette." *A History and Criticism of American Political Address*. Vol. 2. Edited by W. N. Brigance. New York: Russell and Russell, 1960.
———. "Robert Marion La Follette as Public Speaker and Political Leader." Ph.D. dissertation, University of Wisconsin, 1939.
Ranney, Austin. *Curing the Mischiefs of Faction: Party Reform in America*. Berkeley: University of California Press, 1975.

Selected Biographies

La Follette, Belle Case, and La Follette, Fola. *Robert M. La Follette*. 2 vols. New York: Hafner Publishing Company, 1971.
Thelen, David P. *The Early Life of Robert M. La Follette, 1855–1884*. Chicago: Loyola University Press, 1966.
———. *Robert M. La Follette and the Insurgent Spirit*. Boston: Little, Brown, 1976.

CHRONOLOGY OF MAJOR SPEECHES

See "Research Collection and Collected Speeches" for source codes.

"Iago," Iowa City, May 7, 1879; *LFP*.

Speech against oleomargarine, U.S. House of Representatives, Washington, D.C., June 3, 1886; *LFP*.

"Menace of the Political Machine," Chicago, February 22, 1897; *LFP*; *PPRL*, pp. 27–29, 53–57.

"Representative Government," often delivered from 1897 to 1922; *LFP*.

"The Undermining of Democracy," Philadelphia, Pennsylvania, February 2, 1912; *LA*, pp. 342–62.

"Free Speech in Wartime," U.S. Senate, Washington, D.C., November 6, 1919; *LFP*; *APA*, pp. 244–48.

"Peace without Victory," U.S. Senate, Washington, D.C., November 18, 1919; *LFP*; *PPRL*, pp. 260–68.

JOHN LLEWELLYN LEWIS
(1880–1969), labor leader

RICHARD J. JENSEN

The history of the United Mine Workers of America (UMW) in the twentieth century in many respects is the history of one man, John Llewellyn Lewis. During the first two decades of the century, UMW leaders were often unable to control their membership, but Lewis broke that tradition. Upon assuming the union's presidency in 1920, he immediately became its dominant force. Saul Alinsky described the relationships between Lewis and the membership of the UMW: "The mine workers union would only be united by some man who would know not only the economics of coal but the miners and their self-destructive hatred. It would have to be a man far tougher and much more ruthless than all of them put together. It would have to be, as the miners said, 'something of a man.' "

Lewis was born on February 12, 1880, in Lucas, Iowa, the son of a coal miner. As a young man Lewis traveled throughout the West. Those travels, he claimed, taught him of the suffering of workers and the need for organization: "Laboring in isolated communities, where they are often denied even food and shelter; handicapped and persecuted by the almost satanic ingenuity of the shameless agents of the non-union coal operators; insulted, abused, beaten and offered every personal indignity by murderous mine guards, their lot is far from being an easy one."

By 1909 Lewis and many other members of his family had settled in Panama, Illinois, where he became president of a UMW local. In 1911 he was appointed by Samuel Gompers as a traveling American Federation of Labor (AFL) organizer, a position he occupied for six years. His years as an organizer gave him a solid foundation in unionism. In 1917 he was appointed to the position of statistician of the UMW. In announcing his appointment, the *UMW Journal* described Lewis as "a man of strong personality, a gifted orator." Through a series of appointments, he became acting president in 1919. In 1920 Lewis won election to the presidency, an office he occupied until he retired in 1959.

JOHN L. LEWIS AS LABOR ORATOR

By the time Lewis had consolidated his power in the UMW, he had built an efficient union political machine to run the organization, but that was not his only means of maintaining strength. Lewis was a powerful orator who was able to maintain control over the miners at conventions and meetings through emotionalism, sarcasm, anecdotes, and patriotism. If a delegate at a UMW convention challenged Lewis, he had ready ripostes. For example, Melvin Dubofsky reports in his biography that Lewis rebuked an Irish-American militant: ''I happen to know that while Mike is a stern unyielding exponent of Irish freedom that he does his fighting for Ireland in America. Even though the Irish people may be compelled by force of circumstances and the rule of the British Empire to continue their fight for an additional 700 years, you will still find Mike in America.''

Lewis's training as an orator began as a young man. He practiced his speaking as an amateur actor in the Lucas Opera House. During his acting career, he became familiar with the plays of Shakespeare and several lesser playwrights. Lines and allusions from drama later appeared in his oratory. Dubofsky stated that early in life, Lewis ''knew that impressive classical allusions could be drawn from *Bartlett's Familiar Quotations* and the even-more-familiar Bible. Later in life he evinced no deep interest in literary classics, preferring instead military history, western adventures, formula magazines, and . . . *American Heritage*, a popularized, easy-to-read version of the national past.'' C. K. McFarland stated in *Roosevelt, Lewis and the New Deal, 1933–1940* that as an AFL organizer, Lewis apparently learned from Gompers ''that a large part of the labor leader's function was showmanship; and a showman he became.'' In his biography of Lewis, C. L. Sulzberger even claimed that Lewis was such a great speaker that a Chautauqua company offered him $25,000 to speak three times a week, but Lewis declined.

According to Dubofsky, by the time Lewis assumed the presidency of the union, he had mastered two different but equally effective styles of speaking. When emotion and sentiment were needed, he used carefully prepared and re-hearsed biblical and Shakespearean allusions that impressed his union audiences. Never at a loss for words, even during the most tempestuous debates, he mastered the caustic comment and the ad hominem argument. He could also change from a dramatic orator to professional union leader when necessary. As a union leader, he could marshal facts and figures to convince his audience. As Dubofsky stated, ''When he needed to Lewis applied lessons drawn from the Old Testament, Shakespeare, and Machiavelli, he mixed clarity with vengeance; he cajoled and he roared; he played the lion and the fox.''

Lewis's physical stature and voice helped him as an orator. Dubofsky states, ''Having mastered the imperatives of public speaking in the premicrophone age, Lewis's voice alternately bellowed and modulated, crooned and cursed. He charmed and cajoled his audiences, entertained and taught them, agitated and pacified them. So fine was his voice modulation, so smoothly could Lewis change moods, that listeners became hypnotized by him and cheered platitudes, inap-propriate classical allusions, and outright solecisms.'' The miners listened and were proud that their leader could speak so well. Lewis's style of speaking was so popular among the miners that other union leaders attempted to copy him.

Although he had a proved reservoir of materials, Lewis did not write his own speeches or essays. He relied on Ellis Searles, K. C. Adams, and W. Jett Lauck,

UMW employees who served Lewis virtually his entire career as writers and advisers.

In his role of union leader, Lewis gave numerous speeches that attracted the attention of the public. Many of those speeches supported or opposed political candidates. On October 17, 1928, Lewis spoke over national radio under the auspices of the Republican National Committee. He argued that the Republican nominee for president, Herbert Hoover, had established a new economic order where higher wages, greater consumer power, and a rising standard of living created prosperity: "Industry and trade must be released from the restrictions of the anti-trust laws so that the maximum economics in production and distribution may be made possible." In order to continue the economic order, he called for Hoover's election.

Two years later in March 1930, Lewis faced serious opposition from insurgents at the union's convention in Indianapolis. After two weeks of ferocious battle, Lewis spoke some of his most-often quoted lines to the miners, claiming he had "pleaded their case from the pulpit and the public platform, in joint conference with the associated operators of the country, before the bar of state legislatures, in the councils of the President's cabinet, and in the public press of this nation— not in the quavering tones of a feeble mendicant asking alms, but in the thundering voice of the captain of a mighty host, demanding the right to which free men were entitled." He went on to define his role as labor orator: "As an individual my opinion and my voice is of no more consequence in our world of affairs or in the coal industry . . . than the voice or opinions of any passerby upon the street. It is only when I am able to translate your dreams and aspirations into words which others may understand that my tongue possesses any strength or my hand any force."

Although Lewis had supported Republicans in the 1920s, he found himself linked to the Democrats in the 1930s. Franklin Delano Roosevelt's support of legislation such as section 7A of the National Recovery Act made it possible for labor to organize and bargain collectively. Under these favorable laws, the UMW grew, and Lewis began to plan strategies to organize workers in the steel and automotive industries where the AFL had little success. He sought to organize those workers along industrial lines (where all workers in the industry belong to a single union) rather than craft lines, as the AFL did. Lewis attempted to work within the AFL but broke with it in 1935 and eventually formed the Congress of Industrial Organizations (CIO). He became the first CIO president. On November 28, 1935, in a radio address, he explained that the establishment of industrial unions in mass production industries "offers the only way to emancipation from industrial autocracy—to economic and political freedom to those who work by hand and brain." His actions brought him into conflict with William Green, president of the AFL, but in typical fashion, Lewis attacked Green: "Your lament is that I will not join you in a policy of anxious inertia. . . . Candidly, I am tempermentally incapable of sitting with you in sackcloth and ashes, endlessly intoning, 'O tempora! O Mores.' . . . For myself I prefer to err on the side of America's underprivileged and exploited millions, if erring it be.''

On July 6, 1936, Lewis inaugurated a campaign to organize steelworkers. In a broadcast speech, Lewis stated: ''I salute the hosts of labor who listen. . . . My voice tonight will be the voice of millions of men and women unemployed in America's industries, heretofore unorganized, economically exploited and inarticulate.'' He then attacked the owners of the steel industry for not allowing workers to organize and improve their standard of living.

Successes in steel and among autoworkers brought the CIO to great heights in 1937. With the large increase in union members, labor and Lewis secured tremendous political and economic power.

Although Lewis and Roosevelt had formed an alliance during the first Roosevelt administration to improve the lives of workers, a series of disagreements led to a split between these two strong individuals. That split became final after Roosevelt condemned both labor and management during a coal strike. Roosevelt's statement led to a famous rebuke by Lewis in a speech on September 3, 1937: ''Labor, like Israel, has many sorrows. Its women weep for their fallen and they lament for the future of the children of the race. It ill behooves one who has supped at a labor's table and who has been sheltered in labor's house to curse with equal fervor and fine impartiality both labor and its adversaries when they are locked in deadly embrace.'' Lewis also opposed Roosevelt because he saw the country moving toward another European war, a war to be fought by the sons of the laboring class. In a Labor Day radio address in 1939, Lewis stated: ''Labor in America wants no war nor any part of war. Labor wants the right to work and live—not the privilege of dying by gunshot or poison gas to sustain the mental errors of current statesmen.''

Lewis refused to support Roosevelt for a third term and may even have considered running for president himself on a third party ticket. On October 25, 1940, he made a long-awaited announcement in a speech broadcast over three national radio networks. He charged Roosevelt with seeking personal power at the expense of the American public: ''The spectacle of a President who is disinclined to surrender that power, in keeping with traditions of the Republic. . . . Personal craving for power, the overweening abnormal and selfish craving for increased power, is a thing to alarm and dismay. . . . America needs no royal family.'' Lewis then recommended that workers vote for Wendell Willkie: ''He is not an aristocrat. He has the common touch. He was born in the briar and not to the purple. He has worked with his hands, and he has known the pangs of hunger.'' Workers apparently ignored Lewis and voted for Roosevelt. For the rest of Roosevelt's presidency, Lewis opposed the president and his policies.

In 1940 Lewis resigned the presidency of the CIO and spent the rest of his career leading the UMW. During World War II, he led a series of unpopular strikes and became one of the most hated men in the United States. An editorial in *Stars and Stripes* captured the essence of Lewis's negative image among many

Americans: "Speaking for the American soldier, John L. Lewis, damn your coal-black soul."

Roosevelt was not the only politician Lewis attacked. In 1939 when Vice-President John Nance Garner helped conservatives undermine the Roosevelt administration's wages and hours law, Lewis ridiculed him as a "labor-baiting, whiskey-drinking, evil old man." Lewis's label stuck with Garner for the rest of his career. In 1947 Lewis had a disagreement with Secretary of the Interior J. A. Krug. At a congressional hearing, Lewis referred to Krug as a "great modern Hercules with a number twelve shoe and a number five hat."

In 1944 Lewis faced his last internal challenge in the UMW. At that year's convention, Lewis demonstrated that the passing years had not dimmed his ability to strike. In the September 13, 1944 issue, the *New York Times* quoted Lewis saying of his opponent: "There isn't any mincing, lackadaisical, lace-painted gigolo going to dethrone John L. in his own convention." The challenge was beaten back.

Lewis led only one strike after World War II. As years went on, he assumed the role of a labor statesman presiding over a union that declined in membership and power as the consumption of coal decreased.

Throughout his career, Lewis was revered by the miners, who were proud that their leader could speak so well. According to Dubofsky, they "liked hearing their dreams, their problems, their suffering cloaked in Biblical phrases. . . . They felt proud that a workers' leader could use so many educated words with such obvious fluency, and they were pleased and a little flattered by hearing their own fate discussed in such rolling periods and such dramatic phrases." The miners also saw Lewis as one of them and not as a bureaucrat in Washington, D.C. In his rhetoric, Lewis built that identification with the workers: "The thing that gives me strength is the fact that I am able correctly to interpret the aims of my people. I know the psychology of the coal miner. I know about his dreams and his ideals and trials and tribulations. I have lived with coal miners. I am one of them."

INFORMATION SOURCES

Research Collections and Collected Speeches

Most of Lewis's papers are housed in the State Historical Society of Wisconsin, Madison; included are typescripts of Lewis's major speeches. There is also a collection of Lewis material housed at the office of the United Mine Workers, Washington, D.C. Copies of the *United Mine Workers Journal* during the years of Lewis's leadership contain his speeches and writings.

The American Labor Movement. Edited by Leon Litwack. Englewood Cliffs,   *ALM*
    N.J.: Prentice-Hall, 1962.
John L. Lewis and the International Union: United Mine Workers of Amer-
    ica. Edited by Rex Lauck. Washington, D.C.: International Exec-
    utive Board of the United Mine Workers of America, 1952.

Speaking Out: An Oral History of the American Past. Edited by Philip Reed   *SO*
    Rulon and William H. Lyon. 2 vols. Minneapolis: Burgess, 1981.
State Historical Society of Wisconsin.   *SHSW*
United Mine Workers Journal.   *UMWJ*

Selected Critical Studies

Gallagher, Mary Brigid. "John L. Lewis: The Oratory of Pity and Indignation." *Today's Speech* 9 (1961): 15–19, 29.

Rothman, Richard M. "Name-Calling And Its Results: A Vignette." *Today's Speech* 10 (1962): 11.

———. "On the Speaking of John L. Lewis." *Central States Speech Journal* 14 (1963): 177–85.

———. "A Case Study in Critical-Historical Research: Effects of Mythical Speech." *Speech Monographs* 34 (1967): 95–97.

Selected Biographies

Alinsky, Saul D. *John L. Lewis: An Unauthorized Biography*. New York: Vintage Books, 1949.

Dubofsky, Melvyn, and Van Tine, Warren. *John L. Lewis: A Biography*. New York: Quadrangle/New York Times Book Co., 1977.

McFarland, C. K. *Roosevelt, Lewis, and the New Deal, 1933–1940*. Fort Worth: Texas Christian University Press, 1970.

Sulzberger, C. L. *Sit Down with John L. Lewis*. New York: Random House, 1938.

CHRONOLOGY OF MAJOR SPEECHES

See "Research Collections and Collected Speeches" for source codes.

"Hoover's Tonic Safest for Industry," Washington, D.C., October 17, 1928; *SHSW*.

Speech to Commonwealth Club, San Francisco, October 10, 1934; *UMWJ*, November 15, 1934, pp. 10–14.

"The Future of Organized Labor," Washington, D.C., November 25, 1935; *SHSW*; *UMWJ*, December 15, 1935, pp. 20–21.

"Industrial Democracy in Steel," Washington, D.C., July 6, 1936; *SHSW*.

"Labor and the Nation," Washington, D.C., September 3, 1937; *UMWJ* September 15, 1937, pp. 3–4; *Vital Speeches of the Day*, 3 (1937), pp. 731–33.

Speech to American Youth Congress, Washington, D.C., February 10, 1940; *SHSW*.

Speech to the nation, Washington, D.C., October 25, 1940; *SHSW*; *UMWJ*, November 1, 1940, pp. 4–6.

HUEY PIERCE LONG, JR.
(1893–1935), governor of Louisiana, U.S. senator

_____ PAUL C. GASKE

A prominent Louisiana opponent of Huey Long gave the following assessment of Long's oratorical skill: "Huey Long is the best stump speaker in America. He is the best political radio speaker, better even than President Roosevelt. Give him time on the air and let him have a week to campaign in each state, and he can sweep the country. He is one of the most persuasive men living."

Long's political and public speaking careers are entwined. His high school forensics experience in debate and declamation led him to adopt the extemporaneous, natural, free-wheeling style that was to become a political trademark and a fundamental basis of his mass appeal. His observant study of effective regional orators and their dealings with the "hillbillies" and "rednecks" of his area planted the seeds for a rhetorical stance that allowed him to be one of the boys yet clearly differentiated from them—a delicate balance needed to acquire their loyalty, support, and respect.

Long's rhetoric was the foundation for a significant political program, the Share Our Wealth movement. Through a series of national radio broadcasts, he was able to articulate a simplistic yet appealing program for radical social and economic change. His speeches purposively aligned him with the program, so that "Share Our Wealth" and "Huey Long" became perceptually one and the same. When Long was able to enlist the support of 800,000 of Share Our Wealth societies within one month of announcing the program and some 7 million by the time of his assassination eighteen months later, he was transformed from a regional to a national force. James Farley, Franklin D. Roosevelt's chief political strategist, confided in 1935 that Huey Long as a third-party presidential candidate might have the balance of power in the 1936 election.

The study of Long's rhetoric has generated considerable insight into knowledge of rhetorical theory and practice. First, his Share Our Wealth broadcasts enrich an understanding of the evolution of social movements. Recurring patterns, themes, and images emerge in his discourse that help to explain the popularity of Share Our Wealth and tie it directly to its context, the Great Depression. Second, in a related manner, an analysis of Long's rhetoric informs our understanding of the relationship of the audience, speaker, and situation that may define a genre of oratory called demagogic discourse. Third, an examination of Long's speeches and method of delivery reinforces the notion that there is not one best way to compose or deliver political oratory. Unlike Franklin Roosevelt and most other contemporary politicians, Long did not utilize speech writers, almost always spoke without notes or text, and violated nearly every normative prescription regarding appropriate speech content. In spite of (or partially because of) his deviance from the norm, Long was among the most effective political orators in the century.

LONG'S RHETORIC AND THE AMERICAN POLITICAL SYSTEM

The significance of Huey Long's rhetoric on the U.S. political system was substantial. Initially, it should be noted that Long demonstrated the force of quantity of speech on the floor of the Senate through the filibuster. On several occasions after his 1932 election (he was elected governor of Louisiana in 1928 after a strong third-place showing in the 1924 primary), Long took on legislation practically singlehandedly. Once he filibustered for fifteen and a half hours consecutively against the extension of the National Recovery Act, leaving the floor only twice for ten minutes apiece during quorum calls. On another occasion, he led a filibuster against a banking reform bill for nearly three weeks, at one point speaking for nearly three consecutive days without interruption. Although the bill eventually passed the Senate, it died in committee in the House, killed by a senator "with a front of brass and lungs of leather." These extended discourses were hardly rhetorical masterpieces, but they won Long the attention of the public. They established him as an individual of substantial power and attractive philosophic ideals, a combination that set the stage for another substantial rhetorical impact on the political system: Long's use of the radio in his series of national broadcasts.

As a stump speaker, Huey Long gained a strong regional following. Noted for his bellicose attacks against opponents and his rapier-like wit, he drew large and generally supportive crowds, although he was perceived by more traditional political figures as something of a clown. Upon his election to the Senate, he recognized that a national audience was required to make a national impact and that a national medium was required to carry that message. In fact, Long was the first politician to reach a national audience. He actually purchased airtime from the National Broadcasting Company to speak in support of his senatorial bills. Five days after President Roosevelt's first fireside chat, Huey Long was provided free time by NBC (under a policy of providing access to members of Congress, on request) and delivered the first of eleven national radio broadcasts.

From these radio broadcasts, two additional effects on the political system may be discerned. First, the speeches demonstrated radio to be the most powerful medium of Long's day. The 800,000 individuals who joined the Share Our Wealth Society within one month from Long's announcement of the program on the February 23, 1934, "Every Man a King" address is but one example of the persuasive power of the radio. Another example was Long's radio address of March 7, 1935. Long had come under strong attack during a March 4th radio speech by General Hugh Johnson, the controversial and colorful World War I director of the Selective Service and architect and former director of the National

Recovery Administration, a flagship program of the New Deal. Long demanded equal time to answer Johnson from NBC, which granted him thirty minutes of response time. When every radio station in the NBC network ordered the broadcast, Long was able to wrangle an additional fifteen minutes of airtime.

An audience estimated at 25 million awaited an extended Long outburst against Johnson and Roosevelt. Instead he calmly observed, "It will serve no purpose to our distressed people for me to call my opponents more bitter names than they call me. Even were I able, I have not the time to present my side of the argument and match them in billingsgate or profanity." For forty minutes, Long explained the Share Our Wealth program to his largest audience ever. Presenting information in a calculatingly restrained manner, "he appeared as a man of reason and calm and made his opponents seem to be men of unreason. A perceptive correspondent . . . wrote that Johnson and Roosevelt between them had managed to transform the Kingfish 'from a clown into a real political menace.' " Without the radio medium, such remarkable transformations would not have been possible. As FDR himself ironically noted concerning Long and Father Coughlin, "In normal times the radio and other appeals by them would not have been effective. However, these are not normal times; people are jumpy and very ready to run after strange gods."

A second impact of Long's rhetoric generally and the national radio broadcasts specifically was that they reinforced the effectiveness of the common man strategy in political rhetoric. Rather than distance himself from his Louisiana farming roots, Long chose to identify himself with those most directly disenfranchised by the Great Depression. His speeches were characterized by simple and direct language and sentence structure, estimated at fourth-grade level by the Flesch readability formula. This does not imply that Long was uneducated, merely that understanding by his target audience was a critical concern. Adding to the common man strategy was Long's extemporaneous delivery of his radio speeches, his rapid rate of delivery, clear articulation, modest regional dialect, and effective phrasing. These delivery components created a combination of self-assuredness, intensity, and conviction that made Long's amalgam of populism, technocracy, the Bible, and Share Our Wealth, especially appealing. As Bormann observed, "He talked to his national radio audience as he might have talked to a group of men on the streets of Winnfield, Louisiana. His listeners heard the familiar idioms, the familiar figures of speech, the familiar grammar that they were hearing at their work and in their homes."

A third remarkable impact of Huey Long's rhetoric was its role in furthering understanding of demagogic discourse and in illumining understanding of the demagogue as a political figure. Initially Long's radio broadcasts and other speeches recast the demagogue into a rhetorical mode, not a personality mode. An analysis of Long's speeches reveals that the defining features of the demagogue are not a set of personality traits but a set of features created largely through public discourse.

The demagogue shares several elements common to a revered public figure;

both are mass leaders, are charismatic, and are public heroes. But what distinguishes the demagogue from the revered public figure is illumined by an analysis of Long's rhetoric. First, a single issue dominates the demagogue's rhetoric. Issues peripheral to the redistribution of wealth and the Share Our Wealth program were rarely raised independently by Long; they were integrated into his program, deemphasized, or dropped entirely. Second, the essence of Long's rhetoric was confrontational, not conciliatory. For example, Long's creation of the enemy, the cause of the maldistribution of wealth (for example, the Rockefellers, Morgans, and FDR), was a dominant and consistent theme in his radio broadcasts. Thus the demagogue's rhetoric polarizes public support, exciting "violent antithetical emotions in people, even in those not closely associated with him." Finally, although the public figure may spearhead a movement, the demagogue is the movement. That is, the demagogue is a symbolic figure, inextricably weaving himself and his issue so that they become synonymous. In much the same manner as Joseph McCarthy and the red menace were isomorphic, so too were Huey Long and Share Our Wealth. Long deliberately created this linkage through his radio broadcasts in the hope that the surge of pent-up emotions resulting from the frustrations of the depression would sweep him into the White House.

A second contribution of Long's rhetoric to an understanding of demagoguery was an identification of context and circumstance that made demagoguery most appealing. The roots of audience response to Huey Long were the economic dislocation of the depression that significantly disrupted the life-style of a substantial number of citizens. This dislocation was coupled with a pronounced societal move toward fundamentalism and spiritualism, a deemphasis on individualism and an increased search for community, and a rejection of science and intellectualism in favor of the spirit and anti-intellectualism. The domination of heart over mind is consistently reinforced in Long's Share Our Wealth addresses as he seized appropriately religious themes to identify enemies and propose his programs as cures for the nation's ills. Thus the appeal of Long's rhetoric helps us better to understand the conditions under which demagoguery is likely to flourish.

Third, an analysis of Huey Long's rhetoric identifies key features of demagogic discourse structure. Long's speeches typically followed a particular motivational pattern of action described in Kenneth Burke's *Permanence and Change*: a procession from guilt to victimization to redemption to salvation. Long's radio broadcasts typically began with the creation of guilt in his audience: guilt for being impotent and ill equipped to deal with their own problems, guilt for being poor and denying their children basic necessities. This guilt would then be transferred to a "sacrificial offering"—an enemy—in the persona of the conspiratorial wealthy and the individual ultimately responsible for decisions affecting the poor, Franklin Roosevelt. The victimization process would include not only the identification of the enemy but its demonic and sinister features, the extent and threat of its power, and the justifiable and necessary retribution that must be taken against it.

Long's next structural step was to supply the means to eliminate the enemy, to cleanse the audience's guilt and justify persecution of the enemy. Long's redemptive plan was Share Our Wealth, and joining Share Our Wealth societies was the behavioral commitment to the means of grace. Both the features of Share Our Wealth and the necessity to join Share Our Wealth societies were key elements of Long's radio broadcasts.

Finally, the salvation step served to link the speaker with the successful implementation of the program. To do so, the leader must not merely be an authority figure but a god figure. Gerald L. K. Smith, a chief Long aide, remarked, "No great movement has ever succeeded unless it has deified some one man. The Share-the-Wealth movement consciously deified Huey P. Long." The parallels between Jesus's humble origins and simple parables and Long's rhetorically created common man image with a vision for a heaven on earth (Share Our Wealth) cannot be lightly dismissed. As he observed in his February 23, 1934, address: " 'Every Man a King.' Every man to eat when there is something to eat; all to wear something when there is something to wear. That makes us all a sovereign."

A fourth contribution of an analysis of Long's rhetoric to understanding of demagogic discourse is that it facilitates identification of key features of demagogic discourse content. Recognizing that the structural dimension is given force through the content dimension, several features warrant comment and illustration. First, one finds extensive, even dominant, reliance on Scripture to justify Long's attacks against the wealthy throughout his radio broadcasts, to justify retribution against them, to legitimize Share Our Wealth. In his January 19, 1935, speech, he observed, "Here is what He said: 'The profit of the earth is for all.' Ecclesiastes: chapter 5, verse 9." His March 7, 1935, address linked Share Our Wealth directly to the Scriptures: "Such is the Share Our Wealth movement. What I have stated to you will be found to be approved by the law of our Divine Maker. You will find it in the Book of Leviticus, from the twenty-fifth to the twenty-seventh chapters. You will find it in the writings of King Solomon. You will find it in the teachings of Christ." And the retribution against the wealthy is sanctified by the Scriptures: " 'Go to now, ye rich men, weep and howl for your miseries that shall come upon you. . . . Your gold and silver is cankered; and the rust of them shall be a witness against you, and shall eat your flesh as it were fire." The linkage between program and Scripture, given the societal move toward spiritualism and away from intellectualism, was important.

Additionally, a common feature of Long's rhetoric was simplification—of the workability of Share Our Wealth, of the causes of the problem of inequitable income distribution, of the nature of the economic system. While Long's analysis may have been simplistic, it was nonetheless appealing. In fact, the presence of complexity in arguments was cited by Long as devious strategy by his detractors to obscure the merits of his program: ''Let no one tell you that it is difficult to redistribute the wealth of this land. . . . The law of God shows how it has been done throughout time. Nothing is more sensible or better understood than the redistribution of property.'' The simplicity of Long's message was carried out in large part by his ability to use analogies and parables skillfully. For example, Long often used light/dark metaphors to drive home the sinister image of the conspiratorial wealthy ''who bask in the splendor of sunlight and wealth, casting darkness and despair and impressing it on everyone else.'' His vivid use of analogy was often a successful vehicle to justify his program: ''The United States is like a fool carrying a loaf of bread under his arm and starving to death at the same time. We propose to Share Our Wealth.'' And Long was a master story-teller, using the parable to simplify, yet enrich, his arguments: ''Well, ladies and gentlemen, America, all the people of America, have been invited to a barbecue. . . . God called: 'Come to my feast.' Then what happened? Rockefeller, Morgan, and their crowd stepped up and took enough for 120,000,000 people and left only enough for 5,000,000 for all the other 120,000,000 to eat. And so many millions must go hungry and without these good things God gave us unless we call on them to put some of it back. I call on you to organize share-our-wealth societies. Write to me in Washington if you will help.''

In short, the context of the depression and its coincident spiritual, heart-over-mind movement among the disenfranchised made the content of Long's speeches take on a nearly messianic quality. At the same time, his rhetoric sparked violent antithetical emotions in the nonbelievers, focused attention exclusively on the redistribution of wealth issue, and symbolically linked Huey Long and the Share Our Wealth society as a single, unified, driving force.

Long's oratorical career suggests that rhetorical features, not personality characteristics, define the demagogue and that a genre of demagogic discourse is revealed in structure and content through a systematic examination of Long's speeches, a genre optimally successful in specific economic and sociological climates. Finally, Long's mastery of the radio demonstrates the significant impact of that medium and became a vehicle for his representation as the champion, if not the messiah, of the common man. Huey Long resisted classifying himself, claiming he was one of a kind. Clearly, as a twentieth-century American orator, that assessment may well be accurate.

INFORMATION SOURCES

Research Collections and Collected Speeches

Tape recordings of several of Long's radio speeches are collected in the Museum of Broadcasting, New York City. Texts of his radio addresses are reprinted in the *Congressional Record*. Important research collections include the Huey Long Scrapbooks, the Huey P. Long Papers, and the T. Harry Williams Papers (Long's major biographer) at the Louisiana State University Library at Baton Rouge and the Perkins Library, Duke University, Durham, North Carolina.

American Rhetoric from Roosevelt to Reagan: A Collection of Speeches and   ARRR
    Critical Essays. Edited by Halford Ross Ryan. Prospect Heights:
    Waveland Press, 1983.
Congressional Record.   *CR*

Selected Critical Studies

Abernathy, Elton. "Huey Long: Oratorical 'Wealth-Sharing.' " *Southern Speech Communication Journal* 21 (1955): 87–102.

Bormann, Ernest G. "A Rhetorical Analysis of the National Radio Broadcasts of Senator Huey P. Long." *Speech Monographs* 24 (1957): 233–57.

Gaske, Paul C. "The Analysis of Demagogic Discourse: Huey Long's 'Every Man a King' Address." In *American Rhetoric from Roosevelt to Reagan*. Edited by Halford Ross Ryan. Prospect Heights, Ill.: Waveland Press, 1983.

Mixon, Harold. "Huey P. Long's 1927–28 Gubernatorial Primary Campaign: A Case Study in the Rhetoric of Agitation." In *The Oratory of Southern Demagogues*. Edited by Cal M. Logue and Howard Dorgan. Baton Rouge: Louisiana State University Press, 1981.

Selected Biographies

Brinkley, Alan. *Voices of Protest*. New York: Alfred A. Knopf, 1982.

Long, Huey P. *Every Man a King*. New Orleans: National Books, 1933.

———. *My First Days in the White House*. Harrisburg, Penn.: Telegraph Press, 1935.

Williams, T. Harry. *Huey Long*. New York: Alfred A Knopf, 1969.

CHRONOLOGY OF MAJOR SPEECHES

See "Research Collections and Collected Speeches" for source codes.

"Every Man a King," national radio broadcast, February 23, 1934; *ARRR*, pp. 39–48; *CR*, March 1, 1934, pp. 3450–53.

"Redistribution of Wealth," national radio broadcast, January 1935; *CR*, January 14, 1935, pp. 410–12.

"Economic Conditions," national radio broadcast, January 19, 1935; *CR*, January 23, 1935, pp. 790–92.

"Our Plundering Government," national radio broadcast, February 10, 1935; *CR*, March 4, 1935, pp. 2832–34.

"Our Blundering Government," national radio broadcast, March 7, 1935; *CR*, March 12, 1935, pp. 3436–39.

"The St. Vitus' Dance Government," national radio broadcast, May 2, 1935; *CR*, May 7, 1935, pp. 7048–50.

DOUGLAS MacARTHUR
(1880–1964), general of the U.S. Army

———————————————————————— BERNARD K. DUFFY

Although several former military commanders have figured in U.S. political history and a few made memorable speeches, none was more flamboyant or controversial than Douglas MacArthur. Unlike George Washington, Andrew Jackson, Ulysses S. Grant, Teddy Roosevelt, and Dwight Eisenhower, Mac-Arthur did not become part of the political establishment. He remained an outsider, remembered as much for his fierce opposition to President Harry Truman as for serving as army chief of staff, liberating the Philippines, leading the occupation of Japan as Supreme Commander of the Allied Powers, engineering the remarkably successful Inchon landing, and aspiring to the presidency in the 1952 primaries. His other accomplishments, though less well known, are also significant. He graduated first in his class from West Point; brilliantly commanded the Rainbow Division in World War I, attaining the rank of brigadier general at the age of thirty-eight, as a War Department public relations officer helped sell the draft to the public; became superintendent of West Point after the war; and headed the U.S. Olympic team in 1928. His superb military leadership and his distinctive rhetoric shaped MacArthur's public persona.

MacArthur gained the public's awareness as an orator in 1945 when he spoke to the nation after the Japanese surrender, in 1951 when he defended his views on the Far East before a joint session of Congress after Truman had recalled him, in 1952 when he delivered the keynote address at the Republican National Convention, and on countless other occasions when he stood behind the rostrum to praise the military, the nation, his soldiers, or the cadet corp, such as his 1935 speech to the Rainbow Division or his speech accepting the Thayer Award at West Point in 1962. MacArthur enjoyed a considerable reputation as an orator throughout his life, although not everyone would agree that he deserved it. MacArthur biographer William Manchester admits that intellectuals had reason to criticize his rhetoric: "Despite occasional gleams of Churchillian eloquence he usually spoke poorly." But the histrionics that offended the intellectuals who heard or read his speeches fascinated and persuaded his audiences and helped make MacArthur an intensely public figure. As Manchester observes: "He had the Cyrano gift for feeling the pulse of the audience." Neither the West Texas Military Academy nor West Point specifically prepared MacArthur for his role as a public speaker. More than his formal education, MacArthur's aristocratic conviction that a military leader should be liberally educated and capable of writing and speaking skillfully distinguished him from officers who were merely specialists in the arts of war. MacArthur followed both Mars and Minerva.

MACARTHUR AS PUBLIC ENCOMIAST AND POLITICAL SPEAKER

MacArthur approached each of his speeches with the characteristic flair for which he became renowned. While MacArthur said of Eisenhower that he was the "best clerk I ever had," Eisenhower, who had been on MacArthur's staff, facetiously claimed to have "studied dramatics under him [MacArthur] for five years in Washington and four years in the Philippines." One role MacArthur seemed especially to relish was that of the encomiast, who spoke in response to an occasion. One of his best-remembered speeches in this genre is "Duty, Honor, Country," delivered at West Point in 1962, a time when, in MacArthur's words, the "shadows" were "lengthening" for him. The speech borrowed heavily from one he had delivered in 1935 to the veterans of the World War I Rainbow Infantry Division he had commanded. Even a cursory comparison of the two speeches reveals that MacArthur used many of the sentences, and in fact, entire paragraphs from the earlier speech in the later one, though the organization is not the same. Both speeches indirectly praised their audiences by celebrating the values that underlie the military. In the Rainbow Division speech, MacArthur spoke of "the military code which . . . has come down to us from even before the age of knighthood and chivalry," while in the West Point speech he rendered the same theme as "duty, honor, country," the motto of the cadet corp. Reminiscent of Greek funeral orations, both of MacArthur's speeches described in identical language the hardships of war and the valor of the soldier: "However horrible the incidents of war may be, the soldier who is called upon to offer and to give his life for his country is the noblest development of mankind."

In both speeches MacArthur addressed contemporary political issues. In the 1935 speech, he counseled against the disarmament policy the United States had adopted as a result of the new isolationism of the 1930s. Yet MacArthur said the sole function of the military was to preserve or regain the peace. In the West Point speech, he ironically articulated a litany of his own political views at the same time he admonished cadets against taking any role in politics: "Let civilian voices argue the merits or demerits of our processes of government: Whether our strength is being sapped by deficit financing indulged in too long, by Federal paternalism grown too mighty . . . by politics grown too corrupt." Of course, MacArthur's celebrated difficulties with the Truman administration had been caused precisely by his inability to keep his political views out of the newspapers and his failure to discriminate between military and political decisions. The problem, quite simply, was MacArthur's persistent belief, as he said again at West Point, that "in war there is no substitute for victory." It was a belief he could not act upon in Korea, a war seriously limited by political considerations.

Among MacArthur's best remembered and least controversial speeches was the one he delivered on September 2, 1945, on the U.S.S. *Missouri* as the nation listened on radio to his comments after the signing of the Japanese surrender instrument. Displaying a balance, simplicity, and forcefulness of biblical diction, the speech began: "My fellow countrymen, today the guns are silent. A great tragedy has ended. A great victory has been won. The skies no longer rain death—the seas bear only commerce—men everywhere walk upright in the sunlight. The entire world is at peace." Although MacArthur used a portion of the speech to condemn the Japanese leaders for oppressing their people and denying them basic freedoms, on balance the tone of the speech was not one of moral condemnation. Rather, as one war correspondent, Shelley Mydans, described it, the speech was olympian. It was the proclamation of a proconsul. MacArthur used the occasion to reflect on the war and to warn of the future: "Various methods through the ages have attempted to devise an international process to prevent or settle disputes between nations. . . . Military alliance, balance of power, League of Nations all in turn failed, leaving the only path to be by way of the crucible of war. . . . We have had our last chance. If we do not now devise some greater and more equitable system Armageddon will be at our door."

The Korean conflict created for MacArthur a unique military challenge and significant rhetorical problems. Militarily MacArthur achieved momentary victory, which was quickly replaced by a stalemate. His Inchon landing not only resulted in a successful UN offensive and the recapture of Seoul but gave further proof of MacArthur's brilliance as a military strategist. But when he led his troops to the Yalu River, which bordered on Manchuria, the Chinese intervened and forced him to order a retreat. MacArthur's political rhetoric while he commanded the UN forces met with less success than his military ventures and led to greater controversy. Not long into the conflict, MacArthur began making statements at odds with the Truman administration's foreign policy. He sent a widely publicized letter to the Veterans of Foreign Wars strongly expressing his view that Formosa was essential to the defense of the Pacific region. It came at a time when President Truman was attempting to defuse as many of the potentially explosive areas in the Far East as possible. Infuriated by the unauthorized statement, which MacArthur had innocently assumed would meet with Washington's approval, Truman considered replacing MacArthur. MacArthur's Yalu offensive created even greater problems because he deliberately violated an order from the Joint Chiefs of Staff that he use only South Korean troops when he approached the Yalu. Washington reasoned that the Chinese would be less likely to intervene if foreign troops were not used near their border. Furthermore, just at the moment the State Department had decided to suggest a truce to the communists, MacArthur issued a statement in which he declared the Chinese incapable of waging a war should it be extended to their territory and expressed his willingness to negotiate with the enemy, essentially about their capitulation. Around the same time MacArthur wrote a letter to Republican Congressman Joe Martin supporting his view that Chiang-Kai-shek's forces on Taiwan should be unleashed to bring a quick end to the Korean conflict. This series of events led ineluctably to Truman's extremely unpopular decision to relieve MacArthur of all his commands in the Far East. It also set the stage for a public altercation between MacArthur and Truman that endured until MacArthur's death in 1964.

MacArthur returned from Korea to a hero's welcome in San Francisco, where he delivered a brief speech, in Washington, D.C., and in New York City. He spent most of the flight from Korea working on the speech to the joint session of Congress, which he would deliver on April 19, 1951, and would be broadcast over radio and television. MacArthur's speech was remarkable less for what he said than for fulfilling the dramatic potential of the situation. In the speech he had delivered after MacArthur's recall, Truman had unwittingly enhanced the drama of MacArthur's return by failing to explain the precise reasons why the general had been dismissed and instead defended Secretary of State Dean Acheson's foreign policy. Concerned about the content of MacArthur's speech, Truman asked to see an advance copy, read it, and declared: "It was nothing but a bunch of damn bullshit."

The substance of the speech was predictable from much of what MacArthur had said previously. He argued for the importance of defending Asia against what he perceived to be a monolithic communist threat. While other generals such as General George Marshall held that U.S. military resources should not be diverted from Europe, MacArthur asserted that the challenge must be met on two fronts. He defended his military leadership in Korea by blaming his inability to win a decisive victory on the intervention of Chinese troops and the reluctance of the Truman administration to allow him the military means to win the war. He proposed a four point program: an economic and naval blockade of China, air reconnaissance over Chinese territory, and the employment of Chiang-Kai-shek's forces against the Chinese. He refuted allegations that he was a warmonger by quoting the admonition against a future war he had expressed on the U.S.S. *Missouri*. Yet he argued against a policy of appeasement for which he implicitly held the Truman administration responsible: " 'Why,' my soldier asked of me, 'surrender military advantages to an enemy in the field?' I could not answer."

MacArthur played effectively on the dramatic situation created by his recall, as some of the responses to his speech reflected. In his introduction, MacArthur told his audience he was "in the fading twilight of life with but one purpose in mind—to serve my country." He concluded even more melodramatically: " 'Old soldiers never die; they just fade away.' And like the old soldier of that ballad, I now close my military career and just fade away—an old soldier who tried to do his duty as God gave him the light to see that duty." The House chamber was packed when MacArthur spoke, and the audience responded with applause at least thirty times. Many people were moved to tears. Those who commented on the speech did not agree on its quality, but its admirers often exceeded MacArthur himself in their hyperbole. Oxford-educated Congressmen Dewey Short declared: "We saw a great hunk of God in the flesh, and we heard the voice of God." *The Quarterly Journal of Speech* published a symposium of criticism in which congressman Joe Martin opined that the speech surpassed

Roosevelt's first Inaugural and Winston Churchill's speech before the joint session of Congress. According to Karl Mundt, the speech was "destined to become one of the classics of the English language." Some speech professors felt the same enthusiasm. In a separate article Paul Beall expressed his belief that it might even become a "world classic in oratory." Journalists such as Richard Rovere, who recorded their views in the symposium, were less sure: "MacArthur has eloquence of a kind, but it strikes me as a rather coarse eloquence." Quincy Howe wryly observed: "By a coincidence, rare in the history of drama, the man who acted the part of the old soldier happened himself to be an old soldier whose experiences precisely resembled the experiences of the old soldier whose part he was enacting." MacArthur had spent a lifetime learning how to use his ethos rhetorically, and the joint session of Congress was surely his greatest platform.

Later that day Washington turned out for a parade to celebrate MacArthur's homecoming, and the general gave a brief speech at the Daughters of the American Revolution Congress held at Constitution Hall, which the women called the most important event in its history. Following a seven-hour parade in New York City, MacArthur settled into his apartment in the Waldorf Astoria, which would become home base for an extensive speaking tour. On May 3 the Hearings on the Military Situation on the Far East were convened in the Senate. Despite the protestations of Republicans wishing to capitalize on MacArthur's fame and political views, the hearings were not open to the press; expurgated transcripts were made available.

MacArthur also stayed in the public spotlight by giving several speeches across the country throughout 1951 and 1952. The majority of these speeches restated or elaborated on the positions MacArthur had expressed in his speech to Congress, but they tended to be more specific in indicting the administration's policies and in seeking vindication. In a speech he delivered on June 13, 1951, in Austin, Texas MacArthur warned of appeasing the Soviet Union, a policy he believed would invite war, and of continuing the Korean conflict "indecisively and indefinitely." A year and a half later, during December 1952, MacArthur would propose to President Eisenhower that if the conflict could not be ended by negotiating with the Soviets, nuclear weapons should be deployed in North Korea and radioactive material should be strewn to close supply and communication lines. In a speech before the Massachusetts legislature on July 25, 1951, MacArthur questioned the principle of an unswerving allegiance to the commander-in-chief: "I find in existence a new and heretofore unknown and dangerous concept that the members of our armed forces owe primary allegiance and loyalty to those who temporarily excercise the authority of the executive branch of government." He also referred to the "abitrary nature of the decision to replace him."

MacArthur adopted most of the themes of Truman's Republican critics. Some of the political themes expressed in MacArthur's speeches had little to do with his experiences as a military leader, though he would say in his speech to the Michigan legislature on May 15, 1952: "There is no politics in me, nor none intended in what I say.'' In addressing such diverse issues as the burden of taxation, corruption in government, and the growth of the federal bureaucracy, MacArthur began sounding like a presidential candidate. Like other Republicans, he feared internal conspiracy, declaring in his Boston speech, ''It is not of any external threat that I concern myself but rather of insidious forces working from within. . . . This evil force, with neither spiritual base nor moral standard, rallies the abnormal and subnormal elements among our citizenry and applies internal pressure.'' In a September 6 speech in Cleveland he criticized the increased power of the State Department and suggested that the centralization of government was part of the ''drift toward totalitarian rule.'' A committed anticommunist, MacArthur asked, ''Are we going to preserve the religious base of our origin, our growth and our progress or yield to the devious assults [*sic*] of atheistic or other anti-religious forces? Are we going to maintain our present course toward state socialism?'' In the same speech MacArthur showed that he had not forgotten the humiliation of his recall. He criticized the administration for reacting violently to ''the citizens voice when raised in criticism of those who excercise political power.'' He lambasted Truman implicitly for ''abusive language and arbitrary action [which] challenges the concept of free speeches [*sic*] and is an attempt at direct suppression through intimidation of . . . public criticism.'' In a speech on October 17, 1951, delivered to the National Convention of the American Legion in Miami, MacArthur embellished this point: ''Americans will not be fooled by the bombast of propaganda and vulgar language which inevitably meets every honest criticism directed at the Government.'' MacArthur's bitterness toward Truman did not go unobserved in the press and undoubtedly affected the general's public image.

MacArthur's speeches led to speculation that he was a presidential candidate. In fact, MacArthur revealed his willingness to run for the presidency, but in the end he supported Robert Taft. One story has it that Taft offered to give his votes to MacArthur if a second ballot was required to select a presidential candidate at the Republican convention. Taft had prevailed upon MacArthur to present the keynote address, and MacArthur agreed. It was one occasion where his oratory failed miserably to hold the attention of the audience. Critics have attributed the failure both to the banality of the content and to MacArthur's delivery, which lacked the control of his earlier speeches. He periodically rose up on his toes and pointed toward the ceiling, and his voice became high pitched and cracked when he spoke of God. Even if his delivery had been unflawed, MacArthur's speech left much to be desired. He spoke in such generalities and with so few specifics that his long speech bored the delegates, who began to talk among themselves when he was no more than half finished.

The Republicans had used MacArthur as a cause célèbre to help bring down Truman, and MacArthur had been only too eager to vent his wrath against the man who had sullied him. Although he had said in his speech to Congress that he spoke ''with neither rancor nor bitterness . . . but . . . to serve my country,'' his speaking tour and repeated attacks on Truman led many to believe that his motivations were impure. His speech to the Republican convention proved finally that politics was not a profession to which he was well suited. Although MacArthur was no doubt delighted to see Truman turned out of office, his reputation might have been better preserved if he had adopted the course he described in his speech to Congress and faded away. A few months after the convention, MacArthur assumed a new role as chairman of Remington Rand, but he continued to make his political views known to the public throughout his life. MacArthur never forgot or forgave Truman.

MacArthur was larger than life, and his speeches immodestly reflected his awareness of this fact. Few other speakers could have carried off the outsized corncob pipe, the squashed hat with resplendent gold embroidery, and, in his earlier days, the riding crop and raccoon coat. MacArthur's rhetoric was as self-conscious as his appearance. According to William Manchester: "Most intellectuals, wincing at his William Jennings Bryan speeches, thought him a ham." Similarly, Theodore White observed: "He was outrageous in his rhetoric; and any sophisticated scholar can make him look like a fool in his moments of transport, when, indeed, he was a fool." His rhetorical style tended toward the grandiloquent and often came too close to poetry. For example, in his speech to the Rainbow Division, he said of the doughboys: "They have gone beyond the mists that blind us here. . . . In chambered temples of silence the dust of their dauntless valor sleeps, waiting." His speeches contain remarkable examples of hyperbole. Of losing Asia to communism, he said in his Republican convention keynote address: "Such a tragedy would return civilization to the darkness of the Middle Ages and the ideal of human liberty might perish from the earth." There was no situation too dramatic for MacArthur's oratory. Immersed in the drama of the moment, MacArthur could stir great emotion; reading the same speech long after the event, one might wonder what he had said that made his audiences cheer, applaud, and weep as they did when he addressed Congress. Although MacArthur's rhetoric often dripped with metaphor and melodrama, it was also quite effective. As D. Clayton James suggests, "His 'purple prose,' at its best possessed an old fashioned eloquence and vividness that surely distinguished it from the pedestrian writings of most generals."

MacArthur enjoyed writing his speeches, and most of the evidence suggests that he relied very little on the help of others. After 1944, General Courtney Whitney wrote drafts of speeches for MacArthur, but those that survive in the MacArthur archives were not delivered in the form that Whitney wrote them. Apparently MacArthur merely used them as inventional aids, although in the case of a draft Whitney wrote for the speeches delivered on the U.S.S. *Missouri*, there are some thoughts and a few words that correspond with what MacArthur finally said. If MacArthur did deliver the speeches Whitney wrote, it might be difficult to tell because both men thought and wrote similarly, though Whitney's rhetoric is more restrained.

MacArthur possessed qualities that other public speakers covet. First, he was a quick study. Eisenhower reported, "Reading through a draft of a speech or paper once, he could immediately repeat whole chunks of it verbatim.'' In addition to his commanding presence and noble bearing, MacArthur was blessed with a resonant voice. Speaking with an upper-class eastern accent, he could use his voice skillfully to achieve emphasis and convey emotion. In his speech before Congress, for example, he paused dramatically prior to uttering the final two words in ''they just fade away,'' and virtually whispered ''Goodbye.''

Not in this century or perhaps in any other has the United States produced a general who was more charismatic or rhetorically gifted. It is, on the other hand, difficult to see his contribution to the anticommunist hysteria of the 1950s and his long-lived vindictiveness toward Truman, not to mention his willingness to use nuclear weapons to end the Korean conflict, in any but a negative light. Whatever ethical assessment one might make, MacArthur's distinctive rhetoric deserves careful study if only because of the pivotal roles he played in U.S. history.

INFORMATION SOURCES

Research Collections and Collected Speeches

The MacArthur Archives, Norfolk, Virginia, contains an extensive collection of MacArthur's speeches, copies of which may be obtained by mail. The first speech in the collection is from 1932, and according to an explanation in the inventory, fewer of the speeches before 1942 are represented because so much material was destroyed when Manila fell. There are only final drafts of most speeches, but the collection contains some preliminary drafts, including a few General Whitney wrote. Although *Representative Speeches of General Douglas MacArthur*, available from the archives, contains the general's major addresses, many are printed in *Vital Speeches*, and his speech before Congress is in the *Congressional Record*.

Congressional Record.	CR
MacArthur, Douglas. *A Soldier Speaks: Public Papers and Speeches of General Douglas MacArthur*. Edited by Vorin E. Whan Jr. New York: Praeger, 1965.	SS
Vital Speeches.	VS
U.S. Congress. Senate. *Representative Speeches of General Douglas MacArthur*. 88th Cong., 2d sess. Doc. 95. Washington, D.C.: Government Printing Office, 1964.	RSDM

Selected Critical Studies

Beall, Paul R. "Viper-Crusher Turns Dragon Slayer." *Quarterly Journal of Speech* 38 (1952): 51–56.

Dyer, Armel. "The Oratory of Douglas MacArthur." Ph.D. dissertation, University of Oregon, 1968.

Haberman, Frederick, ed. "General MacArthur's Speech: A Symposium of Critical Comment." *Quarterly Journal of Speech* 37 (1951): 321–31.

Phillips, William S. *"Douglas MacArthur: A Modern Knight-Errant*. Philadelphia: Dorrance, 1978.

Robb, Stephen. "Fifty Years of Farewell: Douglas MacArthur's Commemorative and Deliberative Speaking." Ph.D. dissertation, Indiana University, 1967.
Wylie, Philip. "Medievalism and the MacArthurian Legend." *Quarterly Journal of Speech* 37 (1951): 473–78.

Selected Biographies

James, D. Clayton. *The Years of MacArthur*. 3 vols. Boston: Houghton Mifflin, 1970–1985.
MacArthur, Douglas. *Reminiscences*. New York: McGraw-Hill, 1964.
Manchester, William. *American Caesar*. Boston: Little, Brown, 1978.
Rovere, Richard H., and Schlesinger, Arthur M. Jr. *The MacArthur Controversy*. New York: Noonday, 1951.
Spanier, John W. *The Truman-MacArthur Controversy*. New York: Norton, 1959.
Whitney, Courtney. *MacArthur: His Rendezvous with History*. New York: Knopf, 1956.

CHRONOLOGY OF MAJOR SPEECHES

See "Research Collections and Collected Speeches" for source codes.

Speech to the Veterans of the Rainbow (42d) Infantry Division of World War I, Washington, D.C., July 14, 1935; *RSDM*, pp. 1–6; *SS*, pp. 67–75.

Address upon signing the surrender instrument by Japan aboard the U.S.S. *Missouri*, Tokyo Bay, Japan, September 2, 1945; *RSDM*, pp. 8–10; *SS*, pp. 150–52; *VS*, 11 (1945), 707–08.

"Don't Scuttle the Pacific," speech before Joint Session of Congress, Washington, D.C., April 19, 1951; *RSDM*, pp. 14–20; *SS*, pp. 243–54; *CR*, April 19, 1951, pp. 4123–25; *VS*, 17 (1951), 430–31.

Speech to the Texas legislature, Austin, Texas, June 13, 1951; *RSDM*, pp. 20–26; *SS*, pp. 262–72; *VS*, 17 (1951), 546–49; *U.S. News & World Report*, June 22, 1951, pp. 76–78.

Speech to the Massachusetts legislature, Boston, July 25, 1951; *RSDM*, pp. 27–33; *VS* 17 (1951), 652–55.

Speech to the citizens of Cleveland, Cleveland, Ohio, September 6, 1951; *RSDM*, pp. 33–39; *SS*, pp. 2763–82; *VS*, 17 (1951), 713–16.

Speech before the American Legion Convention, Miami, Florida, October 17, 1951, *RSDM*, pp. 39–46; *VS*, 18 (1951), 36–40.

Speech to the Mississippi legislature, Jackson, Mississippi, March 22, 1952; *RSDM*, pp. 51–58; *VS*, 18 (1952), 389–92.

Speech to the Michigan legislature, Lansing, Michigan, May 15, 1952; *RSDM*, pp. 58–65; *VS*, 18 (1952), 529–32.

Keynote address at the Republican National Convention, Chicago, July 7, 1952; *RSDM*, pp. 65–74; *VS*, 18 (1952), 578–82.

"Duty, Honor, Country," speech at the United States Military Academy, West Point, New York, May 12, 1962; *RSDM*, pp. 100–3; *VS*, 58 (1962), 519–21.

JOSEPH RAYMOND McCARTHY
(1908–1957), U.S. senator from Wisconsin

ROBERT P. NEWMAN

Joseph McCarthy was born on a farm near Appleton, Wisconsin. He was unusually ambitious as a boy, raising chickens successfully, running a grocery store, and taking a full four-year high school course in one year. Bored with small-town life, he enrolled at Marquette University, entering as a freshman of twenty-one in 1930. At Marquette he was an active boxer, played much poker, held part-time jobs to see himself through, and thus got only average grades. He developed his persuasive abilities as a salesman; friends said he could sell anything. He continued at Marquette, in law school, earning his degree in 1935.

He began practice in Waupaca, Wisconsin, hustling every kind of job a fledgling lawyer in the depression might handle for a few dollars. McCarthy was then a New Dealer; when he moved to Shawano in 1936, he began serious political activity as chairman of the Young Democrats and as a fund raiser for the second Roosevelt campaign. Less than a year after settling in Shawano, he ran for district attorney as a Democrat; the Republican won easily, but Joe had established name recognition. Three years later, in a campaign marred by McCarthy's below-the-belt attacks on the incumbent circuit judge in the Sawano-Appleton area, Joe won his first office. It was as circuit judge that he first showed clearly the extent to which he would bend the rules to achieve his objectives. Quickie divorces, sanitized trial records, and extensive illegal gambling were all part of the repertoire.

After Pearl Harbor, he recognized that a war record would be politically necessary and enlisted in the marines. He did not resign his judgeship but waived his judicial salary. After three years as an intelligence officer in the South Pacific, he had sent home enough press releases to establish himself as a war hero. The phoniness of his claims was not well known at the time; he took his record with him on a month's leave of absence from the marines to run against Senator Alexander Wiley in the 1944 Republican primary. Wiley won, but McCarthy had laid the foundation for his successful race two years later, when he beat Robert La Follette in the Republican primary and defeated Democrat Howard McMurray in the fall. McCarthy entered the U.S. Senate in 1946.

McCARTHY AS ARCHDEMAGOGUE OF THE 1950s

Joe McCarthy was probably the most successful peddler of devil insurance in U.S. history. At a time of great public anxiety, he produced simple and attractive answers to people's fears. The spread of communism in Europe and Asia, early

Soviet acquisition of nuclear weapons, the breakdown of the pax Americana so soon after the resplendent U.S. victory in World War II, the arrest and conviction of high-level spies, the defeat of the U.S. Eighth Army in Korea—all of these disasters he attributed to one simple cause: treason of the Democrats who had been in power so long. Eliminate these traitors, give his anticommunist crusade the green light, and all would be well. The country was ready for this gospel, and McCarthy had the skills to sell it.

McCarthy was familiar with the force of anticommunist ideology long before his celebrated Wheeling speech. He had damned his detractors in several Wisconsin elections by smearing them as reds. What made his February 9, 1950 speech to the Republican Women's Club of Wheeling, West Virginia, so incendiary was the specificity of his claims of subversion and the eminence of his targets. Dozens of Republican orators had red-baited the Democrats before Wheeling; McCarthy did not just hint darkly about treason, he boldly (and falsely) charged that the Department of State had 205 traitors working for it at the moment and that Secretary of State Dean Acheson tolerated this.

It took several days for the Wheeling speech to achieve national circulation; when it did, McCarthy gained universal recognition as the foremost anticommunist rhetor. His speech at Wheeling was a mishmash of unverified and inaccurate charges; no transcript or recording has survived. He repeated somewhat the same charges but with different numbers in other parts of the country. Reporters who questioned him got the brush-off; his supporting documents, he said, were on the plane or in his other briefcase. The media at the time were not conditioned to view statements by government officials skeptically as they are now, and since what a U.S. senator said was news, they faithfully reproduced it. Many scholars believe that had the media been as skeptical and probing as they were during Watergate, McCarthy's crusade could not have achieved the momentum it did.

Shortly after the Wheeling speech, on February 20, 1950, McCarthy addressed the full Senate. Democratic Majority Leader Scott M. Lucas had let it be known that no votes would be taken the night of McCarthy's speech, so only a handful of senators were present. The press gallery, however, was in business. McCarthy began by describing the first of what he claimed would be eighty-one cases of subversives in the State Department. He had an old list compiled by a House of Representatives investigator, and he altered, exaggerated, and extrapolated these cases to the point where it sounded as if the State Department were indeed a nest of subversives. The few Democrats in the chamber heckled him, which played to his strength. He was a skillful alley fighter. He began his speech at 5:30; at 7:30, after he had covered fourteen cases, majority leader Lucas moved to adjourn. Republicans voted this down, which led to an agreement to compel the attendance of absent senators. In forty minutes, a quorum was present, and McCarthy went on until 11:42 P.M. Senator Robert Taft called it a ''perfectly reckless performance.'' The most prominent news coverage next day was of case number 99, who was not in the Department of State at all but was a strongly anticommunist speech writer on President Truman's staff. The February 20 speech generated so much heat that the Senate Democratic leadership agreed to appoint a subcommittee of the Foreign Relations Committee to investigate McCarthy's charges. Conservative Millard Tydings of Maryland was named chairman; his group held hearings from March 8 to June 28, 1950. McCarthy thrived on the publicity. He early displayed the brawling, insulting tactics that four years later, during the Army-McCarthy Hearings, led many Americans to condemn him; but the Tydings hearings were not televised, and reporters did not convey to their readers the virulence of McCarthy's demagoguery.

His first major target while testifying to the Tydings committee was Judge Dorothy Kenyon of New York. With his usual indifference to the facts, McCarthy claimed that she held "a high State Department position" and belonged to at least twenty-eight communist front organizations, nine of them listed as subversive by the attorney general. Reporters soon learned that she was never a State Department employee and noted that McCarthy mentioned only twenty-four organizations. They later discovered that only four were ever on the attorney general's list, and only one was cited at the time she belonged to it. This one tainted organization, the National Council of Soviet-American Friendship, also enrolled Albert Einstein, Harold Urey, and four U.S. senators. Judge Kenyon appeared before Tydings to answer the charges and was a most effective witness. The Kenyon case collapsed speedily.

But it was part of McCarthy's rhetorical technique to ignore embarrassing failures and to rush on to new accusations before truth could catch up with his old ones. He attacked Ambassador-at-Large Philip Jessup, a pillar of the eastern foreign affairs establishment and a former isolationist. His scenario here was similar to that with Kenyon; McCarthy went far beyond the documented facts about Jessup's memberships and opinions, and the ambassador turned the tables on him.

The Lattimore case was his salvation. Professor Owen Lattimore was never a State Department employee, but he was a prominent Asian scholar who believed that the United States should make peace with the People's Republic of China. McCarthy had never met Lattimore, never even heard of him until he was soliciting suggestions for potential targets from members of the China lobby. With his usual disdain for truth, McCarthy told the Tydings committee in executive session (it soon leaked) that Lattimore was the top Soviet spy in the United States, the boss of the whole ring of which Alger Hiss was a part. So confident was McCarthy of the vulnerability of this new target that he scheduled another major speech to the Senate on March 30, the sole topic to be Lattimore. By the time of the speech, however, some of his saner advisers, possibly including J. Edgar Hoover, had persuaded him that there was no evidence whatever that Lattimore had been a spy, so he dropped this claim and halfway apologized for it. But the rest of the speech was vintage McCarthy. It started at 2:05 and rambled on until 6:18, by which time even the press gallery was beginning to empty. McCarthy had by now fully developed his virile self-image; the pro-communist (and pro-Lattimore) crowd would ruin anyone who attempted to expose them; he had been warned that he would be subject to smears and vilification if he attacked Lattimore; but he was doing battle for 140 million God-fearing Americans against the forces of evil. He was a fighter, and he would not quit.

This speech too, crammed with dubious superlatives ("fantastic") and exaggerations (he attacked Lattimore "only after the most deep and painstakingly thorough study"), did not stand up against Lattimore's rebuttal testimony a week later. Many observers thought McCarthy was now completely washed up. He had, however, promised to produce a witness with first-hand testimony that Lattimore was a communist, and shortly after he did. This witness was Louis Francis Budenz, raised a Catholic, for ten years a communist spy and editor, and by 1945 a Catholic again. Budenz lied artfully about Lattimore; but he had Monsignor Fulton Sheen, Cardinal Spellman, and (until the FBI completed its investigation of Lattimore) J. Edgar Hoover behind him. Budenz brought Lattimore's anticommunism into doubt, thus rescuing McCarthy, who went on to hundreds of other targets, polarizing the country, activating nativists and anti–New Dealers, claiming the defeat of Scott Lucas and Millard Tydings in the 1950 elections, and eventually taking on the U.S. Army and President Dwight Eisenhower. The politics nurtured by McCarthy were not normal pragmatic American exchanges; the only label that fits is *witch-hunt*.

When McCarthy's assistant, Roy M. Cohn, bullied the army into giving preferential treatment to Cohn's side kick, G. David Schine, the establishment finally got its back up. Millions of Americans saw the Army-McCarthy Hearings in 1954 and realized how nasty and demagogic McCarthy was. On December 2, 1954, acting on the report of a censure committee headed by Senator Arthur V. Watkins of Utah, the Senate condemned McCarthy's tactics. He then ceased to be news, his crusade collapsed, and he drank himself into cirrhosis and death.

In mid-career, more than half the American people told pollsters that they supported McCarthy. The Catholic press (except for *Commonweal* and *America*, which later was silenced by the Vatican) and the Hearst, McCormick, and Scripps-Howard papers backed McCarthy strongly. Attacks on him by liberal journalists got nowhere. Barnet Baskerville's brilliant and highly accurate "Joe McCarthy, Briefcase Demagogue" (*Today's Speech*, September 1954) was little noticed. Television and the Senate establishment brought McCarthy down but only after terrible damage to the lives of thousands of people. As with Watergate, there is still argument as to whether in this case the system worked, or whether, as Senator Stuart Symington said, the people just got tired of McCarthy.

Like much else about him, McCarthy's location on the ideological spectrum is still controversial. Since he was supported throughout his career by the conservative Asia-first block of senators, by the conservative press, by Texas oilmen and many big corporations, by the American Legion, and by Roosevelt haters in and out of politics, he is often classed as conservative himself. This is an error. The most trenchant analysis of McCarthy's politics was made by conservative scholar Peter Viereck:

Basically McCarthy is a type of left wing Populist or Jacobin agitator who, by an infallible instinct, has been subverting those institutions which are the most organic and conservative. As the revolutionary of "plebs" (and "plebs" include certain primitive millionaires of the West), he satisfies the resentments of his followers because his sincerest hatred is always against the oldest, the most deeply rooted, and the most patrician aspects of our society. His attacks have ranged against the Constitution, our most decorated military leaders (Marshall, Eisenhower, Taylor, Zwicker, and even MacArthur), the most ancient of our universities, the leaders of our most strongly established religion, and finally members of our best educated families (Lodge, Conant, Acheson, Stevenson).

How, then, did they creep under the mantle of conservatism? Primarily by providing simplistic answers to America's problems, answers that could be distorted to fit into the anti-Roosevelt coalition. By 1950, the (mostly Republican) Roosevelt haters were spastic in their frustration, shut out of executive power for eighteen years by Roosevelt's four presidential elections, and robbed of their certainty of recapturing power in 1948 by a Missouri haberdasher. After 1948, this Republican party, having lost with a moderate, bipartisan foreign policy and a me-too domestic issues stance, was desperate to find an issue with which to return to power. McCarthy's issue, treason, was that royal road to power. The Republican elites used him and then discarded him when he became embarrassing. But not even Eisenhower discarded his issue totally; Ike, too, as his loyalty-security program showed, was anxious to defenestrate Democrats by labeling them soft on communism.

McCarthy found not a single communist, but he left a legacy of hostility and suspicion that affected U.S. policy for decades. It was fear of a revival of McCarthyism that underwrote the Kennedy-Johnson foray into Vietnam. The imperative of their survival, as phrased by Daniel Ellsberg, was "This is not a good year for this Administration to lose Vietnam to Communism." Nixon, as one of the foremost rhetors of the "Democrats are soft on communism" school, could not be outflanked on the Right, and he seized the opportunity to promote détente with the Soviet Union and to slap backs and bubble pleasantries in Peking. For this, Nixon lost the support of the visceral anticommunists. Only with Reagan did the McCarthyites find their true ideological leader, immovable in his contempt for the Soviet Union, and with a positive program, such as McCarthy never had, finally and for all time to roll back the Rooseveltian revolution.

INFORMATION SOURCES

Research Collections and Collected Speeches

There is no single archive of outstanding value on McCarthy. His papers are at Marquette University, Milwaukee, Wisconsin, but will remain closed indefinitely. The consensus among scholars is that these papers are mostly news clippings and trivia. Probably the best collections of material about McCarthy are at the Wisconsin State Historical Society, Madison, which has the papers of Senator William Benton (who sued McCarthy), of Senators Alexander Wiley and Ralph Flanders, of Thomas C. Reeves, biographer of McCarthy, and other sources.

The only collection of his speeches is an early, and largely unobtainable, government publication.

Congressional Record.   *CR*

Lomas, Charles W. *The Agitator in American Society.* Englewood Cliffs: *AAS*
    Prentice-Hall, 1968.

*Major Speeches and Debates of Senator Joe McCarthy, Delivered in the
    United States Senate, 1950–51,* Washington, D.C., Government
    Printing Office, 1952.

Selected Critical Studies

Adams, John G. *Without Precedent: The Story of the Death of McCarthyism.* New York:
    W. W. Norton & Co., 1983.

Baskerville, Barnet. "Joe McCarthy, Brief-Case Demagogue." *Today's Speech* 2 (1954):
    8–15.

Bayley, Edwin R. *Joe McCarthy and the Press.* Madison: University of Wisconsin Press,
    1981.

Buckley, William F., Jr., and Bozell, L. Brent. *McCarthy and His Enemies.* Chicago:
    Henry Regnery, 1954.

Crosby, Donald F., S.J. *God, Church, and Flag: Senator Joseph R. McCarthy and the
    Catholic Church, 1950–57.* Chapel Hill: University of North Carolina Press, 1978.

Fried, Richard M. *Men against McCarthy.* New York: Columbia University Press, 1976.

Griffith, Robert. *The Politics of Fear: Joseph R. McCarthy and the Senate.* Lexington:
    University Press of Kentucky, 1970.

Newman, Robert P. "Arch Demagogue of the Fifties." *Reviews in American History* 11
    (1983): 282–88.

Rogin, Michael Paul. *The Intellectuals and McCarthy: The Radical Specter.* Cambridge:
    MIT Press, 1967.

Viereck, Peter. "The Conservative Case against McCarthyism." *Pacific Spectator* 9
    (1955): 256–62.

Selected Biographies

Anderson, Jack, and May, Ronald W. *McCarthy: The Man, the Senator, the "Ism."*
    Boston: Beacon Press, 1952.

Cohn, Roy. *McCarthy.* New York: Lancer Books, 1968.

Cook, Fred J. *The Nightmare Decade: The Life and Times of Senator Joe McCarthy.*
    New York: Random House, 1971.

Oshinsky, David M. *A Conspiracy So Immense: The World of Joe McCarthy.* New York:
    Free Press, 1983.

Reeves, Thomas C. *The Life and Times of Joe McCarthy.* New York: Stein and Day,
    1982.

Rovere, Richard H. *Senator Joe McCarthy.* New York: Harcourt Brace, 1959.

CHRONOLOGY OF MAJOR SPEECHES

See "Research Collections and Collected Speeches" for source codes.

Wheeling speech, Wheeling, West Virginia, February 9, 1949, no text available.

Lattimore speech, Washington, D.C.,March 30, 1950; *CR*, March 30, 1950, pp. 4375–93.

Speech to the Senate, Washington, D.C., February 20, 1950; *CR*, pp. 1952–81.

"The Story of George Catlett Marshall," U.S. Senate, Washington, D.C., June 14, 1951; *CR*, June 14, 1951, pp. 6556–6603.

Republican National Convention speech, Chicago, July 9, 1952; *New York Times*, July 10, 1952, p. 21 (not a complete text).

"The Red-Tinted Washington Crowd," Appleton, Wisconsin, November 3, 1952; *AAS*, pp. 155–62.

MALCOLM X
(1925–1965), spokesman for black liberation and human rights

THOMAS W. BENSON

Malcolm X was killed because he spoke his truth. It must be seen as a central fact of the history of American oratory that the two most eloquent black speakers of the twentieth century—Malcolm X and Martin Luther King, Jr.—were assassinated. Their messages and their methods differed, however. King was a messenger for redemption and reconciliation through nonviolence, whereas for most of his short career Malcolm X was perceived as an agitator for rebellion through potentially violent self-defense. King held a doctorate from Boston University; Malcolm had educated himself in prison. King was the leader of a national movement of direct action that changed the laws, customs, and attitudes of a nation; Malcolm was an influence upon but not a direct participant in the civil rights movement itself. King was awarded the Nobel Peace Prize; Malcolm was often seen as a thrilling but curious anomaly, threatening a fantasy of armaggedon. And yet Malcolm X has come to be regarded as a unique and essential contributor to the rhetoric that defines America's racial agony. He was an original American spokesman, and it is partly a measure of his achievement that every serious discussion of American racism must come to terms with Malcolm's uncompromising challenge.

MALCOLM X AS PILGRIM AND PREACHER

Malcolm's life is the story of a series of conversions, to which he gave witness in his rhetoric as a process of change impelled by a consistent motive: to break the bonds of racism.

Malcolm X was born Malcolm Little on May 19, 1925, in Omaha, Nebraska. Before his twenty-first birthday, he was in prison, serving an eight- to ten-year sentence for burglary that came at the end of a cycle of dope selling, robbery, and hustling as Detroit Red in Harlem and Boston. In prison, he began his self-education by voracious reading of the classics and a painstaking copying of the dictionary. Malcolm experienced a mystical conversion while reading a letter from his brother Reginald that described Elijah Muhammad's Lost-Found Nation of Islam. After his release from prison in 1952, he devoted his life to the Lost-Found Nation, rapidly becoming a minister, organizing mosques in Boston and Philadelphia, and then assuming leadership of Mosque No. 7 in Harlem. Malcolm was the Lost-Found Nation's most effective spokesman and was generally regarded as Elijah Muhammad's heir apparent.

From the Harlem mosque, Malcolm, who had dropped his former "slave name'' of *Little* in accordance with the Lost-Found Nation's practice and assumed the name *Malcolm X*, undertook leadership of a congregation of highly disciplined and family-centered converts who lived by a rigorous code of upright conduct. He also became a streetcorner preacher who walked unafraid throughout the ghetto, speaking a compelling message of dignity and a cynical rejection of white hypocrisy. He became widely noticed by the white press and mass media and was a frequent speaker on radio and television and at white colleges and universities, where he effectively raised the specter of black revolution—sometimes in debates with more moderate black leaders, whom he delighted in confounding with his brilliance as a debater.

In 1964, Malcolm broke with Elijah Muhammad and undertook a pilgrimage to Mecca, from which he returned as a Sunni Muslim and with the revelatory news that whites must no longer be regarded as the devil. He founded a religious and a political organization, the Muslim Mosque, Inc., and the Organization of Afro-American Unity, and adopted a Muslim name, El-hajj Malik El-shabazz. While preaching to his followers, he was assassinated on February 21, 1965. Later in 1965, Grove Press published *The Autobiography of Malcolm X*, which brought the story, and the rhetoric, of Malcolm before a worldwide audience.

Malcolm's career as an orator was brief. He assumed leadership of Harlem Mosque No. 7 in 1954, broke with Elijah Muhammad in March 1964, and was killed less than a year later. An assessment of Malcolm's rhetoric is further complicated by the unfamiliarity of his message to many Americans, by the range of topics that he spoke about, and by the changes in his views that occurred after he left the Black Muslims. Although most of his speaking took place while he was a minister for Elijah Muhammad, a large percentage of the texts available for study are from his last year.

Malcolm's speeches during his years with the Black Muslims are marked by two chief features. As a minister, Malcolm preached the millennarian theology of Elijah Muhammad, a tale that identified the white race as the devil and predicted the imminent destruction of the white world. The Black Muslims claimed that they were devout Muslims, but in addition they had a unique doctrine that Elijah Muhammad traced to his teacher, Wallace D. Fard: that a great manmade mother ship shaped like a wheel and accompanied by fifteen hundred smaller ships would destroy the earth with bombs and that only blacks who had separated from the white race and joined the Muslims would survive.

Malcolm also preached the lesson of black nationalism, and he did so in a direct and factual way that was in startling contrast to the supernatural doctrines of the Lost-Found Nation. On this theme, Malcolm spoke compellingly, underscoring in direct language the fact of American racism; excoriating the hypocrisy of America's unfulfilled promise of freedom, justice, and equality; and threatening that blacks who were denied their rights were increasingly ready to fight in their own self-defense. This message was persuasive to many Americans of different views. To black Americans impatient with the deferral of justice, Malcolm's cynicism about whites and the simple clarity of black nationalism was not simply appealing but sensible. To a generation of idealistic white college students, Malcolm's accusations of white hypocrisy seemed painful but just. To those white Americans still unwilling to acknowledge the rights of black Americans, Malcolm's threat of violence fit their own worst fears. In a debate at Cornell University in 1962, Malcolm argued that if the United States would not permit its blacks to return to Africa, it should give blacks a separate section of the United States for their own black state. His defense of the proposition illustrates his matter-of-factness about the history of racism:

Some of you may say, Well, why should you give us part of this country? The Honorable Elijah Muhammad says that for four hundred years we contributed our slave labor to make the country what it is. If you were to take the individual salary or allowances of each person in this audience it would amount to nothing individually, but when you take it collectively all in one pot you have a heavy load. Just the weekly wage. And if you realize that from anybody who could collect all of the wages from the persons in this audience right here for one month, why they would be so wealthy they couldn't walk. And if you see that, then you can imagine the result of millions of black people working for nothing for 310 years. And that is the contribution that we made to America. Not Jackie Robinson, not Marian Anderson, not George Washington Carver, that's not our contribution; our contribution to American society is 310 years of free slave labor for which we have not been paid one dime. We who are Muslims, followers of the honorable Elija Muhammad, don't think that an integrated cup of coffee is sufficient payment for 310 years of slave labor.

After his break from Elijah Muhammad, Malcolm's views changed, but he did not become an integrationist. As a speaker, he faced the difficulties of reconsidering his own religious and political commitments and finding a way to present them so as not to appear completely inconsistent with his former views. Perhaps Malcolm's greatest rhetorical work was not a speech at all but the eloquent *Autobiography*, whose prose rings with the cadences of Malcolm's voice and which makes principled change a central theme of Malcolm's life.

The most widely known speech of Malcolm's last year is "The Ballot or the Bullet," delivered with slight variations as his standard speech. In this speech, Malcolm redefined black nationalism. No longer calling for a return to Africa or for a separate state in the New World, Malcolm said that "the political philosophy of black nationalism means that the black man should control the politics and the politicians in his own community; no more." In interviews given during his last days, Malcolm acknowledged that he had formerly been dogmatic in his usage of *black nationalism*, since the phrase focused on skin color rather than actions.

In "The Ballot or the Bullet," Malcolm rejected the phrase *civil rights* in favor of *human rights*, since civil rights confined blacks

to the jurisdiction of Uncle Sam. No one from the outside world can speak out in your behalf as long as your struggle is a civil-rights struggle. Civil rights comes within the domestic affairs of this country. All of our African brothers and our Asian brothers and our Latin-American brothers cannot open their mouths and interfere in the domestic affairs of the United States. And as long as it's civil rights, this comes under the jurisdiction of Uncle Sam. But the United Nations has what's known as the charter of human rights, it has a committee that deals in human rights. . . . When you expand the civil-rights struggle to the level of human rights, you can then take the case of the black man in this country before the nations of the U.N. You can take it before the General Assembly. You can take Uncle Sam before a world court.

Malcolm's career as a speaker was not only brief, it was clearly unfinished, cut off in the midst of a search that was in its courage and integrity as much a part of his rhetorical appeal as the particulars of his evolving political and religious views. Malcolm's dignity, his sincerity, and his unique ability to combine a vividly evoked street-level experience of American racism with a world perspective framing his demand for freedom, justice, and equality create for him a unique place in the history of American oratory.

INFORMATION SOURCES

Research Collections and Collected Speeches

For an excellent guide to the literature on Malcolm X, see *Malcolm X: A Selected Bibliography*, compiled by Lenwood G. Davis (Westport, Conn.: Greenwood Press, 1984).

Lomax, Louis. *When the Word Is Given*. New York: Signet, 1964.   *WWG*

Malcolm X. *Malcolm X Speaks*. Edited by George Breitman. New York: *MXS*
Grove Press, 1966.

Malcolm X: The Man and His Times. Edited by John Henrik Clarke. New   *MHT*
York: Collier Books, 1969.

The Rhetoric of Black Americans. Edited by James L. Golden and Richard   *RBA*
D. Rieke. Columbus, Ohio: Charles E. Merrill, 1971.

The Rhetoric of the Civil-Rights Movement. Edited by Haig A. Bosmajian   *RCRM*
and Hamida Bosmajian. New York: Random House, 1969.

The Rhetoric of Racial Revolt. Edited by Roy L. Hill. Denver: Golden Bell   *RRR*
Press, 1964.

The Voice of Black Rhetoric. Edited by Arthur L. Smith and Stephen Robb.   *VBR*
Boston: Allyn and Bacon, 1971.

Selected Critical Studies

Benson, Thomas, W. "Rhetoric and Autobiography: The Case of Malcolm X." *Quarterly Journal of Speech* 60 (1974): 1–13.

Campbell, Finley C. "Voices of Thunder, Voices of Rage: A Symbolic Analysis of a Selection from Malcolm X's Speech, 'Message to the Grass Roots.' " *Speech Teacher* 19 (March 1970): 101–110.

Eakin, Paul John. "Malcolm X and the Limits of Autobiography." *Criticism* 3 (1976): 230–42.

Epps, Archie. "The Theme of Exile in the Harvard Speeches." In *Language, Communication, and Rhetoric in Black America*. Edited by Arthur L. Smith [Molefi Asante]. New York: Harper & Row, 1972.

Illo, Joseph. "The Rhetoric of Malcolm X." In *Language, Communication, and Rhetoric in Black America*. Edited by Arthur L. Smith [Molefi Asante]. New York: Harper & Row, 1972.

Mullen, Robert W. *Rhetorical Strategies of Black Americans*. Washington, D.C.: University Press of America, 1980.

Rich, Andrea L., and Smith, Arthur L. *Rhetoric of Revolution: Samuel Adams, Emma Goldman, Malcolm X*. Durham, N.C.: Moore Publishing Company, 1971.

Scott, Robert L., and Brockriede, Wayne. *The Rhetoric of Black Power*. New York: Harper & Row, 1969.

Smith, Arthur L. *Rhetoric of Black Revolution*. Boston: Allyn and Bacon, 1969.

Selected Biographies

Essien-Udom, E. U. *Black Nationalism: A Search for an Identity in America*. Chicago: University of Chicago Press, 1962.

Franklin, John Hope. *From Slavery to Freedom: A History of Negro Americans*. 3d ed. New York: Alfred A. Knopf, 1967.

Goldman, Peter. *The Death and Life of Malcolm X*. New York: Harper & Row, 1973.

Malcolm X, with the assistance of Alex Haley. *The Autobiography of Malcolm X*. New York: Grove Press, 1965.

Wolfenstein, Eugene Victor. *The Victims of Democracy: Malcolm X and the Black Revolution*. Berkeley: University of California Press, 1981.

CHRONOLOGY OF MAJOR SPEECHES

See "Research Collections and Collected Speeches" for source codes.

Speech at Harvard University, Cambridge, Massachusetts, [no day or month given] 1960; *WWG*, pp. 128–35.

"Unity," New York City, ["early in the spring"] 1960; *WWG*, pp. 128–35.

Speech at Yale University, New Haven, Connecticut, [day not given] October, 1960; *WWG*, pp. 153–67; *RRR*, pp. 304–17.

"University Speech," given on various university campuses, 1961–1962; *WWG*, pp. 136–46.

Speech at Queens College, Flushing, New York, n.d.; *WWG*, pp. 147–52.

Debate at Cornell University between James Farmer and Malcolm X, Ithaca, New York, March 7, 1962; *RCRM*, pp. 59–88; *RBA*, pp. 422–39.

"The Ballot or the Bullet," Cory Methodist Church, Cleveland, Ohio, April 3, 1964; *MXS*, pp. 23–44; *VBR*, pp. 214–35.

"Black Revolution," New York City, April 8, 1964; *MXS*, pp. 45–57; *VBR*, pp. 235–50.

Appeal to African Summit Conference, Cairo, Egypt, July 17, 1964; *MXS*, pp. 72–77.

[J. H. Clarke, in *MHT*, pp. 288–93, identifies this text as a speech, but Breitman refers to it as a memorandum presented to the conference.]

"Prospects for Freedom in 1965," New York City, January 7, 1965; *MXS*, pp. 147–56; *VBR*, pp. 250–63.

RICHARD MILHOUS NIXON
(1913–   ), thirty-seventh president of the United States

CELESTE MICHELLE CONDIT

The career of Richard M. Nixon demonstrates both the great potentials and severe limitations of public oratory. Raised in a family where voluble political argument was common, he refined his speaking skills in debate and intramural political contests throughout his school years. This competitive experience shaped his public discourse, making the primary focus of his oratory to win, using whatever strategies were available. After graduating from Duke Law School in 1937, Nixon honed these skills throughout his career, evolving from what critics have called a rough and immature extremist into an effective presidential orator.

His first major political battle was the campaign against Jerry Voorhis for California's Twelfth District congressional seat in 1946. The major theme of his political life, anticommunism, was established here. Its emotional application led to his victory and gave him the House Un-American Activities Committee as a platform from which to emerge as a national figure by exposing Alger Hiss as a communist espionage agent. He successfully used the same harsh anticommunist appeals in his next major race, against Helen Gahagan Douglas for the U.S. Senate in 1950. He was soon selected by Dwight Eisenhower as the Republican vice-presidential candidate, and the ticket won in 1952 and 1956, propelling Nixon into the Republican nomination for the presidency in 1960. After losing this close race to John F. Kennedy, he ran for governor of California in 1962, a contest he also lost. Always "Mr. Republican," he continued to work diligently for the party and to learn to use the medium of television more effectively. He emerged again in 1968 as the Republican presidential nominee, winning the presidency after a bitter campaign only to face the divisive issue of the Vietnam War. During this term, he laid the groundwork for several international achievements, but facing a hostile Congress and a divided nation, he was unsuccessful in many of his domestic goals. He was reelected over George McGovern for the presidency in 1972. This election, however, occasioned the Watergate break-in. As a consequence of his participation in the Watergate cover-up, he was compelled to resign from office after losing the confidence of his party and the public.

NIXON AS POLITICAL PERSUADER

Nixon's most natural speaking milieu was probably that of his many political campaigns, where the rules of the game emphasized personal victory. He used extremely careful preparation of background materials and tireless, intensive campaigning to make effective attacks on his opponents, mostly through claims that they supported, represented, or indirectly served international communism. The campaigns against Voorhis in 1946 and Douglas in 1950 exemplified these techniques. Through innuendo and a guilt by association tactic, he depicted them as linked with communist interests. Nixon himself, in his memoirs, indicated that his claims were perhaps overstated, although he relied on his favorite excuse—that others were doing the same. Biographers and critics often have described the tactics as vicious, emotional, and unwarranted. They were nonetheless successful.

Perhaps because of the reputation and skills gained from these activities, in the vice-presidential campaign of 1952 Nixon was assigned the hatchet job of partisan attack. His themes were corruption, communism, and Korea, and he campaigned vigorously. This persona made him highly vulnerable to counterattack, and consequently, when he was charged with having a secret campaign fund, the "dump Nixon" movement gained force rapidly. Before the largest national television audience in history to that date, he replied to these attacks with the "Checkers" speech of September 23, 1952 (which he called "My Side of the Story"). The speech was one of the most successful public orations in U.S. history, resulting in over 2 million supportive telegrams, telephone calls, and letters; it was the salvation of Nixon's career.

Although critics have agreed that Nixon failed to use sound argument or evidence to address the major issue in this speech, they have generally nominated it as a paradigm of the development and use of ethos. Nixon projected sincerity and homeyness, using the simplified expression that was characteristic of his style. Other hallmarks, including the personalization of the event, the use of innuendo, and the predisposition toward attack, were also evident. Nixon's preparation of the speech was typical of his early speaking. He wrote multiple draft outlines of the speech, drawing material from minor impromptu speeches he had given in the days before the event. He delivered the speech extemporaneously, which allowed him to project sincerity. In his decision to speak directly to the people rather than through the news media, the speech also represented Nixon's continual, eventually almost obsessive, distrust of the press. Ultimately the speech vindicated Nixon the man but perhaps at the cost of making him appear too simple, immature, and "unpresidential."

In the presidential campaign of 1956, Nixon sought a new image as vice-president and presented more positive campaign themes: "peace, prosperity, and progress." His good baritone voice, dynamism, and general mastery of the skills of the platform orator were fully developed by this time. In 1960, this new Nixon ran on his own, facing a dramatically new type of campaign, dominated by the mass media. The nationally televised Republican convention featured much skilled oratory, evoking a positive response to Republicanism in general. Nixon's speech provided the ultimate performance of the convention. He had learned to project sincerity and maturity with stature through the new medium.

The seasoned fighter continued his stump oratory throughout the country, giving over 180 prepared speeches and as many informal ones, but 4 televised debates with his opponent, John Kennedy, captured most public interest and presented him directly to the largest number of people—tens of millions for each debate.

Most commentators judged Kennedy the winner in the crucial first debate. Nixon and the commentators have attributed this to the fact that appearance is more important than substance in the television medium. Often cited is the fact that some radio audiences preferred Nixon to Kennedy. However, the radio audiences probably consisted of rural and older voters predisposed to favor Nixon, and they were perhaps influenced by Nixon's superior voice qualities. Furthermore, stump speeches had always made appearances important. Nixon's loss in the first debate is more likely accounted for by the fact that television, because it features a mass, nonpartisan audience and because of its visual focus, demanded a different type of image than earlier media. The partisan, attack-oriented Nixon fulfilled the demands less naturally than did a more confident Kennedy. In any case, the debates are attributed with changing a small margin of votes, a factor perhaps significant in his narrow loss, and Nixon in his two future presidential campaigns refused to debate on television again. He learned, however, more lessons about the new medium and was to apply them diligently in later campaigns.

Nixon's heart was probably not in his gubernatorial contest in 1962, but his efforts at rebuilding the party were both sincere and well calculated to gain him the Republican party's 1968 nomination for the presidency. In 1960, Nixon had attempted to appeal to small-town middle America through close personal identification on the stump in all fifty states. In 1968, Nixon and his staff worked hard to find new ways to use television to appeal to a broader audience in a less personal style. His speech writing had changed dramatically from the early days. Although he would always take primary responsibility for major addresses (in campaigns and in the presidency), he now had a large, sophisticated, and skilled speech-writing staff that he relied on heavily. The staff included at various periods Patrick Buchanan, William Safire, Ray Price, and more than a dozen other writers, researchers, and editors. The staff was extremely sensitive to television as a medium. At one point they reviewed many television tapes of Nixon, concluding that he was best in spontaneous question and answer formats. The ''man in the arena'' commercial campaign evolved from these conclusions. In addition, in 1968 the Republicans also handled the televising of the conventions far more skillfully than the Democrats (who were plagued by controversial demonstrations in Chicago), and Nixon's acceptance speech was again extremely successful.

By the 1972 campaign, Nixon's strategy and style had evolved even further from the partisan slugger who was just a common man. Nixon not only relied on others to write his speeches but now to deliver them as well. He campaigned very little in person, sending dozens of surrogates to speak for him around the nation. He appeared on radio and television late in the campaign, and adopted a presidential image throughout. His tactic was powerfully effective, contributing to a victory over George McGovern by one of the largest margins in history.

Nixon's campaigning is of interest as an example of both the evolution of campaigning between two different periods (that of platform public address and mass mediated public address) and of the evolution of an orator—from vicious partisan to national leader. It is also of interest, of course, because it produced a highly controversial presidency. Nixon's major concern as president was foreign policy. Although his summit meetings with the Soviets and his diplomatic initiatives to China and the Middle East have received most foreign policy attention, his oratory on the Vietnam War—bridging the domestic and the international realms—has received the most attention from rhetorical critics. Nixon's first major speech on Vietnam as president, the "Vietnamization" address of November 3, 1969, was his most controversial and has spawned an enduring debate about the nature and purposes of rhetorical criticism. Most critics agree that the speech was highly effective; it garnered a 77 percent public approval rating for Nixon's handling of Vietnam. It was well designed to appeal to the silent majority, the middle audience that Nixon clearly targeted. The style was clear and simple, allowing him to create a public understanding of difficult matters in a way that led to acceptance of his policy. Critics, however, have also noted that Nixon applied his standard political tactics of polarizing the audience and casting some of the nation's citizens as an unacceptable extremist group, thereby dividing the country against itself. The speech also relied on weak logic, including heavy dependence on either-or fallacies. This speech was thus like his many earlier partisan efforts, effective in gaining him what he wanted—in this case, majority public support to carry on the war until he could negotiate a graceful exit—but at the price of divisiveness.

The later speeches on the Vietnam War, particularly the April 30, 1970, address defending the invasion of Cambodia and the May 8, 1972, speech announcing the mining of Haiphong Harbor, relied on fairly similar strategies although with less dramatic public response. In the Vietnam speeches, Nixon emphasized the need to protect allies and to achieve a "just" peace without shame to the United States. He villified and blamed the enemy for the failure of negotiations, he suggested his willingness to make the hard decisions to continue the fighting, and he provided historical descriptions to buttress his interpretations. In the long run, these speeches were perhaps most firmly supported by the clever policy they announced. Pulling out Americans while maintaining an anticommunist stance through material support satisfied the most central demands of the major national factions.

Nixon's most eloquent statement of his goals for peace and freedom came not in his Vietnam War speeches but in his First Inaugural Address. This address has been attacked by critics as mediocre and as having attempted and failed at greatness. While it is true that several of Nixon's phrases—"we will be as strong as we need to be as long as we need to be" or "I know the heart of America is good''—seem to fall short of the sonorous heights of John F. Kennedy's Inaugural, the speech compensates for these minor weaknesses in sentence construction by offering Americans a fresh dose of high ideals. Nixon began by calling attention to the "orderly transfer of power" that allows Americans to "celebrate the unity that keeps us free.'' He asked Americans to turn away from merely material concerns to "build a great cathedral of the spirit.'' He offered every American the path to greatness through the simple tasks of "helping, caring, doing.'' Most forcefully, he applied Archibald MacLeish's depiction of the earth from space—"small and blue and beautiful in that eternal silence where it floats''—as a compelling metaphor for the necessity of peace. Nixon's Inaugural Address, although spoken through the words of a common man, not a poet, was loftily delivered and offered Americans the broadest vision they had heard in a long time. Enhanced by the majestic setting, the public reception was extremely positive. The negative response of the critics is traceable to the fact that they judged the man who delivered the phrases as incompetent for such promises. Even when transcending in word the partisan style of his past, the partisan slugger's ethos continued to limit his larger effectiveness.

Although domestic issues did not garner most of his interest, Nixon delivered many important speeches on these issues, and they were generally well crafted. His clear and forceful "Energy Emergency" speech of November 7, 1973, for example, called for balanced responses to a complex situation. Comparing it, for example, to President Jimmy Carter's far less effective efforts on similar topics suggests Nixon's great skill in using the rhetorical power of the presidency to gain public support and action.

Nixon's greatest rhetorical challenge, however, was presented by the Watergate incident, and in that case, not even his seasoned and artful skill was adequate to surmount the obstacles. The long ordeal of Watergate began for the public on June 17, 1972, when political spies, acting on the authority of the Committee to Re-elect the President, were caught breaking into the Democratic party's Watergate office complex. In the next two years, revelations of improper wiretaps, break-ins, and political dirty tricks would add to the Watergate story. In addition to Nixon's self-admitted general responsibility for these acts, the crucial blow to his public confidence was the revelation, through tapes made in the White House itself, that Nixon had actively participated in a cover-up of these activities.

Nixon made what he calls his first formal address on Watergate on April 30, 1973. In his memoirs, he admits that for the sake of simplicity, he chose to claim falsely that he had not been involved personally in the cover-up. He announced the resignation of his top advisers, insisted on his determination to get to the truth and bring the guilty to justice, and tried to explain the events. He concluded by urging the country to forget Watergate and get on to the "vital work to be done'' for the country. The speech was well designed in most respects. Unfortunately, it followed too well his long-established speaking patterns, relying on ethos and neglecting evidence. In this case, and increasingly throughout the year, counterevidence presented in other media (often with admittedly partisan frenzy) thoroughly impugned his character. Gradually he was forced to recognize this.

His adaptation is evident in the "Watergate Investigation" speech of August 15, 1973. The address repeated much of the earlier strategies but also emphasized a higher principle in the president's actions. If the facts had been other than they were, this might have been recorded as a truly great speech. Nixon clearly and forcefully elaborated the principle of confidentiality. Moreover, he argued eloquently for the need to "clean up politics" because Americans needed to "show a renewed respect for the mutual restraints that are the mark of a free and a civilized society."

The facts, however, once again betrayed Nixon's words. At the time of this speech, he was already ranked at an all-time low in the polls, and the speech, because it could not counter with evidence of innocence, did little to change the public's opinion. The man did not exemplify his words. The words that were taken as a truer sign of his character were those finally revealed in his last major Watergate policy address on April 29, 1974. After losing a Supreme Court test, Nixon finally admitted that it was necessary to waive executive privilege. Ultimately, executive privilege protects the actions of a president in the national interest, not the personal interests of a person who wishes to win or maintain the presidency. In this final speech, Nixon tried skillfully to recharacterize what the nation would hear in the tapes that were to be released. He carefully contextualized damaging phrases and emphasized those lines that might redeem him. The nation, however, would see the full transcripts of the tapes, and these revealed a profane, extremely partisan, ethically lax person, a man who operated without the mutual restraint necessary to a civilized society. The Congress and the public, and most important the Republican party leaders, denied this man their confidence.

The denouement came with Nixon's resignation speech of August 8, 1974, and the White House Farewell of August 9, 1974. Nixon's resignation speech was dignified and appropriate; once defeated, the partisan rose to good grace in leaving the arena. The speech has been criticized as failing to meet the demands of the genre of apologia, but it did not really attempt to provide an apology. Nixon explained the reason for his resignation as a loss of a political base that would allow him to govern effectively and then provided a fairly standard presidential Farewell Address. The address does not provide a fully satisfactory response to the situation, but Nixon's situation had long gone beyond the ability of oratory to "make all come right," as he himself noted in his memoirs. Only the sad and maudlin personal farewell to the White House staff remained. This was an address appropriately full of pathos but one that should not have been open to the public. Nixon—the common man, the personal partisan, the emotional orator—reappeared here; the man who rose to the presidency with the rise of television was its captive even in his private farewell.

There is no doubt that Richard M. Nixon was one of the most skillful of

America's modern-day political rhetors. He learned to adapt to changing media and roles. In the end, however, his discourse and its effectiveness were shackled by the partisan nature of the creature who constructed and delivered the rhetorical creation.

INFORMATION RESOURCES

Research Collections and Collected Speeches

Much of Nixon's private papers were donated to the National Archives. In 1987, the Nixon Presidential Library is scheduled to open in San Clemente, California. The public documents and speeches from his presidency are available in the *Weekly Compilation of Presidential Documents*.

Bremer, Howard F. *Richard M. Nixon: 1913–*. Dobbs Ferry, N.Y.: Oceana   *RMN*
 Publications, 1975.
Singer, Aaron. *Campaign Speeches of American Presidential Candidates:*   *CSAPC*
 1928–1972. New York: Frederick Ungar Publishing Co., 1976.
Weekly Compilation of Presidential Documents. Washington, D.C.: Gov-   *WCPD*
 ernment Printing Office, 1969–1974.

Selected Critical Studies

Alexander, Frederick G. "Richard M. Nixon and Nelson A. Rockefeller." *Quarterly Journal of Speech* 46 (1960): 245.
Baskerville, Barnet. "The New Nixon." *Quarterly Journal of Speech* 43 (1957): 38–43.
Campbell, Karlyn Kohrs. "Richard M. Nixon: 'Vietnamization: The President's Address on the War,' " *Critiques of Contemporary Rhetoric*. Belmont, Calif.: Wadsworth, 1972.
Harrell, Jackson; Ware, B. L.; and Linkugel, Wil A. "Failure of Apology in American Politics: Nixon on Watergate." *Communication Monographs* 42 (1975): 245–61.
Harris, Barbara Ann. "The Inaugural of Richard Milhous Nixon: A Reply to Robert L. Scott." *Western Journal of Speech Communication* 34 (1970): 231–34.
Hart, Roderick P. "Absolutism and Situation: Prolegomena to a Rhetorical Biography of Richard M. Nixon." *Communication Monographs* 43 (1976): 204–28.
Hill, Forbes I. "Conventional Wisdom—Traditional Form: The President's Message of November 3, 1969." *Quarterly Journal of Speech* 58 (1972): 373–86.
Newman, Robert P. "Under the Veneer: Nixon's Vietnam Speech of November 3, 1969." *Quarterly Journal of Speech* 56 (1970): 168–78.
Rosenfield, L. W. "A Case Study in Speech Criticism: The Nixon-Truman Analog." *Communication Monographs* 35 (1968): 435–50.
Scott, Robert L. "Rhetoric That Postures: An Intrinsic Reading of Richard M. Nixon's Inaugural Address." *Western Journal of Speech Communication* 34 (1970): 46–52.
Smith, Craig R. "Richard Nixon's 1968 Acceptance Speech as a Model of Dual Audience Adaptation." *Communication Quarterly* 19 (1971): 15–22.
Trent, Judith S. "Richard Nixon's Methods of Identification in the Presidential Campaigns of 1960 and 1968: A Content Analysis." *Communication Quarterly* 19 (1971): 23–30.

Wilson, Gerald L. "A Strategy of Explanation: Richard M. Nixon's August 8, 1974 Resignation Address." *Communication Quarterly* 24 (1976): 14–20.

Selected Biographies

Brodie, Fawn. *Richard Nixon: The Shaping of His Character*. New York: W. W. Norton, 1981.

Mazo, Earl, and Hess, Stephen. *Nixon: A Political Portrait*. New York: Harper & Row, 1968.

Nixon, Richard. *RN: The Memoirs of Richard Nixon*. New York: Grosset and Dunlap, 1978.

―――. *Six Crises*. Garden City, N.Y.: Doubleday and Company, 1962.

CHRONOLOGY OF MAJOR SPEECHES

See "Research Collections and Collected Speeches" for source codes.

"Checkers" speech, Los Angeles, September 23, 1952; *RMN*, pp. 85–94.

Acceptance speech, Chicago, July 15, 1960; *CSAPC*, pp. 307–18.

First Inaugural Address, Washington, D.C., January 20, 1969; *RMN*, 96–100; *WCPD*, 5, no. 4, pp. 150–53.

"Vietnamization" address, Washington, D.C., November 3, 1969; *WCPD*, 5, no. 45, pp. 1546–55.

"Cambodian Invasion," Washington, D.C., April 30, 1970; *WCPD*, 6, no. 18, pp. 596–601.

"Mining Haiphong Harbor," Washington, D.C., May 8, 1972; *WCPD*, 8, no. 20, pp. 838–42.

First Watergate Address, Washington, D.C., April 30, 1973; *WCPD*, 9, no. 18, pp. 433–38.

"The Watergate Investigation," Washington, D.C., August 15, 1973; *WCPD*, 9, no. 33, pp. 984–91.

"The Energy Emergency," Washington, D.C., November 7, 1973; *WCPD*, 9, no. 45, pp. 1312–18.

"Subpoena of Presidential Tapes," Washington, D.C., April 29, 1974; *WCPD*, 10, no. 18, pp. 450–58.

Resignation Address, Washington, D.C., August 8, 1974; *RMN*, pp. 232–36; *WCPD*, 10, no. 32, pp. 1014–17.

RONALD REAGAN
(1911–   ), fortieth president of the United States
————————————————————————— RONALD H. CARPENTER

Ronald Reagan is called the Great Communicator. Well into his second term as president of the United States, Ronald Reagan remains in a unique position. His personal popularity and public approval of his performance have not diminished. For some presidents, prior stature as a hero in itself was sufficient to secure election initially and ensure esteem throughout years in the White House, regardless of communicative ineptness or political misfortunes or both. Dwight Eisenhower exemplifies that immensely popular military hero who in the public mind could do no wrong as president, and other Americans before him capitalized politically on earlier, heroic images to attain the presidency and function effectively therein. But Ronald Reagan neither drew upon such a resource initially nor capitalized on it subsequently to an appreciable extent. He was elected and remains effective to a large degree because of his abilities as a communicator.

Reagan's communication prowess evolved from substantial experience prior to formal entry into politics as governor of California from 1967 to 1974. Prominent among these are his professional vocations of sports announcer on radio from 1932 to 1937, Hollywood actor from 1937 to 1966, and years of pragmatic experience as a platform speaker. Beginning in 1954, with his role as host of television's "G.E. Theatre," Ronald Reagan contributed extensively for almost ten years to General Electric's public relations program by speaking to national business conventions, state chamber of commerce meetings, and weekly luncheon clubs. Ideal preparation for the presidency might be political experience in successively more significant roles to the point of attaining the status of public servant at the least or statesman at the most, or the role of military hero is an appropriate background if the candidate is regarded as capable of dealing successfully with other leaders internationally, or leading armed forces' campaigns of epic proportions. But Reagan's political success is derived mainly from communication skills honed and perfected before cameras and microphones for years prior to his entry into the political arena. Some presidents become actors in their jobs, but Reagan's job as actor helped him become president. To understand this oratorical success, one must consider the societal evolution of the United States from the nineteenth century to what it became in the 1960s and 1970s, the set in which this man began to play his most important role.

RONALD REAGAN AS PRESIDENTIAL ORATOR-SPOKESMAN

Americans were once a vocal if not oratorical people who spoke often in Grange halls or town meetings, and nineteenth-century education helped them become communicators. Colleges and universities taught rhetoric as the art of writing and speaking for situations in which people participated. Moreover, rhetoric taught for writing and speaking was read and heard often, notably in the Scriptures.

Before the Civil War, one American in four was a townsman; now nine of ten Americans live in cities and urban sprawls. After tiring rides home in rush-hour traffic, they are not so likely to go out again and participate in discourse. Some read from mass circulation magazines and daily newspapers that proliferated with their congregations into cities; more, however, are viewers and listeners in a vast communication mosaic of pervasive (and persuasive) electronic mass media. Writers and speakers became readers and listeners, with more of the latter, and many Americans now begin formal discourse by saying with complete conviction, "Unaccustomed as I am to public speaking..." But for all their communication ineptness, Americans still wanted their ideals stated— and bestowed political leadership on people more adept as communicators who could say well what they wanted said well.

Watergate briefly altered the expectations of Americans for the presidency. After the trauma of Richard Nixon's resignation, what Americans wanted most in the White House was honesty. Jimmy Carter fulfilled that expectation effectively in 1976. A wide range of television commercials, including those with the candidate in farmer's garb as a man of the soil, underscored a basic campaign promise that he would "never lie" to us. For virtue and trustworthiness in the White House, voters overlooked Carter's communication liabilities such as unnatural pause patterns and tendencies toward slips of the tongue. His ineptness as the nation's surrogate communicator became more apparent and more detrimental, however. During the 1980 presidential campaign, Jimmy Carter, the inarticulate incumbent, stood in stark contrast to the challenger Ronald Reagan, whose communication skills Americans wanted in the presidency to dispel effectively their fears for the present and articulate well their hopes for the future.

In 1964, with a speech endorsing Barry Goldwater's campaign for the presidency, Ronald Reagan emerged as a prominent spokesman not only for Republicans but for growing numbers of other Americans. His recurring international issue became an anti-Soviet rhetorical stance calling for U.S. strength aginst communism. Early in his political career, particularly in platform speeches for conservative groups, Reagan was emphatic, if not strident, about communism's threat to the United States. As president, typically on television to wider, national audiences, he also urges military strength to counter communism. Nevertheless, because public opinion polls show Americans in a nuclear age more inclined toward improved relations with the Soviet Union, Reagan met amiably with Soviet Premier Gorbachev in Geneva. Reagan did so, however, only with Americans' understanding that he would deal with Soviet "savagery" from a position of military strength; the result, as Robert Ivie observed, is the public's impression of his commonsense approach to international issues.

The president's rhetorical stance on domestic issues began evolving approximately ten years before his October 27, 1964, speech endorsing Barry Gold-water, during the extensive speaking schedule in his public relations role for General Electric. The broad theme of an address delivered over and over was encroaching government controls and dangers of "a Big Brother or paternalistic government" instead of limited government whereby "problems would all be solved if the federal government would return to the states and communities some of the sources of taxation the federal government has usurped for itself." Reagan's consistent attacks on big government became, in Kurt Ritter's assessment, "the speech" on free enterprise from which Reagan never varied significantly over the years. For both domestic and international themes, however, Reagan also seeks audience approval consistently by linking his position with such cultural values as faith in the family and the belief that through hard work individuals can and do succeed; and his 1980 acceptance address to the Republican National Convention was eminently successful, in Henry Scheele's estimate, because Ronald Reagan emphasized a return to those cherished values.

A political orator who appeals effectively to basic values and adjusts to changing public opinion is not unique, however. To appreciate President Reagan's success as orator-spokesman, a helpful orientation is the exception principle, whereby the speaking skills of interest are not those that the orator utilizes in common with other communicators but rather those by which the speaker differs from them, quantitatively or qualitatively. From this frame of reference, what Reagan says is not exceptional; as candidate and then as president, he succeeds more because of how that content is delivered. When classical theorists wrote about the art of persuasive discourse, they organized their commentaries into canons of rhetoric. One was *actio*, the canon of delivery, or how orators manage voice and body to be effective in discourse. For a communication context in which many Americans are inarticulate themselves, someone who speaks particularly well has an advantage.

For presidential discourse on television, Reagan's prowess with delivery is perhaps unequaled. Only an occasional lapse mars his performance with scripts or when extemporizing. During the first television debate with Walter Mondale in 1984, for instance, disfluencies occurred in some answers, and the president's meandering and stumbling through his concluding illustration were disconcerting. For the second debate, though, he bounced back to customary performance levels perfected during years of practice on Hollywood sets and in television studios, and observers of presidential discourse for the most part acclaim Reagan's mastery of voice and body while speaking. Conducing to that admirable *actio* are a particularly well-modulated baritone voice capable of controlled variation between restrained forcefulness and an almost hushed whisper, eye contact, meaningful and well-timed gesture, physical poise, and a superb sense of when to pause for clarity, emphasis, and emotional affect. From a dramatic perspective, only Reagan as candidate could carry off so well his acceptance address conclusion to the Republican convention in 1980: "I'll confess that I've been a little afraid to suggest what I'm going to suggest. [beat] I'm more afraid not to. [beat]

Can we begin our crusade joined together in a moment of silent prayer?'' Add the president's well-timed, characteristic nod of the head with clenched teeth and pursed lips between some words, and the paramessage of facial gesture reinforces an impression of determination. In combination with physical poise that bespeaks both unflappable stature and that coolness so suitable for television, Reagan's rhetorical management of voice and body warrant acclaim for *actio* and the controlled flexibility and polished delivery of his lines. Indeed, for the vocal aspects of skillful delivery, no other president likely has matched Ronald Reagan since Franklin Roosevelt through the medium of radio.

Acclaim is not warranted, however, for Reagan's command of the classical canon called *elocutio*, or how orators manage word choice and word arrangement stylistically to achieve the most effective sentences. Other presidents assured places in posterity with eloquent phrases and sentences, such as Abraham Lincoln's "government of the people, by the people, for the people," Franklin Roosevelt's "The only thing we have to fear is fear itself," and John Kennedy's "Ask not what your country can do for you—ask what you can do for your country." No comparable eloquence comes from Reagan. We notice and remember his quip about sending a film hero, Rambo, to solve a problem or an on-mike slip about when World War III will start, but this president does not gain esteem for language and style in discourse. He is not eloquent in part because of consistent attempts, as Roderick Hart observes, to use homespun, everyday language that does not call attention to itself. Thus, characteristic contractions such as "we're," "it's," "we've," and "we'll" transform what could be elevated discourse into idiomatic expression. Moreover, he is particularly fond of a conversational and stylistically inept "well" or "now" to begin sentences, as in his First Inaugural and the 1984 State of the Union Address: "Well, I believe we the Americans of today are ready to act" or "Now, I believe there is . . . " Those colloquial interjections are verbal filler to accompany nods of the head with pursed lips, but this is not the lofty, elevated expression that finds its way on monuments. Consider what is lost in Reagan's Second Inaugural by saying, "Well, with heart and hand, let us stand as one today." Similarly, in a solemn speech after visiting a German military cemetery, what could have been an incisive epigram was undermined by an idiomatic interjection: "Some old wounds have been reopened, and this I regret very much, because this should be a time of healing." Other shortcomings appear even in overt attempts at eloquent statements. To create one of America's memorable lines, Martin Luther King, Jr., began successive sentences with the same words (*anaphora*) and emphasized an optimistic "I have a dream. . . . I have a dream. . . . I have a dream." But to amplify upon "the will and moral courage of free men and women," Ronald Reagan says, "It is a weapon our adversaries in today's world do not have. It is a weapon that we as Americans do have." Discounting grammar by which the plural "will and moral courage" become the singular "it," the words "it is" are unworthy of emphasis. While describing a security shield in his Second Inaugural, the president said, "It wouldn't kill people, it would destroy weapons. It wouldn't militarize space, it would help demilitarize the arsenals of earth. It would render nuclear weapons obsolete.'' Great Britain's spokesman, Winston Churchill, reinforced key words in, ''We shall fight on the beaches, we shall fight on the landing grounds, we shall fight in the fields and in the streets, we shall fight in the hills.'' We do learn what is repeated for us, and through style Reagan would have Americans learn a word devoid of rhetorically potent connotation, *it*.

In final appraisal of Ronald Reagan as presidential orator-spokesman, the ultimate question is what determines greatness as a communicator in the White House. For an age in which many Americans are inarticulate readers and listeners more than writers and speakers, an aptly named silent majority appreciates a skilled speaker to express their fears and hopes. In his extraordinary ability to deliver lines well, Reagan meets that expectation, but the visual and auditory stimuli of his body and voice are fleeting, preserved for our collective consciousness only on videotape. Eloquent words that become a nation's persuasive maxims during a president's tenure in office (and endure after) have not been forthcoming from Ronald Reagan or his speech writers. Cast as a formula, *actio*, or admirable delivery of lines, minus *elocutio*, or eloquent word choice and word arrangement, equals a less-than-great communicator after all. For truly great presidential orator-spokesmen, actions of voice and body do not speak louder than the style of the best words in their best orders.

INFORMATION SOURCES

Research Collections and Collected Speeches

American Rhetoric from Roosevelt to Reagan: A Collection of Speeches and   ARRR
    Critical Essays. Edited by Halford Ross Ryan. Prospect Heights,
    Ill.: Waveland Press, 1983.
New York Times.   NYT
Vital Speeches.   VS
Weekly Compilation of Presidential Documents.   WCPD

Selected Critical Studies

Carpenter, Ronald H. ''Ronald Reagan and the Presidential Imperative to Stylize: A −
    E = < GC.'' *Speaker and Gavel* 20 (1982–1983): 1–6.
———. ''The Symbolic Substance of Style in Presidential Discourse.'' *Style* 16 (1982):
    38–49.
Hart, Roderick P. *Verbal Style and the Presidency: A Computer-Based Analysis*. Orlando:
    Academic Press, 1984.
Ivie, Robert L. ''Speaking 'Common Sense' about the Soviet Threat: Reagan's Rhetorical
    Stance.'' *Western Journal of Speech Communication* 48 (1984): 39–50.
Ritter, Kurt W. ''Ronald Reagan and 'The Speech': The Rhetoric of Public Relations
    Politics.'' *Western Journal of Speech Communication* 32 (1968): 50–58.

Scheele, Henry Z. "Ronald Reagan's 1980 Acceptance Address: A Focus on American Values." *Western Journal of Speech Communication* 48 (1984): 51–61.

CHRONOLOGY OF MAJOR SPEECHES

See "Research Collections and Collected Speeches" for source codes.

"Free Enterprise," speech to the National Association of Manufacturers, New York City, December 8, 1972; *ARRR*, pp. 265–77; *VS*, January 15, 1973, pp. 196–201.

Acceptance address to the Republican National Convention, Detroit, Michigan, July 17, 1980; *VS*, August 15, 1980, pp. 642–46.

First Inaugural Address, Washington, D.C., January 20, 1981; *VS*, February 15, 1981, pp. 258–60.

State of the Union Address, Washington, D.C., January 26, 1982; *VS*, February 15, 1982, pp. 258–62; *ARRR*, pp. 278–89.

State of the Union Address, Washington, D.C., January 1984; *WCPD*, January 30, 1984, pp. 87–94.

Second Inaugural Address, Washington, D.C., January 21, 1985; *VS*, February 1, 1985, pp. 226–28.

Address at Bitburg, Germany, May 5, 1985; *New York Times*, May 6, 1985.

ANNA ELEANOR ROOSEVELT
(1884–1962), social reformer and humanitarian

BETH M. WAGGENSPACK

Eleanor Roosevelt was given the title First Lady of the World in honor of her lifelong involvement with causes covering every conceivable aspect of social welfare and reform: civil rights, labor, housing, progressive education, youth rights, public health, child welfare, and political reform. As a speaker for the dispossessed, she was a prominent advocate for social and civil rights. Like her husband, Franklin D. Roosevelt, she represented a resolute struggle to overcome handicaps while in full public view. Critics called her an innocent idealist or worse, a "Brownie Scout run amok," yet none could deny that her rhetoric was marked by selflessness and inspiration. Despite the fact that she had no outstanding talent for speaking, no brilliant mind, little special training, and no artistic genius, she still stood apart from others and became both a symbol and an institution. Eleanor Roosevelt's rhetorical hallmarks were her abilities to see herself in perspective and to see the humanity in all; her oratory recommended equality because that was how she perceived a perfect world would be attained.

ELEANOR ROOSEVELT AS SOCIAL REFORMER

U.S. entry into World War I gave Roosevelt the opportunity to enter the public view in support of social causes. Her early years had been dominated by an unhappy childhood and her marriage, which sublimated her public activities to her husband's growing political career. Supervising Red Cross activities and visiting hospitals exposed her to the horrors of war and the neglect in hospitals. After FDR's unsuccessful 1920 vice-presidential campaign, she became active in the League of Women Voters, the Settlement House movement, and the National Consumers' League. Each group provided Roosevelt with new insights—the desire for excellence, the complexity of urban problems, and the role of reformer as educator who boldly states the facts.

With FDR's 1921 polio attack, Eleanor's public life expanded as she became his personal representative in the political area, especially as in intermediary between FDR and Al Smith. Her talent for combining partisan political activity with a devotion to many reform issues came from a conviction that politics was the handmaiden of reform.

With FDR's election to the presidency in 1932, she began twelve years as First Lady, during which she shattered precedent and made her role influential. The first break was her decision to hold press conferences. On March 6, thirty-five women reporters (restricted to women in order to encourage the employment of newspaper women) assembled at the first White House press conference by a First Lady. Roosevelt stipulated that no political questions could be asked, although that restriction soon vanished. When a reporter cautioned her about an answer that could cause trouble, she said, "Perhaps I am making these statements on purpose to arouse controversy and thereby get the topics talked about." Bess Furman, an AP correspondent, contrasted FDR and Eleanor's styles: "At the President's press conference, all the world's a stage; at Mrs. Roosevelt's all the world's a school." The press conference soon served as a testing ground for many of her later columns and speeches.

Many of Roosevelt's early White House speeches revolved around the theme of women's role in reform if the country was to come through the depression. She interlaced advice on child rearing and budgeting with pleas to join and support trade unions and peace movements. In a 1935 address to the Conference on the Cause and Cure of War, she told women to take leadership roles. "We women who have intuition, who have tact . . . should transfer that skill to a larger field . . . to bring about a better understanding in our own nation in regard to the troubles of other nations." Her speech called for the building of a new world, and in simple words and homely stories, she said that "if only we can get back to the feeling that we are responsible for each other, these years of depression would have been worthwhile."

Fundamentally Roosevelt was not a politician; she was a woman with a deep sense of spiritual duty. She toured the country for FDR, surveyed local conditions, and spoke for the underprivileged. In 1934 she resumed the radio addresses that she had given up two years earlier, and in 1935, she signed with W. Colston Leigh to do two lecture tours per year at a fee of $1,000 per lecture. She had five topics: "Relationship of the Individual to the Community," "Problems of Youth," "The Mail of a President's Wife," "Peace," and "A Typical Day at the White House." Her speeches were marked by naturalness and spiritual energy, though the themes were simple and her presentation style distracting. The lectures and radio shows led naturally to her career as a columnist, and through these media, she reached millions. She became, as one critic noted, a "Cabinet Minister without portfolio, the most influential woman of our times."

In 1936, Roosevelt resigned from the Daughters of the American Revolution over its defense of racism when it refused to allow Marian Anderson, a black singer, to sing in Constitution Hall. Addressing a meeting of the National Negro Congress to commemorate the signing of the Emancipation Proclamation, Roosevelt called upon the United States to finish the job Lincoln had begun. She also predicted that "this vast issue [is] taking shape and every day is coming closer" and that citizens had to answer the urgency of the race issue in unprecedented ways.

Roosevelt actively promoted many liberal causes, and although none of her speeches are immortalized, her support for youth movements and programs such as the National Youth Administration and the Youth Congress, civilian defense, and New Deal social welfare programs is well documented. Her 1940 Democratic convention speech in support of FDR's choice of Henry Wallace as a running mate served as party peacemaker. The speech's theme was that there was a possibility that a third term would be too much of a strain on FDR. She told delegates that by their asking FDR to run again, they assumed the burden of supporting his decisions: "No man who is a candidate . . . can carry this situation alone. This is only carried by a united people who love their country. You will have to rise above considerations which are narrow and partisan." Again, one of her standard themes—selflessness for the good of all—subdued angry feelings, and the convention was united.

After FDR's death in 1945, President Harry Truman named Roosevelt a delegate to the United Nations. There she argued for creation of the Universal Declaration of Human Rights, which passed the UN General Assembly on December 10, 1948. As the declaration's key advocate, Eleanor embodied the inalienable civilized standards of the human rights cause.

Roosevelt resigned her UN post in 1953 and for the next ten years traveled the world extensively speaking on the cause of world peace and human rights. She actively campaigned for Democratic politics, speaking at conventions and traveling for the party's liberal and reform wings. The bulk of her later years' work went toward the American Association for the United Nations, where she attempted to bolster public support for the UN. In her last ten years, Roosevelt traveled around the world three times, once visiting the Soviet Union, where she held a two-and-one-half-hour interview with Premier Khrushchev, covering topics of disarmament, the Marshall Plan, and Mideast policy. Her death in 1962 stilled a voice made legend as the spirit of humanity and selflessness.

Eleanor Roosevelt's oratory was most noted for her verbal delivery, which at the start of her speaking career was extremely poor, and her distinctive approach to her audience. In early addresses, Roosevelt's vocal delivery was characterized by a falsetto voice, which disconcerted her listeners; indiscriminate use of inflections and emphasis; and as political adviser Louis Howe pointed out, a tendency to giggle for no apparent reason. Despite Howe's attempts to alter her delivery by constant criticism and long practice sessions, it was not until February 1938 that Roosevelt found a teacher-critic who was able to provide her with constructive help. Elizabeth Fergeson von Hesse, a New York City speech teacher, heard Roosevelt at Chautauqua "lose an audience of 5,000 within ten minutes." von Hesse wrote Roosevelt, telling her that she could teach her control. Through forty-four hours of study over a two-week period, Roosevelt learned breath and diaphragm control, which gave her voice focus and eradicated the falsetto; tone projection and placement, which provided resonance and lowered her voice four major tones; a freedom in gestures; and a new walk that made her appear more confident and less like a mincing schoolgirl. In addition, Roosevelt was given a card to carry on her travels that reminded her, "The Creator has never as yet made a woman who can talk and laugh at the same time becomingly."

A close student of the changes reported in 1941 that Roosevelt's vocal assets were a pleasing change in pace, rapid in narration yet slower in theoretical material; a variation in emphasis, using greater force in main points; and the clear-cut articulation of a cultured easterner. Perhaps even more of an indication of her verbal changes exists in the *Movie and Radio Guide*'s 1940 grading of the top radio orators. Roosevelt was given good marks on voice quality, delivery, and poise, with a total score of 93. This made her second behind the top-ranked FDR with a score of 97.

What made Eleanor Roosevelt an outstanding orator was not her mastery of vocal technique but her constant awareness of her unseen audience. She consciously attempted to envision her listeners in their diverse situations and tried to remember they were weighing her words against their own experiences. She made the listeners' interests and problems her own and tried out of her own experience to speak meaningfully and simply. She was able to identify with her listeners, to illustrate her thesis with personal and homely stories, and to advance her point of view in a kindly fashion. Eleanor Roosevelt did not like to speak if she did not have something affirmative to say. She told public speaking students that when speaking, one should "be conciliatory, never antagonistic, toward your audience, or it may disagree with you no matter what you say."

Her simple approach to the audience was often the target of her detractors. Her speeches were often banal, characterized by pedestrian style, trivia, and platitudes, such as "No problem is ever solved until you try," or "A vote is never an intelligent vote when it is cast without knowledge." Eleanor Roosevelt did not feel she was a philosopher. Her lack of college education gave her a disadvantage in analyzing and judging competing intellectual claims; thus her speeches were criticized as lacking concrete proposals and forwarding hazy, long-term goals. But Eleanor Roosevelt's concerns were the ends rather than the means. Her role was more of a clarion who pointed listeners toward desired objectives.

Two other characteristics mark Eleanor Roosevelt's rhetoric: simplicity and brevity. Her custom in addressing live audiences was to speak from a single page of notes, which she felt kept her speeches fresh and kept her from becoming bored. Her advice to speech students was, "Have something to say, say it and sit down. At first write out the beginning and the end of a speech. Use notes and think out a speech, but never write it down." She despaired that people would ever understand that "simple things don't require a tremendous amount of verbiage."

The recurring theme in Roosevelt's oratory was one of constructive activism as a response to threatening challenges. She created unprecedented ways of interceding on the behalf of the underprivileged by becoming an intermediary among the President, New Deal bureaucrats, cabinet members, and public. Because she did not consciously solicit votes, she was more a political force than a politician; her human touch gave people confidence in governmental bureaucracy. Her three fundamental motivating principles were to do her best; to indulge less in herself and more in others; and to find gratification in giving and in bringing happiness to others.

Roosevelt's contributions to U.S. political democracy are marked by pragmatic idealism; her ideas took shape as new circumstances arose. With the depression, she stressed social and economic causes; World War II caused her to reemphasize the U.S. world leadership role and racial equality; problems at the UN caused her to see domestic issues as inseparable from world conditions. She had no conscious program or preplanned tools or many outstanding addresses. She adopted causes as they arose, and at times, too many causes caught her spirit, so her role in them was often superficial. While an examination of Eleanor Roosevelt's oratory reveals contradictions, naiveté, oversimplifications, and an absence of analysis, the major value of her statements rested in her constant emphasis on social responsibility, human rights, and human dignity. Eleanor Roosevelt's oratorical strength lay in inspiring and exhorting, and her speeches held her listeners because they reflected her own efforts to think about what was right and true.

INFORMATION SOURCES

Research Collections and Collected Speeches

The most useful source of materials for studying Eleanor Roosevelt is the Franklin D. Roosevelt Library, Hyde Park, New York. Six boxes contain Mrs. Roosevelt's unedited speeches and articles from 1924 until her death. Bound volumes of her column, "My Day," also contain unedited, diary-like articles, presenting her innermost thoughts on issues. The president's personal file is of special relevance for the Eleanor Roosevelt researcher; it contains correspondence and newspaper articles that shed additional light upon her role and how critics viewed her. Eleanor Roosevelt's *It's Up to the Women* (New York: Frederick A. Stockes Co., 1933) presents a compilation of her early speeches and articles, focusing on woman's role in home and politics. Other collections, most notably those in the Schlesinger Library of Radcliffe College, Cambridge, Massachusetts, and in the Library of Congress's papers from the National Consumers' League and the National Women's Trade Union League, present correspondence that indicates Roosevelt's views and activities.

Eleanor Roosevelt Papers. Franklin D. Roosevelt Library.   ERP
Representative American Speeches: 1939–1940. Edited by A. Craig Baird.   RAS 1939
    New York: H. W. Wilson, 1940.
Representative American Speeches: 1956–1957. Edited by A. Craig Baird.   RAS 1956
    New York: H. W. Wilson, 1957.
Treasury of Great American Speeches. Edited by Charles Hurd. New York: TGAS
    Hawthorn Books, 1959.
Women's International League for Peace and Freedom Papers. Swarthmore   SCPC
    College Peace Collection, Swarthmore, Pennsylvania.

Selected Critical Studies

Berger, Jason. *A New Deal for the World: Eleanor Roosevelt and American Foreign Policy.* New York: Columbia University Press, 1981.
Bilsborow, Eleanor J. "The Philosophy of Social Reform in the Speeches of Eleanor Roosevelt." Ph.D. dissertation, University of Denver, 1957.

Hareven, Tamara K. "The Social Thought of Eleanor Roosevelt." Ph.D. dissertation, Ohio State University, 1965.

Kretsinger, Geneva. "An Analytical Study of Selected Radio Speeches of Eleanor Roosevelt." Master's thesis, University of Oklahoma, 1941.

Ranck, Gloria V. "A Study of Selected Speeches by Mrs. FDR on Human Rights." Master's thesis, University of Washington, 1952.

Wamboldt, Helen J. "Anna Eleanor Roosevelt: A Descriptive and Analytical Study of the Speaking Career of AER." Ph.D. dissertation, University of Southern California, 1952.

———. "Speech Teacher to the First Lady of the World." *Today's Speech* 12 (1964): 5–7.

Selected Biographies

Hareven, Tamara K. *Eleanor Roosevelt, An American Conscience*. Chicago: Quadrangle Books, 1968.

Kearney, James R. *Anna Eleanor Roosevelt: The Evolution of a Reformer*. Boston: Houghton Mifflin, 1968.

Lash, Joseph P. *Eleanor Roosevelt: A Friend's Memoir*. Garden City, N.Y.: Doubleday, 1964.

———. *Eleanor and Franklin*. New York: W. W. Norton, 1971.

———. *Eleanor: The Years Alone*. New York: W. W. Norton, 1971.

Roosevelt, Eleanor. *The Autobiography of Eleanor Roosevelt*. Boston: G. K. Hall, 1984.

CHRONOLOGY OF MAJOR SPEECHES

See "Research Collections and Collected Speeches" for source codes.

1928 campaign speech; *ERP*.

"Women in Politics," City Club, New York City, November 21, 1931; *Quarterly* (January 1930): 71.

Speech before the Conference on the Cause and Cure of War, Washington, D.C., January 10, 1935; *SCPC*.

"Civil Liberties—The Individual and the Community," Chicago, March 14, 1940; *RAS 1939*, pp. 173–82.

Address before the Democratic National Convention, Chicago, July 18, 1940; *ERP*.

"The United Nations and Its Future," Chicago, July 23, 1952; *TGAS*, pp. 297–302.

Address before the Democratic National Convention, Chicago, August 31, 1956; *RAS 1956*, pp. 109–13.

FRANKLIN DELANO ROOSEVELT
(1882–1945), thirty-second president of the United States

HALFORD R. RYAN

Oratory was an integral and important factor in the career and political advancement of Franklin Delano Roosevelt. At Groton preparatory school, he debated in the forensic society, and at Harvard University he took courses in public speaking. Roosevelt used these skills to practical advantage in learning and mastering campaign speaking in his successful Democratic bid for the New York State Senate in 1910 and again in 1912. After serving as assistant secretary of the navy from 1913 to 1920, he improved his campaign speaking and assumed national stature as the vice-presidential running mate for James M. Cox in 1920. Cox and Roosevelt lost to Warren G. Harding and Calvin Coolidge.

Although stricken with polio in 1921, Roosevelt was able to maintain contacts with national Democratic leaders, largely through the efforts of his wife, Eleanor Roosevelt, and Louis Howe, who was something of the man behind FDR. Consequently he twice nominated fellow New Yorker Al Smith for the presidency, once in 1924 with the famous "Happy Warrior" speech and again in 1928. This caused Will Rogers to quip in the 1932 campaign that FDR was the man "who has spent a lifetime nominating Al Smith." Roosevelt successfully honed his campaign and speaking techniques in the New York gubernatorial races of 1928 and 1930. During his governorship, FDR began to use speech writers, and he also initiated his fireside chats to the people of New York in order to counter the conservative press in upstate New York. Both of these practices were to serve him well in the White House. During these pre–White House years, Roosevelt had developed and matured his speaking and campaigning skills, and they in turn propelled him to increasingly important political offices. When he ran for the presidency in 1932, he had already mastered the persuasive techniques of the orator-politician.

FDR AS PRESIDENTIAL PERSUADER

President Roosevelt was an archetype for modern rhetorical presidents. He changed the presidency from a posture of relative aloofness from the people to one of intimacy with the people. Although he was not the first chief executive to use speech writers, his successful reliance on them led to the institutionalization of the presidential speech-writing team. Henceforth professionals would help the president to persuade the people. Although some captious critics might cavil at presidential reliance on so-called ghostwriters, FDR was open about using them, and he sought to deceive no one. Samuel Rosenman, who had signed on as a speech writer for the 1928 gubernatorial campaign, continued in a central role throughout most of Roosevelt's presidency. Other writers included Harry Hopkins, Robert Sherwood, Donald Richberg, Tommy Corcoran, Archibald MacLeish; and Louis Howe usually had his hand in the process, too, until his death in 1936.

Although not the first president to speak over the radio, FDR was quick to recognize radio's potential while he was governor of New York; and thereafter the rise of radio and Roosevelt were inextricably linked. President Roosevelt realized that the radio, as an instrument of the rhetorical presidency, allowed him to persuade his national listeners in the immediacy and intimacy of their homes. Consequently he took to the airwaves for his important speeches, and he used the fireside chats, which he had developed at Albany, to reinforce his image as a forthright, optimistic, and genuinely caring presidential communicator. Indicative of his persuasive acumen was the fact that Roosevelt presciently perceived that television—the 1939 New York World's Fair was the occasion for the first presidential address to a television audience—had an even greater persuasive potential than radio, but World War II cut short television's development and his utilization of it.

Although not the first president to hold press conferences, FDR was a pioneer in elevating them to high persuasive-political art. He manipulated the press conferences in order to guide the press, as best he could, to print the news to his liking. In his first press conference, the president told the members of the press that they could not quote him directly, that they would be given background information that could not be attributed to the White House, and that certain information would be off the record, confidential information that could not be shared. Of course, there were times when the president desired to be quoted, and he made those instances clear to the reporters. For instance, in his press conference on the Supreme Court in 1935, his famous "horse and buggy definition of interstate commerce" comment gave a searing condemnation, in language the layman could understand, against a conservative Court. Another efficacious example of his press conference artistry was the language of his famous "neighbor's garden hose" analogy for Lend-Lease in 1940, with which he successfully obfuscated the intricate legalities of his proposal to help Great Britain before U.S. entry into World War II. His availability to the press, blended with candor, coyness, and circumlocution as necessary and prudent, produced a useful symbiotic relationship for him, the press, and the American people.

The president also enjoyed a symbiotic relationship with the motion picture newsreels, the precursor of the television news broadcast. Ensconced in the movie palaces of the day, the average American could easily empathize with the larger-than-life image on the screen as FDR portrayed buoyancy that the New Deal would solve the depression, compassion for the ordinary citizen, anger at the moneychangers, and nothing but contempt for Mussolini and Hitler. In sum, FDR installed the modern presidential practice of using the media to appeal directly to the people for their support of his legislative programs in the Congress.

He institutionalized a persuasive troika: professional writers who helped him draft his messages and fireside chats; direct presidential radio addresses, in conjunction with the newsreels, to the nation; and presidential press conferences to manage the reception of his persuasive communications. These presidential persuasive practices are still in evidence in the Oval Office, and FDR's use of them remains a benchmark by which to judge its successive incumbents and practitioners of the rhetorical presidency.

As a political communicator, Franklin Roosevelt excelled in all of the genres of presidential discourse. The First Inaugural Address—with its famous "the only thing we have to fear is fear itself" statement—was his best Inaugural, certainly one of the best speeches he ever delivered, and probably one of the top three or four presidential Inaugurals. In that speech, he successfully used three rhetorical devices. First, he used the scapegoat device to blame the bankers and Wall Street for the depression: "The rulers of the exchange of mankind's goods have failed through their own stubbornness and their own incompetence, have admitted their failure, and have abdicated. Practices of the unscrupulous money-changers stand indicted in the court of public opinion, rejected by the hearts and minds of men." In order to rally the country behind his leadership, he next deployed military metaphors: "If we are to go forward, we must move as a trained and loyal army, willing to sacrifice for the good of a common discipline, because without such discipline no progress can be made, no leadership becomes effective. . . . With this pledge taken, I assume unhesitatingly the leadership of this great army of our people dedicated to a disciplined attack upon our common problems." Third, he waved the carrot and stick before the Congress in order to motivate it to pass his New Deal program: "But in the event that the Congress shall fail to take one of these two courses, in the event that the national emergency is still critical, I shall not evade the clear course of duty that will then confront me. I shall ask the Congress for the one remaining instrument to meet the crisis: broad executive power to wage a war against the emergency, as great as the power that would be given to me if we were in fact invaded by a foreign foe."

Many critics would also denote as a great address his Second Inaugural, with its famous phrase, "I see one third of a nation ill-housed, ill-clad, ill-nourished," which communicated the president's belief that the New Deal had accomplished much but that more would be mounted in his second term. In his Third Inaugural, for which he wrote in longhand a first draft of two and one-half pages, he compared the nation's needs to the mind, body, and spirit of humanity. One also finds a revealing political philosophy in the short but personally eloquent Fourth Inaugural, wherein Roosevelt reaffirmed his faith in "our essential democracy," quoted Ralph Waldo Emerson on friendship, and used Dr. Endicott Peabody's (Peabody was FDR's headmaster at Groton) philosophy that "civilization itself . . . always has an upward trend" in order to communicate to the nation that he had led it upward through peace and war.

Among his presidential nomination speeches, the 1932 one, in which he symbolically flew to Chicago personally to address the Democratic convention in order to pledge a New Deal to the country, and the 1936 one, in which he again declared war on the ''economic royalists'' by reminding the nation that ''this generation of Americans has a rendezvous with destiny,'' are models of that genre. In the 1940 campaign, Roosevelt poked fun at ''Martin, Barton, and Fish''—three Republican congressmen who had voted against the repeal of the embargo of arms for the Allies—at Madison Square Garden in New York, and when he appeared at Boston two days later, he had only to mention ''Martin'' and the audience yelled ''Barton and Fish'' in response. The paramount example of his campaign oratory was his 1944 Teamsters' Union speech wherein he deadpanned Republican attacks, when he said ''now include my little dog, Fala [much audience laughter and applause]. . . . I don't resent attacks . . . but Fala *does* resent them [prolonged audience applause and laughter]. You know, Fala is Scotch [more audience uproar].'' FDR was so successful with the Fala technique that Republican Senator Richard Nixon, running for the vice-presidency in 1952, borrowed the ploy in his famous ''My Side of the Story'' speech, in which he referred to his dog, Checkers (by which name that speech is often called), to evoke sympathy for himself and his family. Other examples of FDR's campaigning include the 1936 speech in Chautauqua, New York, in which he stated, with utmost sincerity and gravity, ''I have seen war. . . . I hate war,'' and the never-to-be-forgotten, ''We have only just begun to fight'' speech at Madison Square Garden in New York City during the same campaign.

In his function as the nation's First Orator, FDR delivered some monumental and moving addresses. In 1941, he prophetically pledged to the nation and what was left of the free world his ''Four Freedoms'': freedom of speech and expression, freedom to worship God, freedom from want, and freedom from fear. ''Yesterday, December 7, 1941—a date which will live in infamy'' began his war message to Congress. He eloquently employed anaphora—''Last night Japanese forces attacked''—to emphasize Japan's concerted and premeditated attack on American lives and interests. He emotionally ended his speech with one of his great perorations: ''With the confidence in our armed forces, with the unbounding determination of our people, we will gain the inevitable triumph, so help us God.''

Yet for all of his rhetorical masterpieces and persuasive accomplishments, President Roosevelt was unsuccessful in three major instances in which he undertook to change the nation's prevailing attitudes and beliefs. First, he made a serious blunder in the so-called attempt to pack the Supreme Court of the United States in 1937. He bungled the rhetorical timing of the announcement by literally springing it on the Congress and the nation without laying his usual and necessary prior persuasive groundwork; he created a bogus issue centering on the ''nine old men,'' which backfired almost immediately by angering both liberals and conservatives; and then he had to change the attack by finally affirming the real issue of a conservative Court that was thwarting liberal New Deal legislation by judicial fiat. But it was in vain. Even the eloquence of one of his greatest speech conclusions in the Victory dinner address—complete with parallelism at the beginning and ending of seven rhetorical clauses, "Here are . . . NOW," which was delivered with consummate timing and phrasing—and his more reasoned approach in the fireside chat on the judiciary, which he delivered five days later, failed to obtain passage of his judicial reorganization bill. In the latter speech he told his radio audience that "the Court has been acting not as a judicial body, but as a policy-making body," explained the bill with the assertion that "this plan will save our national Constitution from hardening of the judicial arteries," and defended himself against his accusers with the promise that "you who know me can have no fear that I would tolerate the destruction by any branch of government of any part of our heritage of freedom." Consequently he lost his air of invincibility, some of his persuasive credibility, and much of his ability to control the Congress. Second, FDR was unsuccessful in the series of campaign speeches he gave during the 1938 purge. His efforts to rid the Democratic party of conservatives who would not support his legislative program did not work. As a function of the rhetorical presidency, it is evidently acceptable for the chief executive to exhort the people on national matters but not to meddle in local affairs and politics. Third, while Roosevelt strove emotionally and eloquently in the late 1930s to garner public opinion for U.S. intervention in Europe, he could not bring this about. In great addresses like the 1937 quarantine speech at Chicago, in which he used that metaphor to try to contain "the epidemic of world lawlessness," in the pathos of the 1939 fireside chat on war in Europe, and in "the hand that held the dagger has struck it into the back of its neighbor"— FDR delivered this line in almost perfect iamb—speech at Charlottesville, Virginia, against Mussolini in 1940, he valiantly tried, but failed, to persuade the people. In fairness to Roosevelt, though, a strong case can be made that his failure to convince Americans of the dangers of isolationism lay with their unwillingness to be persuaded rather than with their president's earnestness or rhetorical talents. Aristotle, in his *Rhetoric*, did recognize, as he argued metaphorically in such cases, "that it is possible to give excellent treatment even to those who can never enjoy sound health."

Consideration is also due Roosevelt's effective delivery skills. The public reaction file, running the gamut from humorous to caustic letters and telegrams, attests to the fact that his delivery—whether in person, over the radio, or in the important movie newsreels—always affected his audiences, and in most cases the effect was positive. Roosevelt had a good tenor voice, and he consciously managed and modulated it for vocal variety and emphasis. A Kentucky newspaperman was moved by FDR's voice in the 1936 acceptance speech: "Your voice carried more conviction, more strength, more confidence than at any time since the spring of 1933." FDR used only moderate changes in pitch and volume (as juxtaposed with the dramatic cadences and often shrill tones of the Longs, Coughlins, and Hitlers of his time), and his phrasing of important words and thoughts was superb. By broadcast standards of 175 words per minute (wpm), FDR's rates of 120 wpm for the fireside chats and 100 wpm for his major addresses were too slow; however, his measured pace was calculated to communicate trust, authority, and control to his listeners, attributes that were requisite images for a depression-era chief executive and a war-era commander in chief. A woman from Long Island, New York, wrote that FDR's second fireside chat "was like the intimate confidence of a father to his family" and after the 1939 fireside chat on war in Europe, a man from Omaha, Nebraska, wrote to FDR: "The calm tone of the address in the face of great world emotion, as well as the logic of the speech, were truly remarkable".

Notwithstanding his constraint of platform movement at the podium due to his polio handicap, FDR could and did gesture often and vigorously with his arms and to some degree with his upper torso. His best and most effective gestures were the tilt, nod, and punctuation of an ever expressive facial visage. Two examples illustrate the range of FDR's facial gestures. On March 4, 1933, the president was grim and unsmiling, and he often thrust out his chin in order to communicate a certain pugnaciousness that reinforced the militant language of his First Inaugural Address. On the other end of the spectrum was the president's playful performance before undergraduates at the University of North Carolina at Chapel Hill for his famous "Grilled Millionaire" speech on December 5, 1938, when he screwed up his face—to the great delight of his college audience—to look like an ogre when he said: "You undergraduates who see me for the first time have read your newspapers and heard on the air that I am, at the very least, an ogre . . . and that I breakfasted every morning on a dish of 'grilled millionaire.' '' His audiences always responded to his earnestness, sincerity, and dynamism—and his playful sense of humor when he was in the mood—with applause and laughter, at his political opponents' expense.

Roosevelt prepared his speeches carefully in close conjunction with his speech team. The drafts of his speeches are replete with Roosevelt's personal emendations and yield valuable insights into his thinking on political matters at important junctures in U.S. history. By closely examining the progression of speech drafts with an eye toward what FDR dictated and deleted, one can reach reasonable conclusions concerning his political philosophy and practice. For instance, the point has been demonstrated that the rhetorical techniques of the scapegoat, military metaphor, and carrot and stick, which were used in FDR's First Inaugural Address, were his. He also personally penned the famous phrase, "I see one-third of a nation ill-housed, ill-clad, ill-nourished," on the second draft of his Second Inaugural Address. On the other hand, one can make the case that a significant reason for FDR's persuasive successes with his audiences was due to his intimate involvement with his speech team in the speech composition process. A case in point is his Fourth Inaugural Address, for which he selected Robert Sherwood's submitted draft over Rosenman's and MacLeish's submissions because Sherwood had more closely followed FDR's dictated thoughts. Roosevelt personally edited the drafts from 779 words down to 560 in order to keep the speech and ceremonies brief in recognition of wartime exigencies. The words of the speech were ultimately Roosevelt's; consequently, he knew the address so well that he could concentrate on delivering an oratorical masterpiece.

Among political orators and among presidential communicators, FDR historically stands in the first rank, an equal among equals. He was an effective rhetorical president. Through his oratory, he talked and led a peacetime nation into a war on the depression, and he talked and marshaled a wartime nation into a war on the Axis powers. He accomplished these feats with a talented team of speech writers, but Roosevelt deserves considerable credit for his own contributions to the process. He continued the traditional practice of addressing the mass live audience, but he wisely realized he could reach the entire national audience by radio, and his political opponents wisely feared his abilities to persuade over this direct and intimate medium. He recognized that the press often filtered or distorted presidential discourse for editorial and political reasons, so he countered by attempting to flatter, cajole, and orchestrate the news media in his press conferences. His was a considerable oratorical achievement.

INFORMATION SOURCES

Research Collections and Collected Speeches

Researchers can rely on the resources of the Franklin D. Roosevelt Library, Hyde Park, New York. Oratorical-political researchers will find the following sources particularly useful: successions of speech drafts up to the final reading copies on which FDR often made even last-minute emendations; sound recordings and motion picture films of his addresses and fireside chats; an indexed photographic file; and the public reaction mail, which uniquely gauges FDR's persuasive impact on his national audiences. Additionally, the library maintains valuable secondary materials, such as insightful oral histories, valuable diaries from the New Dealers, theses and dissertations on FDR and his era, and helpful finding aids to the other pertinent holdings.

American Rhetoric from Roosevelt to Reagan: A Collection of Speeches and Critical Essays. Edited by Halford Ross Ryan. Prospect Heights, Ill.: Waveland Press, 1983.   ARRR

Nothing to Fear. Edited by B. D. Zevin. Boston: Houghton Mifflin, 1946.   NF

Roosevelt, Franklin D. *Complete Press Conferences of Franklin D. Roosevelt.* Introduction by Jonathan Daniels. 12 vols. New York: Da Capo Press, 1972.

———. *The Public Papers and Addresses of Franklin D. Roosevelt.* Edited by Samuel I. Rosenman. 13 vols. New York: Random House, 1938–1950.   PPA

The World's Great Speeches. Edited by Lewis Copeland and Lawrence W. Lamm. 3d enlarged ed. New York: Dover Publications, 1973.   WGS

Selected Critical Studies

Benson, Thomas W. "Inaugurating Peace: Franklin D. Roosevelt's Last Speech." *Speech Monographs* 36 (1969): 138–47.

Brandenburg, Earnest. "The Preparation of Franklin D. Roosevelt's Speeches." *Quarterly Journal of Speech* 35 (1949): 214–21.

Brandenburg, Earnest, and Braden, Waldo W. "Franklin D. Roosevelt." In *A History and Criticism of American Public Address*. Edited by Marie Kathryn Hochmuth. New York: Longmans, Green, 1955.

Crowell, Laura. "Building the 'Four Freedoms' Speech." *Speech Monographs* 22 (1955): 266–83.

Ryan, Halford Ross. "Roosevelt's First Inaugural: A Study of Technique." *Quarterly Journal of Speech* 65 (1979): 137–49.

———. "Roosevelt's Fourth Inaugural Address: A Study of Its Composition." *Quarterly Journal of Speech* 67 (1981): 157–66.

———. "Roosevelt's Second Inaugural Address." Paper presented at the annual meeting of the Speech Communication Association, Washington, D.C., 1983.

———. "Roosevelt's Third Inaugural Address." Paper presented at the annual meeting of the Speech Communication Association, Chicago, Illinois, 1986.

Stelzner, Hermann G. " 'War Message,' December 8, 1941: An Approach to Language." *Speech Monographs* 33 (1966): 419–37.

Winfield, B. H. "Franklin D. Roosevelt's Efforts to Influence the News during his First Term Press Conferences." *Presidential Studies Quarterly* 11 (1981): 198–99.

Selected Biographies

Alsop, Joseph. *FDR 1882–1945*. New York: Viking Press, 1982.

Burns, James MacGregor. *Roosevelt: The Lion and the Fox*. New York: Harcourt, Brace, 1956.

Freidel, Frank. *Franklin D. Roosevelt Launching the New Deal*. Boston: Little, Brown, 1973.

Leuchtenburg, William E. *Franklin D. Roosevelt and the New Deal: 1932–1940*. New York: Harper & Row, 1963.

Miller, Nathan. *FDR, An Intimate History*. Garden City, N.Y.: Doubleday, 1983.

Rosenman, Samuel I. *Working with Roosevelt*. New York: Harper and Brothers, 1952.

Sherwood, Robert E. *Roosevelt and Hopkins: An Intimate History*. New York: Harper and Brothers, 1948.

Tully, Grace. *F. D. R. My Boss*. New York: Charles Scribner's Sons, 1949.

CHRONOLOGY OF MAJOR SPEECHES

See "Research Collections and Collected Speeches" for source codes.

Acceptance speech, Chicago, July 2, 1932, *NF*, pp. 1–12; *PPA, 1928–1932*, pp. 647–59.

First Inaugural Address, Washington, D.C., March 4, 1933; *ARRR*, pp. 1–5 (this text is authoritative and includes audience applause); *NF*, pp. 12–17; *PPA 1933*, pp. 11–16; *WGS*, pp. 508–12.

Acceptance speech, Philadelphia, Pennsylvania, June 27, 1936; *PPA, 1936*, pp. 230–36.

Second Inaugural Address, Washington, D.C., January 20, 1937; *NF*, pp. 87–92; *PPA 1937*, pp. 1–6.

Victory dinner address, Washington, D.C., March 4, 1937; *PPA, 1937*, pp. 113–21.

Fireside chat on the reorganization of the judiciary, Washington, D.C., March 9, 1937; *NF*, pp. 94–104; *PPA, 1937*, pp. 122–33.

Quarantine speech, Chicago, October 5, 1937; *NF*, pp. 111–15; *PPA, 1937*, pp. 406–13.

"Grilled millionaire" speech, Chapel Hill, North Carolina, December 5, 1938; *PPA, 1938*, pp. 613–21.

Commencement address, University of Virginia, Charlottesville, Virginia, June 10, 1940; *PPA 1940*, pp. 259–64.

Four Freedoms speech, Washington, D.C., January 6, 1941; *NF*, pp. 258–76; *PPA 1941*, pp. 663–72.

Third Inaugural Address, Washington, D.C., January 20, 1941; *NF*, pp. 268–71; *PPA, 1941*, pp. 3–6.

War message to Congress, Washington, D.C., December 8, 1941; *ARRR*, pp. 23–34; *NF*, pp. 302–03; *PPA 1941*, pp. 514–15; *WGS*, pp. 531–32.

Fourth Inaugural Address, Washington, D.C., January 20, 1945; *ARRR*, pp. 25–26 (this text is authoritative); *NF*, pp. 438–39; *PPA 1944–45*, pp. 523–25.

THEODORE ROOSEVELT
(1858–1919), Twenty-sixth president of the United States

WALDO W. BRADEN

Theodore Roosevelt was a many-sided personality who packed his life full of activities and accomplishments. Albert Shaw called him the "most influential and representative American of his generation." In addition to holding political office, he won recognition as author, journalist, naturalist, historian, rancher, big game hunter, explorer, and diplomat. Born in New York City on October 27, 1858, Roosevelt came from a well-to-do family. He graduated from Harvard University in 1880 and was elected to Phi Beta Kappa, but he received no training in public speaking.

During the first phase of his career prior to 1900, he rose to prominence, serving for three terms in the New York State legislature (1881–1884), as a delegate to the National Republican Convention (1884), as an unsuccessful candidate for the mayor of New York City (1886), as a member of the U.S. Civil Service Commission (1889–1895), as a Commissioner of the New York City Police Department (1895–1897), as assistant secretary of the navy (1897–1898), as a colonel in the Volunteer Cavalry (Rough Riders) in the Spanish-American War (1898), and as governor of New York (1898–1900).

Before 1900 he had published thirteen titles, including two biographies, five books on hunting, and his famous *Winning of the West* (4 volumes).

The second phase of TR's career (1900–1908) opened with his election as vice-president to William McKinley (1900). When the president was assassinated, Roosevelt succeeded to the presidency on September 14, 1902, and then won a second term (1904). He made vigorous statements on trustbusting, U.S. responsibilities abroad, the building of the Panama Canal, and the U.S. role as a world power.

The third phase of his busy career (1908–1915) started with a big game hunting trip to Africa and lecturing abroad. In 1912 he espoused the progressive cause and subsequently ran for president on a third party ticket (Bull Moose) in 1912, polling over 4 million votes.

During the anticlimactic fourth and final phase of his life, Roosevelt talked about preparedness and unsuccessfully sought a command in the U.S. Army in France.

TR AS PREACHER MILITANT

TR often referred to himself as a preacher, to his speeches as "lay sermons," and to the presidency as a "bully pulpit." In a lecture at Harvard on December

14, 1910, he stated that the orator's duty was "to preach realizable ideals." Typical of what Roosevelt presented at public ceremonies, fairs, and university functions are two of his most widely quoted and anthologized lay sermons: "The Strenuous Life," delivered April 10, 1899 to the Hamilton Club of Chicago, and "The Man with the Muckrake," delivered April 14, 1906, at the laying of the cornerstone for the Congressional Office Building, Washington, D.C.

The first speech, delivered while he was governor, expresses his basic philosophy: "I wish to preach, not the doctrine of ignoble ease, but the doctrine of the strenuous life, the life of toil and effort, of labor and strife." Speaking to an exclusive midwestern Republican club, he adroitly shaped his presentation to fit the predispositions of his listeners, many of them self-made businessmen who believed the Horatio Alger myth. Operating from a two-valued orientation, he denounced "slothful ease," "timid peace," and "the cloistered life." He said:

The timid man, the lazy man, the man who distrusts his country, the over-civilized man, who has lost the great fighting, masterful virtues, the ignorant man, and the man of dull mind, whose soul is incapable of feeling the mighty lift that thrills, "stern men with empires in their brains"—all these, of course, shrink from seeing the nation undertake its new duties; shrink from seeing us build a navy and an army adequate to our needs; shrink from seeing us do our share of the world's work, by bringing order out of chaos in the great, fair tropic islands from which the valor of our soldiers and sailors has driven the Spanish flag. These are the men who fear the strenuous life.

Honor, hard work, and manliness, virtues that he often lauded, brought "victorious effort," "virile qualities," and "the stern strife of life." Herein he played upon motive appeals that encouraged his listeners to support his major premises concerning a buildup of the armed forces, the construction of a canal, and an advancing imperialism. "If we seek merely swollen, slothful ease and ignoble peace," the Rough Rider warned, "stronger peoples will pass us by, and will win for themselves the domination of the world." He used a line similar to what Albert J. Beveridge argued in his famous "The March of the Flag."

By far his best-known speech is the second, which takes its striking title and theme from John Bunyan's *The Pilgrim's Progress*. Made while he was president, he blasted the yellow journalists who in his view had become excessive in their exposure of corruption. "The man who never does anything else [muckrake], who never thinks or speaks or writes, save of his feats with the muckrake, speedily becomes, not a help, but one of the most potent forces for evil," said the militant preacher. This presentation showed masterful rhetorical technique. In his presentation, he appeared to be the relentless foe of the muckraker, and this feint may have misled the superficial listener; however, he wanted to avoid the extremes of the muckrakers. "Any excess is almost sure to invite reaction," he said. To achieve his goal he qualified his denouncements through some rhetorical subtleties in order to preserve what A. C. Baird characterized as a "nondemagogic and intermediate stand," a tendency often implanted in the Roosevelt rhetoric.

His staying on middle ground is often shown in his use of cleverly constructed compound and complex sentences that lessen the sting of his censure. For example, he argued: "The men with the muckrake are often indispensable to the well being of society; but only if they know when to stop raking muck." In the element following the coordinating conjunction *but*, he altered his position. Some additional examples show TR's strategy:

Expose the crime and hunt down the criminal; but remember that . . . if it is attacked in a sensational . . . fashion, the attack may do more damage . . . than the crime itself.

The fool who has not sense to discriminate between what is good and what is bad is well nigh as dangerous as the man who does discriminate and yet chooses the bad.

Bad though a state of hysterical excitement is, . . . yet a sodden acquiescence in evil is even worse.

We can no more and no less afford to condone evil in the man of capital than evil in the man of no capital.

The forces that tend for evil are great and terrible, but the forces of truth and love . . . are also stronger than ever before.

These sentences also suggest Roosevelt's delight in aphorisms. The preacher almost assumed the pose of the prophet of old, giving out moral instruction to his followers, a pose that never seemed to embarrass self-confident Teddy.

What is often ignored in this bifurcated speech is the second part, which made pleas for "a progressive tax on all fortunes" and for "more regulation of all large corporations engaged in interstate business." The power of the analogy between muckrakers and "the wild preachers of unrest and discontent" caused many to overlook Roosevelt's constructive case. It is possible that TR, as a skillful rhetorian, may have welcomed this misdirection of focus.

On March 4, 1905, after winning by the largest popular vote in history, Roosevelt made a formal inaugural address, speaking with manuscript in hand, for no more than six or seven minutes. The large crowd, probably more interested in seeing the president than hearing him, endured the threatening dark day, and he respected the precedents of the inaugural ceremonies; consequently he appeared conventional and subdued. Nevertheless, his tenor of optimism suggested that he had not forsaken his "bully pulpit," telling his fellow Americans how fortunate they were to have achieved "so large a measure of well-being and of happiness." Pursuing a hortatory objective, he returned to a recurring theme concerning the American mission, developed earlier by Daniel Webster, Abraham Lincoln, and others: "Upon the success of our experiment much depends, not only as regards our own welfare, but as regards the welfare of mankind. If we fail, the cause of free self government throughout the world will rock to its foundations, and therefore our responsibility is heavy, to ourselves, to the world as it is today, and to the generations yet unborn.'' His short speech was adequate for the occasion but not one of his better efforts.

Any assessment of Roosevelt public addresses must consider his campaigning, which showed his vigor and openness as well as his ability to relate face to face to thousands. In 1912, no longer restrained by ties to the Republicans and his conservative friends, he turned his enthusiasms to popular reform. He campaigned as a presidential candidate on the Progressive ticket (Bull Moose). Before 16,000 cheering supporters in Madison Square Garden in New York City, October 30, 1912, he concluded the canvass with ''a farewell manifesto'' (''The Purpose of the Progressive Party''), which turned into more of a statement of his own political philosophy than a definition of party issues. ''We war against the forces of evil, and the weapons we use are the weapons of right,'' said the moralizing crusader. Once more in a statement of a familiar theme, he said, ''The doctrines we preach reach back to the Golden Rule and the Sermon on the Mount. They reach back to the Commandments delivered at Sinai. All that we are doing is to apply those doctrines in the shape necessary to make them available for meeting the living issues of our own day.'' Roosevelt declared the Progressive platform ''a covenant with the people of the United States.'' (Notice the religious implications of the use of the word *covenant*.) In his sermonizing, he made the campaign a holy struggle between ''righteousness'' and ''evil.'' Implying that he stood on high—almost sacred—ground, he claimed for himself (and the Progressives) morality, truth, justice, honesty, and ''real brotherhood,'' and to the opposition he attributed selfishness, arrogance, envy, greed, privilege, lawlessness, and treachery.

Another side of the speaking of TR is evident in a eulogy that he delivered February 9, 1909, at the laying of a cornerstone and the dedication of a structure to cover the Lincoln cabin at Hodgenville, Kentucky. Contrary to his usual practice, he read this one from manuscript. In less than ten minutes, Roosevelt offered a moving picture of the rail-splitter, one of his favorite sources:

He [Lincoln] grew to know greatness, but never ease. Success came to him, but never happiness, save that which springs from doing well a painful and vital task. Power was his, but not pleasure. The furrows deepened on his brow, but his eyes were undimmed by either hate or fear. His gaunt shoulders were bowed, but his steel thews never faltered as he bore for a burden the destinies of his people. . . . As the red years of war went by they found him ever doing his duty in the present, ever facing the future with fearless front, high of heart, and dauntless of soul. Unbroken by hatred, unshaken by scorn, he worked and suffered for the people. Triumph was his at the last; and barely had he tasted it before murder found him, and the kindly, patient, fearless eyes were closed forever.

Roosevelt's short, graphic sentences showed his mastery of direct but emotional language and polished style. Quoted in full in the leading newspapers, this sincere statement about the ''mightiest of the mighty men who mastered the mighty days'' is one of Roosevelt's most eloquent speeches.

Attracting interest abroad, Roosevelt was a welcome lecturer before university audiences at Oxford, Cambridge, Berlin, and the Sorbonne. Before the Cambridge Union on May 26, 1910, he fit into the jovial atmosphere of the debating society. What he ended up doing was preaching on the theme that success depended upon developing character. "You don't need any remarkable skill," he told the British students. "All you need is to possess ordinary qualities, but to develop them to a more than ordinary degree." Unlike in many of his other speeches, he included in this one apt illustrations.

A distinctive characteristic of Roosevelt's rhetoric was his delight in platitudes and moral imperatives, supported with no more than his own ethos. To his admirers, statements such as the following were accepted without question:

"The liar is no whit better than the thief."

"An epidemic of discriminate assault upon character does no good; but very great harm."

"The foundation stone of the national life is, and ever must be, the high individual character of the average citizen."

"The men who wishes to do his duty . . . must be imbued through and through with the spirit of Americanism."

"Tame submission to foreign aggression of any kind is a mean and unworthy thing."

"Preparation for war is the surest guaranty for peace."

"We hold work not as a curse, but as a blessing."

"The poorest way to face life is to face it with a sneer."

"To admire the gift of oratory without regard to the moral quality behind the gift is to do wrong to the republic."

Through his speeches, he lauded honesty, hard work, manliness, efficiency, and achievement, as well as Americanism (nationalism), imperialism, Christianity, common sense, and what the founding fathers and particularly Washington and Lincoln had stood for. He seldom missed opportunities to preach the Christian virtues and the Ten Commandments.

Although he seldom strayed far from his pulpit, Roosevelt was often adroit in walking a narrow line and in balancing his idealism with practical politics. "The citizen must have high ideals," he told listeners at the Sorbonne on April 23, 1910, "and yet he must be able to achieve them in practical fashion." "In practical fashion" to Roosevelt meant keeping a working understanding with political bosses, men of great wealth, and business leaders even at moments when he supposedly was wielding the big stick. Critics have censured him for inconsistency in such matters.

Not a trained speaker, Roosevelt perfected his rhetorical skills in hundreds of speeches in the New York assembly, on the campaign trail, on the lecture circuit, and as president. Because he appeared so often, many of his speeches were impromptu or extemporaneous, particularly in the canvasses of 1900, 1904, and 1912; consequently, some critics have suggested that he talked too often and without deep thought. However, he did prepare his important addresses with care. After outlining one, he might write it out in his own hand or dictate it to a stenographer and submit it to one or more advisers. He had an excellent vocabulary and facility in his writing. He might rewrite and revise a manuscript several times. Even at his busiest times he did not turn to ghost writers.

In his mature period, he sometimes spoke from manuscript, but he was never fastened to what he had written, and seldom did he simply read a manuscript. He did not attempt a grand manner; instead he was often informal and direct, sincere, confident and earnest. He did not have a pleasant voice, but he could be heard and understood by large gatherings. One authority has called him a "conversational, yet dynamic, vigorous speaker."

Paramount in the assessment of Roosevelt's public address is to account for certain extrinsic persuasive factors that increased the motive power of his rhetoric. He arrived in the public eye at the right time to gain the admiration of many Americans who sought a leader to quiet their anxieties about the closing of the frontier, the growth of big cities, the emergence of great monopolies, the planting of the flag on farflung islands, and responsibilities of being a world power. They wanted someone to answer the alarming voices of industrialists, labor leaders, reformers, journalists (muckrakers), suffragists, socialists, and even anarchists.

They found Teddy attractive because of his stable background (a good family man), his self-assurance, his often boyish bravado, and his open stands on morality, American ideals, and the work ethic.

Cartoons, photographs, and newsreels contributed to his appeal. Well built, stocky, and active, he appeared in aggressive stances, standing in center stage, leaning forward, making sweeping gestures, defying the opposition. He was easy to caricature with his broad smile, big round face, great glasses, open mouth, big teeth, and broad-brimmed hats. Cartoonists characterized him as a gladiator, a Samson, a lion hunter, a cowboy, a military hero—in uniform, beating a drum, leading a parade, riding a horse or even an elephant, charging up San Juan Hill, fighting off Indians, or roping steers. He was always shown in motion, usually orating, but seldom in repose. In one famous drawing, mighty Teddy was holding a great globe of the world in one hand and waving a big club in the other.

Roosevelt's literary and rhetorical output was tremendous, including numerous magazine articles and editorials (more than 2,000 titles). His collected works filled twenty volumes, which preserved 160 speeches. Constantly on the public platform, he was in demand as a campaigner, a lecturer, and an occasional speaker. During the summer and fall of his 1900 campaign for the vice-presidency, he delivered 673 talks in 567 towns in 24 states, traveling 21,206 miles. For at least thirty years, he was perhaps the best-known American, probably facing more listeners than any other speaker of his era with the possible exception of William Jennings Bryan.

A final judgment of Roosevelt's speaking suggests that it was ephemeral. Nevertheless prior to 1915, thousands of Americans identified with this robust activist who confirmed what they wanted to believe. Perhaps their acceptance of his rhetoric tells us as much about them as the speaker. Today what he said and how he said it is likely to seem trite, stilted, simplistic, and even sentimental. Roosevelt was a powerful advocate during his active years, but he did not possess the lasting qualities of a great speaker.

INFORMATION SOURCES

Research Collections and Collected Speeches

The T. R. Roosevelt papers, including "Addresses Scrapbooks" (revision of speeches and stenographical reports), are in the Library of Congress, Washington, D.C., and Harvard University Library, Cambridge, Massachusetts.

American Public Addresses. 1740–1952. Edited by A. Craig Baird. New   APA
    York: McGraw Hill, 1956.
The Works of Theodore Roosevelt. Edited by Herman Hagedorn. National   TRW
    Edition. 20 vols. New York: Scribner's, 1926.

Selected Critical Studies

Behl, William A. "Theodore Roosevelt's Principles of Speech Preparation and Delivery."
    Speech Monographs 12 (1945): 112–22.
———. "Theodore Roosevelt's Principles of Invention." *Speech Monographs* 14 (1947):
    93–110.
Betz, Linda. "Theodore Roosevelt's 'Man with the Muckrake.' " *Central States Speech
    Journal* 20 (1969): 97–103.
Dallinger, Carl A. "Theodore Roosevelt: The Preacher Militant." In *American Public
    Address.* Edited by Loren Reid. Columbia: University of Missouri Press, 1961.
Lucas, Stephen E. "The Man with the Muck Rake." *Quarterly Journal of Speech* 59
    (1973): 452–73.
Murphy, Richard. "Theodore Roosevelt." In *A History and Criticism of American Public
    Address.* Edited by Marie K. Hochmuth. Vol. 3. New York: Longmans, Green,
    1955.
Silvestri, Vilo N. "Theodore Roosevelt's Preparedness Oratory." *Central States Speech
    Journal* 20 (1969): 178–86.

Selected Biographies

Bishop, Joseph Bucklin. *Theodore Roosevelt and His Times Shown in His Own Letters.*
    2 vols. New York: Scribner's, 1920.
Morris, Edmund. *The Rise of Theodore Roosevelt.* New York: Coward, McCann &
    Geoghegan, 1979.
Pringle, Henry F. *Theodore Roosevelt.* New York: Harcourt Brace, 1931.
Shaw, Albert. *A Cartoon History of Roosevelt's Career.* New York: Review of Reviews,
    1910.

CHRONOLOGY OF MAJOR SPEECHES

See "Research Collections and Collected Speeches" for source codes.

"The Strenuous Life," Hamilton Club, Chicago, April 10, 1899; *TRW*, 13:319–31.

Inaugural Address, Washington, D.C., March 4, 1905; *TRW*, 15:267–69.

"The Man with the Muckrake," Washington, D.C., April 14, 1906; *TRW*, 16: 415–24; *APA*, 211–19.

"Abraham Lincoln: Centenary Address," Hodgenville, Kentucky, February 12, 1909; *TRW*, 11: 210–14.

"The Purpose of the Progressive Party," New York City, October 30, 1912; *TRW*, 17: 334–40.

ANNA HOWARD SHAW
(1847–1919), woman suffrage orator

WIL A. LINKUGEL

Anna Howard Shaw's vocation was oratory. She first demonstrated speaking skill as a debator, reader, and orator at Big Rapids, Michigan, high school, which she attended at the age of twenty-four years because life in the Michigan wilderness had left little time for formal education. At Albion College, where she enrolled in 1873 after two years of secondary education, young Anna delivered temperance lectures and preached an occasional sermon from the pulpit of some liberally minded Methodist minister. She left college after two years and earned a theological degree at Boston University Seminary. Subsequently the Reverend Shaw spoke from a parish pulpit for seven years at East Dennis, Massachusetts. While there, she commuted to Boston for three years to study medicine at the Boston University Medical School and earned her M.D. in 1886. Now equipped to treat both soul and body, Dr. Shaw resigned her pastorate, not to practice medicine but to preach the gospel of women's rights. She was appointed national lecturer by the American Woman Suffrage Association in 1888, and two years later the newly merged National American Woman Suffrage Association gave her the same post. From that time forward until the adoption of the Nineteenth Amendment, Shaw was an advocate of woman's suffrage.

For forty years, Shaw proclaimed woman's right to national suffrage in every U.S. state and in most European countries. Her resonant voice and majestic presence left the English, the Swedes, and the Germans spellbound. She addressed leading U.S. colleges and universities; presided at packed meetings in Carnegie Hall and Cooper Union; and pleaded with numerous congressional committees and state legislatures. She delivered several hundred speeches a year, often speaking as many as eight times a day. In 1915 she gave 204 speeches in New York State alone. Shaw normally spoke without notes, and she adapted her message to the immediate context. Her ideas were similar, but they were arranged differently in each speech.

Shaw's woman suffrage rhetoric was characterized by a strongly logical, constructive argument that was grounded in principle; by trenchant refutation; by piquant humor; and by dynamic extemporaneous delivery.

SHAW AS WOMAN SUFFRAGE CAMPAIGNER

The belief that a "republican form of government is desirable," Shaw argued, is "the whole ground of contention that woman should be enfranchised." The consequences of woman suffrage, she said, were not germane. On January 25,

1915, she told New Jersey legislators at a hearing that "whether all women vote once they receive the ballot or no women vote, whether all women vote right or all women vote wrong, whether women will love their husbands after they vote or forsake them, whether they will neglect their children" or be loving and attentive mothers—the results of women voting, good or bad—were irrelevant to the fundamental issue. Having thus eliminated expediency as a suitable ground for arguing the woman suffrage question, she proceeded to a constructive analysis of "a republican form of government" in most of her speeches.

Shaw usually began by inquiring into the essential components of a democracy. For an answer, she turned to the writings and sayings of the founding fathers. With delight, she quoted such able advocates of democracy and the rights of man as James Otis, Benjamin Franklin, and Samuel Adams. From the words of these patriots she drew great principles describing the nature of democracy: "No taxation without representation"; "The voice of the people is the voice of God"; "Under God, the people rule." From these axioms of the founding fathers, Shaw concluded that the essence of a republican form of government was that laws were made by representatives of the people. In her Birmingham speech on April 16, 1915, she supported her reasoning with a dictionary definition. If women were people, she concluded, they should be represented in the lawmaking and governing processes.

People, as distinguished from other animals, according to Shaw, were generally acknowledged to have souls. She often inquired whether women indeed had souls. For an answer she referred to a seventh-century church council that by a very small majority had decided that women did have souls. Mirthfully Shaw remarked at San José in 1895, "How thankful we should be for that decision, for unless it had been reached there is no telling what we would have been decided to be by this time." Then with mock surprise, she pointed out that a Massachusetts court had even declared women to be "persons" in the eyes of the law in an 1883 opinion. If women were people—even persons in the eyes of the law—they should have the same political privileges as men, and to deny them their rights would abridge the fundamental principles of a republican form of government.

Shaw thus arrived at her conclusion through an argument from genus. By inquiring into the nature of democracy, she revealed that it was a form of government that guaranteed certain unalienable rights to its people; by legal definition, she established that women were persons, thus making them people; and by logical inference, she concluded that the rights of the whole must be predicated to all its parts. As long as a woman was denied the right of the ballot because she was a woman, democracy could not exist.

Shaw continued her reasoning by applying the fundamental principles of a republican form of government to existing conditions, only to discover that the status quo did not fit the definition of a democracy. Laws were being made in the United States by half the human family. Women had no voice in the government, yet they were expected to obey all its laws and pay taxes to support it. This was not democracy but tyranny—as the Revolutionary fathers had so ably proclaimed. In a true democracy, voting qualifications must be uniform. The only restrictions that the nature of democracy decreed were that people be rational beings susceptible of ideas and capable of reasoning upon them. Age or residency were qualifications that could be met by all humans alike. But sex, she said, was not a qualification, but an insuperable barrier. To place this barrier on women was by definition to place them with criminals, idiots, children, and the insane—all excluded because of irresponsibility.

Upon completing the constructive part of her argument, Shaw commonly turned to refutation of antisuffrage contentions. She relied upon three refutative techniques: the exposition of inconsistencies, the reduction of opponent's arguments to absurdity, and an attack on the evidence of the opposition.

Exposing inconsistencies was Shaw's deadliest tactic. She often maintained that the beauty of the antisuffragists' arguments was that they came in pairs: they would spend five minutes developing an argument and then proceed to present a second argument so contradictory in nature that it thoroughly refuted the first one. Once when asked to answer an antisuffrage debater, she replied, "What's the use? Divide up their literature and let them destroy themselves." With eyes twinkling, Shaw pointed out that one minute the antisuffragists contended that it was no use for women to vote for they would vote like their husbands, even if they had no husbands; in the next breath, these same speakers said that great discord, broken homes, and divorce would be the consequences of equal suffrage. A similar argument was the one that women do not want the ballot, and if it were given to them, they would not use it. Later these same antisuffragists argued that women would neglect their homes and families because of the great amount of time spent in voting—as though voting would take several hours out of every day of the year.

Shaw showed her skill in reducing an opponent's argument to absurdity by her response to the argument that women should not be given the ballot because it would be adding large numbers of ignorant voters to the electorate. To begin with, she would assert, the nation would also be adding a large number of intelligent voters; as a matter of fact, the proportion of intelligent voters among women was considerably higher than among male voters. Indeed, she thought it strange that an objection to woman suffrage should be made on the ground of female ignorance since such painstaking effort was made to protect male illiteracy. In order to avoid corruption, the Australian ballot was imported to the United States, but a voter needed to be able to read to vote this ballot. Large numbers of men, however, could not read. To remedy matters, a rooster was placed in front of the candidates of one party and an eagle in front of the other. Since all illiterate men could tell the difference between the rooster and the eagle, ignorant males were able to vote. Shaw suggested that ignorant women also could tell the difference between a rooster and an eagle, and if not, the eagle could be changed to a hen, then they certainly would be able to differentiate.

Frequently Shaw attacked the evidence of the opposition. Antisuffragists cited large numbers of statistics in support of their stand, but according to Shaw, all they proved was that liars could figure. For example, in dry states antisuffragists offered statistics to show that women would legalize liquor if given the vote, and in wet states they presented figures to show that women would vote the state dry.

Equal to refutative skill was Shaw's capacity for the clever retort in heckling situations. At Wichita in 1912, an antisuffragist informed her that suffrage was bad because her husband had voted for her. Shaw retorted that she did not believe it, since no man could vote for another and for himself too. Turning to another antisuffragist who contended that she controlled her husband's vote, Dr. Shaw said she doubted that also, for no woman who had a fool for a husband would publicly announce it. The crowd was delighted.

A rare sense of humor enlivened Dr. Shaw's refutation. Anecdotes, odd conceits, wit, and amusing comparisons abounded in her campaign speeches. Early in her career, Shaw was prone to sarcasm, but later she sweetened her satire and modified it with a gracious smile. In her eulogy of Dr. Shaw, Carrie Chapman Catt said that "as the cause gained she put aside . . . ridicule and sarcasm and assumed a gentler and sunnier humor." Instead of scolding man for his shortcomings, Shaw poked fun at him in a manner that made him laugh with her. Even the man who quivered under her blows usually smiled, applauded, and admired her. Her touch of quiet humor tended to keep even the crustiest listeners on pleasant terms with her.

Newspapers reporting Shaw's speeches as a rule noted the crispness of her logic but then called special attention to her sense of humor. *The Nebraska State Journal* of October 2, 1906 asserted, "Greater entertainment is seldom enjoyed than that delivered from the address of the Rev. Anna Howard Shaw." Certainly Shaw's infectious humor was an important goodwill device in her suffrage speeches and as such was one of her most important avenues to persuasion.

Shaw delivered most of her speeches in a lively, extemporaneous manner. Friends chided her for writing her speeches on the tips of her fingers because she named each of her fingers for her major points. The few times she delivered speeches from manuscript, her delivery suffered badly. Upon assuming the presidency of the National American Woman Suffrage Association, she wrote out and read her first two presidential addresses at the national convention, but reading so detracted from her delivery that association members asked her to speak extemporaneously thereafter. The delegates looked to Shaw's addresses for inspiration and failed to be uplifted when she read her speech.

Dr. Shaw's extemporaneous style of speaking allowed her to adapt to difficult situations. Sometimes she discarded her speech on the spur of the moment and spoke completely impromptu; on other occasions she totally reshaped her speech to fit the needs of the occasion. For example, on Shaw's first trip to Europe after graduation from theological school, she preached to a group of sailors aboard a gospel ship. The officiating clergyman, disliking women ministers, gave the Reverend Shaw an unfavorable introduction. As she rose to speak, she realized that her audience of sailors was hostile to her, so she discarded her sermon on "The Heavenly Vision" and preached on a text not found in the Bible: "Blessed are the homesick, for they shall go home." Thoughts of home, uppermost in the sailors' minds, generated favorable emotional responses. After the sermon, the homesick sailors came up to shake her hand.

The language of Shaw's woman suffrage rhetoric was that of a debater: vigorous, hard hitting, somewhat commonplace, and largely devoid of rhetorical devices. Figures of speech occasionally occurred in her speeches, but she used hardly any carefully contrived sentences or balanced phrases. Personal anecdotes, on the other hand, abounded in Shaw's rhetoric. Due to her many and varied experiences, she had a good story for every occasion. When she found a story that illustrated a point especially well, she used it repeatedly. Shaw's theological background provided her with biblical quotations, allusions to biblical characters, and scriptural phraseology. In Shaw's mind, she was carrying out a divine plan, and so she presented her message with zeal and inspiration. Movement and energy characterized her speeches; her thoughts marched along at a rapid rate.

A debate concerning genetics took place among American feminists at the turn of the century. Three points of view—best represented by Charlotte Perkins Gilman, Elizabeth Cady Stanton, and Anna Howard Shaw—prevailed. Gilman held that genetic deterioration had occurred in the female due to her restricted environment since savage society, and because woman's inferiority was the product of evolution, only through consciously directed evolution could she ultimately regain genetic equality. To this end, Gilman advocated reform measures that in her day seemed revolutionary, such as communal kitchens. Elizabeth Cady Stanton, like Gilman, grounded her argument in anthropology. She too believed that in the primitive stage, women were equal to men, but Stanton did not concur with Gilman that long ages of male dominance had caused women to deteriorate genetically; rather, women's present inferiority, Stanton said, was a cultural inheritance. Thus what to Gilman was a product of evolution, to be changed only by further consciously directed evolution, was to Stanton a product of education, to be corrected by truer education and by educational devices such as the ballot. Anna Howard Shaw, however, admitted to no such inferiority and declared herself and her sex fully equal to men. Such a belief, of course, demanded that Shaw enact equality to men in her rhetoric. She herself needed to be the proof of her argument. As Karlyn Kohrs Campbell and Kathleen Hall Jamieson point out in *Form and Genre, Shaping Rhetorical Action*, rhetorical enactment occurs when "the speaker incarnates the argument."

Nineteenth-century male-dominated society assumed fundamental and natural differences in the mental and emotional characteristics of the sexes. Men presumably reasoned—they used logic and evidence—whereas women relied on intuition. The male mind was given to rationality, the female mind to emotionality. In direct contrast to these beliefs, Shaw's force as a speaker stemmed from her inexorable logic, her ability to refute the contentions of opponents in the framework of good humor, and her extraordinary ability to extemporize her speeches fluently and effectively. Her skill as a speaker demonstrated an essential equality with men. In fact, few men ever dared to debate her. Anna Howard Shaw stood as a great bulwark against the charge that women were frail, emotional, and irrational. Her argument had the perspicuity of reason and of governmental philosophy that characterized a qualified voter.

Newspapers, large and small, praised Shaw's oratory profusely. "A magnificent speaker," "brilliant, clever, and humorous," "The foremost orator of her generation," "Queen of the platform" were typical journalistic plaudits. The *North American* of Philadelphia the day after her death proclaimed, "Dr. Shaw was without equal as an orator among women. She is generally conceded as the greatest woman speaker who ever lived. Some believed her to have been without peer in either sex among orators of her day." Carrie Chapman Catt and Nettie Shuler in *Woman Suffrage and Politics* state that Shaw won more for equal suffrage than any other advocate. Shaw herself may well have been the proof of her argument.

INFORMATION SOURCES

Research Collections and Collected Speeches

Shaw's private papers are found at Radcliffe Women's Archives, Cambridge, Massachusetts. A few texts of speeches, correspondence, and other historical documents are included in this collection. Various speeches can also be found in proceedings of international women's councils of Shaw's time, in the record of congressional hearings on woman suffrage, and in scattered newspapers. They have all been collected and edited in the two following works.

Linkugel, Wilmer A. "The Speeches of Anna Howard Shaw, Collected and   SAHS
    Edited with Introduction and Notes." Ph.D. dissertation, University
    of Wisconsin, 1960.
We Shall Be Heard. Edited by Patricia Schleppi Kennedy and Gloria   WSH
    O'Shields. Dubuque, Iowa: Kendall Hunt, 1983.

Selected Critical Essays

Linkugel, Wil A. "The Speech Style of Anna Howard Shaw." *Central States Speech Journal* 13 (1962): 171–78.
———. "The Woman Suffrage Argument of Anna Howard Shaw." *Quarterly Journal of Speech* 49 (1963): 165–74.
———. "The Distinguished War Service of Dr. Anna Howard Shaw." *Pennsylvania History* (October 1961): 372–85.
McGovern, James R. "Anna Howard Shaw: New Approaches to Feminism." *Journal of Social History* 3 (1969): 135–54.

Selected Biographies

Shaw, Anna Howard, in collaboration with Elizabeth Jordan. *A Story of a Pioneer.* New York: Harper & Brothers, 1915.

CHRONOLOGY OF MAJOR SPEECHES

See "Research Collections and Collected Speeches" for source codes.

"Woman's Right to Suffrage," Chautauqua, New York, August 8, 1892; *SAHS*, 2: 88–104.

"The Fate of Republics," Chicago, 1893; *WSH*, 197–208; *SAHS*, 2:388–401.

"The Nature of Democracy," hearing before Committee on Woman Suffrage, U.S. Senate, Washington, D.C., April 26, 1913; *SAHS*, 2:757–74.

"We Demand Equal Voting Qualifications," hearing before New Jersey Legislature, Trenton, New Jersey, January 25, 1915; *SAHS*, 2:789–816.

"The Other Half of Humanity," Birmingham, Alabama, April 16, 1915; *SAHS*, 2:207–46.

"The Fundamental Principle of a Republic," Ogdenburg, New York, June 21, 1915; *SAHS*, 2:258–92.

"A Republican Form of Government," New York State, 1917; *SAHS* 2:302–52 (exact location of where speech was given is unknown).

FULTON J. SHEEN
(1895–1979), Roman Catholic archbishop

MICHAEL P. RICCARDS

Unlike many Protestant denominations, the Catholic church in the United States has had no strong tradition of revivalism or evangelical rhetoric over the years. Part of the reason for this separate development is the church's emphasis on hierarchy and ritual and a downplaying of enthusiasm and sermonizing. Few Catholic priests have established a widespread reputation for oratorical skills, even as the ranks of the clergy grew considerably with the increasing numbers of European immigrants and their descendants. One major exception to this oversight, however, has been the career and popular appeal of Fulton J. Sheen.

Born over a hardware store in El Passo, Illinois, on May 8, 1895, Peter John Sheen grew up in a traditional Midwest family with a strong commitment to Catholicism. He later took his mother's maiden name, Fulton, as his first name and went from a local Catholic college to a seminary. Ordained a priest in 1919, Sheen did graduate work at the Catholic University, Washington, D.C., and began to preach and assume some parish responsibilities. After several years, Sheen moved to the University of Louvain in Belgium and later taught dogmatic theology in London, also preaching frequently at Westminster Cathedral and becoming friends with the great translator of the Bible, Ronald Knox. By 1923, he had earned a Ph.D. from Louvain, and two years later, the prestigious *agrégré en philosophe*. Quickly becoming recognized for his brilliance, Sheen was offered teaching positions at both Columbia and Oxford universities. Instead the young priest obeyed the order of his local bishop in Peoria, Illinois, and returned home to assume pastoral duties in a declining city parish, where he stayed until 1926. Convinced of his obedience and loyalty, the local bishop finally approved Sheen's transfer to the Catholic University in Washington. Sheen was recognized from the first as a fine popular speaker, a superb but rather aloof college lecturer, and a charming dinner guest on the capital social circuit. By 1930, he made a major move from the communion breakfasts and the seasonal sermon circuit and took responsibility for the Catholic Hour, a devotional radio show. His early use of radio encompassed a series of talks on rather traditional church themes: the doctrines of the Catholic church, the existence of God, and the inspired wisdom of the Scriptures.

In his use of radio, though, Sheen had been preceded by another priest, one whose influence was extraordinarily powerful, Father Charles Coughlin, the pastor of the Shrine of the Little Flower in Royal Oak, Michigan. In the early and mid–1930s, Coughlin had preached a message of political protest that was a mixture of Scripture, right-wing rhetoric, and often crude stereotypes. He acquired a large and faithful following and eventually became a bitter critic of the incrementalist liberal reforms of Franklin D. Roosevelt's New Deal. Under pressure from the president, Francis Cardinal Spellman secured approval from the Vatican to force Coughlin to give up his radio show.

Sheen's reputation as a public orator was quite different from Coughlin's, and he reflected in part the changing style of midcentury America and the message that its people wanted to hear. Where Coughlin was belligerent, Sheen was polished; where Coughlin spewed forth a crazy-quilt of reform and scapegoat rhetoric, Sheen carefully crafted his speeches with humor and unobtrusive learning. His popularity began in the late 1930s and reached its peak in the 1950s when a great deal of public concern focused on the threat of communism and on the even more intense private concerns of personal adjustment and professional advancement in postwar America.

SHEEN AS A TELEVISION PERSONALITY

Marshall McLuhan has written that each new medium is started by people who recapitulate the themes and techniques acquired from previous media. Sheen's radio presentations were developed from his college lectures and sermons, and some stations felt at first that his talks were too scholarly and didactic. But the response to his shows was clearly positive. In one three-month period alone, over 70,000 people wrote to the priest. For nearly twenty-two years, Sheen remained a regular with the Catholic Hour, and in that period, he traveled throughout the United States and parts of Asia, gaining recognition as a spellbinding speaker and bringing the message of Catholic orthodoxy.

Besides his radio shows, Sheen also kept up his preaching and for twenty years gave a series of highly regarded Lenten addresses each year in New York City until his final falling out with Cardinal Spellman. After World War II, Sheen became increasingly well known because of his role in the religious conversion of several prominent figures. In 1945, he was credited with the return of former communist editor Louis Budenz to the Catholic church. In 1946, Claire Boothe Luce, former congresswoman, playwright, and wife of *Time* magazine editor Henry Luce, began meeting with Sheen and later joined the Catholic church. Sheen was also involved in convincing the great violinist Fritz Kreisler to return to the Catholic church, and he personally converted auto magnate Henry Ford II and writer Heywood Broun.

By 1952, the new television industry had incorporated the major radio stars into the new medium, and Fulton Sheen began a series, "Life Is Worth Living." For the first time, large audiences saw the popular priest, and Sheen became acutely aware of the need to add a touch of the dramatic to his own superb voice. By today's standards, the long-lasting series was simply a collection of homilies given by a standing speaker for about half an hour. Sheen was placed opposite both Milton Berle, the comedian who so dominated early television that he was called "Mr. Television," and Frank Sinatra, the most durable of American singers. Rather remarkably though, Sheen proved to be a spectacular success, and the Dumont network that carried his show was overwhelmed, with mail averaging about 10,000 letters a week.

When Berle's rating sharply dropped, the comedian attributed that decline to Sheen and quipped, "If I'm going to be eased off TV by anyone, it's better that I lose to the One for Whom Bishop Sheen is speaking." In 1952, when Sheen received an Emmy award, he thanked his writers: Matthew, Mark, Luke, and John. By 1954, Sheen had a following of about 25 million viewers, an incredible number of people, considering the less than universal availability of television in American homes then and the nature of his show.

An admirer, the actress Loretta Young, called Sheen the greatest orator of his time. His presence did seem to dominate the small screen of the black and white television of that period. Aware of the importance of voice control in the medium he had chosen, Sheen rose early in the morning and delivered sermons and orations as he walked around the area in which he lived. His voice contained little of the flat cadence of his Midwest origins. Instead, in a finely modulated baritone voice, Sheen's speech seemed to betray a touch of Irish brogue with a pleasant mixture of Oxford and standard American accents. As his biographer, D. P. Noonan has noted, Sheen's range went from a "spine-tingling whisper to an Old Testament fury." Although not a tall man, Sheen wearing a bishop's cassock, a *zucchetto* or skullcap, and a flowing cape appeared much larger than his size as he presented his sermons and public speeches. As he spoke, he would touch the chain of a cross that hung around his neck and deliberately walk over to a chalkboard where he frequently wrote down major points or terms from his talk. Then out of range of the camera, a stagehand would wipe the blackboard clean; Sheen referred to him as "my little angel," and soon the angel's presence became a running gag on the show. Sheen used no other props, spoke without notes or cue cards, and timed his talks exactly for the time period at his disposal. After a commercial message given by others, the bishop returned to give a few parting remarks, usually concerning the plight of the world's poor. Although he spoke without notes, he did not speak without preparation. Sheen often gave his television lectures as homilies in Italian or French to admirers in New York City before his final presentation on Tuesday night television.

Besides his superb voice and his dramatic flourishes, Sheen's major rhetorical asset was his eyes. With deeply set, almost hypnotic eyes, Sheen's piercing expression provided him with even more of a commanding presence. Aware of this impression, he had the television studio tone down the lights aimed at his eyes, thus accentuating his fixating gaze. A first-rate scholar and long-time university professor, Sheen was able to deal with fairly complicated intellectual concepts, concentrating his strongest attacks for years on Marxism and Freudian psychoanalysis. But his presentations were laced with stories, anecdotes, and shop-worn jokes that tended to lighten the critiques. By 1955, his television program was carried by 170 stations in the United States and 17 in Canada, and his ratings were strong among Jewish and Protestant households as well as with Catholics.

He assumed in 1950 the role of national director of the Society for the Propagation of the Faith, the major Catholic missionary effort, and helped to raise some $200 million. In addition to his public presentations and fund-raising efforts, Sheen extended his popular audience with his major written works as well, including his *Life of Christ* and numerous volumes on spiritual renewal, the follies of communism, and the joys of life within a Christian perspective.

Sheen observed in one sermon on Marx that was later reprinted, "No more miserable, unhappy, distraught, and disturbed people exist in the world than communists. Did they but know it, their unhappiness is due to the Finger of God stirring their souls, making them restless." Against that ideology, he posed the vision of Jesus Christ who survived the greatest trial in history and the terrible death on the cross. "But if He is not only Man, but God, then He is primarily a Redeemer and can take the worst the world has to offer and, by the Power of God, rise above it. Thus He did teach a noble army to bear the worst this life has to offer and to regard all its trials as: the shade of His hand outstretched caressingly until the final vindication of the Final Easter of the world!"

Sheen seemed to move effortlessly from pulpit to the mass media, from being a sparkling professor of philosophy to popular star and best-selling author. In the late 1950s, however, Sheen became involved in a bitter conflict with Francis Cardinal Spellman, his one-time mentor and later jealous rival for preeminence in the American church. Sheen accused Spellman of trying to bill the Society for the Propagation of the Faith for milk supplies that Spellman had received free of charge from the U.S. government. The controversy led to a showdown meeting with Pope Pius XII, a long-time friend of Spellman and also an admirer of Sheen's worldwide reputation and fund-raising abilities. The pope's sources found that Sheen had indeed been correct in his charges. Spellman, realizing that he had lost considerable credibility with the pope, told Sheen that he would get even, no matter how long it took. Consequently Spellman forbade Sheen from continuing his famed Lenten sermons at St. Patrick's Cathedral, and he warned young priests to avoid Sheen and not to emulate his disobedient ways. By 1957, Sheen's show was discontinued—some thought because of Spellman's pressure. Two years later, however, Sheen returned to television with a group of lectures on the life of Christ and with another series in 1964, "Quo Vadis, America."

In 1966, Sheen was appointed by Pope Paul VI bishop of Rochester in upstate New York, where he tried to emulate the new humanitarianism of the previous pope, John XXIII. He proved to be a brilliant idea man but a poor administrator with little follow-through. And although he was a master of the media of television and radio, he rarely handled the press well, seeming often condescending and cool. Within three years, he announced his resignation and tearfully concluded, "I was too young for the old people, and too old for the young persons."

After his retirement, Sheen was interviewed by television reporter Mike Wallace, who asked why he had never reached higher in the Church hierarchy and been made a cardinal. Sheen paused and reflected, "I refused to pay the price," and then declined to elaborate. His biographer and other writers maintain that Sheen was referring to his refusal to submit to the will of Cardinal Spellman and to the demand that he submerge his integrity and substantial ego to the most powerful American clergyman of his day. Sheen had learned that in the contemporary church, the greatest temptation is not lust but ambition. His autobiography is less than revealing about his own turmoil and feelings during this period; it is instead an uneasy chronicle of a proud and gifted man celebrating the virtues of simple Christian humility.

Yet as an orator, Sheen remained almost without peer in his own time. He moved with remarkable ease from the pulpit and classroom to radio and finally television. And unlike most other media clergymen, his show was not consigned to Sunday morning. Sheen competed with the most popular and durable entertainers, bested them on their own ground, dealt with serious ideas seriously, and established himself as a pioneer and a major practitioner of electronic missionary work.

INFORMATION SOURCES

Research Collections and Collected Speeches

The major depository of Fulton Sheen's papers and speeches is the Colgate-Rochester Divinity School, Rochester, New York. Sheen's voice has been preserved in a series of talks that have been taped and are available from Keep the Faith, 810 Belmont Avenue, North Haledon, New Jersey 07508.

Best Sermons, 1949–50 Edition. Edited by G. Paul Butler. New York: Harper   *BS*
    and Brothers, 1949.
Fulton Sheen Reader. St. Paul: Carillon Books, 1979.   *FSR*
Sheen, Fulton J. *Footprints in a Darkened Forest.* New York: Meredith
    Press, 1967.
———. *Life Is Worth Living.* New York: McGraw-Hill, 1953–1957.   *LWL*
———. *Thinking Life Through.* New York: McGraw-Hill, 1955.   *TLT*
———. *Way to Inner Peace.* Garden City, N.Y.: Garden City Books, 1955.

Selected Critical Studies

Breig, J. "And Now a Word from His Sponsor." *U.S. Catholic* 45 (1980): 24–28.
Chandler, Daniel Ross. "Protestant Preaching and the Liberal Tradition." *Today's Speech*
    21 (1973): 39–44.
Ducharsky, D. "Bottom Line Theology." *Christianity Today* 21 (1977): 8–11.
Palmer, James C., Jr. "An Analysis of the Themes of Bishop Fulton J. Sheen's TV
    Talks." *Southern Speech Journal* 30 (1965): 223–30.

Selected Biographies

Cooney, John. *American Pope: The Life and Times of Francis Cardinal Spellman*. New York: New York Times Books, 1984.

Noonan, D. P. *Missionary with a Mike: The Bishop Sheen Story*. New York: Pageant Press, 1968.

————. *The Passion of Fulton Sheen*. New York: Dodd, Mead and Co. 1972.

————. *Treasure in Clay: The Autobiography of Fulton J. Sheen*. Garden City, N.Y.: Doubleday, 1980.

CHRONOLOGY OF MAJOR SPEECHES

See "Research Collections and Collected Speeches" for source codes.

"The Greatest Trial in History," n.d.; *TLT*, pp. 190–204.

"My Four Writers," n.d.; *FSR*, pp. 1–10.

"The Psychology of a Frustrated Soul," January 4, 1948; *BS*, pp. 28–34.

"What History the Stones of Notre Dame Cry Out," n.d.; *LWL*, 5th series, pp. 150–59.

"The Three Great Confessors of History," n.d.; *FSR*, pp. 112–22.

ALFRED EMANUEL SMITH
(1873–1944), governor of New York and U.S. presidential candidate

———————————————————————— G. JACK GRAVLEE

Born on New York City's Lower East Side, the grandson of Irish immigrants, Alfred Emanuel Smith will be remembered as the first Roman Catholic to win the nomination of a major party for president. Although an adequate student, a champion orator of city parochial schools, and a serious amateur actor, his father's untimely death in 1886 forced him to leave school to take a job supporting his mother and sister, though he had not even completed the eighth grade. Ambitious and hard working, Smith would thereafter claim that he earned his "F.F.M." degree as a graduate of the Fulton Fish Market. He became known as a talker who could negotiate his way out of difficulty, a skill particularly valuable for a young man raised in a tough neighborhood.

After his marriage in 1900, Smith became seriously interested in Democratic politics and migrated quite naturally toward Tammany Hall. He was elected to the state assembly in 1903, became Democratic leader of the assembly in 1911, and speaker in 1913. In 1915, he became New York county sheriff; in 1917, he was elected president of New York City's board of aldermen; in 1918, he became governor. After losing the governorship in the national Republican landslide of 1920, he was reelected in 1922, 1924, and 1926 before being selected the Democratic nominee for president in 1928.

Ironically Smith persuaded a reluctant Franklin Roosevelt to run successfully for the governorship in 1928 while he lost the presidency. Furthermore, it paved the way for Roosevelt's journey to the White House, a circumstance that Smith later scornfully opposed. In his first gubernatorial campaign, FDR wisely exploited the strength of Governor Smith's legislative programs: workmen's compensation, limitation of hours for women and children in industry, the forty-eight hour week, farm relief, road construction, health provisions, improved housing, pensions for the aged, increased appropriations for education, care of orphans, development of state water power resources, development of parks and parkways, and the reduction of 187 state boards into 19 organized departments. Governor Smith achieved these reform programs despite resistance from usually balking Republican-controlled legislatures. Although he vetoed such partisan measures as a loyalty test for teachers, neither his vetoes nor his appointees were ever overturned. An achiever who confronted adversity optimistically, Al Smith became forever branded by the "Happy Warrior" sobriquet that Franklin Roosevelt borrowed from Wordsworth:

> This is the happy Warrior: this is he
> That every man in arms should wish to be.

SMITH AS A POLITICAL DEBATER

With so little formal education, it was necessary for Smith to determine how he could succeed in the political arena. Early in his career, he determined to become totally informed on every pressing legislative issue. In each new office, he methodically consumed all available material on a given subject: newspaper clippings, government documents, minutes of lengthy meetings, discussions with assorted experts. No one was better acquainted with the record. He became a champion of the fact. Thus whenever he declared, "Let's look at the record," a phrase that became an enduring rhetorical trademark, he demonstrated an impressive grasp of an otherwise complicated topic. As a new member of the assembly, he attempted to study the laws passed during the previous session. He was often overwhelmed by the legalistic terminology: "In the Fulton Fish Market I could tell a hake from a haddock by the color of his eyes, but if I studied this stuff all night, I couldn't tell it from a bale of hay." He acquired the reputation of being the only member of the New York state legislature to read an appropriation bill thoroughly before voting on its contents. On one occasion, a reporter asked Governor Smith how he knew that a disputed passage was missing from a bill. "I read the bill last night," he explained. But even so, "How could you practically memorize a bill of that length?" Smith jokingly replied, "Maybe it is because my mind never was cluttered up by an education."

Smith's biographers sometimes contend that he never read a book in his life, as if to imply that he was vacuous and unsophisticated. Most public officials probably spend little time in recreational reading. Smith was no different. He devoted business hours as well as his private time to those ephemeral topics that kept the political pot boiling. But unlike many other public officials, he usually had total control of the basic facts of a subject before he rose to participate in the debate. As described in his 1930 article, "Spellbinding," he routinely saved clippings from newspapers, "particularly of speeches made by prominent men of the opposition party at times other than campaign periods." He pasted these in scrapbooks or placed them in envelopes "with a word or two written on the back to describe the contents." Then his keen memory later recalled this information at crucial moments in subsequent debates. These constituted a permanent speech file that he used repeatedly over a lifetime. Although he made different speeches on the same subject, these envelopes always were subject to revision or to be cast aside in favor of updated replacements.

Smith attributed much of his ultimate success to the value of outdoor speeches early in his career where he had to adjust to every adversity: the weather, noisy vehicles, fickle crowds, hecklers, crying babies, impromptu agendas. For the young beginner, there was no pressure to be either a great orator or an instant success. The ability to hold these audiences required a commanding voice, strong lungs, and an impressive appearance. Smith's voice, variously described as hoarse, raucous, thick, powerful, elastic, harsh, resonant, and rough, carried at least a block away. He had "a trick of bringing out the last word in a sentence like the crack of a whip." Later he made peace neither with the awkward microphones of the period, which he called "pie plates," nor with amplifiers, which gave a disconcerting "metallic, tinny sound to the voice." His gestures were free, vigorous, and sometimes awkward. He often leaned forward "like a perspiring evangelist," but on more formal occasions, his physical delivery could be charming and dignified. "To his admirers the mannerisms were endearing; to his opponents they were gross and alien." Nevertheless, his personality was so engaging that one Republican politician declared, "If everybody in New York State had a personal acquaintance with Al Smith, there would be no votes on the other side."

Smith preferred the direct clash and rebuttal of the debate format and resisted written speeches and manuscript speakers. "A speaker takes what the other fellow says, tears it to pieces and shows you how impossible it is. Then he sets up his own house and shows you how easy it is to live in. That is the speaker to whom I like to listen." If the argument was to be presented only by a single speaker, the debate approach still might prevail by refuting this opposition's main argument. With this debate format in mind, Smith arranged the facts in the order he wanted to deliver his arguments. He usually dictated the text and, if time allowed, tested the content on various confidants. When the day of presentation arrived, he rehearsed in the afternoon, released an advance copy if the press requested one, but he "almost never followed the advance copy strictly" in the presentation that evening. He relied on fragmentary notes, scribbled in his own hand on envelopes, that constituted an easy-to-read speech outline. Sometimes three or four envelopes were adequate to sustain him for sixty to ninety minutes. Often numbered points outside the envelope corresponded to numbered material within the envelope that was pulled out as he declared, "Let's look at the record." Biographies include samples of a few extant envelopes. For each of his four gubernatorial inaugural addresses, Smith boasted that he "had no notes and no prepared material." These utterances might have been lost to posterity except for some stenographic reports by enterprising journalists.

Smith employed the accent of New York's East Side to deliver language that was plain, direct, and peppered with metaphors and similes. FDR was the friend of the "common man" but never common. Smith was from the common man and was content to remain so. One wealthy landowner objected vehemently to a Smith proposal: "That parkway will bring the rabble out here!" "The rabble!" Smith bellowed, "I am the rabble!" Concerning his 1924 GOP gubernatorial opponent, Theodore Roosevelt, Jr., Smith declared, "If bunk was electricity, young Roosevelt would be a powerhouse." Elements of style and pronunciation that endeared him to New York constituents possibly alienated him from other sectors of the country. In *The American Language*, H. L. Mencken pointed to Smith's use of "rad-dio" for *radio*, "foist" for *first*, "thoid" for *third*. Also, Smith preferred "horse-pital" for *hospital* and introduced such terms as "bal-oney" for *buncombe*, "alphabet soup" to describe the many New Deal agencies, and "off the record" to avoid attribution. "Baloney!" Smith would thunder into the microphone, "No matter how thin you slice it, it's still baloney!" He also freely used *crackpot* and *crackerloo*. Given his background, he favored visceral terms that were instantly intelligible.

Humor was another weapon in Smith's stylistic arsenal. At the 1915 constitutional convention, he opposed a move to require voter literacy tests by asserting that writing ability is no indication of character: "I refer to the number of sojourners at Sing Sing Prison who were not only able to write their own names, but found their way in there because of their ability to write somebody else's." The literacy test was laughed down following this attack. On another occasion, Smith employed humor unintentionally. Soon after his election as governor, he visited Sing Sing and addressed the inmates. He started, "My fellow citizens," then remembered that the audience technically lost their citizenship. Then, he said, "My fellow convicts." That was not fitting, so finally he said, "Well, anyhow, I'm glad to see so many of you here."

Smith's rhetorical career divides itself into three distinct periods. First, as an elected local and state politician prior to 1928, his discourses illuminated precise problems and usually offered specific solutions. Second, during the famous presidential candidacy, his rhetoric slipped in quality proportionally as it departed from the problem-solution formula. In attempting to sound presidential, his pronouncements lost their focus, their vigor, their rationale. Third, his latter period into the 1930s and 1940s affected the persona of the wealthy statesman, aloof from the fray, whose sole mission was to dispense unsolicited advice to national administrations.

Some of the best extant examples of speeches from the initial rhetorical period were delivered soon after Smith's second election to the governorship. In a speech to the New York State League of Women Voters at Albany in January 1923, Smith advocated the need for more efficiency in state government, a topic much discussed at the time. His tactic was to ask a question, explore its alternatives, and offer an answer: "Why should the state elect a state treasurer?" "Why should the state maintain four or five engineering departments?" He proceeded to consider prisons, the Board of Parole, state purchasing, the Canal Board, the Highway Department, and several other areas. A lengthy speech, it easily could have been dull and disorganized. It was neither. Although the issues have faded after more than sixty years, the speech retains a fresh vitality that suggests the personality of its author. It is rife with detail, has a debater's regard for opposing arguments, directs attention to future action, and sizzles with humorous sarcasm. The speaker, immersed in the record, is committed to resolving problems.

The second rhetorical period encompasses the presidential campaign of 1928. Some researchers, such as Silva, attempt to prove that religion was not the foremost issue, while others, such as Lichtman, directly refute that claim. Nevertheless, scurrilous anti-Catholic literature surfaced early and abundantly. Some items reflected pseudo-intellectual trappings; others were simplistic and heavy-handed. Even the venomous writings of Georgia's Tom Watson, who died in

1922, were resurrected in 1928. Handlin contends, "Smith encountered the religious issue in the campaign of 1918; and it plagued him in every election thereafter." If true, he betrayed little skill in dealing with it over the decade. Even if 1928 was a Republican year and any Democrat would have lost, Smith's rhetorical effort was unimpressive. He later condemned "old-fashioned, old time" political oratory wherein the speaker avoids issues, "claims credit for his party for all the good . . . and blames all the bad on the opposition." Unknowingly he described his disastrous acceptance speech of 1928. His only memorable presentation of the campaign, delivered in Oklahoma City on September 20, concentrated on religion. Obviously angry, he identified his enemies explicitly and fearlessly developed a speech that argued in behalf of true religious freedom. But as a single address on the topic, it came too early in the campaign to make a lasting impression, its substance was too localized to Oklahoma, and its intensity faded from lack of repetition. Any anticipation that the campaign might continue to treat such a real issue soon dissolved under the steady progression of humdrum discourses. Smith later despaired over being ignored by his opponent yet he squandered the best of all issues for provoking national debate.

During those last fifteen years, with all of his superb talent and experience, Smith should have been at his rhetorical best. But at the time of FDR's 1933 inaugural, he urged the Democratic party to rid itself of "bigots, fanatics, populists, demagogues, mountebanks and crackpots." It was a risky recommendation for someone who claimed to be the rabble. As his successor, Governor Roosevelt did not seek Smith's advice, keep him apprised of confidential developments, or retain his appointees. Furthermore, Smith thought that he deserved another chance at the presidency in 1932, entered the race too late, and then was never invited to join the new administration. He supported Alf Landon in 1936 and then left the ranks again in favor of Wendell Willkie in 1940. He burned most of his Democratic bridges in a national radio address on January 25, 1936, before the wealthy, ultra-Right American Liberty Leaguers. He called for a return to the Democratic platform of 1932 and tossed in several farfetched assertions: "At the end of three years we are just where we started"; "it is all right with me if they want to disguise themselves as Karl Marx or Lenin"; "there can be only one capital, Washington or Moscow." Smith relied on metaphors, such as "The young brain trusters caught the Socialists in swimming and they ran away with their clothes." But only a pale imitation of his earlier New York State discourses, the speech contained little substantive argumentation. Three days later, the administration responded with a brilliant broadcast rebuttal by Senator Joseph T. Robinson, Smith's 1928 vice-presidential running mate. He called on Smith to "look at the record," used similar biblical undertones, and characterized the Happy Warrior as a former battler for the masses who for greed and "thirty pieces of silver" had defected to the other side. The once-effective debater was devastated by a rebuttal from a former colleague.

There were other speeches, but without the stimulation of working-class audiences, Smith's speeches grew stale and inconsequential. Espousing the moneyed interests of the Liberty League, he appeared petty and resentful over his exclusion from the inner circle of the New Deal. He was at his rhetorical best when debating the merits of a proposal that ultimately was his responsibility to resolve. He was at his rhetorical worst when, detached from direct involvement, he sanctimoniously second-guessed those in power.

INFORMATION SOURCES

Research Collections and Collected Speeches

No Smith correspondence, speech drafts, or private papers are available. His gubernatorial messages are recorded in his *Public Papers* (2 volumes, Albany, 1920) and Henry Moskowitz, ed., *Progressive Democracy* (New York, 1928). His edited presidential campaign addresses are contained in *Campaign Addresses* (Washington, D.C., 1929). Stenographic reports of his speeches probably offer the most accurate record of his utterances. Otherwise researchers must rely upon assorted anthologies, *Vital Speeches*, and contemporary newspaper accounts.

Contemporary Forum: American Speeches on Twentieth-Century Issues.   CF
    Edited by Ernest J. Wrage and Barnet Baskerville. Seattle: University
    of Washington Press, 1962.
Modern Speeches. Edited by Homer D. Lindgren. New York: F. S. Crofts   MS
    & Co., 1926.
Smith, Alfred E. *Campaign Addresses.* Washington, D.C.: Democratic Na-   CA
    tional Committee, 1929.

Selected Critical Studies

Gravlee, G. Jack. "The New Deal." In *America in Controversy: History of American
    Public Address.* Edited by DeWitte Holland. Dubuque: Wm. C. Brown, 1973.
Jones, James L. "Alfred E. Smith, Political Debater." *Quarterly Journal of Speech* 54
    (1968): 363–72.
Lichtman, Allan J. *Prejudice and the Old Politics: The Presidential Election of 1928.*
    Chapel Hill: University of North Carolina Press, 1979.
McClerren, Beryl F. "Southern Baptists and the Religious Issue during the Presidential
    Campaigns of 1928 and 1960." *Central States Speech Journal* 18 (1967): 104–
    12.
Silva, Ruth C. *Rum, Religion, and Votes: 1928 Re-examined.* University Park: Penn-
    sylvania State University Press, 1962.
Smith, William David. "Alfred E. Smith and John F. Kennedy: The Religious Issue
    during the Presidential Campaigns of 1928 and 1960." Ph.D. dissertation, South-
    ern Illinois University, 1964.

Selected Biographies

Handlin, Oscar. *Al Smith and His America.* Boston: Little, Brown, 1958.
Josephson, Matthew, and Josephson, Hannah. *Al Smith: Hero of the Cities.* Boston,
    Houghton Mifflin, 1969.
Moses, Robert. *A Tribute to Governor Smith.* New York: Simon and Schuster, 1962.

Smith, Alfred E. "Spellbinding." *Saturday Evening Post*, May 24, 1930, pp. 3–5, 141, 144.

———. *Up to Now: An Autobiography*. Garden City, N.Y.: Garden City Pub. Co., 1929.

CHRONOLOGY OF MAJOR SPEECHES

See "Research Collections and Collected Speeches" for source codes.

Address before the New York State League of Women Voters, Albany, New York, January 16, 1923; *MS*, pp. 490–506.

Address at Oklahoma City, September 20, 1928; *CA*, pp. 43–59.

"Come Back to Your Father's House," American Liberty League Dinner, Washington, D.C., January 25, 1936; *CF*, pp. 168–78.

ADLAI EWING STEVENSON
(1900–1965), U.S. statesman

LLOYD E. ROHLER

Although Adlai Stevenson held only one elected office for a single four-year term and was twice nominated and twice defeated for the presidency, he achieved national and international renown as an eloquent spokesman for American liberalism. Born into a political family devoted to public service, this grandson and namesake of Grover Cleveland's second vice-president met and heard such important orators as William Jennings Bryan, Woodrow Wilson, Theodore Roosevelt, and Franklin Roosevelt. At Choate, he edited the school newspaper and joined the dramatic society. At Princeton, he managed the newspaper and joined the Whig Debating Society. Although he had no formal training in public speaking, his education followed the classic precepts of listening to good models, writing, and practice.

Stevenson first achieved recognition as a public speaker as president of the Chicago Council on Foreign Relations with his graceful and witty introductions of guest speakers. During this period, he developed the style that won him so much praise during the 1952 campaign: a self-deprecating humor, involved syntax, elevated diction, frequent use of parallelism, and a choppy delivery. Called to Washington in July 1941 to serve as assistant to the secretary of the navy, Frank Knox, he wrote the many speeches and statements before congressional committees that Knox gave. Later, as a member of the State Department, he attended both the San Francisco and London plenary sessions of the United Nations where he had major responsibility for briefing the press about U.S. policy. When he returned to Chicago to practice law, his friends persuaded him to run for governor of Illinois in 1948 on a reform ticket. He won by over 500,000 votes and gained national attention.

STEVENSON AS SPOKESMAN AND STATESMAN

Most Americans first heard Stevenson speak when he welcomed the Democrats to Chicago during the 1952 convention. This speech and his subsequent acceptance address established Stevenson's reputation as an independent, thoughtful, and courageous spokesman for American liberalism. In welcoming the delegates, he rose above the usual partisan attacks and political clichés and challenged them to meet their responsibilities by deliberating the important issues, adopting a platform, and choosing a candidate who had the vision to comprehend the revolutionary forces of the time. He returned to the same theme in his acceptance speech. Abjuring the conventional pieties of politics, Stevenson reminded the party that responsible leadership involved educating the electorate about the great issues confronting the United States in a revolutionary world. In a passage destined to be quoted again and again, Stevenson stressed the fundamental belief that would become the major theme of his political career: "The ordeal of the twentieth century—the bloodiest, most turbulent era of the Christian Age—is far from over. Sacrifice, patience, understanding and implacable purpose may be our lot for years to come. Let's face it. Let's talk sense to the American people."

Taking his own advice, he told one of the major pressure groups in politics, the American Legion, "I get so sick of the everlasting appeals to cupidity and prejudice of every group which characterize our campaigns. There is something finer in our people." He used this opportunity to attack those who use *patriot* as a club for attacking nonconformity and to affirm his belief that patriotism is "not short frenzied outbursts of emotion but the tranquil and steady dedication of a lifetime." His address at the Liberal party Convention showed Stevenson's wit as he tweaked the Republicans for imitating the Democrats and "borrowing many phrases from past Democratic platforms." He also claimed they "would rather battle Democrats than Communists any day and like the Communists their favorite sport is prophesying our imminent doom." Against such criticism, he affirmed his belief "that an authentic humility, an awareness of the complexity of men's choices, a tolerance for diverse opinions, and a recognition for brave experimentation are the heart of any liberal faith." Perhaps the peroration to his foreign policy address given in San Francisco on September 9, 1952, best conveyed Stevenson's message in the campaign: "I say that America has been called to greatness."

Neither a national hero nor a well-known figure before the campaign, Stevenson had barely three months of intensive campaigning following the convention to make his case. The themes he chose—a defense of the liberal state, a call for tolerance and understanding in the midst of the frustrations of the cold war, and a recognition of the need for international cooperation in dealing with the revolutionary forces of the twentieth century—captured the enthusiastic attention of only part of the electorate. After the returns were in, Stevenson ended his concession speech by characteristically choosing a Lincoln story about a little boy who stubbed his toe: "He was too old to cry but it hurt too much to laugh."

Following the election, Stevenson found himself cast in the role of spokesman for his party. He scheduled a world tour, met with many foreign leaders, gave speeches, and wrote. Perhaps his most important speech during this period was in Miami. On the eve of Joseph McCarthy's censure by the Senate, Stevenson presented the case against McCarthy in such forceful terms that the speech influenced public opinion to support the Senate action.

In 1956, Stevenson had to fight for the Democratic nomination through the primaries against Senator Estes Kefauver. Stung by criticism that his 1952 campaign had been too amateurish and his speeches too intellectual for the voters, Stevenson hired a professional campaign manager and broadened the appeal of his speeches. There are notable differences in style and content between the two campaigns, and these can be explained by the need to adapt to changed political realities. In 1952, Stevenson did not have to fight for the nomination and thus could pose as an independent to distance himself from an unpopular president while defending the record of achievement of the Democratic party. In 1956, the situation had changed. His was the party out of power, and the Republicans under Eisenhower were running on their record. Now he had to attack, and attacks usually sound less high minded than a defense of solid accomplishments. In 1956, he took seriously the advice not to talk over the heads of his audience and incorporated more material about bread-and-butter issues.

Stevenson gave the most important speech of the 1956 campaign to the American Society of Newspaper Editors before he was the official candidate of the party. In a speech devoted almost entirely to foreign policy, Stevenson reviewed the Eisenhower administration's conduct of foreign policy against its professed purposes and pronounced it a resounding failure. He reviewed the convergence of revolutionary forces in the twentieth century—technical, political, and ideological—that produced "violent, sudden change" and charged that the administration's policies were "no longer adequate in a new situation." It was an impressive performance demonstrating Stevenson's deep understanding of the fundamental problems facing the nation. More important, he ended the speech with a reasoned appeal to halt atmospheric testing of nuclear bombs and a challenge to "regain the initiative; to realize the warm creative energies of this mighty land; it is time to resume the onward progress of mankind in pursuit of peace and freedom." Unfortunately, Stevenson accepted the analysis of his advisers and chose to make domestic policy the centerpiece of the campaign. The resulting program, a "New America," which he announced in his acceptance speech, anticipated many of the programs later initiated by the Kennedy and Johnson administrations.

There is a myth about the Stevenson campaigns that the candidate wrote his own speeches. As with all other myths, this one contains a seed of truth. Perhaps no other candidate in recent memory worked as hard or took as much pride in his speeches as Stevenson did. Reporters accompanying him on the campaign uniformly wrote that Stevenson could be seen scribbling over speech texts up to the moment of delivery. But the demands of a contemporary campaign are so great that no candidate could write all the speeches he or she has to deliver. In 1952, Stevenson's speech-writing staff was a mirror image of the campaign: amateurish, dedicated, improvised. Stevenson's core staff, in addition to his personal aide, Carl McGowan, included Arthur M. Schlesinger, Jr., W. Willard Wirtz, Robert Tufts, and David Bell. Other notables—John Kenneth Galbraith, John Fischer, Bernard DeVoto, Herbert Agar, and Sydney Hyman—assisted for varying lengths of time. Usually Carl McGowan acted as a conduit, conveying Stevenson's requests for speeches to the staff and relaying texts from the writers to Stevenson. McGowan frequently rewrote drafts extensively before Stevenson rewrote them again. A major speech might go through as many as nine drafts before the candidate was satisfied with it, and he would still probably rework it up to the moment of delivery. In 1956, the Stevenson campaign was more professionally managed, and the speech staff reflected this difference. Drawing on his experience from 1952, Stevenson saw the need for more research and more deliberation than could be done under the pressure of a political campaign. To lay the groundwork for the 1956 campaign, he met with Thomas K. Finletter, Chester Bowles, and George Kennan in October 1953 to establish the nucleus of a study group that would provide research and policy alternatives to the Eisenhower administration. When the 1956 campaign began, the study group had been functioning for almost two years and had produced a variety of position papers and supporting research that became the basis for the Stevenson campaign. During the primaries, Harry Ashmore and John Bartlow Martin provided drafts of speeches for Stevenson. In the fall campaign, Schlesinger again joined the staff full time along with such veterans of the 1952 campaign as Willard Wirtz, Bill Blair, and Newton Minow. Bob Tufts and William Lee Miller were added later on a part-time basis along with Thomas Finletter.

In his campaign speeches, Stevenson utilized extremely effective introductions designed to gain the goodwill of the audience by humorous references and, especially, self-deprecating remarks. Once the introduction was over, Stevenson regarded fidelity to his prepared text as more important than adapting the text to the specific audience. The main body of the speeches relied extensively on ethical proof, but artistic proofs such as parallelism, historical comparisons, enthymemes, and maxims abound. His humor ranged from the folksy anecdote told on himself or borrowed from Lincoln to biting satire and sarcasm. Perhaps Stevenson's reputation as a witty speaker was derived from his effectiveness in relating the humor to the issue at hand to make a telling point rather than adding it as an unrelated device to gain audience response.

Neither an original nor a systematic thinker, Stevenson in his speeches reflected ideas basic to the U.S. political tradition: a faith in democracy, a belief in the universality of the American experience, and a profound concern for the moral values of the society. He derived his faith in democracy from Jefferson and Lincoln. He accepted their faith that the common man could decide the issues of the day if given adequate information. He believed that history demonstrated the correctness of this belief. He often cited Lincoln as an example of a courageous president whose leadership depended on his faith in the people. He felt a special kinship with Lincoln. Stevenson's maternal great-grandfather used the family newspaper to champion Lincoln early in his career and suggested the famous debates with Douglas. Equally important to Stevenson was a fundamental faith in the universality of the American experience. The United States was the city on a hill that demonstrated to the rest of the world that democracy could work. The Wilsonian ideal that the United States could lead the world to freedom and democracy through its own moral example guided Stevenson's approach to foreign affairs and influenced his diplomacy at the United Nations. Stevenson's speeches frequently concerned the larger moral purposes of society. Like the

Puritan preacher of old, he worried about the state of souls. What ideals motivate us? What visions do we have? Coming from a family devoted to public service and steeped in the reform tradition from Bryan to Roosevelt, Stevenson's vision of a new America was not bounded merely by material gains but included a fresh vision of the possibilities of American life.

Stevenson ended his political career as U.S. ambassador to the United Nations. In that important forum, his great talents were utilized not in making policy but in defending policies made by others. Although he expressed private reservations about his role, he valued the institution of the United Nations so highly that he performed his tasks in an exemplary manner. Perhaps his greatest moment came in 1962 during the debate over the Cuban missile crisis when he presented the U.S. case with all the moral indignation of a prosecutor in a courtroom. He challenged Soviet ambassador Zorin to deny that "the USSR has placed and is placing medium and intermediate-range missiles and sites in Cuba." Stevenson called for an immediate answer: "Don't wait for the translation. Yes or no?" When Zorin lamely replied that Stevenson would "receive the answer in due course," Stevenson indignantly proclaimed his willingness to "wait for my answer until hell freezes over." Throughout this period, he continued to speak about the necessity for establishing a genuine world community and to speak against those who would turn their backs on the United States' international responsibilities for stability and world order. A good example of these speeches is the speech given to a UN Day Rally in Dallas on October 24, 1963, during which Stevenson was heckled by right-wing demonstrators.

Although Stevenson produced great deliberative speeches as a candidate for president and demonstrated great skill as an advocate for his country at the UN, perhaps his talents were best displayed in the ceremonial, or epideictic, speeches he made. In this genre, where the speaker celebrates the values of the society and praises individuals who exemplify them, Stevenson's awareness of the tradition of American political culture produced speeches of unquestioned eloquence. In his 1963 Notre Dame patriotism address, he defined the role of patriotism in a world divided into two blocs, each armed with nuclear weapons. Basing his claims on the American dream of freedom, human rights, and equality before the law, Stevenson argued that this tradition "must give our patriotism a universal aspect." He gave the name *patriot* to "those who love America enough to wish to see her as a model for mankind."

Perhaps the most enduring of his speeches will be his eulogies for friends who joined with him in the struggle for a decent world. His speeches in this genre are models of brevity and style, expressing deep feelings of grief for the loss of a colleague or friend and placing the life of the individual within a broader context of the ideas and values that animated it. Eleanor Roosevelt was a personal friend and political supporter of Stevenson. His eulogy of her at the UN on November 9, 1962, contains the memorable phrase, "She would rather light candles than curse the darkness." Addressing the UN General Assembly on the death of John Kennedy, he said: "Now he is gone. Today we mourn him.

Tomorrow and tomorrow we shall miss him.'' At a memorial service for Winston Churchill, he expressed dismay that ''the voice that led nations, raised armies, inspired victories and blew fresh courage into the hearts of men is silenced.'' He told the mourners: ''Our world is thus poorer, our political dialogue is diminished and the sources of public inspiration run more thinly for all of us. There is a lonesome place against the sky.''

In summation, both the 1952 welcoming address and the acceptance speech provide the context for evaluating Stevenson's influence on the American public. In both speeches he made clear his faith in the capacity of the common man in a democratic society to understand the issues and to make an informed choice. In both speeches he affirmed his intention to talk sense to the people, not to talk down to them or to mislead them by slogans or simplistic formulas. But the speeches themselves, with their elevated style and their wit, may have defeated his purpose. The speeches appealed to many Americans, but many others either did not listen to him or would not make the effort to understand him. But if he failed at his primary purpose of stimulating public debate and winning votes, he succeeded in establishing an agenda for the later Kennedy-Johnson administration. The 1956 campaign, with its emphasis on the quality of American life and its proposals on education, defense, medical care, and nuclear testing, anticipated the issues that Kennedy would dramatize in the 1960 campaign. More important, Stevenson inspired a generation to public service. Many of the men and women who later staffed the Kennedy administration testified that their political awakening came when they first heard Stevenson speak and realized that public service could be an honorable occupation for an intelligent person. Stevenson represents the traditional devotion to public service of an American elite that shares a vision of the possibilities of American life combined with a recognition of American responsibilities to world order. A cosmopolitan man, he had the breadth of vision to see Americans' problems and concerns as part of a larger pattern of global concerns.

INFORMATION SOURCES

Research Collections and Collected Speeches

The Stevenson papers are indispensable for any research into Stevenson's writings and public speeches. Those dealing with his early life and the years as governor are in the Illinois State Historical Library, Springfield, Illinois. The papers from his presidential campaigns and his years as spokesman for the Democratic Party are in the Firestone Library, Princeton University. The official papers from the years as ambassador at the United Nations are in the Department of State Archives. Both the Illinois State Historical Library and the Firestone Library have recordings of his speeches available. Stevenson's speeches are available in a number of published collections.

An Ethic for Survival: Adlai E. Stevenson Speaks on International Affairs,   ES
     1936–1965. Edited by Michael H. Prosser. New York: William Mor-
     row, 1969.
Representative American Speeches: 1963–1964. Edited by Lester Thonssen.   RAS
     New York: H. W. Wilson, 1964.

Stevenson, Adlai E. *Looking Outward: Years of Crisis at the United Nations.*   LO
    Edited by Robert L. and Selma Schiffer. New York: Harper & Row,
    1963.
———. *Major Campaign Speeches of Adlai E. Stevenson, 1952.* New York: MCS
    Random House, 1953.
———. *The New America.* Edited by Seymour E. Harris, John Bartlow   NA
    Martin, and Arthur Schlesinger, Jr. New York: Harper & Brothers,
    1957.
———. *The Papers of Adlai Stevenson.* Edited by Walter Johnson, Carol   PAS
    Evans, and C. Eric Sears. 8 vols. Boston: Little, Brown, 1972–1979.
———. *What I Think.* New York: Harper & Brothers, 1956.   WIT

Selected Critical Studies

Baird, A. Craig, et al. "Political Speaking in 1952: A Symposium." *Quarterly Journal of Speech* 38 (1952): 265–300.
Brownlow, Paul C., and Davis, Beth. " 'A Certainty of Honor.' The Eulogies of Adlai Stevenson." *Central States Speech Journal* 25 (1974): 217–24.
Larsch, Albert. "Rhetoric and the Campaign of 1956: Stevenson." *Quarterly Journal of Speech* 43 (1957): 34–39.
Murphy, Richard. "Adlai Stevenson: Part I. Stevenson as Spokesman." *Today's Speech* 8 (1960): 3–5.
———. "Adlai Stevenson: Part II. Stevenson and His Audience." *Today's Speech* 8 (1960): 12–16.
Windes, Russel R., Jr., and Robinson, James A. "Public Address in the Career of Adlai E. Stevenson." *Quarterly Journal of Speech* 42 (1956): 225–33.
Yeager, Raymond. "Stevenson: The 1956 Campaign." *Central States Speech Journal* 12 (1960): 9–15.

Selected Biographies

Davis, Kenneth S. *The Politics of Honor: A Biography of Adlai E. Stevenson.* New York: G. P. Putnam's Sons, 1967.
Martin, John Bartlow. *Adlai Stevenson of Illinois.* Garden City, N.Y.: Doubleday, 1976.
———. *Adlai Stevenson and the World.* Garden City, N.Y.: Doubleday, 1977.
Muller, Herbert J. *Adlai Stevenson: A Study in Values.* New York: Harper & Row, 1967.
Sievers, Rodney M. *The Last Puritan? Adlai Stevenson in American Politics.* Port Washington, N.Y.: Associated Faculty Press, 1983.

CHRONOLOGY OF MAJOR SPEECHES

See "Research Collections and Collected Speeches" for source codes.

Welcoming address to the Democratic National Convention, Chicago, July 21, 1952; *PAS*, 4:11–14; *MCS*, pp. 3–10.

Acceptance speech, Chicago, July 26, 1952; *PAS*, 4:16–19; *MCS*, pp. 7–10.

"Nature of Patriotism," American Legion Convention, New York City, August 27, 1952; *PAS*, 4:49–54; *MCS*, pp. 17–22.

"Faith in Liberalism," Liberal party Convention, New York City, August 28, 1952; *PAS*, 4:60–64; *MCS*, pp. 30–34.

"World Policy," San Francisco, September 9, 1952; *PAS*, 4:79–86; *MCS*, pp. 91–99.

Concession speech, Springfield, Illinois, November 4, 1952; *PAS*, 4:187–188; *MCS*, pp. 319–320.

"Crusades, Communism and Corruption," Miami, Florida, March 7, 1954; *PAS* 4:327–333; *WIT*, pp. 64–71.

Address to American Society of Newspaper Editors, Washington, D.C., April 21, 1956; *PAS*, 6:110–121; *NA*, pp. 17–27.

Acceptance speech, Chicago, August 17, 1956; *PAS*, 6:182–89.

Statement to UN Security Council, New York City, October 23, 1962; *PAS* 8:309–25, *LO*, pp. 79–99.

Second statement to UN Security Council, New York City, October 25, 1962; *PAS*, 8:325–29; *LO*, pp. 100–06.

Confrontation with Soviet Ambassador Zorin, UN Security Council, New York City, October 25, 1962; *PAS*, 8:330–34; *LO*, pp. 107–12.

Eulogy of Eleanor Roosevelt, UN Security Council, New York City, November 17, 1962; *PAS*, 8:339–40.

Eulogy of Eleanor Roosevelt, Cathedral of St. John the Divine, New York City, November 17, 1962; *PAS*, 8:342–46; *LO*, pp. 290–95.

"The United Nations: Hope for the Future," UN Day Rally, Dallas, Texas, October 24, 1963; *ES*, pp. 379–92.

Eulogy of John F. Kennedy, UN General Assembly, New York City, November 26, 1963; *RAS*, pp. 30–33.

Eulogy of Winston S. Churchill, National Cathedral, Washington, D.C., January 28, 1965; *PAS*, 8:686–88.

EUGENE TALMADGE
(1884–1946), four-time governor of Georgia

CALVIN M. LOGUE

Eugene Talmadge was a politician with an uncanny ability to manipulate public audiences by means of the spoken word. He was dissatisfied working as a teacher and a lawyer. Thus, in 1926 he enticed J. J. Brown, a powerful commissioner of agriculture of Georgia, into a debate at the challenger's home town of McRae. Using the debate skills he learned while a student at the University of Georgia, Talmadge ambushed the incumbent at the polls. Having defeated Brown by attacking the man and his practices unmercifully, Talmadge began a twenty-year political career based primarily on a strategy of uninhibited defamation of character and institutions. He characterized J. J. Brown as an untrustworthy person who abused the public. Talmadge won the 1926, 1928, and 1930 elections for commissioner of agriculture and the 1932, 1934, 1940, and 1946 elections for governor by entertaining rural audiences with a public rowdiness seldom matched in politics. While in office, he helped satisfy the business community by espousing policies that prevented government from interfering with their transactions.

TALMADGE'S DISCOURSE OF DOMINANCE

Talmadge campaigned and governed as if he believed in a monocracy. He felt his decisions were infallible and his preferences were decrees. His persuasion refracted this posture of imperiousness into campaign appeals and governing edicts. Talmadge's 1926 campaign strategy was an apostrophe to his self-esteem. The "economic, moral and political welfare" of Georgians "depends absolutely" on Talmadge's being elected to office. Talmadge marketed himself as the rescuer of a working class enslaved by big business and a callous government. The dominant theme in his rhetoric was his trustworthiness. He presented himself as a man the people could believe. Although Talmadge's public speeches were laden with excessive appeals to raw feelings of economic suffering and regional pride, his "battle cry"—as he called it—claimed the credibility of a good man "proving all things." Many voters believed the brassy lawyer. Others winced at or criticized his tyrannical tendencies.

Rather than cultivate a partnership with officials, Talmadge as governor preferred to act unilaterally. When anyone opposed his decisions, he attempted to bludgeon them into submission or retreat. On June 20, 1933, the *Atlanta Constitution* called Governor Talmadge a "dictator of virtually all functions of State government." On one occasion, Talmadge activated the National Guard to oust a Highway Board with which he disagreed. In his Second Inaugural Address, on January 17, 1935, one that he said would be an impromptu talk to the legislature, Talmadge discussed his controversy with the old highway board but did not mention his use of national guardsmen in ousting them. In that same 1935 speech, Talmadge also ignored what was said to have been "the most controversial issue before the assembly—prohibition, repeal or modification."

Talmadge warned blacks to stay in their place. He influenced the Georgia Board of Regents to fire Dean Walter D. Cocking of the University of Georgia, and, when that institution lost its accreditation, he bragged that he would not back off but would continue "looking for any more professors that teach a doctrine of racial equality," placing his prejudice above the welfare of the youth of the state. He promised to be "hunting more Cockings" to fire. With each of his rash acts, Talmadge returned to the masses with requests for understanding and support.

Talmadge offered simplistic, understandable, and, to many, attractive-sounding solutions to bothersome social and economic problems. He attacked government's "bacchanalia of spending," prescribing cuts in government income as the primary cure for Georgia's problems. He was proud of reducing the cost of customers' electric bills, telephone and freight rates, and automobile tags. Talmadge explained to a Waycross, Georgia, audience why what he perceived to be excessive freight rates hurt both the railroads and agriculture: The "products of the farm" were "decaying in the fields, because they cannot profitably be transported to market." Thus, "there is no buying power on the farm. Consequently there is no freight to be hauled from factory and city to the country." He would "put the unfair competition of trucks and buses off the highway." In an editorial supporting Talmadge's economic practices, the *Augusta Chronicle* on September 1, 1940, provided an explanation of how the governor's cuts had helped Georgians:

When a political candidate mounts the stump to extol his virtues . . . the average citizen, if he is smart, will want to know what benefits *HE* has derived. . . . Political speeches studded with pleasant generalities usually sound good. But the voters like these things reduced to facts—facts which are applicable to him. . . . It will be of particular interest to Richmond County citizens to cite a few of the impressive savings achieved for them as the result of policies formulated during the period of 1933–1937. . . . For instance, in 1936 Richmond County's registered automobiles numbered 10,217. When Governor Talmadge reduced the price of the license tag on the ordinary family car from average of $11.25 to the flat rate of $3, it produced an annual saving of $8.25 on each car . . . an aggregate of $84,290.25 in savings each year for the people of Richmond County alone. . . . In 1935 Georgia had 98,823 family telephones. This does not include those for business. . . . With the Talmadge reorganization of the Public Service Commission, telephone rates were scaled down more than $729,268 per year. This was about $7.30 annually for each telephone. . . . You could develop interesting figures [also] with respect to reduced light and power rates, which constitute an equally impressive argument in Talmadge's favor.

Although he worked to reduce the cost of government expenses for citizens, at the same time Talmadge promised to meet the basic requirements of education for children and needs of the elderly. He consistently insisted that schools would get whatever money they needed, particularly the rural institutions and vocational facilities. He would seek relief for dairymen and provide hospital care throughout Georgia. Talmadge assured the voters that he would never abandon the veterans of the Confederacy. He was particularly effective personalizing the needs of veterans. He said in his First Inaugural delivered in Atlanta on January 10, 1933: "To meet and shake hands with these old soldiers makes you realize how old they are getting. . . . They need their money sorely." In 1942, he specified four principles of interest to Georgians: "white supremacy, state's rights, Jeffersonian Democracy, and old time religion."

At times Talmadge seemed to work magic on audiences with his quick mind and tongue. Hoping to attract as many supporters as possible, he appeared capable on occasions of convincing persons with conflicting interests that his policies would benefit both parties. To placate working men and women, for example, Talmadge criticized "banking and industrial interest." At the same time, he offered to abolish "useless bureaus and boards" of government, a decision that appealed to successful businessmen and bankers who preferred as few regulations limiting their investments as possible. To businessmen who had been "hounded" by federal restrictions, Talmadge advised, "You have one thing that'll match John D. Rockefeller. That's your ballot."

Many of the remedies that Talmadge promised would relieve the economic burdens of the citizens were as shallow in plan of action as was his language colorful. Often he treated conditions oppressing the working class far too lightly, introducing innocuous solutions contrived to give supporters something to cheer. For example, to regulate surplus farm crops, Talmadge advocated following the Bible with a holiday each seven years. In his Second Inaugural Address delivered in Atlanta on January 16, 1935 he offered the following advice for improving ethics in government: The "only way to have an honest government is to keep it poor."

Talmadge depicted himself as a courageous leader ready to fight for farmers and urban workers who were impoverished by policies that favored government bureaucrats and successful bankers. In a frenzied, boisterous, and often effective rhetoric, Talmadge stressed the urgent need for immediate social and economic changes in government that would allow the working people to prosper. The "waves look rocky to me," he shouted, dramatizing the hardships of farmers and laborers to a fever pitch. He insisted that something must be done, that actions had to be taken immediately. To Talmadge, however, the content of an issue was less important than its selling potential. After the Supreme Court ruled that blacks could vote in primaries, Talmadge made what he called race talk dominant in the 1946 gubernatorial election. But in his 1933 gubernatorial inaugural address, he named one "emergency" facing Georgians—the need to reduce the fee for automotive vehicles to three dollars, a reduction that pleased a majority of voters attending Talmadge's speeches and owners of large trucks that damaged the state's roads.

Talmadge was particularly skillful in creating a political persona poised to defeat people and policies he said were harmful to the working class. The potent verbs in his public discourse pictured a man at war with enemies of a deprived group of citizens. In a rhetorical strategy conceived to place opponents on the defensive, to win votes, to marshal support for his policies, and to legitimize his rowdy behavior, Talmadge claimed that he would stay on the neck of the politicians and government officials opposed to his views and hang at their "throats." He would slash government payrolls, lick taxes, and whack utility rates as a means of lifting the financial burdens from a deprived citizenry.

Cultivating a public image of a brave warrior and drawing precepts from a blend of Bible morality and common experience, Talmadge said in speeches what many Georgians felt in their families. When critics said that Talmadge had never actually farmed, he rebutted that workers in his audiences had "seen me plowing," and many in the crowds nodded affirmatively. Even more effective, however, was Talmadge's skill in speaking messages in language with which farmers and laborers were comfortable. He talked in his First Inaugural about "good men, women and children" being dressed so "raggedly and barefooted" that some are "ashamed to go to church and . . . to school." While serving as governor, he insisted that a "cow barn" be maintained "on the mansion grounds." In his First Inaugural Address, he drew examples from the experience of farmers, chastising railroads for charging "as much for hauling a $35 mule as they used to charge for hauling a $300 mule."

Talmadge sensed that working people were tired of struggling to pay bills and bowing to a wealthy class, and he took steps to capitalize politically on these economic and social frustrations. Talmadge told the downtrodden that he would dismantle the political "conspiracy" that deprived them of their fair share of Georgia's resources and end the "orgy of waste" in government. Matching the intensity of his criticism with the level of response of the crowds who heard him, he tried to intimidate political opponents and to ridicule policies he found offensive. He employed vituperative language as a means of defeating the opposition, using *sinister, shameful, jackasses, arrogant dictation, pernicious, corrupt, sinister, alien influences, lightheaded, oily boys,* and *plunderbund politician.* With his aim on increased taxes for government programs, Talmadge called Franklin D. Roosevelt's New Deal administration "crazy" and a "boondoggling crowd." Early in the New Deal, Talmadge criticized virtually all federally sponsored programs. He scorned Roosevelt for supporting a policy that promised to "create a scarcity to provide, of all things, the abundant life." By 1946, however, Talmadge said he would work to bring in Georgia's proportion of federal money.

After 1944, when the court ruled white-only elections to be unconstitutional and many Georgians were fearful of blacks voting and campaigning for office, Talmadge made racial topics dominant in public discussion. He complained of "wilder and wilder experiments" with a variety of forms of "racial equality." Specifically, Talmadge argued that if he were not elected to office, white citizens would be forced to "mix with Negroes in restaurants, hotels, schools, and other places." Blacks who did not kneel to Talmadge's racist plans were said to be communists.

Talmadge won seven statewide elections in Georgia in part by criticizing all persons and parties who refused to join his personal struggle for political power. But not all Georgians approved of his methods of campaigning and governing. Increasingly after observing Talmadge's persuasive antics for a number of years, many newspersons attempted to expose Talmadge's coercive maneuvers and abuse of authority. Editorials compared "Talmadgeism" with Nazism. In some elections, voters rejected his peculiar behavior in office and his blatant attacks on opponents. He was defeated by Richard B. Russell and Walter George in separate elections for the U.S. Senate. Relatively few Georgians approved his tasteless portrayal of a crippled Roosevelt and ridicule of badly needed New Deal programs. When Talmadge in a speech in Canton, Georgia, on July 4, 1935, promised to help defeat Franklin Roosevelt, "on state affairs his audience was with him pretty generally," but on "national affairs he received repeated applause from certain sections of the crowd" and "silence from others." In a widely reported comment made before the Atlanta Post of the American Legion on June 23, 1933, Talmadge apparently referred to forestry camp workers employed under the Civilian Conservation Corps as "loafers and bums." The public outcry was so great that Talmadge was forced in a speech in Albany, Georgia, on July 4 to claim that what he actually said was that the men were being asked to do "useless work." During the 1942 election that followed the loss of the University of Georgia's accreditation, moderate Ellis Arnall defeated Talmadge in a race for governor. Many persons, however, remained loyal to the "wild man" of Georgia until the end. Voters reelected Talmadge governor in 1946, but he died before taking office.

INFORMATION SOURCES

Research Collections and Collected Speeches

Because most of Talmadge's official papers were burned and his personal materials not preserved, to study his public performances one must rely primarily on government documents in Georgia and press reports. Newspaper coverage of Talmadge's campaign speeches and gubernatorial addresses was extensive. Because some editors supported Talmadge and others opposed him, researchers can identify and weigh a variety of accounts of speeches and of judgments concerning the man's public persuasion.

Atlanta Constitution   *AC*

Selected Critical Studies

Anderson, William. *The Wild Man from Sugar Creek: The Political Career of Eugene Talmadge*. Baton Rouge: Louisiana State University Press, 1975.

Cobb, James Charles. "Eugene Talmadge and the Purge: The Georgia Senatorial Campaign of 1938." Master's thesis, University of Georgia, 1972.

Crooks, Mary Glass. "The Platform Pledges of Governor Eugene Talmadge and Resulting Statutes." Master's thesis, University of Georgia, 1953.

Dykeman, Wilma. "The Southern Demagogue." *Virginia Quarterly Review* 33 (1957):558–68.

Gibson, Chester. "Eugene Talmadge: A Case Study in the Use of Common Ground during the 1936 Gubernatorial Campaign in Georgia." Master's thesis, University of Georgia, 1967.

Gilbert. G. M. "Dictators and Demagogues." *Journal of Social Issues* 11 (1955):51–53.

Larson, Allan Louis. *Southern Demagogues: A Study in Charismatic Leadership*. Ann Arbor: University Microfilms, 1964.

Lemmon, S. M., "Governor Eugene Talmadge and the New Deal," in *Studies in Southern History*. Edited by Joseph Carlyle Sitterson. Chapel Hill: University of North Carolina Press, 1957.

———. "The Public Career of Eugene Talmadge: 1926–1936." Master's thesis, University of North Carolina, 1952.

Logue, Cal M. "The Coercive Campaign Prophecy of Gene Talmadge." In *The Oratory of Southern Demagogues*. Edited by Cal M. Logue and Howard Dorgan. Baton Rouge: Louisiana State University Press, 1981.

Luthin, Reinhard H. *American Demagogues*. Boston: Beacon Press, 1954.

Steinberg, Alfred. *The Bosses*. New York: Macmillan, 1972.

CHRONOLOGY OF MAJOR SPEECHES

See "Research Collections and Collected Speeches" for source codes.

First Gubernatorial Inaugural Address, Atlanta, Georgia; *AC*, January 11, 1933, p. 7.

Second Gubernatorial Inaugural Address, Atlanta, Georgia; *AC*, January 17, 1935, pp. 1, 3. (This may be a rare impromptu inaugural address.)

Speech to "Grass Roots Convention," Macon, Georgia; *AC*, January 30, 1936, pp. 1, 2.

Third Gubernatorial Inaugural Address, Atlanta, Georgia; *AC*, January 15, 1941, p. 5.

HARRY S TRUMAN
(1884–1972), thirty-third president of the United States
_____ HALFORD R. RYAN

Harry S Truman had the distinct rhetorical disadvantage of following one of the greatest presidential persuaders in U.S. history, Franklin D. Roosevelt. Although Truman was not as eloquent as his predecessor and would always thereby suffer in comparison, he was nevertheless an effective speaker as president of the United States.

Truman was not unacquainted with oratorical skills upon ascendancy to the Oval Office. He began his speaking career by addressing Masonic lodges in Missouri. He ran for judge of the Jackson County Court as a Democrat in 1922, and he appealed effectively to the veteran voters from World War I. But many of his close friends and political pals agreed that he was not a particularly effective orator. He lost the judgeship race in 1924 due to a national Republican sweep into power from the presidency, with Calvin Coolidge, right down to Jackson County, Missouri. Truman, however, was elected Jackson County presiding judge in 1926, and he was never thereafter defeated in a political race. Voter loyalty to the Democratic party and to its candidates probably accounted more for Truman's elections than did his oratory. Although his speeches were not stirring or stylistic, they were characterized by a straightforward style that stressed the facts and the issues at hand. This rhetorical habit of plain speaking served him well in the presidency.

Just being a Democrat in the 1934 Senate race helped Truman win his seat. Truman ran against the Republican conservative incumbent and for Franklin D. Roosevelt and his popular New Deal. During the depression, the choice was abundantly clear to the voters. Truman was not a noted orator in the Senate, nor were his speeches widely printed or closely read; however, he was a conscientious worker on senatorial committee business.

The campaign for his Senate seat in 1940 was arduous, often bitter, and close. He emerged from the primary by a narrow margin of 8,000 votes and beat the Republican candidate by some 44,000 ballots. Truman had to campaign extensively, and, again, he was somewhat helped by being a New Deal Democrat. His political prominence on the national level increased under his leadership of the Truman committee, which investigated what could be called today the seamy side of the military-industrial complex of World War II. Indeed Truman was chosen as FDR's running mate in 1944 not so much for his oratorical abilities as for his loyalty to FDR and to the New Deal and for his popular and praiseworthy work on the Truman committee. Truman campaigned as the vice-presidential candidate, but Roosevelt won the votes. And then, on April 12, 1945, Harry S Truman became president of the United States.

TRUMAN AS A RHETORICAL PRESIDENT

President Truman relied on persuasive presidential oratory to articulate his key administrative policies and to seek support for them. In this category of significant policy speeches were the Truman Doctrine, the Korean war, and the firing of General MacArthur. In addition to these addresses, the miracle of 1948 merits special mention: his convention acceptance speech, his whistle-stop campaign, and his Inaugural Address. His valedictory speech appropriately summarizes his seven-year tenure in the White House.

One of President Truman's most important addresses was his so-called Truman Doctrine speech to a joint session of Congress on March 12, 1947. This speech was Truman's economic, political, and rhetorical response to mounting communist infiltration and subversion in Greece and Turkey, and it also was the impetus for his containment policy and cold war rhetoric. He organized his speech around four main ideas: (1) Greece needed economic and political aid in order to survive as a democracy, (2) so did Turkey, (3) the United States was the only power capable of meeting that need, and (4) Congress needed to approve the specific funds. Truman used a number of logical appeals in the form of factual examples to underline the urgent situation, and he employed numerous emotional appeals—centering around pity and indignation for the embattled Greeks and Turks and focusing on fear, righteousness, and anger against the communists—to bolster his argument. As an example of the cold war rhetoric, Truman polarized his language: the United States was portrayed as good and the communists as bad. This hard-line speech was generally well received by the American people and even by some newspapers that did not normally support Truman, and a bipartisan Congress passed the enabling legislation. The cold war containment policy, which was enunciated in the Truman Doctrine speech, was one of Truman's major legislative accomplishments.

President Truman delivered several important addresses on the Korean war, which was uppermost in his and America's thoughts for most of his last two years in office. North Korean forces invaded South Korea in June 1950, and Truman delivered his first rhetorical response on July 19, 1950. In his usual manner, he went directly to the facts of communist "aggression," "contempt," and "challenge." He gave a short history of how the crisis arose, which was narrated in the cold war polarity between good (the United Nations and the United States) versus the bad (the Soviet Union). He bolstered his justification for sending U.S. troops to Korea by citing letters from Generals Collins and MacArthur. In the latter part of the speech, he dealt with the economic and military measures he sent to the Congress for enactment, and he tried to still domestic fears about shortages of food and rationing of materials. He indicated in his speech that the war aim was "to put down lawless aggression" and "to stop the fighting in Korea.'' The rationale for these responses to the Korean intervention was based on the lessons one learned from the 1930s: ''Appeasement leads only to further aggression and ultimately to war.'' The same general themes were stressed in his speech at the War Memorial Opera House in San Francisco on October 17, 1950, where he made his famous statement, ''The only victory we seek is the victory of peace.''

Suddenly, however, the military situation changed dramatically when the Chinese communists entered the fray to help the North Koreans who were losing the war. Truman took to the airwaves on December 15, 1950, to announce a national emergency. He again stressed the themes of nonappeasement and no more Munichs, and he clearly identified the Soviet Union as the real culprit. The rest of the speech dealt with domestic issues on how Americans should respond to the Korean setback in their new emergency situation.

In these speeches, President Truman gave good reasons for U.S. involvement in the Korean war. However, his main problem was that he used the term *victory* in a nebulous sense. A close reading of his speeches suggests a realistic victory goal as the *status quo ante bellum*. But many Americans probably did not listen or read that closely, and so they inferred that Truman meant an all-out military victory in its traditional sense rather than a holding action. As the Korean war wore on without significant battlefield progress, Truman became the target of political attacks from the Republicans, who had their eyes on the 1952 presidential election, and from General Douglas MacArthur. The general became combative under his constitutional constraints; he made unauthorized statements about the conduct of the war—unwise and improper as he saw it—and he finally wrote a letter, which was insubordinate to Truman, to Congressman Joseph Martin, who read it on the floor of the House. Truman's rhetorical problem was that he never adequately prepared Americans for a new kind of war in which there was no traditional victory, and his political enemies capitalized on that rhetorical mistake. In the atomic age, Truman wanted to avoid another world war, and perhaps it was too much to ask of the man that he should persuade others to believe that the United States probably could not win another world war, assuming it could even be won, at a price the United States would be willing to pay.

Fortunately for the country and for its principle of civilian control over the military, Truman occupied the Oval Office when it was necessary to remind America's would-be Caesar, General MacArthur, that he was a general only. In his constitutional role as commander-in-chief, Truman fired MacArthur for actions of insubordination, but as chief executive, he wanted to explain his presidential action to the country. For his radio speech on April 11, 1951, Truman chose between two sets of speech drafts. One came from the State Department, and it stressed Secretary of State Dean Acheson's belief that the now-unpopular Korean war was being waged to avoid a world war III. The other draft was produced by Truman's own speech team of David Bell and Charles Murphy, who stressed MacArthur's insubordination to the president as the reason why he was fired. From a rhetorical perspective, it was unfortunate that Truman used Acheson's State Department draft, which mentioned only obliquely in a few sentences toward the end of the speech why MacArthur was fired. The strategy was not overly successful with the radio audience. Americans expected to hear why Truman fired MacArthur, a popular World War II hero; instead they heard why soldiers should remain fighting an unpopular war. Support for the president's speech was weak as gauged by the caustic White House reaction mail: "Your speeches stink and you stink," "Your lousy speech over the radio trying to clear yourself of the blundering mistakes you made at the expense of General MacArthur are as stupid and dumb as your daughter's sand paper singing voice." Truman also continued to cast his language in cold war rhetoric with phrases such as "Communist doubletalk" and "Commie language." Although the president had every right to sack MacArthur, this speech was one in which Truman did not successfully communicate the real basis for his legitimate action but chose instead to try to defend the Korean war. That rhetorical strategy was unwise because he did not meet audience expectations.

The conditions under which President Truman delivered his 1948 convention acceptance address, which some critics believe was his most stirring speech, would not ordinarily be conducive to such an oratorical achievement. The weather in Philadelphia was hot and humid; the Dixiecrats had walked out, and the "doves of peace"—pigeons, actually, that were released into the hall—caused a commotion in the convention, and some even dove for Speaker Sam Rayburn's bald head. Finally, at 2:00 A.M. on July 15, Truman began to address the exhausted delegates. He delivered his speech from a bare-bones outline of twenty-one pages, which allowed him to extemporize in vivid interpolations and emotional ad-libs. Truman was not a good manuscript speaker, but off-the-cuff Truman soon had the weary delegates on their feet and applauding his remarks. He told the delegates that he and vice-presidential nominee Senator Alban Barkley would "win this election and make the Republicans like it—don't you forget that!" because "they are wrong and we are right." He reminded the working man and the farmer that they should vote Democratic, or else they would be "the most ungrateful people in the world!" Then Truman ticked off the legislation he had requested, unsuccessfully, from the Republican Eightieth Congress—price controls, housing, minimum wage—and he reminded the delegates what he got, "Nothing. Absolutely nothing." He then ripped into the Republican platform, which promised the legislation its Congress had refused him, and he asserted: "I wonder if they can fool the people of the United States with such poppycock as that!" The president administered his rhetorical coup de grâce to the Republicans when he pledged to call the Eightieth Congress back into session in order to pass the Republican platform. That was the high point of his rousing speech, and the convention audience greeted his adroit political move with thunderous approval. In his conclusion, he aptly stated the theme of his speech, and indeed the theme of the coming campaign, in his parting sentence: "The country can't afford another Republican Congress."

The speech statistics for the 1948 campaign suggest the role his oratory played in persuading the people: 26 addresses in major cities and approximately 250 whistlestop talks. These talks, from the rear platform of a railroad observation car, were actually quite refined in their rhetorical technique. Truman would speak for about five minutes or so on local interests and issues, then introduce Mrs. Truman as "the Boss," and then finally his daughter Margaret. This folksy touch drew the crowds and pleased the people. But the substance of his rhetoric persuaded the voters. Truman ran against the "Do-Nothing Eightieth Congress," and this gave the voters a scapegoat on which to vent their frustrations rather than on him. He made specific appeals on economic issues that touched the voters' lives, such as at Worcester, Massachusetts, on October 27: "The Republicans believe in what they call the 'trickle down' theory. They want the big, rich, and wealthy, the privileged special interest groups to get the lion's share of the income and let the scraps fall down for the rest of us." He never failed to call for specific action, such as to an audience in New York City on October 28: "Now I want to say this to you, that if you believe in government of, by, and for the people, if you believe in your own self-interest, the best thing for you to do on November 2d is to go to the polls early and vote the straight Democratic ticket, and then the country will be safe for another 4 years." In truth Truman outhustled his complacent opponent, Governor Thomas Dewey.

On January 20, 1949, President Truman delivered his Inaugural Address. He and his speech writers turned their attention from the domestic issues of the past campaign to foreign affairs, for which the speech would serve as a state paper. In typical Truman style, the address was arranged around several points—this time four. The importance of these four points is that to some degree they still guide U.S. foreign policy. First, Truman pledged support for the United Nations and its peacekeeping function. The Korean war was a logical extension of that commitment. Second, he promised support for world economic recovery and continued help for war-ravaged Europe. Third, he pledged U.S. efforts to strengthen freedom-loving countries against aggression with the NATO security plan. Last, he offered American science and industry to help the underdeveloped nations. The speech contained his usual cold war rhetoric, but it was toned down for the occasion. Truman merely juxtaposed democratic values with their communistic counterparts in order to tell his audiences, domestic and foreign, that only the United States and its allies stood for peace against communist aggression.

Truman's Valedictory Address, delivered to the nation on January 15, 1953, was a personal and sometimes poignant statement of his major trials and triumphs in the Oval Office. The speech is particularly useful in revealing the motivations of the president's major policies in his own language. Two main issues concerned him. The first was the beginning of the containment policy, begun in Greece and Turkey in 1947, and expanded to the Marshall Plan, the Berlin airlift, and NATO. The second issue was his nemesis: Korea. Truman repeated in this speech the same kind of rhetorical reasoning he had used in his other major speeches on Korea. He decided, on the basis of his knowledge of European political leaders' unwise appeasement policies in the era of the 1930s for Hitler, Mussolini, and the Japanese, that that kind of appeasement should not be repeated in areas threatened by communist aggression and takeover, especially in the case of Korea. However, Truman's claim that the UN forces had successfully met and repelled the aggression there sounded hollow to some Americans who were accustomed to traditional military victories. From Truman's viewpoint, however, the assertion was warranted because his goal of limited war, as earlier delineated, was a useful political and military response to the realities of the time, but many people failed to perceive it that way. Nor was Truman particularly successful in persuading them to that viewpoint. There was also a certain soberness in the later part of the speech in which he tried to reassure the country that the cold war would cease when the communist world collapsed. The speech reveals that Truman had come to terms with that unsolvable cold war problem but that American people, then as now, had difficulty in adjusting to that uncomfortable reality.

Truman was famous for public profanity. He wrote to a Methodist minister who complained about the chief executive's language but decided not to mail the letter; that emphatic language was a prerogative the president would never forgo. Truman in private was Truman in public. Some critics objected to such honesty in speech, but something must be said for his lack of duplicity. In hindsight, Americans now know that he was little better or worse than his predecessors or his successors in using profane language; they just hid it from view. That seems to be Truman's major mistake: he was not a hypocrite.

The effectiveness of President Truman's delivery seemed to depend on whether he spoke from a prepared text or extemporaneously—he called it off the cuff. By most accounts, Truman was not an effective manuscript speaker. What happens to most other manuscript speakers happened to him: his rate was too fast, his phrasing was poor, his pitch tended to be unvarying, he often slurred and mispronounced words, and his voice was faintly nasal. In short, he did not have FDR's wonderfully modulated radio voice. Although his speech staff tried repeatedly to coax him to change his delivery habits, Truman apparently had little motivation or willingness to do so. On the other hand, he was effective as an extemporaneous campaign speaker or any other time he spoke without relying on a written text. In this area, he was probably FDR's superior. Freed from the obligation of saying words on paper, HST was able to be his greatest asset, himself, because he could communicate energetically, enthusiastically, and effectively with his live audiences. Freed from the constraints of a written manuscript style, Truman communicated in a direct conversational style. He maintained the dignity of his position, yet he was able—through a folksy style, coupled with direct eye contact and vigorous gestures—to appeal to the issues on the listeners' minds. This common man, with his common language, made the voters believe their best interests were served by the man communicating with them. President Truman's delivery in the 1948 whistlestop campaign was one of the vital elements in its and his success. The direct and vigorous style of delivery—but not finely polished or presented—that Truman had learned and practiced on the Missouri stump in his early political career served him well in campaigning, often from the rear platform of an open-air railroad observation car. Voters saw and heard a feisty, scrappy, and unpretentious president who talked with them in a straightforward and down-to-earth fashion and who earnestly and sincerely delivered his political remarks. They liked what they saw and heard.

Truman's rhetorical style was plain. He believed he should communicate in clear, unadorned, and ordinary language, and he instructed his speech writers to compose his major addresses accordingly. Consequently his rhetoric is practically devoid of the "purple patches of prose" one might associate with FDR or JFK. No memorable Truman lines come to mind. Truman was also fond of the debater-like first, second, and third method of signposting his major points, and his speeches read more like lawyers' briefs than eloquent orations.

Truman was not an ideal presidential orator. Yet he was a major political orator, if not an eloquent one, who persuaded Americans to accept or tolerate ideas that have had a lasting legacy in postwar American political thought and action.

INFORMATION SOURCES

Research Collections and Collected Speeches

The Harry S Truman Library, Independence, Missouri, is a rich repository of rhetorical artifacts for the speech scholar. Truman's home, burial site, and museum are also located there. The materials in the library are typical of the holdings of the other presidential libraries. There are copies of the speech drafts up to Truman's reading copy, and many of these contain his emendations; one can utilize the sound recordings and motion picture films to criticize his delivery; there is a photographic file; and the White House kept the invaluable public reaction mail to the president's major speeches and addresses. The library also holds the usual secondary materials: oral histories, diaries of Truman's contemporaries, theses and dissertations, and other germane research guides and aids. The Harry S Truman Library Institute makes available a number of grants-in-aid for scholarly investigation of Truman and his presidency.

American Rhetoric from Roosevelt to Reagan: A Collection of Speeches and   ARRR
    Critical Essays. Edited by Halford Ross Ryan. Prospect Heights,
    Ill.: Waveland Press, 1983.
The Public Papers of the Presidents: Harry S. Truman. 8 vols. Washington,   PPP
    D.C.: Government Printing Office, 1964.

Selected Critical Studies

Brembeck, Cole S. "Harry Truman at the Whistlestops." *Quarterly Journal of Speech*
    38 (1952): 42–50.
Brockreide, Wayne, and Scott, Robert L. *Moments in the Rhetoric of the Cold War.* New
    York: Random House, 1970.

Hensley, Carl Wayne. "Harry S. Truman: Fundamental Americanism in Foreign Policy Speechmaking, 1945–46." *Southern Speech Communication Journal* 40 (1974): 180–90.

McKerrow, Ray. "Truman and Korea: Rhetoric in the Pursuit of Victory." *Central States Speech Journal* 28 (1977): 1–12.

Ryan, Halford Ross. "Harry S Truman: A Misdirected Defense for MacArthur's Dismissal." *Presidential Studies Quarterly* 11 (1981): 157–66.

Underhill, William R. "Harry S Truman: Spokesman for Containment." *Quarterly Journal of Speech* 47 (1961): 268–74.

White, Eugene E., and Henderlider, Clair R. "What Harry S. Truman Told Us about His Speaking." *Quarterly Journal of Speech* 40 (1954): 37–42.

Selected Biographies

Donovan, Robert J. *Tumultuous Years: The Presidency of Harry S. Truman, 1949–1953.* New York: Norton, 1982.

McCoy, Donald R. *The Presidency of Harry S. Truman.* Lawrence: University Press of Kansas, 1984.

Miller, Merle. *Plain Speaking: An Oral Biography of Harry S. Truman.* New York: Putnam, 1974.

Truman, Harry S. *Memoirs.* 2 vols. Garden City, N.Y.: Doubleday, 1955–56.

Underhill, Robert. *The Truman Persuasions.* Ames: Iowa State University Press, 1981.

CHRONOLOGY OF MAJOR SPEECHES

See "Research Collections and Collected Speeches" for source codes.

"Truman Doctrine," Washington, D.C., March 12, 1947; *ARRR*, pp. 80–85; *PPP*, pp. 176–80.

Inaugural Address, Washington, D.C., January 20, 1949; *PPP*, pp. 112–19.

Special message to Congress on Korea, Washington, D.C., July 19, 1950; *PPP*, pp. 527–36.

Address at the War Memorial Opera House, San Francisco, October 17, 1950; *PPP*, pp. 673–79.

"Far Eastern Policy," Washington, D.C., April 11, 1951; *ARRR*, pp. 86–91; *PPP*, pp. 223–27.

Valedictory, Washington, D.C., January 15, 1953; *PPP*, pp. 1197–1202.

GEORGE CORLEY WALLACE
(1917–   ), spokesman for segregation

———————————————————————————————— JOHN J. MAKAY

George C. Wallace is an important spokesman in U.S. history because of his strong vocal and highly visible opposition to the civil rights movement in the 1960s.

Wallace won his first political race at the age of sixteen when his father took him to Montgomery to run for page in the state senate. In 1937 he entered the University of Alabama in Tuscaloosa and earned a bachelor's degree and a law degree. He left the University of Alabama in 1942 and promptly joined the U.S. Army Air Corps. Wallace returned home from the service in 1946 and served as Alabama's assistant attorney general.

Wallace became active in politics first by becoming a state legislator and then a circuit court judge. To obtain a seat in the legislature, he campaigned from sunup until almost midnight, every day of the week, and he was elected by a wide margin over his two opponents. In 1958, he made his first attempt to win the governorship, but his primary Democratic challenger, John Patterson, defeated him by a vote of 314,000 to 250,000. Reportedly Wallace announced to other Alabama politicians, "John Patterson out-nigguhed me, and boys, I am not going to be out-nigguhed again." He pledged to prevent desegregation of Alabama schools, and he acted on it in his attempt to bar Vivian Malone and James Hood from registering at the University of Alabama. On that occasion he told his audience: "I stand before you today in the place of thousands of other Alabamans whose presence would have confronted you had I been derelict and neglected to fulfill the responsibilities of my office." Federal officials enrolled the two black students, but Wallace had kept his campaign promise to stand in the doorway to support racial segregation in public education.

After the nationally televised drama of his stand at the University of Alabama on June 11, 1963, Wallace's office was deluged with mail from all parts of the country, most of it supporting the governor. He received a tremendous number of speaking invitations from outside the South, and he and his aides became convinced Wallace had a national constituency.

Some regard Wallace as an angry demagogue whose speeches and policies inflamed both blacks and whites. Yet his supporters called him a hero who spoke out courageously for the individual rights of the white working class. Throughout the period in which he was an active speaker on the national scene, Wallace struggled to change his national image as a racist orator, an image that lingered in the minds of millions of people who favored integration.

WALLACE AS A SEGREGATIONIST SPEAKER

To describe how George Wallace carved his place in history, one must begin with his first inaugural address as governor in which he declared: ''Let us rise to the call of freedom-loving blood that is in us and send our answer to the tyranny that clanks its chains upon the South. In the name of the greatest people that have ever trod this earth, I draw the line in the dust and toss the gauntlet before the feet of tyranny. And I say: Segregation now! Segregation tomorrow! Segregation forever!'' This declaration became the cornerstone for Wallace's political speaking, and although he always denied he was a racist, he supported segregation until political reality made it necessary for him to support integration.

Before the 1964 presidential primaries, the newspapers speculated that Wallace would do poorly in all states. Confounding predictions that he would receive no more than 100,000 votes in Wisconsin, Wallace received 240,000 votes, and in Indiana he earned almost 30 percent, or 172,000 votes. He was most successful in Maryland, where in spite of difficulties and barriers he won almost 43 percent of the vote—with a majority of the votes cast by whites.

Wallace relied on three major rhetorical strategies in his oratory. The strategies, or the major maneuvers, methods, and appeals he used to achieve victory at the polls, were illusion, image substitution, and fear.

The strategy of illusion was Wallace's plan to create an impression that he was conducting an intense and highly active campaign. Because state and local campaign officials tried to discourage and block the governor's appearances, he was unable to schedule the number of speeches he wanted to deliver. Moreover, one of his top aides, Bill Jones, reported that the most difficult task he had in managing Wallace's political speaking was protecting the governor from harm. The campaign planners carefully scheduled Wallace to speak to selected audiences where he could be provided with the best protection. Rather than following a heavy speaking schedule, Wallace relied considerably on extensive newspaper advertising to create the illusion of a comprehensive campaign.

Wallace's campaign slogan, ''Stand Up for America,'' characterized his strategy of illusion. He made a strong effort in his oratory to exchange his image as a southern racist for the image of a patriotic champion of the common person, who comprised the hard-working white middle class. He did not deal explicitly with race in his public speaking, but it remained a dominant feature of his public persona. For example, he told his audience in Cambridge, Maryland:

If you believe the liberal left-wingers in this country, you're supposed to believe that George Wallace is immoral. As I have said on many occasions, I have never made a statement against any man because of his race, color, or national origin. Never have I made a statement intended to incite violence on anyone. . . . The excuse of those who are pushing the so-called civil rights bill which would destroy the American concept of government is an excuse in the name of civil rights, and it is nothing but an extension of federal power—not civil rights. I am against the bill.

While Wallace was speaking, angry black citizens in Cambridge were marching from the black neighborhoods toward the campaign rally. Wallace spoke as if he were concerned with preserving constitutional rights and not supporting segregation, but civil rights supporters interpreted his statements as racist rhetoric. A Wallace speaking engagement was usually a rally with bands, flags, songs, and prayer—the ingredients for a highly patriotic and a rousing political get-together. His speeches were devoted to opposing federal efforts to pass civil rights legislation and to declaring he was not a racist. His defense of segregation and angry opposition to the civil rights movement was so dramatic that an effective image substitution was almost impossible.

The strategy of fear was designed to create anger and insecurity and to arouse negative emotions about the threat of racial integration. Attacking the civil rights bill being debated in Congress, Wallace charged that its passage would cost whites job seniority and white purity in their neighborhoods. He often spoke in a code that members of the press referred to as the "oriental junket." For instance, in Cambridge, Maryland, on May 11, 1964, Wallace told his audience: "If a man's got one-hundred Japanese Lutherans working for him and there's a hundred Chinese-Baptists unemployed, he's got to let some of the Japanese-Lutherans go so he can make room for some of the Chinese-Baptists." Wallace obviously implied that passage of the civil rights bill would mean whites would be fired and blacks would be hired. Wallace was either careless in his interpretation of the bill, generalizing about its potential, or he purposefully distorted its meaning to serve his rhetorical ends.

Wallace and his staff decided after the 1964 primaries to mount a major presidential campaign in 1968. They created the American Independent party to spearhead a movement to support his candidacy. In 1968 the governor, while reiterating the positions with which he had become identified, enlarged his platform to include statements on foreign policy and the Vietnam War.

For the 1968 campaign, Wallace used three rhetorical strategies: unification, differentiation, and substitution. First, Wallace attempted to unify himself strongly with the common person struggling against the elitist bureaucrats in Washington, the "pointy-headed" university professors promoting socialist ideas, and the greedy big businessmen. His anti–civil rights stand would unify whites against blacks seeking equal opportunities and further integration. Wallace attracted a huge, intensely loyal following during his presidential campaigns. The Wallacite was characterized as usually nonideological but considerably extreme in positions associated with Wallace's oratory and undecided about whether the political action to resolve national problems should be liberal or conservative. The bonds that unified Wallace supporters were opposition to the civil rights movement, distrust of the federal government, and a fundamental pessimism. Wallace told his supporters in Toledo, Ohio, on October 3, 1968:

This business of integration such as schools and hospitals, and seniority of local labor unions is costing you taxpayers several hundred million dollars, and this is going to be now spent on the defense of our nation and we're going to cut out this expenditure in the next four years. Let me say this to you about law and order. I use it in every speech about law and order, but we don't have to illuminate on it too much tonight because you have seen the breakdown of law and order in your State. And according to the decisions of the Supreme Court, if you go into the streets tonight and are attacked and a policeman knocks the person in the head, he'll be let out of jail before you get into the hospital, and they'll go and try the policeman about it.

The strategy of differentiation portrayed Wallace as a distinctive choice over Richard Nixon and Hubert Humphrey, both of whom Wallace viewed as being about the same. In his speeches, he argued there was hardly any difference between the two major parties and their candidates, while his third party offered a genuine alternative to solving the important problems facing the nation. He told his Toledo audience:

I might point out that just a few nights ago the Republicans and Democrats, joined by Mr. Nixon and Mr. Humphrey, called for Congress to pass a law that goes into effect after the election that will put you in jail without a trial by jury—of the federal court for denying the sale of your own home and property. . . . I can say here tonight that when two national parties such as the Republican and the Democratic parties succumb to the anarchists in the streets and destroy society, then they are not fit to lead the American people during the next adminstration.

Wallace claimed he, more than Nixon or Humphrey, would protect the citizenry and would get tough with criminals and anarchists.

In 1968 Wallace knew that in order to be a serious candidate, he must create a patriotic states' rights image to replace the racist one that seemed inescapable. He sidestepped the racial issue and avoided any direct references to the plight of black Americans in his speeches. By delivering them in the midst of an emotionally charged and patriotic political rally, he tried to shift attention from his image as a segregationist to his image as a champion of the common person. Rather than explicit references to race, Wallace focused his opposition on efforts at integration by addressing the issue of busing children to establish racial balance in public schools. He told his audiences: "The busing of your little school children to bring about social schemes of pointy-headed psuedo-intellectual snobs violates the rights of every man, woman, and child of every race and color in this land. Most of those psuedo-intellectuals don't even have the sense to park a bicycle straight and yet they're tellin' you they're gonna use federal tax money to bus your little child where you don't even want him." This claim was part of Wallace's strategy to reinforce his image as a states' rights, conservative political leader.

Americans in 1968 were preoccupied with U.S. participation in the Vietnam War. Wallace needed to speak in a way that would make him appear to be an effective commander in chief who could end the war with honor. He told his audience in Toledo, for example:

We are in Vietnam whether you like it or not. And American serviceman are committed to this war and are between life and death. And I desire peace and to bring the troops home as soon as possible. But we have learned a few things about our involvement in this confrontation. We should learn that we never should have gone in there by ourselves. And we should have looked our European allies in the face and said to them: We built your factories and defended you and unless you help us in Vietnam and stop trading with the North Vietnamese we're going to cut off every dime of foreign aid you're getting and let you take care of yourselves.

Wallace placed retired Air Force General Curtis LeMay on the ticket with him, but he made a mistake because most Americans suspected or feared that LeMay, if given the opportunity, would be too quick to widen the war. Wallace sensed the public apprehension about LeMay and therefore spoke in moderation about how he could handle foreign policy and the fighting in Southeast Asia. The Alabama governor won over 13 percent of the total popular vote in 1968. He polled 4 million of his nearly 10 million votes outside the South. His political speaking was the major force in one of the most successful third party campaigns in U.S. history.

His next major campaign was the 1972 presidential race. The campaign was shortened when Wallace was shot and seriously wounded in an assassination attempt. He was confined to a wheelchair, and his health prevented him from mounting a significant campaign in 1976. In the 1980s, Wallace prepared to regain his seat in the governor's office in Alabama, a seat he eventually won.

As a national political speaker, Wallace stands as a charismatic and controversial spokesman who primarily appealed to the emotions of a segment of the American population who constituted a white backlash to the civil rights movement and were pessimistic about the federal government. He presented powerful speeches bound to attract both affection and hatred. During the years he was highly visible, millions of citizens regarded him as either a demagogue or a hero. He now speaks as an official who has come to accept integration as preferable to segregation in Alabama and elsewhere, but the racist image lingers for those who know his past.

INFORMATION SOURCES

Research Collections and Collected Speeches

Obtaining copies of George Wallace's speeches is not easy because his rhetoric has not been included in nationally published collections of speeches. The Alabama State Archives, Montgomery, contains material on Wallace's political activity, and additional material can be obtained from the Office of the Governor. Researchers may have to rely considerably on press copies and newspaper accounts of Wallace's oratory. Copies of Wallace's speeches can be obtained by contacting this writer, who secured audio recordings and press releases of speeches from the 1960s. Other authors of dissertations and published articles can also be contacted for speech materials.

Makay, John T. "The Speaking of Governor George C. Wallace in the 1964   *GW*
Maryland Primary." Ph.D. dissertation, Purdue University, 1969.
————, and Brown, William R. *The Rhetorical Dialogue: Contemporary*   *RD*
Concepts and Cases. Dubuque: Wm. C. Brown, 1972.
Office of the Governor, Montgomery, Alabama.   *OG*

Selected Critical Studies

Carlson, Jody. *George C. Wallace and the Politics of Powerlessness.* New Brunswick,
N.J.: Transaction Books, 1981.
Crass, Philip. *The Wallace Factor.* New York: Mason/Charter, 1976.
Freeman, Dorothy Elaine. "A Critical Analysis of the Rhetorical Strategies Employed
in the Speaking of George C. Wallace in the 1968 Presidential Campaign." Ph.D.
Dissertation, Indiana University, 1981.
Haun, Martha J. "A Study in Demagoguery: A Critical Analysis of George Corley Wallace
in the 1968 Presidential Campaign." Ph.D. Dissertation, University of Illinois,
1971.
Hogan, J. Michael. "Wallace and the Wallacites: A Reexamination." *Southern Speech
Communication Journal* 50 (1984): 24–28.
Makay, J. J. "George C. Wallace: Southern Spokesman with a Northern Audience."
Central States Speech Journal 19 (1968): 202–08.
————. "The Rhetorical Strategies of Governor George Wallace in the 1964 Maryland
Primary." *Southern Speech Communication Journal* 36 (1970): 164–75.
————. "The Rhetoric of George C. Wallace and the 1964 Civil Rights Law." *Today's
Speech* 18 (1970): 26–33.
Ramish, Donald Roseman. "The Rhetoric of a Rebel: George Corley Wallace: Campaign
Themes and Consistency Responses." Ph.D. Dissertation, University of Califor-
nia, 1975.
Raum, Richard D., and Measell, James S. "Wallace and His Ways: A Study of the
Rhetorical Genre of Polarization." *Central States Speech Journal* 25 (1974): 28–
35.
Rosenfield, Lawrence. "George Wallace Plays Rosemary's Baby." *Quarterly Journal
of Speech* 55 (1969): 36–44.
Wallace, George C. *Hear Me Out.* Anderson, S.C.: Droke House, 1968.

Selected Biographies

Dorman, Michael. *The George Wallace Myth.* New York: Bantam Books, 1976.
Frady, Marshall. *Wallace.* New York: World Publishing, 1968.
Greenhaw, Wayne. *Watch Out for George Wallace.* Englewood Cliffs, N.J.: Prentice-
Hall, 1976.
Jones, Bill. *The Wallace Story.* Montgomery, Ala.: American Southern Publishing, 1966.

CHRONOLOGY OF MAJOR SPEECHES

See "Research Collections and Collected Speeches" for source codes.

Inaugural Address, Montgomery, Alabama, January 14, 1963; *OG*.

Proclamation at the University of Alabama, June 11, 1963; *New York Times*, June 12, 1963, p. 20.

1964 presidential primary speech, Cambridge, Maryland, May 11, 1964; *GW*, pp. 177–81.

1968 presidential campaign speech, Toledo, Ohio, October 3, 1968; *RD*, pp. 243–48.

HENRY AGARD WALLACE
(1888–1965), thirty-third vice-president of the United States
_____ MICHAEL WEILER

The fame and significance of Henry A. Wallace as an orator derive from his advocacy of important if unsuccessful ideas and from what the failure of those ideas meant in a particular historical context.

Before joining the Franklin Roosevelt administration in its first term, Wallace had become a successful agricultural businessman in his native Iowa. He built a multimillion dollar seed business in the 1920s and published and edited the *Wallace Farmer*, a regional agricultural journal. In 1933, Roosevelt appointed him secretary of agriculture, a post his father had held in the Harding administration. He served for eight years, presiding over a revolutionary New Deal farm policy, which included an ambitious crop price support program and the Soil Bank program of subsidies to discourage overproduction. In 1940, Roosevelt picked him as his running mate, and Wallace became vice-president in the third term. But Harry Truman replaced him in 1944, and he rejoined the cabinet as secretary of commerce for the final Roosevelt term. Truman fired him two years later, and in 1948 Wallace opposed Truman for the presidency, running as a candidate of the Progressive Citizens of America party.

Henry Wallace's importance as an American orator stems from his leadership role in two lost causes of the years following World War II. First, he fought against the triumph of the corporate business state over the principles of nineteenth-century liberal ideology. Second, he opposed the rise of the national security state and involvement in the cold war.

HENRY WALLACE AS NINETEENTH-CENTURY LIBERAL

An irony of Henry Wallace's career is that he was viewed widely as a socialist and by some even as a communist. In fact, he was wedded to the liberal tradition of the nineteenth century in its uniquely American version. Wallace's political philosophy reflected his background as a farmer-businessman. He regarded the farming experience as the most desirable model for individual character development. For Wallace as for traditional liberalism, the central concern was the formation of that character in ways consistent with both capitalism and the general welfare.

In a speech in Los Angeles in 1944, "What America Wants," Wallace identified the elements of farm life that together made up this ideal individual. "The farmer," he said, "is not only a worker, but also a manager, a capitalist, a trader, and a debtor. Farmers know what it is to labor with their own hands . . .

farmers also know what it is to risk money in their own businesses. . . . Farmers are the ultimate bridge between capital and labor.'' The Jeffersonian yeoman farmer was Wallace's ideal, but by the 1930s and 1940s, this ideal had little to do with economic reality. The farm sector in the United States had endured several decades of depressed prices, and millions had left farming to seek employment in the cities, joining throngs of recent immigrants mostly from Southern and Eastern Europe to form a vast pool of industrial wage workers. Wallace knew this yet continued to advocate a philosophy of individual character based in the work-life experiences of a rapidly shrinking minority.

This emphasis of the farming ideal was not simply a product of Wallace's responsibilities as secretary of agriculture. Early during the Roosevelt administration, Wallace had become a major spokesman not just for the farmer but for the New Deal generally. By the beginning of the war, many considered him liberalism's chief advocate, more faithful to the cause than even Roosevelt himself.

Wallace was a vigorous supporter of the New Deal's social welfare initiatives, but he never lost sight of what to him such programs were supposed to be, not just palliatives for symptoms of deprivation but liberating devices that could remove barriers to the realization of each individual's potential. Social welfare was only a preliminary step to securing the general welfare, for the latter depended on the willingness of each person to look beyond his own interests to those of the group. Good policies could help to make good people, and good people would create the good society.

Wallace outlined his concept of the general welfare in a 1940 essay, "The Price of Freedom." "Nowhere have I defined 'the general welfare,' " he reminded, "In a democracy, every individual ought to develop his own definition. For the success of democracy depends on each individual endeavoring to discover his unique capacities insofar as they are related to the common good."

To this individualist approach, Wallace added a religious element. He was deeply religious, and his simultaneous commitment to capitalist principles made him an example of the ideological combination Max Weber called *The Protestant Ethic and the Spirit of Capitalism*. "The Price of Freedom" continued that "modern capitalism derives its inmost essence, in large measure, from orthodox Judaism and Protestant Christianity. Men who can deny themselves, who can save, and who can pursue their purposes relentlessly make the best capitalists," and he might have added, the best Christians.

These sentiments are not remarkably original. They lie at the heart of the American liberal tradition. Nor were they unusual for their time. However radical some New Deal programs might have appeared initially, the philosophy undergirding them was not socialism but Millian liberalism, at least for most New Dealers. Nonetheless, Wallace's rhetorical career is important as the final battle in the liberal tradition's unsuccessful struggle against the triumph of the corporate business state.

If the New Deal is defined simply as a set of social welfare programs, it appears to have been a historical success. Many of these programs have survived and expanded significantly during the postwar period, but the New Deal was more, at least for Wallace. It was a defense of the small-scale entrepreneur, whether independent farmer or businessman, against the relentless onslaught of the huge corporation.

In 1943, Wallace wrote that corporate "cartels have acquired a degree and range of arbitrary power, which threatens the very existence of small business and stifles the creative energy of our people. It must be our resolve," he urged, "that small business shall not become the No. 1 casualty of this war."

Like most other liberals, Wallace recommended vigorous enforcement of antitrust legislation as the way to protect the independent entrepreneur. He assumed that small business could hold its own if the alleged anticompetitive practices of large-scale enterprises were curbed. He did not understand that the comparative advantages of size were considerable, even in a competitive environment, or that antitrust laws were a cumbersome and ineffective method to control the concentrations of economic power he condemned.

Wallace tended to see politics as a struggle between good and evil men. The threat he perceived was not structural; its source was the individual wrongdoer. Wallace wrote an article for the *Saturday Evening Post* in October 1943 entitled "We Must Save Free Enterprise." He cautioned that "numerous attacks have been made on capitalism without distinguishing between capitalist institutions and their abuses. If criticism is to be constructive, it must realize that there are other ways to cure a headache than by decapitation."

Wallace knew that how an individual made his living had much to do with his or her chracter. He understood the connection between independent entrepreneurship and development of the group of traits he admired: discipline, sobriety, risk taking, and delayed gratification. He could see that as more Americans shifted from self-employment to wage labor and the scale of business enterprise increased, the individualist ethic of the liberal tradition would become increasingly irrelevant. Yet the very ideology that led him to this appreciation of the problem precluded his discovering an effective solution.

Wallace conceptualized business interests in individual terms. The checks on business power he proposed were appropriate to individual abuses. But corporations are not individuals, and though they are managed by individual executives, no one person is responsible in a moral sense for corporate policies. Corporate managers are expected to maximize profits, not to practice civic virtue. Moreover, the impact that corporate expansion has had on small business is not primarily a result of illegal anticompetitive practices but of the economic and political advantages of scale.

Wallace's predicament was the liberal tradition's. Nineteenth-century liberalism was founded on a suspicion of concentrations of power. The liberation of bourgeois capitalism from the control of church and state was an effective way, initially, to diffuse political and economic power, but by the late nineteenth century, business itself had become a threat to the principle of divided power.

Liberalism's individualist bias prevented its advocates from analyzing this problem structurally. By the 1940s, Henry Wallace's political rhetoric was no longer relevant to economic reality. Indeed it was the liberal tradition's last gasp. A decade later, liberals would come to accept, and some even to glorify, the large corporation. The individualist ethic, so close to Wallace's heart, would be monopolized by conservatives alert to its usefulness in attacking the social welfare programs of the New Deal.

The increasingly positive image that the corporation came to enjoy in the postwar period was due in large part to the war itself. World War II eclipsed much of the dialogue about domestic economic issues. Controversies that had been intense during the depression receded rapidly. It seemed unpatriotic to complain about corporate power when this power was being applied vigorously toward Allied victory. At war's end, this positive image persisted, especially as economic conditions improved and the depression did not return.

A new national debate predominated. The issue was what role the United States should play in the postwar international arena. Wallace had begun to address this question a few years earlier. He delivered his best-known wartime speech, "The Price of Free World Victory," on May 8, 1942, to a meeting of the Free World Association, an international organization advocating foreign policies based on anti-imperialism. Wallace echoed these principles as he assured that "everywhere the common people are on the march." He prophesied a day when "no nation will have the God-given right to exploit other nations. Older nations will have the privilege to help younger nations get started on the path to industrialization, but there must be neither military nor economic imperialism."

At one level, Wallace did no more than restate the oft-heard anti-imperialist attacks on the Axis powers, but he wished also to preclude the United States from replacing Germany and Japan as the new imperialist nation of the postwar period. "We ourselves in the United States are no more a master race than the Nazis," he stressed, and "we cannot perpetuate economic warfare without planting the seeds of military warfare."

Wallace was especially mindful of a series of articles that *Time/Life* editor Henry Luce had written in the 1940s. These predicted an "American century" based on U.S. economic and military dominance on terms of its own choosing. "The Price of Free World Victory" rejected this attitude. "Some have spoken of the American Century," Wallace admitted, "but I say that the century which will come out of this war can and must be the century of the common man."

Wallace's anti-imperialist rhetoric received relatively little attention during the war except as strictly an attack on U.S. enemies. Not until the war had been won was Wallace viewed widely as a major spokesman for a distinct and dissenting view of U.S. foreign policy. Of course the context had changed. Now the United States was fighting a cold war, and its enemy was its recent ally, the Soviet Union.

In 1945 and 1946, Wallace saw U.S. policy become increasingly anti-Soviet.

He opposed this trend, believing that only a more conciliatory approach could preserve the postwar peace. Truman, he believed, was open-minded and reasonable. Wallace hoped to use his position in the cabinet and his public prominence as liberalism's champion to influence the administration away from confrontative policies.

Wallace favored sharing the secrets of the atomic bomb with the Soviets, providing them with substantial economic aid relatively free of restriction, and accepting Soviet influence in Eastern Europe. Such concessions, he believed, would allay Soviet suspicions of the West and would facilitate peaceful relations in the long term. The administration rejected all of these views, and Wallace's advocacy of them irritated many in it. Matters came to a head in September 1946 when in a speech at Madison Square Garden, New York City, Wallace argued that "we have no more business in the political affairs of Eastern Europe than Russia has in the political affairs of Latin America, Western Europe, and the United States. . . . Whether we like it or not, the Russians will try to socialize their sphere of influence just as we try to democratize our sphere of influence."

The spheres of influence doctrine, though accepted widely among *realpolitik* political scientists from the 1950s onward, was not popular in 1946. It conceded to the Soviets what was theirs in real military terms but what American political rhetoric had denied them consistently: permanent domination of Eastern Europe. Moreover, Wallace's remarks appeared not just to recognize this reality but to legitimize it. Truman reacted swiftly. Wallace was fired on September 20, 1946.

A short stint as editor of the *New Republic* followed. Wallace's foreign policy views were more extreme than the publishers of this mainstream liberal periodical might have wished, but he was considered still the leading symbol of New Deal liberalism, especially amid doubts of the strength of Truman's commitment to its principles.

For anyone in agreement with Wallace's foreign policy views, 1947 was a bad year. The Truman Doctrine, announced in April, amounted to a formal declaration of the cold war. The Marshall Plan followed. Though it invited Soviet participation, Wallace considered its conditions unfair to the Soviets and was not surprised when they declined to join. Wallace's national radio speech of December 29, 1947, announcing his independent candidacy for the presidency of the United States, would argue that "the Truman Doctrine and the Marshall Plan as applied divide Europe into two warring camps. With the Truman Doctrine at its core, the European Recovery Program is a plan to interfere in the social, economic, and political affairs of the countries receiving aid."

Many liberals, some in the Truman administration, had doubts about the Truman Doctrine, with its broad commitment to oppose communist subversion anywhere in the world, but few agreed with Wallace about the Marshall Plan. Most considered the restoration of Western European economies an urgent necessity, and if the United States was to foot the bill, a little interference in the affairs of these nations seemed appropriate.

Wallace's weekly column was dropped from the *New Republic*, and he became increasingly isolated from the Democratic liberal mainstream. By the end of 1947, Wallace had concluded that the Democratic party would not adopt an acceptable foreign policy program. His only recourse, he felt, was to seek a platform outside the party. He, with Senator Glen Taylor of Idaho, agreed to form the national ticket of the Progressive Citizens of America party.

The Progressive party was a loose conglomeration of disaffected Democrats, radical labor leaders, socialists, and communists. From its beginning, it suffered from its association in many minds with communism. Wallace, however, refused to limit or discourage communist participation. At an anti–Truman Doctrine rally in Los Angeles on May 19, 1947, he had proclaimed, "I am not afraid of Communism. If I fail to cry out that I am an anti-Communist, it is not because I am friendly to Communism, but because at this time of growing intolerance, I refuse to join even the outer circle of that band of men who stir the stormy caldron of hatred and fear."

This explanation was unsatisfactory to most people, especially as it became obvious that communists dominated much of the decision making at the 1948 national Progressive party nominating convention. Most doubted Wallace was a communist but saw him as a dupe whose honorable intentions could not compensate for the threatening elements within his movement.

Wallace's rhetoric did little to allay these fears. His speeches were an unfamiliar combination of religious and revolutionary diction. He was fond of biblical allusions. His candidacy announcement proclaimed his following "a Gideon's Army where for every fearful one who leaves, there will be a thousand to take his place." Other speeches contained references to "the people's revolution" throughout the world or glowing descriptions of the ideals of the Russian Revolution. At one campaign stop in 1948, he described communists as "the closest thing to the early Christian martyrs." When asked about the similarities of the Progressive and American Communist party platforms, Wallace replied that the latter had "a good platform."

Wallace characterized his rhetorical style as "the old-fashioned American doctrine of standing up, speaking your mind, and letting the chips fall where they may." Indeed, few other American politicians could equal his candor. Wallace crusaded not only for a conciliatory foreign policy but for domestic policies that accorded with his liberal views. He traveled through the South demanding civil rights for blacks and refusing to speak in segregated halls. He attacked Truman's Federal Employee Loyalty Program as subversive of civil liberties. He condemned "the Wall Street–military team that is leading us toward war."

At times, political ineptness combined with his radical-sounding rhetoric. At one campaign appearance, he was asked how families squatting on federal land set aside for conservation could be persuaded to leave. "People who live on that kind of land," he suggested, "have no right to have children." Later he apologized, but such gaffes underscored his image as a crank, and perhaps even a dangerous radical. One critic dubbed him "Stalin's Mortimer Snerd."

Unsurprisingly the Wallace campaign was a failure. Initially it was expected to split the Democratic liberal vote. In fact, it may have aided Truman's candidacy by allowing him to distinguish clearly his anticommunist credentials from Wallace's alleged connection with communism. Wallace became the focus of anticommunist sentiment in the campaign. By attacking him, Truman could deflect Republican criticism of administration policies to deal with the communist threat. Wallace, who for a decade had stood at the front of liberal ranks, was consigned in the end to their radical fringes. Wallace's 1948 defeat ended his active participation in politics. In later years he supported the formation of NATO and U.S. entry into the Korean war, believing that the opportunity for U.S.-Soviet reconciliation had been lost.

Henry Wallace was not a politically sophisticated orator. The biblical element in his rhetoric gave it an archaic tinge. His radical diction conjured up alarming images. His extreme statements caused audiences to question his political judgment and even his patriotism. Wallace is an important figure in American oratorical history because of his intimate identification with the two major ideological casualties of the postwar period: nineteenth-century liberalism and anti-imperialist isolationism. The first was supplanted by the corporate state in its domination of economic life. The second gave way to the national security state and the cold war.

Wallace's rhetoric provides reference points by which to chart these significant developments. By comparing their advocates' claims to Wallace's, we see more clearly the ways in which persuasion helped bring about ideological change. By taking Wallace's political philosophy as a historical standard, we understand more insightfully the nature of the postwar political consensus in the United States.

INFORMATION SOURCES

Research Collections and Collected Speeches

An extensive collection of Henry Wallace's manuscripts, diaries, and other records is housed in the Special Collections Department of the University of Iowa Libraries, Iowa City, Iowa. Wallace's correspondence as vice-president is in the Franklin D. Roosevelt Library, Hyde Park, New York. The Oral History Office of Columbia University, New York City, has compiled an extensive oral memoir of Wallace's career. Most of these materials are indexed and on microfilm. Additional materials are available in the Library of Congress, Washington, D.C.

Democracy Reborn. Edited by Russell Lord. New York: Reynal and Hitch-   DR
    cock, 1944.

Primary Sources

Wallace, Henry A. *The American Choice*. New York: Reynal and Hitchcock, 1940.
———. *The Century of the Common Man*. New York: Reynal and Hitchcock, 1943.

————. *The General Welfare*. Chapel Hill, N.C.: University of North Carolina Press, 1937.

————. *The Price of Freedom*. New York: National Home Library, 1940.

————. *Sixty Million Jobs*. New York: Reynal and Hitchcock, 1945.

————. *Statesmanship and Religion*. New York: Round Table Press, 1934.

————. *Toward World Peace*. New York: Reynal and Hitchcock, 1948.

————. *Whose Constitution?* New York: Reynal and Hitchcock, 1936.

Selected Critical Studies

Kingdon, Frank. *Henry Wallace and Sixty Million Jobs*. New York: Reader's Press, 1945.

MacDonald, Dwight. *Henry Wallace: The Man and the Myth*. New York: Vanguard Press, 1947.

MacDougall, Curtis. *Gideon's Army*. Vols. 1–3. New York: Marzini and Munsell, 1965.

Markowitz, Norman. *The Rise and Fall of the People's Century: Henry A. Wallace and American Liberalism, 1941–1948*. New York: Free Press, 1973.

Ross, Irwin. *The Loneliest Campaign*. Westport, Conn.: Greenwood Press, 1968.

Schmidt, Karl M. *Henry A. Wallace: Quixotic Crusade, 1948*. Syracuse, N.Y.: Syracuse University Press, 1960.

Walker, J. Samuel. *Henry A. Wallace and American Foreign Policy*. Westport, Conn.: Greenwood Press, 1976.

Walton, Richard J. *Henry Wallace, Harry Truman, and the Cold War*. New York: Viking Press, 1976.

Selected Biographies

Blum, John Morton. *The Price of Vision: The Diary of Henry A. Wallace, 1942–1946*. Boston: Houghton Mifflin, 1973.

Lord, Russell. *The Wallaces of Iowa*. Boston: Houghton Mifflin, 1947.

Schapsmeier, Edward L., and Schapsmeier, Frederick H. *Henry A. Wallace of Iowa: The Agrarian Years*. Ames: Iowa State University Press, 1968.

————. *Prophet in Politics: Henry A. Wallace and the War Years, 1940–1965*. Ames: Iowa State University Press, 1970.

CHRONOLOGY OF MAJOR SPEECHES

See "Research Collections and Collected Speeches" for source code.

"Capitalism, Religion and Democracy," Pacific School of Religion, Berkeley, California, February 24, 1938; *DR*, pp. 137–44.

"The Price of Free World Victory," Free World Association, New York City, May 8, 1942; *DR*, pp. 190–96.

"What America Wants," Los Angeles, Feburary 4, 1944; *DR*, pp. 17–24.

"What America Can Have," Los Angeles, February 7, 1944; *DR*, pp. 24–30.

"America Can Get It," Los Angeles, Feburary 9, 1944; *DR*, pp. 30–40.

"The Way to Peace," Madison Square Garden, New York City, September 12, 1946; reprinted in *New Republic*, September 30, 1946, pp. 401–06.

"I Shall Run in 1948," national radio address, New York City, December 29, 1947; *Vital Speeches of the Day*, January 1, 1948, pp. 172–74.

WOODROW WILSON
(1856–1924), twenty-eighth president of the United States

ROBERT A. WALLER

As an accomplished academic, domestic reformer, and international statesman, Woodrow Wilson relied heavily on his oratorical skills. His effect on audiences contributed to his election as president of Princeton University in 1902, as governor of New Jersey in 1910, and as president of the United States in 1912 and 1916. In contrast, his inability to persuade the American people and the U.S. Senate of the value in joining the Leage of Nations led to his most tragic defeat.

Wilson, the son of a Presbyterian minister, was born in Staunton, Virginia, on December 28, 1856. He never attended a public school but was privately tutored, mostly by his father, in the Reconstruction South. In an October 28, 1916, interview with Ida M. Tarbell in *Collier's*, President Wilson reminisced about the importance of his father's early advice to stress simplicity in both speaking and writing: "Don't shoot at your meaning with bird shot and hit the whole countryside; shoot with a rifle at the thing you have to say."

During his youth Wilson longed to be a political orator in the pattern of his idols, Gladstone and Burke. First as an undergraduate at Davidson College, then at Princeton University, later as a law student at the University of Virginia, and finally as a graduate student in political economy at Johns Hopkins University, Wilson joined the literary societies and engaged in their debates.

Debate, with its emphasis on organization and logic, significantly influenced Wilson's speaking style. As a faculty member at Wesleyan University and Princeton University, he promoted debating societies. Although he never wrote about the art of public address, some impressions can be gleaned from his articles on orators and from his personal practice. His most important precept was that content was fundamental to eloquence. Using Edmund Burke as his model, Wilson wrote in an article contained in his *Public Papers*: "Eloquence consists not in sonorous sound or brilliant phrases. *Thought* is the fibre, thought is the *pith* of eloquence. Eloquence lies in the thought, not in the throat. . . . It is persuasion inspired by conviction." As a professor Wilson practiced what he preached; the Princeton students frequently elected him their most popular lecturer.

WILSONIAN ORATORY IN PEACE AND WAR

Wilson's background, personality, and position inclined him to make argumentative speeches. Because of his moral bent and religious background, he advocated abstract principles rather than specific policies. Although his speeches offered ample support of his positions, only rarely did they incorporate statistical evidence. The speech teachers of his day were thrilled with the models he presented, in part because they helped instruct their students in the value of both previewing and summarizing the body of a speech. Many of his addresses, like "The Meaning of the American Flag," found their way into the style books of the 1910s and 1920s only to be replaced in the 1930s with the less formal ones of Franklin D. Roosevelt.

Wilson's oratorical style differed markedly from his political contemporaries, especially William Jennings Bryan, Robert M. La Follette, and Theodore Roosevelt. He studiously avoided the emotionalism and bombast of his rivals. Beset with numerous health problems, Wilson's frail physical constitution left him little choice but to adopt in his speeches a reserved and statesmanlike approach, which his detractors criticized as schoolmarmish. Although he acquired a reputation for coolness and aloofness, he swayed his listeners with the strength of his convictions, the high purpose of his message, the logic of his argument, and the religious correctness of his position.

For one frequently depicted as dour, distant, and disdainful, Wilson possessed a puckish sense of humor, which tempered the impression created by his great personal ambition, strong religious convictions, and keen intellect. His sense of humor enabled him to laugh at himself and to make light of serious issues. He frequently used limericks as a rhetorical device. He was skillful at mimicry and dialect stories, though these were minor weapons in his oratorical arsenal. As an orator, Wilson could coin the masterful phrase on which to hang his concept. As both a writer and an orator, he loved to use alliteration to embellish his style. As a student of oratory, he could employ a variety of rhetorical devices, but he also knew which ones he should avoid.

Wilson shunned the pompous and impetuous in his delivery. Moving pictures of the time portray a bespectacled public figure standing very erect using modest gestures, most notably an index finger waving in the manner of a schoolmaster. His presence was serene and sensible in contrast to the arm-waving antics of Teddy Roosevelt. His voice was better suited to the auditorium than the outdoor platform. Recordings suggest a well-modulated tenor voice but not an overpowering one. His platform manner was pleasant and inviting but also scholarly and subdued. It was calculated to convey the efficacy of the principles involved.

In the days before the widespread use of presidential ghost writers, Woodrow Wilson was the initiator of the ideas, the outliner, the organizer, and the stylist. After mentally organizing the material, he made a shorthand outline, then a shorthand draft, and finally a typewritten draft he personally picked out on his typewriter. Time permitting, he shared the drafts with his wife, secretary, or various confidants, depending on the issue. Inaugural addresses, congressional speeches, and policy statements were prepared with meticulous attention to detail including nuances of phrasing. *The Public Papers of Woodrow Wilson* and the even more comprehensive *Wilson Papers* now being published offer insights into the thought processes as the final version unfolded. Once the ideas were developed, he frequently dictated a rough draft to a stenographer. Too often in less formal settings, his advisers thought, Wilson relied heavily on his ability to speak impromptu, which he developed as a Chautauqua speaker. Extempore phrases like "too proud to fight" and "watchful waiting" were subject to varying and sometimes embarrassing interpretations. Fortunately for the student of Wilsonian rhetoric, the stenographic notes of Charles Lee Swem have been preserved for numerous campaign and ceremonial speeches of an impromptu nature.

Mindful of the importance of public opinion and confident of his own abilities, Wilson initiated on March 14, 1914, a series of semiweekly press conferences as a vehicle for furthering his programs. These sessions were open to all accredited White House correspondents (about twenty then). Although subsequent presidents have been more masterful in managing the news, Wilson used his knowledge of communication skills to ensure a favorable press.

Wilson most deserves an important place in the history of American public address for his memorable expression of ideas. As a professor turned politician, he transformed his ideas and ideals into platforms and programs. While he illustrated his oratorical prowess as an educational leader and a progressive governor, he delivered his most memorable speeches as president. His well-expressed phrases became rallying points for major shifts in legislative and public opinion.

Before transcontinental transportation and telecommunication, a party's presidential standard-bearer was expected to accept the presidential nomination at his front porch. At Sea Girt, New Jersey, reporters were treated to a calm, well-organized, and closely reasoned address. Speaking from a prepared text, Wilson championed progressive reform, philosophized about the nature of government, and stirred the masses concerning a need for change. It was not until later in the campaign, however, that he coined the expression "New Freedom" to encompass his domestic reform promises. The day following his being notified of his nomination, he advised reporters that "the rest of my speeches will be delivered as I like to deliver a speech—right out of my mind as it is working at the time." Throughout the 1912 campaign, he relied on an extempore style to carry his message to the electorate. The tactic proved effective, for he became the first Democratic president since Grover Cleveland.

In his First Inaugural, the new president expressed his desire for national unity after the three-party contest: "This is not a day of triumph; it is a day of dedication." He compellingly outlined the promises to be redeemed by the Congress in promoting social justice by destroying the power of invisible government. One of the shortest inaugural addresses in U.S. history (only 1500 words), it was simple and sincere. In retrospect this was the finest speech of his political career, for Congress enacted as law the "work of restoration" he sought.

As a confident and a consummate orator, Wilson reintroduced the practice of delivering his messages to Congress in person. Thomas Jefferson, who was a better writer than speaker, began the practice of sending written messages to the

Congress to be read by its clerk. Confident that his effective delivery and personal presence would contribute to the persuasiveness of his message, Wilson returned to the tradition of George Washington by appearing personally, a practice followed by all of his successors. The editor of the *New York Times* commented that Wilson "probably has no equal in this country as an effective speaker." Besides addresses to Congress, Wilson frequently appealed directly to the people to rally support for his programs. For example, his Jackson Day address in 1915 encouraged the business interests and independent voters to foster the congressional teamwork necessary to overcome legislative obstinance. During his eight years in the Oval Office, the president used his oral proficiency to advantage.

Wilson had hoped to concentrate on domestic reform, but his energies were diverted to the international situation. The advent of World War I in Europe thrust him into the role of impartial observer and then reluctant associate. Initially the president asked the nation to be "neutral in fact as well as in name" and to be "impartial in thought as well as action." As the pressures for involvement mounted, his ideal proved impractical and then impossible. On April 2, 1917, Wilson appeared before a joint session of Congress seeking a declaration of war against Germany because "the world must be made safe for democracy." The chief executive deftly distinguished from a propaganda standpoint between the acts of the German government regarding the resumption of unrestricted submarine warfare and those of the German people. Declaring that "the right is more precious than peace," he spoke to that larger audience, the American people, expressing their hopes and enlisting their support. The address was intended not only to bring about a declaration of war with Germany but also to justify past policies and to explain the shift from neutrality to belligerence. In a dispassionate request to the Congress, Wilson sought to convert a war he hated into a crusade for nobler ends.

As a spokesman for civilization, Wilson stated in idealistic terms the hopes for a world of peace and tranquillity. His memorable address to Congress laid the basis for an armistice by sketching the Fourteen Points on which the peace should be built. This foundation included "open covenants of peace, openly arrived at," freedom of the seas, economic interchange, arms reduction, territorial adjustments, and (most important to Wilson) "a general association of nations." When the Central Powers appeared reluctant to pursue peace on these terms, the president enunciated four principles on which the United States was pursuing this "war of emancipation." The essential condition was "self-determination" for all subject peoples. These aims reached fruition at the end of the war when Wilson offered the Covenant of the League of Nations to be incorporated in the Treaty of Versailles. In presenting the report at the peace conference, the president, become international diplomat, described the proposal and the terms as a "vehicle of life" for the world. Wilson's rhetoric had achieved its widest audience.

Wilson's oratorical skills served him well until the last few years of his second administration. On two important occasions, his appeals were rebuffed. Just before the off-year elections in November 1918, he had urged the voters to return a Democratic Congress to express confidence in his administration of the war. Making partisan what had been regarded as a bipartisan effort backfired with a vengeance. Tired of meatless days, wheatless days, fuelless days, and manless households, the electorate returned a House and Senate with Republican majorities. Wilson's calculated call for a vote of confidence had failed. His hand at the Versailles peace conference and his support of a League of Nations were both weakened. Analysts disagree about the reason for the miscalculation, but all acknowledge the consequences were great.

Congressional resistance to the peace treaty and the international organization drafted at Paris began to mount. Confident of his ability to communicate the nation's need for a role in world affairs, Wilson vowed to take his case to the people. He began a whistle-stop tour across the country delivering thirty-three major addresses to stem the tide of isolationism sweeping the country. In his first informal report to the people in Columbus, Ohio, Wilson described the whole proposal a "measurable success" in redeeming promises made and in preventing future catastrophe. Three weeks later at Pueblo, Colorado, the president endeavored to answer criticisms of the treaty by stressing the positive features of a "people's treaty." Although he met with modest success, he so exhausted his frail body that he suffered a paralytic stroke from which he never recovered. Without his commanding leadership to convince the public, the treaty, with or without reservations, was doomed to defeat.

Wilson was a versatile orator whose career as professor of politics had prepared him to mold public opinion, to implement his ideas, and to foster his ideals. His oratory was characterized by logical form, effective style, and intense conviction. His speeches were noted for their intellectual content, persuasive argumentation, and homespun interpretation. Even taking into account his defeats in the November 1918 election and the ratification of the Treaty of Versailles with its provision for a League of Nations, the objective analyst must conclude that the power of his technique, the persuasiveness of his ideas, and the permanence of his reputation dictate that he be included among the great orators of the twentieth century.

INFORMATION SOURCES

Research Collections and Collected Speeches

Original source materials for Wilson are available in the Library of Congress Manuscripts Division for the Wilson Papers (they are arranged in two chronological files, one for speeches and one for correspondence) and those of his contemporaries. These materials can be procured on microfilm, but substantial portions of these works have been published. *The Papers of Woodrow Wilson* are being collected, edited, and published by Arthur S. Link et al. (Princeton: Princeton University Press, 1966-). The collection currently stands at forty-five volumes. The best published bibliography with 1,248 entries is *Woodrow*

426 American Orators of the Twentieth Century

Wilson: A Selected Bibliography of His Published Writings, Addresses, and Public Papers, compiled by Laura S. Turnbull (Princeton: Princeton University Press, 1948).

A Crossroads of Freedom: The 1912 Campaign Speeches of Woodrow Wilson. Edited by John Wells Davidson. New Haven: Yale University Press, 1956. CFCS

The Public Papers of Woodrow Wilson. Edited by Ray Stannard Baker and William E. Dodd. 6 vols. New York: Harper and Brothers Publishers, 1925–1927. PPWW

Selected Critical Studies

Cornwell, Elmer E., Jr. "The Press Conferences of Woodrow Wilson." *Journalism Quarterly* 39 (1962): 292–300.

Craig, Hardin. "Woodrow Wilson as an Orator." *Quarterly Journal of Speech* 38 (1952): 145–48.

Henderlider, Clair R. "Woodrow Wilson's Speeches on the League of Nations, September 4–25, 1919." *Speech Monographs* 13 (1946): 23–34.

Hendrix, J. A. "Presidential Addresses to Congress: Woodrow Wilson and the Jeffersonian Tradition." *Southern Speech Journal* 31 (1966): 285–94.

Ivie, Robert L. "Presidential Motives for War." *Quarterly Journal of Speech* 51 (1974): 337–45.

McEdwards, Mary G. "Woodrow Wilson: His Stylistic Progression." *Western Speech* 26 (1962): 28–38.

McKean, Dayton D. "Woodrow Wilson." In *A History and Criticism of American Public Address*. Edited by William Norwood Brigance. New York: McGraw-Hill, 1943.

Oliver, Robert T. "Wilson's *Rapport* with His Audience." *Quarterly Journal of Speech* 27 (1941): 79–90.

Osborn, George C. "Woodrow Wilson as a Speaker." *Southern Speech Journal* 22 (1956): 61–72.

Reid, Ronald F. "The Young Woodrow Wilson's Political Laboratories." *Southern Speech Journal* 28 (1963): 227–35.

Runion, Howard L. "An Objective Study of the Speech Style of Woodrow Wilson." *Speech Monographs* 3 (1936): 75–94.

Snell, John L. "Wilsonian Rhetoric Goes to War." *Historian* 14 (1952): 191–208.

Wilson, John F. "Rhetorical Echoes of a Wilsonian Idea." *Quarterly Journal of Speech* 43 (1957): 271–77.

Selected Biographies

Baker, Ray Stannard. *Woodrow Wilson: Life and Letters.* 8 vols. Garden City, N.Y.: Doubleday, Doran, 1927–1939.

Bragdon, Henry W. *Woodrow Wilson: The Academic Years.* Cambridge, Mass.: Belknap Press of Harvard University Press, 1967.

Hirst, David W. *Woodrow Wilson, Reform Governor: A Documentary Narrative.* New York: D. Van Nostrand Company, 1965.

Link, Arthur S. *Wilson.* 5 vols. Princeton: Princeton University Press, 1947–1965.

Osborn, George C. *Woodrow Wilson: The Early Years.* Baton Rouge: Louisiana State University Press, 1968.

Weinstein, Edwin A. *Woodrow Wilson: A Medical and Psychological Biography*. Princeton: Princeton University Press, 1981.

CHRONOLOGY OF MAJOR SPEECHES

See "Research Collections and Collected Speeches" for source codes.

Acceptance speech, Sea Girt, New Jersey, August 7, 1912; *PPWW*, *College and State*, 2:452–74; *CFCS*, pp. 15–37.

First Inaugural Address, Washington, D.C., March 4, 1913; *PPWW*, *The New Democracy*, 1:1–6.

Flag Day address, Washington, D.C., June 15, 1914; *PPWW*, *The New Democracy*, 1:131–34.

"American neutrality," Washington, D.C., August 18, 1914; *PPWW*, *The New Democracy*, 1:157–59.

Jackson Day address, Indianapolis, Indiana, January 8, 1915; *PPWW*, *The New Democracy*, 1:236–51.

Address seeking declaration of war, Washington, D.C., April 2, 1917; *PPWW*, *War and Peace*, 1:6–16.

Fourteen Points speech, Washington, D.C., January 8, 1918; *PPWW*, *War and Peace*, 1:155–62.

Four Principles speech, Washington, D.C., February 11, 1918; *PPWW*, *War and Peace*, 1:177–84.

Presentation of the Covenant of the League of Nations, Paris, France, February 14, 1919; *PPWW*, *War and Peace*, 1:413–29.

First speech in support of League of Nations membership on Western tour, Columbus, Ohio, September 4, 1919; *PPWW*, *War and Peace*, 1:590–605.

Last speech in support of the League of Nations, Pueblo, Colorado, September 25, 1919; *PPWW*, *War and Peace*, 2:399–416.

BASIC RESEARCH SOURCES IN AMERICAN PUBLIC ADDRESS

"Information Sources," the section at the end of each essay in this book, lists the pertinent books and articles about each speaker and where texts of the speaker's most important speeches may be found. Here we provide an outline of the information sources readily available to students and critics of speech making in twentieth-century America.

A milestone in the scholarly study of public address is *A History and Criticism of American Public Address*, published in three volumes. William Norwood Brigance edited the first two volumes (1943), and Marie Hochmuth (Nichols) edited the third (1955). The complete work stands as a monument to American oratorical criticism and remains one of the standard sources for the criticism of America's leading political orators. These volumes are often cited in "Information Sources" for orators discussed in this book. Although *A History and Criticism* contains critical essays on orators, it does not offer any speech texts. That void was filled with the appearance of two other books that collected important speeches.

Wayland Maxfield Parrish and Marie Hochmuth (Nichols) published a collection of speeches, *American Speeches*, in 1954. This book was an archetype for future collections of speeches because it prefaced the text with biographical information, the occasion of the oration, and information about the nature of the original source of the speech text. Hochmuth's essay "Lincoln's First Inaugural" is a classic in the field of rhetorical criticism, and Parrish's "The Study of Speeches" informed much of the rhetorical criticism published for a decade. The other important collection of speech texts is A. Craig Baird's *American Public Addresses, 1740–1952* (1956). Like Parrish and Hochmuth, Baird added a seminal ingredient, his chapter, "The Study of Speeches," in which he answered the important questions of why one should study political oratory and how one should study speeches.

Succeeding books on the criticism of American oratory seemed to follow these early leads. Several successive works have served the needs of students and critics by supplying collections of significant public addresses. Ernest J. Wrage and Barnet Baskerville edited *Contemporary Forum: American Speeches of Twentieth Century Issues* (1962). They expanded the kinds of speech texts offered by including less significant but nevertheless important figures in American politics and culture. Lesser-known figures such as Eugene Debs, Al Smith, Burton Wheeler, and Roy Wilkins assumed their rightful places alongside the Roosevelts and Trumans of the period. *Contemporary American Speeches: A Source-*

book of Speech Forms and Principles (4th ed., 1978), edited by Wil Linkugel, R. R. Allen, and Richard Johannesen, contains standard speech texts but also includes texts from lesser-known speakers on a wide range of subjects; additionally the editors included speeches delivered by college students. *Critical Anthology of Public Speeches* (1978), edited by Kathleen Jamieson, is a pamphlet-length collection of interesting speeches, arranged by genre. Jamieson also briefly discusses each genre. For the study of female oratory, one may advantageously turn to Judith Anderson's *Outspoken Women: Speeches by American Women Reformers 1635–1935* (1984). Anderson has included hard-to-find texts of speeches by women orators and by orienting the critic of feminist rhetoric with a fine historical overview of the role and successes of American women on the political platform. *The World's Great Speeches*, (3rd enlarged ed., 1973), edited by Lewis Copeland and Lawrence Lamm, contains the texts of many lesser-known speakers in addition to the standard ones on a wide range of interests and topics, from legislative to courtroom to after-dinner speaking.

An innovation in the field was John Graham's important *Great American Speeches, 1898–1963* (1970). Graham combined in one book the texts of important addresses with critical essays about those speeches, previously published in scholarly journals. Graham pointed the way for students and critics to read a speech and a critic's response to it and then to form a personal critical judgment. That idea was carried forward in Halford Ryan's *American Rhetoric from Roosevelt to Reagan: A Collection of Speeches and Critical Essays* (1983). Ryan's collection was the first to anthologize such speakers as Huey Long, Father Coughlin, and Jerry Falwell in addition to supplying case studies on particular speeches. Karlyn Kohrs Campbell's *Critiques of Contemporary Rhetoric* (1972) provides texts of nine speeches of the late 1960s and early 1970s, as well as Campbell's critiques of five of these speeches. Charles W. Lomas wrote and edited a useful work on speakers who are problematical in American society, *The Agitator in American Society* (1968), in which he combined texts of speeches by individuals such as Eugene Debs, Joseph McCarthy, Billy James Hargis, and Stokley Carmichael with a perceptive analysis of the role of agitation in the United States.

The initial volume covered the year 1937–1938, but *Representative American Speeches* (succeeded by the dates of the respective years) has been published every year since. First edited by A. Craig Baird and later edited by Lester Thonssen, then by Waldo Braden, and currently by Owen Peterson, the complete set of volumes is a significant source of speech texts. *Vital Speeches of the Day*, published since 1934, is a periodical devoted to printing the texts of timely and important speeches.

In the specialized field of presidential rhetoric, Theodore Windt has met the needs of researchers with two important books. Windt was the first to collect only the speeches of the nation's chief executives in *Presidential Rhetoric (1961 to the Present)* (3d ed., 1983). In addition to collecting the significant presidential addresses from Kennedy to Reagan, Windt incorporated a seminal essay on the nature of presidential rhetoric. His second book, edited with Beth Ingold, is *Essays in Presidential Rhetoric* (1983). Windt selected important critical essays about the uses and abuses of presidential persuasion from Kennedy to Reagan. Two particularly important essays are "The Rise of the Rhetorical Presidency," which commends itself to the serious scholar of presidential rhetoric, and Windt's own "The Presidency and Speeches on International Crisis: Repeating the Rhetorical Past," which helps to explain why and how presidents commit the country to military adventures. Although the so-called rhetorical presidency probably begins with Theodore Roosevelt and Woodrow Wilson, and most certainly includes all the presidents from Franklin Roosevelt forward, Windt's two books serve the post-Kennedy era effectively. For those who seek a more comprehensive treatment of twentieth-century presidential speaking, they may find *The President in the Twentieth Century* (1983), edited by Louis Filler, useful. Filler anthologizes significant presidential orations from William McKinley to Lyndon Johnson, although only one of Johnson's speeches is included. This book is particularly useful for those who wish to research presidential rhetoric before Franklin Roosevelt.

Researchers of religious rhetoric should examine DeWitt Holland's edited volumes, *Preaching in America* (1971) and *Sermons in American History* (1969). *Preaching* is an excellent source for essays that place in perspective the theological issues of the times and the responses of various orators-preachers to religious and political concerns. *Sermons* contains, along with brief biographical materials, important historical sermons on a wide variety of topics by America's leading preachers. Holland serves readers and critics well by including sermons on important religious issues.

General readers may find Karl Wallace's *A History of Speech Education in America* (1954) a helpful overview of the educational and cultural heritage in which the study of oratory has flourished in U.S. colleges and universities.

The study and criticism of American political oratory is ongoing, and the productive results of scholarly research are published in a variety of scholarly journals. *Presidential Studies Quarterly*, under the auspices of the Center for the Study of the Presidency, increasingly devotes space for critical essays on all aspects of presidential rhetoric. Book reviews on topics of rhetorical transactions are also included. The Speech Communication Association publishes several significant journals that regularly treat American political oratory: *Quarterly Journal of Speech*, *Communication Monographs*, and *Critical Studies in Mass Communication*. Regional speech associations also routinely publish articles on political oratory: *Southern Speech Communication Journal*, *Western Journal of Speech Communication*, *Central States Speech Journal*, and *Communication Quarterly*. All of the speech journals are indexed in *Index to Journal in Communication Studies through 1979* (1980), compiled by Ronald J. Matlon, a good beginning point for research on American public address. Articles contained in the speech journals are also listed in the bibliography published annually in *Communication Monographs*.

Speaker and Gavel, published by the national speech honorary society, prints timely articles on American oratory, particularly since 1960, and *Exetasis* prints critical essays on recent speeches.

There are a number of commercially produced disk and cassette audio recordings of speeches. Among these, the Listening Library has produced *The Presidents Speak Cassette Library* (1976), which includes speeches from Calvin Coolidge forward, *F.D.R. Inaugural Addresses* (1976), *Kennedy Nixon Debates* (1976), and *Great Debates of 1976* (1977). The Visual Education Corporation has produced *Speaking for America: Six Presidents Talk about Their Visions for America* (1975), which includes audio recordings of presidents from Hoover to Johnson, and Caedmon has produced an excellent series, *Great American Speeches*, of which volume 2, 1931–1947, and volume 4, 1950–1963, have good selections of speeches by important speakers of this century. There is also *John Fitzgerald Kennedy 1917–1963: A Memorial Album* produced by Diplomat Records. In addition, all of the presidential libraries will, upon request, dub cassette copies of audio recordings of speeches from master recordings and mail them to researchers.

Although the presidential libraries and other major research collections of major American spokesmen also have film and video recordings, Alliance for Great Speeches has produced a commercial videotape, *Great Speeches*, vol. 1 (1985), which includes great speeches by several of the most important contemporary American orators.

LIST OF BASIC RESEARCH SOURCES IN AMERICAN PUBLIC ADDRESS

Collections of Speech Texts

American Public Address: 1740–1952. Edited by A. Craig Baird. New York: McGraw Hill, 1956.

American Speeches. Edited by Wayland Maxfield Parrish and Marie Hochmuth. New York: Longmans, Green, 1954.

Contemporary American Speeches: A Sourcebook of Speech Forms and Principles. Edited by Wil A. Linkugel, R. R. Allen, and Richard L. Johannesen. 4th ed. Dubuque: Kendall/Hunt, 1978.

Contemporary Forum: American Speeches on Twentieth Century Issues. Edited by Ernest J. Wrage and Barnet Baskerville. New York: Harper, 1962.

Outspoken Women: Speeches by American Women Orators, 1635–1935. Edited by Judith Anderson. Dubuque: Kendall/Hunt, 1984.

Presidential Rhetoric (1961 to the Present). Edited by Theodore Windt. 3d ed. Dubuque: Kendall/Hunt, 1983.

The President in the Twentieth Century. Edited by Louis Filler. Englewood: Jerome S. Ozer, 1983.

Representative Speeches 1937/1938 [and successive annual volumes]. Edited by A. Craig Baird 1937/38–1950/59; Lester Thonssen 1959/60–1969/70; Waldo Braden 1970/71–1979/80; Owen Peterson 1980/81–. New York: H. W. Wilson.

Sermons in American History. Edited by Dewitte Holland. Nashville, Tenn.: Abingdon Press, 1971.

The World's Great Speeches. Edited by Lewis Copeland and Lawrence Lamm. 3d enlarged ed. New York: Dover, 1973.

Collections of Speeches and Critical Essays

American Rhetoric from Roosevelt to Reagan: A Collection of Speeches and Critical Essays. Edited by Halford Ross Ryan. Prospect Heights, Ill.: Waveland Press, 1983.

Campbell, Karlyn Kohrs. *Critiques of Contemporary Rhetoric*. Belmont, Calif.: Wadsworth, 1972.

Critical Anthology of Public Speeches. Edited by Kathleen Jamieson. Chicago: Science Research Associates, 1978.

Great American Speeches, 1898–1963. Edited by John Graham. New York: Meredith, 1970.

Lomas, Charles W. *The Agitator in American Society*. Englewood Cliffs, N.J.: Prentice-Hall, 1968.

Collections of Critical Essays

Essays in Presidential Rhetoric. Edited by Theodore Windt with Beth Ingold. Dubuque: Kendall/Hunt, 1983.

Preaching in American History. Edited by DeWitte Holland. Nashville, Tenn.: Abingdon Press, 1969.

Audio Recordings

F.D.R. Inaugural Addresses. Cassette. Listening Library, CX 367/2, 1976.
Great American Speeches. Vol. 3, 1931–1947. Record. Caedmon, TC 2033, n.d.
Great American Speeches. Vol. 4, 1950–1963. Record. Caedmon, TC 2035, n.d.
Great Debates of 1976. Cassette. Listening Library, CX 368/4, 1977.
John Fitzgerald Kennedy, 1917–1963: A Memorial Album. Record. Diplomat Records, n.d.
Kennedy Nixon Debates. Cassette. Listening Library, CX 366/4, 1976.
The Presidents Speak. Cassette. Listening Library, CXL 520, 1976.
Speaking for America: Six Presidents Talk about Their Visions for America. Cassette. Visual Education Corporation, 5101, n.d.

Video Recordings

Great Speeches. Vol. 1. Alliance Video for Great Speeches Inc., 1985.

General Sources and Indexes

A History of Speech Education in America. Edited by Karl R. Wallace. New York: Appleton-Century-Crofts, 1954.
Index to Journals in Communication Studies through 1979. Compiled by Ronald J. Matlon. Annandale, Va.: Speech Communication Association, 1980.

Journals

Central States Speech Communication Journal.
Communication Monographs.
Communication Quarterly.
Critical Studies in Mass Communication.
Exetasis.
Presidential Studies Quarterly.
Southern Speech Communication Journal.
Speaker and Gavel.
Western Journal of Speech Communication.
Vital Speeches.

GLOSSARY OF
RHETORICAL TERMS _____

ad hominem argument   "to the man"; an appeal to one's prejudices rather than to reason or intellect.

ad-libbed   slang for *ad libitum*, "as one desires or wishes"; to insert or delete words from a prepared speech text.

alliteration   the repetition of the same sound at the beginning of consecutive words or near one another, as in "from dripping dusk to drizzling dawn" (General MacArthur's "Duty, Honor, Country").

analogy   a form of argument in which it is advanced that if two things agree with one another in some respects, then they will probably agree in other respects as well.

anecdote   a brief, interesting, and often amusing story or event; used for humorous effect in a speech or for support of a persuasive point.

antithesis   an opposition of ideas emphasized by the positions of the contrasting words, as in "We observe today not a victory of party but a celebration of freedom" (John Kennedy's Inaugural Address).

argument from authority   occurs when a speaker offers evidence from accepted or supposed experts to substantiate a point.

argument from definition   occurs when a speaker employs legal or moral meanings to formulate an appeal, as in "every American citizen must have an equal right to vote" (Lyndon Johnson's "The Right to Vote").

audience   the person(s) assembled to hear a speech; can also denote those who listen (by radio or television) or read (by newspapers).

audience adaptation   how the speaker adjusts the style of word choice, the kinds of gestures, the nature of the reasoning and analysis, the impact of the emotional appeals, and so on, in order to meet the needs of an audience or different audiences.

audience analysis   the act of discerning the attitudes and beliefs of an audience by means of polls, sampling, questionnaires, and other means. These data can help the speaker in audience adaptation.

auditor   the person(s) who hear a speech; synonymous with *audience*.

Burkean cluster analysis   after Kenneth Burke, *A Grammar of Motives* and *a Rhetoric of Motives*, in which situations are described by act (what was done); scene (when or where it was done); agent (who did it); agency (how it was done); and purpose (why it was done).

call and response   indigenous to certain kinds of pulpit oratory and carried over into the political arena, in which an orator skillfully uses cadences of words and rhythm to evoke vocal responses from the members of the audience, as in Martin Luther King's "I Have a Dream" speech.

ceremonial speeches   addresses, often in an elevated style, delivered on formal occasions such as inaugurals, eulogies, dedications, and commencements. See *epideictic oratory*.

chiasmus   the inversion of parallel phrases or words, as in "Let us never negotiate out of fear. But let us never fear to negotiate" (John Kennedy's Inaugural Address).

Ciceronian speech pattern   an organizational pattern for the development and arrangement of a speech, discussed in Cicero's *De Inventione*; consists of an introduction (*exordium*), a narration (*narratio*) of the events under consideration, the division (*partitio*) of the main points in the speech, the arguments (*confirmatio*) that support the orator's thesis, the refutation (*refutatio*) that addresses arguments from the opposition, and the conclusion (*epilogus*) that summarizes the points of the speech and calls for action by the audience.

classical canons of rhetoric   codified by Cicero in *De Inventione*; consists of invention (*inventio*), the art of discovering arguments to persuade an audience; arrangement (*dispositio*), the art of arranging and organizing the arguments in the speech; the style (*elocutio*), the art of selecting language effectively; delivery (*pronuntiatio*), the art of delivering the speech with an effective voice, gestures, and so forth; and memory (*memoria*), the art of recalling or remembering the speech at the time of its delivery.

deduction   a reasoning from known or accepted principles or premises to a specific conclusion. See *induction*.

deliberative oratory   delineated in Aristotle's *Rhetoric*; consists of political speaking in legislative bodies, toward action (or nonaction) in the future, aimed at expediency. See *epideictic oratory*; *forensic oratory*.

discourse   denotes formalized speech making, the words of the speech, the complete speech as delivered.

disjunctive syllogism   a kind of syllogism in which alternatives are posited and then negated to state a conclusion; Richard Nixon used this rhetorical device in his "Cambodia" speech. See *syllogism*.

disposition   the ancient art of arranging the arguments and words of the speech for maximum persuasive appeal. See *Ciceronian thought pattern*; *classical canons of rhetoric*.

dissonance   occurs when speakers use language appeals that run against accepted attitudes and beliefs in order to create psychological imbalance or mental tension in their audience's minds, which can then be reduced or resolved by adopting the speaker's proposal.

emotional appeal   a rhetorical or persuasive argument that stirs the emotions—love, hate, anger, fear—of the audience. See *pathos*.

enthymeme   a rhetorical argument from probabilities; enthymematic reasoning occurs when the speaker bases an argument on generally held beliefs without expressing the premises, as in General MacArthur's "In war there is no substitute for victory"; the full argument might be: "The end of war is victory; Korea is a war; therefore, the end of the Korean war is victory."

epideictic oratory   expounded in Aristotle's *Rhetoric*; consists of ceremonial speaking before the populace, toward establishing honor and virtue through praise or blame while focusing on the present. See *deliberative oratory*; *forensic oratory*.

epithets   words, usually disparaging, used to characterize persons or things, as in Father Coughlin's kindly epithet—"Roosevelt or ruin"—in 1933 to his unkindly one in 1936—"Roosevelt and ruin."

ethos   one of the three rhetorical appeals adduced in Aristotle's *Rhetoric*; the speaker's character or goodwill, good sense, and good moral character are judged by the audience in terms of the audience's foreknowledge of the speaker's credibility and how the speaker utters the address. See *logos*; *pathos*.

eulogy   an instance of epideictic oratory; a speech of tribute in which the orator praises in elevated language the decedent's past life as an exemplar for the living. See *epideictic oratory*.

exordium   the introduction of a speech in which the speaker tries to make the audience receptive to the speaker and to the cause. See *Ciceronian speech pattern*.

extemporize   to deliver a speech with little preparation or notice; also to speak without memorizing the address; "extempore remarks" usually denotes a speech drawn from the immediate time and occasion; "extemporaneous speaker" usually indicates a speaker who, with little or no prior preparation, delivers a noteworthy speech. See *impromptu speaking*.

forensic oratory   expounded in Aristotle's *Rhetoric*; consists of legal courtroom oratory, toward establishing justice, with regard to the past. See *deliberative oratory*; *epideictic oratory*.

genre   a kind of oratory or speech in which similarities and differences distinguish certain speeches from others; for example, within the genre of epideictic oratory are eulogies, inaugurals, and commencements, among others.

identification   the rhetorical process in which the speaker tries, via language and delivery, to make the audience believe the speaker believes, feels, and acts as the audience does so that the audience will accept the speaker and give assent to the speech.

imagery   descriptions and figures of speech, as in "One hundred years later, the Negro lives on a lonely island of poverty in the midst of a vast ocean of material prosperity" (Martin Luther King's "I Have a Dream" speech).

impromptu speaking   occurs when a speaker delivers an address with no preparation or deliberation. See *extemporize*.

induction   reasoning from particular examples to a general conclusion. See *deduction*.

irony   a rhetorical method by which words are used in an opposite sense to their intended meanings or in a manner not expected or usually appropriate, as in "For man holds in his mortal hands the power to abolish all forms of human poverty and all forms of human life" (John Kennedy's Inaugural Address).

jeremiad   a kind of speech with religious overtones that condemns a social evil as a crisis and proposes a solution by returning to traditional values held by the audience as a chosen people.

logical appeal   a rhetorical argument based on statistics, testimony, facts, and other data that appear rational and reasonable to the audience as proof for the speaker's claims. See *emotional appeal*.

logos   described in Aristotle's *Rhetoric*; the persuasive arguments and materials presented by the speaker in the speech to prove a truth or an apparent truth. See *ethos*; *pathos*.

maxim   a statement of a general truth or rule of conduct, used rhetorically to display the speaker's possession of good judgment and character.

metaphor   a figure of speech implying comparison by a word or phrase of one meaning applied to another, as in ''Now the trumpet summons us again—not as a call to bear arms, though arms we need—not as a call to battle, thought embattled we are'' (John Kennedy's Inaugural Address).

oral outlining   a rhetorical technique in which the orator indicates the structure and organization of the speech, as in ''My first point is,'' and ''In summary, let me say.''

orator   denotes a practiced, accomplished, and eloquent speaker; synonymous with *speaker*.

parallelism   the beginning of successive phrases or sentences with the same word or words, as in Franklin Roosevelt's ''I see millions'' in the Second Inaugural Address and ''Last night'' in his war message; sometimes termed *anaphora*.

pathos   one of the three rhetorical appeals postulated in Aristotle's *Rhetoric*; a persuasive means by which the orator stirs the emotions of the audience in order to persuade them, appeals to the heart. See *ethos*; *logos*.

peroration   the conclusion of a speech; usually connotes one of high artistry or exceptional elegance and force.

persona   the rhetorical role and language assumed by a speaker for a persuasive purpose, as in the president of the United States as commander in chief (war messages), head of the party (campaign oratory), and head of state (inaugurals and state occasions).

pitch   the musical-like tone or note level at which an orator speaks, usually varied within a range for vocal emphasis and variety.

proof, artistic and inartistic   from Aristotle's *Rhetoric*; artistic proofs or appeals were generated by a knowledge and application of the art, as in how to make oneself appear credible to the audience; inartistic proofs—contracts, wills, evidence—existed before the speech and were merely used by the speaker as proof for an argument.

public discourse   oratory delivered from the public platform; synonymous with *public speaking* and *public oratory*.

rate   refers to the words-per-minute (wpm) in a spoken discourse; an average rate is around 125–175 wpm.

rhetor   from the Greek, meaning ''to speak''; denotes one knowledgeable in the art of persuasion and skilled in the practice of speaking persuasively; synonymous with *speaker* and *orator*.

rhetorical genre   the different kinds of speeches, forensic, deliberative, and epideictic address. See *genre*.

rhetorical premises   the principles, attitudes, and values on which an address rests; the argumentative assumptions that support the orator's appeals and proofs.

rhetorical question   a question asked for persuasive effect; ordinarily the speaker phrases the question to elicit the desired response from the audience; occasionally the audience may respond vocally, but usually the audience members mentally supply the answer to themselves, as in "Do you think that when I or any other senator makes a political speech, has it printed, should charge the printing of that speech and the mailing of that speech to the taxpayers?" (Richard Nixon's "My Side of the Story").

rhetorical strategies   the appeals, arguments, organizational patterns, techniques, delivery skills, and so on that a speaker can employ to persuade an audience.

satire   a rhetorical use of ridicule and sarcasm to attack persons or objects, as in "this pompous diplomat in striped pants, with a phony British accent [Secretary of State Dean Acheson]" (Joseph McCarthy, speech to U.S. Senate).

sermon   a kind of speech not accounted for in Aristotle's *Rhetoric*; a persuasive speech, delivered in a religious or moral setting, with the aim of changing, committing, or reinforcing moral or religious beliefs and actions.

speech writer   a person who writes, usually for hire, speeches or who extensively helps the employer to compose speeches; the pejorative term is *ghost writer*; the practice is as old as ancient Greece where men such as Lysias were known as logographers, literally "word writers."

syllogism   in rhetoric, the arguing from the general to the specific; an argument in which two premises are made and a logical conclusion made from them. Example: "All rhetors are successful speakers; X is a rhetor; therefore, X is a successful speaker."

theme   the main idea, argument, thesis, or proposition of an address.

volume   the loudness level at which an orator speaks, usually varied for emphasizing points and stressing ideas.

SUBJECT INDEX ————————————

Page numbers of actual entries appear in **boldface**.

SPEAKER AND SPEECH INDEX ⎯⎯⎯⎯⎯⎯⎯⎯⎯⎯⎯⎯⎯⎯⎯⎯⎯

CONTRIBUTORS _____

RICHARD E. BAILEY, Professor of Speech Communication, University of Rhode Island, Kingston, teaches courses in rhetoric and communication theory and has published articles on J. William Fulbright and religious communication theory.

THOMAS W. BENSON, Professor of Speech Communication, Pennsylvania State University, University Park, teaches courses in rhetorical criticism and has published widely on the rhetoric of Malcolm X. He is the 1983 recipient of the Robert J. Kibler Memorial Award of the Speech Communication Association and a former editor of *Communication Quarterly*.

WALDO W. BRADEN, Boyd Professor Emeritus of Speech, Louisiana State University, Baton Rouge, has published numerous articles in speech and history journals. His latest book is *The Oral Tradition in the South* (1983).

BERNARD L. BROCK, Professor of Speech Communication, Wayne State University, Detroit, teaches courses in rhetorical criticism, political communication, and contemporary public address. He has published on Spiro Agnew and is coauthor of *Methods of Rhetorical Criticism: A Twentieth-Century Perspective*.

EUGENE BROWN, Associate Professor of Political Science, Lebanon Valley College, Annville, Pennsylvania, teaches courses in international relations and U.S. foreign policy. He is the author of *J. William Fulbright: Advice and Dissent* and is writing a textbook on international relations.

CARL R. BURGCHARDT, Assistant Professor of Speech Communication, Colorado State University, Fort Collins, teaches courses in critical methodology and the history and criticism of American public address. He has a special interest in protest rhetoric and has published articles on communist pamphlets and the political discourse of Robert M. La Follette, Sr.

RONALD H. CARPENTER, Professor of English, University of Florida, Gainesville, teaches courses in speech writing, rhetorical theory, and language and image in political communication. He has received a Fellow of the Huntington Library Award, a National Endowment for the Humanities Fellowship, a University of Florida President's Scholar Award, and a 1984 Speech Communication Association Golden Anniversary Monograph Award.

DANIEL ROSS CHANDLER, Minister, United Methodist Church, New York City, for the past fifteen years has held assistant professorships in speech communication in the state and city universities of New York and at Rutgers University. His published books are *The Reverend Dr. Preston Bradley* and *The Rhetorical Tradition*.

CELESTE MICHELLE CONDIT, Assistant Professor of Speech Communication, University of Illinois, Urbana, teaches courses in political communication and does research and has published in contemporary public communication.

CHARLES R. CONRAD, Associate Professor of Speech Communication, University of North Carolina, Chapel Hill, teaches courses in organizational communication and rhetorical theory. He won the Karl L. Wallace Memorial Award in 1984 for his research on religious political rhetoric and has published an article on the Moral Majority in the *Quarterly Journal of Speech*.

RICHARD E. CRABLE, Professor of Communication, Purdue University, West Lafayette, teaches courses in argumentation, rhetorical theory and criticism, public relations, issue management, and corporate advocacy. He has written several essays on Dwight D. Eisenhower.

L. PATRICK DEVLIN, Professor of Speech Communication, University of Rhode Island, Kingston, teaches courses in political communication and public address. He is an archivist and analyst of presidential campaign television commercials, the author of numerous articles in political communication and *Contemporary Political Speaking*, and the editor of *Political Persuasion in Presidential Campaigns*.

HOWARD DORGAN, Professor of Communication Arts, Appalachian State University, Boone, North Carolina, teaches courses in the history of American public address and in southern oratory and has published numerous articles in the fields of southern rhetoric and Appalachian studies. He is a coeditor of and contributor to *The Oratory of Southern Demagogues* and *Public Discourse in the Contemporary South*.

BERNARD K. DUFFY, Associate Professor of Speech and Coordinator of the Speech Program, Clemson University, Clemson, South Carolina, teaches courses in rhetorical theory and American public address and publishes in the fields of rhetorical theory and political rhetoric.

SUSAN DUFFY, Assistant Professor of Speech, Clemson University, Clemson, South Carolina, teaches courses in public speaking, history and criticism of broadcasting, and oral interpretation of literature. She is compiling a bibliography of works by and about Shirley Chisholm.

KAREN A. FOSS, Associate Professor of Speech Communication, Humboldt State University, Arcata, California, teaches courses in women and communication and contemporary rhetoric and is coeditor of *Women's Studies in Communication*.

ROBERT V. FRIEDENBERG, Professor of Communication, Miami University, Hamilton, Ohio, teaches courses in the history and criticism of American public address and political campaign communication. He is coauthor of *Political Campaign Communication: Principles and Practices* and has published widely on political communication. He has also served as a speech writer, media consultant, and manager in over seventy political campaigns and as a campaign communications specialist for the Republican National Committee.

HAL W. FULMER, Assistant Professor of Communication, Mississippi State University,

Starkville, teaches courses in public speaking, rhetorical and communication theory, and persuasion. He is currently analyzing Billy Graham's radio sermons.

PAUL C. GASKE, Associate Professor of Speech Communication, San Diego State University, San Diego, California, teaches courses in argumentation and political communication. He is a contributor on Huey Long to *American Rhetoric from Roosevelt to Reagan*.

G. JACK GRAVLEE, Professor of Speech Communication, Colorado State University, Fort Collins, teaches courses in the history and criticism of American and British public address and in contemporary American television. He has written essays for *America in Controversy* and *The Oratory of Southern Demagogues*.

J. JUSTIN GUSTAINIS, Assistant Professor of Communication, State University of New York, Plattsburgh, teaches courses in rhetorical theory and rhetorical criticism.

JOHN C. HAMMERBACK, Professor of Speech Communication, California State University, Hayward, teaches courses in the history, criticism, and theory of public communication. His published scholarship on Chicano discourse includes, with Richard J. Jensen, *A War of Words: Chicano Protest in the 1960s and 1970s*.

DAVID HENRY, Professor of Speech Communication, California Polytechnic State University, San Luis Obispo, teaches courses in rhetorical theory, public discourse, critical thinking, and small group communication. He is currently at work on a critical analysis of Ronald Reagan's campaign communication for a book on the president's rhetoric.

RICHARD J. JENSEN, Associate Professor of Speech Communication, University of New Mexico, Albuquerque, teaches courses in rhetorical criticism, the rhetoric of dissent, and Southwest rhetoric. His scholarly works on Chicano rhetoric include, with John C. Hammerback, *A War of Words: Chicano Protest in the 1960s and 1970s*.

LOCH K. JOHNSON, Associate Professor of Political Science, University of Georgia, Athens, has been an American Political Science Association Congressional Fellow, an aide to Senator Frank Church, and staff director of the Subcommittee on Oversight, Committee on Intelligence, in the House of Representatives. His publications on Senator Frank Church include *The Making of International Agreements: Congress Confronts the Executive* and *A Season of Inquiry: The Senate Intelligence Investigation*.

WILLIAM LASSER, Assistant Professor of Political Science, Clemson University, Clemson, South Carolina, teaches courses in U.S. politics and public law. His publications include articles in the *Journal of Politics* and *Technology Review*.

PETER AUGUSTINE LAWLER, Associate Professor of Political Science, Berry College, Mount Berry, Georgia, teaches a variety of courses in U.S. politics and political philosophy. He is editor of *American Political Rhetoric: A Reader* and has published widely on U.S. political thought.

DALE G. LEATHERS, Professor of Speech Communication, University of Georgia, Athens, teaches courses that focus upon the persuasion of the Far Right and Far Left movements. He has published articles on Billy James Hargis.

RICHARD W. LEEMAN, Instructor in Speech, Clemson University, Clemson, South Carolina, teaches courses in persuasion and argumentation. He has a research interest in the Iranian hostage crisis and has published on terrorism as rhetoric.

WIL A. LINKUGEL, Professor of Communication Studies, University of Kansas, Lawrence, teaches courses in American public address and has developed courses in the rhetoric of black Americans and women's rights. He has published books on public speaking and is coeditor of *Contemporary American Speeches*, now in its fifth edition.

CALVIN M. LOGUE, Professor of Speech Communication, University of Georgia, Athens, teaches a seminar in rhetorical criticism. He contributed to *Oratory in the New South*, edited with Howard Dorgan, *Oratory of Southern Demagogues*, and *Public Discourse in the Contemporary South: A New Rhetoric of Diversity*. He received the Creative Research Medal from the University of Georgia Research Foundation for his continuing criticism of southern discourse.

MICHAEL DENNIS MCGUIRE, Associate Professor of Speech Communication, University of Georgia, Athens, teaches courses in rhetorical theory, criticism, and history.

JOHN J. MAKAY, Associate Professor of Communication, Ohio State University, Columbus, teaches courses in presentational speaking, rhetorical theory, and rhetorical criticism. He has written on George Wallace.

ALLEN H. MERRIAM, Associate Professor of Communication, Missouri Southern State College, Joplin, teaches courses in political and social communication and international communication. He wrote *Gandhi vs. Jinnah: The Debate over the Partition of India* and an article on racism in American oratory that appeared in *Phylon*.

ROBERT P. NEWMAN, Professor of Rhetoric Emeritus, University of Pittsburgh, Pittsburgh, Pennsylvania, teaches courses in evidence, deliberation and decision making, historiography, and the rhetoric of Joseph McCarthy. In 1982 he was the co-winner of the Winans-Wichelns Prize for distinguished scholarship in rhetoric. He is the author of *Recognition of Communist China? A Study in Argument* and coauthor of *Evidence*.

JAMES S. OLSON, Associate Professor of History, Sam Houston State University, Huntsville, Texas, is the author of five books, including *Herbert Hoover and the Reconstruction Finance Corporation* and *The Historical Dictionary of the New Deal*.

JOHN H. PATTON, Associate Professor and Chair, Department of Communication, Tulane University, New Orleans, Louisiana, has served on the editorial board of the *Quarterly Journal of Speech* and other journals and was a recipient of the Speech Communication Association's Karl L. Wallace Memorial Award for scholarship in rhetoric and public address. He teaches courses in American public discourse, persuasion, presidential rhetoric, rhetorical theory, and criticism.

WILLIAM D. PEDERSON, Associate Professor of Political Science and Director of American Studies, Louisiana State University at Shreveport, teaches courses in U.S. government, the U.S. Congress, and the presidency.

JAMES R. PENCE, Associate Professor of Speech Communication, University of North Carolina, Chapel Hill, teaches courses in the history and criticism of American public address and in southern oratory. He is conducting research on the relationship between culture and the rhetoric of religious conversion.

DOROTHY LEE PENNINGTON, Associate Professor of Communication Studies and African Studies, University of Kansas, Lawrence, teaches courses in the rhetoric of black Americans and intercultural communication. She has researched and written on strategies in black rhetoric.

BEATRICE K. REYNOLDS, Associate Professor of Speech Communication, University of Houston-Victoria, Texas, teaches courses in rhetorical theory, political communication, and persuasion. She has published an article on Ti-Grace Atkinson and is editor and translator of *Spokesmen of the French Revolution: 1790–1794*.

MICHAEL P. RICCARDS, President of St. John's College, Sante Fe, New Mexico, specializes in the areas of the American presidency, political theory, and political behavior. He has been a Fulbright Fellow to Japan, a National Endowment for the Humanities Fellow at Princeton University, and a Henry Huntington Fellow at the Huntington Library in California. He is the author of *The Making of the American Citizenry: An Introduction to Political Socialization* and a forthcoming study of the early American presidency.

LLOYD E. ROHLER, Assistant Professor of Speech Communication, University of North Carolina at Wilmington, teaches courses in persuasion and the history and criticism of American public address and writes on political communication.

HALFORD R. RYAN, Professor of Public Speaking, Washington and Lee University, Lexington, Virginia, teaches courses in American public address and presidential rhetoric. He is writing a book on Franklin Delano Roosevelt's presidential rhetoric.

EDWARD L. SCHAPSMEIER, Distinguished Professor of History, Illinois State University, Normal, teaches a course on great figures in U.S. history and coauthored *Dirksen of Illinois: Senatorial Statesman*.

MARTIN W. SLANN, Professor of Political Science, Clemson University, Clemson, South Carolina, teaches courses in comparative politics and political philosophy. He is coauthor of *The American Republic: Politics, Institutions, Policies*.

CRAIG ALLEN SMITH, Assistant Professor of Speech Communication, University of North Carolina, Chapel Hill, teaches courses in political communication and deliberation. He is coauthor of *Persuasion and Social Movements*, author of several articles on the rhetoric of American social movements, and has studied the rhetoric of the International Workers of the World.

DONALD K. SPRINGEN, Professor of Speech, Brooklyn College of the City University of New York, teaches courses in the history and criticism of American public address. He is a contributor to *The Rhetoric of Protest and Reform, 1878–1898* and in 1980 was awarded the Winans-Wichelns Prize for distinguished scholarship in rhetoric and public address.

HERMANN G. STELZNER, Professor of Communication, University of Massachusetts, Amherst, teaches courses in rhetorical criticism. He has been editor of *Communication Quarterly* and the *Quarterly Journal of Speech*.

BETH M. WAGGENSPACK, Assistant Professor of Communication Studies, Virginia Polytechnic Institute and State University, Blacksburg. Her teaching encompasses the field of rhetoric and public address, particularly the areas of persuasion and rhetorical criticism. She conducts research into the rhetoric of the women's movement, impression management, and political rhetoric.

ROBERT A. WALLER, Professor of History and Dean of the College of Liberal Arts, Clemson University, Clemson, South Carolina, pursues teaching, research, and publication interests in twentieth-century U.S. history.

MICHAEL WEILER, Assistant Professor of Communication at the University of Pittsburgh, Pittsburgh, Pennsylvania, specializes in political rhetoric, particularly rhetorical analysis of contemporary political ideologies. He is the author of "The Rhetoric of Neo-Liberalism," *Quarterly Journal of Speech*. Currently he is working on a study of neoconservative rhetoric and its relationship to problems of legitimacy in the American welfare state.

CHARLES HENRY WHITTIER, Specialist in Religion and Public Policy, Congressional Research Service, Library of Congress, Washington, D.C., has worked with Father Charles Coughlin's papers and has lectured widely on public speaking.

THEODORE O. WINDT, JR., Associate Professor of Political Rhetoric, University of Pittsburgh, Pittsburgh, Pennsylvania, teaches courses in presidential rhetoric and in cynicism. He is the editor of *Presidential Rhetoric: 1961 to the Present*, and is coeditor with Beth Ingold of *Essays in Presidential Rhetoric*. He is the weekly commentator on presidential politics for KDKA-TV, Pittsburgh, a professional political consultant and speech writer, and a consultant to the ABC-TV News department, New York City.

DAVID ZAREFSKY, Professor of Communication Studies and Associate Dean of the School of Speech, Northwestern University, Evanston, Illinois, teaches courses in American public discourse, both historical and contemporary, and in theories of argumentation. He has written a series of essays and a book on the rhetoric of the Johnson presidency. In 1984–1985, he was the Van Zelst Research Professor of Communication at Northwestern University and is preparing a book on the Lincoln-Douglas debates.